CW01544314

THE SOVIET UNION AND EUROPE IN THE COLD WAR, 1943–53

The Soviet Union and Europe in the Cold War, 1943–53

Edited by

Francesca Gori
Feltrinelli Foundation
Milan

and

Silvio Pons
Department of Historical and Social Sciences
Bari University

FONDAZIONE GIANGIACOMO FELTRINELLI
FONDAZIONE ISTITUTO GRAMSCI

Selection and editorial matter © Francesca Gori and Silvio Pons 1996
Text © Macmillan Press Ltd 1996

All rights reserved. No reproduction, copy or transmission of
this publication may be made without written permission.

No paragraph of this publication may be reproduced, copied or
transmitted save with written permission or in accordance with
the provisions of the Copyright, Designs and Patents Act 1988,
or under the terms of any licence permitting limited copying
issued by the Copyright Licensing Agency, 90 Tottenham Court
Road, London W1T 4LP.

Any person who does any unauthorised act in relation to this
publication may be liable to criminal prosecution and civil
claims for damages.

The authors have asserted their rights to be identified as the authors of
this work in accordance with the Copyright, Designs and Patents Act 1988.

Published by
PALGRAVE
Houndmills, Basingstoke, Hampshire RG21 6XS and
175 Fifth Avenue, New York, N.Y. 10010
Companies and representatives throughout the world

PALGRAVE is the new global academic imprint of
St. Martin's Press LLC Scholarly and Reference Division and
Palgrave Publishers Ltd (formerly Macmillan Press Ltd).

ISBN 0–333–65316–5

This book is printed on paper suitable for recycling and
made from fully managed and sustained forest sources.

A catalogue record for this book is available
from the British Library.

Transferred to digital printing 2002

Published with the financial support of CNR
(Consiglio Nazionale delle Ricerche)

Contents

List of Abbreviations	viii
Preface	xii
Notes on the Contributors	xiii
Introduction	xviii

PART I   THE SOVIET UNION AND THE POST-WAR EUROPEAN ORDER

1. Problems of Post-War Construction in Soviet Foreign Policy Conceptions during World War II   3
   Aleksei M. Filitov

2. Stalin's Plans for Post-War Germany   23
   Wilfried Loth

3. The Soviets and the Christian Democrats: the Challenge of a 'Bourgeois' Party in Eastern Germany, 1945–9   37
   Norman M. Naimark

4. The Soviet Union and the Berlin Crisis, 1948–9   57
   Michail M. Narinskii

5. The Soviet Liberation of Poland and the Polish Left, 1943–5   76
   Anita J. Prazmowska

6. The Soviet Union and Finland after the War, 1944–53   89
   Jukka Nevakivi

7. The Limits to Soviet Influence: Soviet Diplomats and the Pursuit of Strategic Interests in Norway and Denmark, 1944–7   106
   Sven G. Holtsmark

8. A Balkan Union? Southeastern Europe in Soviet Security Policy, 1944–8   125
   R. Craig Nation

9. The Soviet Union and 'the Greek Question', 1946–53: Problems and Appraisals   144
   Artiom A. Ulunian

10. The Soviet Union and the Italian Communist Party, 1944–8   161
    Elena Aga-Rossi and Victor Zaslavsky

11	Stalin and the Prospects for Post-War Europe: a Comment on Chapters 1, 2 and 7 *Alexander Dallin*	185
12	How much of the Cold War was Inevitable? A Comment on Chapters 4, 6, 8 and 9 *William Taubman*	191

PART II THE COMINFORM AND THE SOVIET BLOC

13	Stalin's Foreign Policy and the Cominform, 1947–53 *Nataliia I. Egorova*	197
14	The Marshall Plan and the Founding of the Cominform, June–September 1947 *Anna Di Biagio*	208
15	The Soviet–Yugoslav Conflict and the Soviet Bloc *Leonid Ia. Gibianskii*	222
16	A Challenge Let Drop: Soviet Foreign Policy, the Cominform and the Italian Communist Party, 1947–8 *Silvio Pons*	246
17	Vittorio Vidali and the Cominform, 1947–53 *Joze Pirjevec*	264
18	Revolution Released: Stalin, the Bulgarian Communist Party and the Establishment of the Cominform *Vesselin Dimitrov*	272

PART III THE RELATIONS BETWEEN THE SOVIET UNION AND WESTERN EUROPE

19	From 'Ally' to Enemy: Britain's Relations with the Soviet Union, 1941–8 *Geoffrey Warner*	293
20	General de Gaulle and the Soviet Union, 1943–5: Ideology or European Equilibrium *Georges-Henri Soutou*	310
21	Britain and the Death of Stalin *Antonio Varsori*	334
22	The Soviet Union and Germany in the Late Stalin Period, 1950–3 *Gerhard Wettig*	356
23	Soviet–Italian Relations, 1945–8 *Nina D. Smirnova*	375

24	Negotiating a Settlement for Italy and the Minor Axis Powers: Peace Diplomacy and the Origins of the Cold War, 1945–7 *Ilaria Poggiolini*	383
25	The Search for Symmetry: a Tentative View of Trieste, the Soviet Union and the Cold War *Giampaolo Valdevit*	395
26	Security and Perceptions of Threat in Italy in the Early Cold War Years, 1945–53 *Leopoldo Nuti*	412

Index 431

List of Abbreviations

ARCHIVES

AAN	Archiwum Akt Nowych (Warsaw)
ACS	Archivio Centrale di Stato (Rome)
AJ–CK SKJ	Arhiv Jugoslavije, Centralni komitet Saveza komunista Jugoslavije (Belgrade)
AJBT–KMJ	Arhiv Josipa Broza Tita–F. Kabinet Maršala Jugoslavije (Belgrade)
AN	Archives Nationales (Paris)
ANM	Arhiv Notranjega Ministrstva Republike Slovenije (Ljubljana)
APC	Archivio Partito Comunista Italiano, Fondazione Istituto Gramsci (Rome)
AP RF	Arkhiv Prezidenta Rossiiskoi Federatsii (Moscow)
ARL	Archivum Ruchu Ludowego (Warsaw)
ASMAE	Archivio Storico Ministero degli Affari Esteri (Roma)
ASSIP-PA	Arhiva Saveznog sekretarijata za inostrane poslove–Političa arhiva (Belgrade)
AUSSME	Archivio Ufficio Storico Stato Maggiore Esercito (Rome)
AVP RF	Arkhiv Vneshnei Politiki Rossiiskoi Federatsii (Moscow)
FO	Foreign Office
GARF	Gosudarstvennyi Arkhiv Rossiskoi Federatsii (Moscow)
HIA	Hoover Institution Archives (Stanford)
MAE	Archives du Ministère des Affaires Etrangères (Paris)
NA	National Archives (Washington, D.C., and Suitland, Md.)
PRO	Public Record Office (London)
RTsKhIDNI	Rossiiskii Tsentr Khraneniia i Izucheniia Dokumentov Noveishei Istorii (Moscow)
SAPMO-BA	Stiftung Archiv der Parteien und Massenorganisationen der DDR im Bundesarchiv (Berlin)
TsDA–TsPA	Tsentralen d'rzhaven arkhiv–Tsentralen partien arkhiv (Sofia)
ZPA	Zentral Parteiarchiv (Berlin)

List of Abbreviations

INSTITUTIONS, POLITICAL ORGANIZATIONS AND OTHERS

ACC	Allied Control Commission
AFH	Allied Force Headquarters
AFSOUTH	Allied Forces South
AK	Armia Krajowa (Home Army)
AL	Armia Ludowa (People Army)
AP	Associated Press
BCh	Bataliony Chłopskie (Peasant Battalion)
BRP(k)	B'garska rabotnicheska partiia (komunisti) (Bulgarian Workers' Party (Communist) (up to December 1948)
CCS	Combined Chiefs of Staff
CDU	Christlich-Demokratische Union (Christian Democratic Union)
CFLN	Comité Français de Libération Nationale (French Committee of National Liberation)
CFM	Council of the Foreign Ministers
CGIL	Confederazione Generale Italiana del Lavoro (Italian General Confederation of Labour)
CIA	Central Intelligence Agency
CIG	Central Intelligence Group
CINCSOUTH	Commander in Chief, South
CKL	Centralny Komitet Ludowy (Central People's Committee)
CLNAI	Comitato di Liberazione Nazionale Alta Italia (Committee for the Liberation of Northern Italy)
CPSU	Communist Party of the Soviet Union
CSU	Christlich-Soziale Union (Christian Social Union)
DBD	Demokratische Bauernpartei Deutschlands (German Democratic Farmers' Party)
DC	Democrazia Cristiana (Christian Democratic Party)
DDR	Deutsche Demokratische Republik (German Democratic Republic)
ELAS	Ethnikos Laikos Apeleftherotikos Stratos (National Popular Liberation Army)
EMMO	Europa Meridionale/Mediterraneo Occidentale (South Europe/West Mediterranean)
FBI	Federal Bureau of Investigation
FRUS	*Foreign Relations of the United States* (Washington, D.C.)
FTT	Free Territory of Trieste
GSUSA	General Staff, United States Army
JSSC	Joint Strategic Survey Committee

KKE	Kommunistiko Komma Ellados (Communist Party of Greece)
KPD	Kommunistische Partei Deutschland (German Communist Party)
KPJ	Komunistička partija Jugoslavije (Communist Party of Yugoslavia)
KPP	Communistyczna Partja Polski (Polish Communist Party)
KRN	Krajowa Rada Narodowa (Homeland National Council)
KSČ	Kommunistická strana Československa (Communist Party of Czechoslovakia)
LDP	Liberal Demokratische Partei Deutschlands (Liberal-Democratic Party)
MID	Ministerstvo Inostrannykh Del (Ministry of Foreign Policy)
MMIA	Military Mission to the Italian Army
MTO	Mediterranean Theater of Operations
NATO	North Atlantic Treaty Organization
NDPD	National Demokratische Partei Deutschlands (National-Democratic Party of Germany)
NKID	Narodnyi Komissariat Inostrannykh Del (People's Commissariat of Foreign Affairs)
NKVD	Narodnyi Komissariat Vnutrennykh Del (People's Commissariat of Internal Affairs)
OBWPI	*OMGUS Berlin Weekly Political Intelligence Report*
OMGUS	Office of the Military Government of the United States
OSS	Office of Strategic Services
PAL	Polska Armia Ludowa (Polish People's Army)
PCF	Parti Communiste Français (French Communist Party)
PCI	Partito Comunista Italiano (Italian Communist Party)
PKSh	Partia Komuniste e Shqipërisë (Communist Party of Albania)
PHPS	Post-Hostilities Planning Staff
PPR	Polska Partja Robotnicza (Polish Workers Party)
PPR-Lewica	(Polska Partja Robotnicza-Lewica (Polish Workers Party – the left-wing faction)
PPS	Polska Partia Socjalystyczna (Polish Socialist Party)
PSI	Partito Socialista Italiano (Italian Socialist Party)
PWB	Psychological Warfare Branch
RJD	Rada Jedności Narodowej (Council of National Unity)
SACEUR	Supreme Allied Commander in Europe
SACMED	Supreme Allied Command in the Mediterranean

List of Abbreviations

SED	Sozialistische Einheitspartei Deutschland (Socialist Unity Party of Germany)
SHAPE	Supreme Headquarters Allied Powers in Europe
SKK	Sowjetische Kontrol Kommission (Soviet Control Commission)
SL	Stronnictwo Ludowe (Peasant Party)
SM	Stato Maggiore (General Staff)
SME	Stato Maggiore Esercito (General Staff of the Army)
SPD	Sozial-Demokratische Partei Deutschlands (German Social Democratic Party)
SVAG	Sovetskaia Voennaia Administraciia v Germanii (Soviet Military Administration in Germany)
UDB	Uprava Državne Bezbednosti (State Security Office)
VdgB	Vereinigung der Gegenseitigen Bauernhilfe (Agricultural Cooperatives)
WRN	Wolność, Równość i Niepodległość (Party of 'Freedom, Equality and Independence') (Poland)
ZPP	Zwiázek Patriotow Polskich (Union of Polish Patriots)

Preface

This volume contains revised versions of papers originally read at the international conference on 'The Soviet Union and Europe in the Cold War (1943–1953)' (Cortona, 23–24 September 1994). The conference was held in collaboration with the Institute of World History of the Academy of Sciences, Moscow, and with the support of the Italian National Research Council and the Italian Ministry of Foreign Affairs.

We are greatly indebted to the various people and institutions who contributed to the success of the conference – in particular to Igor Lebedev, Director of the Archives of Foreign Policy of the Russian Federation, and to Kirill Anderson, Director of the Russian Centre of Conservation and Study of Records for Modern History. We wish also to thank the scholars who were members of the Scientific Committee of the conference, together with the editors of the volume: Aleksander Chubarian (Institute of Universal History, Russian Academy of Sciences), Ennio Di Nolfo (University of Florence), René Girault (University of Paris I, Sorbonne), Jonathan Haslam (Corpus Christi College, Cambridge), Mikhail Narinskii (Institute of Universal History, Russian Academy of Sciences), Victor Zaslavsky (Memorial University of Newfoundland, LUISS Rome).

FONDAZIONE GIANGIACOMO FELTRINELLI
FONDAZIONE ISTITUTO GRAMSCI

Notes on the Contributors

Elena Aga-Rossi is Professor of Contemporary History at the University of Aquila, Italy. Among her publications are *Operation Sunrise* (with Bradley F. Smith) (1979); *Gli Stati Uniti e le origini della guerra fredda* (1984); *Italia nella sconfitta* (1985); and *Una nazione allo sbando* (1993).

Alexander Dallin is Professor Emeritus of History and Political Science at Stanford University and Senior Fellow of the Institute for International Studies. He is the author, among other works, of *Political Terror in Communist Systems* (1970); *German Rule in Russia, 1941–1945* (1981); and editor of *The Soviet Union: From Crisis to Collapse* (1995).

Anna Di Biagio is researcher at the Department of History at the University of Florence, Italy. She is the author of several essays on the history of Soviet Russia, of the volume *Le origini dell'isolazionismo sovietico. L'Unione Sovietica e l'Europa dal 1918 al 1928* (1990), and co-editor of *The Cominform. Minutes of the Three Conferences 1947/1948/1949* (1994).

Vesselin Dimitrov teaches in the Department of Government at the London School of Economics and Political Science, after finishing a doctorate on the establishment of the communist system in Eastern Europe at the University of Cambridge.

Nataliia I. Egorova is senior researcher at the Institute of World History of the Russian Academy of Sciences. Among her publications are *Isolation and European Policy of the USA, 1933–1941* (1995) and *'Iranian Crisis' 1945–1946: A View from the Russian Archives/Cold War: New Approaches, New Documents* (1995).

Aleksei M. Filitov is senior researcher at the Institute of World History of the Russian Academy of Sciences. Among his publications are *Cold War: Historiography of Discussion in the West* (1991) and *German Question: From the Split to Union* (1993).

Leonid Ia. Gibianskii is research fellow and head of Group of the Institute for Slavic and Balkan Studies at the Russian Academy of Sciences. He is the author and editor of several publications on the history of Yugoslavia, of Soviet foreign policy and of international problems in Eastern Europe in the twentieth century.

Sven G. Holtsmark is senior research associate at the Norwegian Institute for Defence Studies. His publications include *A Soviet Grab for the High North? USSR, Svalbard and Northern Norway 1920–1953* (1993) and *Norway and the Soviet Union 1917–1955: A Foreign Policy Documentation* (1995, in Norwegian, Russian edition forthcoming).

Wilfried Loth is Professor of Modern History at the University of Essen and President of the Kulturwissenschaftliche Institut. Among his works are *Geschichte Frankreichs im 20. Jahrhundert* (1987); *The Division of the World 1941–1955* (1988); *Der Weg nach Europa. Geschichte der europäischen Integration 1939–1957* (1990); and *Stalins ungeliebtes Kind. Warum Moskau die DDR nicht wollte* (1994).

Norman M. Naimark is Robert and Florence McDonnell Professor in East European Studies and Chairman of the Department of History at Stanford University. He is the author of *The History of the 'Proletariat': The Emergence of Marxism in the Kingdom of Poland, 1870–1887* (1979); *Terrorists and Social Democrats: The Russian Revolutionary Movement under Alexander III* (1983); and *The Russians in Germany: A History of the Soviet Zone of Occupation, 1945–1949* (1995).

Mikhail M. Narinskii is Chief of the Chair of International Relations of the Moscow State Institute of International Relations (MGIMO) and Deputy Director of the Institute of Universal History, Russian Academy of Sciences. A specialist of international relations and the history of twentieth-century Europe, he has participated in publishing a number of collective works (among them *Allies at War*, 1994) and is the author of *England and France in Post-War Europe* (1972); *Classes and Parties in France* (1983); and *Komintern and the Second World War. Part 1* (1994).

R. Craig Nation is Professor of International Relations and coordinator of Russian Area and East European Studies at the Johns Hopkins University Bologna Centre, Paul H. Nitze School of Advanced International Studies. His publications include *War on War: Lenin, The Zimmerwald Left and the Origins of Communist Internationalism* (1989) and *Black Earth, Red Star: A History of Soviet Security Policy 1917–1991* (1992).

Jukka Nevakivi is Professor of Political History at the University of Helsinki. Among his publications are *Britain, France and the Arab Middle East 1914–1920* (1969) and *The Appeal That Was Never Made – The Allies, Scandinavia and the Finnish Winter War 1939–1940* (1976).

Leopoldo Nuti is Associate Professor of History of International Relations at the University of Catania, Italy. He is the author of *L'esercito ital-*

iano nel secondo dopoguerra, 1945-1950. La sua ricostruzione e l'assistenza militare alleata (1989) and the editor of *I missili di ottobre. La storiografia americana e la crisi cubana del 1962* (1994). He is presently completing a book on the USA and the 'opening to the left' in Italy.

Joze Pirjevec is Professor of History of Eastern Europe in the Faculty of Political Sciences at Padua University. His main works are *Storia della Russia del XIX secolo* (1984); *Tržaški vozel, 1945-1980* (1984); *Il gran rifiuto. Guerra calda e fredda tra Tito, Stalin e l'Occidente* (1990); *Il giorno di San Vito. Jugoslavia 1918-1992. Storia di una tragedia* (1993); *Serbi, Croati, Sloveni. Storia di tre nazioni* (1995); and *Jugoslavija 1918-1992. Nastanek, razvoj ter razpad Karadjordjeviceve in Titove Jugoslavije* (1995).

Ilaria Poggiolini is researcher of the history of international relations of the Department of Political Sciences at the University of Sassari, Italy. Among her publications are *Diplomazia della transizione. Gli Alleati e il problema del trattato di pace italiano* (1990) and, as a contributor, 'The Enemy/Ally Dilemma and Military Limitations' (in Fred Tanner (ed.), *From Versailles to Baghdad: Post-War Armament Control of Defeated States* [1992]); 'Italian Revisionism after World War II: Status and Security Problems 1947-1956 (in Rolf Ahmann (ed.), *The Quest for Stability. Problems of Western European Security 1918-1957* [1993]); and 'Some Reflections on Post-World War II Peace-Making Practices (1947-51)' (in A. Varsori (ed.), *Europe 1945-1990s: The End of an Era?* [1995]).

Silvio Pons is a researcher in contemporary history at Bari University, Italy. He is a collaborator of the Gramsci Foundation, Rome. His works include *Il sistema di potere dello stalinismo. Partito e Stato in URSS, 1933-1953* (1988, co-author); *L'età dello stalinismo* (1991, co-editor); *The Cominform. Minutes of the Three Conferences 1947/1948/1949* (1994, co-editor) and *Stalin e la guerra inevitabile, 1936-1941* (1995). He has written articles about the Soviet system under Stalin and in the post-Stalin era, Stalin's foreign policy, Communist politics in the 1930s and in the 1940s.

Anita J. Prazmowska is Lecturer in the Department of International History at the London School of Economics. Among her publications are *Britain, Poland and the Eastern Front, 1939* (1987); and *Britain and Poland 1939-1943. The Betrayed Ally* (1995).

Nina D. Smirnova is senior researcher at the Institute of World History of the Russian Academy of Sciences. Among her publications are

Balkan Politics of Fascist Italy 1936–1941 (1969) and *Italian Politics in Balkan 1922–1935* (1979).

Georges-Henri Soutou is Professor of Contemporary History at the University of Paris-Sorbonne (Paris-IV); his field is the history of international relations in the twentieth century. Besides numerous articles, he has published *L'Or et le Sang. Les buts de guerre économiques de la Première guerre mondiale* (1989) and he wrote the chapter on France in David Reynolds (ed.), *The Origins of the Cold War in Europe* (1994). He is currently publishing the articles by Raymond Aron in *Le Figaro*: Raymond Aron, *Les articles de politique internationale dans Le Figaro de 1947 à 1977*, Vol. I, *La Guerre froide (juin 1947 à mai 1955)* (1990); Vol. II, *La Coexistence (mai 1955 à février 1965* (1994).

William Taubman is Betrand Snell Professor of Political Science at Amherst College. He is the author of *The View from Lenin Hills* (1967); *Governing Soviet Cities* (1973); *Stalin's American Policy* (1982); co-author of *Moscow Spring* (1989); and editor/translator of *Khrushchev on Khrushchev* by Sergei N. Khrushchev. He is currently writing a biography of Nikita S. Khrushchev.

Artem A. Ulunian is senior researcher at the Institute of World History of the Russian Academy of Sciences. Among his publications are *National-Liberation Front of Greece (EAM) 1941–1944. History, Ideology, Politics* (1991) and *Communist Party of Greece* (1995).

Giampaolo Valdevit is researcher of Contemporary History at the Department of Geographical and Historical Sciences, University of Trieste, Italy. Among his publications are *La questione di Trieste. Politica internazionale e contesto locale (1941–1954)* (1986); *Gli Stati Uniti e il Mediterraneo. Da Truman a Reagan* (1992); and *Trieste 1953–1954. L'ultima crisi?* (1994).

Antonio Varsori is Associate Professor of the History of International Relations and Jean Monnet Chair of the History of European Integration at the Faculty of Political Sciences of the University of Florence. He is the Italian representative in the Liaison Committee of Historians at the EU Commission, member of the editorial board of the *Journal of European Integration History* and deputy-editor of the journal *Storia delle relazioni internazionali*. Besides numerous articles in international journals and miscellaneous volumes, his publications include *Gli Alleati e l'emigrazione democratica antifascista (1940–1943)* (1982) and *Il Patto di Bruxelles (1948): tra integrazione europea* *e alleanza atlantica* (1988). He is the editor of *La politica estera italiana nel secondo dopoguerra (1943–1957)* (1993) and *Europe 1945–1990s: The End of an Era?* (1995).

Geoffrey Warner is a supernumerary fellow in Modern History at Brasenose College, Oxford. He has written widely on post-war international history and the cold war, including the chapter on Ernest Bevin in Gordon Craig and Francis Loewenheim (eds), *The Diplomats, 1939–1979* (1994).

Gerhard Wettig is Director of International Relations and International Security Studies at the Federal Institute of East European and International Studies, Cologne, Germany. His publications include *Broadcasting and Détente* (1977); *Das Vier-Mächte-Abkommen über Berlin in der Bewährunsprobe* (1981); *Diplomacy and Public Action in Soviet Foreign Policy* (1989); and *Changes in Soviet Policy Towards the West* (1981).

Victor Zaslavsky is Professor at the Memorial University, St John's, Canada. Among his recent publications are *From Union to Commonwealth* (with G. Lapidus) (1992); *The Neo-Stalinist State. Class, Ethnicity and Consensus in Soviet Society* (2nd edn, 1994); and *Storia del sistema sovietico. L'ascesa, la stabilità, il crollo* (1995).

Introduction

The end of the Cold War presents historians with a twofold opportunity. Firstly it makes it possible to take up a more detached attitude over the ideological and political disputes at issue – not least the question of who was to blame for the state of Cold War itself. We may justifiably hope that in the next few years historical contributions to understanding will emphasize the complexity of the questions regarding the origins of the Cold War, the mechanisms which kept it going, the costs it involved, and the influence it exerted. Secondly, the ending of the Cold War has led to the opening up of Soviet archives. Until recently, the Cold War has in fact been studied exclusively via Western sources – whereas now it is possible to examine what has always been the more secret and enigmatic side of things: Soviet foreign policy. These two opportunities will bear their full fruit only with time (always assuming, of course, that international politics play no tricks on us, and that the – still incomplete – opening-up of Soviet archives goes ahead according to plans). Nonetheless, the first results are already visible.

There has been much research and discussion over the role played by the USSR in the Cold War. Russian and Western historians have exchanged views, archival documents have been published, there has been considerable debate over crucial moments of the Cold War.[1] Collections of essays on the historical origins of the Cold War have devoted considerable space to the Soviet Union.[2] The reawakening of Russian historiography which got off the ground in the late 1980s has so far devoted far less attention to international politics than to home affairs: when Russian historians do get round to giving it more attention, we can certainly expect new stimuli. Even now, however, they have made decisive contributions in the re-examination of Soviet foreign policy – where the Cold War was not the only issue, but certainly had a central place.[3]

The present book is part of this series of research initiatives which are finally clarifying the USSR's part in the Cold War. The essays it contains discuss the relationship between the Soviet Union and Europe in the years between the last phase of the Second World War and the death of Stalin. This choice of limits requires a little explaining, perhaps especially regarding the geographical confines. But first let us say something about the chronology. As is well known, periodization of the Cold War has not raised long-standing controversy. The long post-war epoch has often been divided into sub-periods, but today there is broad consensus that the Cold War should be placed in the years between the end of the Second World War, or the immediate post-war years (1945–7), and the end of the Soviet Union, heralded by the fall of the Communist regimes in Eastern and Central Europe (1989–91). Agreement is almost as general that the classic phase of the Cold War ran from the Conferences of Yalta and Potsdam up until Stalin's death – although many historians also see 1947 as a turning point, with the launching of the Marshall Plan and the founding of the Cominform. It has also been suggested that in order to understand the origins properly, we need to go back further in time to the latter years of the war.[4] Different periodizations do not seem to be necessarily linked to particular interpretations of the origins or nature of the conflict. In any case, our decision to focus on the period 1943–53 does not necessarily indicate any particular definition of the Cold War. It simply means reexamining the classic period of the conflict – which is that which has been most intensely studied – in the light of the Soviet dimension.

With regard to politico-geographical area, we decided to exclude the superpower context on which most research in recent years has focused. This book concentrates on the European dimension, seen in its relationship with Soviet policy. The essays are thus part of the revival of interest in the European dimension of the Cold War.[5] Historians have sometimes seen Europe in a reductionist manner as just one among many strategic arenas of the conflict. However, the Cold War was ended in Europe, and this cannot but make us re-think its origins. The need to link up this trend in research with the Soviet dimension is the real justification for the present book. The contributors are scholars who have worked on Russian archive material from various points of view, but all focusing on connections between Europe and the Soviet Union in the post-war years, or who have worked on Western sources regarding the European dimension of the Cold War. With regard to methodology, political and diplomatic history inevitably dominates the scene in these first studies of the Soviet side of things, although other perspectives will need to be developed later – especially the connections between international history and domestic contexts.

The essays focus on three major topics: the Soviet Union and the post-war European order; the Cominform and the Soviet Bloc; the relations between the USSR and Western Europe. All of the main strategic areas of post-war Europe are covered by the book – with the aim of avoiding excessive concentration on the admittedly crucial area of Eastern Europe.[6] Particular attention is given to the German Question in all its aspects, since this goes to the heart of the Cold War in Europe. So the essays discuss Soviet post-war plans for Germany, Soviet attitudes over the issue of unity or division of Germany up until the last years of Stalin's rule, Soviet policies in the occupied zone, the USSR in the 1948–9 Berlin crisis (Filitov, Loth, Naimark, Narinskii, Wettig). The essays also tackle the themes of relations between the USSR and

Western Europe (Warner, Soutou, Varsori), including post-war peacemaking (Poggiolini), and with special reference to Italy as one of the crucial political theatres of the Cold War in Europe (Aga-Rossi and Zaslavsky, Smirnova, Valdevit, Nuti); Soviet policy towards the Scandinavian countries as a case study of Soviet planning for post-war Europe (Holtsmark); the peculiarities of the relationship between the USSR and Finland (Nevakivi); Soviet policy towards the Balkans, including the question of the Greek civil war (Nation, Ulunian); the analysis of Stalin's plans and the problem of how inevitable the Cold War was (Dallin, Taubman); the links between Soviet foreign policy, the Cominform and the formation of the Soviet Bloc in Eastern Europe (Prazmowska, Egorova, Dimitrov), including the problem of the conflict between the USSR and Yugoslavia (Gibianskii); Soviet reactions to the Marshall Plan and the creation of the Cominform, including its repercussions for the Western Communist parties (Di Biagio, Pons, Pirjevec). Essays dealing with the last two areas also complement the publication of the proceedings of the three conferences of the Cominform, which have recently come out in the *Annali* of Feltrinelli Foundation.[7]

It is not possible in this introduction to summarize the content of individual essays in this book – we will simply indicate the main concerns which the contributors have in common, and the main differences in approach. This seems appropriate especially if we bear in mind that research on the Soviet dimension of the Cold War does not have the benefit of the thirty years of studies which have honed studies of the American dimension to a fine pitch of sophistication in their analyses and their use of the sources. Research on relations between the USSR and Europe during the Cold War are in some ways at a pioneer stage. Nonetheless, it is legitimate to ask what stance the authors of this volume, Russians included, take up (explicitly or implicitly) towards the differing schools of American historiography on the Cold War – whether 'orthodox', 'revisionist' or 'post-revisionist'. It seems to us that the tendency is to opt for the first or third of these schools, which place more weight on the effects of Soviet policy. The 'orthodox' perspective in fact sees the prime cause of the Cold War as Soviet expansionism, especially in Europe; whereas the 'post-revisionists' focus on Soviet conduct in the framework of the security dilemma, paying attention to the way the USSR responded to American strategy in its attempt to maintain reciprocity. This same distinction between expansionism and security as different keys to understanding Soviet behaviour, also emerges in some of the first monographic studies to be published after the opening up of Soviet archives.[8]

It should be said at once that it would be misleading to classify the interpretations which have been made up till now as necessarily falling neatly into one of these two camps. As with recent historiography on the Cold War, the main tendency is not so much to take up one side or another, but rather an inclination towards more nuanced approaches. Many scholars share similar assumptions even when their viewpoints differ. This does not mean that any general consensus has emerged.[9] Even a label like 'post-revisionism' does not signify any unified perspective, since historians of this tendency have, in quite varied ways, focused on Soviet security strategies. If we can talk of two emblematic differing viewpoints, they would probably be those associated with (on the basis of American documentation) John L. Gaddis and Melvyn P. Leffler.[10] In other words, the issue which is still under debate is whether or not the prevailing unilateral tendency of Soviet security strategy allowed at least room for flexibility, and thus whether the West was justified in adopting a policy of containment, or whether it might not have been more appropriate to adopt a more reassuring policy. Tackling this issue directly on the basis of Soviet documents does not seem to resolve the question unambiguously in one way or the other.

However, direct study of the Soviet dimension does permit us to qualify the traditional controversies and render them more precise. What the essays do is to set a series of questions for historical research, recurrent questions which are now better defined in the light of substantial archive evidence. Firstly, let us consider Soviet policy towards the Western 'sphere'. We need to ask ourselves what meaning is to be attributed to the growing evidence of a relative restraint of the Soviet Union outside its sphere of influence, and of Stalin's caution in the management of crises in the years following the war (or at least of his tendency to take only calculated risks, and willingness to make U-turns, as far as Europe was concerned). Secondly, about Soviet policy towards Eastern Europe. The main issue probably remains: to what extent was Soviet policy already decided on before 1947–8? This must now be seen in the context of the knowledge that, from the years of the war on, the Soviet leadership definitely tended to view Eastern Europe as its own exclusive 'sphere of influence'. The question raised by Charles S. Maier therefore remains pertinent: if the Soviet tendency to dominate Eastern Europe is taken as given, need this necessarily have implied such a repressive and oppressive security zone model?[11] However, this question now needs to be asked in the light of our realization that Soviet strategy was more complex than had been imagined – and was not simply based on reacting to Western moves. The third point concerns the relationship between Soviet policy and the Communist movement. The closeness of the links between Moscow and the European Communist parties emerges clearly (even after the break-up of the Comintern); but this is not the sole point. For it is far less obvious to what extent Stalin thought the European Communist parties had an essential role to play in Soviet foreign policy in the post-war period. On examination of the documents, it turns out in fact that even the setting up of the Cominform does not resolve this question. In any case, different attitudes of the Soviet leadership emerge towards Communist policies in Western and in Eastern Europe.

Finally, what impact did Western actions and circumstances in Europe have on Soviet policy *vis-à-vis* the Cold War? This is a highly complex question, which can now be split up into consideration of a number of more specific areas – as is done in the essays in this book. On a few of these areas, major work has already been published since the opening of Soviet archives. This is true of Soviet occupation policy in Germany, and for the effects of this on the international conduct of the USSR.[12] Soviet assessments of atomic diplomacy and of its effects on the war of nerves in Europe have also been analyzed.[13] Alongside these issues, others are of course at the centre of discussion. In particular, there has been consideration of the Soviet perception of the outside world and Soviet leaders' feeling of being under threat as an element of continuity with the inter-war experience.[14] We are forced to ask ourselves how much the Soviet leadership was capable not only of being flexible in its conduct and strategy, but also how capable it was of reviewing its basic political culture, how able it was to avoid falling back into the pre-war mentality of the Security State, and the old isolationist instincts. One point of interest is the connection between this question and the issue of how reconcilable each side's perception of the other was with its counterpart.

Consideration of all these issues runs up against the limits of the documentation available. The basic problem is that we do not have documents allowing us to piece together adequately the decision-making process in the Soviet leadership. Many examples could be cited. With regard to the plans worked out during the war for the shape of post-war Europe, we know virtually nothing of the relationship (if any) between the strategic planning and political decision. The real intentions underlying Stalin's policy towards Germany remain uncertain, which is reflected in the very diverse positions taken up on this question by authors in this book. We have only limited understanding of essential aspects of what the Soviet leadership was aiming at when it set up the Cominform. In more general terms, with regard to the strategic thinking and the underlying concepts of Stalin's foreign policy, new evidence emerges with regard to the importance of a geostrategic perspective – giving prominence to power politics and to unilateral considerations of security – in the positions of Soviet policy-makers. This will perhaps add weight to the arguments put forward by supporters of a geopolitical interpretation of the Cold War. However, it does not resolve the specific question of the interaction in Soviet thinking between a geopolitical approach and an ideological vision of the capitalist world – not least, the influence exercised on policy by the doctrine that war was inevitable. Finally, it is particularly difficult to decide whether the hypotheses put forward by Western scholars regarding the presence of latent (or actual) conflicts among Soviet leaders over post-war foreign policy should be dismissed or not.[15] On this point, all scholars are very cautious, and among Russian scholars caution borders on scepticism. So we are still a long way from having a satisfactory panorama of the European foreign policy of Stalin's USSR, in the years when the Cold War was getting under way.

And yet we are closer to the objective than we were. The wider knowledge we now have sometimes just confirms previous hypotheses and suppositions; sometimes it is not sufficient to resolve the question we have. But it certainly helps us to formulate better questions. In any case our knowledge of Soviet views, plans and aims *vis-à-vis* post-war Europe has been enriched. If we can say that it has pushed discussion in any one direction, we might say that the paradigm of stabilization has been put to the test, and to some extent cast in doubt. The Cold War in Europe has sometimes been portrayed retrospectively in a way which makes it seem as though right from the end of the Second World War there was a tendency for stability to emerge, a stability which was to develop around the balance of deterrence and polarization into two political and military blocs.[16] This kind of view no longer appears acceptable, not even for Eastern Europe.

We now have a more definite picture of the extent to which the Soviet and the Western spheres developed in step with each other, and of the similarities and differences in the processes which led to their formation. The years between 1943 and 1947 were in many ways a shifting period of uncertainty and ambivalence, from the point of view of Soviet as well as of Western conduct. In several cases, the limits of Soviet ability to exercise influence on European affairs are in evidence. Soviet policy remained much more hemmed in by ideological rigidity than was American or British policy, formulated by decision-making groups which were far smaller, more closed and hierarchical. But this policy was not completely immobile, nor without diverse tendencies; nor was it completely immune to reactions in the countries occupied. This is not to challenge the difference between a hegemonic sphere which was constructed in large part 'by invitation', as the Western sphere was, and a sphere imposed by force. However, we can now see that Soviet foreign policy towards Europe – the context in which the Eastern Bloc was moulded – was not entirely pre-determined in all its features. The new evidence confirms, on the other hand, the decisive acceleration of a crystallization process in the Soviet sphere, at the same time as the same process was occurring in the West. In the USSR, this had its own predominant ideological features. In the years of late Stalinism, this crystallization led to the setting up in East-Central Europe of an extreme form of political uniformity, militarization and authoritarianism – which, in its turn, contributed to the lengthening of the Cold War in the wider sense of the politics of the long post-war period up till 1989. One final remark. It has been persuasively argued that the more we understand the origins of the Cold War, the more they seem to recede into the years of the Second World War.[17] We may safely say that study of the Soviet dimension reinforces this viewpoint. For this reason too, study of the Soviet side of things seems indispensable if we are to place the Cold War in the history of our century – whether we see the Cold War as marking the end of the period of European civil wars, or whether we see it as the last of such conflicts.[18]

Notes

1. The most important forum for recent studies and publications on the Cold War is without doubt the *Bulletin* of the Cold War International History Project (Woodrow Wilson International Centre for Scholars, Washington, D.C.). The CWIHP, in collaboration with the Institute of General History of the Russian Academy of Sciences and with the Storage Centre for Contemporary Documentation, organized the first conference on the Cold War based mainly on new materials from the Russian archives. This was held in Moscow, 12–15 January 1993. On the classic phase of the Cold War, see, in particular, the contribution to this conference by S.D. Parrish, M.M. Narinsky, 'New Evidence on the Soviet Rejection of the Marshall Plan, 1947: two Reports', CWIHP, Working Paper No. 9, March 1994. Several papers from the conference have been published in Russia as *Kholodnaia voina: novye podkhody, novye dokumenty* (Moscow: RAN, Institut Vseobshchei Istorii, 1995).
2. See D. Reynolds (ed.), *The Origins of the Cold War in Europe: International Perspectives* (New Haven: Yale U.P., 1994); M.P. Leffler, D.S. Painter (eds), *Origins of the Cold War. An International History* (London and New York: Routledge, 1994). See also M.J. Hogan (ed.), *The End of the Cold War. Its Meaning and Implications* (Cambridge: Cambridge U.P., 1992).
3. Apart from contributions by Russian scholars in *Kholodnaia voina*, see also *Sovetskaia vneshniaia politika v gody 'kholodnoi voiny' (1945–1985). Novoe prochtenie* (Moscow: Mezhdunarodnie otnosheniia, 1995). Also *Sovetskaia vneshniaia politika v retrospektive 1917–1991* (Moscow: Nauka, 1993); *Sojuzniki v vojne 1941–1945* (Moscow: Nauka, 1995). These last two collections of essays have also been published in English: G. Gorodetsky (ed.), *Soviet Foreign Policy, 1917–1991. A Retrospective* (London: Frank Cass, 1994); D. Reynolds, W.F. Kimball, A.O. Chubarian (eds), *Allies at War: the Soviet, American, and British Experience, 1939–1945* (New York: St. Martin's Press, 1994).
4. On Soviet policy, see, in particular, V. Mastny, *Russia's Road to the Cold War. Diplomacy, Warfare, and the Politics of Communism, 1941–1945* (New York: Columbia U.P., 1979).
5. See D. Reynolds, 'The European Dimension of the Cold War', in *Origins of the Cold War*, pp. 125–38.

6. On the specific theme of relations between the Soviet Union and the countries of Eastern Europe in the early years after the Second World War, see L. Gibianskii (ed.), *U istokov 'sotsialisticheskogo sodruzhestva': SSSR i vostochnoevropeiskie strany v 1994–1949 gg.* (Moscow: Nauka, 1995). On the general issue of the Soviet presence in Eastern Europe in the decades following the war, see O.H. Westad, S. Holtsmark, I.B. Neumann (eds), *The Soviet Union in Eastern Europe 1945–1989* (London: Macmillan, 1994).
7. See G. Procacci (ed.), G. Adibekov, A. Di Biagio, L. Gibianskii, F. Gori, S. Pons (co-eds), *The Cominform. Minutes of the Three Conferences 1947/1948/1949*, Fondazione Feltrinelli, *Annali*, XXX (Milan: Feltrinelli, 1994).
8. For two very different approaches in recent works on the USSR and the origins of the Cold War, the one centred on expansionism, the other on security as the major sources of Soviet conduct, see: R.C. Raack, *Stalin's Drive to the West 1938–1945. The Origins of the Cold War* (Stanford: Stanford U.P., 1995); C. Kennedy-Pipe, *Stalin's Cold War. Soviet Strategies in Europe, 1943–1956* (Manchester and New York: Manchester U.P., 1995).
9. See R. Crockatt, 'The Origins of the Cold War and the Problems of Synthesis: A Review of Recent Work', *Contemporary European History*, 4 (1995) 383–92; F. Romero, 'La guerra fredda nella recente storiografia americana. Definizioni e interpretazioni', *Italia contemporanea*, 200 (1995) 397–412.
10. J.L. Gaddis, *Strategies of Containment: A Critical Appraisal of Postwar American National Security Policy* (Oxford and New York: Oxford U.P., 1982); M.P. Leffler, *A Preponderance of Power. National Security, the Truman Administration, and the Cold War* (Stanford: Stanford U.P., 1992).
11. C.S. Maier, 'After the Cold War: Introduction to the 1991 Edition', in Id. (ed.), *The Cold War in Europe. Era of a Divided Continent* (New York: Markus Wiener, 1991) pp. 9–10.
12. N.M. Naimark, *The Russians in Germany. A History of the Soviet Zone of Occupation, 1945–1949* (Cambridge, Mass.: Harvard U.P., 1995).
13. D. Holloway, *Stalin and the Bomb. The Soviet Union and Atomic Energy 1939–1956* (New Haven and London: Yale U.P., 1994).
14. See M. McGwire, 'National Security and Soviet Foreign Policy', in *Origins of the Cold War*, pp. 53–76.
15. See W.O. McCagg, Jr., *Stalin Embattled, 1943–1948* (Detroit: Wayne State U.P., 1978); G.D. Ra'anan, *International Policy Formation in the USSR: Factional 'Debates' During the Zhdanovshchina* (Hamden: Archon Books, 1983).
16. See A.W. DePorte, *Europe Between the Superpowers. The Enduring Balance* (New Haven and London: Yale U.P., 1979).
17. See D. Reynolds, 'Beyond Bipolarity in Space and Time', in *The End of the Cold War*, pp. 245–56. A recent study on the perspective of the division of Europe is: L.C. Gardner, *Spheres of Influence. The Partition of Europe, from Munich to Yalta* (London: John Murray, 1993).
18. For these different viewpoints see respectively: C.S. Maier, 'I fondamenti politici del dopoguerra', in P. Anderson, M. Aymard, P. Bairoch, W. Barberis, C. Ginzburg (eds), *Storia d'Europa*, vol. I (Turin: Einaudi, 1993) pp. 311–72, and M. Walker, *The Cold War and the Making of the Modern World* (London: Vintage, 1994).

Part I

The Soviet Union and the Post-War European Order

1 Problems of Post-War Construction in Soviet Foreign Policy Conceptions during World War II
Aleksei M. Filitov

The question of how the Soviet leadership conceived of the post-war world is one of the most disputed and least investigated in historiography. In our country there prevailed for a long time a scheme according to which the USSR's war-aims were consistently democratic, were directed against interference in the internal affairs of other countries and peoples, and were opposed to the West's plans to divide the world into spheres of influence and partition Germany.[1] Western writers, on the other hand, wrote that the USSR planned 'the export of revolution', if not into the whole of Europe, at least into a considerable part of it, and accordingly its policy aimed at dividing Europe into hostile blocs.[2] Sometimes Soviet policy was seen as being guided by a mixture of motives and positions, with persons like Molotov and Dekanozov, viewed as exponents of a 'hard line', counterposed to the representatives of a soft line (with Litvinov alone named) who had less influence on the key decision-maker, Stalin.[3]

The logic of both treatments of Soviet policy, the 'ideological' and the 'non-ideological', led to the conclusion that the partition of Germany was something predetermined, inevitable. Only very recently has the idea appeared in Western historiography that a possibility did exist for a non-confrontational, compromise solution of the German question, on the basis of preserving the unity of the German state. I have in mind primarily the monograph by the West German historian Wilfried Loth, *Stalins ungeliebtes Kind*, in which the author shows, convincingly it seems to me, that, for the Soviet leadership, the creation of the GDR was not the optimal, preferred way to solve the German question, that it reverted to this only after all alternatives had been eliminated.[4] Agreeing with this book's basic thesis does not, however, mean that there is nothing in it to be criticized.

With the collapse of the myths of the 'Cold War' period a temptation naturally arises to replace the previous black-and-white appraisals with others that are diametrically opposite, but just as black-and-white. Loth appears not to have escaped that temptation. Stalin's ideas about Germany appear in his book as too static, too rectilinear, monolithic and free from contradictions. To some extent this was dictated by the sources he used. His basic source was Pieck's notes on his conversations with Stalin. Yet Stalin distrusted not only enemies but also 'friends' (as foreign Communists were called in Soviet parlance) and it is hard to say with whom he was more insincere. One cannot, of course, discover what the Soviet ideas on post-war construction really were without examining the materials of those departments of the Soviet foreign-policy apparatus which were specially set up to work out these ideas.

There were three such departments: the Commission of Questions of the Peace Treaties and Post-War Construction ('the Litvinov Commission'), the Commission on Armistice Problems ('the Voroshilov Commission'), and the Commission on compensation for the losses inflicted on the Soviet Union by Hitlerite Germany and its Allies ('the Maisky Commission', sometimes known for short as 'the Reparations Commission'). They were formally 'under the People's Commissariat of Foreign Affairs' but were actually broader, extra-departmental in character – for example, the Maisky Commission was made up not only of I.M. Maisky and G.P. Arkad'ev, from the Foreign Commissariat, but also of representatives of the State Planning Commission (first V.V. Kuznetsov, then M.Z. Saburov and N.M. Siluianov), of the Foreign Trade Commissariat (E.I. Babarin) and of the Academy of Sciences (E.S. Varga). The Litvinov Commission was more homogeneous: apart from Academician E.V. Tarle and D.M. Manuilsky, all of its members were officials of the Foreign Affairs Commissariat (G.Ia. Surits, S.A. Lozovsky, B.E. Shtein and G.F. Saksin, who was later replaced by M.M. Iudin). The Armistice Commission consisted mostly of military men.[5] The Litvinov and Voroshilov Commissions were formed in September 1943, the Maisky Commission later.[6]

It is interesting that, at first, Litvinov (to whom, of course, after his stay in the USA in the summer of 1943, was assigned the task of presenting preliminary proposals for the organization of preparatory measures for the post-war settlement) had in view a quite different pattern of organization. He wanted a Committee of 'authoritative representatives of the Government and the Party' (he named Molotov, Zhdanov, Mikoian, Shvernik and Vasilevsky) who were to act as 'the overall leadership, to consider the fundamental questions of principle, the most important proposals and aspects', and four Commissions – a *political* one (mandate: 'the territorial status and state structure of the conquered and occupied countries, the principles and organizational forms of international co-operation'), and a *military* one, one for *establishing the state frontiers of the USSR*, and one for *economic and legal questions*. Litvinov was ready to act as deputy head of the first of these commissions, which he proposed should be headed by A.Ia. Vyshinsky.[7]

This scheme was not adopted. Also rejected were the recommendations which he made after the three-commissions scheme had been adopted: for closer co-ordination of their work (to this end he proposed that Maisky be deputy head of his, Litvinov's, commission, while he himself would serve on the other two) and on the priorities of this work (he had in mind the urgent need to prepare a memorandum on the Baltic States, so as to secure, as quickly as possible, recognition under international law that they belonged to the USSR). The composition of his commission that he proposed was changed slightly, the German specialist Professor A.S. Erusalimsky being replaced by two old Comintern functionaries, Lozovsky and Manuilsky.[8]

The impressive list of 'questions the Commission has to deal with' which Litvinov presented soon after was, apparently, approved, though it could hardly be regarded as a working document in the sense of a concrete programme of action. Mingled in it were major and minor questions, real problems and hypothetical ones (for instance, the Cyprus question was to be examined 'in case of some straining of relations between Britain and ourselves', and the reason why the section on Italy included a sub-section 'Sicily' was that Litvinov did not consider excluded 'an attempt by Britain to separate Sicily from Italy'). Finally, neither in the text itself nor in the extensive commentary on it was anything said about the order in which the matters set out were to be considered.[9]

Not until the session of 7 November 1943 was an attempt made to decide priorities in the work. Of the eight subjects, three concerned Germany and there was one each for France, Finland and Sweden. Extremely short periods of time were assigned for the necessary work on them – between ten days and a fortnight. These deadlines were not, of course, met.[10] The first memorandum, 'The treatment of Germany', was not ready until 9 March 1944. It was discussed at a plenum of the Commission on 14 March, and on 16 March the memorandum and the minutes of the discussion were sent to Molotov. The second memorandum, 'The treatment of France', was sent on 25 March, to be followed by a series of others.

After this a certain stagnation set in where the Commission's work was concerned. Litvinov gave the reason for this in a letter to Molotov on 31 March 1944: 'Owing to my isolation from current diplomatic negotiations and even from the work of the European Advisory Commission which is discussing matters that fall within the competence of my commission, I find it difficult to plan the further priority of these questions and will await the appropriate instructions from you.'[11]

In his concluding report on the work of the Commission Litvinov observed, not without bitterness, that 'the programme for the Commission which was planned and approved by the CC had been fulfilled almost completely. If I say "almost", this is only because some of the questions included in the programme either fell into the competence of the other commissions or turned out not be of topical concern, i.e. they would not be on the agenda of any expected or likely international conferences.'[12]

A certain 'academic' character of the work of the Litvinov Commission was reflected not only in the slowness with which it prepared materials and the extraordinary dispersion in its selection of these for study and the proffering of advice. The present writer has been able to see only a few of this Commission's documents, but even the most analytically rich of them (such as 'The treatment of Germany', 'The treatment of France' and, especially, 'The prospects and possible basis for Soviet–British co-operation', dated 15 November 1944) are somewhat disappointing. In each, the largest part consists of the historical survey, to which are added materials from the Western press: the conclusions often consist of an extrapolation of the past into the present or the opinions of a single Western observer on the entire policy of his country. This is connected with the Commission's method of work. I shall come back to the results of that work, but first turn to the work of the Maisky Commission, the materials of which I have been able to see.

It seems that the work of this commission, even before it was formally constructed, proceeded more efficiently and purposefully, and produced results sooner. On 10 November 1943, 'The basic outline of a plan of work' was ready, containing not only a list of subjects for study but also a finished conception for the solution of the reparations problem.[13] Subsequent memoranda developed this conception consistently and with persistence. Its fundamental principle was formulated quite unambiguously: 'To take from Germany and its allies everything that can be taken,' with the qualification 'allowing for the "famine minimum".'[14] The maximum value of the equipment, goods and services to be secured was 75 milliard dollars, 80 per cent of this to be got directly from Germany. In negotiations with the Allies the Soviet Union had to insist that its share of this amount must be 50–80 per cent. How the proportion between different forms of reparation was conceived we can judge from one of the calculations of reparation claims to be presented to Germany. It was proposed that 17 milliard dollars be obtained by a one-off deduction from Germany's national wealth, 6 milliard by procurements from current production over a period of ten years, and 35–40 milliard by employing the labour of German workers and specialists in the USSR, also over a period of ten years. The average 'net product' of one German 'labour-unit' was calculated to be 750 dollars a year, from which it was deduced that the annual quota of German workers to be sent to the USSR was 5 million, or about a third of the total workforce in pre-war Germany.[15]

With praiseworthy frankness Maisky wrote in his very first memorandum:

> Their work must be conceived as compulsory service: Germany and its satellites must give the USSR a definite quantity of labour units of particular skills (including the highest) which, in the form of something like labour armies, will carry out tasks assigned to them under the command of the NKVD.[16]

Maisky was not only the author of this scheme for a 'super-Gulag'. It was over his signature that was sent to Molotov, as early as 11 January 1944, the very first and most detailed document setting out Soviet war aims, an exposition that was not at all for propaganda purposes, being intended for the eyes of the 'initiated'.[17] It is worth dwelling on its contents because it was the first such document, because it was detailed, and also because it frees us to a considerable extent from the need to reproduce and comment on the materials of the 'Litvinov Commission'. The latter merely developed (with some elaborations and additions about which we shall speak) the propositions of Maisky's memorandum of 11 January 1944.

In the introductory section of the memorandum the fundamental aim in the post-war period was defined as 'to create a situation which will guarantee for a long period the security of the USSR and the maintenance of peace, at least in Europe and Asia.' The concept 'a long period' was explained as meaning 'a period long enough for (a) the USSR to become sufficiently strong to fear no aggression in Europe and Asia, and so that no power or combination of powers in Europe and Asia could even think of such aggression, and for (b) Europe, or at least continental Europe, to become socialist, thereby excluding the possibility of wars occurring in this part of the world.'

From what follows we can conclude that the period indicated in (a) would be completed in ten years while that in (b) would take between 30 and 50 years.

The second section sets out the primary conditions for realizing this fundamental aim: 'It is above all necessary that the USSR should emerge from the war with favourable strategic frontiers.' Concretely, this meant the frontiers of 1941 with the following 'amendments':

> (a) the Petsamo area must be brought within the USSR; (b) South Sakhalin must be returned to the USSR; (c) the Kurile island chain, which cuts the USSR off from the Pacific Ocean, must be ours ...; (d) in whatever circumstances (even if our frontiers with Poland and Romania are modified) we must have a common frontier with Czechoslovakia; (e) between the USSR, on the one hand, and Finland and Romania, on the other, long-term pacts of mutual

assistance must be concluded, with granting to the USSR, on the territory of these countries, of the necessary bases – military, naval and air-force; (f) the USSR must be guaranteed free and convenient use of transit routes across Iran and the Persian Gulf ...

In the next section ('Germany') it was noted that 'the question of Germany's future is, of course, fundamental for our interests.' To solve this question were proposed: 'occupation of strategic points for not less than ten years'; 'breaking Germany up into a number of more or less independent state formations'; disarmament – 'military, industrial and ideological'; reparations (here the role of 'reparations in labour' was re-emphasized); severe punishment of war criminals, including 'not only persons who committed crimes on the battlefield or in occupied areas but also the members of the SS, the SA, the Nazi Party apparatus and wide circles of the military, naval and air-force leaderships.'

In the section on 'The rest of Europe' the main thesis is: 'What would be most to our advantage would be that in post-war Europe there should be only one strong land power, the USSR, and only one strong sea power, Britain.' Proceeding from this, France (dealt with in the next section) should not be allowed to reappear as a great power, especially as, according to Maisky, that country was incapable of playing such a role unless 'the course of events leads to a real proletarian revolution.' About Italy it is said (in the following section) that it

> was never and will never be a serious threat to the peace of Europe. A long time after the war will be needed to heal the wounds it suffered during the war. Nevertheless, Italy must be made to understand that the Allies, and the USSR in particular, have not forgotten its role in this war. Concretely, while Italy must be guaranteed its possessions in Europe, including Sicily and Sardinia but excluding all of its previous possessions in the Balkans, its African possessions must be completely liquidated. The USSR need not play an active role here: it will be enough to prevent Britain and the USA from disposing of Italy's African possessions at their exclusive discretion.

About Spain and Portugal:

> Negrin [the former head of the government of Republican Spain– A.F.] told me more than once in London that he would be ready to sign a pact of mutual assistance and military alliance with the USSR. How practically expedient it would be to conclude such an agreement with Spain is open to question.

About Poland:

> The USSR's aim must be to create an independent and viable Poland, but we are not interested in creating a Poland too large and

too strong. In the past Poland was always Russia's enemy: will the future Poland be a true friend of the USSR? ... No-one can answer for certain ... [We must] very carefully shape post-war Poland within frontiers as narrow as possible, strictly observing the principle of ethnicity. [In the East] the 1941 frontier or something like it (for example, the Curzon Line, though L'vov and Vil'na must remain within the USSR). In the West the whole of East Prussia can be included in Poland (or, perhaps, the greater part of it), plus a part of Silesia, but with resettlement elsewhere of the German inhabitants.

Czechoslovakia 'can be an important transmitter of our influence in Central and South-Eastern Europe'.

About Hungary: 'the USSR is not interested in creating a strong Hungary. For the first few years after the war, at least, it must be kept in a state of international isolation ...'

The Balkans: (a) Romania (repetition of the idea of a pact with the USSR–A.F.): (b) Yugoslavia: 'will probably want to conclude a long-term pact of mutual assistance with the USSR. The USSR should accede to this wish by the democratic forces of Yugoslavia ...': (c) 'In Bulgaria, too, after the liquidation of the present ruling circles, which will become inevitable at the end of the war, a powerful tendency will arise in favour of concluding a pact of mutual assistance with the USSR. We should agree to this ...': (d) 'The problem with Greece is somewhat more complicated. The USSR is much less interested in Greece than in the other Balkan countries, while Britain, on the contrary, is extremely interested ... If a democratic Greece, following the example of the other Balkan countries, should also want to conclude a pact of mutual assistance with the USSR, we should have no grounds for discouraging that. However, if the conclusion of such a bilateral Greco–Soviet pact were to give rise to complications with Britain, we might try to solve the problem by way of concluding a three-sided pact of mutual assistance between Britain, Greece and the USSR (as in the case of Iran).'

It was proposed that Greece be given the Dodecanese, while Bulgaria should receive an outlet to the Aegean Sea at Dedeagach. 'Bulgarian possession of Dedeagach might be in the USSR's interest in the event of the conclusion of a Soviet–Bulgarian Pact ...'

As a compromise, in case of opposition from Britain, the principle of 'triple' pacts could be extended to all the Balkan countries, except Romania. 'A three-sided pact with Yugoslavia or Bulgaria would in practice signify strengthening Soviet influence in those countries.'

Scandinavia, Holland, Belgium: It may be that Denmark will demand its pre-1864 frontier [with Germany]. There is no reason for us to object ... Iceland, of course, will not want to return to Danish rule. In

fact, it will probably become something like a dominion of the USA.'
In Maisky's view, the interests of the USSR in Northern Europe were
confined to ensuring 'that no sort of Scandinavian federation is formed
after the war'.

... It is not out of the question that, after the war, Britain (and also, possibly, the USA) will want to have bases on the Atlantic coast of Norway. Such intentions by the Anglo-Americans would probably meet with support from Norwegian ruling circles (this conclusion can be drawn from some talks I had in London with the Norwegian leader Trygve Lie). From the USSR's point of view it would be desirable to prevent such an agreement. Should this prove impossible, however, the following variant is conceivable: bases on Norway's Atlantic coast to be granted not only to Britain and the USA but also to the USSR ...

It is highly likely that Britain will want to have bases (military, naval and air-force) in Belgium and Holland, and also pacts of mutual assistance with these countries. The USSR would have no reason to object ...

Turkey: we must 'utilize all available means to weaken Turkey's position as "sentinel" on the Straits ...'

Iraq, Arabia, Syria, Lebanon, Palestine, Egypt: these countries, for Maisky, were of interest from the standpoint of ensuring the USSR's outlet to the Mediterranean Sea, 'avoiding Turkey and the Straits'.

Japan:

The USSR is not interested in engaging in war with Japan, but it is very much interested in the military defeat of Japan ... From the USSR's point of view it would be much more advantageous to leave the 'honour' of defeating Japan to the British and Americans. That would spare us losses in men and materials, while, instead, the USA and Britain would be forced to squander some of their human and material resources. Thereby the USA's imperialist ardour in the post-war epoch would be somewhat dampened ... This would also be our revenge for the Anglo-Americans' position on the second-front question ...

On the future state structure of the enemy countries and those now occupied by the enemy.

The USSR is interested in seeing to it that the state structure of these countries shall be based on principles of broad democracy, in the spirit of the people's-front idea. There are grounds for supposing that in such countries as Norway, Denmark, Holland, Belgium, France and Czechoslovakia these principles will be adequately realized without any pressure from without. The situation is different with such countries as Germany, Italy, Japan, Hungary, Romania, Finland, Bulgaria, Poland, Yugoslavia, Greece and Albania. There it may be necessary in order to secure the establishment of democratic regimes, to apply various measures of intervention from outside, by the USSR, the USA and Britain. One must not shrink from these 'interferences in internal affairs' ... because democracy in countries' state structures is one of the essential safeguards for lasting peace ...

An extremely important role will be played here by the position to be adopted by the USA and Britain. Hitherto the USA has taken a retrograde position on the future structures of the European countries. Very influential elements in the State Department and outside it (especially the American Catholics) dreamt of creating a conservative-clerical bloc in Europe ... At the present time, as is shown by the establishment of the Consultative Council on Italian questions, Washington seems to be inclined to orient its European policy on more democratic elements.

As for Britain, it has from the outset manoeuvred on these questions more flexibly and cunningly than the USA. Eden told me more than once that he envisioned creating in the countries of post-war Europe 'national front' governments which should include all the major progressive parties in each state. He appreciated that to wager on the reactionary elements would be a bad and quite unrealistic policy. The British, knowing Europe better and having more political experience, have made substantially fewer mistakes than their allies in European affairs. The main thing is that they have known how to take account of facts, regardless of whether they like them or not (Yugoslavia) ...

There are grounds for thinking that, where democratization of the regime in post-war Europe is concerned, it will be possible for the USSR, the USA and Britain to co-operate, though this will not always be easy.

The idea of counterposing Britain to the USA, put forward in this section, becomes more definite in the concluding section of the memorandum ('Prospects'). Proceeding from the premises that the USA represents 'dynamic imperialism' whereas Britain represents the 'conservative' variety, Maisky concludes that the latter will function as a factor of 'stability and order' in the post-war world. The chief threat to peace and tranquillity, he gives his readers to understand, can result from premature revolution:

> If the initial post-war period leads to the unleashing of proletarian revolutions in Europe, relations between the USSR, on the one hand, and the USA and Britain, on the other, are bound to become tense and even acute. If, however, no proletarian revolution takes place in

the immediate future in Europe there are no grounds for expecting that these relations will be bad.

Furthermore, Maisky thinks quite probable the prospect of an Anglo-Soviet coming-together *against* the USA.

The logic of things must press Britain closer to the USSR, because its fundamental struggle in the post-war period will be against the USA... I am also inclined to think that in this period, it will be to the USSR's interest to keep Britain as a strong power: in particular, it will be interested in Britain's retention of a strong navy, for such a Britain can be needed by us to counterbalance the USA's imperialist expansion (Britain will never be a strong power on land, it lacks the traditions, customs, inclinations and needs). And although it is not likely that we can expect any specially unpleasant surprises from Washington in the immediate post-war years, we cannot rule them out for the more distant future.

Among Maisky's alarming 'scenarios' for future Soviet-American relations was loss ('in the more distant future') of the invulnerability of USSR territory from American aircraft and the possibility of a bloc of the USA with defeated Germany and Japan, with France and even with China.

In conclusion Maisky sets out the following 'line for a possible and desirable foreign policy for the USSR in the post-war period':

strengthening friendly relations with the USA and Britain; utilizing the Anglo-American antagonisms in Soviet interests, with the prospect of ever-closer contact with Britain; increasing by every means Soviet influence in China; transformation of the USSR into a centre of attraction for all genuinely democratic middle-sized and small countries, especially in Europe; maintenance of the international helplessness of Germany and Japan until when and if these countries show more sincere strivings to take the path of real democracy and socialism.

To turn now to the work of the 'Litvinov Commission'. As mentioned above, it was clearly influenced by the conceptions set out in Maisky's memorandum: One cannot, of course, say for certain that Litvinov knew what this contained, but the fact is that the memoranda on Germany and France prepared in his Commission differ only in their greater detail from the Maisky document (in relation to Germany, a plan to divide Germany into seven or eight states; in relation to France, a survey of the history of relations between that country and Russia/USSR from which it emerges that France was almost always the latter's main enemy).[18]

Deserving of more detailed examination is the Commission's memorandum of 15 November 'On the prospects and possible basis for

Soviet-British co-operation'.[19] In this, Litvinov, proceeding from the same ideas as Maisky's – the Anglo-American antagonisms as the basic feature of the post-war world and the resultant opportunities for Soviet-British co-operation – sets out a plan for ensuring security in Europe which was the first and perhaps the only such plan produced during World War II. Litvinov writes:

> The sole important contradiction in Anglo-Soviet relations which the post-war epoch will inherit from the past may result from the idea of the balance of power in Europe. This contradiction may even become more acute owing to the increased strength of the USSR, which, after the defeat of Germany and the weakening of France and Italy, will be the only strong power on the Continent. But the very acuteness of this question may impel Britain to come to an understanding with us. Such an understanding could be achieved only on the basis of an amicable delimitation of security spheres in Europe, according to the principle of relative proximity. The maximum sphere of interest for the Soviet Union can be defined as Finland, Sweden, Poland, Hungary, Czechoslovakia, Romania, the Slav countries of the Balkans, and also Turkey. The British sphere can certainly embrace Holland, Belgium, France, Spain, Portugal and Greece.
>
> This delimitation will mean that Britain must undertake not to enter into specially close relations with, or make any agreements against our will with the countries in our sphere, and also not to have military, naval or air-force bases there. We can give the corresponding undertaking with regard to the British sphere, except for France, which must have the right to join an Anglo-Russian treaty directed against Germany. The third, neutral sphere will include Norway, Denmark, Germany, Austria and Italy, wherein both sides will co-operate on the same footing and with regular mutual consultation.

Litvinov foresees 'objections by Britain with regard to Norway, Yugoslavia and Turkey, which it will want to include in its own sphere, even though Norway and Turkey are geographically closer to the USSR than to Britain. Also, it may insist on guarantees concerning the internal regime and independence even of the countries in the Soviet sphere.' Nevertheless, Litvinov is optimistic. First, because leaving the USSR 'complete freedom of action' may seem to the British even more dangerous, especially in view of the worsening of their relations with the USA which is forecast and, secondly, because the USSR could promise them that it would not penetrate Afghanistan and Southern Iran and would 'agree to co-ordinate the actions of both sides in Afghanistan and Sinkiang'.

The first impression we get from these documents by Maisky and Litvinov is unambiguously negative. The Great-Power attitude shown in them sometimes goes so far as outright cynicism, and many of the appraisals and forecasts are superficial and groundless. This applies not only to particular cases – for example, the assumption that the *status quo ante* Franco will be restored in Spain or the alleged wish of the Belgians to be absorbed into France – but also to the more cardinal subjects on which their entire argument is based. Notably, the level of the Anglo-American antagonisms and the role these were to play in the post-war world is obviously exaggerated. Still, we ought to try to find something positive, some rational kernel, in these plans. And it is there.

In the first place, the documents are completely free from the idea of 'exporting revolution'. In Maisky's there is, to be sure, something like the idea of 'exporting democracy'. The documents divide countries quite artificially into those which can be democratized without external intervention and those which will require such intervention. Also open to criticism is the comparison between the British Government and the American as regards their negative attitudes to the idea of 'broad democracy in the spirit of the people's front'. The progressive Roosevelt might have been more of an ally in that context than the conservative Eden.

In any case, however, no claim is made here for the Soviets to have a monopoly in deciding what constitutes democracy and how to achieve it, and the idea that a democratic Europe – on the basis of the generally accepted interpretation of that concept! – would be the best guarantee of peace seems quite sound.

Not too much weight should be given to the expressions, scattered through Maisky's memorandum, of attachment to the prospect of socialist revolution. More important, in my view, is his plain hint that in the first years after the war such a revolution would complicate the international situation.

Litvinov's document lacks both the theme of revolution and that of democracy. So far as the latter is concerned, this is a defect. More on that later, but attention must first be paid to the highly *non-ideological* character of both documents.

In the second place, we must certainly see as positive that both Maisky and Litvinov, when defining particular political tasks, proceed from *state interests* and put *ensuring security* first among these interests. One can, of course, ask to what extent those interests required 'an outlet into the Mediterranean' or bases in Norway, but it is highly probable that such claims were conceived merely as maximum demands, withdrawal of which could be made conditional on getting concessions from the other side.

In the third place, the plan to build European security on the basis of a 'three spheres' idea was very promising. It was not the same as the conception of dividing Europe into opposed blocs. We see here, rather, a certain echo of the concept that lay behind the guarantee pacts of the 1920s – supplementing the 'Western Locarno' with an 'Eastern' equivalent – such as Barthou had in mind. The legitimacy and even usefulness of an 'Eastern security sphere' was acknowledged by many in the West in 1944 – from Walter Lippmann and anonymous leader-writers in the London *Times* (to whom Litvinov referred) to the future president of France, Vincent Auriol.[20] Comparatively new was the idea of a 'central belt', and there was nothing bad in that, either, rather the contrary – it would make Europe more stable.

Nevertheless Litvinov's plans, or, more precisely, the way in which it was proposed to put them into effect, had serious defects. Not just the extremely wide interpretation of the 'Soviet sphere' but also the circumstance that in only three of the countries to be included in it – Czechoslovakia, Yugoslavia and Bulgaria – was support to be expected for the conclusion of pacts of mutual assistance with the USSR (with Czechoslovakia a pact of this type existed already). Poland (and let us recall what was said about that country in Maisky's memorandum!) constituted a problem, and this was no less the case with Romania and Finland.

Ways of solving these problems were only implicit in Maisky's document, but in Litvinov's they were set out more clearly, though still somewhat veiled. They amounted to intervention in the internal political life of the USSR's neighbours, and this not so as to establish 'broad democracy' but in order to put into power those politicians who would be willing to orient themselves 'Eastward'.

Could it be expected that such a line of action would not lead to confrontation with the West? Litvinov, as we have seen, expressed concern that Britain 'may insist on guarantees regarding the internal regime and independence' of the countries to be included in the 'Soviet sphere'. But we have also seen that he thought it quite possible to neutralize that danger – first, by playing upon the Anglo-American contradictions, and second, by offering Britain generous bribes. Not only, moreover, on the plane of 'co-ordinating' actions in Iran, Afghanistan and Sinkiang but also in Europe. Litvinov's memorandum contains, for example, this argument:

> We may assume that, faced with the facts, Britain will be reconciled to a division of spheres of *influence* [my emphasis, A.F.] in the Balkans. After securing control of the Mediterranean coast of the Balkan Peninsula, i.e., including in its zone of influence Greece and, if possible, *Yugoslavia* [my emphasis, A.F.], Britain will probably not refuse to recognise a preponderant influence for the USSR in Romania and Bulgaria, but will merely endeavour to ensure that no-one gets control of the outlets from the Balkans into the Aegean and Adriatic Seas. With that aim it will, probably, oppose giving

Bulgaria an outlet on the Aegean and will try to include Albania in its sphere of influence, either directly or through annexing it to Greece.[21]

All the priorities and limits for possible 'trade' are indicated plainly enough here. Provided that Britain shuts its eyes to what the Soviet Union does in Romania and Bulgaria, it will be guaranteed retention of its monopolistic domination of the Mediterranean and may even receive a sizeable chunk of what had been marked down for the 'Soviet zone' (Yugoslavia, and Albania as well!).

Leaving aside the moral aspect, were these calculations well-founded and realistic? In the first place, the line of establishing 'spheres of influence' through deals and through coercion of nations if they did not agree to occupy the places 'assigned' to them plainly ran counter to the idea of democratizing Europe as the chief way of ensuring its security, and essentially turned that idea into empty propaganda. In the second place, it ignored the role of the USA – there were no grounds for that state to sanction such deals. In the third place it overlooked the simple consideration that although Britain, for the sake of strengthening its position, might *temporarily* agree to some sort of 'delimitation', *subsequently* it might refuse to conform to this and so confrontation would merely have been postponed.

There was also a profound contradiction inherent in Litvinov's plan. This concerned the German question. Was it possible to ensure German neutrality by transforming that country into an economic and political vacuum? If a conflict should arise between the Allies it would be enough for one side to raise the slogan of unity and economic restoration for Germany and the Germans would at once rally to that side in the conflict, which would then become irreversible. And how could the German people be democratized if they were to be subjected to such coercion?

Perhaps the supporters of the 'punitive approach' to Germany were confident that there would be no conflict with the Western Allies and so they could 'crush' the Germans with impunity? Not at all. In the papers of the 'Litvinov Commission' there are the minutes of the session at which they discussed the information-note 'On the treatment of Germany' (14 March 1944). One of those who spoke, B.E. Shtein, recalled that not only Bismarck but also Marx was for the unity of Germany, and said that the Germans would not reconcile themselves to dismemberment. In reply Litvinov admitted that he, too, was worried by that possibility. Disarmament and control – stricter than in the post-Versailles period – might constitute an adequate safeguard against revival of militarism and *revanchisme*, but these measures presupposed continued unity between the victor powers, and since one could not count on that, there was no alternative to dismemberment.[22]

It is difficult to understand Litvinov's logic here. Advocating the principle of dismemberment could have some sense given two conditions, or with one, at least, of them present: if this idea was popular among the Germans themselves and if there was an absolute consensus for it in the West (or if it was considered there to be less questionable than disarmament and control). But precisely those conditions were lacking! As regards the attitude of the Germans themselves, Litvinov agreed with Shtein, and as regards the West's position there was plenty in Litvinov's materials and Maisky's as well as show that the West was far from sharing the concept of dismemberment. It was not difficult to forecast that, with any worsening of relations with the USSR, opposition to that concept would increase still further. It may be that Litvinov and Maisky had obtained their notion that the concept of dismemberment was accepted in Western ruling circles from their contacts as ambassadors with such individuals as Sumner Welles in the USA and Robert Vansittart in Britain, but they were already yesterday's men in politics.

As for the problems of combining a punitive approach to the Germans with the task of re-educating them, this does not appear to have concerned Litvinov particularly. An interesting though somewhat curious suggestion for solving it was put forward by Maisky. Arguing for the advantage of using German labour as the principal form of reparations he advanced this consideration: 'The Germans and others who have passed through the school of work in the USSR will, at least to some extent, return home with sounder views and attitudes, especially if we, on our part, adopt the appropriate measures as regards education and propaganda'.[23] Forced labour as a method for restoring health to German society – here was a truly remarkable recipe!

To what extent and in what way was the work of the Litvinov and Maisky commissions received by the highest Soviet leadership? Did they accept it or reject it? Did they pay any attention to it at all?

We can at least say definitely that, where the reparations problem was concerned, there was a very active 'dialogue' between 'customer' and 'supplier', though this was not always pleasant for the latter. As has been mentioned, the first memorandum on the reparations question was completed on 10 November 1943 and, only ten days later, Maisky, referring to a conversation he had had with Molotov, sent him a letter answering criticisms. Significantly, one of the points which evoked a critical reaction from the head of the Foreign Commissariat was that which related to forced labour. In his reply Maisky wrote:

> You say that I overemphasise labour as a form of reparations. Perhaps so. Yet it is still difficult to say what role labour will play in the total amount of reparations. The future will show. If, however, I

gave too big a place in my plan to the section on labour, that was mainly because this question is less indisputable than that concerning equipment [that is, about taking equipment from German enterprises as reparations].

While admitting the disputability of his thesis, Maisky nevertheless does not think of withdrawing it. He stipulates only one condition under which he might agree to revise it: 'The plan proposed by me is, of course, based on the assumption that the war will not lead to a real proletarian revolution in Germany. Should such a revolution occur, the entire plan would fall.'[24]

Over a year later an episode occurred in which Maisky himself figured as critic, with the object of his criticism none other than... Stalin himself! In a communication addressed to Stalin personally, Maisky writes:

Comrade Dekanozov has passed to me today your instruction to compose a memorandum for submission to the European Advisory Commission in London on our demand for reparations to the value of five milliard dollars ... The figure of five milliard which you give seems to me too small ... The sum of five milliard will have little effect on Germany's war-potential and its economic disarmament, of which you speak in your address of 6 November [1944], will not be very effective.'[25]

Judging by the fact that at the Yalta conference the Soviet delegation put forward the figure 10 milliard dollars as the sum due to the USSR as reparations from Germany, this criticism succeeded. We can only guess at Stalin's motive in originally naming (according to Dekanozov) a sum half that size. When, at Yalta, the British objected to the USSR's plan for reparations, Stalin came out with: 'Churchill pities the Germans.'[26] The reproach was unfounded and, of course, no such feelings were to be suspected in Stalin's case. Nevertheless, he was capable of a certain flexibility, and even more so than Maisky.

Unfortunately I have not managed to find any traces of the reaction by the top leadership to Maisky's memorandum of 11 January 1944 (if there was any). As for the materials of the Litvinov Commission, the only signs of such reaction are notes (usually in blue pencil) in the margins and on the text of the documents sent 'up'. These are especially numerous in the concluding section of the memorandum of 15 November 1944, where Litvinov sets out his plan for 'three spheres' in Europe. This is understandable: not long before that date negotiations with Churchill had taken place in Moscow precisely in the spirit of 'division of spheres of influence', and the 'philosophical' basis for the corresponding political line, along with the problems that might arise and the possible ways of solving these could not fail to interest the top leadership.

It is difficult to say how the interaction between the planners and the decision-takers was arranged. Did the material in the memoranda influence the opinions of the latter, or did those who composed the memoranda adjust their content to the opinions already formed 'up above', which they either knew about or could guess? It would seem that the list of 'amendments' to the frontier of the USSR complied by Maisky did to a considerable extent determine the official Soviet position and was put into practice, but does this mean that Maisky was their original author? There is much here that we do not yet know. In any case there was *not* complete coincidence between the views of the planners – the Maisky and Litvinov commissions – and the political actions of practical diplomacy.

A question of principle on which there seems to have been considerable difference of opinion was: unity or partition for Germany? Some new facts that I have found show that, in its practical, everyday activity, Soviet diplomacy, including the leadership, proceeded on the basis of maintaining Germany as one state. True, there are documents that point the other way: Vyshinsky's letter supporting, in January 1945, Litvinov's recommendations of dismemberment,[27] and Gusev's letter of February 1945 asking for materials and experts to be sent for work in the European Advisory Commission on plans for dismemberment.[28] One gets the impression, however, that these were just hasty 'zigzags' which had no consequences, whereas the basic orientation was different.

Consider, for example, the important question of banknotes for the future occupied Germany, which figured largely in the work of Allied diplomats in January–April 1945. The Soviet position was unambiguous – one currency for all Germany. It was held not only by the Foreign Commissariat but also by the Finance Ministry, which was involved in the study of this question. A proposal for a separate monetary system for the Soviet occupation zone did make its appearance, but only as a means of bringing pressure to bear on the Americans, who at first were unwilling to supply the Soviets with the matrices for printing banknotes.[29] Incidentally, pressure worked in this case, and that may have engendered in the Soviet leadership fatal illusions as to the universal effectiveness of such a method in negotiations. Perhaps, in January–February 1945, the idea of dismemberment was being advanced as a sort of bogy in order to induce the West to make concessions on other matters.

In any case, in the correspondence of the operational department of the Foreign Commissariat responsible for Germany (III European) nothing was mentioned about splitting Germany up. On the contrary, when, for example, this department received from the European

Advisory Commission a query by the British representative Strang regarding the future German economy, the then head of the department, A.A. Smirnov, prepared this reply for Dekanozov, who supervised its work: 'In answering the question raised by the British it would be expedient to uphold the principle of regarding Germany as a single economic entity, regardless of the occupation-zones. This will strengthen our position on the question of control of German industry, which is largely concentrated in the Anglo-American zone.'[30]

The USSR Government's ideas on the post-war world and the European order were developed by way of a complicated and contradictory process. On the other hand, if we compare, say, Maisky's memorandum of January 1944 with Litvinov's of November 1944, it is not difficult to observe a shift of emphasis – from the idea of democratizing Europe to the idea of crude pressure on the peoples by the great powers (USSR and Britain) for the sake of forming 'spheres of influence'. In both cases the aim was to ensure peace and security, in both cases the calculations and arguments used were far from irreproachable, but in the second variant (division into spheres) the contradiction between aims and methods was more marked, so that one can speak of a certain regression.

On the other hand, it is in the second variant (Litvinov's) that first appears the conception of a 'neutral belt' in Europe, with the key idea of neutralizing Germany. It is difficult to account for the appearance of this idea in Litvinov's document: both his and Maisky's ideas on how to solve the German question were, to say the least, far from adequate.

We may suppose that the impetus for a more balanced approach to German affairs came from the group of Foreign Ministry officials who had to do the operational work on them, what was called 'the Smirnov–Semenov group'. It was this group that was distinguished by a high degree of pragmatism where the German question was concerned, pursuing a more or less consistent line for retaining German and Allied unity through compromise and co-operation.

In considering their work and proposals we must, of course, avoid idealization. Pragmatism had its reverse side: behind it lay no big general idea, no 'global approach', such as, undoubtedly, Maisky and Litvinov had. The 'pragmatists' obviously underestimated the extent to which Germany's machinery of state had been deformed by fascism, and overestimated the possibility of simply using or borrowing it for building the new Germany. Here was shown something like the conservatism which led Churchill to favour co-operation with Dönitz's Government (a deliberately exaggerated comparison, of course).

Finally, the most complicated question: what approach was chosen by the Soviet leaders, Stalin and Molotov, and also by Vyshinsky and Dekanozov (in so far as the last two supervised post-war planning for at least part of Germany)? For answer we may quote the old joke about the 'general line', that it is a curve which winds its way between two straight lines, the left and right 'deviations'. That really was the case. The Soviet leaders wavered, improvised, zigzagged in both aims and methods. The question of dismemberment was probably made much of by the Soviets in negotiations with their allies, not as an optimal or even real programme but merely as a bargaining weapon – sometimes as a weapon in blackmail. Bohlen was probably right in supposing that, at Yalta, Stalin merely wanted to 'attach' the Westerners to the idea of dismemberment, so as later to use this in his propaganda in the struggle not with Germany but for Germany. In any case it was not an element in Soviet policy but in Soviet diplomatic *tactics*, one that sometimes succeeded in the sense of getting short-term results, but in the longer view was more counter-productive.

Regarding the general tendency in the planning of policy we can say that, especially in the last phase of war, it favoured the less confrontational scenario. And as a general conclusion we can say that nobody planned the 'Cold War'.

Notes

1. Of the last works of the 'pre-*perestroika*' period, see: A.A. Roshin, *Poslevoennoe uregulirovanie v Europe* (Moscow: 1984); V.Ia. Sipols, *Na puti k velikoi pobede. Sovetskaia diplomatiia v gody 1941–1945gg.* (Moscow: 1985); V.L. Israelian, *Diplomatiia v gody voiny (1941–1945)* (Moscow: 1985), and also the article by the present writer included in the miscellany *Evropa XX veka: problemy mira i bezopasnosti* (Moscow: 1985) pp. 81–114.
2. An interesting discussion between advocates of these two variants, G. Kennan and G. Snell, took place at the beginning of the 1960s. The dispute has not been greatly enriched since then. See *The American Slavic and East-European Review* (April 1961) 284–94, and *Slavic Review* (October 1961) 551–2.
3. See, for example, V. Mastny, *Russia's Road to the Cold War* (New York: 1979).
4. See W. Loth, *Stalins ungeliebte Kind. Warum Moskau die DDR nicht wollte* (Berlin: 1994).
5. The first two commissions were mentioned for the first time in volume 5 of *Istoriia KPSS* (book 1, p. 549), published in 1970. For reasons unknown, nothing was said there about the Maisky Commission. Its title and composition are known to us from Maisky's memorandum to Molotov of 3 March 1944 (AVP RF, f. 06, op. 6, p. 16, d. 168, l. 26) and the decisions of the USSR Council of People's Commissars, 7 January 1944, No. 18 (*ibid.*, l. 9), which deals with changes in the Commission's composition.
6. On 14 November 1943 Maisky merely offered his proposals for the composition of the Commission. See AVP RF, f. 06, op. 6, p. 16, d. 166, l. 9–10.

7. AVP RF, f. 06, op. 6, p. 14, d. 149a, l. 25–9 (without date or signature).
8. Litvinov to Molotov, 3 August 1943, AVP RF, f. 06, op. 6, p. 14, d. 149, l. 1–2.
9. Litvinov to Stalin and Molotov, 9 September 1943, *ibid.*, l. 9–18.
10. Minutes No. 3, 17 November 1943, *ibid.*, l. 33–4.
11. Litvinov to Molotov, AVP RF, f. 06, op. 6, p. 14, d. 145, l. 43.
12. Litvinov to Molotov, 19 November 1945, AVP RF, f. 06, op. 6, p. 14, d. 149, l. 36.
13. Maisky to Molotov, 10 November 1943, AVP RF, f. 06, op. 6, p. 17, d. 169, l. 46–9.
14. Maisky to Molotov, 3 March 1944, AVP RF, f. 06, op. 6, p. 16, d. 168, l. 32.
15. Memorandum No. 1, 27 July 1944, AVP RF, f. 012, op. 5, p. 56, d. 42, l. 101–2, 124–30, 144–6; 'Po voprosy o reparaciiach s Ruminii', 29 August 1944, *ibid.*, l. 46; Maisky to Molotov, 16 October 1944, AVP RF, f. 06, op. 6, p. 17, d. 169, l. 11; Memorandum No. 3, 13 December 1944, *ibid.*, l. 54–5.
16. Maisky to Molotov, 10 November 1943, *ibid.*, l. 48.
17. Maisky to Molotov, AVP RF, f. 06, op. 6, p. 14, d. 145, l. 1–41.
18. 'Obraschenie s Germaniei', 9 March 1944, AVP RF, f. 06, op. 6, p. 14, d. 142, l. 3–110; 'Obraschenie s Francii', AVP RF, f. 06, op. 6, p. 14, d. 146, l. 3–30.
19. AVP RF, f. 06, op. 6, p. 14, d. 143, l. 31–9.
20. See Vincent Auriol's speech in the French National Assembly, in W. Lipgens (ed.), *Europa – Föderationspläne der Widerstandsbewegungen 1940–1945: Eine Dokumentation* (Munich: 1968) pp. 242–3.
21. 'O perspektivakh i vozmozhnoi baze sovetsko-britanskogo sotrudnichestva', AVP RF, f. 06, op. 6, p. 14, d. 143, l. 61.
22. Minutes No. 4, 14 March 1944, AVP RF, f. 06, op. 6, p. 14, d. 142, l. 117–18.
23. Maisky to Molotov, 10 November 1943, AVP RF, f. 06, op. 6, p. 17, d. 169, l. 48.
24. Maisky to Molotov, 14 November 1943, AVP RF, f. 06, op. 6, p. 16, d. 166, l. 12.
25. Maisky to Stalin, 19 December 1944, AVP RF, f. 06, op. 6, p. 17, d. 169, l. 73.
26. *Sovetskii Soiuz na mezhdunarodnykh konferentsiiakh perioda Velikoi Otechestvennoi voiny 1941–1945gg. Krymskaia konferentsiia rukovoditelei trekh soyuznykh derzhav–SSR, ShA i Velikobritanii, 4–11 fevralia 1945g.* (Moscow: 1984) p. 169.
27. Vyshinsky to Molotov, 12 January 1945, AVP RF, f. 07, op. 10, p. 16, d. 212, l. 1.
28. Gusev to Litvinov, Vyshinsky, Dekanozov and Molotov, 14 February 1945, AVP RF, f. 06, op. 7, p. 30, d. 416, l. 4–5.
29. AVP RF, f. 06, op. 6, p. 35, d. 425.
30. Smirnov to Dekanozov, 9 August 1944, AVP RF, f. 012, op. 5, p. 61, d. 101, l. 55.

2 Stalin's Plans for Post-War Germany
Wilfried Loth

All along, the aims of Soviet policy on Germany after World War II have been the focus of intense controversy. Did Stalin, drunk with success, believe that sooner or later he would be able to incorporate the whole of Germany in the Soviet sphere of influence? Did he concentrate from the very beginning on establishing a separate Socialist state on the territory of the Soviet zone of occupation? Or did he set his eyes on some kind of arrangement with a bourgeois German nation state? All three views have been put forward.[1] In addition, other interpretations have been developed which assume that different conceptions interplay. Boris Meissner, for example, speaks of a competition between different schools of thinking,[2] while Hans-Peter Schwarz argues that opportunities to extend Soviet influence were taken up opportunistically whenever they presented themselves.[3] However, none of these interpretations could ever be entirely convincing, not least because of the notorious lack of information on Soviet planning. Remarks regarding this matter, which were directly attributable to Stalin, were too rare, were too uncertain in their tradition, and were too unclear in their respective context.

In this matter the notes made by Wilhelm Pieck about his talks with Stalin and the heads of the Soviet Military Administration in Germany[4] allow a qualitative breakthrough. Even though they recapitulate the course of the talks between the Soviet Occupying Authority and the top officials of the SED only fragmentarily and unevenly, they nevertheless cover a period of nearly eight continuous years. Due to their fragmentary character they cannot be easily decoded. Reading the notes in their context, however, and then adding all of the other sources which have now become available for the first time, allows a satisfactory picture of Soviet policy towards Germany to emerge – a picture based on a multitude of sources which is convincing because of its consistency.

For 130 discussions during eight years, Pieck's notes show the same tendency. They are further corroborated by other sources which have been passed on independently. This excludes the possibility that they reflect anything but the actual remarks made by Stalin and his representatives in their talks with the leaders of the German Communists. On this wider source basis it is now possible to show that Stalin really pursued the democratization of Germany under the auspices of the four powers and that he only ended up with a separate Socialist state as a result of the incompetence of the Communists to play the democratic game. While this view has been argued before,[5] it can now be substantiated much more thoroughly and specified further with regard to important details.[6]

I

First of all, the preservation of the unity of occupied Germany was a declared aim of Soviet policy. Indeed, Stalin saw the danger of a division between East and West. 'Perspective – there will be two Germanys, despite all the unity of the Allies,' noted Pieck at the first meeting of the KPD leaders with comrade Secretary General after the end of the war on 4 June 1945 in Moscow. But Stalin always ordered his comrades to oppose such a development. 'Plan to dismember Germany existed with the English-Americans,' notes Pieck at this same meeting. 'Division into Northern and Southern Germany / Rhineland-Bavaria with Austria / Stalin was against it.' Immediately following in the text, measures are ordered which were to avert the East–West division which was seen as a danger: 'Secure Germany's unity through unified KPD / unified Central Committee / unified party of the working people / in the centre unified party.'[7]

When Walter Ulbricht visited Stalin again at the end of January 1946, the aim of German unity was once more made aware to him, this time in connection with French demands for cessions of German territory: 'Germany cannot survive without the Ruhr district / consent not given that ceding, though already demanded by French / unity is right.'[8] One year later, Stalin confirmed this during a talk with Pieck, Ulbricht, Grotewohl, and others: 'Position SED in favour of Germany's unity is right.' He then developed balance of power model within which Germany's resurrection appears as a condition for securing world peace: division would mean weakness, and this would lead to an 'undivided control' of the world market 'by America'. The result would be exploitation by American imperialism, new revanchism of suppressed Germans and a new war.[9]

According to Stalin this united Germany would – at least initially – not be a Socialist or even a Soviet-Communist-type Germany. This is probably the most surprising and most provoking conclusion which can be deduced from Pieck's notes. During a talk with Stalin at the beginning of June 1945 Pieck notes down under the category 'character of anti-Fascist struggle': 'Completion of bourgeois-democratic revolution /

bourgeois-democratic government / overcome the power of landed aristocracy [*Rittergutsbesitzer*] / eliminate the remains of feudalism.'[10] This statement corroborates evidence given by Wolfgang Leonhard. The KPD cadres were told in their exile in Moscow in March and April 1945:

> The political purpose is not to realize Socialism in Germany or to cause a Socialist evolution. On the contrary, this must be condemned and fought as a detrimental tendency. Germany is about a bourgeois-democratic rearrangement which will be a completion of the 1848 bourgeois-democratic revolution according to its content and its nature. What matters is to speak up actively for its completion, but to resist any Socialist mottos, since they would be purest demagogy under present conditions; under these circumstances the idea of Socialism would only be discredited.[11]

During the ideological courses in Moscow particular emphasis was put on the preparation for a possible confrontation with comrades in Germany 'who now wish to establish Socialism'. Responsibility for the 'bourgeois-democratic transformation', it was said, lay with the allied powers:

> The occupation powers were coming to Germany to extinguish Fascism and militarism and to take the necessary measures for a democratic rebirth of the German people. The exact measures of the occupation powers were not yet known in detail, but it could be assumed with certainty that apart from the trial of war criminals, measures against monopolism, a land reform and a reform of the school system were planned. It would be important to cooperate actively in these reforms and to insure their consistent implementation, exactly following any instructions by the Allies.[12]

Pieck's notes verify the fact that this conception of March and April 1945 was still in force after the end of the war. Therefore, the corresponding passages of the well-known appeal of the KPD of 11 June 1945 were not simply the expression of a crude confidence game like they always have been interpreted in the West. Indeed, they conveyed the thoughts of the leadership in Moscow. 'Setting up of an anti-Fascist democratic regime, of a democratic parliamentary republic'[13] indeed meant a Western-type democracy and by no means what was later extolled as 'people's democracy'. It would be inept to assume that Stalin actually had something in mind which was entirely different from the views which, according to all sources, he continuously expressed in talking to the German Communist leaders as well as to his closest advisers.[14] 'One has to tell the people the truth,' Ulbricht declared in Berlin on 12 June 1945 after his return from Moscow. 'It consists of the fact that anti-Fascist Germany is still a capitalist country.'[15]

At first glance, these findings do not accord with all we know about Stalin's imaginations and about the horrors of his dictatorship. But if one tries to put oneself in Stalin's position at the end of the war, it soon becomes clear that rationally he could not have a different programme for Germany after the outcome of the war. In view of the importance of capital and industry for Germany's expansionism – in fact and much more in Stalin's marxist interpretation of national Socialism – security against Germany was not to be gained without control of the industrial Western areas. This control could not be left exclusively to the Western powers: first, because they were unreliable by definition; and, second, because in Stalin's view – which in this case was influenced by Evgenii Varga – there was the threat of expansion of American capitalism into Europe. An alliance of (West) German capital with the expanding American imperialism was in fact the worst Stalin could imagine.

An additional motive to stick to a common allied policy towards Germany was the lasting interest in reparations from West Germany. The persisting insistence of Soviet diplomacy on this point, which can be recognized at all of the allied conferences in the post-war period, makes clear that when the extent of wartime destruction in the Soviet Union became obvious, the prospect of American help for reconstruction decreasing rapidly at the same time, the interest in reparations increased accordingly.

Socialism in Germany, in the given circumstances, was really *cura posterior*, a vague long-term goal, on which more detailed evidence could not be given in the present situation. The Soviet state and the Communist world movement would gain much if the German danger could only be eliminated and the American danger contained at the same time. For that one had to rely on co-operation with the 'eastern occupying powers'. Therefore, only such a programme for Germany could be developed which also could be accepted by the Western occupying powers – a programme to eliminate the authoritarian roots of national Socialism, an idea which was well received among the Western powers, too. Typically enough, nowhere in internal instructions and discussions was the transition to Socialism mentioned. 'Not Socialism is on the agenda, but democracy,' Ulbricht told the comrades of the Social Democratic (SPD) Central Committee at their first meeting on 15 June 1945.[16]

Socialism was not talked about until the winter of 1945–6 when a programme of the new 'united party' of Communists and Social Democrats had to be formulated. In this connection Stalin decided – again, surprisingly, not only for us, but also for the Communist Party's leadership at that time – on a 'democratic way' to Socialism which was to be fundamentally different from the Soviet way. 'Situation quite different,' he explained to Ulbricht in January 1946. 'In Russia shortest way / rule of working class ... / in the West parliamentary traditions /

on democratic way to workers' power / not dictatorship.' Stalin mentioned the following elements of the 'democratic way' (this term was emphasized by Pieck with underlining): 'Purge of apparatus of state, putting firms under the control of the local authorities, expropriation of big landowners'; behind that the term 'Socialism' is mentioned.[17]

At different times Stalin said the same in similar terms to other interlocutors. In April 1945, talking to Tito, he said: 'Today, Socialism is even possible under the English monarchy. A revolution is not necessary everywhere. A short while ago a delegation of British Labour people was over here, and we discussed this.'[18] In August 1946, when Labour already had been in power on its own for more than one year, Stalin, in talking to a delegation of Labour leaders, mentioned the possibility 'of Britain becoming a Socialist country without the stage of dictatorship of the proletariat, violent revolution and oppression of the bourgeois class'. Stalin expressed his belief that the Labour Party in Britain could reach at least the same or even a higher level of Socialist development by comparison with the Soviet Union once she had put her programme of nationalization of industry, transport, finance and so on into practice, following a Socialist foreign and domestic policy. 'It will naturally take longer. Also, a greater degree of patience with the capitalist class is needed, but nonetheless it is possible to establish Socialism with democratic-Socialist methods.'[19] This indicates that to relativize the Soviet way was not a programmatic ruse to tempt the Social Democrats on the way to a united party. It also indicates that it was not a spontaneous inspiration which Stalin soon would have had forgotten. Instead, he made an attempt to bring into accord realistic insights into the necessity of a bourgeois-parliamentary regime in Germany with the ideological certainty of future victory of Socialism.

In this respect, Stalin followed Varga who saw, in the weakening of the monopolistic bourgeoisie in the 'democracies of the new type' with a growing economic state quota, a strengthening of the proletariat and as a result the possibility of an evolutionary way to Socialism. After the election victory of the Labour Party in Britain and the formation of left-wing coalition governments in France, Italy and Belgium, the prominent Soviet economist concluded that the whole of Europe was on its way to Socialism. 'Today,' he wrote in 1947 in his observations on the 30th anniversary of the October Revolution,

> the struggle in Europe is being transformed more and more into a struggle for the pace and the forms of the transition from capitalism to Socialism. Even though, without doubt, the Soviet way, the Soviet system, is the best and fastest method of transition from capitalism to Socialism, historical development shows, as predicted by Lenin, that there are other ways to reach the same aim.[20]

There can be no question that Stalin could have had hopes of a clear way in the whole of Germany after a quick unilateral withdrawal of the American forces. In all the internal reports the presence of the Western powers in Germany appears as a permanent quantity. There are no references to Roosevelt's remark at the Yalta Conference that public opinion in the USA would hardly allow him to keep US forces in Europe for more than two years. A document can even be found for the summer of 1949 which helps verify that the Soviet leadership definitely reckoned on longer periods of the Western Allies' presence: After a talk with Vladimir Semenov, Pieck noted under the headnote 'duration of occupation' an American statement of 10 February 1945 which gave 'ten to one hundred years'; in 1946 remarks by Acheson ('twenty-five at least') and Eisenhower ('a long period') are cited.[21] In January 1947, in talking to the SED leadership, Stalin complained that the Soviet occupying power had 'to stay in Germany for a longer period than we like it' because the conclusion of a peace treaty had been delayed.[22] This shows that he understood the presence of occupying forces as limited to the duration of the necessary democratic reorganization of Germany.

Furthermore, it is possible to show that for a certain period Stalin was worried about the possibility that the common occupation would not be long enough to bring the reorganization of Germany to a satisfactory conclusion. As Byrnes set out to Molotov in September 1945, Stalin had declared in Yalta 'that there was always the danger that, as after the last war, the United States might return home and withdraw from European affairs, at which time the danger of a recrudescence of German aggression might become real.'[23] Ambassador Novikov warned in his telegram of 27 September 1946, sent to the Moscow head office: 'The United States is considering the possibility of terminating the Allied occupation of German territory before the main tasks of the occupation – the demilitarization and democratization of Germany – have been implemented.' He added: 'This would create the prerequisites for the revival of an imperialist Germany, which the United States plan to use in a future war on its side. One cannot help seeing that such a policy has a clearly anti-Soviet edge and constitutes a serious danger to the cause of peace.'[24] Once again this shows that, according to the Soviets, the democratization of Germany was a common allied task which could only jointly be brought to a successful conclusion.

II

The stubbornness with which Stalin stuck to his vision of a unified Germany in the responsibility of the Allies, despite the increasing tensions between them and the diverging developments in the occupation zones, is quite remarkable. He did not regard the result of the conference of foreign ministers in Moscow as a preliminary decision in favour of partition. Instead, as Pieck reported back to the SED party leadership in May 1947, he envisaged 'a kind of transition period until the conference of foreign ministers in November which can be expected to lead to the establishment of the economic and political unity of Germany'.[25] Neither did the Marshall Plan, in Stalin's view, mark a turning point. He expected its failure and, as Tiul'panov's remarked and Molotov's actions proved, concentrated on a successful outcome of the conference of foreign ministers in London in November/December 1947.[26] After this conference also broke off without any results, for a certain moment Stalin may have been irritated, as is suggested by a remark which Milovan Djilas passed on for February 1948: 'The west will make western Germany its own, and we will establish our own state in eastern Germany.'[27] It is also striking that the SED leadership received no directives from Moscow between December 1947 and end-March 1948.

Then, however, when the SED leadership travelled to Moscow at the end of March 1948, there were no 'new decisions on the basis of the new situation', as Pieck had announced one year earlier in the event of a failure of the next conference of foreign ministers.[28] Pieck reported that the Communists were being successful 'in including in the people's congress movement wide circles of the bourgeoisie and in unmasking the policy of Schumacher', and Stalin apparently believed him.[29] At the end of August he explained to the representatives of the three Western powers that the Berlin blockade could only be lifted if 'the fulfilment of the promise of the London Conference [that is the mandate for the West German minister presidents to create a constitutional commission, the *Parlamentarischer Rat*] is delayed until, at a common meeting, the Allies have discussed and agreed upon the most important questions with respect to Germany'.[30]

When in December 1948 the SED leadership presented Stalin with the ideas of a provisional government and a speeding up of the transformation process in the Soviet zone of occupation, they were refused brusquely: 'No expropriation, still too early ..., still no people's democracy, no action against groups of owners ..., not insisting on plan.' As an explanation for the demanded restraint, the German comrades were told that the 'situation' in Germany would not be 'similar to those in the people's democracies': 'Still no unified state / we are not about to assume power.' And once again it was impressed upon them that for the time being it only mattered to establish 'unity' and 'peace' in Germany. The admission to Cominform, to which the SED's party executive formally had applied, was denied.[31]

Even at the height of the Cold War, Stalin still did not wish to know of Socialism in the Soviet occupation zone. The peace treaty remained his strategic aim. When the Western Allies, in a counter-move to the lifting of the blockade, agreed to a further meeting of the Allied Council of Foreign Ministers, he immediately staked on a successful outcome of possible negotiations. Pieck, who at that time was staying in Moscow taking a cure, allowed himself to be infected with the optimism prevailing there, so that, in a preparatory note for a meeting with Molotov, he talked about a possible 'resumption of the work of the Control Commission' and about the creation of a 'united Germany'. He noted down 'peace treaty', and then 'no occupation regime – no separate Western state – no Western government' – and this, it needs to be emphasized, after the Parliamentary Council in Bonn, which had been asked to draft the *Grundgesetz* (basic law), had finished its deliberations.[32] In mid-July 1949 Stalin let the SED leaders know via Semenov that he was expecting 'the next conference of foreign ministers (to take place) in the autumn'. It 'will deal with unity and a peace treaty'.[33] The decision in favour of the creation of the DDR was only taken at the beginning of 1949.[34] Even thereafter, Stalin still did not abandon all hope for a unified Germany. During a further visit of the SED leadership to Moscow in May 1950, Stalin bluntly criticized that the Party's approach towards the West left a lot to be desired. As a result, on 2 June 1950, the SED's Politburo passed an internal 'resolution on intensifying the struggle in West Berlin and West Germany'. It said: 'The Politburo of the SED self-critically emphasizes that the SED's policy and practical work is insufficiently orientated towards the solution of the all-German tasks.' In view of the fact 'that the main task consists in the evolution of an all-German policy', it stated, 'the leading organs of the Party cannot be allowed to restrict themselves to the tasks in the DDR.'[35]

Consequently, also the following diplomatic initiatives to bring about a peace treaty with an all-German Government were undoubtedly meant seriously: the proposal for an all-German Parliamentary Council made by the foreign ministers of the Eastern bloc states on 21 October 1950, the People's Congress appeal to hold 'all-German free elections for a national assembly' of 15 September 1951 and the Soviet note of 10 March 1952. The internal documents repeatedly show that the Soviet side believed in succeeding with their initiatives, but at least hoped for their success. In February 1951, during a conversation with Tschuikov and Semenov, Pieck said: 'The *Bundestag* will not say no.' There might be delays and 'tricks of the Federal Government', but in the end the Parliamentary Council would probably agree to 'deal with the 8 points' conveyed by the *Volkskammer* to the *Bundestag* under the slogan '*Deutsche an einen Tisch!*' (Conciliatory talks between the two German parts).[36] Semenov informed the SED leaders on 1 November 1951 that the demand for a supervision of the elections by the United Nations was 'not a hopeless question'.[37] After the Western note of

25 March 1952, however, the SED leadership was no longer sure that four-power negotiations could actually begin. Pieck reported during his next visit to Moscow on 1 April: 'The proposal of the Soviet Government caused a mass movement putting the Western powers and the Adenauer Government in a predicament.' He also noted: 'For Germany question of elections, without UN Commission, as mass fight to overthrow Adenauer Government.' Nevertheless he asked 'which prospects in this fight; will four-power conference be held; which possible results?'[38]

Stalin's answer during a second discussion one week later clearly shows that he interpreted the Western note of 25 March as a definite rebuff and no longer believed that a success in negotiations was possible in the foreseeable future:

> Com[rade]. Stalin said that the last time W. Pieck raised the question about the prospects for the development in Germany in connection with the Soviet proposals on a peace treaty and the policy of the Americans and British in Germany. Comrade Stalin considers that irrespective of any proposals that we can make on the German question the Western powers will not agree with them and will not withdraw from Germany in any case. It would be a mistake to think that a compromise might emerge or that the Americans will agree with the draft of the peace treaty. The Americans need their army in West Germany to hold Western Europe in their hands. They say that their army is there (to defend) us. But the real goal of this army is to control Europe. The Americans will draw West Germany into the Atlantic Pact. They will create West German troops. Adenauer is in the pocket of the Americans. All ex-Fascists and generals also are there. In reality there is an independent state being formed in West Germany. And you must organize your own state. The line of demarcation between East and West Germany must be seen as a frontier and not as a simple border but a dangerous one. One must strengthen the protection of this frontier.[39]

Obviously, the Western note of 25 March 1952 meant a turning point for Stalin: as his most extensive offer up to then to the Western side and to the Germans had proved ineffectual, he no longer believed in an agreement in the near future. Instead he saw the DDR endangered by the arrangements to raise a West German army. As a result, he strove for the protection and stabilization of the DDR, which until that moment he had obviously considered a provisory solution.[40] Only on these terms did he agree to accepting 'the SED line of pushing forward the build-up of Socialism in the DDR' on 8 July 1952.[41]

Even when, in the beginning of July 1952, Stalin agreed to the proclamation of the 'building of Socialism' in the DDR by Ulbricht, this was still not intended as a final break with his all-German programme. 'He expects', Pietro Nenni noted about a talk in the evening of 17 July 1952, 'that the split between the two Germanys will continue for some time' – that means: not forever. And then he described Germany as 'an area where a long-term approach must be pursued'.[42] In the telegram which the Soviet Communist Party sent to the Second Party Conference of the SED, the future prospect of socialism was not mentioned at all. Instead, Moscow merely wished 'new success ... in the realization of the historical task to create a unified, independent, democratic, and peaceful Germany'.[43]

III

Given Stalin's continuous all-German orientation, how can the creation of the DDR be explained? The decisive reason for the failure of the programme of democratic transformation under the supervision of the four powers is to be seen in the fact that the self-styled leaders of the working class, as a result of their ideological orientation and of Stalinist practices, were incapable of playing the democratic game in realizing this programme. The Soviet occupiers were totally unfamiliar with the traditions of rule of law. As a result, they had great difficulty in putting the directives, which were sent to Zhukov, into practice in a country which they hardly knew. Despite their pluralist programme, the German Communists continued to think of themselves as the only real anti-Fascists. Whenever presented with any such opportunity, they thus tried to gain control over the economic and political process. The Moscow leadership, on the other hand, always sensed the class enemy and was thus easily convinced to sanction developments which in fact were incompatible with the main strategic aim.

Initially, this resulted in a fundamental legal insecurity in the Soviet zone of occupation. On entering Germany, the Red Army committed countless crimes against the civilian population. Some of these could be checked, but rape continued until mid-1946.[44] Equally, arbitrary internments by the NKVD, which were making a mockery of the principles of rule of law and for tens of thousands of innocent people meant endless suffering and, in many cases, death, remained the order of the day.[45] In addition, under the protection of the initially all-powerful SVAG, a system of control by Communist Party liners emerged which did not allow real pluralism in the Soviet zone. In their decision-making the SVAG officers relied almost exclusively on the advice of the German comrades who appeared to be reliable. At the same time they assisted them as far as possible in their confrontation with all other political forces. In parallel, the German Communists continued to use such methods as infiltration, conspirative intrigues and demagogical manipulation to which they had become so accustomed. In order to strengthen their position they also made use of their privileged access to the SVAG and of the latent Soviet threat to use force. Real democrats who participated in the anti-Fascist upheaval were thus put at a disadvantage. Eventually, the system of control reached such an extent that only subordination or expulsion were left as alternatives.[46] In these circumstances the anti-Fascist upheaval went much further than the 'completion of the bourgeois revolution'. For example, de-Nazification was systematically used to establish Communists in key positions in administration, police, justice and schools. Anti-capitalist impulses were largely yielded to with the takeover of unclaimed property and the expropriation of Nazis and 'persons with an interest in the war'. Thus, until spring 1948, 40 per cent of industrial production in the Soviet zone was already nationalized.[47]

Not everyone participated equally in the creeping Stalinization of the Soviet zone. For example, according to Gniffke, Ackermann had spiritualized the aim of 'political unity of Germany on the basis of parliamentary democracy'.[48] On the other hand, Ulbricht chummed up to the occupation administration with his conspirative efficiency, as his confidential remarks to the Social Democrats in the SED leadership illustrate.[49] Semenov was much more aware of the conditions for a success of the all-German concept than the much more dogmatic Tiul'panov. However, no formation of real fractions took place. The fact that the political practice ran counter to the all-German democratic aims and that this strengthened the forces in the West, which anyway wanted a split between the West and the East, was never openly discussed within the SED leadership or during the talks of SED leaders with the SVAG or the Moscow leadership. Stalin himself never realized the contradiction between programme and political practice. Indeed, as a prisoner of his own system he probably couldn't.

The result was a highly schizophrenic policy. Unity was the aim, but in fact division was pursued unwillingly.[50] In the end, the 'German Democratic Republic' came into existence on paper while, in reality, a transition took place from occupation rule to the rule of functionaries. For Stalin, this was a defeat for which, without ever grasping it, he himself was responsible to a large extent. The question remains: What would have happened had the West taken him at his word? As it is impossible to prove whether all-German structures would not perhaps have made it easier for those responsible on the Soviet side to take account of the necessities of their own programme, the barriers which the West erected have to be seen as another factor in the process which led to the establishment of two German states.

Notes

1. Cf. for the first view V. Mastny, *Russia's Road to the Cold War* (New York: 1979), and A. Fischer, 'Die Sowjetunion und die "deutsche Frage" 1945–1949', in *Die Deutschlandfrage und die Anfänge des Ost-West-Konflikts 1945–1949* (Berlin: 1984) pp. 41–57. For the second view H. Graml, *Die Alliierten und die Teilung Deutschlands. Konflikte und Entscheidungen 1941–1948* (Frankfurt: 1985), and also D. Staritz, *Sozialismus in einem halben Land. Zur Problematik und Politik der KPD/SED in der Phase der antifaschistisch-demokratischen Umwälzung in der DDR* (Berlin: 1976); for the third view see notes 2 and 3.
2. B. Meissner, *Rußland, die Westmächte und Deutschland. Die sowjetische Besatzungspolitik 1943–1953* (Hamburg: 1953; 2nd edn 1954); with slightly different emphasis W. Leonhard, *Der Weg nach Pankow. Zur Gründungsgeschichte der DDR* (Munich/Vienna: 1980) pp. 32–42, and B. Bonwetsch, 'Deutschlandpolitische Alternativen der Sowjetunion 1949–1955', *Deutsche Studien*, 24 (1986) 320–40.
3. H.P. Schwarz, *Vom Reich zur Bundesrepublik. Deutschland im Widerstreit der außenpolitischen Konzeptionen in den Jahren der Besatzungsherrschaft 1945–1949* (Berlin/Neuwied: 1966; 2nd edn, Stuttgart: 1980) pp. 201–69.
4. R. Badstübner, W. Loth (eds), *Wilhelm Pieck – Aufzeichnungen zur Deutschlandpolitik 1945–1953* (Berlin: 1994).
5. Cf. W. Loth, *The Division of the World, 1941–1955* (London: 1988) pp. 34–58 and 121–4; see also D. Geyer, 'Deutschland als Problem der sowjetischen Europapolitik am Ende des Zweiten Weltkrieges', in J. Foschepoth (ed.), *Kalter Krieg und Deutsche Frage. Deutschland im Widerstreit der Mächte 1945–1952* (Göttingen: 1985) pp. 50–65.
6. Cf. for a more detailed exposition W. Loth, *Stalins ungeliebtes Kind. Warum Moskau die DDR nicht wollte* (Berlin: 1994).
7. ZPA, NL 36/629, 62–6.
8. ZPA, NL 36/631, 33–4, 49.
9. ZPA, NL 36/694, 3–7.
10. ZPA, NL 36/629, 62–6.
11. W. Leonhard, *Die Revolution entläßt ihre Kinder* (Munich: 1979) pp. 288–9.
12. *Ibid.*, p. 289.
13. *Deutsche Volkszeitung*, 13 June 1945.
14. Insofar the criticism of the results of my study is unfounded. Cf. H.A. Winkler, 'Im Zickzackkurs zum Sozialismus', *Die Zeit*, 17 June 1994; D. Staritz, 'Die SED und Stalins Deutschlandpolitik', *Deutschland-Archiv*, 27 (1994) 854–61.
15. ZPA, NL 182/857, 86–99.
16. E.W. Gniffke, *Jahre mit Ulbricht* (Cologne: 1966) p. 33.
17. ZPA, NL 36/631, 33–4, 49.
18. M. Djilas, *Gespräche mit Stalin* (Frankfurt: 1962) p. 145.
19. Report by Harold Laski to the party leadership, quoted in K. Kaplan, *Der kurze Marsch. Kommunistische Machtübernahme in der Tschechoslowakei 1945–1948* (Munich–Vienna: 1981) p. 91.
20. E. Varga, 'Sotsializm i kapitalizm za tridtsat'let', *Mirovoe khoziaistvo i mirovaia politika*, 10 (1947) 4–5.
21. ZPA, NL 36/735, 204–13.

22. Gniffke, *Jahre mit Ulbricht*, p. 251.
23. *FRUS, 1945*, Vol. 2, p. 268.
24. *Diplomatic History*, 15 (1991) 527–37, here 536.
25. ZPA, IV 2/1/10, 12.
26. Cf. Loth, *Stalins ungeliebtes Kind*, pp. 95–9.
27. Djilas, *Gespräche*, p. 159.
28. ZPA, IV 2/1/10, 12.
29. ZPA, NL 36/695, 2–29.
30. Soviet record minutes of the talk of 2 August 1948, published in *Moskovskie Novosti*, 18 May 1988.
31. ZPA, NL 36/695, 42–7.
32. *Ibid.*, 79–85, 93–9.
33. ZPA, NL 36/735, 204–13.
34. Loth, *Stalins ungeliebtes Kind*, pp. 157–60.
35. ZPA, NL 36/556, 174.
36. ZPA, NL 36/736, 226–9.
37. *Ibid.*, 283–6.
38. ZPA, NL 36/696, 12–5.
39. AP RF, f. 45, op. 1, d. 303, l. 179. I wish to express my gratitude to Prof. M.M. Narinskii for providing me with a copy of this document.
40. For the correct interpretation of the discussions of 1 April and 7 April 1952 it is important to recognize that the creation of the People's Army had been placed on the agenda at short notice. The 'proposals of the Politburo concerning the preparations of the Second Party Conference' of 20 March 1952, to be discussed in Moscow (ZPA, NL 36/654, 1–6), did not include that plan. And as Pieck in Moscow, obviously instructed by the SKK, cautiously touched upon the question of 'taking steps towards the formation of a People's Army instead of police', Stalin immediately corrected him 'No steps, but immediate completion' (ZPA, NL 36/696, 12–5). This and the tenor of the discussions between Pieck and Stalin about the question of a four-power conference exclude the possibility that the discussions concerning stabilization measures for the DDR prove a lack of willingness on the part of Stalin to negotiate (for this view cf. G. Wettig, 'Die Deutschland-Note vom 10. März 1952 auf der Basis der diplomatischen Akten des russischen Außenministeriums', *Deutschland-Archiv*, 26 (1993) 786–805). Neither do Pieck's notes say that the question of elections should be 'organized' as a mass fight. Consequently, there is no basis for the assumption that the Soviet leadership did not want the proposed elections. As a result, there is also no basis for Wettig's assertion that Stalin's note-initiative was neither directed at successful negotiations nor mere propaganda, but 'war with other than military means' (whatever this means).
41. Resolution of the Politburo of the Soviet Communist Party of 8 July 1952, quoted from a resolution of the Soviet Ministerial Council of 27 May 1953, ZPA, 90/699, 27–33.
42. R. Steininger, *Deutsche Geschichte 1945–1961* (Frankfurt: 1983) p. 410. For the context of this document see Loth, *Stalins ungeliebtes Kind*, p. 254.
43. *Protokoll der Verhandlungen der II. Parteikonferenz* (Berlin: 1952) pp. 7–8.
44. Gniffke, *Jahre mit Ulbricht*, p. 177.
45. See lately M. Klonovsky, J. von Flocken, *Stalins Lager in Deutschland 1945–1950* (Berlin–Frankfurt: 1991).

46. For impressive examples see the accounts by Leonhard and Gniffke. As regards personnel policy see H. Weber, *Geschichte der DDR* (Munich: 1985) pp. 104–7.
47. *Ibid.*, pp. 107–15.
48. Gniffke, *Jahre mit Ulbricht*, p. 233.
49. *Ibid.*, pp. 194, 223, 298.
50. See in more detail Loth, *Stalins ungeliebtes Kind, passim*.

3 The Soviets and the Christian Democrats: the Challenge of a 'Bourgeois' Party in Eastern Germany, 1945–9

Norman M. Naimark

There was very little scholarship before 1989 on the relations between the Soviet authorities and the non-socialist parties in Eastern Germany, in particular the large and significant CDU (Christian Democratic Union).[1] Historians in the Federal Republic, not to mention the Anglo-American scholarly world, tended to look at the CDU in the East as a party that had been simply a 'transmission belt' for Soviet needs, writing off the early period of struggle as anomalous and inconsequential. With the fall of the Berlin Wall and the collapse of the Soviet Union, historians have been more willing to explore the political alternatives presented by the past.[2] The selective opening of the Soviet archives for the post-World War II period also make it possible now to examine the extent to which the Soviets were interested in the development of 'bourgeois' parties in the East.

The purpose of this chapter, then, is to review the major episodes of Soviet–CDU relations in the zone with an eye towards understanding the general goals of Soviet policies towards Germany. By identifying the ways in which Soviet attitudes and actions changed over time, this narrative does not assume that one stage necessarily had to follow the other. Just because the Soviets had created a completely supine CDU in the East by the early 1950s does not necessarily mean that such a development was inevitable. Rather, like the emergence of the Cold War itself, the harnessing of the CDU to the wishes of the Soviets and the SED depended on contingency, circumstance and political will on both sides.

THE CREATION OF THE CDU

On 9 June 1945 the Soviet Military Administration in Germany (SVAG) announced its existence in Order No. 1. The real surprise to the Germans and the Western Allies was the fact that Order No. 2, issued the following day, on 10 June, authorized the establishment of political parties in the zone. As a result, a group of former Centre and German Liberal Party politicians, who met on the initiative of Andreas Hermes, Berlin's chief official for Food Acquisition, decided to form a new party 'of the middle', the Christian Democratic Union, which issued a very general programme of democracy, interdenominational unity and social conscience.[3] From the beginning of the Party's existence, the CDU included a strong component of Christian labour union principles, advocated, among others, by Jakob Kaiser and Ernst Lemmer. The Party announced its existence on 26 June, and from that point until the establishment of the DDR in October 1949, the CDU represented a striking paradox of Soviet policy in the zone. On the one hand, the Party was encouraged and guided by Soviet political officers in the zone – in particular by Colonel S.I. Tiul'panov, head of SVAG's Propaganda (later Information) administration, and his deputy for the CDU, Captain (later Major) A. Kratin – to become a contributing member of the anti-Fascist democratic bloc of parties, on which the Soviets relied for political leadership among the German population. On the other hand, the Soviets attacked and bullied CDU leaders in an attempt to contain the Party's influence and independence in the zone.

The enmity of the German Communists to the CDU did not help matters. Soviet officials generally tried to have their cake and eat it too by supporting a strong and progressive CDU (East), which could lead Christian Democrats in all of Germany, and by forcing the CDU to accept blindly any and all Soviet-inspired policies in the zone. The KPD's (later SED's) policies towards the CDU contained no such contradictions. The Christian Democrats were political opponents to be crushed and subordinated. If the Soviets thought they might need the CDU for their all-German policies, the KPD (SED) had no such interests. From the very beginning, the German Communists sought to exclude their CDU bloc 'partners' from any influence in the zone.

The KPD refused to publish the CDU's programme (unlike that of the SPD, or even of the LDP, the Liberal Democrats) because 'the CDU's programme', wrote Wilhelm Pieck to Georg Dertinger, 'did not make sufficient reference to the unity of all democratic forces'.[4] The KPD report on the founding meeting of the German CDU on 6 August 1945, showed just how negatively the communists viewed the new Party's goals:

There was the purest demagoguery in Christian dress. There was Hitlerism [*Hitlerei*] in other terms. There was reaction and the crassest of bourgeois backwardness. There was even militarism in the attempt to make the war heroic. Even the word Socialism was avoided as if it were embarrassing to mention it.[5]

In the Soviet-controlled German Communist press, attacks on the new Party were unremitting. What kind of 'unity front' can we look forward to, the CDU leadership wrote to Pieck on 15 August 1945, when Communist rhetoric leads to 'the poisoning of our political life'?[6]

The KPD's sniping at the CDU intensified at the beginning of September 1945 and throughout the autumn, when the Communist programme for land reform was introduced and implemented. According to the details of the programme, worked out by the Soviets and German Communists in mid-August, all estates over 100 hectares were to be confiscated and redistributed in 5 to 10 hectare parcels to the so-called 'new farmers' (*Neubauern*), mostly landless refugees in the process of being resettled in the Eastern German countryside.[7] The CDU found itself in an extremely difficult position. The Party agreed with the basic principles behind the land reform, thinking it fair and 'Christian' to expropriate the property of Nazi war criminals and supporters of the Hitler regime in order to provide land to needy refugees and poor farmers. Yet CDU officials worried that non-Nazis and even anti-Nazis would be swept up illegitimately in the process and deprived of their lands. (The LDP followed much the same line of argument.) The CDU opposed the KPD's contention that all *Junkers* and large landholders were responsible for the Nazi regime, and the Party insisted that landowners be compensated for their property, especially if the land had been in their family's possession before the Nazi's ascent to power.[8]

When it became clear that the CDU's worries about the land reform were justified, Andreas Hermes and Walther Schreiber expressed 'second thoughts' about the reform, though they continued to endorse 'the expropriation of Nazi criminals and war-mongers'.[9] Hermes also complained in an October 1945 Dresden speech about the brutal fashion in which 'innocent' landholders were driven off their land, without allowing them any time to gather their belongings or inventory their losses.[10] In another speech in Berlin-Lichterfelde, Hermes reminded his listeners that the CDU had supported land reform in the bloc, but he reiterated his belief that it was an injustice to the millions of 'decent people' in Germany to drive uncompromised landowners off their estates with no compensation.[11] Like some SPD critics of the land reform, Hermes questioned the economic viability of breaking up estates and creating so many small farms. As the former President of Germany's Raiffeisen agricultural cooperative movement, Hermes appreciated the advantages of combining resources on the land. As a result, he advocated restraint when dividing up big estates, test farms and forests.[12]

Predictably, the CDU's public criticisms of the land reforms infuriated the German Communists. In the province of Saxony (later Saxony-Anhalt), where the reform was first introduced, KPD province Vice-President Robert Siewert excoriated Walther Schreiber for stating his objections to the reform at a CDU party meeting in Bitterfeld. There could be no talk of compensation for the landholders, Siewert protested. As for Schreiber, 'in his own interests' and in the name of law and order in the province, he 'should leave the province of Saxony by the shortest and quickest route possible'.[13] Hermes was so worried about the frequent political threats against CDU party spokesmen that he appealed personally to Pieck on 1 October to keep his KPD chiefs in line. In a follow-up letter of 8 October, Hermes protested again to Pieck about the repeated interference of KPD provincial functionaries in the meetings of the CDU.[14]

Hermes and the CDU had no chance to alter the basic outlines of the Soviet-inspired land reform. Already during a consultation in Moscow before the authorization of the KPD's 11 July programme, Georgi Dimitrov, representing the interests of the CPSU's Central Committee, insisted that the German Communists allow the so-called kulaks (large independent farmers) to remain on their lands.[15] But the estates of the *Junkers* and large landowners (*pomeshchiki*), who were held responsible for and profited from the Hitler regime, would be confiscated without any compensation. Hermes and the CDU were able to force the KPD into a compromise about teaching religion in the schools of the Eastern zone because the Soviets were ready to make concessions to the Eastern German churches. But the Soviets were ready neither to compromise nor to be challenged on the land reform issue, and the CDU paid dearly for its opposition.

In a September 1946 report to a Central Committee commission, Tiul'panov claimed that he was wary of the CDU from the very beginning. 'We clearly understand that you can't trust a political combination made up of class enemies and that you can't make this Party pro-Soviet.' But he felt that there was enough of a 'mixed-bag of democratic elements' in the Party to warrant working with it. In addition, the policy of his Propaganda administration regarding the CDU was to limit its possibilities of making 'anti-Soviet statements'.[16] By this he meant direct intervention, which included bullying and threatening CDU leaders. Once the CDU contradicted SVAG on the land reform issue, some Soviet officials could barely contain their hostility to the 'bourgeois' origins and attitudes of the Party. One agitated Soviet report from the zone to Dimitrov in Moscow about the CDU bluntly described the situation.

> In point of fact, the political line of the CDU is antidemocratic and in many cases reactionary. This is the line of the big German bourgeoisie, which tries to escape from its responsibility for supporting Hitler and to keep open certain economic and political possibilities for the reemergence of German imperialism.[17]

The same reporter denounced the CDU for its 'chauvinistic and reactionary policies couched in democratic phrases'. Since they could not come out openly against the land reform for fear of being banned in the zone, the Christian Democrats, he claimed, did everything they could 'to destroy and discredit it'. This was made all the more pernicious, the report continued, by Hermes's ties with the Bavarian Catholics and through them the Vatican and even Brüning![18]

Hermes received no help from the SPD for his opposition to the expropriations. (The SPD argued against compensation, though for keeping the former estates together.) By the end of November 1945, the LDP's former leader, Dr Waldemar Koch, had resigned in favour of the more pliable deputy, Dr Wilhelm Külz, whose new deputy, Arthur Lieutenant, was firmly in the Soviet camp.[19] As a result the Soviets felt confident they would not have to face a coalition between the CDU and the LDP on the land reform issue.[20] With the CDU isolated and on the defensive, the German Communists launched a new initiative by publishing the appeal, 'Help the New Farmers' (6 December 1945). The appeal was filled with vague and self-congratulatory formulations about aiding those who had received land and about the accomplishments of the land reform. Pieck's real goal, however, was to demonstrate the effectiveness of the Communist-led bloc of parties. The SPD and the LDP signed the appeal, but Hermes stood firm, protesting that the document was nothing but a political ploy and did not serve the interests of a sensible settlement on the land.[21] There can be little question that Tiul'panov and the Propaganda administration urged Pieck along his path of confrontation with the CDU. (This was also the period in which the Soviets had decided on the course of forcing the SPD to join with the KPD in the new Unity Party.) Whether pressuring the SPD, the CDU or the LDP, Tiul'panov's tactics were the same: to encourage splits in these opposition parties by organizing pressure at the provincial level against the policies of the centres and finding politicians at the centre, who were willing – either out of conviction or ambition or a combination of both – to serve Soviet interests. Local and provincial politicians felt more vulnerable to Soviet (and KPD) machinations and therefore were more susceptible to political 'suggestions' from local officers. The Soviets also kept very careful files on all German politicians, the Communists included, which noted any problems from the past, any ties with the Nazi regime, any weaknesses or bad habits that could be exploited to influence the individual. Tiul'panov was also not above using the fact that many politicians had sons or relatives in prisoners-of-war camps, promising intervention in their cases in exchange for 'friendly' behaviour.[22] In face of the growing popularity of the CDU in the autumn of 1945 and the problems experienced by the KPD, now identified by the population as 'the Russian Party', Tiul'panov decided to launch a campaign against the CDU leadership.[23] As he put it, 'when this Party [the CDU] became a clear threat ... we undertook this combination [*kombinatsiia*] for changing Hermes and bringing in Kaiser.'[24] As outlined by Tiul'panov to his Brandenburg deputy, Mil'khiker, among others, SVAG's plan had several components. First, in an attempt to flush out 'the reactionaries', the Soviets would organize a series of meetings among local CDU groups demanding that the appeal 'Help the New Farmers' be signed by Party officials. Then the supporters of Hermes and Schreiber were to be isolated and removed from positions of local leadership with the aid of Soviet officers. More 'democratic' CDU leaders were to be identified, checked out and their names forwarded to Tiul'panov, so that they could serve in an extended Central Directorate of the Party. Meanwhile, Soviet officers were instructed to follow local reactions to changes in the CDU leadership, making sure that the CDU and the LDP did not form a common bloc against the changes.[25]

Mil'khiker's reports back to Tiul'panov about his activities in Brandenburg provide a good source for understanding the way the Soviets presented their case against Hermes and Schreiber to local CDU 'progressives'. For example, Mil'khiker recounted his discussions with Dr Wilhelm Wolf, leader of the Brandenburg CDU, and his wife Dr Erika Wolf. First, the Soviet officer tried to convince the Wolfs that Hermes and Schreiber were reactionaries because they refused to sign the appeal to help the new farmers. The Wolfs refused to accept this characterization of their Party leaders, insisting that both were proven democrats and reminding Mil'khiker of their anti-Nazi pasts. The Wolfs were ready to sign the appeal, they said, but they would not organize the petition drive against Hermes and Schreiber that Mil'khiker wanted. Then the Soviet officer argued that Hermes was 'objectively' a reactionary because 'he is the symbol around whom all reactionary elements are uniting'. In Mil'khiker's words, 'he [Hermes] has created a rift in the bloc of parties and this makes possible the activities of reactionaries'. Both Wolf and his wife resisted Mil'khiker's logic. It was not Hermes's fault, they argued, that reactionaries sought to use his principled stand for their own purposes. Hermes may have committed a political error by not signing the appeal, they conceded, but he was a democrat through and through.[26] If Mil'khiker got no help from the Wolfs, he managed to make some headway with Willi Heller, head of the CDU organization in Cottbus, who was identified by the Soviets as opposed to Hermes's position on signing the appeal. Mil'khiker handed to Heller a letter of protest against Hermes's actions addressed to the CDU leadership and signed by several CDU members. Heller should write just such a letter, Mil'khiker urged, and send it 'openly, like a democrat', to SVAG. Mil'khiker warned Heller (as he had the Wolfs) that reactionaries were gathering around Hermes, and he made the case that Hermes's refusal to sign the appeal 'contradicts all Christian ethics'. Heller agreed to write a letter of protest, but suggested that he send it directly to Hermes and the CDU rather than to SVAG. He also asked to wait until the Cottbus Party met and discussed the issue before drafting the letter. Mil'khiker responded that there was no need to wait; as head of the Cottbus organization Heller could go ahead and send the letter. Heller agreed (or gave in) and Mil'khiker got the protest letter he wanted, a copy of which was forwarded by the Brandenburg military Government to SVAG headquarters in Karlshorst.[27]

In addition to Tiul'panov's version of 'salami tactics', the Soviets put direct pressure on Hermes to conform. In what was clearly a 'last chance' for Hermes to keep his position in the zone, Marshal Zhukov summoned him and Kaiser to a meeting on 12 December. The subject of the meeting was ostensibly a conference of the CDU in Bad Godesberg, which Hermes wanted to attend along with a delegation from Berlin. But the real goal of the meeting, according to an American Military Intelligence report of its conversations, was to test Hermes's resolution on the issue of signing the appeal.

> *Zhukov* asks why the CDU did not come out openly with their objections [to the conditions of the appeal] and why they did not cooperate with other political parties.
> *Hermes* replies that the CDU will not submit to the dictatorship of one party.
> *Zhukov*: 'What dictatorship?'
> *Hermes*: 'The actions of the KPD, which has but little popular support, amounts to a dictatorship.'
> *Zhukov* (pleasantly): 'I am most interested in inter-party cooperation. If the CDU does not cooperate, it will harm the CDU.' (very temperamentally) 'The land reform will be carried out without fail.'
> *Hermes* states that they too are in favor of the land reform but feel that private property should be respected.
> *Zhukov* agrees except for the private property of the *Junkers*. He elaborates on the war guilt of the *Junkers* and states that he is aware of the fact that private property has to be respected in Germany, but not that of the *Junkers*.
> *Hermes* calls attention to the case of the widow of a July 20 [1944] victim who has been expropriated.
> *Zhukov* promises that he will intervene in individual cases to avoid undue and undeserved hardships.
> *Hermes*: 'Summarizing, I may assume that you insist on your refusal to grant the visa for Godesberg because of the CDU attitude toward land reform.'

Zhukov confirms this and states that the account is now balanced.
Hermes: 'In other words, you refuse because we did not sign the land reform appeal.'
Zhukov ignores this remark.
Smirnov: 'This is a provocation.'
Zhukov: 'That was a risky statement, Herr Hermes.'[28]

THE KAISER CDU

By Christmas 1945, Hermes and Schreiber had been removed as heads of the CDU by the Soviets, based ostensibly on the mounting evidence of dissatisfaction, like Heller's letter, that had been collected from the provinces. In January 1946 the Party got a new and more provincially based 'Central Directorate', and Jakob Kaiser and Ernst Lemmer replaced Hermes and Schreiber as Party leaders. Kaiser was aware of how hard it would be to maintain the integrity of the CDU, and he was reluctant to step quickly into Hermes's shoes. At a sad farewell meeting between the two, Kaiser asked that Hermes understand his difficult position. According to Elfriede Ebgen, Kaiser's companion, Hermes answered: '"Herr Kaiser, I have thought through everything one more time, come with me to the West." Kaiser was startled a moment, but dismissed Hermes's offer with friendly words.'[29]

The new Kaiser leadership of the CDU underlined the Christian Socialist emphasis in the Party, one which advocated class peace and social reform, while rejecting Marxism and materialism. These ideas found some resonance in the Soviet Military Administration, given its momentary toleration of the SED's ideas about 'the German road to Socialism'.[30] First articulated by Anton Ackermann in an article in the German Communist journal, *Einheit*, 'the German road to Socialism' served as a tactical concession to the Western Allies, a recruitment device to get SPD members to join the KPD in the new Unity Party, and as an ideological honeypot for attracting support from the rest of Germany for the bloc of parties in the East.[31] Kaiser's own ideas that the CDU and Germany could serve as 'a bridge between East and West', and his commitment to good relation with the Russians made him an appealing alternative to Konrad Adenauer's CDU politics, which called for West German ties with the Atlantic community and repudiated efforts to deal with the Russians and even with Germans east of the Elbe.

Paradoxically, the possibility of a serious *demarche* between SVAG and the CDU was undermined by the latter's popularity among the citizens of the Soviet zone. Despite all the efforts and special campaigns mounted by the KPD and later SED, the CDU continued to gain adherents among women and youth, two groups seen as critical by the Soviets. In part, because of the German Communists' inability to control the extent and pace of dismantling, workers, too, increasingly turned to the CDU for defence. The Party also enjoyed a solid base of support among the middle class, despite the fact that it had to be more careful about admitting former Nazis into its ranks than either the KPD or SPD.[32] With local and provincial elections approaching in the early autumn of 1946, Tiul'panov embarked on another of his campaigns to undermine the support of the CDU in the provinces. In July 1946 he sent out instructions to his subordinates to find ways to hinder the growth of the CDU among women and the youth. He urged his officers to foster the development of opposition groups within the CDU and to gather compromising material on 'reactionary' CDU elements in city and local governments. Tiul'panov also insisted that his officers openly challenge the CDU's political rhetoric about standing for the rights of workers.[33] Moreover, the CDU should no longer be allowed to make 'provocational' statements about reparations or the Oder–Neisse border:

> from this moment on, there will be no discussion at all of the Eastern borders, we will not permit any party [to do so], and if the bourgeois parties – the CDU and LDP – start to speak [about the borders], then we will close down these meetings. We'll pick them up on the same day.[34]

Tiul'panov's attacks on the CDU in the summer and autumn of 1946 encouraged the SED to use its own growing control of the German administration to deny CDU members jobs in government bureaucracies and to deprive the CDU of access to newsprint, meeting rooms and radio.[35] Moreover, Tiul'panov artificially supported the development of the LDP, hoping to provide a 'counterweight' to the CDU. (As Tiul'panov later realized, this tactic failed: 'we have suckled a snake at our own breast.'[36]) But Kaiser refused to buckle under. Although he was unable to attack Soviet interference in Party affairs, he made it clear in his campaign speeches that the SED sought to re-establish a Nazi-like dictatorship and that it was little more than a pathetic clone of the CPSU.[37] At a rally in Thüringen in October 1946, Kaiser stated: 'We want a democracy and not the repetition or the second edition of a dictatorship.' Federalism, he claimed, was one of the only ways to protect Germans from the crushing weight of a centralized authority to which the SED aspired. 'We want to protect ourselves against becoming again the *Befehlsempfänger* of a certain totalitarian party.'[38] Meanwhile, Kaiser worried privately that the CDU could not overcome the obstacles placed in front of it and that it would be impossible to hold free elections in the zone.[39]

For all of Tiul'panov's blustering and bullying, the results of the elections of the autumn of 1946 were interpreted by the Central Committee of the CPSU as a major setback for the SED and the Soviets, and as a victory for the bourgeois parties. The LDP, in particular, did much better than expected in the large industrial cities of Saxony. But it was also true that the CDU more or less controlled the countryside, especially in Mecklenburg, despite open discrimination against their candidates, and they did extremely well in Greater Berlin.[40] Tiul'panov's Propaganda administration was held responsible for the election defeat, and the SED was roundly attacked as incompetent and out of touch with the German working class.[41] Tiul'panov was on the defensive and there were signs in the winter of 1946–7 – among them plans for the re-establishment of the SPD in the East – that the Soviets were intensifying their search for a new political solution to the German Question, one that would bolster Kaiser's attempts to bridge East and West.[42] But by the spring of 1947, relations between the Soviets and Americans deteriorated again. On 12 March, Truman announced his policy of containment; at the beginning of April, the Moscow foreign ministers' Conference collapsed without agreement; and in June the Marshall Plan was announced. By the time of the Paris foreign ministers' Conference, held at the end of June, beginning of July 1947, Cold War tensions had reached a breaking point.

At a series of provincial meetings in the summer of 1947, Kaiser went on the offensive, defending the Marshall Plan and questioning the need for further reparations and dismantling in the East. He also posed questions that were on every German's mind: why was it necessary to arrest so many German young people; when would the prisoners of war return from Soviet camps; how were the Allies going to assure the unity of Germany?[43] But Kaiser could only go so far in his speeches, and this became painfully apparent during the preparations for the Second Congress of the CDU held in Berlin, 6-7 September 1947. According to Tiul'panov's self-serving account of the meeting, his Information administration had 'stimulated the formation of an opposition' within the CDU, which made it possible to contain Kaiser's 'anti-Soviet' tendencies.[44]

It is more likely that Marshal Sokolovsky's stern warnings to Kaiser in a pre-Congress meeting gave the CDU leader a clear sense of the limits of Soviet tolerance. In his speech, Kaiser made no mention of the Marshall Plan and underlined the importance of bloc policies. He emphasized the fact that the totalitarian bent of the SED was the problem in the zone and left the Russians out of the picture altogether. The role of the CDU, he emphasized, was to break the waves of 'dogmatic Marxism' in the zone. According to Tiul'panov, Kaiser made no mention of 'Christian Socialism' as a concession to his American and Vatican sponsors.[45] Tiul'panov also noted that a provocative speech by the CDU leader Karl Arnold from Rheinland-Westphalen threatened to disrupt the Congress until his officers made sure that the CDU (East) speakers who followed understood the implications of supporting the West German's call for all four zones to join the Marshall Plan. 'This would mean that members of the CDU [East] would not be able to be ministers or responsible functionaries of the German administrations.' According to Tiul'panov, the threat was clearly understood, as a series of speakers criticized Arnold and expressed, in Tiul'panov's words, 'a unique zonal patriotism'.[46] All in all, Tiul'panov felt gratified that the Congress passed a resolution that contained no anti-Soviet utterances, 'did not include the demand for the revision of the Eastern borders', and was silent about the Marshall Plan.[47]

With the Congress concluded, Tiul'panov launched a characteristic campaign to remove Kaiser and Lemmer from the leadership of the CDU. As in the case of Hermes, he looked to foster opposition groups in local and provincial Party organizations that would demand the ouster of its leaders. Our job, he stated, 'is to prepare the expulsion from the Central Directorate of the Party of reactionaries, supporters of Kaiser and the obvious henchmen of the Americans, at the head of whom is Kaiser'.[48] In Thüringen, Hugo Dornhofer and Georg Schneider were removed on the initiative of the Soviets. In Brandenburg, 'by means of well-known pressure, and then other means', the opponents of Kaiser were promoted in the provincial organization.[49] The SED was also encouraged to join the attack. Ulbricht suggested in a 26 November 1947 *Tägliche Rundschau* article that Kaiser had veered sharply to the right and now seemed to be taking his orders from General Clay.[50] Kaiser himself understood that his hope that Germany could serve as a bridge between East and West had become little more than a Utopian pipedream in a period in which the powers threatened to tear Germany apart.[51] Tiul'panov also saw the removal of Kaiser in the context of the developing Cold War, as contributing to 'the general discrediting of American policies and propaganda' in Germany.[52]

In November 1947, Tiul'panov and the SED devised the People's Congress movement as a tactic to appeal to the London Conference of foreign ministers on behalf of a 'national' German representation, supported by the anti-Fascist bloc. Kaiser opposed the CDU's participation in the People's Congress because, without the inclusion of the SPD and CDU in the West, it could only exacerbate the divisiveness of German politics. According to Tiul'panov's rendition of events, when the issue of signing the appeal of the People's Congress came to a head at the 11 December meeting of the CDU's Central Directorate, Otto Nuschke 'surprised' the 'Kaiserites' with the demand that Kaiser resign, a demand that was backed up by a gathering of representatives of the provincial CDU organizations. But Kaiser would not back down without a struggle. Even at a closed meeting with Lt Colonel Nazarov (head of Tiul'panov's political parties' section) and Captain Kratin (the CDU liaison officer), Kaiser insisted that he was legally still Chairman of the CDU until removed by the Central Directorate, a narrow majority of whose members still supported his position. Finally, two years after the removal of Hermes and Schreiber, Tiul'panov gave the orders to remove 'the Kaiserites' 'by one means or another'. Kaiser was forbidden to give speeches in the East in early January 1948, and he wisely chose to remain in West Berlin.[53]

THE CDU AS A BLOC PARTY

The tribulations of the CDU between the fall of Kaiser and the establishment of the DDR constitute one of the most interesting phases of Party history in the zone. Tiul'panov did not move immediately to establish a new leadership, but turned the Party over to a broadened provincial representation that included the future Party leaders Otto Nuschke and Georg Dertinger (who Tiul'panov claimed had been 'our man' since 1947).[54] When the Soviets' Mecklenburg CDU confidant, Reinhold Lobedanz, wavered, Tiul'panov bought him off with a special allocation of newsprint. Dr Siegfried Witte, also from Mecklenburg, was made a minister in order to ensure his co-operation. There was a long list of Tiul'panov's cynical manipulations of provincial CDU organizations. These policies were undertaken, Tiul'panov wrote, so that 'all the organizational lines of the Party agree with us' and provided both accurate information and reliable leaders, whether through the electoral process or 'administrative measures'.[55] Tiul'panov's immediate target was clear: a CDU that would co-operate in the bloc with the SED on the question of building 'democracy' in the zone and in all of Germany. His medium-range goal was to foster a CDU that would advocate close co-operation with 'new democracies' and the Soviet Union, while influencing the CDU/CSU in the West.[56]

However, it was too early in the spring of 1948 for Tiul'panov to celebrate a victory over the CDU. Part of Tiul'panov's problem was that the Central Committee of the CPSU rejected his tactics and was repelled by the extent of his manipulation of CDU internal affairs. The Central Committee secretaries understood only that Jakob Kaiser was the last prestigious and independent bourgeois politician in the Soviet zone who was ready to co-operate with the Soviets, and Tiul'panov had conspired to remove him. Central Committee representatives accused Tiul'panov of bullying elected German Party leaders and of taking crude 'administrative measures' when reason and argument would have sufficed. Soviet officials were so upset by Tiul'panov's behaviour in the zone that they recommended his censure and removal. Although Tiul'panov remained in his position until the autumn of 1949, he did temporarily change his public stance towards the CDU as a result of the Central Committee critique. At the congress of the Thüringen CDU in December 1948, he unexpectedly made conciliatory remarks about the Christian Democrats and urged Party members to 'take full advantage' of their opportunities for political development in the zone.[57] But Tiul'panov had gone too far in eviscerating the leadership of the Party for CDU members to take politics seriously. Many Party members were passive and rarely attended meetings at all. As one of Tiul'panov's deputies wrote him (12 April 1948):

> The majority of the old, pro-Kaiser functionaries ... have been removed from political life ... Their supporters avoid speaking, fearful of the consequences, and the newly assembled progressive functionaries are not qualified enough to inspire lively discussions and activism about major political problems.[58]

The new leaders of the CDU, Nuschke and Dertinger, were also not as pliant as Tiul'panov, at least, would have liked. While both immediately signed on to the People's Congress Movement, they were less than comfortable with accepting the new Two-Year Plan, developed by SVAG and the SED. Nuschke also complained constantly to Grotewohl (the 'good cop' to Ulbricht's 'bad cop') about the dangers of being 'overrun' by the SED in the bloc. Nuschke had been placed in the impossible position of trying to maintain the integrity of his Party while CDU members were being systematically eliminated from important government jobs and responsible posts in the economy. To his credit, Nuschke also warned – in vain as it turned out – of the dangers of a 'police dictatorship' in the zone, given the SED's penchant to turn the civil, criminal and barracked police into purely Communist operations.[59] Dertinger, too, could never be completely trusted. Even when he was named the first Foreign Minister of the DDR Government, Grotewohl assured his comrades in the SED that their man, Anton Ackermann, would follow his every step.[60] No matter how thoroughly the CDU leaders conformed to Soviet (and SED) expectations, they could never be fully trusted.

Another 'wild card' in the development of the CDU in the spring and summer of 1948 was the situation of Ernst Lemmer, who, unlike Kaiser, had remained active in the Eastern zone, though removed from the leadership of the CDU. The Soviets saw Lemmer as a moderating influence on Kaiser during the crisis of the autumn of 1947, and they felt that Lemmer had acted with restraint during the period of Kaiser's removal. Especially after the ban on Kaiser in the Eastern zone and the rain of criticism from the Central Committee about bullying the CDU leaders, Tiul'panov and his men did everything they could to keep Lemmer happy.[61] During February 1948, the Soviet-run occupation newspaper, *Tägliche Rundschau*, made favourable references to Lemmer's role in the CDU, and fellow CDU politicians were urged by the Soviets to support Lemmer's reintegration into the Party's affairs.[62] On 11 March, Lemmer engaged in extensive conversations with Captain Kratin about the possibility of rejoining the CDU leadership as second to Nuschke. In Kratin's transcript of those conversations, recently discovered by Stefan Creuzberger, Lemmer came close to acceding to the Soviet demands that he distance himself from Kaiser, join the People's Congress Movement and work to free the Berlin trade union from 'Kaiserite' influence.[63] But it quickly became clear that Lemmer, for all his desire to work with the Soviets while keeping the CDU at the centre of all-German politics, could not abandon his principles. On 6 April 1948, Kratin noted that 'Lemmer has not fulfilled a single one of his ... promises'.[64] By the end of the summer 1948, *Tägliche Rundschau* again attacked Lemmer, along with Hermes and Kaiser. The CDU and labour union veteran gradually withdrew from politics altogether. In April 1949, Lemmer left his home in Kleinmachnow for West Berlin.

Although Tiul'panov got the CDU leaders he wanted (and deserved), the rank and file of the Party remained sullen and angry. The military authorities arrested and sentenced to long prison terms 25 Kaiser supporters from the CDU in June 1948 for alleged 'spying, anti-Soviet propaganda and the forming of illegal organizations', only intensifying the hatred in the CDU of the SED and the Soviets.[65] When the names of Nuschke and Dertinger were mentioned at a 4–6 June 1948 CDU meeting in Saxony, a storm of whistles and howls greeted the speakers. When Nuschke himself greeted delegates at a 12–14 June meeting in Schwerin, the crowd yelled at him '[Say] dear Party friends', 'Why don't you say Comrades!'.[66] In fact, what had happened to the CDU, as General Kolesnichenko of Thüringen complained to Central Committee secretary Ponomarev, was that the 'destruction of Kaiser and his friends' had led to the 'popularization' of his ideas among the rank and file of the Party and to their spread among the working class.[67]

Removing the Kaiser leadership had backfired on Tiul'panov, and he was faced with the problem of cutting the CDU down to size and reducing its ability to influence local policy. As a result, with the approval of the Central Committee, he devised the tactic of creating two new parties that would weaken the CDU's electoral and social base. First of all, during the spring of 1948, he and the SED prepared the bases for creating a new Democratic German Farmers' Party (DBD). Recognized formally by SVAG on 2 June 1948, the fundamental idea behind the DBD was to reduce the influence of the CDU in the countryside by unleashing the class struggle against the 'big farmers' from the CDU, eliminating their influence in the VdgBs (the agricultural co-operatives) and recruiting VdgB farmers to the new Party. Similarly, after several months preparation, on 16 June 1948, SVAG recognized the existence of the National Democratic Party of Germany (NDPD). The NDPD was known as the party of 'small Nazis' and was designed to gain adherents from the middle and lower middle classes and especially from the ranks of returning prisoners of war. In the case of both the DBD and the NDPD (in contrast to the CDU and LDP), leading cadres were recruited directly from the SED, so that there was never any question about who was really in charge. Not only were the two parties intended to reduce the influence of the 'bourgeois' parties in society, they also made it much more difficult for the SED's leadership to be challenged in the bloc.[68]

From the autumn and winter of 1948 until the early 1950s, when the CDU faced another series of arrests and political trials, the CDU settled into an uncomfortable compromise position with the Soviet authorities and the SED. Clearly, the CDU would not criticize the Soviet Union, nor would the Party contradict Soviet policy imperatives in Germany. Both Nuschke and Dertinger visited Moscow in November 1948 and returned with glowing reports of Soviet progress and Stalin's commitment to unified Germany. Yet, the CDU continued to criticize the shortcomings of the SED, though increasingly these criticisms focused on tactics and means rather than on the determination of the Communists to join the fold of people's democracies.

The extent to which the CDU remained a potential independent force and a worrisome thorn in the side of the SED was evident during the planning for the establishment of the DDR in September and October 1949. Vladimir Semenov warned the CDU not to stand in the way of the creation of the new democracy in the East; otherwise they would face the possibility of complete disbandment.[69] The SED understood, as well, that they could not face elections immediately after the foundation of the new state; the potential drawing power of the CDU was too strong. As a result, through Semenov, they made sure that the Christian Democrats would agree that there would be no call for elections until the new state institutions of the DDR had time to influence the electorate to support the 'new democracy'.[70] In short, if the CDU wanted to be a part of the political spectrum of the DDR, it would have to agree to be a junior partner, and a supine junior partner at that.

CONCLUSIONS

In the end, the Soviets used the CDU in its German policy for purely decorative purposes. After the establishment of the DDR, the all-

German function of the Party was reduced to the minimum. To be sure, within the DDR, the CDU served important roles for transmitting Soviet and SED policies to middle-class and professional groups and for channelling the energies of Christians and Christian Socialists into useful and non-threatening directions. The CDU became a party of preachers and professionals, thoroughly penetrated by the State Security Service, but able to exert some marginal influence on behalf of Christian tolerance and welfare in Eastern Germany.

This bleak picture of the fate of the CDU should not colour our image of Soviet policy towards the Party in the immediate post-war period. To be sure, Tiul'panov's goals were unambiguous. He was a Sovietizer out of both ideological conviction and personal inclination. For him, the CDU was an enemy object to be stormed, a relic of independence and autonomy to be reduced, a threat to be eliminated. In this sense, his actions were ultimately affirmed by the course of Soviet policy in the East. But his incessant intrigues in the CDU leadership alienated his Central Committee superiors, who sought to keep their options open for Germany. An independent 'progressive' CDU in the East, friendly to the Soviet Union, might be used to resolve the German Question. For the Central Committee secretaries, Tiul'panov's scheming undermined the Soviets' chances of gaining genuine support within the Party's rank and file. Despite repeated calls in Moscow for Tiul'panov's removal, he remained at his post. In all likelihood, Stalin felt that Tiul'panov's approach to the development of politics and institutions in the Eastern zone was one of a number of legitimate alternatives for Soviet policy in Germany.

Contemporary arguments in Germany about the extent to which the SPD aided the perpetuation of the SED regime in the East or the level of collaboration of the CDU (East) in keeping Communism afloat in the DDR tend to obscure the complexity of politics in the Soviet zone of occupation. Seen from the perspective of the post-war years rather than from that of the post-1989 period, the CDU fought a valiant battle to keep the hopes of democracy and unity alive in the East. First Hermes and then Kaiser did everything they could to satisfy sometimes contradictory Soviet demands, while maintaining the political integrity of their Party. That the CDU continued to attract adherents in the East long into the 1950s attests to the appeal of the slogan 'Socialism out of Christian Responsibility', to which Kaiser, in particular, gave real content. In the end, the CDU was harnessed to the chariot of the new German People's Democracy, but the Party and its leaders can hardly be blamed for caving in without resistance. If CDU party notables like Lemmer and Nuschke held on to unrealistic dreams of unity and of the withdrawal of occupation forces from Germany longer than they should have, it is well to remember that they were not alone. Not only that, looked at from the perspective of post-war Europe, it was not impossible for diplomacy to have bridged the growing tensions between the Soviets and the Western Allies about Germany. That it did not do so does not mean that unity was an impossible short-term goal. The CDU in the East lost the gamble that it could play a positive role in the process. But it wasn't a bad gamble, and there was no other game in town.

Notes

1. For the exceptions, see: W. Conze, *Jakob Kaiser: Politiker zwischen Ost und West* (Stuttgart: 1969), and S. Suckut, 'Christlich-Demokratische Union Deutschlands', in M. Broszat, H. Weber (eds), *SBZ Handbuch: Staatliche Verwaltung, Parteien, Gesellschaftliche Organizationen ...* (Munich: 1990) pp. 515–39. See also the memoirs by former CDU (East) activists: Peter Bloch, Ernst Lemmer and J.B. Gradl. Some of the background material for this essay is developed in my book *The Russians in Germany: A History of the Soviet Zone of Occupation* (Cambridge, Mass.: Harvard University Press, 1995).
2. See M. Richer, *Die Ost-CDU, 1948–1952: Zwischen Widerstand und Gleichschaltung* (Düsseldorf: 1990), and, especially, A. Fischer, 'Der Einfluss der SMAD auf das Parteiensystem in der SBZ am Beispiel der CDUD' ['Parteien in der SBZ/DDR: Anhörung der Enquete-Kommission'], *Deutschland Archiv*, 2 (February 1993) 266–72.
3. 'Address of Dr. Andreas Hermes at the first meeting of the Christian Democratic Union of Germany', Berlin, 22 July 1945, HIA, Lerner, box 72, folder 9.
4. SAPMO-BA, ZPA, NL 36/722, (Pieck), b. 1.
5. Report of Dr Krämer, 17 August 1945, SAPMO-BA, ZPA, NL 36/722 (Pieck), b. 5.
6. SAPMO-BA, ZPA, NL 36/722 (Pieck), b. 14.
7. *Bodenreform: 'Junkerland in Bauernhand'* (Berlin: Verlag Neuer Weg, 1945) pp. 3–16.
8. See the documents on land reform in SAPMO-BA, ZPA, NA 36/722 (Pieck), bb. 30, 38–9, 55–7. See also the KPD Central Committee's 18 October 1945 account of the land reform, *ibid.*, IV, 2/7/227, bb. 55–68.
9. SAPMO-BA, ZPA, NL 36/722 (Pieck), b. 30.
10. Tugarinov to Dimitrov, 'O politicheskom polozhenii v Germanii', 3 November 1945, RTsKhIDNI, f. 17, op. 125, d. 321, l. 106.
11. SAPMO-BA, ZPA, NL 36/722 (Pieck), bb. 38–9.
12. *Ibid.*, b. 40.
13. SAPMO-BA, ZPA, NL 36/722 (Pieck), bb. 23–4. See also 'Political Trends in Saxony', 15 November 1945, NA, RG 84, CGC, box 17, folder 4.
14. SAPMO-BA, ZPA, NL 36/722 (Pieck), bb. 42, 45.
15. Dimitrov diary entry, 9 June 1945, RTsKhIDNI, f. 146, op. 2, d. 15, l. 62.
16. 'Stenogramma soveshchaniia v upravlenii propagandy SVAG', 17–18 September 1946, RTsKhIDNI, f. 17, op. 128, d. 149, l. 158–9.
17. Tugarinov to Dimitrov, 15 November 1945, RTsKhIDNI, f. 17, op. 125, d. 321, l. 15.
18. *Ibid.*, l. 15.

19. LDP leaders are analyzed in 'Spravka o Liberal'no-Demokraticheskoi partii sovetskoi zony okkupatsii', 28 April 1948, RTsKhIDNI, f. 17, op. 128, d. 569, l. 45–61.
20. Tiul'panov to Lt Col Mil'khiker (Brandenburg), 31 December 1945, GARF, f. 7077, op. 1, d. 203, l. 45.
21. Pieck to Hermes, 6 December 1945; Hermes to Pieck, 6 December 1945, SAPMO-BA, ZPA, NL 36/722 (Pieck), bb. 66, 67.
22. Hermes's son Peter was used in an unpleasant game to influence the CDU leader. At one point, he was actually released from prisoners of war camp and brought to Potsdam, but then was sent back to Russia again when his father refused to co-operate. For this and other similar cases, see OBWPI, No. 22, May 2–8, 1947, NA, RG 57, 740.00119, Control (Germany), 5–1347. M. Gräfin Dönhoff, *Von Gestern nach Übermorgen* (Munich: 1984) p. 67.
23. GARF, f. 7077, op. 1, d. 203, l. 25.
24. 'Stenogramma soveshchaniia', 17–18 September 1946, RTsKhIDNI, f. 17, op. 128, d. 149, l. 158.
25. Tiul'panov to Mil'khiker, 29 December 1945, GARF, f. 7077, op. 1, d, 186, l. 28. Elsewhere, Tiul'panov talked about the way he had 'provoked' the reactionaries to come out in the open. 'Stenogramma soveshchaniia', 17–18 September 1946, RTsKhIDNI, f. 17, op. 128, d. 149, l. 159.
26. Transcript of the conversations between Mil'khiker and the Wolfs, GARF, f. 7077, op. 1, f. 186, l. 19–21. Wilhelm died in 1948 and Erika fled to the West in 1950. Yet both were known for their willingness to deal with the Soviets.
27. Transcript of conversation between Mil'khiker and Heller, GARF, f. 7077, op. 1, d. 186, l. 23–4. See also letter of Maj. Gen. Sharov to Lt Gen. Bokov, 16 December 1945, *ibid.*, l. 22.
28. G-2, Berlin District, Current Political Intelligence, December 21, 1945, pp. 2–4, NA, RG 57, 740.00119, Control (Germany), 11–346.
29. Conze, *Jakob Kaiser*, p. 50.
30. It should be added, however, that the CDU's claims to being a 'workers' party' made some SVAG officials very nervous. Reports of Col Valiugin and Lt Col Rozentsvaig, Eberswalde, 9 March 1946, GARF, f. 7077, op. 203, l. 51–2. 'Dokladnaia zapiska o s'ezde Khristiansko-Demokraticheskogo soiuza v Berline', 2 July 1946, RTsKhIDNI, f. 17, op. 128, d. 146, l. 8.
31. A. Ackermann, 'Gibt es einen besonderen deutschen Weg zur Sozialismus?', *Einheit*, 1 (1946) 23–42. By September 1948, Ackermann was forced to recant his 'mistaken' theories as concessions to anti-Soviet sentiments among the Germans. *Neues Deutschland*, 24 September 1948.
32. Valiugin, Rozentsvaig report, Eberswalde, 9 March 1946, GARF, f. 7077, op. 1, d. 203, l. 51.
33. 'Plan meropriiatii tsentral'noi voennoi komendatury g. Berlina po podgotovke k kommunal'nym vyboram, July-August 1946', RTsKhIDNI, f. 17, op. 128, d. 151, l. 114.
34. 'Stenogramma soveshchaniia', 17–18 September 1946, RTsKhIDNI, f. 17, op. 128, d. 149, l. 131.
35. HIA, Sander, box 2, folder 6.
36. 'Stenogramma soveshchaniia', 17–18 September 1946, RTsKhIDNI, f. 17, op. 128, d. 149, l. 160.

37. 'Auszug aus der Rede von Jakob Kaiser', Friedrichstadtpalast, 16 November 1947, SAPMO-BA, ZPA, NL 36/722 (Pieck), b. 173.
38. Jakob Kaiser speech at Gera, 16 October 1946, *ibid.*, b. 82.
39. Murphy to Secretary of State, 3 August 1946, NA, RG 59, 740.00119, Control (Germany), 8–346.
40. In Berlin, the SED finished only in third place; the SPD received 1 015 609 votes (48.7 per cent), the CDU 462 425 (22.2 per cent), the SED 412 582 (19.8 per cent) and the LDP 194 722 (9.3 per cent). The CDU received 37.1 per cent of the votes in Mecklenburg, in percentage terms its highest provincial totals. H. Weber, *Geschichte der DDR* (Munich: 1985) pp. 142–3. See also Conze, *Jakob Kaiser*, pp. 107, 268.
41. 'Stenogramma soveshchaniia', 17–18 September 1946, RTsKhIDNI, f. 17, op. 128, d. 149, l. 125–7.
42. See especially the Soviet account of the SED's visit to Moscow at the end of January and beginning of February 1947, RTsKhIDNI, f. 17, op. 128, d. 1091, l. 43–52. In a 31 January 1947 conversation with Stalin, the SED leaders were chided for being afraid of legalizing the SPD in the Eastern zone. This account is supplemented by Pieck's notes on the meeting, SAPMO-BA, ZPA, NL 36/694 (Pieck), bb. 1–7, which were also published by R. Badstübner in *Utopie kreativ*, 7 (March 1991) 105–7.
43. 'Informatsionnaia svodka o s'ezde KhDS sovetskoi zony okkupatsii Germanii', 9 September 1947, RTsKhIDNI, f. 17, op. 128, d. 360, l. 231.
44. *Ibid.*
45. *Ibid.*, l. 233.
46. *Ibid.*, l. 237.
47. The resolution was reviewed first by the Information administration, *ibid.*, l. 239.
48. *Ibid.*, l. 242.
49. Tiul'panov, 'Polozhenie v CDU', 3 May 1948, RTsKhIDNI, f. 17, op. 128, d. 568, l. 81.
50. W. Ulbricht, 'Jakob Kaiser's Wandlung', *Tägliche Rundschau*, 26 November 1947, SAPMO-BA, ZPA, NL 36/722 (Pieck), b. 180.
51. 'Jakob Kaiser auf der Sitzung des Erweiterten Vorstandes der Union der Ostzone und Berlins in Berlin am 12. Juli 1947', HIA, Kaiser 13, p. 1.
52. 'Polozhenie v CDU', 3 May 1948, RTsKhIDNI, f. 17, op. 128, d. 568, l. 92.
53. 'Polozhenie v CDU', 3 May 1948, *ibid.*, l. 70–86. See also the accounts of Kratin's meetings with Kaiser in Conze, *Jakob Kaiser*, p. 202, in Murphy to Secretary of State, 14 December 1947 (telegram), NA, RG 59, 740.00119, Control (Germany), 12–1447, and in Berlin to Secretary of State, 29 December 1947 (telegram), NA, RG 59, 740.00119, Control (Germany), 12–2947.
54. 'Polozhenie v CDU', 13 May 1948, RTsKhIDNI, f. 17, op. 128, d. 568, l. 70.
55. *Ibid.*, l. 69, 90.
56. *Ibid.*, l. 69.
57. Lt Col Makariushin to Tiul'panov, 15 December 1948, GARF, f. 7184, op. 1, d. 166, l. 259.
58. Blestkin to Tiul'panov, 12 April 1948, GARF, f. 7184, op. 1, d. 165, l. 215.
59. Nuschke to Grotewohl, 13 August 1948, Materials on Meeting in Aschersleben 19 July 1948 (sent by Nuschke to Pieck), and other materi-

als forwarded by Nuschke to Pieck, SAPMO-BA, ZPA, NL 36/722 (Pieck), bb. 204–9, 223.
60. SAPMO-BA, ZPA, IV 2/1/38, Parteivorstand Protocol (9 October 1949), b. 80.
61. 'Polozhenie v CDU', 13 May 1948, RTsKhIDNI, f. 17, op. 128, d. 767, l. 101. Here, Tiul'panov draws a picture of Lemmer as someone who had co-operated for a long time with SVAG. When Lemmer complained to Kratin about being under-appreciated by the Soviets in May 1948, SVAG responded by turning over additional food rations to him. At the September 1947 meeting with the Central Committee commission, Tiul'panov claimed that the military Government had documents which showed that Lemmer worked for Goebbels's ministry, but that these documents could not be used against him any more. Instead, the Soviets exploited the fact that 'he dreamed of a high post in the future Government' and that he was 'unusually ambitious'. 'Stenogramma soveshchaniia', 17–18 September 1946, RTsKhIDNI, f. 17, op. 128, d. 149, l. 114.
62. See S. Creuzberger, 'Opportunism or Tactics? Ernst Lemmer, the Soviet Occupation Authority, and the Treatment of New "Key Documents"' (draft conference paper), May 1994, pp. 2–3.
63. *Ibid.*, p. 5.
64. Cited in *ibid.*, p. 6.
65. Richter, *Die Ost-CDU*, p. 106.
66. *Ibid.*, p. 87
67. Kolesnichenko to Ponomarev, 29 November 1948, RTsKhIDNI, f. 17, op. 128, d. 572, l. 70–1.
68. On the DBD and NDPD, see the chapters by B. Werner-Tietz and D. Staritz in the *SBZ Handbuch*, pp. 574–95.
69. Richter, *Die Ost-CDU*, p. 193.
70. SAPMO-BA, ZPA, NL 36/695 (Pieck), b. 112.

4 The Soviet Union and the Berlin Crisis, 1948–9
Michail M. Narinskii

With the defeat of the Fascist aggressors and so the disappearance of the common enemy, the chief bonds holding together the anti-Hitler coalition began to disintegrate. Far-reaching changes in the distribution of roles between the great powers in the international arena and in the relations of strength between them, radical differences in social and political structure, value-system and ideology of the Soviet Union, on the one hand, and the West, especially the USA, on the other, became powerful factors for breaking up the victors' alliance and transition to antagonism between the USSR and the Western powers. This was obviously bound to happen in one way or another.

It is another question, however, whether the form that this antagonism took – the Cold War, meaning acute military and political confrontations, fraught with crises and conflicts – was inevitable. I think that we have to answer this question affirmatively if we take account of the moods of thought and systems of ideas of the leaders and ruling circles of the principal victor powers. It seems to me that on neither side (meaning mainly the USSR and the USA) was willingness shown to recognize and accept the reality of the post-war world and adapt its political line thereto.

Their wartime experience caused the leaders of the great victor powers to over-emphasize military strength as the instrument for deciding socio-political, territorial and other international problems. Highly characteristic was Stalin's irritated reply: 'The Pope? How many divisions has he got?'

On their part, the leaders of the USA also provided evidence enough of their endeavour to pursue a policy from a position of strength, and unwillingness to seek consistently for mutually acceptable decisions at the conference table: the actual relation of strength in the first post-war years was plainly favourable to the USA. At the end of the war the USA was the biggest industrial power in the world (responsible for about half of the world's total industrial production) and it had a monopoly of the atom bomb. America's rulers appreciated perfectly well the weakness of the huge Red Army. On 21 August 1945 France's diplomats in Washington informed their Minister of Foreign Affairs, Georges Bidault, that:

the Russians have emerged tired from this war. The contacts that the American authorities have had with the Soviet troops in Germany have convinced them of the undeniable superiority of the American army. All the officials who went to Potsdam came back with the same idea. The Russians have the men, but their technique is inadequate.[1]

Under conditions of an unfavourable relation of strength, Stalin and his circle considered that time would work for the Soviet Union. The Soviet leaders proceeded from confidence that there would inevitably come a new economic crisis in the West, and particularly in the USA. Thus academician E. Varga wrote, in a memorandum of 24 June 1947 for V. Molotov: '... Of decisive significance for the promotion of the Marshall Plan was the economic situation in the USA. The Marshall Plan was intended, primarily, as a means of mitigating the next economic crisis, the approach of which nobody in the USA denies.'[2]

Stalin showed mistrust, suspicion and profound hostility towards the West. As early as January 1945, in a conversation with Dimitrov, he contemplated the possibility of a future conflict with his Allies in the anti-Hitler coalition:

The crisis of capitalism found expression in a division of the capitalists into two factions – one fascist, the other democratic. An alliance came about between us and the democratic faction of the capitalists because they were concerned not to tolerate Hitler's rule, since its harshness would have driven the working class to extremes and so to the overthrow of capitalism itself. We are now with one faction against the other, but in the future we shall be against that capitalist faction too.[3]

The most important aim of Stalinist leadership was to strengthen the position of the USSR in international politics, and, in the first place, to consolidate its control over the Soviet sphere of influence. This was required for the performance of several tasks: ensuring the USSR's security, increasing its weight in international affairs, and not allowing the positions of Britain and the USA to grow too strong. It was from the standpoint of struggle for its sphere of influence that the Stalinist leadership approached the joint decisions of the Allies on post-war construction. In a conversation with Dimitrov in August 1945, Molotov summed up thus the decisions of the Potsdam Conference, with particular reference to Bulgaria and the Balkans: 'Basically, these decisions are good for us. To all intents and purposes this has been recognized as our sphere of influence.'

The USSR's policy on the German question became a component in the Kremlin's drive to create and consolidate a Soviet sphere in post-war Europe. The Stalinist leadership sought to establish complete control over the Soviet occupation zone and to extend its influence over the situation in Germany as a whole. They considered that implementation of the Allies' decisions on de-Nazification, demilitarization and democratization was bound to strengthen those German political groups which leant towards the Soviet Union. In order to ensure the payment of Germany's reparations in kind to the USSR they demanded Soviet participation in control over the Ruhr. Moscow's negative reaction to the American proposal for a treaty on German disarmament, put forward in September 1945, was typical. After seeing the draft of the treaty the Soviet side concluded that its purpose was to end as soon as possible the military occupation of Germany, and that it was restricted to military disarmament and demilitarization, ignoring the most important prerequisites for Germany's economic disarmament and democratization. Marshals G. Zhukov and V. Sokolovsky, together with V. Semenov, the political adviser to the Soviet Military Administration in Germany, wrote to the People's Commissariat of Foreign Affairs that:

> in the form proposed the American plan is unacceptable, and at the present moment we are not at all interested in co-operating in any way with possible American moves to end the occupation of Germany in the near future, since we cannot, after such a war, allow the task of disarming and democratizing Germany to be abandoned half-way.[4]

In his political tactics Stalin at first showed notable caution. Thus, in June 1945 he advised the German Communists to work for the establishment of an anti-Fascist democratic parliamentary regime and not to advocate the Soviet system for Germany.

In 1947, however, acute aggravation was observable in the international situation: crushing of the opposition in several countries of South-Eastern Europe, proclamation of the Truman Doctrine, ineffectual outcome of the Moscow meeting of the Council of Foreign Ministers, beginning of the implementation of the Marshall Plan, refusal by the USSR and the countries friendly to it to participate in this plan, creation of the Cominform. All these events heralded the coming of the Cold War.

In the autumn of 1947 Moscow's ruling circles began to show disquiet with regard to the increasing contradictions between the former Allies over the German problem. In a memorandum of 3 October to his Minister, Molotov, the head of the 3rd European Department of the USSR Ministry of Foreign Affairs, A. Smirnov, drew attention to new factors in the Western powers' policy on the question of the peace settlement with Germany, pointing towards further departure from the Potsdam decisions, with a view to a separate solution of the German problem. This was confirmed by the practical measures being carried out by the USA and Britain in Germany, aimed at preparing the way for such a separation procedure:

> Analysis of the materials available to us and of the practical measures being undertaken in Germany by the USA and Britain gives grounds for concluding that this is no mere propaganda trick or political blackmail but a real threat to partition Germany politically and economically and to include the Western part of the country, with all its resources, in the Western bloc which the USA is forming.[5]

The Soviet leadership tried to prevent this undesirable development. Basing itself on the decisions of the Yalta and Potsdam Conferences, it sought to retain complete control over the Soviet occupation zone while at the same time not losing the possibility of influencing the situation in Germany as a whole. In the directives to the Soviet delegation to the London meeting of the Council of Foreign Ministers, which were approved by the Politburo on 21 November 1947, what was put in the forefront was the conclusion of a peace treaty with Germany, linked with the task of restoring 'a united democratic Germany'. These directives stressed the importance of getting accepted in London the Soviet proposals on two questions:

> (a) the creation of a democratic government for the whole of Germany, in accordance with the Potsdam decisions; (b) the convening of a peace conference of representatives of the neighbouring Allied states, together with other Allied states which participated with their armed forces in the common fight against Germany, while rejecting the American proposal for a peace conference embracing all the countries which declared war on Germany ...[6]

However, this London meeting of the Council of Foreign Ministers (25 November–15 December 1947) ended in complete breakdown. Utilizing acute differences which arose in the discussion of German reparations, the US Secretary of State, George Marshall, broke off the meeting, which ended without exhausting its agenda. No date was set for the next meeting of the Council, and it was unclear whether it would be able to resume its labours. The only real outcome of the meeting was the open break between the three Western powers and the Soviet Union. During the meeting France agreed in principle to merge the French occupation zone with 'Bizonia', so creating 'Trizonia'. On 19 December Washington announced the State Department's decision to cease reparations deliveries to the Soviet Union. Germany was to be divided, then drawn into the Cold War.

Part of this process was preparation for the introduction of currency reform separately in West and East Germany. The problem of currency reform in Germany had already been discussed in the Control Council in 1946. The Soviet representatives had insisted that the new banknotes be issued separately for the Western occupation zones, in Berlin, and for the Soviet zone, in Leipzig, 'under the same international control'. The US representatives had strongly opposed this. Special importance was accorded, in the discussion of the intended currency reform, to the question of the right to issue banknotes. The Western representatives insisted on the creation of an all-German banking mechanism under the Control Council, to which should also be entrusted the issuing of banknotes. As Minister of Finance A. Zverev pointed out in a memorandum of 21 January 1947 to the CC of the CPSU(B), the Western powers were trying by this means 'to bring under their control the volume of our expenditure on occupation and reparation charges', and this was quite unacceptable to the Soviet side. The Minister noted that it was necessary ' to take account of the fact that the Allies do not agree to allow the command of the Soviet occupation zone the right to issue banknotes to cover occupation and reparation expenses'.[7] The Minister expressed fear that the Western powers might utilize the absence of agreement on the question of an issuing mechanism as a pretext for carrying out a separate currency reform in the Western zones, which would entail further economic isolation of the Soviet occupation zone. Zverev considered that the Western powers' proposals could be agreed to on condition that they, on their part, guaranteed 'complete coverage of our occupation costs and expenditure in connection with reparations, including reparation payments from current production'.[8] This document gives further evidence of the importance that the Soviet leadership accorded to the reparations problem.

The four powers failed to agree on a co-ordinated introduction of currency reform in Germany. In September 1947 the head of the Soviet Military Administration in Germany, Marshal V. Sokolovsky, informed Moscow that, given the active preparation by the American authorities for carrying out a separate currency reform in West Germany, it would be necessary to prepare new banknotes for the Soviet zone. On the initiative of Sokolovsky and Semenov the USSR Council of Ministers took a decision 'on new banknotes for the Soviet occupation zone in Germany'.[9] Taking account of the possible implementation of a separate currency reform in the Western zones, the Soviet Government authorized the Soviet military administration in Germany 'to manufacture new German banknotes for the Soviet occupation zone'. A decision of the USSR Council of Ministers required the Gosznak factory in Moscow to manufacture 400 million new German banknotes, to the value of 5 million marks, by 1 July 1948. (By a decision of the USSR Council of Ministers on 5 May 1948 this deadline was put off to 25 August,[10] evidently owing to technical hitches.)

Meanwhile, the Western powers were engaged in direct preparation for the establishment of a West German state. 'The Yalta era is over,' wrote the *New York Herald Tribune* on 20 December 1947. 'The partition of Germany gives us freedom of action to include West Germany in the Western state system.'[11]

Between 23 February and 6 March 1948 a conference on the German problem was held in London between representatives of the USA, Britain and France, together with Belgium, the Netherlands and Luxembourg. The decisions of this London conference of six Western countries signified that a course had been taken towards including West Germany in the Marshall Plan and preparing for the creation of a West German state which would be integrated into the Western bloc.

These decisions disturbed the Soviet Government, which began looking for methods of countering the West's policy in Germany. On 9 March 1948 Semenov and Sokolovsky were urgently recalled to Moscow for discussions.[12] The documents now available allow us to suppose that at this time a plan had been worked out in Moscow for interrupting Berlin's communications with the Western occupation zones. In any case, in mid-April Semenov and Sokolovsky's deputy, Lieutenant-General M. Dratvin, informed Molotov and the Minister for the Armed forces, Bulganin: 'The plan drawn up, according to your instructions, for restrictive measures to be taken regarding communications between Berlin and the Soviet zone with the Western occupation zones is applied from 1 April, except for restrictions on communication by air, which we intend to introduce later.'[13] This shows that Moscow had prepared a special plan for exerting pressure on the Western Allies in Berlin.

Those who evidently took part, in one way or another, in the discussion and adoption of the plan, were Stalin, Molotov, Malenkov, Bulganin, Sokolovsky and Semenov. The devising of the measures for Soviet resistance to the realization of the Western powers' London decisions proceeded in strictest secrecy and involved a very narrow group of people. The matter was not discussed in the Politburo and this supreme Party organ took no official decision on it. There can be no doubt that Stalin himself played the chief role in the taking of such an important political decision.

The telegram from Dratvin and Semenov shows also that the Soviets' original plan envisioned the introduction of restrictions on communication by air as well, but no practical attempts were made to put that part of the plan into effect. Evidently it was thought in the Kremlin that to take measures against the American 'air-bridge' would be too risky. The relation of strength where air-power was concerned was clearly not in the USSR's favour. It was not accidental that on 1 July 1948 the Politburo passed a resolution for reorganizing the country's system of anti-aircraft defence.

When Sokolovsky and Semenov were summoned to Moscow on 12 March 1948, Smirnov, the head of the 3rd European Department of the USSR Foreign Ministry, sent Molotov a memorandum headed 'On our measures in relation to Germany in the immediate future'. This document noted that the USA and Britain had refused to settle the German problem on the basis of the Yalta and Potsdam decisions and 'are carrying out preparatory measures for the creation of a West German state with which they intend to conclude a separate peace treaty'. The London meeting of the Western powers on the German problem was taken as proof that 'the Western powers are turning Germany into their *point d'appui* and including it in the military–political bloc they are creating which is directed against the Soviet Union and the new democracies'.[14]

Smirnov proposed that the Western powers' German policy be resisted more resolutely.

> In the conditions that have been created we can no longer confine ourselves to protests to the Western powers about their separate actions which seriously encroach on our interests in Germany and in Europe ... We need, therefore, to take measures which would not merely restrict separate actions by the USA, Britain and France in Germany but would actively disrupt their plans to put together a Western bloc including Germany.[15]

In his memorandum Smirnov formulated the following proposals: (1) to convene a meeting of the Foreign Ministers of the USSR, Poland, Yugoslavia, Czechoslovakia and Albania with invitations to attend, as observers, being sent to Hungary, Romania, Bulgaria and Finland, together with the German People's Congress: this meeting to adopt a declaration concerning the behaviour of the Western powers in Germany; (2) after this meeting, the Soviet Union to take the initiative in convening a fresh meeting of the Council of Foreign Ministers in order to consider the German question. 'If the USA, Britain and France accept this proposal, that will undermine the basis for their action to put together a Western bloc including Germany. If our proposal is rejected it will be clear that those powers have finally decided against settling the German question on the basis of the Potsdam decisions.'[16]

After that, the Soviet Union was to declare that, by their actions, the Western powers had destroyed the Allied Control Council and the Council of Foreign Ministers, and consequently the existing agreements on an Allied control mechanism and on zones of occupation had lost their force. The Soviet Government would therefore be obliged to close off completely its occupation zone, introducing the appropriate financial measures, organizing frontier defence, and so on.

In my view, Smirnov's memorandum was not prepared on the initiative of the 3rd European Department. It reflected the views of the Soviet top leadership, and of Molotov in particular, and set the measures for restricting Berlin's communications with the Western zone in the wider context of a political–propaganda campaign against the conduct of the Western powers on the German question. The entire plan set out in the memorandum was put into effect in one form or another.

On 20 March 1948 Marshal Sokolovsky demonstratively walked out of a meeting of the Allied Control Council, and for all practical purposes the activity of this organ came to an end.[17] On 25 March Sokolovsky issued an order 'On strengthening control on the demarcation line of the Soviet occupation zone in Germany', by which the head of the transport department of the Soviet Military Administration was instructed to reduce to a minimum the movement of passenger traffic and the transports of American, British and French troops.[18] This order was followed on 27 March by an order 'On strengthening control on the external borders of Greater Berlin', which tightened control over the movement of persons and freight through the city's outer limits. On 1 April various restrictions were imposed on communications between Berlin and the Western zones.

Moscow received information testifying to the seriousness of the confrontation around Berlin. Thus, in a survey of the German morning papers sent from Berlin on 2 April:

> The American State Department has announced that the USA's armed forces will remain in Berlin. In Washington diplomatic circles the Soviet measures are seen as the beginning of an attempt to oust the Western powers from Berlin. In their view Berlin is the place where the resoluteness of American and Russian foreign policies will be tested.[19]

Nevertheless, the leaders of the Soviet Military Administration in Germany were in determined and optimistic mood. Dratvin and Semenov, informing Moscow on 17 April about the realization since 1 April of the restrictions on Berlin and the Soviet zone's links with the Western zones, reported triumphantly: 'Our measures have dealt a serious blow to the prestige of the Americans and British in Germany. The German population considers that "the Anglo-Americans have retreated before the Russians" and that this shows how strong the Russians are.'[20]

The Soviet Military Administration in Germany clearly underestimated both the determination of the Western Allies to oppose the Soviet pressure on Berlin and the means to do this that were at their disposal. In that same telegram they claimed that 'Clay's attempts to create an "air-bridge" between Berlin and the Western zones have failed. The Americans have realized that this is too costly a venture.'[21]

Dratvin and Semenov proposed that the pressure on the Western powers be intensified by further tightening of the regime controlling Berlin's communications with the Western zones. Goods trains should be allowed to proceed from Berlin to the Western zones only if their freight was licensed by the Soviet Military Administration, and a new procedure was introduced for postal communication with the Western zones. Later, on the pretext of safeguarding security, flights of aircraft between Berlin and the Western zones should be restricted.[22]

In moving into a serious confrontation with the Western powers over Berlin, Stalin's Government sought above all to secure the possibility of negotiating on the German problem from a position of strength. It was supposed that the difficulties in Berlin would force Washington, London and Paris to be more tractable and to give up their plans to create a West German state. The Soviets' pressure should also increase the German population's lack of confidence in the Western powers. If the latter were not willing to make serious political concessions, the Soviet leaders would try to oust them from Berlin and absorb the city into the Soviet zone. During a conversation between Stalin and the leaders of the Socialist Unity Party of Germany on 26 March 1948, W. Pieck remarked that the results of the elections due to be held in Berlin in October were not likely to be better for his Party than those of 1946. Later, he said that 'they would be glad if the Allies left Berlin,' Stalin commented: 'Let's try with all our might, and maybe we'll drive them out.'[23]

Between April and June 1948 the Soviet Military Administration in Germany continued to exert pressure on the Western powers in Berlin. On 23 April Semenov reported to the Foreign Ministry that there were signs that the administrative staffs of the Western powers in Berlin were leaving for the Western zones, and expressed the view that the 'smoking out' of the Western powers would not be made easier by this, since the latter would perhaps now have greater freedom of action in 'resisting our pressure'.[24]

On 11 June he reported that, 'according to plan,' further measures were being taken to restrict traffic, and expressed hope that these measures would give 'another jolt to the prestige' of the Western occupying powers in Berlin.[25] Thus, the Soviet occupying authority in Berlin were doing their utmost to cause difficulties for the Western powers and undermine their influence in the city.

Meanwhile, in both West and East Germany preparations continued for introducing separate currency reforms. On 18 May the Soviet Government adopted a decision 'On introducing currency reform in the Soviet occupation zone of Germany'. This required the Soviet Military Administration in Germany, in the event of the carrying-out of a separate currency reform in the Western zone, immediately to put a currency reform of their own into effect in the Soviet zone. The Government required 'the Soviet Military Administration to allow circulation in the entire area of Greater Berlin exclusively to the new banknotes of the Soviet occupation zone.'[26] This restricted sharply the Military Administration's scope for manoeuvring. The Soviet Government was trying to include all Berlin in the financial and economic system of the Soviet zone, and this meant giving a new twist to the developing Berlin crisis.

On 18 June the commanders of the occupying forces of the USA, Britain and France, Generals Clay, Robertson and Koenig, informed Marshal Sokolovsky of the introduction, as from 20 June, of a currency reform in the Western zones of occupation. It was proposed that currency reform be not extended to the Western sector of Berlin. However, on 19 June the Soviet authorities announced that 'banknotes issued in the Western occupation zones will not be allowed to circulate in the Soviet zone or in "Greater Berlin", which is situated in the Soviet zone and is economically a part thereof.'[27] Negotiations between financial experts from the four powers on 22 June proved fruitless. The Soviet representative said: 'We give notice to you and to the German population of Berlin that we shall apply economic and administrative sanctions which will ensure that only one currency will circulate in Berlin – the currency of the Soviet zone.'[28]

Having carried out separate currency reforms in Germany, and with the Soviets trying to include Berlin financially in their zone, both sides now deliberately moved to sharpen the situation. Reporting to Moscow on the letters from the Western commanders about the introduction of the currency reform and its non-extension to the Western sector of Berlin, the head of the Soviet Military Administration observed: 'It is obvious, however, that the new currency for the Western zones will be introduced in the Western sectors of Berlin after the announcement of our introduction of the Soviet zone's banknotes for the whole of Berlin.'[29] On the other hand, representatives of the French military authorities in Germany warned their American and British partners of the seriousness of the threatening international crisis. On 23 June the French General Ganeval declared:

> As we proceed to application of the counter-measures provided for in the event of a Soviet currency reform, the French Government draws its Allies' attention to the incalculable consequences that will follow the introduction of the Western zones' currency into our sectors – consequences which will undoubtedly not be confined to Berlin.'[30]

On 22 June Marshal Sokolovsky informed Generals Clay, Robertson and Koenig of the introduction of currency reform in the Soviet zone and Greater Berlin. On 23 June the occupation authorities of the three Western powers decided to extend the currency reform which had been introduced in West Germany into the Western sectors of Berlin. On 24 June the Soviet occupation authorities completely closed land communications between the Western occupation zones and Berlin, 'for technical reasons'.

The Soviet Military Administration reported to Moscow on the growing difficulties endured by the Western powers in Berlin and the certainty that they would have to retreat on the German question. As was mentioned later in a memorandum written by a member of the USSR's diplomatic mission to the GDR, M. Senin, 'our leading comrades in Germany assumed that, as a result of the difficulties which could arise from the restrictions imposed by us in Berlin, the Western powers would be forced to retreat, to surrender their positions in Berlin to the Soviet Union'.[31]

The situation in which the Western powers found themselves was indeed far from simple. There were no documents valid in international law that guaranteed their communications with Berlin. An attempt to break the Soviet blockade by force would mean so serious an escalation of the conflict, fraught with such unforeseeable consequences, that it was very hard to decide on such a step. Georges Bidault, the French Foreign Minister, considered, at the end of June, that the Western powers could hold out in Berlin for no more than a few weeks. In a telegram to the French Embassy in Washington on 27 June he wrote: 'The way the situation in Berlin is developing shows that the Western powers will find it very difficult to stay there for more than a few weeks unless there is a radical change in relations with the Soviet authorities.'[32]

For all the acuteness of the international political crisis over Berlin, those involved assumed that neither side was aiming at a large-scale armed conflict. The American, British and French military and political leaders were unanimous in considering that the Soviet Union was not ready for a war at that time and was not trying to start one.[33] The French military command in Germany summed up the position of the Americans and British on 24 June thus: 'Their attitude is based on absolute certainty that the Russians do not want war.'[34]

On its part, the Soviet leadership followed closely the development of the West's position on the Berlin crisis. After analysing the USA's reaction to the Soviet note of 14 July, the USSR Foreign Ministry came to this conclusion: 'After some hesitation and sounding-out of the firmness of the Soviet position, the USA's leading circles have decided not to proceed, for the present, to a further aggravation of the Berlin question.'[35] All the Soviet actions were aimed at exerting military and political pressure on the West so as to obtain political concessions, relying on the West's prudence and unwillingness to provoke war.

The fundamental mistake made by the Soviet leadership was that they underestimated the resolution of the Western powers to resist

Soviet pressure and to press on with realization of the decisions on the German question taken by the London conference of representatives of six countries. On 3 July Sokolovsky announced that the restrictions on transport would be maintained until the Western powers gave up their plan to create a West German government. General Clay saw this as the Soviets' first admission of the true reason for the blockade.[36]

The Western powers organized and extended their 'air-bridge' between the Western zone and Berlin. At the same time, after a fruitless exchange of notes, the American leaders decided to seek a personal meeting between the ambassadors of the three Western powers in Moscow and Stalin himself. On 30 July these ambassadors called on V. Zorin, the Soviet deputy Foreign Minister, and handed him memoranda, couched in identical terms, requesting that he arrange a meeting with the head of the Soviet Government, 'in order to discuss the situation in Berlin and its wider implications'.[37]

On 31 July the ambassadors had separate talks with Molotov in which they discussed what should be covered in the proposed negotiations. The Foreign Minister emphasized that 'the Soviet Government considers it impossible to separate discussion of the Berlin question from that of four-power control of Germany as a whole'.[38] The Western ambassadors broadly agreed with this approach. On 2 August they were invited to meet Stalin.

The head of the Soviet Government vigorously set out his position to the Western ambassadors.

> Comrade Stalin spoke of two factors – the special currency in Berlin and the decisions of the London conference. He thought that it was those decisions which gave rise to the restrictive measures under discussion ... Comrade Stalin said that ... simultaneously with the rescinding of the restrictions on transport applied by the Soviet Military Administration the special currency (the 'B' mark) introduced by the three powers in Berlin should be withdrawn and replaced by the currency circulating in the Soviet zone, the *Deutschemark*. That was the first point. Secondly, assurance should be given that application of the London conference's decisions would be postponed until representatives of the four powers had met and negotiated on all the basic questions concerning Germany.[39]

Stalin stressed that he was opposed to the formation of a West German state and to the unification of the three Western zones. He repeatedly insisted: 'Stop applying the London decisions and withdraw the "B" mark. There will be no difficulties. It could be done tomorrow. Think about it.'[40]

Coming up against the firm refusal of the West's representatives to give any official assurance that application of the London decisions would be halted, Stalin made a concession. He did not demand this as a condition for rescinding the Soviet restrictions on communications, but asked to register the urgent desire of the Soviet Government that decision on the question of a West German government be postponed. On their part, the representatives of the Western powers agreed to the introduction into Berlin of the currency in circulation in the Soviet zone and withdrawal of the 'B' mark from the city's Western sectors. It was agreed that simultaneously with this measure the restrictions on transport between Berlin and the Western zones would be lifted.[41]

During the conversation Stalin admitted that the Soviets had brought pressure to bear on the Western powers, but tried to present this as a necessary defensive measure. 'Comrade Stalin replied that he did not deny that pressure had been exerted, but this was due to the pressure exerted by the London Conference. That constituted pressure on the Soviet Union, an attack on its currency in Germany.'[42] Stalin set out his position altogether very logically, consistently and vigorously.

The basic task of the Soviet leaders was to get the Western powers to renounce realization of the London decisions and abandon preparation for the establishment of a West German government. To this theme Molotov returned again and again during his meetings with Western representatives in August 1948. Thus, on 6 August he stressed the need 'to put aside the decisions of the London Conference. The Soviet Government does not insist on this being done at once, since it would be difficult for the representatives of the three powers. But it regards it as desirable, and this is the Soviet Government's firm wish.'[43]

As their fall-back position Stalin and Molotov tried to obtain recognition of the Soviet zone's currency as the only currency for Berlin in exchange for lifting the Soviet restrictions on the city's links with the Western zones. Thereby they would have achieved, *de facto*, the inclusion of all Berlin in the financial and economic system of the Soviet zone, under their control. This would have substantially strengthened their position in Berlin and weakened that of the West. Later the second secretary of the USSR's diplomatic mission in the GDR, Senin, was to write in his memorandum on the Berlin question:

> What was most important for us was to restore the economic unity of Berlin, to include all Berlin in the economic system of the Soviet zone and also to restore unified administration of the city. That would have served as basis for winning over the population of West Berlin, and would have created the pre-conditions for completely ousting the Western powers from Berlin.[44]

I think the Western powers made a tactical error in going for a meeting between their representatives and Stalin. He felt that he was the master of the situation, exerted vigorous pressure, demanded, insisted.

He took the evasive diplomatic answers of the Westerners as a sign of weakness, of readiness to make concessions. These illusions formed by Stalin and Molotov were reflected in the Soviet project for a joint communiqué by the governments of France, Britain, the USA and the USSR on German questions, which was confirmed by the Politburo during the Berlin crisis.

The proposed joint communiqué provided for the lifting on 15 August of all the transport restrictions introduced after the announcement of the currency reform in the Western zones, while at the same time the Soviet zone's Mark would become the sole currency for Berlin, with regulation of all monetary matters in the city to be exercised by the Soviet zone's German Bank of Issue. It was proposed that there should be a meeting in the near future of representatives of the four powers, along the lines of the Council of Foreign Ministers, or else a separate meeting of these representatives 'to discuss (a) any outstanding questions affecting Berlin and (b) any other outstanding problems affecting Germany as a whole'.

But that was not yet all. The Soviet document contained the following important paragraph:

> In the negotiations which have taken place the representatives of the four powers considered the Soviet Government's wish that implementation of the decisions of the London conference on the creation of a West German government be put off until the results of the proposed meeting of representatives of the four powers become clear. The representatives of the three Western powers have announced that the governments of these powers will not, for the present, take up the question of creating a government for West Germany.[45]

Clearly, acceptance of such a document would have meant a clear victory for Stalin, signifying that the blockade of Berlin and the pressure on the Western powers had succeeded. The Politburo's approval of it showed that they hoped to secure a settlement of the Berlin crisis which would be highly favourable to the USSR. It sharply restricted the chances for Soviet diplomacy to achieve a compromise. The Stalinist leadership made a serious political mistake in underestimating the readiness of the Western powers to resist Soviet coercion and continue the confrontation.

The hardening of the position of the Western powers' representatives during the negotiations in August 1948 was received very negatively by the Soviet side. They were disappointed by the convening on 1 September of a Parliamentary Council to draw up a constitution for West Germany, an action which clearly demonstrated that the Western powers were continuing to prepare for the establishment of a West German state. In a conversation between Stalin and representatives of the Western powers on 2 August Molotov had remarked 'that there would be nothing to negotiate about if the decisions of the London conference were to be put into effect'.[46]

It would appear that it was because the Parliamentary Council began its work that negotiations between the commanders-in-chief of the four occupying armies failed at the beginning of September.

The Soviet leadership's mistaken estimate of the general military and political situation and of the intentions and resources of the Western powers led to rejection of compromise solutions in August–September 1948 and the dragging-out of the Berlin crisis.

On 31 August Molotov had sent to Berlin instructions for the Soviet side in the negotiations between the commanders-in-chief 'in which he prescribed that there was to be no retreat from the decisions agreed in Moscow, especially as regards extension of the powers of the financial commission'.[47] In accordance with a general directive of the four governments, drawn up in Moscow, a finance commission of representatives of the four commanders-in-chief in Germany had been formed, to see to the practical implementation of measures connected with the introduction of a single currency in Berlin. The question of the functions and powers of this commission became one of the chief 'stumbling-blocks' in the negotiations between the commanders-in-chief that were held in Berlin on 1–7 September.

It appears to me that the representatives of the Western powers were willing to accept a sensible compromise. At their meeting with Molotov on 18 September they showed that their commanders-in-chief did not want to interfere in the financial affairs of the Soviet zone. During these talks the US ambassador in Moscow, Smith, declared that 'no attempt was made by the representatives of France, Britain and the USA to extend control by the finance commission over the German Bank of Issue in respect of any matters other than those relating to Berlin'. He went on to say that 'the representatives of the three powers have always recognized that control by the Finance commission must be so exercised as not to encroach on the responsibility of the Soviet administration for the circulation of currency in the Soviet occupation zone'.[48]

Unfortunately, the Soviet leadership failed to seize this chance to arrive at a fairly favourable compromise. They evidently gambled on expectation that the American 'air-bridge' could not function normally in the autumn and winter of 1948. The Soviet representatives carefully collected and reported to their leaders all information that pointed to increasing difficulties being experienced by the organizers of the 'airbridge', and the inevitability of its breakdown. Typical in this connection was the report by an official of the Soviet delegation to the general Assembly of UNO, on his talk with the French deputy head of UNO's press department on 20 November 1948. According to this report an official of the American delegation had told the Frenchman that

> the position of the 'air-bridge' in Berlin is extremely difficult. The American military say that in the approaching winter conditions flights will be very complicated and the personnel are so exhausted that great efforts have to be made to make the pilots go on flying. The *matériel* will soon be worn out. This American said that the American army command and the State Department fear that the 'air-bridge' will cease to operate in the very near future.[49]

Expecting failure of the 'air-bridge' and surrender by the Western powers on the Berlin question, the Soviet leaders adopted the line of dragging-out diplomatic discussions.

All the diplomatic battles and manoeuvres on the Berlin question during the autumn and winter of 1948 – the debate in the Security Council of UNO, the attempt by the Chairman of the Security Council to mediate, the work of a technical committee of experts from six neutral countries – all proved fruitless.

Meanwhile, the general political situation concerning Berlin underwent change. First, the four powers took further steps towards the partition of Germany: Berlin's united city council ceased to exist, and in both West and East of the country preparations went ahead for the creation of two German states. Second, and this may have been the most important factor, the American 'air-bridge' succeeded in functioning successfully in the winter conditions. The Soviet leadership was obliged to admit the defeat of its attempt to blockade Berlin. A political–propaganda failure had been suffered.

On 31 January 1949 Stalin's replies to questions put by the General European director of the American International News Service, Kingsbury Smith, were published. Stalin connected the lifting of all the transport restrictions solely with the convening of another meeting of the Council of Foreign Ministers. The question of a single currency for Berlin was avoided.[50]

After that, in mid-February 1949 negotiations for settling the Berlin question began, on American initiative, between the deputy representative of the USA in the Security Council, Jessop, and the Soviet representative at UNO, Malik. These talks continued until the beginning of May 1949. On 4 May agreement was reached in New York, by which all restrictions on communications, transport and trade between Berlin and Western countries, between the Soviet zone and the Western zone of Berlin, and also between the Western and Soviet zones of Germany were to be abolished on 12 May. Article 3 of the agreement provided that 'eleven days after the ending of the restrictions mentioned in articles 1 and 2, i.e., on 23 May 1949, a meeting of the Council of Foreign Ministers will be held in Paris to examine questions concerning Germany and problems arising from the situation in Berlin, including the question of a currency for Berlin'.[51] This agreement was put into effect. On 12 May all the restrictions on communications, transport and trade between Berlin and the Western zones which had been introduced after 1 March 1948 were lifted.

Unfortunately, I have at my disposal no documents that reveal what the Soviet leaders' motives were in ending the blockade of Berlin or how they arrived at their decision. There is only the following appraisal by Senin, of the Soviet mission in the GDR, who noted the negative consequences of the 'air-bridge' for the USSR, from the political, propaganda and strategic points of view. ' The Soviet Government could not, of course, tolerate the existence of this airway into Berlin for the military aircraft of the Anglo-American imperialists,' wrote Senin in 1950. 'In order to liquidate this aggressive "installation" and its negative consequences, and, in general, to strike from the imperialists' hands any excuses, arising from the introduction of restrictions, for kindling anti-Soviet propaganda among the Germans and for war-propaganda, in May 1949 the Soviet Government proceeded to lift the restrictions on transport, communications and trade.'[52] In this way it was obliquely admitted that the USSR had suffered defeat on the Berlin question.

The Paris meeting of the Council of Foreign Ministers did not arrive at genuine agreements. Berlin remained a divided city with different currencies. In West and East Germany alike preparations were completed for the creation of two German states.

Analysis of the conduct of the Soviet leadership during the Berlin crisis of 1948–9 enables us to say that, for them, it was a struggle to widen the Soviet sphere of influence. Moscow was trying not to allow a West German state to be formed and included in the Western bloc. The blockade of Berlin was intended to create a situation in which the USSR could negotiate on the German problem from a position of strength. In the event of the Western powers refusing to offer serious political concessions, an attempt would be made to oust them from Berlin and include the entire city in the financial and economic system of the Soviet zone.

The fundamental miscalculation by the Soviet leadership was to underestimate the determination of the Western powers, and of the USA in the first place, to pursue their line of creating a West German state, and to underestimate also the financial–economic and military–technical resources possessed by the West. The successful functioning of the American 'air-bridge' resulted in the Soviet Union suffering a political and propaganda defeat. Stalin showed once again that, when met with serious resistance in his foreign-policy actions, he was able to retreat. At the Paris meeting of the Council of Foreign

Ministers in May 1949 the Western powers enabled the Soviet leaders to 'save face' by agreeing to compromise. An important feature of this very acute international crisis of the Cold War era was the unwillingness of both sides to 'fire the first shot' and unleash a large-scale military conflict. In that sense the participants correctly understood each other's intentions and showed wise restraint.

Notes

1. Note sur la politique américaine en Europe Orientale. Le 21 août 1945, AN, Archives privées de M. Georges Bidault, fonds 457, carton AP80.
2. Note of Varga to Molotov, 24 June 1947, AVP RF, f. 6, op. 9, p. 18, d. 213, l. 2.
3. Quoted in M. Narinskii, 'Sovetskaia vneshnaia politika i proiskhozhdenie kholodnoi voiny', in *Sovetskaia politika v retrospektive, 1917–1991* (Moscow: 1993) p. 122.
4. AVP RF, f. 489, op. 24g, p. 19, d. 1, l. 172.
5. Note of Smirnov to Molotov, 3 October 1947, AVP RF, f. 082, op. 34, p. 146, d. 7, l. 1.
6. Protokol zasedaniia Politburo TsK VKP(b) ot 21.XI.1947g., RTsKhIDNI.
7. 'Germanskii vopros vo vzaimootnosheniiakh SSSR, SShA, Anglii i Frantsii v period ot Berlinskoi konferentsii do obrazovaniia dvukh germanskikh gosudarstv'. Obzor, ch. 3, AVP RF, f. 048/3, op. 11zh, p. 70, d. 17, l. 433.
8. *Ibid.*
9. Postanovlenie Soveta Ministrov SSSR ot 10.XII.1947g., APRF, f. 3, op. 64, d. 789, l. 1–2.
10. Postanovlenie Soveta Ministrov SSSR ot 7.V.1948g., *ibid.*, l. 32.
11. *New York Herald Tribune*, 20 December 1947.
12. 'Germanskii vopros', AVP RF, f. 048/3, op. 11zh, p. 70, d. 17, l. 435.
13. Telegram of Dratvin and Semenov to Molotov and Bulganin, 17 April 1948, APRF, f. 3, op. 64, d. 789, l. 23.
14. 'Germanskii vopros', AVP RF, f. 048/3, op. 11zh, p. 70, d. 17, l. 436.
15. *Ibid.*
16. *Ibid.*, l. 437.
17. See *Sovetskii Soiuz i Berlinskii vopros (Dokumenty)*, vypusk 1 (Moscow: USSR Ministry of Foreign Affairs, 1948) pp. 22–5.
18. 'Germanskii vopros', AVP RF, f. 048/3, op. 11zh, p. 70, d. 17, l. 439.
19. Telefonogram from Berlin to Moscow, 2 April 1948, APRF, f. 3, op. 64, d. 789, l. 13.
20. Telegram of Dratvin and Semenov to Molotov and Bulganin, 17 April 1948, APRF, f. 3, op. 64, d. 789, l. 25.
21. *Ibid.*, l. 24.
22. *Ibid.*, l. 28.
23. 'Zapis' besedy tov. I.V. Stalina s rukovoditeliami Sotsialisticheskoi Edinoi Partii Germanii V. Pikom i O. Grotevolem', 26 March 1948, AP RF, f. 45, op. 1, d. 303, l. 34.
24. 'Germanskii vopros', AVP RF, f. 048/3, op. 11zh, p. 70, d. 17, l. 449.
25. *Ibid.*, l. 451.

26. Postanovlenie Soveta Ministrov SSSR ot 18 marta 1948g., AP RF, f. 3, op. 64, d. 789, l. 33, 35.
27. *Sovetskii Soiuz*, p. 30.
28. 'Germanskii vopros', AVP RF, f. 048/3, op. 11zh, p. 70, d. 17, l. 454.
29. Telefonogram of Sokolovskii and Semenov to Molotov, 18 June 1948, AP RF, f. 3, op. 64, d. 789, l. 45.
30. Général Ganeval à G. Bidault, le 24.6.1948. Télégramme arrivée, AN, Archives privées de M. Georges Bidault, fonds 457, carton AP 18.
31. M. Senin, 'Zapiska po Berlinskomu voprosu. 1950g.', AVP RF, f. 082, op. 37, p. 216, d. 112, l. 21.
32. G. Bidault à AmbaFrance, Washington, le 27.VI.1948. Télégramme au départ, AN, Archives privées de M. Georges Bidault, fonds 45, carton AP 18.
33. See A. Shlaim, *The United States and the Berlin Blockade, 1948-1949. A Study in Crisis Decision-Making* (Berkeley, Ca.: University of California Press, 1983) pp. 216, 232, 248, *passim*.
34. Télégramme reçu de Berlin, le 24 Juin 1948, AN, Archives privées de M. Georges Bidault, fonds 447, carton AP 18.
35. 'Pozitsiia SShA v otnoshenii otvetnoi noty SSSR ot 14 iiuliia o polozhenii v Berline (Spravka)', AVP RF, f. 082, op. 35, p. 165, d. 32, l. 28.
36. See L. Clay, *Decision in Germany* (Melbourne–London–Toronto: 1950) p. 367.
37. US Department of State, *The Berlin Crisis. A Report on the Moscow Discussions* (Washington, D.C.: 1948) pp. 15–16.
38. 'O peregovorakh predstavitelei SShA, Velikobritanii i Frantsii s V.M. Molotovym po voprosu o polozhenii v Berline i drugim germanskim voprosam v avguste-sentiabre 1948g. (Spravka)', AVP RF, f. 7, op. 11zh, p. 1, d. 2, l. 22.
39. 'Beseda tov. I.V. Stalina s amerikanskim poslom Smitom, britanskim predstavitelem Robertsom i frantsuzskim poslom Shaten'o'', 2 avgusta 1948g., AVP RF, f. 07, op. 21zh, p. 43, d. 1, l. 7, 11.
40. *Ibid.*, l. 17.
41. *Ibid.*, l. 21.
42. *Ibid.*, l. 18.
43. 'Iz dnevnika V.M. Molotova. Priem amerikanskogo posla Smita, frantsuzskogo posla Shaten'o i predstavitelia Bevina Robertsa', 6 avgusta 1948g., AP RF, f. 3, op. 64, d. 789, l. 105.
44. AVP RF, f. 082, op. 37, p. 216, d. 112, l. 21.
45. Vypiska iz protokola No. 65 zasedaniia Politbiuro TsK VKP(b). Reshenie ot 7 avgusta 1948g., AP RF, f. 3, op. 64, d. 789, l. 119–21.
46. AVP RF, f. 07, op. 21zh, p. 43, d. 1, l. 18.
47. 'Germanskii vopros', AVP RF, f. 048/3, op. 11zh, p. 70, d. 17, l. 467.
48. AVP RF, f. 07, op. 11zh, p. 1, d. 2, l. 11.
49. 'Iz dnevnika G.M. Ratiani. Zapis' besedy s zamestitelem nachal'nika otdela pressy OON Odenom, 20 noiabria 1948g.', AVP RF, f. 082, op. 35, p. 165, d. 32, l. 62.
50. See *Sovetskii Soiuz i berlinskoi vopros (Dokumenty)*, vypusk 2 (Moscow: 1949) pp. 8–9.
51. 'Germanskii vopros', AVP RF, f. 048/3, op. 11zh, p. 70, d. 17, l. 492–3.
52. AVP RF, f. 082, op. 37, p. 216, d. 112, l. 34.

5 The Soviet Liberation of Poland and the Polish Left, 1943–5
Anita J. Prazmowska

In November 1943 the Polska Partja Robotnicza (PPR – Polish Workers Party) publicized its programme in Nazi-occupied Warsaw. Entitled 'What we are fighting for?' it laid down the basic principles for the future struggle. The organization was little known and, among wartime underground movements, it was, at the time of the publication of the programme, an entirely irrelevant political grouping.[1] The two first drafts of the PPR's declaration had been prepared by Pawel Finder, the Secretary of the Central Committee of the PPR, and the third one was prepared by Władysław Gomułka, the First Secretary of the Warsaw Party cell.[2] The final draft was agreed with Georgi Dimitrov, the head of the Comintern. Within the context of conspiratorial politics of the time the publication of a programme constituted a bid for the leadership of left-wing underground organizations. It was nevertheless a situation abundant with paradoxes. The PPR, although set up by a group of Polish ex-Communist Party members who were parachuted from the Soviet Union to Poland in December 1941, was not allowed to refer to its Communist past. The Komunistyczna Partja Polski (KPP – Polish Communist Party), had been accused of sectarianism and as a result had been disbanded by the Comintern in 1938. Subsequently, in all its activities, and most notably in its programme, the PPR sought to break links with the KPP and to assert continuity with the Socialist and peasant movement in Poland.[3] In its published programme the PPR was reticent about any identification with revolutionary objectives. The programme referred broadly to the need to create a new governmental structure in Poland after the war. This meant the creation of democratic institutions, the guaranteeing of national liberty and guarantees of equality before law for all citizens. In the economic sphere state involvement in a progressive programme of industrialization was proposed. Agriculture was to be modernized and improved, but a certain vagueness was apparent in references to land reform. In 1943 the PPR confined itself to hoping that property of collaborators – land which had been taken from Poles in the course of the war, and estates belonging to 'landowners' – would be distributed among peasants and the landless. The size of the estates which were to be broken up, was not defined.[4] Both in its detail and its general statements the programme radiated a commitment to private property, elected institutions and the defence of the Polish nation's interest.

The initiative to establish the PPR and to publicize its programme reflected the insecurity of its leadership in relation to the Soviet decision-makers. According to Gomułka it was an attempt to force the Soviet authorities to back the Polish Communists in Poland. He admitted to having become acutely aware in 1943 that Dimitrov's decision to despatch to Poland a nucleus of the future Polish Communist movement was a minor initiative and likely in due course to be sidelined by Stalin's preference for bringing into Poland his own Poles whose political profiles could be manipulated to convey a message more in tune with Stalin's policies towards his allies. The diplomatic break at the end of April 1943, between the Soviet Union and the Polish Government-in-exile which was based in London, was swiftly followed by the announcement of the creation of a new Polish authority in the Soviet Union, the Związek Patriotów Polskich (ZPP – Union of Polish Patriots). This signalled to the Warsaw-based Polish Communists the possibility of Stalin embarking on a policy of direct intervention in Poland.[5]

At the same time the PPR leadership was only too well aware of its own lack of support in Poland. In April 1943 the left wing of the Polska Partja Socjalistyczna (PPS – Polish Socialist Party) made a bid for the leadership of the disparate left-wing, trade union and progressive movements. Everything suggested that they were likely to be successful. The PPR's attempts to become a pivotal organization in the debates taking place within the reformist and progressive organizations were doomed to failure. Earlier attempts to split the Stronnictwo Ludowe (SL – Peasant Party) and to attract its more radical sections to the PPR had not been successful. The leadership of the SL in spite of its criticism of the pre-war regime now remained steadfastly loyal to the Government-in-exile. As would be inevitable in wartime conditions, the issue was not only about political alliances. The PPR, mindful of its weak base in the villages, was also seeking the collaboration of the peasant military units. It was hoped that the peasant partisan movement the Bataliony Chłopskie (BCh – Peasant Battalions), which collaborated uneasily with the Armia Krajowa (AK – Home Army), the resistance movement recognized by the Government-in-exile, could be attracted by the PPR's programme to join the Gwardie Ludowe (GL – People's Guard) units, the partisan movement of the PPR. Thus the PPR's November declaration signalled an attempt to create an umbrella organization, with democratic and progressive objectives, and emphatically Polish in character, but most importantly, broadly based and embracing left-wing and centre parties. Since the PPR was unable to attract enough support to establish a strong position in its negotiations with the AK and the SL, its next proposal was to work through conspiratorial organizations in which it could merge with others and not have to get involved in divisive debates on the subject of the Soviet Union and its territorial aims.[6]

The PPR followed the publication of its political programme with the declaration that it was supporting the establishment of the Krajowa Rada Narodowa (KRN – Homeland National Council), in effect a proposal to establish a network of local councils which would bring together various local parties and organizations committed broadly to a progressive programme based on the PPR's objectives. For Gomułka, who had replaced the arrested Finder as Party Secretary, this appeared to be a victory of the national programme. The attitude of the Comintern and the Soviet leadership to the announcement of the KRN programme was unknown, because of the Gestapo's success in discovering the PPR's radio communications with the Soviet Union. The new Party Secretary embarked on a policy of negotiating with other left-wing and Liberal parties in order to bring them into the KRN fold. The Communists hoped to benefit from divisions in the two main parties, the PPS and SL. By the end of 1943, divisions within the ranks of the Socialist movements had become open and the AK's aggressive policy of incorporating the armed peasant units into its ranks had caused further controversy. It would seem that the PPR hoped to be able to benefit from these controversies, and opened a new initiative with the announcement of a conciliatory programme and its proposal for the establishment of the national councils. In particular, they had persuaded themselves that the rank and file of the PPS and SL were critical of their leaders' inactivity and subservience to the London Poles and were looking for new initiatives. Publishing their progressive programme would, the PPR believed, encourage dissidents within the Socialist and peasant movement to voice their opposition to the Government-in-exile.

Among the left-wing parties of the inter-war period the PPS had the highest membership. However, its political influence was negligible. A number of factors had contributed to this. The Party had represented the full gamut of left-wing ideas frequently pre-dating the establishment of the independent state of Poland. The Socialist leadership's policy of supporting the Pilsudski regime divided the Party further. In the late 1930s the PPS suffered political trials and imprisonment. As the war broke out a number of its leaders decided to leave Poland together with the departing Government. They subsequently joined the Government-in-exile, frequently disagreeing with its policies, nevertheless preferring to remain within its ranks rather than outside. Inside occupied Poland an unusual decision had been made to disband the Party. The officially stated reason for this was so that the occupation forces would not identify and imprison PPS leaders.[7] An alternative suggestion was that those who chose to go into exile did not want to see a new leadership emerging within Poland. During the years that followed, the London based PPS sought to limit the influence of the left wing of the Party in occupied Poland. A new organization, dedicated to conspiratorial activities, was created by the PPS.[8] This was named Wolność, Równośća i Niepodległość (WRN – Freedom, Equality and Independence). In March 1943 the infighting within the ranks of the Socialist movement in the country and in exile was resolved uneasily by a message brought by a courier from London. The instruction was that the left-wing Socialist who had represented the movement on the Political Consultative Committee, an underground political forum which accepted the authority of the Government-in-exile in London, was to be replaced by a WRN delegate.[9] This freed the left-wing of the PPS to voice its ideological differences with the main stream Socialists openly and to proceed with building an alternative grouping on the left.

Furthermore, during the first two years of the war, the PPS was inactive. In London its leaders concentrated on exile politics. In Poland Socialists were encouraged to support the Government-in-exile's policy of concentrating on fighting two enemies, namely Nazi Germany and the Soviet Union. It was hoped that by doing this the Party would not dwell on divisive issues, such as the responsibility for the September *débâcle*, co-operation with pre-war politicians who had imprisoned Socialists, the role of trade unions in the present struggle. In this way, the Socialists were to avoid fuelling damaging splits within the nation. The same attitude prevailed in relation to the armed struggle. Socialists were encouraged to join the military organizations loyal to the Government-in-exile, and no effort was made to create a left-wing partisan movement, nor to train workers for the anticipated national uprising. In 1941 WRN formulated and published its programme. In it the organization stated its hope for a republican–democratic political system in Poland after the war. References to land reform were vague. In particular it was not clear what would be the criteria for deciding which landed estates would be taken over and redistributed. Industrial capacity which was deemed 'ready for nationalization' would be taken over and handed over to co-operatives.[10] WRN was committed to fighting the Nazi as well as the Soviet enemy. It also identified the Jews as a source of Poland's economic problems, committing itself to taking away from them what was described as their excessive influence in finance and trade. This was an unusual comment. No anti-Semitic sentiments of this sort appear in the political programmes of other left-wing movements. Inevitably, individual activists tried to rebuild the Socialist movement on both a local and national level. Simultaneously, political differences resurfaced in spite of WRN's attempts to limit them. One such group became associated with the conspiratorial publication *Barykada Wolności* (Barricade of Freedom), which started appearing in the spring of 1940. In September 1941 those associated with the *Barykada Wolności* organized a national meeting of the left wing of the PPS. In order to distance themselves from the inactivity of the WRN leadership those attending the meeting elected to call themselves Polscy Socialisci (PS – Polish Socialists). In their Political Declaration members of the new group committed themselves to an unambiguously left-wing programme of post-war reconstruction.[11] The Polish Socialists stated clearly their belief that the war would result in a political change, as a result of which the working masses would have a decisive say in the creation of a new society. Social equality, the socialization of the instruments of labour and the right of peasants to take over the land were stated as the key elements of the PS programme. In addition, the new section of the PPS (for that was all it considered itself to be at present) called for a positive attitude towards the Soviet Union and its fight against the Nazis.[12] The Central Committee of the PS had arranged for its programme to be conveyed to the London-based leadership of the PPS by a courier. In its communication the PS Central Committee reaffirmed its opposition to 'Bolshevik methods' but in support of resolving Polish–Soviet differences and a united fight against the Nazi regime.[13]

At the beginning of 1943 the Polish Socialists decided to make a break with the PPS. At a founding congress which took place in March 1943 a new party was officially named. It assumed the name Robotnicza Partia Polskich Socjalistów (RPPS – Workers' Party of the Polish Socialists). Unlike the PPS and WRN publications the RPPS programme and constitution did not avoid Marxist phraseology. The RPPS paid homage to the achievements of the Soviet Revolution but disagreed with the pace of industrialization and collectivization which caused the workers and peasants to be oppressed.[14] The Soviet Union was criticized for having abandoned the goal of world revolution and instead subjugating the policies of Communist Parties to its needs. As the RPPS programme stated, this had limited the 'revolutionary strategy of the European proletariat'.[15] While recognizing the Soviet Union's contribution to fighting Hitler's Germany, the Party clearly stated that 'it wished to take the matter of the revolution and that of the achievement of Socialism in Poland, into its own hands'.[16]

The RPPS's programme committed its membership to fostering a revolution in Poland. Power was to be taken over in the last stages of the war by a temporary Government of workers and peasants. The workers were to be armed in order that they take over factories which would then be run by factory committees. Committees of poor peasants and landless agricultural workers were to take over land which would then be distributed justly.[17] A period of consolidation of power would follow during which, according to the RPPS, the Government would have extensive powers to fight the counter-revolutionary forces. What would follow would be a Socialist Republic in which the power of the propertied classes and the Catholic Church would be destroyed. That republic would be classless and 'all society's efforts would be directed towards the common good'.

The RPPS created a military wing. After briefly toying with the idea of calling its partisan units the Armia Ludowa (AL – People Army) in July it was decided to call the units loyal to the RPPS Polska Armia Ludowa (PAL – Polish People's Army). This was done in order to distinguish its units from the PPR military units, the Gwardia Ludowa, which were in the meantime being consolidated into an army and would be called Armia Ludowa.[18] It was hoped that the Bataliony Chlopskie loyal to the peasant movement would unite with the PAL units, forming a strong military counterbalance to the AK.

The entry of the ex-Communists onto the political scene in occupied Poland had been hampered by the fact that they had been forced to build a new organization from scratch. Nor were its objectives clear, beyond generally stated ideas of rallying those opposed to the Nazi aggressor. Neither the individuals empowered by the Comintern to incorporate the Polish Communists to the new party, nor Dimitrov himself, were very clear where this new organization would fit into the context of political debates taking place in occupied Poland. The PPR's objectives had been, from the outset, to form an anti-Fascist bloc abroad. The leader of the first group parachuted from the Soviet Union, Marceli Nowotko, identified the PPS and SL as the two potential allies. In June 1942 Nowotko wrote optimistically to Dimitrov that contact had been made with the Polish Socialists and expressed the hope that it was possible to think of joint action.[19] On the 29 June Nowotko reported that the *Barykadowcy* (the name given to those associated with *Barykada Wolności*) had a radical programme, 'nearly Soviet'. He noted that the left wing of the PPS, unlike the right PPS sections and the SL, did not look to London.[20] Nowotko continued in his optimistic belief that the PPR could enter into political agreements with other political groups. On 31 July he reported again to Dimitrov that the PPR's contact with the masses was increasing. He appeared to be convinced that, unlike the KPP, which he described as '80 per cent Ukrainian, Belorussian and Jewish', the PPR would not become a sectarian organization lacking contact with the masses.[21]

Nowotko was assassinated on 28 November 1942 by the brother of another of the PPR leaders in circumstances that are to this day unclear. When Pawel Finder became the First Secretary he continued the task of building bridges with other anti-Fascist political organizations. He was hampered in this by Soviet instructions and expectations. The Party was not entirely free to adjust its programme. Dimitrov made it clear in March–April 1943, when first attempts were made by the PPR to formulate its post-war programme, that they had to stick to a popular front programme. He forbade them to use the phrase 'the establishment of the authority of workers and peasants'. He instructed that the basic principles of the PPR's programme should be (1) the defeat of the enemy, (2) the winning of national independence and (3) the establishment of genuine national democratic authority, and not that of workers and peasants.[22] In these circumstances the PPR had limited freedom to negotiate with dissidents from the ranks of PPS and other left-wing groups on the basis of any other programme. A paradoxical situation emerged. While the PPR was commonly believed to be a revolutionary party, a perception it tried to dispel, other potential left-wing partners were unabashed about their radical post-war aims, which they stressed differed from those of the Communists because the non-Communist left would not allow Poland to become the Soviet Union's seventeenth republic. Whereas the RPPS's programme was revolutionary and Socialist, the PPR was fixed firmly to a democratic popular front platform required of them by Dimitrov.

In 1943 both sides sought to investigate the possibility of co-operation. It is not entirely clear why this proved impossible. Gomułka subsequently claimed that the RPPS was anti-Soviet and that it viewed the PPR as no more than Soviet stooges.[23] One of the RPPS leaders recorded a different story. He pointed out that the organization represented a variety of views and that only one section was hostile to the Soviet Union. The real reason for the RPPS's leadership's reluctance to support the PPR and join the KRN, according to Mulak, was the feeling that a direct association with the PPR would discredit the RPPS at a time of deep internal ideological and leadership struggles. The RPPS was willing to consider supporting the PPR but came to the conclusion that it was necessary first to complete talks aimed at co-operation with SL.[24] This decision, confirmed at the Third Conference of the RPPS in September 1943, caused a split within the organization. The group led by Edward Osóbka Morawski, which supported direct co-operation with the PPR, was isolated.[25] Co-operation between the two organizations on a national level proved impossible, though the RPPS suggested that the PPR join in forming factory committees and trade unions. This limited platform for joint work was accepted by the PPR.[26]

The RPPS was the key organization in unifying disparate left-wing groups opposed to the Government-in-exile in London. Although its membership was small, it was respected by other Socialist, radical and syndicalist groups. Its key role was confirmed in February 1943 by the creation of the Centralizacja Stronnictw Demokratycznych, Socjalistycznych i Syndykalistycznych (CSDSiS – The Centralization of Democratic, Socialist and Syndicalist Parties). Its executive organization was the Centralny Komitet Ludowy (CKL – Central People's Committee). The failure to draw the Peasant Party into the new umbrella organization immediately qualified its long-term success. This meant that once more the RPPS had to look to its own resources.

From June 1944 the RPPS decided to adopt the historic name PPS-Lewica (Polish Socialist Party – The left-wing faction). (A faction of the PPS under that name had gone in to make up the first Polish Communist Party in 1920.) The 18-point programme reaffirmed the PPS–Lewica's commitment to the establishment of a workers' and peasants' state after the war.[27] In addition to making references to parliamentary institutions guaranteeing equality of political and civil rights, the programme referred to local self-government and factory and village councils and co-operatives as a means of people's power. The destruction of the capitalist system was identified as the most pressing objective in Socialist Poland. The expansion of co-operatives was seen as a way of securing supplies without allowing exploitation. The programme did not confine itself to purely internal Polish matters. Revolutionary objectives included the destruction of the world capitalist system. Compared with the earlier programme of the RPPS, the PPS-Lewica was even more precise in its political credo. It was Marxist and internationalist in a clear and uninhibited manner, in contrast with the programme put forward by the PPR to gain popular acceptance.

By the summer PPS-Lewica resumed talks with the aim of joining the KRN. According to Gomułka the PPR became increasingly keen to bring the CKL into the KRN. As was bluntly admitted, the CKL was an umbrella organization bringing together real, even if not the most powerful or numerous left-wing parties. The leadership of the PPR knew that the organizations in KRN were fictitious so that their claim to represent various social and political groups was also a fiction.[28] Without the CKL's co-operation or external support, the PPR's attempts to influence developments in post-war Poland would be difficult, if not outright impossible. In co-operation with the CKL, the PPR was more likely to draw the SL into joint planning. PPR–CKL unity was a precondition for securing the goodwill of the peasant movement.

During talks which the CKL conducted with PPR representatives in the spring of 1944 the former put forward a suggestion that the two could join the Rada Jedności Narodowej (RJD – Council of National Unity) which had been set up in January 1944. This was a form of underground parliament which brought together the four main political movements loyal to the Polish Government in London: the Peasant Party, the Socialists, the Party of Labour and the National Democrats.

The CKL tried to persuade the PPR that they could form a left-wing opposition bloc within the RJD.[29] When the Communists appealed to Moscow for advice they were told not to accept the CKL proposal and instead to continue with their policy of drawing parties into their KRN organization. This enquiry coincided with the visit of a KRN delegation to Stalin on 19 May 1944, as a result of which the KRN was assured that it would have a greater say in the establishment of a provisional government in Poland than the ZPP and the Communists, who were in the Soviet Union.[30]

The outbreak of Warsaw Uprising on 1 August and the participation of the PPS-Lewica's military section, the PAL, in fighting in Warsaw led to destruction of its Warsaw organization and the loss of its precariously achieved military potential. Since the most important and successful conspiratorial cell of the PPS-Lewica had been established in Warsaw, and the main power base of the PAL had been in the Warsaw factories, this spelled the end of the independent Polish left-wing alternative to the Communists. As the Red Army entered Polish territories, in some cases PAL units joined the AL loyal to the PPR, in other cases united with the peasant guerrillas in the Bataliony Chłopskie (BCh).

The disintegration of the autonomous left-wing movement in Poland was completed as much by an internal confusion as by the repression of the Gestapo. PPS leaders who had spent the war years in the Soviet Union had decided to join the Soviet-sponsored ZPP. This meant that they entered Lublin and continued their activities in liberated territories together with the Lublin authorities. The PPS organization in the Soviet Union had not conducted its own policies and had instructed Socialists to join the ZPP.[31] The PPS organization in liberated Poland was to be dominated by those who had returned to Poland with the Red Army and the Osóbka Morawski group which had earlier dissented from the RPPS decision not to join the KRN.

The need to secure the support of the peasant movement was obvious to all conspiratorial political and military organizations. The Government in London, the Socialist movement and the PPR, when it entered the scene in 1942, went to great lengths to secure the support of the peasants. Unlike the Socialist movement the most influential Peasant Party was able to establish near total control over its membership and by 1940 had already a well-organized nationwide network.[32]

The Stronnictwo Ludowe-'Roch' (SL-Roch, Peasant Party's movement using the pseudonym 'Roch') had, in addition, well-established contacts with the Sikorski Government, which the exile leaders supported. After Sikorski's death the position of Prime Minister was taken over by Stanisław Mikołajczyk, the leader of the SL. The AK was dependent on the support of the SL since more than half of the partisan units loyal to the Government-in-exile were in fact Bataliony Chłopskie which had been formed by the SL. The AK leadership was not happy about the independence of the peasant units. They would have preferred to see all partisans united under its leadership. General Rowecki, who was in charge of the united underground units from 1940, found the independence of the SL particularly irksome.[33]

It was inevitable that relations between the leadership of the AK and the peasant movement were going to be difficult. The SL leadership pointed out to Rowecki that the peasants deeply resented the AK's contempt for them, that they felt that the most important military and political positions were retained by the supporters of the pre-war Government.[34] With time the question of control over arms and complaints about the AK's unwillingness to take action, so as to conserve resources for the planned national uprising, was to cause sufficient disaffection among the BCh who were associated with the AK, for them to seek alternative allegiances.

In one of his first reports to Dimitrov, Nowotko assessed the peasant movement as decentralized but strong in the regions. He wrote that their political programme was vague, 'neither capitalist nor socialist'. He assessed their attacks on the Soviet Union as 'moderate' in tone.[35] In their leaflets addressed to 'workers, peasants and the intelligentsia' the PPR stated that it stood for a free Poland in which 'land would belong to the peasants'.[36] It would appear that these general appeals had no effect on the peasant movement, in particular because of the peasants' strong loyalties to their own organizations.[37] During the remaining years of the war, couriers who carried reports from Poland to London and PPR activists both admitted that the peasants and their leaders simply distrusted political movements based on the workers. They were not Socialist and had no feeling of class solidarity with the town. That factor, possibly more than anything else, stood in the way of the PPR's partisan groups establishing anything more lasting than vague co-operation based on temporary expedience.[38]

Towards the end of 1943, when the PPR opened a debate on the subject of the post-war order followed, in December 1943, by the establishment of the KRN as a form of popular parliament under its control, the PPR attitude towards the peasant movement altered. Attempts were now made to divide the rank and file of the movement from their leadership and to attract them towards joint action, with promises of availability of arms and action with the Communists. Frustration with the inactivity of the AK was in effect the only motive for members of the BCh changing their allegiance and joining the AL units.

Like the PPS leadership, the SL was divided according to where sanctuary was obtained during the war. The SL leader Mikołajczyk became the Prime Minister of the Government-in-exile in London, where the SL was the largest political group participating in the

Council of National Unity, the quasi-parliamentary exile authority. But there were also SL leaders who had ended up in the Soviet Union. On Polish territories a small group of dissident SL members grouped themselves around the publication *Wola Ludu* (The People's Will). They were willing to associate with the KRN. In the Soviet-occupied territories a rival SL leadership joined the ZPP and subsequently the Lublin authority.[39] A common ideology and programmes which would define the movement's broad aims were the obvious casualties of such divisions. Until the end of the war, in spite of its impressive organizational structure, the movement was deeply divided and, most importantly, unclear about the nature of the land reform which it sought.

In their dealings with the peasant movement the PPR and the military leaders of the AL units were quick to realize that the supply of arms would be a decisive factor. Away from Warsaw, relations between local commanders of BCh and AK units varied widely. By 1943, where difficulties arose, these tended to relate to the BCh commanders' frustration with the AK policy of conserving its resources for the planned national uprising. In some cases, the AK officers' high-handed treatment of the peasant partisans and their collaboration and familiarity with unpopular local landowners made for a potent mix of disappointment and anger. These were circumstances in which the rank and file of local BCh units were occasionally willing either to join outright AL units, or to enter into fraternal agreements with them. Rarely did the BCh partisans turn to the AL because of an appreciation of the PPR's political programme. This would suggest that, had the AL been able to secure regular supplies of arms, they would have been able to exploit disaffection with the AK and to establish closer relations with the peasant movement. This in turn would have made it more likely that the Socialist movements would have been more willing to enter into agreements with the PPR.

Unfortunately, in spite of being to all intents and purposes Soviet agents in Poland, the PPR had little influence over decisions made in Moscow. According to Gomułka the PPR and the AL were never able to count on regular supplies of arms. The suspicion was not only that Dimitrov's influence on the Soviet leadership was minimal, but that he himself did not want to see the emergence of an independent Communist movement firmly rooted in Polish underground politics.[40]

The difficulties experienced by the PPR leadership in establishing itself within the Polish underground movement are illustrated by the reports which the PPR activists and AL commanders send to the Central Committee. For example, in March 1943 the PPR received a report from the Lublin district. Its writer stated that PPR's slogans were making little impression in the area, though availability of weapons would change this state of affairs, and would be a decisive factor in attracting people to the Party.[41] By April 1944 reports from the Lublin area optimistically stated that BCh partisans were transferring to the AL. In one particular incident two units, training with the AL, joined it when the AK decided to confiscate arms from the BCh partisans.[42]

Unfortunately for the PPR leadership, the Soviet Union retained total control over most supplies sent to Poland. This meant that the PPR's negotiating position in relation to the SL and BCh partisans was always constrained. Although at the end of hostilities all efforts were made to encourage BCh men to transfer to the Polish People's Army, the political advantages that might have been gained from closer association during the occupation were never fully exploited.

CONCLUDING REMARKS

The purpose of this chapter has been to signal areas of future research. It is clear that a study of internal politics and exchanges between the PPR, on the one hand, and the Socialist movements conspiratorial organizations and the peasant movement, on the other, is not adequate in explaining the limited success of the PPR in its policies. As has been suggested, there existed in Poland political groups which were determined to pursue a revolutionary or at least a radical programme. Nevertheless, the Soviet Union would not support such a programme for Poland. Its policy towards Poland went against establishing the basis of a future Communist system. While such a system might have been a consideration in the policies of the Comintern, or a group within that organization, it was not an option which was pursued with any consistency by the Soviet authorities. By ignoring, for pragmatic reasons, opportunities to facilitate the PPR's search for a base in Polish society, the Soviet Union made it all the more difficult for the Polish Communists to build a base in Polish society after the war.

Notes

1. K. Przybysz, *Wizje Polski. Programy polityczne latwojny i okupacji 1939–1944* (Warsaw: Elipsa, 1992) pp. 265–80.
2. F. Tych (ed.), *Archiwum Ruchu Robotniczego*, Vol. 1 (Warsaw: Ksiáźka i Wiedza on behalf of Centralne Archiwum KC PZPR) pp. 223–83.
3. Przybysz, *Wizje Polski*, pp. 278–91.
4. *Ibid.*, pp. 268–9.
5. W. Gomułka, *Pamiętniki*, Vol. 2 (Warsaw: Polska Oficyna Wydawnicza «BGW», 1994) pp. 340–1.
6. A. Werblan, *Klasowe in narodowe aspekty myslipolitycznej PPR in PZPR* (Warsaw: Panstwowe Wydawnictwo Naukowe, 1987) pp. 131–5.
7. This argument is put forward by most of the PPS leaders, for example A. Pragier, K. Puźak.

8. J. Mulak, *Polska Lewica Socjalistyczna 1939–1944* (Warsaw: Ksiáźka i Wiedza, 1990) pp. 38–41.
9. J. Lerski, *Emisariusz Jur* (Warsaw: Oficyna Wydawnicza Interim sp. z o.o., 1989) pp. 103–4.
10. AAN, WRN, 205/1, pp. 1–4a, 1941.
11. *Ibid.*, pp. 318–19.
12. *Ibid.*
13. AAN, Polscy Sociališci, 340/t. 1, pp. 2–3n.
14. AAN, RPPS, 196/1, p. 3c.
15. *Ibid.*
16. *Ibid.*
17. *Ibid.*, p. 4a.
18. Mulak, *Polska*, p. 445.
19. AAN, PPR, 190/I–13, 11 June 1942.
20. AAN, PPR, 190/I–13, 29 June 1942.
21. AAN, PPR, 190/13–1, 31 July 1942.
22. AAN, PPR, 190/I–13, 1 March 1943.
23. Gomułka, *Pamiętniki*, pp. 336–8.
24. Mulak, *Polska*, p. 459.
25. *Ibid.*, pp. 479–83.
26. AAN, RPPS, 198/1, pp. 17–19, 9 October 1943.
27. AAN, RPPS, 198/1.
28. Gomułka, *Pamiętniki*, p. 411.
29. *Ibid.*, p. 412.
30. *Ibid.*, pp. 414–16.
31. AAN, CKW PPS at the ZG ZPP, Moscow 428/2, 22 September 1945.
32. E. Duraczyński, *Kontrowersje i konflikty 1939–1941* (Warsaw: Państwowe Wydawnictwo Naukowe, 1979) pp. 334–5.
33. ARL, KG–11, 4 December 1942.
34. *Ibid.*
35. AAN, PPR, 190/I–13, 29 July 1942.
36. AAN, PPR, 190–I–1, January 1942.
37. M. Nadolski, *Komunišci wobec chłopów w Polsce 1941–1956* (Warsaw: Ošrodek Badań Społecznych, 1993) p. 31.
38. *Ibid.*, pp. 33–4.
39. J. Coutouvidis, J. Reynolds, *Poland 1939–1947* (Leicester: Leicester University Press, 1986) pp. 141–2.
40. Gomułka, *Pamiętniki*, pp. 385–6.
41. AAN, PPR, XII–10, 1 March 1943.
42. AAN, PPR, XII/10, 12 April 1944.

6 The Soviet Union and Finland after the War, 1944–53
Jukka Nevakivi

Stalin's attitude to Finland was a rather controversial one. In order to make the Finns bow to his demands he allowed the Red Army to invade the country in November 1939. He was by then using the invitation by a Soviet-installed 'Finnish People's Government' led by O.V. Kuusinen to camouflage this aggression as an act of international solidarity assisting Finnish 'Democrats' in distress. But as the Finns resisted and as the Western powers appeared to intervene in the resulting Winter War, the Kremlin dropped the puppet cabinet and negotiated a peace treaty with the Government in Helsinki.[1]

One cannot fail to observe the reasonable character of this arrangement despite the severity of its terms for Finland. In fact, far from being a surrender, the Moscow Peace Treaty of 12 March 1940 allowed Finland to keep its army and even to strengthen its defences provided that this did not take place in an alliance with a third power. The territorial concessions also, as serious as they were, did not extend at that time to the Petsamo region on the Arctic coast, which Finland had controlled since 1920, allowing the country continuous access to open seas and to the outer world.

Even when the embittered Finns joined Hitler's Barbarossa Operation in order to take revenge for the Winter War, Stalin was prepared to come to terms with them, obviously wanting to neutralize their war effort. Having finally accepted a negotiated peace from them he refrained from conquering the country, employed no pretext for occupying it even after the armistice, and did not back the Finnish Communists to take over or even rescue them when the People's Democrats were ousted from Government in July 1948 by their countrymen.

Stalin was satisfied with the Finnish Government's signing of a friendship treaty with the Soviet Union, the name of which was the same as that of the treaties concluded by Moscow with the other Eastern and Central European countries in its sphere of influence. But he did not mind the contents of this treaty being different and even allowed a mention of Finnish endeavours to stay outside great powers' conflicts. Correspondingly he also gave Finland the chance to avoid the status of a people's democracy by allowing it, as the only exception among the European neighbours of Russia, to preserve its traditional political system based on the Constitution of 1919 and its market economy.

Why did the dictator make this exception to the process of Sovietizing all the other countries concerned in 1945–8? Did he have some sentimental or personal motives in allowing Finland to survive, or did he leave this country out for particular *raisons d'état*? These questions will only be answered, if ever, after the most confidential Presidential Archives are opened in Moscow. Even so, some trends, if not causes and consequences, of the Soviet policy towards Finland during Stalin's last years can be traced from the evidence revealed by the declassified parts of the archives of the Soviet Communist Party Central Committee, and of the Soviet Ministry for Foreign Affairs. One suggested argument for the Soviet policy towards Finland is the fact that Lenin had, in co-operation with Stalin – the then Commissar for Nationalities – recognized Finnish independence on the last day of the year in 1917. Both men had, during their underground activities, been hiding or travelling in Finland on several occasions, and though most of the Finns known by Stalin during that time were no longer to influence him during World War II and after it, he might have retained some of his former impressions when dealing with the Finns. The Finnish spirit of resistance, not least that of winter 1939–40, seems to have left him with an open wound.

The position of Finland in the post-war European order had been sketched as early as December 1941 when the British Foreign Secretary Anthony Eden had visited Moscow for the first time. Stalin had been adamant that the Finns would not get a peace on better terms than those they were given in March 1940 when they signed the Moscow treaty ending the Winter War. On the contrary, he had made it clear that the Soviet Union would claim from them an additional region, Petsamo, and 'some kind of military alliance which would give the Russians right to maintain naval and military bases on Finnish territory'.[2]

'We had agreed to these terms,' concludes the official historian of British foreign policy and citing Eden's own comments on the Finnish Armistice terms in 1944, continues:

> Although we hoped that Finland would be left with some real independence – at least in cultural and economic matters – and a parliamentary regime, Russian influence would be predominant in the country. We need not, and indeed could not, contest such influence.[3]

In fact, after the Teheran Conference, where the American President together with the British Prime Minister had appealed to Stalin for a more lenient treatment of Finland, the Soviet Government had ceased to ask the Finns for unconditional surrender. It had then received a Finnish offer to negotiate, at the same time as Moscow radio, on the 29 February 1944, claimed that Finland had never been asked to accept such serious terms. Nevertheless, once the Red Army had succeeded in breaking the Finnish defence lines in the Karelian isthmus, the Soviets appear to have prepared themselves for the occupation of the whole country. According to a document draft discovered recently in the archives of the Soviet Foreign Ministry, Finland was to be subjugated under a rigorous military administration; the plan included among other items the arrest of the members of the paramilitary Civil Guards, the *Suojeluskunnat*.[4]

Although the Soviet answer to the Finnish peace offer transmitted to Helsinki on 22 June 1944, after the fall of Viborg, was interpreted as a further demand that Finland surrender unconditionally, and as the claim was subsequently rejected, the Kremlin did not insist on it but accepted a negotiated armistice in the following September. How this agreement was put into practice was seen during the following three-year period preceding the final Peace Treaty of Paris, which came into force, after its ratification, by September 1947.

The Party leader in Leningrad, Andrei Alexandrovich Zhdanov, had emerged since the eve of World War II as one of the most prominent protagonists of Finnish affairs in the Soviet Communist Party Central Committee. Having taken an active part in the preparations and even in the execution of the Winter War, he was, with Foreign Minister V.M. Molotov and the military representative Brigadier A.M. Vasilevsky, the third signatory to the Peace Treaty of Moscow in 1940. Promoted to Colonel General and appointed as the representative of the Allied (Soviet) High Command when the Armistice was being negotiated with the Finns after the Continuation War, his role as a signatory was even more significant. He alone put his name under the conditions on behalf of both the Soviet and British Governments. As a consequence, he was sent to Finland after the armistice to chair the Allied Control Commission. The arrival in Helsinki after the armistice of 1944 of the man who had directed the Sovietization of Estonia in 1940 and organized the defence of Leningrad as the leading political officer during the years 1941–4, was seen as an ominous sign that the Kremlin had decided to settle its account with Finland. His position as the highest executive of the Soviet Union's Finnish policy was emphasized by the fact that he was known to be Stalin's trusted ideologist and was, besides his continued formal position at the head of the Allied Control Commission in Helsinki, to be charged in 1946 with the guidance of the new Department of Foreign Affairs of the Soviet Party Central Committee which was established in 1946 under the direction of Mikhail Suslov.[5] Zhdanov was a top-ranking Soviet figure, a confidant of Stalin who executed his master's instructions in policy-making word-for-word and reported on his own activities directly to the Kremlin. What he marked down about his sayings and doings must have been in conformity with the goals of the Soviet Government. Correspondingly, his papers are to be considered as an exceptionally valuable primary source in seeking Soviet intentions in Finland in the years 1944–7.

The collection of A.A. Zhdanov, kept at the Russian Centre of Conservation and Study of Records for Modern History in Moscow,[6] is very rich in contents and well preserved. The part of the collection which is related to Zhdanov's activities as the Chairman of the Allied Control Commission in Helsinki contains 88 folders, altogether about 3000 pages.

The Zhdanov Papers provide an opportunity to study the Soviet postwar policy on Finland through the peephole offered by the Allied Control Commission in Helsinki and to compare it with the practice followed in the other European countries which fell under Moscow's influence as a result of the war.

My hypothesis for the first period is that the line that the ACC followed in Finland until the peace-making of 1947 corresponded to the principles which the Soviet Union tried to maintain in comparable countries. The Baltic States were treated exceptionally after their 'liberation' as Soviet member states. Other exceptions were, of course, Albania, Bulgaria and Yugoslavia, which did not have a common border with the USSR, but which were nevertheless declared as people's democracies even before 1947.

The basis of Soviet policy immediately after the war was the ideological *détente* adopted after the dissolution of the Comintern in May 1943. As it happened, the supervisory role of Moscow over the former Comintern member parties never ended. Even though the Executive Committee had been disbanded, its Secretary General G.M. Dimitrov had been appointed head of the new Department of International Information of the Soviet Communist Party Central Committee in July 1944 which had taken over the bulk of the functions of the former organization.[7]

Stalin, as we know, was preparing himself for the war resulting in the partition of Eastern and Central Europe into those spheres of influence which would be inherited by the powers whose troops were the first to reach the territory concerned. He had reason to fear that local Communists would by their umcompromising attitudes create difficulties when mobilizing the Eastern European and Balkan countries against the Germans and adapting their populations to Soviet domination.

Even more, after the dissolution of the Comintern the Soviets seem even to have played for a while with the naïve idea that Socialism would find its way into the most conservative political systems through parliamentary methods: 'Today Socialism is possible even under the English monarchy,' Stalin is reported as having said to Tito when the Yugoslav leader was visiting Moscow in April 1945. 'Revolution is no longer necessary everywhere. Just recently a delegation of British Labourites was here, and we talked about this in particular. Yes, there is much that is new. Yes, Socialism is possible even under an English king.'[8]

The parliamentary method instead of a revolutionary seizure of power was the model which Zhdanov, too, wanted to offer as instrument of policy to the local Extreme Left soon after he settled down in Helsinki. Meeting on 1 December 1944 with a delegation of the newly legalized Finnish Communist Party, he was told by one of the new leaders, Hertta Kuusinen, that people regarded it as a mistake 'that Soviet tanks had not arrived in Helsinki'. Zhdanov's comment to this was significant: 'We do not bring anybody abroad at our expense.'[9]

Zhdanov indeed ignored what had happened some five years earlier, in 1939–40, when the Red Army had attempted to bring the father of his interlocutor, the head of the 'Finnish People's Government', by force of arms to Helsinki. On the contrary, he tried to argue for what had happened in Russia during the Great Patriotic War: 'Nor did we have another Red Army to rescue us [had the old one fallen],' he said and added: 'Victory is a victory only when you gain it on your own initiative.' Zhdanov's message to Finnish Communists was clearly worded: if they were strong enough to challenge power in the country, it would be up to them to do so – but they should not base their calculations on Soviet assistance.

The Soviet leadership was aware that the Finnish Communist Party – which for 25 years had been forced to live underground – was in bad shape. In September 1944 it hardly had 2000 active members. Even so, the Soviets had it difficult to understand that Finnish Communists had not been able to create any serious resistance against their wartime Government and even after the armistice did not know what to do. 'I regret to say that Communists have been until now so scarce that, instead of legalizing their Party without delay, they run around here in the Commission to enquire whether it is allowed,' Zhdanov said scornfully.[10]

Instead, Zhdanov found it politically astute that the 'reactionary' Finnish Government in power had acted at the right moment and taken the peace initiative into its own hands. Even more, as he had characterized the Finnish Government's peace policy as a 'manoeuvre', the newly appointed head of the political department of the Allied Control Commission, P.D. Orlov – who had been Soviet envoy to Finland after the Winter War in the years 1940–1 – had the courage to praise its Premier's (Antti Hackzell) radio speech on the occasion of the armistice as one of 'unparalleled' constructiveness and optimism. According to Orlov, the Government had been 'exceptionally wise' in starting the peace negotiations in time.[11]

Meeting his Allied Control Commission personnel for the first time on 5 October 1944, the Chairman took the opportunity to emphasize that the purpose of the Commission was to control the putting into practice of the Finnish armistice treaty, nothing more. It had to have dealings only with the legal Finnish Government which the Soviet Union had recognized *de facto* when concluding with it the armistice treaty. 'We have not to give the Finnish Communists any advice, we consider it as an internal Finnish matter,' Zhdanov added. 'We do not have two policies, we have only one – the most serious official policy based on the conditions of the armistice treaty.'[12] When pressuring the Finnish Government to fulfil the armistice terms, the Allied Control Commission collided inevitably with the Marshal of Finland, C.E.G. Mannerheim, the then President of the republic, who was at the same time still the Finnish Commander-in-Chief. At first, Zhdanov obviously had in mind to squeeze him to do what the Soviets wanted. The Marshal's responsibility for Finland entering the war on Germany's side in 1941 was so evident, the Chairman said, that if anyone were to be brought into a trial over Finnish responsibility for the war, 'the first one would be Mannerheim'.[13] Revenge on those who had been responsible for Finland's wartime policies was so strongly present in Zhdanov's thoughts that, arriving for the first time in Helsinki, he even spoke of 'executing all the war criminals'! Even so, Mannerheim's co-operation in fulfilling the armistice conditions and in reorienting the country back from its pro-German policies to a new world order defined by the United Nations, was found all the same necessary.

The Kremlin was very severe in expecting the Finns to fulfil the armistice conditions. Once Prime Minister Hackzell had omitted to say in his radio speech on 2 September that Finland would begin compliance with the conditions by breaking relations with Germany, the Soviets reacted by ceasing fire not on 4 September, as agreed and as the Finns did, but on 5 September. The decision to prolong the war by 24 hours was understandably motivated by the will to punish.[14]

The acid test of Finnish sincerity was the second article of the armistice conditions, the obligation imposed on Finland to 'disarm' and 'intern' the German forces which remained on Finnish territory after 15 September, and to hand their personnel over to the Soviet High Command as prisoners of war. In Zhdanov's words, it was up to the Finns to show whether they were in earnest or 'only scraped the fiddle'.[15] In consequence, German troops having been summoned to leave by their High Command, evacuated the whole of southern Finland. Only the 20th Mountain Army operating in the northern front as far south as Oulu (Finland's 'waistline') was unable to leave the country in the time requested. It had at its disposal nine divisions, altogether over 220 000 men, heavily armed and well-trained in arctic war conditions. In order to avoid a clash with it, the Finnish HQ had come with the Mountain Army Staff to a secret understanding on German withdrawal on good terms. Though Mannerheim as the Commander-in-Chief of the Finnish Army was personally responsible for this arrangement, he was forced by the Allied Control Commission to order his forces to pursue the withdrawing Germans, thus breaking with the terms of the agreement. The obligation to open hostilities against the Germans was a burdensome one since Finland had, according to Article 4 of the armistice agreement, also undertaken to place its army on a peace footing within two and half months from the day of signing the treaty. This meant that, in principle, northern Finland had to be cleared of Germans before the beginning of December when some 500 000 troops, in other words over 90 per cent of the total Finnish wartime strength, had to be demobilized.[16]

As a consequence, when meeting with Mannerheim for the first time on 7 October, two days after his arrival in Helsinki, Zhdanov was far from happy with the Finnish fulfilment of the second article of the Armistice Treaty. Instead of bowing to the Chairman, the Marshal hinted at the impossible character of the article obliging the Finns to disarm the withdrawing Germans. He referred to the stipulation included in the same article according to which the Soviet Government would help the Finnish Army to put the disarmament into effect.

The Soviets did not respond to Mannerheim's appeal. All the land fighting in clearing Finnish territory had, in consequence, to be done by the Finns themselves at the expense of over 1000 troops killed and nearly 3000 wounded, in addition to which the whole province of Lapland was destroyed totally by Germans before their withdrawal. Zhdanov himself warned on 16 October that the Finnish Government and High Command had to do their duty, otherwise 'the Allied High Command has the obligation to take the measures which it sees necessary'. In spite of the fact that Rovaniemi, the capital of Lapland, was recaptured by the Finns the following day, the Marshal was nervous that the Soviets were perhaps preparing for the occupation of Finland.

In the light of the material discovered from the Allied Control Commission's papers, Zhdanov's *ukaz* was only meant to frighten Mannerheim. In fact Stalin had precisely at that time ordered his six to seven divisions concentrated in Petsamo to continue their offensive to the north of Norway, and the Soviet Army would consequently hardly have had enough troops to occupy Lapland, let alone the whole of Finland.[17]

Typically enough, Stalin responded to Mannerheim's proposal, a Soviet move against the German flank at Ivalo, as much as 12 days later, stating that it had been made too late and was no longer 'realistic'. The Finnish forces were, nevertheless, requested to continue their operations northwards although, according to the armistice treaty, they had to begin to demobilize their units onto a peace footing at the same time. The only way the Soviets helped in pursuing the Germans in Lapland was by their air force reconnaissance and bombing operations, the results of which, however, are still unclear.[18]

The real purpose in forcing the Finns to fight the withdrawing German army was to lead them into conflict with their former friends. This is shown by Zhdanov's blood-thirsty argument to his Allied Control Commission personnel, on 5 October 1944: 'We must strive for it that they kill some dozen Germans ... and that once they start ... their former channels to the Germans will be closed.'[19] The more important operations which had started in Poland and in the Baltic in July–August 1944 absorbed the Soviet military potential with the result that, once Finland was knocked out of the war, Stalin, instead of trying to occupy the country merely for political reasons, preferred to save his troops for the main fronts where the fate of the war in Europe was to be decided.[20]

Finland in addition gave many promises that it would be willing to do its best to carry out the conditions of the armistice. One of the most important conditions, which related to the poor state of the Soviet economy, was to start to make a serious effort to pay off the war reparations. The Russian railways and inland water transport, which had suffered heavy losses during the war, were given a type of first-aid in the form of additional rolling stock and a number of boats, which the Finns delivered as indemnities by the last quarter of 1944. Finnish industry was nearly intact despite the Soviet bombings of the previous winter, and was fully operational after the demobilization of the armed forces in December 1944. It was in a position to begin war reparation production without delay, delivering most goods desired to Russia – even responding to special 'tailor-made' orders. Finnish reparations, the original total being $300 million at the 1938 price level, were of the same amount as those demanded from Romania. They were relatively small but at least during the first two or three years quite significant. During the winter of 1944–5 the only reparations received by the Soviet Union were from Finland. As the Romanian, Hungarian and even German industries were largely destroyed and were consequently unable to produce reparations in any large quantities – and the Americans for their part closed down the lend and lease programme and even imposed an embargo on the Soviet Union – Finnish deliveries were of importance.

The Control Commission was thus anxious to preserve a good labour climate in Finland and to counteract any move which might cause serious disruption to production. This was no doubt an important consideration in Moscow's decision to dissuade and even disapprove of local Communists in their desire for taking over in Finland. This was clear from the outset when, during the conversation mentioned between Zhdanov and the representatives of the Finnish Communist Party, Hertta Kuusinen suggested that anti-Fascist volunteers (deserted soldiers and leftists who had been freed from jails after the armistice) should be organized and armed to fight the Germans. Zhdanov disapproved of the proposal and said sourly that it came too late: the Germans were already nearly out of Finland.

Probably one of the main reasons why Finland was not obliged, like Romania, to join the full-scale war against Germany and was allowed to bring its men home, starting the reconstruction of the country eight or nine months earlier than the future Kremlin satellites, was an economical one. Political considerations, too, may have motivated the Kremlin's unwillingness to encourage Finland to move openly to the Allied side. When Kuusinen adverted to the question claiming that the Finnish Government should declare war on Germany, Zhdanov said pointedly: 'People do not wish to think of a new war.'[21] Moreover, when in the final stage of the European war, on 3 March 1945, the Finnish Government made a declaration according to which Finland was considered to have been in a state of war with Germany since 15 September 1944 – the deadline given to the German troops to leave the country – the act seems not to have made any impression on the Soviets.[22] Instead, Zhdanov surprised the Kremlin with his readiness to conclude a military alliance with Finland. Surprising enough, the initiative for this arrangement, which foreshadowed the Friendship, Co-operation and Mutual Assistance Agreement of 1948, came from the Finnish President.

In January 1945 the Allied Control Commission insisted that the demobilization should cover the Finnish Navy and coastal artillery to the extent that the Finns should remove all the guns from their southern coastal batteries exceeding 120 mm calibre. Mannerheim then made his own proposal to conclude a regional defence treaty between Finland and the Soviet Union, asking Zhdanov's permission to leave the Finnish coastal defence intact as long as German forces were operating in the Baltic. 'His starting point was the fact that Finland and Russia should, after 250 years of animosity, have a total change in their relations,' Zhdanov reported him as stating. Mannerheim said that 'he is convinced that no defence measures against the Soviet Union are of any use unless we have good relations between the two countries'.[23]

Zhdanov received Mannerheim's surprising initiative well and commented on it positively to Moscow on 19 January. The proposal, however, had no follow-up, nor has it been explained why the energetic

Allied Control Commission Chairman did not revert to the question. In fact, he was called into order by Moscow. In an angry telegram the Foreign Minister criticized Zhdanov the very next day 'for speeding up events' and 'for trying to solve all the problems during one discussion'. The Chairman was reminded of 'the simple fact' that the USSR no more than other allied powers had diplomatic relations with Finland and could not conclude any treaties with that country. Molotov also warned him of 'not frightening him [Mannerheim] with too radical proposals'.[24]

President Mannerheim was certainly not used sparingly when asked to carry out other armistice conditions in addition to the military clauses. The most difficult for him was no doubt Article 13 on the condemnation of the war criminals -- in other words, those responsible for war. A retrospective law criminalizing their actions was, for Mannerheim, a traumatic experience. Unable to satisfy the Soviets, he fell ill and obliged Prime Minister J.K. Paasikivi as acting President to bring this unpleasant task to a conclusion.

Despite his age and poor health President Mannerheim played an important role in 1944–6 in conserving the state machine from the infiltration of Extreme Left radicals. One representative of the Finnish Communist Party, Yrjö Leino, was accepted in the first post-war cabinet formed by Paasikivi on the 17 November 1944 on the grounds that his presence would please the Soviets and satisfy domestic demands for enlarging the Government to include the Extreme Left. Since the subsequent parliamentary election in March 1945, the radicalization of the Finnish society was a fact, the Finnish Communist Party with its allies having won a quarter of all the seats in the Diet. The Communists had to be allowed to have a more concrete share in the Government. Mannerheim tried again to resist but had finally to yield. Even after the new Paasikivi cabinet had taken office on 17 April 1945, the President of the republic controlled the actions of the leftist ministers closely through his right of appointment. Especially Leino, who had changed his post of Minister for Social Affairs to that of the Interior, complained often to Zhdanov that the old President was getting annoying and hindered the 'democratization' of the administration in many ways.[25]

Once the Soviets understood that Mannerheim would no longer be of any use to them, and that Paasikivi as a well-established conservative leader could replace him, they saw no reason for him to stay in power but encouraged him to resign. The way they did it was nevertheless significant. Mannerheim was to be assured that he would not have to face a war crimes trial even if he were no longer head of state. The Allied Control Commission Chairman, who was by then in Moscow, instructed his deputy to go to see the Marshal and to deliver the following message drafted word-by-word by Zhdanov himself: 'If Mannerheim is obliged to resign, he may take into consideration that Russia will allow nobody to arrest him, since he has concluded the peace between Finland and the Soviet Union.' Note the word 'Russia' instead of the 'Soviet Government'[26]: it was certainly meant to have a particular effect in the mind of a former Russian officer, as Mannerheim was!

Meanwhile, with the success of the newly established Communist-controlled People's Democratic Union in the March election, Zhdanov's behaviour had changed. Outspoken when stressing the Communists' role, Zhdanov by now supported an alliance, which he called the 'Democratic Bloc', between the People's Democrats and the other two big parties, the Social Democrats and the Agrarian Party. His original idea was to make the latter two partners in accepting a radical Communist Party programme in which nationalization was to be a prime means of changing Finnish society. In the final analysis Zhdanov planned nothing less than to test Finland as a model Soviet satellite, up to three years before the Communists took the upper hand in the future people's democracies by these tactics.

Disregarding his earlier principles of non-interference in Finnish internal affairs, the Soviet boss now encouraged the Communist ringleaders to claim without hesitation that the People's Democrats be allowed three key ministries in the Government: those of Foreign Affairs, Defence and the Interior.[27] This even succeeded, with the exception that in Foreign Affairs they had to be content to share the portfolio with the 'reactionary' Carl Enckell who was the President's man. Somewhat rashly, forgetting his own rules of play as the Allied Control Commission Chairman, Zhdanov induced Leino, the brand-new Minister of the Interior, to deliver to the USSR a group of 20 arrested emigrants and other people, who were wanted as suspects for wartime anti-Soviet activities. Precisely this episode motivated the Finnish Parliament later, in May 1948, to pass a vote of no-confidence in Leino and to have him dismissed.

In a sudden euphoria, imagining that the leftist seizure of power could take place more or less legitimately behind the parliamentary curtain, Zhdanov was by the spring of 1946 ready for far-reaching schemes of nationalization as well, recommending them to the Finnish Communist Party and, through it, to the three-party bloc's programme.[28] Despite his interests in Finnish culture and history, Zhdanov was obviously not familiar enough with the Finnish mentality. Though he had been very impressed by the Finns' military records, he was inclined to underestimate the strength of their political resistance. Even in 1948, having left Finland, he explained the failure of his plans by accusing the Finnish Communists of being unable to do what their comrades had done elsewhere: 'The biggest of all their failures has been the fact that they have not succeeded in breaking up the Social Democratic Party.'[29] By then, the first half of 1948, Zhdanov was still to receive from the Finnish Communist Party, at least on two separate occasions, an appeal for Soviet assistance and permission for direct action against its domestic enemies, but it seems that these fell on deaf ears. Thus, finally, Zhdanov too returned willy-nilly to his original non-committal line on Finland. Did the Finnish Communists receive any plausible explanation from him why he left them outside the Cominform in 1947?

'The Control Commission has followed a very soft compromising policy towards Finland,' Zhdanov observed at the end of 1945 to the representatives of the big three parties. He continued: 'I am unable to name any country where a corresponding control commission would have acted in a similar fashion. Perhaps I am personally at fault. Maybe in this respect I shall incur heavy criticism among democrats both in Finland and elsewhere...'[30] If we believe Milovan Djilas, however, the ex-boss of the Helsinki Allied Control Commission still regretted in 1948 that the question of Finland had not been dispatched by occupying the country, when that would still have been possible.[31]

An interesting question for future research would be whether Zhdanov adopted his more aggressive policy in Finland after having been criticized at home. The Commission was indeed occasionally under heavy fire from Moscow for what was said to be exaggerated leniency towards Finland. A leading critic was an official of the People's Commissariat for Foreign Affairs, Mikhail Vetrov from the Department Europe 5. This part of the Ministry, which included the *Referentura Finlandii*, was supervised by Deputy Minister V.G. Dekanozov.

Vetrov's attacks, especially at the beginning of the Commission's activity in Helsinki, were mainly directed against the political representative, Pavel Orlov. Though the Chairman was seldom mentioned, the ultimate addressee was obviously Zhdanov himself. In this controversy, there are probably even motives of higher political rivalry, since Zhdanov was a presumed successor of Stalin and Dekanozov a well-known representative of Lavrenti Beria's secret police. Even Molotov, who had once personally criticized Zhdanov for his dealings with Mannerheim, must have given his blessing to Vetrov's vitriolic memoranda on the ACC's behaviour in Helsinki.[32]

The inconsistent, vague and rather 'liberal' policy conducted by Zhdanov in Finland is partly explained by his long periods of absence from the country, when he was away in Moscow. After making six or seven trips to the Soviet capital during his 14-month stay in Finland, he took up permanent residence in Moscow by December 1945. He did not return to Helsinki until February 1947 on the occasion of the conclusion of the final peace treaty, which gave the signal for the departure of the Allied Control Commission. Meanwhile, he focused his attention on his political activities in the Central Committee of the

CPSU and ran the Allied Control Commission in Helsinki only as a side-show. Though Zhdanov had lost his position in the mainstream of the Party during the war, he managed to return to prominence by March 1946 and was again regarded as the third-ranking man in the Soviet Union. Consequently, the harsh criticism directed from Moscow against his Finnish policy began to abate.

To protect himself from his critics, Zhdanov came up with a radical programme for the Finnish Communist Party in spring 1946. As soon as it became clear that the Finns were unlikely to take the road to becoming a people's democracy, he washed his hands of the matter and shifted the responsibility for the failure to the Finnish Communists. He did not dare to assist the latter even in 1948 when plans were made to tie Finland into the Soviet sphere of influence by treaty arrangements. After the death of Zhdanov that same year, Soviet relations with Finland were conducted with even less attention to ideology. Lt Gen. G.M. Savonenkov, Zhdanov's deputy at the Allied Control Commission, tried to continue a hard line after he became the Soviet envoy in Helsinki in 1948. Following the principle that it was his responsibility to protect the Finnish Extreme Left by recourse to Article 7, the so-called non-discrimination article of the Peace Treaty of 1947, Savonenkov several times drew Moscow's attention to what was considered to be violation of this treaty. Savonenkov's pressure was maintained until 1950, or as long as the Social Democratic minority Government of K.A. Fagerholm remained in power. Still, as the following episode indicates, Moscow's policy line was not consistent in principle. Savonenkov had been angered by dismissal of the Director-General of Finnish Radio Broadcasting, Hella Vuolijoki, a well-known pro-Soviet writer, and proposed to his Foreign Ministry that the Finnish Government be sent a protest note. This, however, was not acceptable to Molotov who on 15 July 1949 personally dictated the order that Savonenkov should be told that the measure he had suggested 'would mean interfering in Finnish internal affairs'.[33]

The Helsinki Legation under Savonenkov's guidance sent more and more alarming reports to Moscow on increasing Western influence in Finland. The Soviets were most worried about the Anglo-American cultural hegemony in news transmission, the book and film market and in the scholarship programmes with universities. They noticed that the Americans had agreed to establish a cultural exchange fund with the Finns which would be financed by Finland's debt payments to the USA.

The Russians of Savonenkov's type seem to have been bitter about the fact that their country was after all losing the struggle for Finnish sympathy. The Soviet economy was still in such a weak condition that the Kremlin had no resources for a larger campaign against Western influence. There was insufficient money to subsidize even the Finnish

Extreme Left which was in difficulties keeping its overgrown press alive. When, for instance, the editors-in-chief of the main organs of the Finnish Communist Party and the People's Democratic Union complained in March 1952 to the new Soviet Ambassador, V.Z. Lebedev, about their lack of resources, the diplomat could only recommend the restriction of weekly issues and the number of pages of the newspapers.[34]

In 1952 especially, Soviet–Finnish relations were in all respects heading towards normalization. The non-Communist Government under the premiership of Kekkonen inspired Soviet trust. Finland's return to the international community – still complicated because of the Soviet veto against Finnish membership of the United Nations – gained in confidence since Helsinki had been able to stage the Olympic Games. The war reparation deliveries were completed in September the same year. Thus, Stalin's death in the following March did not cause, but was already witnessing, a period of *détente* in Soviet policy towards Finland.

Once Stalin had succeeded in convincing the Finns to sign the Treaty of Friendship, Cooperation and Mutual Assistance in 1948, though in a moderate and flexible form, he had in practice gained all he wanted from Eden in 1941. Since the Finns had resisted a more advanced form of satellization of their country, Stalin had carefully abstained from implementing it by force. He had proved right the hypothesis of President Paasikivi that the Soviet Union had less ideological than strategical interests in Finland.

Adam B. Ulam considers that Finland, though the most menaced of all the neighbours of Russia, escaped by sheer chance from being Sovietized and integrated within the Stalinist empire. The author no doubt simplifies the issue when arguing that the Kremlin's moderation at this time may be explained by American reactions to Soviet aggression against Finland in 1939–40 – which might have been repeated had the country been threatened again. Even more peculiar is Ulam's claim, presented in his latest book, that finally, 'the Communist dictator in Belgrade helped save Finnish democracy'.[35]

Moscow had had reasons, even before the open conflict with Belgrade, to restrain the panicked Finnish Communists. The Treaty of Friendship, Cooperation and Mutual Assistance signed on 5 April was still waiting for Finnish ratification. Opinion in the West was still alarmed by the events of Czechoslovakia. Though the Finnish Communist Party had evaluated the political situation in Finland before the July parliamentary elections as 'unfavourable' to the Communists, the Kremlin found it wiser to handle it with kid gloves rather than a mailed fist. Without letting a large-scale strike movement (protesting at the dismissal of Minister Leino from the cabinet) at the end of May trouble the country and hinder the elections, the Soviets advised that it be stopped.[36] Instead, they tried to influence the mood of the voters by cutting the remaining Finnish war reparations sum by half (from $147 m. to $73.5 m.) on 3 June.

Indeed, we have no proof that this decisive event occurred because Tito had meanwhile been ostracized from the Soviet camp at the end of June. In fact, Moscow would have had several pretexts for making an end of Finland's emancipation from Soviet guardianship during the year running from spring 1947 to spring 1948 – take only the anti-Communist campaign of the Social Democrats and the considerable evidence for the existence of a large-scale armed resistance organization in the country. But significantly, no great store was ever set by these questions.

Colonel J.H. Magill, who was the leading British military representative in the Allied Control Commission in Helsinki, reveals in his memoirs that since late autumn of 1944 he had himself considered a Soviet military occupation of Finland unlikely. The only concrete danger occurring was, according to him, a Communist *coup d'état*.[37] Even this, as we know now, would hardly have been possible without Soviet permission and, above all, assistance – which were never given.

Notes

1. The diplomatic background of the Winter War has by now been documented on the Soviet side by the volume of the documents of Foreign Policy for the year 1939 published in 1992. See *Dokumenti vnehsnei politiki 1939*, tom XXII, 2 (Moscow: 1992), in particular, the dealings with the 'Finnish People's Government', pp. 355–8. On the Winter War in general, see the present writer's monograph *The Appeal That Was Never Made – The Allied, Scandinavia and the Finnish Winter War, 1939–1940* (London: 1976). The following text is based on my article 'The Decisive Armistice 1944–1947: Why Was Finland not Sovietized?', *Scandinavian Journal of History*, 19 (1994).
2. Sir L. Woodward, *British Foreign Policy in the Second World War*, Vol. 3 (London: 1971) p. 130.
3. *Ibid.*, pp. 134–5. On the reference to Eden's memorandum, 9 August 1944, cf. my article 'Finland and the Cold War', *Scandinavian Journal of History*, 10, 3 (1985) 212, and the source mentioned there.
4. The document discovered by Dr M. Turtola and published (in Finnish translation) in the periodical *Seura*, 51–52 (1993) 14–17.
5. According to N.I. Egorova's paper 'From the Comintern to Cominform: Ideological Dimension of the Cold War Origins (1945–48)', presented at the conference 'New Evidence on the Cold War History' (Moscow, 12–15 January, 1993), p. 5.
6. RTsKhIDNI.
7. Egorova, 'From the Comintern', p. 2.
8. M. Djilas, *Conversations with Stalin* (London: 1962) p. 104.
9. On the mentioned meeting, see RTsKhIDNI, f. 77, op. 3, d. 48, l. 44.
10. RTsKhIDNI, f. 77, op. 3, d. 39, l. 21.
11. *Ibid.*

12. *Ibid.*
13. *Ibid.*
14. According to the passage of the memoirs of Marshal Meretskov as quoted in A.A. Komarov's paper 'Finland's Withdrawal from the Second World War', in J. Nevakivi (ed.), *Finnish–Soviet Relations 1944–1948 – Papers of the Seminar organized in Helsinki, March 21–25, 1994, by the Department of Political History, University of Helsinki, in cooperation with the Institute of Universal History, Russian Academy of Sciences, Moscow* (Helsinki: 1994) p. 35, note 25.
15. RTsKhIDNI, f. 77, op. 3, d. 41, l. 1. Moreover, see the Article 2 of the Armistice Agreement: the text in T. Polvinen, *Between East and West – Finland in International Politics 1944–1947* (Minneapolis, Mn.: 1986) p. 289.
16. On the 1944 war in Lapland, see *ibid.*, pp. 37–54.
17. See, for example, K.A. Meretskov, *Na sluzhbe naroda. Stranitsy vospominanii* (Moscow: 1969) p. 324.
18. RTsKhIDNI, f. 77, op. 3, d. 39, l. 4. The Russian flights over the 20th Mountain Army theatre of operations were at first insignificant but increased rapidly after the start of the Soviet offensive on Petsamo, with a clear purpose to disturb the German reserve transports from Finland to the Petsamo front. Thus, according to what the present writer has seen in the Finnish Air Force reports, already on 7 October the number of Russian flights was greater than that of the German ones. A week later, when the Finns were about to surround Rovaniemi, the number of their planes observed in the theatre was 43 a day.
19. RTsKhIDNI, f. 77, op. 3, d. 39.
20. Zhdanov was personally aware of the Finns' fears and wanted to maintain the belief that their country could be occupied at any time, if they did not strictly adhere to the terms of the armistice. Zhdanov himself was informed that the Soviet troops concentrated along the Finnish borders, south of the theatre of operations of German forces, were in September–October 1944 quite insufficient to attempt to penetrate Finland. The Finns had still deployed during the first week of October the bulk of their troops, altogether 11 divisions and 5 brigades, along the Soviet borders south from the 'waistline' (see RTsKhIDNI, f. 77, op. 3, d. 39, l. 4). Thus Mannerheim's Head Quarters probably still had more troops at their disposal at the frontier than the Soviet Leningrad and Karelian fronts combined.
21. RTsKhIDNI, f. 77, op. 3, d. 48, l. 40–1.
22. See, for example, the *aide-mémoire* by the British Political Representative in Helsinki, Francis Shepherd, 'Interview with Mr. Orlov', 8 March 1945, PRO, FO 371/47367/N/2314.
23. RTsKhIDNI, f. 77, op. 3, d. 54, l. 1. Moreover, see Polvinen, *Between East*, pp. 116–18.
24. RTsKhIDNI, f. 77, op. 3, d. 54, l. 1–2; Polvinen, *Between East*, pp. 119–20.
25. RTsKhIDNI, f. 77, op. 3, d. 63, l. 3–4, 7–8, 11, 32, 50.
26. RTsKhIDNI, f. 77, op. 3, d. 73, l. 36.
27. *Ibid.*, l. 39.
28. As it appears from the f. 77, especially from the d. 53.
29. RTsKhIDNI, f. 77, op. 3, d. 88, l. 28.
30. Quoted by Y. Leino in his memoires, *Kommunisti sisäministerinä* (Helsinki: 1991) p. 101.

31. Djilas, *Conversations*, p. 140. According to the Yugoslav leader, Zhdanov had praised the Finns' punctuality in delivering reparations, as if by this fact the Soviets would have lost a pretext to intervene in Finland. 'We made a mistake in not occupying Finland,' he concluded. 'Everything would have been fine if we had.' Molotov's comment to this was significant: 'Ach Finland – that is a peanut.'
32. See, in general, AVP RF, f. 0135, op. 28, p. 155, d. 4.
33. In general, the year report in 1949 of the Soviet Legation in Helsinki, RTsKhIDNI, f. 17, op. 137, d. 134, l. 86–7, and RTsKhIDNI, f. 77, op. 3, d. 88. On the Vuolijoki episode, see a random note dated 15 July 1949 by Molotov on a draft letter by A.N. Abramov, and Molotov's meeting minutes of the same date in AVP RF, f. 0135, op. 33e, p. 182a, d. 7.
34. In general, the year report in 1949 of the Soviet Legation in Helsinki, especially pp. 71–7. On the advice on press affairs, see V.Z. Lebedev's Diary, 22 March 1952, RTsKhIDNI, f. 17, op. 137, d. 938, l. 40.
35. A.B. Ulam, *The Communists – The Story of Power and Lost Illusions: 1948–1991* (New York: 1992) p. 23.
36. A piece of information provided personally by Dr K. Rentola, the author of a history of the Finnish Communist Party.
37. J.H. Magill, *Tasavalta tulikokeessa – Muistelmia Suomesta kuuman ja kylmän sodan vuosilta* (Mikkeli: 1981) pp. 117–19.

7 The Limits to Soviet Influence: Soviet Diplomats and the Pursuit of Strategic Interests in Norway and Denmark, 1944–7

Sven G. Holtsmark

INTRODUCTION

World War II, and not least Nazi Germany's use of Norwegian territory for attacks on the lines of communication between the Soviet Union's Western Allies and the ice-free ports in Northern Russia, brought the Scandinavian countries closer to the centre of Soviet strategic interests in Europe. As the war in Europe drew to a close, the Scandinavian countries became part of Soviet planning for the post-war order in Europe.

This chapter will examine how the Soviets defined and partly pursued a set of strategic and political objectives in Norway and Denmark from 1944 to early 1947. The focus is on the decision-making process *within one of the bureaucratic structures:* the Commissariat for Foreign Affairs (NKID), renamed the Ministry of Foreign Affairs (MID) in March 1946.[1] In contrast to the established image of effective and deliberate centralization, the picture I will sketch is one of a foreign policy bureaucracy marked by imperfection and indecisiveness, where confusion and flawed information were part of the policy-making process. I will also argue that the NKID/MID to a high degree allowed its middle-ranking staff to generate and pursue their own proposals for foreign policy initiatives. Some of these officials apparently became strongly attached to their pet projects, and continued to argue that they should be implemented, even when confronted with lack of interest or even disapproval on the part of the political leadership.

SOVIET STRATEGIC INTERESTS IN DENMARK: THE BALTIC STRAITS AND BORNHOLM[2]

Denmark attracted Soviet attention because of the country's key location at the entrances to the Baltic Sea. Denmark controlled the Great Belt and the Little Belt, both in Danish territorial waters. Apart from the Kiel Canal, the Danish Belts are the only passages to the Baltic Sea navigable by major warships. It shared the control over the shallow passage of Öresund with Sweden. Soviet strategic interests in Denmark also focused on the island of Bornholm, situated at the approaches to the narrow and westernmost part of the Baltic Sea.[3]

A memorandum from October–November 1940 defined Soviet strategic interests in Denmark in the following simple terms: 'Denmark's strategic significance is defined by its role as the country which virtually controls the shipping through the Straits, which are an important element in the general strategic situation in the Baltic theatre of war.' The powers that controlled the Baltic Straits and the Kiel Canal could decide whether the Baltic should be an open or a closed sea.[4]

In his discussions in November of the same year with Hitler's Foreign Minister, Molotov brought up the Baltic Straits, suggesting some sort of internationalization of the passages. Ribbentrop refused to enter into a discussion of this issue, reminding Molotov that 'Germany is at war with England, and therefore a number of questions cannot be solved now'. Apparently, Molotov made no attempt to press the issue.[5] After the German attack on the Soviet Union in June 1941, the issue of the Baltic Straits became part of the ensuing Soviet discussions about the post-war order in Europe. When Anthony Eden came to Moscow in December 1941, Stalin suggested that he would like 'a guarantee by certain powers as to the entrances to the Baltic Sea'. Apart from the issue of the Straits, Stalin indicated that the Soviets were less interested in Denmark proper, hinting that Great Britain might want to have military bases there after the war. The island of Bornholm was not mentioned in the discussions.[6]

From the very beginning of the formalized Soviet planning process for the post-war order in Europe, the issue of the Baltic Straits figured on the list of topics to be studied. One of the bodies responsible for preparing the Soviet position for the international negotiations which would follow after the end of the war, was the so-called 'Commission for the preparation of diplomatic materials'. This Commission, set up in early 1942 under Molotov's chairmanship, was in 1943 renamed the 'Commission for the preparation of peace treaties and the post-war order', and Maxim M. Litvinov was appointed its chairman. Although the extent of its influence on Soviet policy decisions may be questioned, the topics brought up by the Commission, and the arguments employed, certainly reflected the attitudes of senior members of the foreign policy apparatus.[7]

Although a memorandum on the Baltic Straits was prepared for the Commission in the spring of 1942, it was not until 22 July 1944 that a plenary session of the Commission was convened to discuss Soviet interests in the Baltic Straits and the Western part of the Baltic. The task, according to Litvinov, was to formulate a policy which could create maximum security for the Soviet Baltic coast. The Soviet Union would prefer to have the entrances to the Baltic Sea closed to warships of non-littoral states, and to internationalize the Straits and the Kiel Canal. Litvinov also held that the Aaland Islands ought to be brought under Soviet sovereignty. Litvinov was aware that the Soviet Union would hardly be able to achieve all of this. In particular he was sceptical about the chances of achieving a Straits regime which would close the Baltic Sea to the navies of the Western great powers.[8]

Deputy Commissar Solomon A. Lozovsky argued that the Soviet Union would need military bases[9] on the island of Bornholm. This idea was not mentioned in the original report prepared for the Commission. The Soviet Union, according to Lozovskii, needed additional strongholds in the Baltic Sea between the Kiel Canal and the Aaland Islands. Both Litvinov and Lozovsky realized that it might be difficult to produce a legal basis for the demand for military bases on Bornholm, 'which belongs to Denmark, with which we are not at war'. In the end, it was decided to accept the text of the memorandum which formed the basis for the discussion, with an addition about the possibility of Soviet military bases on the German island of Rügen.[10] A few weeks later, similar views were presented to Deputy Commissar Vladimir G. Dekanozov by the head of the NKID's 5th European Department, Pavel D. Orlov.[11] Orlov stressed the Soviet Union's 'particular interests' in Denmark as the guardian of the entrances to the Baltic Sea. Interestingly, Orlov's memorandum was based on the assumption that the Soviet Union would take part in the military liberation of Denmark from the Nazi forces.[12] The Soviet role in the liberation of Denmark remained unclear: as of December 1944 no decision had apparently been made on the question of whether, or in what way, Soviet forces should take part in military operations there. At that time Dekanozov ordered the NKID's 5th European Department to prepare a memorandum 'on the Danes' attitude towards an Anglo–American occupation of Denmark and our participation in this matter'.[13] Soviet diplomats – among them V.G. Dekanozov and Vladimir S. Semenov, Alexandra Kollontai's deputy at the Soviet legation in Stockholm – repeatedly emphasized in their contacts with Thomas Døssing, the Moscow representative of the Danish Freedom Council, that the Soviet Union was not disinterested in Danish affairs, and that the country's future political order (*ustroistvo*) was of interest not only to the Western powers.[14] From late 1944 and until the end of the war, Mikhail S. Vetrov (the acting head of the 5th European Department), V.S. Semenov, and others, repeatedly urged their superiors in the NKID to implement a more forceful policy towards Denmark. To prepare the ground for Soviet participation in the military liberation of Denmark, they suggested that the Danish Freedom Council should be invited to sign an agreement about jurisdiction and civil administration in liberated areas, similar to the Soviet–Norwegian agreement of 16 May 1944.[15]

Not only the diplomats focused on the importance of the Baltic Straits. In the final months of the war, the issue of security in the Western part of the Baltic Sea was raised in several articles in *Krasnyi flot*, the newspaper of the Commissariat for the Navy. Apart from analysing the significance of the Straits, the articles emphasized the significance of the islands of Bornholm and Rügen in controlling this portion of the Baltic.[16] Then, in mid-March, the idea of seizing Bornholm was raised by Vladimir S. Semenov, who apparently combined his duties in Stockholm with frequent visits to Moscow. In a letter to Dekanozov, Semenov wrote:

> In relation with the evolution of the military operations in Pomerania, it would be appropriate for the Supreme Naval Staff to examine the possibility of landing our troops on the Danish island of Bornholm. Such an operation, if it is possible from the military point of view, would be absolutely justified politically, in view of the fact that the island is occupied by German troops and is used as a base against the USSR. Moreover, by participating in this way in the liberation of Danish territory and having control over the island, we would acquire the same rights as our allies in the settling of all matters in Denmark, participating in the Control ... Commission, if such a body is to be created...
>
> The English persuade Danish politicians, that Denmark, allegedly, is altogether within the Western powers' zone of operations and interest and that the Danish questions are of no concern or interest to the Soviet Union. In reality the delimitation of the occupational zones in Germany and the English control over the Kiel Canal enhance Denmark's significance from the point of view of our Baltic coast.[17]

It seems clear from the available elements of the ensuing correspondence that the issue had not been discussed between Molotov and Dekanozov, the Deputy Commissar primarily responsible for Scandinavian affairs. Dekanozov supported Semenov's proposal. On Molotov's instructions a copy of the letter was sent to N.A. Bulganin, one of the deputy commissars for Defence.[18] Semenov's proposal was supported by Vetrov. On 2 April 1945, in a letter to Dekanozov, the acting head of the 5th European Department, argued that a Soviet military presence on Bornholm would provide the basis for a Soviet–Danish military agreement which would guarantee Soviet influence over Danish political affairs.[19]

The ensuing sequence of events is still unclear. According to a Soviet source, on 23 April the Navy Commissar proposed capturing Rügen and Bornholm to the General Staff. The commander of the Baltic Fleet received the final order to prepare for the capture of Bornholm apparently only on 4 May.[20] On 7 May the Soviets urged the German garrison to surrender. The same day Soviet aircraft bombed the island. When the Germans refused to capitulate to Soviet forces,[21] the bombing was repeated on 8 May. On 9 May, a small Soviet force landed and received the German capitulation, and parts of a Soviet infantry division established themselves on Bornholm.

According to the official Soviet version which the Soviets presented soon after their arrival, Bornholm was seized simply because it lay to the east of the Western limit of the Soviet zone of operations in Germany. Whatever may have motivated the Soviets to bomb and capture Bornholm, the local military commander was instructed to tell the Danes that the Soviet military presence was temporary and that the Soviet troops would be withdrawn when 'the military questions related to Germany' were finally settled. This was done in order to dispel any anxiety the Danes might have had about Soviet intentions on Bornholm.[22]

Declarations to this effect were made during the meetings between the Soviet commanders and the official Danish representatives in the weeks immediately after the Soviets captured the island,[23] and they were repeated in a Soviet note of 24 July.

Two memoranda from July 1945 presented the views of the NKID bureaucracy on Soviet policy towards Denmark. The first, written for the Deputy Commissars A. Ia. Vyshinsky and S.A. Lozovsky, reiterated that the Soviet Union should demand a regime for the Danish Belts, the Sound and the Kiel Canal which would close the Baltic Sea to warships of non-littoral states.[24] Vetrov and A.I. Plakhin, the newly appointed Soviet envoy in Denmark and former head of the NKID's Scandinavian Department, in a related memorandum repeated these recommendations for the Kiel Canal, but proposed a somewhat different solution concerning the Straits. A regime for the Straits, according to Vetrov and Plakhin, could be created by the signing of a Danish–Soviet treaty giving Soviet merchant and naval ships the right to pass through the Straits, while closing these passages to naval vessels of non-littoral states. Such a treaty should include the obligation of the Soviet Union 'to assist Denmark in supervising the regime' which would be established. Other Baltic states should be invited to join the treaty.[25] Finally, in a memorandum from December 1945, Litvinov repeated the arguments and proposals, by recommending that the Soviet Union should try to achieve the internationalization of the Great and Little Belts, the Sound and the Kiel Canal. Only the USSR, Poland, Sweden and Denmark should participate in the control. 'After a certain period of time' Finland and Germany might be invited to take part in the scheme. It was added that any effective control of the Baltic entrances and the Kiel Canal would require the creation of a system of military bases along these waterways.[26]

The idea of establishing permanent Soviet bases on Bornholm reappeared in internal NKID documents throughout 1945, and it seems that the final decision to surrender control of Bornholm to the Danish Government was made only in the winter of 1945-6. In their memorandum to Molotov of 10 July 1945, Vetrov and Plakhin emphasized Bornholm's importance for Soviet security in the Baltic area. The Soviet declarations from May 1945 had served to reassure the Danes about Soviet intentions on Bornholm. Therefore, Vetrov and Plakhin argued, Soviet troops could remain on the island 'for an extended period of time' without any risk of 'political complications'. They suggested reaching an agreement with the Danish Government about the joint Soviet–Danish defence of Bornholm, with Soviet and Danish naval and air bases on the island. Such bases would serve two purposes. They would serve Soviet security interests in the region, but would also be important in securing Soviet 'influence over Denmark's foreign policy'. Negotiations about military bases should be initiated before the Soviet troops were withdrawn – in this situation the Danes could be expected to be more accommodating. The creation of naval and air bases on Bornholm should be complemented by the establishment of bases on Rügen.[27]

In December 1945 Litvinov suggested that hints of possible Soviet demands for military bases on Bornholm and Rügen could be used to make the Western powers more accommodating towards Soviet demands for the internationalization of the Baltic entrances and the Kiel Canal.[28] The Soviet Government's postponement of a planned visit to Moscow in September 1945 by a Danish Government delegation apparently reflected the absence of a clear Soviet stance in the major issues of its policy towards Denmark: the Straits and Bornholm. The available Soviet documents give no direct answer to the reasons for this postponement. A letter of 9 October 1945 from Aleksandr N. Abramov and M.S. Vetrov (Abramov was newly appointed head of the 5th European Department), sheds some light on the Soviet reasoning. The Danish delegation, according to this letter, was supposed to discuss not only trade relations, but also 'political issues, notably the evacuation of Soviet troops from the island of Bornholm' and repatriation questions. The Politburo had decided to defer the delegation's visit until the spring of

1946. The Danish Government nevertheless continued to urge the Soviet Government to receive two of its representatives in Moscow. Abramov, Vetrov and Plakhin, the Soviet envoy in Copenhagen, supported this Danish proposal, partly because it would strengthen the 'democratic forces' as opposed to the 'reactionary' elements in Danish politics. The main reason behind Abramov's and Vetrov's support for the proposal, however, was to bring up with the Danes 'the initiation of an agreement on the joint defence in the Western part of the Baltic Sea (the creation of military bases on the island of Bornholm and the establishment of a regime for the straits).'[29]

The outcome is well known: The Soviets decided not to present to the Danish Government their demands for a revision of the regime over the Straits or for negotiations on the joint defence of Bornholm. Although the issue of passage through the Baltic Straits was brought up by Molotov and Stalin at the Conference of ministers of foreign affairs in Moscow in December 1945, the Soviets made no attempt to press for a solution along the lines suggested in the numerous NKID memoranda. When Stalin expressed anxiety that the Soviet Union would be confined to the Baltic in the event of war, British Foreign Minister Ernest Bevin declared that the British would oppose the establishment of bases in this area. Stalin said that 'he did not refer to bases at all,' and that he only wished to raise the question of free passage through the Straits.[30] Nevertheless, the NKID's 5th European Department produced a draft resolution stipulating that the establishment of a regime for the Baltic Straits should be the task of the Baltic states: the USSR, Poland, Denmark and Sweden.[31] The draft, apparently, was not presented to the British and US representatives.

The decision was taken to withdraw from the island. On 5 March 1946, Molotov received the Danish envoy and delivered this message:

If Denmark is now capable of occupying Bornholm with its own forces and of setting up on Bornholm its own administration without any participation whatsoever of foreign troops or foreign administrators, the Soviet Government will withdraw its troops from Bornholm and hand the island over to the Danish Government.[32]

The Danish Government agreed to the Soviet conditions in a message of 8 March, and the last Soviet troops left the island on 4 April 1946.[33]

SOVIET STRATEGIC INTERESTS IN NORWAY: SVALBARD AND THE NORTHERN BORDERLANDS

The Soviets never tried to coerce the Danish Government to agree to a revision of the regime of the Baltic Straits or a permanent Soviet military presence on Bornholm. Soviet–Norwegian relations evolved differently, and the internal deliberations of NKID bureaucrats resulted in a Soviet attempt to achieve the revision of the internationally recognized regime over the Svalbard archipelago. From November 1944, when Molotov introduced the matter during a conversation with Norwegian Foreign Minister Trygve Lie, to February 1947, discussions of the international status of Svalbard were one of the formative elements in the Norwegian–Soviet relationship. Molotov demanded *inter alia* that Spitsbergen should be transformed into a Norwegian–Soviet condominium, that is come under joint Soviet–Norwegian rule, and that Bear Island should be transferred to Soviet sovereignty. There is no need to repeat the story of the ensuing Norwegian–Soviet negotiations: they have been discussed in detail by various authors.[34] I will limit myself to a discussion of the origin and the evolution of the issue within the Soviet foreign policy apparatus. The idea of changing Svalbard's international status in favour of the Soviet Union had surfaced on the eve of the outbreak of World War II. Until then Soviet interests in the archipelago had been economic, not strategic. By 1939 officials at the Soviet Consulate in Barentsburg on Spitsbergen were arguing in favour of extending Soviet control over the archipelago, in order to prevent the British or the Germans from taking control. At that time their views did not seem to receive much response in Moscow in terms of a profound re-evaluation of Svalbard's significance – whether economic or strategic.[35] The German occupation of Norway in the spring of 1940 gave substance to their warnings, and in the summer of that year the NKID's Scandinavian Department strongly supported the views of the Barentsburg group. In June and July NKID bureaucrats wrote several memoranda on Svalbard, stressing the area's strategic importance and arguing that Norway's claims to the archipelago, and to Bear Island in particular, were weakly founded. The campaign culminated in early August 1940 when Pavel D. Orlov, the acting head of the Scandinavian Department, recommended that the Svalbard archipelago should be occupied 'by units of the Red Army' for the duration of the war and until the 'complete stabilization of international relations'. In this he was seconded by strong appeals from the Soviet Consul in Barentsburg, P.I. Volnukhin.[36]

The efforts of the Soviet Consul in Barentsburg and the Scandinavian Department failed to receive Molotov's support, although they were certainly brought to his attention. One reason for Molotov's lack of interest may have been that the Soviet military authorities were less convinced than the NKID officials of the strategic importance of Spitsbergen and Bear Island. This clearly was the case in the summer of 1941, when Svalbard became an issue in inter-Allied discussions soon after the German attack on the Soviet Union. At the Soviet–Norwegian–British negotiations in July and August, the Soviets did not make any strong efforts to obtain their Allies' agreement to their idea of deploying allied troops to Spitsbergen, and at no point did they hint at the possibility of independent Soviet action on the archipelago. Even the less ambitious idea of arming the Soviet population in Barentsburg evaporated. In the autumn of 1941 the Soviets took part in the evacuation of Norwegian and Russian civilians from Spitsbergen.[37] At the beginning of the discussions Ivan M. Maisky, the Soviet Ambassador to the United Kingdom, had declared to Anthony Eden that the Soviet Government had 'no territorial claims of any kind upon Norway, nor would they ever have'.[38]

Thus, until Molotov's initiative in November 1944, the Soviets had made no formal attempt to change Svalbard's international status in their favour.

> When Molotov finally raised the topic with Lie on 12 November 1944, this appears to have been the outcome of a last-minute decision, and the immediate background was a number of memoranda which argued the necessity of securing a stronger Soviet presence on Spitsbergen and Bear Island. The arguments were summarized by Deputy Commissar Vladimir Dekanozov in a memorandum which seems to have been given to Molotov only hours before his meeting with Trygve Lie. In his memorandum, Dekanozov emphasized the Soviet Union's economic interests on Spitsbergen, but also underlined 'Bear Island's extreme (*iskliuchitel'noe*) strategic importance both for the security of the Soviet mines on Spitsbergen, and for the safety of Soviet communications in the North'. Dekanozov recommended that the Soviet Government should immediately reestablish its legal rights on Spitsbergen, but also 'reach an agreement with the Norwegian Government that would give the Soviet Union the right, if it deems it necessary, to organize one or more naval and air bases ... on the main Spitsbergen archipelago ...' It would also be necessary to agree on the building of a naval base on Bear Island in order to defend our rights on Spitsbergen and to safeguard the movements of Soviet ships of the Northern Fleet.[39]

> The ensuing Norwegian–Soviet negotiations culminated on 9 April 1945, when the Norwegian Ambassador in Moscow delivered to the Commissariat for Foreign Affairs the proposal for a Norwegian–Soviet declaration. Article One of the draft declaration stated that 'the defence of the Archipelago of Svalbard is the joint responsibility of Norway and the Soviet Union'. From April 1945 until Molotov raised the matter again in the summer of 1946, Moscow made no serious efforts to finalize a Soviet–Norwegian agreement on Svalbard. Molotov apparently felt that the Norwegian Government had agreed to his most important demand – Soviet military bases on the islands.

The same group of NKID officials who had been the driving force behind the Svalbard initiative presented and vigorously pursued a set of proposals aimed at securing a military foothold for the Soviet Union in northern Norway. These proposals received much stronger support from the military leadership than the NKID bureaucrats' efforts to convince their superiors of the need to finalize the Svalbard negotiations.

In October 1944 Tatiana Zhdanova of NKID's 5th European Department produced a memorandum which linked the Svalbard issue to Soviet interests in northern Norway. In her view, Spitsbergen constituted

> one side of the channel which connects the Atlantic Ocean with our arctic regions. This channel used to be a very broad one, but it has to a significant degree been 'squeezed' by the evolution of aviation. In this way, the question of reviewing our border with Norway is closely linked with the review leading to a decision on the Spitsbergen question.

The fact that Petsamo (Pechenga) was ceded to the Soviet Union from Finland did not, in Zhdanova's opinion, solve the problem of the 'channel' to the Atlantic. Thus Zhdanova argued along the lines which had been introduced by the Soviet Consul in Barentsburg in 1939 and 1940, but introduced the development of modern aviation as an additional reason to alter the *status quo* in the high North. Zhdanova concluded:

> Taking into account the foreign policy benefit which the Red Army's participation in the liberation of Northern Norway has brought us, it would be appropriate to exploit the Norwegians' need for a counterweight, through friendship with the USSR, to the English attempts to achieve a 'Portugalization' of Norway. In the course of the war England has gained almost complete control over Norway. Thus, it appears that it would not be difficult for us to reach an agreement with the Norwegians on cooperation on the defence of Northern Norway; on the building of naval and air bases, necessary railways etc. Otherwise the English will do this. The creation of this kind of close post-war Soviet–Norwegian cooperation, which would ensure the Soviet Union appropriate permanent influence in Norway, would leave the possibility of raising the problem of a correction to the Soviet–Norwegian border at a more suitable moment.[40]

In the months following the Norwegian draft declaration of 9 April 1945, international conferences and pressing global issues apparently removed the Svalbard question, and Norwegian affairs in general, from the Soviet decision-makers' main agenda. However, while Molotov was concentrating on the more important European and global questions, his subordinates continued to press for a more offensive Soviet policy towards Norway. Officials of the NKID's 5th European Department repeatedly attempted to convince Molotov of the need to finalize the Svalbard discussions. They based their efforts on the Norwegian Government's draft declaration of April 1945, that is on the idea of a joint Soviet–Norwegian defence of Spitsbergen. From early June 1945 onwards, the same officials also took various initiatives to revive Zhdanova's October 1944 proposal for a permanent or semi-permanent Soviet military presence in the northern parts of mainland Norway. The key figure was Mikhail Sergeievich Vetrov, acting head of the Commissariat's 5th European Department.

A letter of 4 June from Rear Admiral Stepan G. Kucherov, the Chief of the Naval Staff (*Glavnyi Morskoi Shtab Voenno-Morskogo Flota*), provided Vetrov with an opportunity to press for a more active Soviet policy. In his letter Kucherov expressed concern about the activity of the significant number of Germans who remained in northern Norway, and about the Norwegian military authorities' subordination to the British. Kucherov proposed that the Soviet Government should 'create a special staff in Norway, which could then immediately start to work on the problems which have been accumulating there'. This staff should include representatives from the Commissariat for Defence, from the Commissariat for the Navy, from the Commissariat for Foreign Affairs, and from General Golikov's repatriation commission which was already working in Norway.[41] It should be noted that Admiral Kucherov did not suggest that the Soviet Union, for strategic or other reasons, should expand its military presence in northern Norway by establishing military bases or by expanding the area controlled by Soviet troops.

> Vetrov, when asked to comment on Kucherov's letter, reached his own far-reaching conclusions. Arguing that the Norwegian–Soviet agreement of 16 May 1944 on jurisdiction and administration in territories liberated by Allied troops 'does not limit the areas which can be occupied by one or other of the Allied powers', he supported Kucherov's plan to create a group of Soviet representatives in Norway. He also suggested, however, that the Soviet Government should 'give instructions to the General Staff of the Red Army to immediately move troops of the 14th Independent Army, which are stationed in Northern Norway, into the North-Western part of Norway, up to and including Narvik'.[42]

On his own initiative Vetrov sent to Molotov a separate memorandum about Svalbard, suggesting that naval units should be sent to Spitsbergen to 'create garrisons' on the island. The aim should be to 'finally resolve the Spitsbergen question'.[43]

Molotov's failure to respond did not discourage his subordinates from taking further initiatives. Vetrov and Zhdanova continued to pursue their pet projects: a solution to the Svalbard question and the creation of Soviet bases in northern Norway. One of their memoranda repeated Zhdanova's arguments from October 1944, concluding that it would be easy to reach an agreement with the Norwegian Government on the joint defence of northern Norway and the creation there of Soviet military bases, strategic railways, and so on. Once permanently established in Norway, the Soviet Government could raise at an appropriate time the question of revising the Soviet–Norwegian border.[44] As for Svalbard, they argued that the agreement with Norway on joint defence of the archipelago should be finalized and implemented.[45]

At this point, Vetrov and his colleagues received welcome support from the General Staff on the matter of necessary changes to the Soviet–Norwegian border. In a letter of 14 July 1945, Lieutenant-General Slavin, an assistant to the Chief of the General Staff, argued 'the necessity of improving our strategic situation' in the northern border region. In view of the need to secure the important Soviet naval bases and ice-free ports on the Kola Peninsula, the optimum solution would be to move the Soviet–Norwegian border to the river Tana and the Tana Fjord – which would mean transferring the whole of the Varanger Peninsula and the area south of the Varanger Fjord to the Soviet Union. Together with the presence of the Soviet military on Bear Island, this would create the preconditions for the establishment of a 'huge land- and sea-based strategic defence area' (*bolshaia sukhoputnaia i morskaia strategicheskaia zona prikrytiia*), stretching from the Spitsbergen archipelago to the Kola Peninsula. The minimum solution would be to lease the Varanger area from Norway for a term of 25–50 years.[46]

When the Soviet Ambassador to Norway, Nikolai D. Kuznetsov, sent Moscow an alarming report about Norwegian activity on Spitsbergen, Vetrov reminded Deputy Commissar Lozovsky of his earlier message to Molotov, to which he had not received any response, and argued that the Soviet Union should 'immediately return to Spitsbergen' in order to establish military garrisons on the island.[47] Little resulted from Vetrov's efforts: Molotov was not prepared to make a decision on the joint declaration on Spitsbergen or on the strategic elements of the various proposals which had been put forward by his subordinates. Thus, as of July–August 1945, the bureaucrats in the Commissariat for Foreign Affairs and the deputy commissars dealing with Norway had produced a number of proposals aimed at a more active Soviet policy for Svalbard and northern Norway. Parts of their efforts had received strong support from the Soviet military authorities, but had failed to kindle Molotov's enthusiasm.

These ideas remained very much alive within the foreign policy bureaucracy. Throughout 1945 and 1946 the group of activist bureaucrats continued to press for a comprehensive solution involving both northern Norway and Svalbard. Their efforts were counteracted by the growing understanding within the foreign policy apparatus that Soviet proposals along the lines urged by Vetrov and his colleagues would have repercussions far beyond the Soviet–Norwegian relationship. Increasingly, Soviet policy towards Norway was becoming caught up in the evolution of East–West relations, and the Soviets gradually realized that their room for manoeuvre was strictly limited. The plans for changing the Soviet–Norwegian border were finally rejected in the winter of 1946, when Molotov issued orders to prepare the demarcation of the new Soviet–Norwegian border corresponding to the pre-war Norwegian–Finnish border. On the bilateral level the Svalbard issue was put to rest in February 1947, when the Norwegian *Storting* (Parliament) rejected the idea of joint Norwegian–Soviet militarization of the archipelago. Although there were proposals, *inter alia* from the Soviet Ambassador to Norway, to accept the Norwegian invitation to start negotiations about a revision of the Svalbard Treaty, Soviet policy towards Svalbard rapidly changed towards the defence of *status quo*.

CONCLUSION

The Soviet Svalbard initiative and the NKID bureaucrats' proposals for an expansionist policy towards northern Norway illustrate the role of the *foreign policy bureaucracy* in Soviet policy towards Norway in the early post-war period. Middle-ranking bureaucrats produced proposals which would have had far-reaching and grave consequences for the Soviet–Norwegian relationship if they had been implemented. Although T.L. Zhdanova certainly wrote her memorandum of October 1944 on the orders of, or at least in full understanding with, her immediate superior, Mikhail S. Vetrov, who was then acting head of the NKID's 5th European Department, I have not been able to find any indication that Zhdanova's and Vetrov's proposals were written in response to signals from their superiors.[48] They were carefully studied on the level of the deputy commissars, and were reflected in the policy proposals which reached Molotov and the other top decision-makers. The circumstances surrounding Molotov's meeting with Norwegian Foreign Minister Trygve Lie on 12 November 1944, and Molotov's behaviour during and after the meeting, leave the distinct impression that this was certainly not Molotov's own project. These ideas did not reflect a 'grand strategy' on the top political level, and never received much attention from Molotov.

The bureaucrats who conceived and elaborated the expansionist schemes had limited access to comprehensive information about the overall priorities of Soviet foreign policy and the political realities in the foreign country in question, that is Norway. This can explain why Molotov did not react to the proposals from 1939 and 1940 to step up Soviet control over, or even occupy, Spitsbergen: Molotov had no desire to annoy the Germans by an adventurist policy in the high north. This pattern repeated itself from 1944 onwards, when the expansionist ideas of the NKID bureaucrats conflicted with overall Soviet foreign policy priorities.

The Svalbard initiative and the plans for northern Norway also illustrate what was apparently a common phenomenon in the Soviet foreign policy-making process: the weak co-ordination between bureaucratic structures. Although the reasoning of the NKID officials was replete with military-strategic terminology, it appears from the available documentation that Molotov *did not* seek the advice of the military authorities before the issue was brought up with the Norwegians in November 1944. The General Staff was asked to present its opinion about the strategic value of Spitsbergen and Bear Island only afterwards, and seems to have been unaware of the Soviet–Norwegian discussions from November 1944 to April 1945.[49] It then turned out that the military leaders were much more interested in northern Norway than the distant Svalbard area, with the possible exception of Bear Island.

The absence of co-ordination between the military and foreign policy bureaucracies weakened the chances of Vetrov, Zhdanova and others of convincing the decision-makers of the need for a more forceful policy towards Svalbard. As for northern Norway, Molotov, as opposed to his subordinates, must have realized that a Soviet initiative along the lines proposed by Zhdanova, Vetrov, Dekanozov and others would have repercussions far beyond the Soviet–Norwegian relationship. Even the fact that the General Staff supported the idea of a system of Soviet military bases in northern Norway, failed to convince Molotov of the need to put aside the political considerations which kept him from raising the issue. The documentation of Soviet deliberations about the strategic significance of the Baltic Straits and Bornholm raises more questions than it answers.[50] There was, apparently, unanimity within the Soviet foreign policy bureaucracy about the need to revise the regime of the Baltic Straits, with the aim of closing the Baltic Sea to warships of non-littoral states. The idea of establishing permanent Soviet naval and air bases on the island of Bornholm meant an additional step in the direction of transforming the Baltic Sea into a Soviet *mare clausum*. The circumstances of the Soviet landing on Bornholm, seen in conjunction with the (however meagre) evidence on the origin of the decision to send Soviet troops to the island, indicate that this decision was primarily motivated by political, not military, considerations.

Soviet policy towards the Baltic Straits and Bornholm reveals the limits of Soviet power and influence in Denmark. Soviet strategic interests in the country were not sufficiently strong to warrant a policy which might impede the fulfilment of more important Soviet aims elsewhere in Europe, *and* have the unintended effect of pushing a frightened Denmark even further into the orbit of the Western powers. The Soviets seemed caught in an insoluble dilemma: The Soviet military presence on Bornholm was motivated by the desire to create a means of influencing the Danish Government. Any hints of Soviet intentions to use their troops in this role, however, would immediately compel the Danes to appeal to the Western powers for help and support. Only the achievement of superior foreign policy or military-strategic aims could warrant the use of military leverage.

Soviet interests in Denmark, as in Norway, were not of this magnitude. The potential threat inherent in the Soviet military presence on Danish and Norwegian soil proved useless. In a letter to Molotov of February 1946, Plakhin, the Soviet envoy to Denmark, hinted that the continued presence of Soviet troops on Bornholm provided the British and the Americans with an excuse to maintain a military presence in Denmark proper.[51] Similarly, the Soviets gradually realized that Soviet demands with regard to Spitsbergen provided the Americans with welcome arguments in support of their efforts to obtain permanent military bases on Greenland and Iceland. Therefore, the pursuit of Soviet offensive strategic objectives in Denmark and Norway gradually gave way to the traditional and basically defensive policy of confining the Western great powers' influence in, and control over, these countries. Soviet diplomatic reports from Denmark and Norway in the early postwar years reveal a curious disparity between the dire description of the Anglo-Saxons' overwhelming influence and activity in these countries, and the less-than-impressive measures proposed to remedy the situation. In February 1947, for instance, Plakhin reported from Copenhagen that British and American post-war policy in Denmark aimed at 'transforming Denmark into a bridgehead against us' and securing full control over the Baltic Straits. To underpin his argument, Plakhin presented examples of the feverish 'Anglo-Saxon' activity in Denmark, in the political, military, economic and cultural fields. Although Plakhin was optimistic about exploiting existing conflicts of interests between Denmark and the Western great powers, his specific suggestions for initiatives which would 'increase our influence in Denmark' clearly reveal that the Soviet envoy realized that the Soviet Union had limited chances of influencing Danish affairs. Of the 15 initiatives recommended by Plakhin, 12 were in the field of 'cultural contacts and propaganda', one was of a strictly formal nature (to elevate the status of the diplomatic missions from legations to embassies), and the final two concerned trade relations. There are no hints that Plakhin at this point was considering stronger measures to counteract the US–British military presence in Denmark, by raising, for instance, the issue of the internationalization of the Baltic Straits or a Soviet or joint Soviet–Danish fortification of Bornholm.[52] The aim of Soviet policy in Denmark, according to Plakhin, should be to strengthen Denmark's ability to resist the British–US influence, and to develop economic contacts between Denmark and the 'democratic' countries.[53] Similar reports came from Soviet diplomatic representatives in Oslo and Stockholm. These limited foreign policy aims were a far cry from the ambitious initiatives which had been discussed by the foreign policymakers in Moscow in the preceding years.

Notes

1. The article is based on newly declassified documents from the Russian Ministry of Foreign Affairs, gathered during numerous and extended visits to the Foreign Policy Archives of the Russian Federation in Moscow. I am indebted to Dr I.V. Lebedev, Director of the Ministry's Department of History and Records, and to his Deputies and the rest of his staff, for help and assistance during my research in the AVP RF.
2. I am indebted to professor B. Jensen, Odense University, for his useful comments to this part of the paper. The historian B. Weil has published an article in a Danish newspaper about Soviet–Danish relations from December 1944 to April 1946 ('Russerne kommer. Diplomater i Moskva ville lade Den røde Häer besäette Danmark – men efter dansk invitation', *Politiken*, 16 October 1994). Unfortunately, Weil's article does not contain archival references to the sources upon which he based his research.
3. Apart from being mentioned in the international literature on World War II and Soviet foreign policy, a number of works by Danish historians discusses the Baltic Straits and Bornholm in Soviet policy. Cf. M. Dau, *Danmark og Sovjetunionen 1944–49* (Copenhagen: 1969); the same author's 'The Soviet Union and the Liberation of Denmark', *Survey. A Journal of Soviet and East European Studies*, 76 (Summer 1970) 64–81; B. Jensen, *Tryk og tilpasning. Sovjetunionen og Danmark siden 2. verdenskrig* (Copenhagen: 1987).
4. AVP RF, f. 085, op. 30, p. 123, d. 24, l. 1–21, Zhdanova's and Adamov's memorandum 'Baltiiskoe more i baltiiskie prolivy', most probably from October–November 1940. Cf. the discussion in T. Miljan, 'The Baltic Sea: *Mare Clausum* or *Mare Liberum*?', *Cooperation and Conflict*, IX (1974) 19–28.
5. Pavlov's minute from Molotov's conversation with Ribbentrop on 13 November 1940, as published in *Novaia i noveishaia istoriia*, 5 (1993) 92–3. The German version of this publication is published in *Documents on German Foreign Policy*, D, Vol. 11, pp. 562–9.
6. Record of Eden's conversation with Stalin on 16 December 1941, PRO, Prem 4 3/8.
7. For the role of the Litvinov commission, cf. A. Filitov's contribution in this volume.
8. Minutes of the Litvinov Commission's 8th meeting on 22 July 1944, AVP RF, f. 0512, op. 2, p. 8, d. 4, l. 89–98.

9. What Lozovskii had in mind was certainly naval or air bases, although this particular document uses the general expression 'military bases' (*voennye bazy*).
10. Minutes of the Litvinov Commission's 8th meeting on 22 July 1944, AVP RF, f. 0512, op. 2, p. 8, d. 4, l. 89–98.
11. In the years covered by this paper (1944–7), Scandinavian affairs were the responsibility of the 5th European Department, under the directors P.D. Orlov, M.S. Vetrov (acting head) and A.N. Abramov.
12. Orlov to Dekanozov, 15 August 1944, AVP RF, f. 085, p. 120, d. 5, l. 17–19. The memorandum commented upon the British note to the Soviet Government of 9 August about the elaboration of a common allied policy during the liberation of Denmark. Orlov emphasized the need to strengthen the authority of the Danish Freedom Council, and to ask this body to take upon itself the administration of the country until the re-establishment of 'constitutional power'.
13. Semionov and Vetrov to Dekanozov, 15 December 1944 [with Dekanozov's handwritten comments], AVP RF, f. 085, op. 28, p. 120, d. 5, l. 22–3.
14. B. Jensen, 'Døssing og Dekanozov – set fra Moskva', in *Struktur og funktion. Festskrift til Erling Ladewig Petersen* (Odense: 1993) pp. 283–4, based on the Soviet minutes of Døssing's conversation with Dekanozov on 17 January 1945. According to Døssing, Dekanozov said that Denmark after the war would become the Soviet Union's 'direct neighbour', and that there would be 'no competitors to the Soviet Union in the Baltic Sea', cf. Jensen, *Tryk og tilpasning*, pp. 48–9. Based on his study of the Soviet documents, B. Jensen questions the reliability of Døssing's reports from his conversations with Soviet diplomats in late 1944 and early 1945.
15. Weil, 'Russerne kommer'.
16. Dau, *Danmark*, pp. 107–9.
17. Semionov to Dekanozov, March 1945, AVP RF, f. 06, op. 7, p. 32, d. 443, l. 2.
18. Podtserob to Bulganin, 12 March 1945, *ibid.*, l. 1.
19. Weil, 'Russerne kommer'.
20. A. Basov, 'Desant na ostrov Bornholm', *Voenno-istoricheskii zhurnal*, VIII, 5 (1966) 29–30.
21. The German forces in Denmark, including Bornholm, capitulated to the British on 5 May. The British, however, deliberately sent no forces to Bornholm to receive the German capitulation.
22. Vetrov and Plakhin to Molotov, 10 July 1945, AVP RF, f. 085, op. 30, p. 123, d. 24, l. 49–60.
23. Dau, *Danmark*, p. 118.
24. Vetrov and Zhdanova to Vyshinskii and Lozovskii, 2 July 1945, AVP RF, f. 085, op. 30, p. 123, d. 24, l. 46–7.
25. Vetrov and Plakhin to Molotov, 10 July 1945, *ibid.*, l. 49–60.
26. Litvinov to Molotov, 18 December 1945, *ibid.*, l. 61–4.
27. Vetrov and Plakhin to Molotov, 10 July 1945, *ibid.*, l. 49–60.
28. Litvinov to Molotov, 18 December 1945, *ibid.*, l. 61–4.
29. Abramov and Vetrov to Novikov, 9 October 1945, AVP RF, f. 085, op. 29, p. 121, d. 8, l. 2.
30. K.E. Eriksen, 'Great Britain and the Problem of Bases in the Northern Area, 1945–1947', *Scandinavian Journal of History*, VII, 2 (1982) 152; and Dau, *Danmark*, p. 122.

31. Draft resolution for the Conference of ministers of foreign affairs, AVP RF, f. 085, op. 30, p. 123, d. 24, l. 66.
32. Minutes of Molotov's conversation with Døssing on 5 March 1946, AVP RF, f. 06, op. 8, p. 33, d. 518, l. 6-10.
33. Prior to their withdrawal, the Soviet troops on Bornholm consisted of one rifle division of 6600 men, with 170 guns and mortars, 7500 tons of munitions and supplies, and a number of transport vehicles. Antonov to Molotov, 14 March 1946, *ibid.*, l. 16.
34. For a more detailed discussion of Soviet policy towards Svalbard and northern Norway during and after World War II, cf. S.G. Holtsmark, 'A Soviet Grab for the High North? USSR, Svalbard, and Northern Norway 1920–1953', in *Forsvarsstudier/Defence Studies*, No. 7 (Oslo: 1993), which contains references to previous research.
35. Holtsmark,'A Soviet Grab', pp. 36-8.
36. *Ibid.*, pp. 38-43.
37. Volnukhin's report about the evacuation is found in AVP RF, f. 0116, op. 23a, p. 123a, d. 1, l. 1-12. Cf. M. Kitchen, *British Policy towards the Soviet Union during the Second World War* (London: 1986) p. 87.
38. O. Riste, 'Svalbardkrisen 1944-1945', in *Forsvarsstudier/Defence Studies 1981* (Oslo: 1982), p. 32.
39. 'Po voprosu o Shpitsbergene i Medvezhem ostrove', 11 November 1944, AVP RF, f. 06, op. 9, p. 62, d. 936, l. 40–8.
40. 'Kratkaia spravka k voprosu o russko-norvezhskoi granitse' [signed by Zhdanova on 27 October 1944], AVP RF f. 0116, op. 28, p. 20, d. 5, l. 1-18.
41. Kucherov to Dekanozov, 4 June 1945, AVP RF, f. 0116, op. 27, p. 127, d. 11, l. 234-6.
42. Vetrov to Lozovskii, 8 June 1945, AVP RF, f. 0116, op. 27, p. 127, d. 10, l. 15.
43. Vetrov to Molotov, 8 June 1945, AVP RF, f. 0116, op. 27, p. 128, d. 22, l. 5.
44. 'Spravka. K voprosu: O sozdanii voenno-morskikh i vozdushnykh baz SSSR v Severnoi Norvegii, kak zvena v obshchei sisteme bezopasnosti', 3 July 1945, AVP RF, f. 0116, op. 27, p. 127, d. 5, l. 33–5.
45. 'Spravka. K voprosu: Ob otmene Parizhskogo Dogovora o Shpitsbergene i o sovmestnoi zashchite Shpitsbergena i ostrova Medvezhii Sovetskim Soiuzom i Norvegiei', 4 July 1945, AVP RF, f. 0116, op. 27, p. 127, d. 22, l. 16-18.
46. Slavin's memorandum of 14 July 1945, AVP RF, f. 0116, op. 27, p. 128, d. 20, l. 10-12.
47. Vetrov to Lozovskii, 21 July 1945, AVP RF, f. 0116, op. 27, p. 128, d. 22, l. 27-8.
48. Most likely Zhdanova wrote her October 1944 memorandum for the Litvinov Commission.
49. This judgement is based on the complete lack of references to the military authorities in the MID documents, and on a letter from the General Staff from January 1945. In this letter the Deputy Chief of the General Staff supposed that the Soviet Union should demand 'long-term lease' of certain Norwegian territories as compensation for Soviet expenses during the liberation of Eastern Finnmark. Although the general included Bear Island on his list of areas where the Soviet Union ought to have military bases, there are no hints in the letter that Antonov was aware of the Soviet–Norwegian negotiations already in progress. Antonov to

Dekanozov, 24 January 1945, AVP RF, f. 012, op. 6, p. 81, d. 168, l. 6–9. Later correspondence between the General Staff and the NKID seems to confirm this impression.
50. This may partly be due to the fragmentary nature of the archival source materials on Soviet policy towards Denmark in the early post-war years. This directly reflects the amount of time the author of this article spent in the AVP RF doing research on Soviet policy towards Norway and Denmark respectively.
51. Plakhin to Molotov, 19 February 1946, AVP RF, f. 06, op. 8, p. 33, d. 512, l. 2–19.
52. Plakhin to Molotov, 16 April 1947, AVP RF, f. 085, op. 31, p. 125, d. 4, l. 8–14.
53. Katalev's '*annotatsiia*' on the legation's report for 1946, 20 June 1947, *ibid.*, l. 17–21.

8 A Balkan Union? Southeastern Europe in Soviet Security Policy, 1944–8

R. Craig Nation

FEDERATIVE OPTIONS IN 1943–5

The idea of a federation of Balkan states is an old one, with roots dating back at least two centuries. In the nineteenth century it became a basic goal of Balkan Socialism, and after 1919 was adopted by the Communist International, which sponsored a Communist Balkan Federation with its seat in Moscow.[1] The goal of federation was revived during the first phase of the World War II, somewhat ironically, by the Greek and Yugoslav Governments-in-exile, with considerable British urging. Little emerged from the initiative, however, which in the understanding of its sponsors was intended to create 'a powerful guarantee against an eventual Bolshevik danger from the Northeast', and which was rejected by the Soviet Union at the foreign ministers conference in Moscow during October 1943 as an attempt to place a new *cordon sanitaire* around the USSR.[2]

During 1943 and 1944 similar projects, but with a very different motivation, grew out of the dynamic of Communist-led partisan resistance. Paul Shoup speculates that in approving a degree of autonomy for the Macedonian provincial committee of the resistance in the autumn of 1942, Tito may already have had in mind the goal of a Balkan federation including a united Macedonia under Yugoslav domination.[3] In February 1943 Svetozar Vukmanović-Tempo arrived in Macedonia as Tito's prefect, where he inspired the founding of an autonomous Macedonian Communist Party and pushed for the creation of a 'Balkan General Staff' to link the region's resistance movements. Tempo engineered a 20 June 1943 agreement, signed by representatives of the Yugoslav, Greek and Albanian Communist Parties, which pledged 'mutual co-operation' and a meeting of 12 July 1943 on Greek territory extended this to a commitment to build a permanent headquarters of the People's Liberation Army of the Balkans 'as the military embryo of a future confederation'.[4]

Tempo's initiative arrived at a moment when the momentum in the military struggle against the axis was shifting. Between January and July 1943 the Yugoslav partisans warded off German offensives in Bosnia and Montenegro and overwhelmed the *Chetnik* forces of the Serbian royalist commander Draža Mihailović. At the battle of Kursk in July 1943 the Soviet armed forces inflicted a crucial defeat upon the *Wehrmacht*, and on 25 July 1943 the Mussolini Government fell in Rome. Tempo's goals seemed designed to contribute to the pressure bearing down upon Hitler's *Reich*, but there were many factors that worked against them. The agreements themselves were only preliminary, the military situation in the Balkans remained chaotic, and at the session of 12 July the Macedonian question had already emerged as a source of discord.[5] Most of all, external sponsorship was lacking. On 22 May 1943 the Soviets announced the disbanding of the Communist International (Comintern) as a gesture of appeasement to the West, and they were in no hurry to revive the spectre of militant international Communism. 'The creation of a "mini-International" in the Balkans,' writes Branko Petranović, 'even on a military level in the struggle against Fascism, did not correspond to Stalin's policy in mid-1943.'[6] On 21 September 1943, opting to prioritize relations with the British, with whom his partisans had only recently established formal contact (the British military liaison officer Fitzroy Maclean arrived at Tito's headquarters in September 1943), Tito informed Tempo that the goal of a federation of Balkan peoples was only an 'agitational' slogan, and ordered him to break off negotiations for a unified Balkan command.[7]

Despite this retreat, Tito encouraged Tempo to reinforce relations with the Greek and Bulgarian resistance forces, and at a session of 16–18 October 1943 the Politburo of the Communist Party of Yugoslavia (KPJ) made the goal of a 'south Slavic federation' a programmatic slogan, and in his report to the session Milovan Djilas evoked a 'federative union of the south Slavic peoples from Trieste to the Black Sea'.[8] These goals would be pursued in the months to come on a bilateral level in relations between the Titoists and the Albanian and Bulgarian Communist movements.

The issue of relations with Albania was sharpened by Italy's capitulation in October 1943. In a dispatch sent by the Central Committee of the KPJ in late January 1944 to the Second Corps Headquarters of the People's Liberation Army of Albania, an option for association was outlined based upon the Yugoslav federal model. The dispatch urged the Albanians to 'further popularize the possibility of other Balkan peoples joining this federation, and the creation of a strong and large Balkan state of equal peoples which would be a major factor in Europe'.[9]

The Kosovo problem remained the key point of dissension. The fourth party congress of the KPJ in Dresden in 1928, in line with what was then the official Comintern line calling for the dismemberment of the Yugoslav federation, had agreed to cede Kosovo to Albania. The Comintern's call for a dismemberment of Yugoslavia was officially abandoned after approval of the Popular Front strategy in 1935, however, and Tito's partisans made clear that any territorial revisions at Yugoslavia's expense were out of the question. At Jajce in November 1943 the Titoists supported a federal Yugoslavia with the right of self-determination for Yugoslavia's constituent 'nations', a status which was, however, not accorded to the Albanian population, officially described as a 'national minority'. A conference of 31 December 1943–2 January 1944 at Bujana in Albanian territory, bringing together representatives of the national liberation forces of Kosovo, Sanjak and Montenegro, contradicted these premises by asserting the will to union with Albania. The gesture was supported by Albanian Communist leader Enver Hoxha in a subsequent pamphlet, but rejected by Djilas as a 'politics of *fait accompli*'.[10] The only hope for a positive solution seemed to lie in some kind of federal system attaching Kosovo to Albania within an enlarged Yugoslavia.[11]

In September 1944 the Soviet Army entered Bulgaria and a Communist-dominated regime under the Fatherland Front came to power. The Front assumed control over a traumatized and defeated nation, badly in need of international support. In the second week of September the Bulgarian Communist leader Georgi Dimitrov, from his wartime base in Moscow, sent several radiograms to Tito urging military co-operation between the Yugoslav partisans and the 'new' Bulgarian army, which, until a week before, had represented the axis as an army of occupation in Vardar Macedonia.[12] From 21 to 28 September Tito was in Moscow, where together with Dimitrov and upon Stalin's urging he approved the terms of a military co-operation agreement.[13] During the return journey, on a stopover in the Romanian city of Craiova, Tito met with Bulgarian officials and signed a pledge to pursue a common fight against Germany.[14]

Macedonia, of course, quickly became a bone of contention. In August 1944 the first session of the Macedonian Anti-Fascist Council of National Liberation asserted the existence of a distinct Macedonian nationality and called for the creation of a unified Macedonia, with implied territorial revindication against Bulgaria and Greece. The Yugoslavs reiterated these positions in their talks with the Bulgarians, and specifically called for a right of self-determination for the Pirin Macedonia region. The Yugoslav conditions were not acceptable to Sofia, which complained of a systematic Yugoslav attempt to 'denationalize' the Bulgarian population of Pirin Macedonia.[15] Despite these frictions, however, there remained some ground for optimism. The victory of Communism in both countries, the need to co-operate in the common war with Germany that was now on the horizon, vague sentiments of Slavic and Balkan cultural affinity, and a common will to association on the part of important forces within the respective leaderships seemed to bode well.

In early November 1944 the Yugoslavs brought dialogue with the Bulgarians to a higher level by sending a concrete project for federation to Sofia by special courier. Between November and January 1945 the Yugoslavs and Bulgarians pursued intense discussions, in the course of which a number of alternative variants for association were developed.[16] The first exchange of proposals during November made basic differences in orientation clear. The Yugoslav side was in general more avid, posing the goal of a 'unitary federal state' and the creation of a joint military command with Tito as commander-in-chief. The proposed agenda was for Pirin Macedonia to unite with Vardar Macedonia in a single federal entity, with the remainder of Bulgaria joining the Yugoslav federation as a seventh republic, a '6+1' approach to federation building that would create an enlarged Macedonia distinct from Bulgaria and reinforce Tito's effective control. The Bulgarian counterproposal emphasized the need for gradualism, posed the more modest goal of strengthening 'bilateral relations', and called for maintaining national armies and command authorities at least until the war's end. The desirability of a federation was acknowledged, but on the basis of a '1+1' approach in which Bulgaria and Yugoslavia would engage as sovereign states and on equal terms.[17] On 22 November 1944 in Moscow, in a discussion with Kardelj and Ivan Šubašić, Stalin approved the Yugoslav variant, though he also proposed waiting before any decisive initiative was undertaken in order to gain a better sense of US and British reactions.[18] On 22 December Kardelj arrived in Sofia, where he was presented by the Bulgarians with a second draft of the federation project. The text called for expanded political, economic and military co-operation leading towards union on the basis of parity, including the attachment of Pirin to Vardar Macedonia once union had been achieved. The proposal was a major concession from the Bulgarian national perspective, but it was not sufficient according to Kardelj, who continued to insist upon a 6+1 approach and noted the lack of references to a joint military command in the Bulgarian draft. In his memoir, Kardelj suggested that the Bulgarians accepted the goal of federation merely 'in principle' and as a result of Soviet pressure, with only the 'super-Stalinist' Vladko Chervenkov prepared to accept a 6+1 approach.[19] Kostov (latter to be hanged as a 'Titoist' for allegedly agreeing to hand over Pirin Macedonia to Yugoslavia) supported the goal of federation but explicitly rejected a 6+1 approach.[20] 'The inclusion of Bulgaria as a seventh republic in the Yugoslav federation', he asserted, 'would mean an abandonment of national sovereignty, a break with the Bulgarian state tradition, and an historically irredeemable blow to Bulgarian national consciousness.'[21]

Negotiations in Sofia led to the drafting of a joint variant of the federation project, based upon the second Bulgarian draft but encompassing changes made by Kardelj, including mention of the union of Pirin and Vardar Macedonia and the creation of a joint command. The document was not entirely satisfactory for either party, however, and the talks broke off non-committally. A subsequent Yugoslav variant, presented to Stalin and Dimitrov in preliminary form by foreign affairs representative Josip Smodlaka, and sent officially to the Bulgarian Government (in two versions) on 5 and 8 January 1945, held uncompromisingly to the 6+1 approach, and included the request that the document be signed within a week. Bulgarian reactions to the proposal were negative, and the Yugoslavs' precipitous haste was not appreciated. In the second week of January a delegation representing the Fatherland Front travelled to Belgrade by special train to present a third Bulgarian variant, and with instructions to slow down the process and to reassert the priority of partnership as a basis for association. The Yugoslavs reciprocated by sending their own high level delegation to Sofia, including Moša Pijade, Veljko Vlahović, and general Vladimir Popović (soon to become the ambassador of Tito's Government to Moscow), on 12 January. These interactions bore witness to seriousness of purpose, but they brought the two sides no closer to agreement.[22]

During talks in Moscow during December with Dimitrov and the Yugoslavs, Stalin seems to have distanced himself from the Yugoslav approach to federation. After Dimitrov argued that a 6+1 approach would 'destroy' the weak Bulgarian Government, Stalin intervened to express 'exasperation' with the Yugoslavs and to recommend a 'two-sided Government on a basis of equality, something analogous to Austria–Hungary.'[23] This inconsistency can be explained in several ways. Stalin does not seem to have been deeply committed to any particular variant of the federative project, and may simply have sought to expedite matters. More likely, however, his somewhat cavalier approach to the issue of Balkan union had begun to clarify as the larger implications of the project became more apparent. On 11–19 September 1944 Roosevelt and Churchill met in Quebec, where the British Prime Minister urged that greater priority be given to military operations in both Italy and the Balkans as a means to block growing Soviet influence in the Mediterranean region. With word of the Yugoslav–Bulgarian dialogue in the air, on 4 December 1944 a memorandum from British Foreign Minister Anthony Eden conveyed London's objections to any kind of Yugoslav–Bulgarian federation to both Moscow and Sofia. Eden expressed concern for the diplomatic isolation of Greece, mentioned the threat posed by 'Slavic hegemonism' to the geopolitical balance of Southeastern Europe, and questioned the legitimacy of a formal association involving the unrecognized interim Government of a defeated belligerent such as Bulgaria. In Belgrade, Fitzroy Maclean expressed similar reservations to the Yugoslavs.[24] Moscow confronted a dilemma, which was predictably resolved on the basis of the strict criteria of Soviet great power interests. In January 1945 the head of the Yugoslav mission to Moscow Andrija Hebrang informed Tito that Stalin was now recommending the conclusion of a Yugoslav–Bulgarian treaty of Friendship, Cooperation and Mutual Assistance for a period of 10–20 years, intended as a basis for movement towards federation, but without any precipitous actions prior to the consolidation of the new regimes and the establishment of legitimate and internationally recognized postwar governments.[25] Texts for the treaty submitted simultaneously by Pijade for the Yugoslavs and Andrei Vyshinsky for the Soviets, and the joint text eventually approved on 27 January, did not contain a single word about the goal of federation. At the end of the month Stalin once again summoned representatives of the Yugoslav and Bulgarian leaderships to Moscow. The Bulgarian delegation (including Dimitrov and Kostov) was on a distinctly higher level that its Yugoslav counterpart (Pijade, Hebrang, Stanoje Simič), perhaps reflecting Tito's displeasure with the direction in which negotiations had been taken. All parties continued to give lip service to the goal of federation, but without establishing any kind of working agenda or timetable.

On 11 April 1945, during the ceremonies accompanying the signing of a Soviet–Yugoslav treaty of Friendship, Cooperation and Mutual Assistance, Stalin threw cold water on hopes to take the process further, asserting that additional initiatives would have to await the end of hostilities.[26] The first phase of negotiations for a Balkan union was concluded. It had produced considerable discussion and some refinement of positions, but no concrete results. The failure of the dialogue of 1944–5 can be ascribed to a number of variables, the most fundamental of them being London's strong opposition. Churchill prioritized Britain's role in Greece, which he would go on to defend with the dispatch of a British expeditionary force to Athens during the 'second round' of the Greek civil war in December. Stalin's October 1944 percentage bargain with Churchill, which assigned 90 per cent influence in Greece to the United Kingdom, was an acknowledgement of the legitimacy of these priorities, with the *quid pro quo* of a guarantee of Soviet predominance in Romania, the one Balkan state with which the USSR shared a common border.[27]

On the regional level, several issues proved to be particularly divisive. The frustrating Macedonian question and the problem of Bulgaria's status within a proposed federation could not be resolved consensually. The Bulgarian leadership rejected a 6+1 approach as incommensurate with national dignity. The Yugoslavs clung to the formula, noting that the Bulgarian national tradition was no more distinct or substantial than those of the Slovenes, Serbs or Croats. While reluctantly accepting the attachment of Pirin to Vardar Macedonia in the context of a federation, the Bulgarians dogmatically refused to acknowledge a Macedonian nationality or language distinct from Bulgarian. Anxious to court Macedonian national feeling in the new Yugoslavia, the Yugoslavs were uncompromising on these points.

Though the most substantial discussions during 1944–5 were conducted between Yugoslavia and Bulgaria, more ambitious variants of the project for a Balkan union included Albania and Greece as well. Albania's dependence upon Yugoslav sponsorship made it a likely candidate for a federative solution, but the 'Land of Eagles' was of great potential strategic value, and Moscow may already have looked askance at the prospect of its absorption by Titoist Yugoslavia. Greece was in the throes of civil war, and it had been defined by the United Kingdom as an area of vital interest. These complications made it unlikely that the federative project could aspire to grow beyond a south Slavic core, at least in the immediate future.

The Greek Communist Party (KKE) had operated without guidelines from Moscow or the Comintern during most of the war.[28] When contacts were re-established, the Soviet Union once again opted to prioritize its status within the grand coalition at the expense of an indigenous Communist movement. The Soviet military mission which arrived at the headquarters of the Communist-led Greek People's National Liberation Army (ELAS) at the end of June 1944 demanded respect for the Lebanon Charter of May 1944, calling for the creation of a unified provisional government. On 15 August, the KKE abandoned its radical rejectionism and accepted the Soviet recommendation.[29] During the fighting in Athens that erupted on 3 December 1944 Moscow remained passive, and it urged acceptance of the 12 February 1945 Varkiza Agreement, a major defeat for the KKE according to which it was required to recognize the British-sponsored successor regime and to disarm ELAS.[30] Peter Stavrakis asserts that Stalin clung to the hope of using the KKE as 'a potential source of political leverage in post-war Greece', but agrees that in 1944–5 Moscow sought to tame the Greek Communists on behalf of its sphere of influence arrangement with the British.[31] All things considered, the issue was of secondary importance in the larger sweep of Soviet diplomacy; C.M. Woodhouse describes Moscow's policy as 'indifferent to Greece and ill-informed about the Balkans during most of the Occupation'.[32]

The Yugoslav partisans had the strongest vested interest in federative solutions. The status of the Albanian population of Kosovo, Montenegro and Macedonia could be stabilized by a formal association with Communist Albania. The unification of the Macedonian people within a single state could also set a positive precedent for Yugoslav territorial revindication in the north, where the call for the unification of the Slovenian peoples within the boundaries of Yugoslavia implied territorial demands against Italy and Austria. But the Titoists were possessed by a swelling sense of self-confidence and ambition, and determined that issues such as that of Macedonia could only be resolved on the terms which they themselves proposed. What Petranović calls Tito's 'megalomanic' conception of federation became a barrier to progress in its own right.[33]

The Soviets' initial support for the idea of federation can be explained in various ways. Stefano Bianchini suggests that, 'in a Yugoslav–Bulgarian accord the Soviet dictator probably saw the possibility of affirming his own hegemony, ideological and political, over the Balkan Communist parties'.[34] Milcho Lalkov perceives Stalin to have manipulated pan-Slavic sentiment on behalf of an ambitious pragmatism 'which saw in Slavic unity and solidarity a basis for strengthening the Soviets' leading position in Eastern Europe'.[35] These perceptions could only have been amorphous ones in the volatile circumstances of 1944–5 however, and, when forced to choose, Stalin was not loath to abandon them. In the end Moscow opted to discourage the dynamic of association, to limit the Yugoslav–Bulgarian dialogue to the terms of a friendship treaty, to accept the KKE's defeat in Athens, and to encourage the logic of the Varkiza accord. The Yalta Conference of February 1945, which devoted very little attention to the Balkan region, marked the conclusion of a first round of discussions of federative alternatives. The opposition of the United Kingdom and the USA to an enlarged, Communist-dominated Balkan union with the potential to subvert Greece, the Soviet decision to prioritize relations with its wartime great power allies, and resistance by a part of the Bulgarian leadership to a Yugoslav agenda that was perceived to threaten the state tradition and autonomy of the Bulgarian people combined to frustrate a hopeful initiative for which circumstances were not yet ripe.

PROJECTS FOR BALKAN UNION IN 1947–8

Between 1945 and 1947 the onset of the Cold War gave new impetus to closer co-ordination among the emerging Communist regimes of the Balkans. The Yugoslav–Bulgarian relationship was once again the key source of dynamism. Collaboration during the final phase of the war, Yugoslav material assistance to Bulgaria, promises of diplomatic support in negotiations leading up to the post-war peace conference, and joint aid to the Greek partisans after the outbreak of the 'third round' of the civil war in the spring of 1946, all provided a foundation for co-operation. Sofia and Belgrade also confronted common tensions in relations with Greece and Turkey. At the Paris Peace Conference in July 1946 the Yugoslavs supported the Bulgarian positions on reparations and on territorial revisions in western Thrace, and in February 1947 Belgrade agreed to annul Sofia's reparations obligations. The culmination of these trends came with the visit of a Bulgarian state delegation to Yugoslavia on 27 July–3 August 1947. Official discussions, conducted at the Slovenian resort of Lake Bled, resulted in the text of a treaty of Friendship, Cooperation and Mutual Assistance of 'unlimited' duration, and three accords covering economic co-operation, reduction of customs barriers, and a more open border regime.[36] Dimitrov described the results as the beginning of a 'new era' in Yugoslav–Bulgarian relations, and Tito also underlined their importance.[37] Although there was no mention of the goal of federation, Western capitals, including Ankara and Athens, were alarmed. In the spring of 1946 a Communist offensive had opened a new round of fighting in the Greek civil war. On 23 June–2 July 1946, Enver Hoxha made his first state visit to Belgrade, where he discussed the prospect of a Balkan federation with Tito, and negotiated the text of an ambitious treaty of Friendship, Cooperation and Mutual Assistance.[38] For some, a Soviet press for hegemony in the Balkans, in the guise of a federation of Communist states, was in the making.

In fact the façade of unity surrounding the Lake Bled agreements disguised important contradictions. The issue of a 6+1 or 1+1 approach remained alive, Yugoslavia continued to seek the attachment of the Pirin region to the Yugoslav republic of Macedonia, and the eventuality of an expanded federation including Albania, Greece and Romania was completely unresolved.[39] The KKE was now engaged in the decisive battles of the civil war, its popular and physical base was more and more concentrated in the 'Slavo-Macedonian' regions of Aegean Macedonia, and the implications of its eventual triumph were disturbing to almost all involved parties. In discussions with Hoxha in Moscow during July 1947, Stalin likewise articulated his 'dissatisfaction' with Yugoslavia's overbearing role in Albania.[40]

Moscow's public response to the Lake Bled accords was a revealing silence. Behind the scenes, the Stalinist leadership reacted strongly to what it perceived to be a lack of prior consultation by its Balkan allies. In a telegram to Tito and Dimitrov immediately after the Lake Bled sessions Stalin criticized the results, and during Dimitrov's sojourn in Moscow for a health cure between August and mid-November 1947, he spoke of 'negative signals' from the West.[41] Although a Yugoslav–Bulgarian treaty of Friendship, Cooperation and Mutual Assistance based upon the Lake

Bled text was signed in Evksinograd (near Varna) on 27 November 1947, Stalin's concern over the implications of a Yugoslav-led *rapprochement* between Balkan states was apparent. 'In the West,' notes Iu.S. Girenko, 'this treaty was perceived as a serious threat to Greece'.[42]

These concerns were aggravated by the dynamic of Yugoslav–Albanian relations. In the autumn of 1947 the head of the Albanian State Planning Commission, Nako Spiru, committed suicide after his expulsion from the Communist Party for protesting Tirana's concessions to Belgrade.[43] With the situation within the Albanian Party unstable, and, in Djilas's words, increasingly nervous that 'the Russians would get the jump on us and "grab" Albania', Tito began to press for rapid movement towards unification.[44] In January 1948, warning of the possibility of Greek aggression, Belgrade announced the intention to move two divisions onto Albanian territory. Informed by Tirana, Soviet Foreign Minister Viacheslav Molotov fired off several critical telegrams to Tito and Kardelj, in response to which the Yugoslav leader opted to back down.[45] At the end of December 1947 Djilas, accompanied by a delegation of military leaders including the chief of the general staff Koča Popović and current head of the army's political administration Vukmanović-Tempo, was called to Moscow for discussions with Stalin. The military leaders, although they were regaled with promises, emerged from consultations deeply disillusioned with Soviet comportment.[46] In his discussions with Djilas, with consummate cynicism, Stalin claimed to support Yugoslav–Balkan policy and noted that 'we have no special interest in Albania. We agree that Yugoslavia should swallow Albania.'[47] These remarks, perhaps calculated to draw out and expose the Yugoslav representative, would be directly contradicted by Soviet actions in the weeks to come.

After returning to Sofia from Moscow in mid-November, Dimitrov temporarily dropped all public references to a federative option. The dynamic of Yugoslav–Bulgarian bilateral ties remained alive nonetheless. During his address upon the signing of the Yugoslav–Bulgarian friendship treaty on 27 November 1947, Tito urged closer economic co-ordination with the goal of creating a full customs union.[48] Between November 1947 and January 1948, Yugoslavia concluded bilateral friendship treaties with Hungary and Romania, and on his travels through Eastern Europe Tito was greeted as a popular hero.[49] On 16 January 1948 Bulgaria also concluded a bilateral treaty with Romania that included a special protocol which foresaw the creation of a customs union. On 18 January 1948, at an impromptu press conference conducted on a special train returning from Romania after the signing of the treaty, an expansive Dimitrov outlined the goal of an Eastern European federation to include 'Romania, Bulgaria, Yugoslavia, Albania, Czechoslovakia, Poland, Hungary and Greece'. The interview appeared in the Bulgarian Communist journal *Rabotnichesko Delo* on 20 January, and immediately provoked a wave of responses in the Western press, which interpreted the initiative as a ploy designed to further Soviet domination of Europe.

On 23 January 1948 *Pravda* published a résumé of the Dimitrov interview without commentary. One day later, however, Stalin sent a telegram to Tito and Dimitrov in which the idea of federation was criticized.[50] A *Pravda* editorial statement of 28 January brought the dissonance into the open, insisting that the Soviet Union was not opposed to the goals of federation or customs union in principle, but asserting that, at the present moment, such goals were premature. The Yugoslav leadership opted to make no official rejoinder. In deference to the Soviet criticism, a Bulgarian Press Agency response of 29 January 1948 abjectly repudiated both the Lake Bled declaration and Dimitrov's interview, asserting that 'neither the Prime Minister nor any other member of the Government has thought or will be thinking about the creation of an Eastern bloc in any form whatsoever'.[51] Despite these disclaimers, on 1 February Moscow summoned both the Bulgarian and Yugoslav leaderships to the Kremlin for a settling of accounts.[52]

In retrospect it is clear that the ensuing summit, conducted on the evening of 10 February 1948, marked a full stop for federative projects in the Balkans in the post-war period. Bulgaria was represented by Dimitrov, Kostov and Kolarov, the Yugoslavs by Kardelj, Djilas and Vladimir Bakarić, and the Soviets by a group of their top leaders, including Stalin, Molotov, Andrei Zhdanov, Georgi Malenkov, Mikhail Suslov and Valerian Zorin.[53] Molotov opened the session with an undisguised attack upon the independent comportment of Belgrade and Sofia, specifically mentioning the implications of the Lake Bled declaration, the Dimitrov press conference and Yugoslav gestures towards Albania. Both Stalin and Molotov blamed their 'fraternal allies' for complicating relations with the West, and reiterated the 'unacceptable' character of the lack of prior consultation with Moscow. Stalin was particularly annoyed by the prospect of a Bulgarian–Romanian customs union, and addressed Dimitrov with shocking rudeness, liking his comportment to that 'of an old woman in the street who says to everyone whatever comes into her head'.[54] Stalin unambiguously rejected the kind of broad Balkan federation that Dimitrov had evoked, and casually dismissed the Communist cause in the Greek civil war as irretrievably lost. He nonetheless urged rapid movement towards the completion of a Yugoslav–Bulgarian union, to which Albania could also be attached eventually.

Although immediately following the session of 10 February the Bulgarian and Yugoslav representatives dutifully assembled to discuss the kind of association that Stalin had recommended, the goal of a Balkan union had in fact become a lost cause.[55] After some hesitation both parties agreed to sign a text submitted by Molotov on 11 February obligating consultation in reaching foreign policy decisions. The Yugoslavs were now wary of Soviet intentions, however, and concerned with the potential for Bulgaria to play the role of what both Kardelj and Tito called a 'Trojan Horse' on behalf of Soviet priorities inside an enlarged South Slavic federation.[56] A special session of the KPJ Politburo on 1 March followed Tito in interpreting the Soviet suggestion for a union with Bulgaria as a form of pressure on Yugoslavia, and agreed that while the Party had supported the federative option in the past, in present circumstances it was no longer appropriate.[57] The Bulgarians, on the contrary, opted to cling to their relationship with the USSR. No doubt revealing the Soviets' real priorities; the Soviet–Bulgarian peace treaty signed on 18 March was accompanied by a private pledge on the part of Sofia to refuse a South Slavic federation with Yugoslavia.[58]

Soviet comportment during the session of 10 February exposed the imperial mentality that dominated the ruling circle in the Kremlin. Stalin's bullying treatment of Dimitrov was shameless. His dismissive reference to the 'naked illusion' of a Greek Communist victory, though not unrealistic, was cruel. Nor was consistency a virtue. While accusing his Balkan lieutenants of provoking the West with loose talk of association, Stalin had already launched into a series of provocations of his own. The creation of the Cominform in September 1947, the confrontational tone of Zhdanov's keynote address, and the prominent role played in published accounts of the sessions by the ultra-radical Yugoslav delegation all served to put the West on warning. Within ten days of the session of 10 February, the coalition Government of Edvard Beneš in Prague was subverted with Soviet connivance, and the stage was set for the transformation of Czechoslovakia into another subservient 'people's democracy'. In June 1948 the blockade of Berlin was begun. A Soviet-dominated regional subsystem was being created in Central and Southeastern Europe whose essential logic was the reinforcement of Soviet control in defiance of the West. Ambitious agendas for regional affiliation with indigenous origins, such as the project for Balkan union as it had unfolded between 1943 and 1948, conflicted with rather than reinforced that logic. Stalin's initiatives at the session 10 February, which buried hopes for federative options in the region indefinitely, made his real priorities quite clear.

THE BALKANS IN SOVIET SECURITY POLICY

Paul Shoup's characterization of the Soviet attitude towards Balkan federalism in the period 1943–8 as 'extremely devious' remains valid.[59] Stalin encouraged the idea of a Yugoslav–Bulgarian federation in

1944–5, at a moment when the Government of the Fatherland Front appeared to be in desperate need of outside support. The Yugoslav–Bulgarian dialogue, which grew out of Tempo's work in Macedonia, generated friction, however, and in the negotiations that followed Moscow did little to facilitate a positive outcome. When accosted by his British Ally, Stalin was quick to reverse himself, and in the end he intervened to block the momentum of the negotiations altogether.

When the idea of federation was revived in 1947–8 the Soviets were already in the process of creating a bloc of people's democracies in Central and Southeastern Europe. The prospect of a 'bloc within the bloc' dominated by an independent-minded national leader such as Tito was certainly not to their liking. The summit of 10 February 1948 was a moment of truth. Although Stalin spoke of the need for a Yugoslav–Bulgarian union, he probably wished only to test his Balkan lieutenants. Was Kardelj correct in describing the role intended for Bulgaria inside a South Slavic federation as that of a 'Trojan Horse' representing the interests of the Kremlin? Did Stalin view a Yugoslav–Bulgarian federation as a possible 'brake' upon Dimitrov's vision of a wider Balkan–Danubian grouping? Did he use the issue of federation hypocritically, in order to play the Bulgarians and Yugoslavs against each other? The answers are not clear. What is certain is that Moscow manipulated the idea of federation instrumentally, playing the issue in different ways at various conjunctures, but never weighing in with decisive support.

There were, of course, important indigenous sources of resistance to federative alternatives in the Balkans. These included traditional territorial disputes, differences over the architecture of a proposed association, and the problem of scale. The substance of federative projects during the post-war years was the idea of a South Slavic union of pro-Soviet Communist Party states. Romania (which from the outset was encouraged to prioritize bilateral relations with the USSR) was never a vital party to the discussions, and the Albanians were represented primarily through their strong dependence upon the Yugoslavs. A Moscow-loyal South Slavic union was anathema to non-Communist and non-Slavic regional powers such as Greece and Turkey. It was strongly opposed by the British, who prioritized their special role in Greece on geostrategic grounds, a position to which the Americans acquiesced, and towards which the Soviets managed to adjust.

Progress towards federative options was also blocked by the confused dynamics of the Greek civil war. The return of Nikolaos Zachariades from incarceration in Dachau to assume the direction of the KKE in June 1945 reinforced Soviet influence over the Greek Communist movement. In view of his cautious approach to the region, Stalin's willingness to acquiesce in the KKE's decision to move from the 'dual strategy' of 1946 towards a reanimation of the armed struggle in 1947–8 seems incongruous.[60] Failure to approve the KKE's decision risked sacrificing influence to the advantage of Tito, however, and Stalin's two key goals, of 'restraining the expansion of the Greek Civil War and preventing the ascendance of Yugoslavia in Balkan affairs', remained essentially defensive.[61] In the documents of the September 1947 founding Conference of the Cominform there was not a single reference to the Greek civil war, which had just entered its decisive phase.[62] The implications of a Communist victory in the civil war, in light both of British opposition and the link between Zachariades and Tito, cannot have been particularly palatable as viewed from Moscow.

Only the determined intervention of Moscow could have forced the issue of Balkan federalism in the post-war years, and such an intervention was not forthcoming. Adam Ulam interprets the Soviets' original support for the ideal of union in terms of ideological motivation: 'the dominant factor must have been the vision of the Balkans united under the aegis of Communism, a testimony to the irresistible march of the Socialist idea, and a promise, perhaps, in the more distant future, of a still greater union of Communist states.'[63] If so, the vision proved to be quite short-lived. Though Stalin may have been intrigued by the possibility of Balkan union at an early stage of peacemaking, he quickly moved away from the idea as the contradictions that surrounded it became clearer. The most important variable restraining Moscow was concern for relations with its wartime Allies, a concern defined not by Communist idealism, but by the national security interests of the Soviet state. In the immediate post-war period Stalin's security policy was focused upon maintaining a limited accommodation within his big three partners, and secondary goals were rigorously subordinated to that purpose. Moscow lent some encouragement to the Yugoslav–Bulgarian dialogue of 1944–5, but the threat to Greece's territorial integrity posed by a Yugoslav–Bulgarian union quickly made the United Kingdom a party to the contest. Rather than argue the point, Stalin acquiesced to Britain's demand for a dominant role in Greece, and embraced a regional sphere of influence arrangement with Churchill.

By the time that the federative project was revived in 1947, Tito's Yugoslavia had emerged as a new source of worry. Stalin had come to perceive the idea of Balkan unity as a function of the ambitions of Tito. Titoist policies called into question the sovereignty of Albania, considered by Moscow to be a useful strategic ally. The offensive thrust of Belgrade's support for the KKE in the third round of the Greek civil war threatened 'international complications' at a moment when Moscow's main priority had become the drawing together of a disciplined bloc as a defensive glacis against the West. With security policy now defined by the priority of retrenchment, the integrity of the bloc became the highest priority. Autonomous initiatives such as the Lake Bled declaration, made 'without consultation' with the masters in the Kremlin, called into question the logic of the hierarchical relations upon which the entire Soviet-led international Communist movement had come to rest. Stalin was probably less concerned with the implications of these initiatives in their own right, given the substantial barriers to their realization, than with the breach of subordination that seemed to inspire them, the gesture of independence that 'threatened the very foundation of the [Soviet] system'.[64]

The break between Stalin and Tito in 1948, the defeat of the Greek Communists in 1949, and the triumph of the Cold War system in Europe sealed the fate of post-war projects for Balkan federation. The Soviets, who had originally toyed with the idea, eventually turned away from it on the basis of a highly conservative international policy tied to traditional conceptions of national interest and unilateral advantage. In the end the goal of Balkan union was used instrumentally, as a lever in the game of power, 'a manipulative device, to be exploited when France, Great Britain or Germany threatened to draw the Balkan states into their sphere of influence, but to be suppressed when Soviet Russia had replaced them as the Great Power dominating the Peninsula'.[65]

Notes

1. The classic study is L.S. Stavrianos, *Balkan Federation: A History of the Movement toward Balkan Unity in Modern Times* (Northampton, Mass.: 1942). On the Balkan Communist Federation see J. Rothschild, *The Communist Party of Bulgaria: Origin and Development* (New York: 1959) pp. 223–54.
2. Cited in B. Petranović, *Balkanska federacija 1943–1948* (Belgrade: 1991) pp. 34–7.
3. P. Shoup, *Communism and the Yugoslav National Question* (New York: 1968) pp. 84–5.
4. Petranović, *Balkanska federacija*, p. 60, and Id., *Dokumenti o spoljnoj politici Socijalističke Federativne Republike Jugoslavije 1943* (Belgrade: 1985) pp. 224 and 228.
5. In his work in Macedonia, Tempo was insistent upon the need to nurture a Macedonian identity within the Yugoslav federation, and on 24 January 1944 Tito officially protested to Moscow concerning a leaflet issued by the Bulgarian Fatherland Front calling for self-determination for an independent Macedonia. Text in S. Clissold (ed.), *Yugoslavia and the Soviet Union 1939–1973: A Documentary Survey* (Oxford: 1975) p. 156.
6. Petranović, *Balkanska federacija*, p. 69.
7. *Dokumenti*, 1943, pp. 233–4. Shoup concludes that in reversing his earlier priorities Tito was 'probably reacting to Soviet pressure'. Shoup, *Communism*, p. 88.
8. Support for the goal of a Bulgarian–Yugoslav federation is reported to have been brought to the session by the Bulgarian emissary Shteria Atanasov (alias Viktor), a message presumably approved by Georgi

Dimitrov in Moscow and perhaps by Stalin as well. Petranović, *Balkanska federacija*, p. 73.
9. Cited in B. Petranović, 'Kosovo in Yugoslav-Albanian Relations and the Project of a Balkan Federation', reprinted from *Serbs and Albanians in the 20th Century* (Academic Conference of the Serbian Academy of Sciences and Arts, Vol. LXI, Department of Historical Sciences No. 20) (Belgrade: 1991) p. 348.
10. Petranović, *Balkanska federacija*, pp. 90–3.
11. Djilas recalls that during his visit to Albania in May 1945 'there was unofficial talk of their joining Yugoslavia as one unit in a future Balkan federation', and notes that during 1945–6 'we all assumed we were heading toward economic and political unity'. M. Djilas, *Rise and Fall* (San Diego, Ca.: 1985), pp. 110 and 113.
12. M. Lalkov, *Ot nadezhda kum razocharovanie: Ideiata za federatsiiata v balkanskiia iugoiztok (1944–1948g.)* (Sofia: 1993), pp. 101–5. On the negotiations between military commands, S. Vukmanović-Tempo, *Revolucija koja teče: Memoari*, 2 Vols (Belgrade: 1971) Vol. 1, pp. 413–26.
13. According to the memoirs of Edvard Kardelj, Stalin encouraged Tito to consider the option of a Balkan federation during these sessions. 'The idea of that federation,' writes Kardelj, 'was given to Tito by Stalin himself in the autumn of 1944, when Tito met him for the first time.' E. Kardelj, *Borba za priznanje i nezavisnost nove Jugoslavije, 1944–1957. Sećanja* (Belgrade: 1980) p. 103.
14. Petranović, *Balkanska federacija*, pp. 118–19, quotes Tito's telegram describing the encounter.
15. Lalkov, *Ot nadezhda*, pp. 76–100. D. Michev, *Makedonskiiat vupros i bulgaro-iugoslavskite otnosheniia, 9 septemvri 1944–1949* (Sofia: 1994) pp. 57–76, offers a Bulgarian national perspective on these events which accuses the Bulgarian Communist leadership of 'national nihilism' in regard to the Macedonian question.
16. The texts of these variants are assembled in Ž. Abramovski, 'Devet projekata ugovora o jugoslovensko-bugarskom savezu i federaciji (1944–1947)', *Istorija XX veka*, 2 (1983) 91–124.
17. The negotiations are carefully analysed in Lalkov, *Ot nadezhda*, pp. 158–63. See also G. Daskalov, 'Problemut za federatsiiata v bulgaro-iugoslavskite otnosheniia (noemvri 1944–april 1945)', *Izvestiia na instituta po istoriia na BKP*, 62 (1988) 5-53, and Petranović, *Balkanska federacija*, pp. 121–30.
18. Lalkov, *Ot nadezhda*, pp. 164–5.
19. Kardelj, *Borba za priznanje*, p. 180.
20. In the signed confession which he publicly repudiated at his show trial in 1949, Kostov was made to describe a conversation with Kardelj during November 1947 in which the latter posed the creation of a Balkan union as a means for blocking Soviet influence in the region on behalf of the 'Anglo-Americans'. 'Iz pokazaniiata na Traicho Kostov pred sledstvenite organi', in *Titovata banda: Orudie na imperialistite* (Sofia: 1950) pp. 486–91.
21. Cited in Lalkov, *Ot nadezhda*, p. 179.
22. Smodlaka's diary claims that on 19 December 1944 Tito showed him the draft of a treaty defining a permanent political, military, and customs union between Yugoslavia and Bulgaria, and states that a similar draft treaty with Albania was also being prepared. J. Smodlaka, *Partizanski dnevnik* (Belgrade: 1972) p. 224.

23. Lalkov, *Ot nadezhda*, p. 184.
24. E. Barker, *British Policy in South-East Europe in the Second World War* (London: 1976) pp. 200–1.
25. Petranović, *Balkanska federacija*, p. 130.
26. Tito nonetheless continued on occasion to speak enthusiastically about prospects for association. See his remarks of 13 June 1945 to the Bulgarian 1st Army in *Dokumenti o spoljnoj politici Socijalističke Federativne Republike Jugoslavije 1945* (Belgrade: 1984) p. 91.
27. The Stalin–Churchill agreement was concluded on 9 October 1944. It allotted influence in the Balkans according to rough percentages: 90 per cent in Greece for the United Kingdom, 90 per cent in Romania and 75 per cent in Bulgaria for the USSR, and a 50–50 per cent split in Yugoslavia. L.Ia. Gibianskii, *Sovetskii soiuz i novaia Iugoslaviia 1941–1947gg.* (Moscow: 1987) pp. 122–4, suggests that the 50–50 per cent division was intended to embody the balance in a new Yugoslav regime between Tito's partisans and the Yugoslav Government-in-exile.
28. Between 1939 and early 1944 the Greek Communist movement received no official communication from either the Soviet Union or the Comintern, and the KKE was not listed among the parties officially informed of the dissolution of the Comintern in May 1943. G. Vaccarino, *La Grecia tra resistenza e guerra civile 1940–1949* (Milan: 1988) p. 63.
29. P.J. Stavrakis, *Moscow and Greek Communism, 1944–1949* (Ithaca, N.Y.: 1989) p. 32, calls this a 'spectacular reversal'.
30. J.O. Iatrides, *Revolt in Athens: The Greek Communist 'Second Round', 1944–1945* (Princeton, N.J.: 1972) pp. 156–7.
31. Stavrakis, *Moscow*, p. 29.
32. C.M. Woodhouse, *The Struggle for Greece 1941–1949* (New York: 1979) p. 23.
33. Petranović, 'Kosovo in Yugoslav–Albanian Relations', p. 348, and Id., *Balkanska federacija*, p. 138.
34. S. Bianchini, *Sarajevo, le radici dell'odio: Identità e destino dei popoli balcanici* (Rome: 1993) p. 214.
35. Lalkov, *Ot nadezhda*, p. 217.
36. See S. Nešović, *Bledski sporazumi: Tito–Dimitrov 1947* (Zagreb: 1979). For the text of the minutes and other documents, *Dokumenti o spoljnoj politici Socijalističke Federativne Republike Jugoslavije 1947*, Vol. 2 (Belgrade: 1986) pp. 84–100.
37. See the comments by Pijade and Dimitrov in *ibid.*, pp. 100–3 and 520–2, and Lalkov, *Ot nadezhda*, p. 245.
38. In a memoir, Hoxha states his conviction that at this moment federation was 'in principle the right way', but that the concept still needed 'a lot of work'. E. Hoxha, *The Titoists: Historical Notes* (Tirana: 1982) p. 328.
39. See the discussion in Lalkov, *Ot nadezhda*, pp. 246–9.
40. D.S. Chubakhin, 'S diplomaticheskoi missiei v Albanii', *Otechestvennaia istoriia*, 1 (1995) 121–2.
41. The telegram is cited in Iu.S. Girenko, *Stalin–Tito* (Moscow: 1991) pp. 325–6. See also N. Ganchovski, *Dnite na Dimitrov, kakto gi vidakh i zapisakh*, 2 Vols (Sofia: 1975) Vol. 1, pp. 494–5.
42. Girenko, *Stalin–Tito*, p. 327. For the text of the treaty, *Dokumenti*, 1947, Vol. 2, pp. 374–6.
43. Hoxha, *The Titoists*, pp. 316–59, and the postscript to Chubakhin, 'S diplomaticheskoi missiei', pp. 131–40.

44. Djilas, *Rise*, p. 148. 'It was an unpleasant thought', continues the author, 'that Moscow might grab the upper hand in Albania, and thereby "encircle" Yugoslavia and prevent unification of the countries.' *Ibid.*, p. 149.
45. Texts in 'Konflikt, kotorogo ne dolzhno bylo byt' (iz istorii sovetsko-iugoslavskikh otnoshenii)', *Vestnik ministerstva inostrannykh del SSSR*, 6 [64] (31 March 1990) 57, 59. See also Girenko, *Stalin–Tito*, pp. 336–8.
46. See the account in Vukmanović-Tempo, *Revolucija*, Vol. 2, pp. 44–59. The Soviet side was equally displeased with their Yugoslav guests. Note the telegram of 7 January 1948 from the Soviet Ambassador in Belgrade A.I. Lavrent'ev to Molotov in 'Konflikt, kotorogo ne dolzhno bylo byt', p. 5.
47. M. Djilas, *Conversations with Stalin* (New York: 1962) p. 143. Djilas claims to have responded that unification was at issue, not 'swallowing', to which Stalin is alleged to have answered, 'Yes, yes, swallowing, here we are in agreement. You must swallow Albania, the sooner the better.'
48. In his address on the occasion Tito praised the display of signs along his route in Bulgaria reading 'We Want Federation'. *Dokumenti*, 1947, Vol. 2, pp. 372–3.
49. V. Zelenin, 'Stalin protiv Tito: Istoki i peripetii konflikta 1948 goda', *Nauka i zhizn'*, 6 (1990) 80–1.
50. L.Ia. Gibianskii, 'K istorii sovetsko–iugoslavskogo konflikta 1948–1953gg.: Sekretnaia sovetsko–iugoslavo–bolgarskaia vstrecha v Moskve 10 fevralia 1948 goda', *Sovetskoe slavianovedenie*, 3 (1991) 15, and Girenko, *Stalin–Tito*, p. 333.
51. Gibianskii, 'K istorii', 3 (1991) 17. In an address to the second congress of the Fatherland Front on 2 February Dimitrov reiterated these comments, claiming that 'we are far from the thought of creating any kind of Eastern bloc in any form whatsoever'. *Ibid.*, p. 18.
52. The summons emphasized the emergence of 'serious differences on foreign policy issues'. Text in 'Konflikt', p. 60.
53. The best description and analysis of the session is the series of articles by Gibianskii, 'K istorii', 3 (1991) 12–23, 4 (1991) 27–36, 1 (1992) 42–56, and *Slavianovedenie*, 3 (1992) 35-51. See also the participants' memoirs by Djilas, *Rise*, pp. 150–1, and Kardelj, *Borba za priznanje*, pp. 111–20.
54. Kardelj, *Borba za priznanje*, p. 113.
55. In Kardelj's recollection of the session of 10 February, Djilas is made to say upon exiting that 'now we must move to a federation with Bulgaria', a conclusion which Kardelj claims to have opposed (Kardelj, *Borba za priznanje*, p. 117). In his most recent account of the episode Djilas argues that Kardelj's decision to oppose a federation with Bulgaria took form only gradually (Djilas, *Rise*, pp. 151–71).
56. Girenko, *Stalin–Tito*, p. 341.
57. *Ibid.*, pp. 343–7, and Vukmanović-Tempo, *Revolucija*, Vol. 2, pp. 60–2.
58. Lalkov, *Ot nadezhda*, p. 284.
59. Shoup, *Communism*, pp. 132–3.
60. The dual strategy, approved at the KKE's second Central Committee Plenum on 12–15 February 1946, included decisions to boycott the March 1946 election and to launch secret preparations for a new round of civil war. The Soviet Union opposed the election boycott, but deferred to Zachariades on behalf of what was still perceived as a defensive strategy. O.L. Smith, 'The Greek Communist Party, 1945–9', in D.H. Close (ed.), *The Greek Civil War, 1943–1950: Studies of Polarization*

(London: 1993) p. 138. Zachariades met with Stalin, Molotov and Zhdanov in Moscow and in Crimea during April 1946 to seek approval of the dual strategy.
61. Stavrakis, *Moscow*, pp. 149–54.
62. The minutes appear in G. Procacci (ed.), G. Adibekov, A. Di Biagio, L. Gibianski, F. Gori, S. Pons (co-eds), *The Cominform. Minutes of the Three Conferences 1947/1948/1949*, Fondazione Feltrinelli, *Annali* XXX (Milan: 1994).
63. A. Ulam, *Titoism and the Cominform* (Cambridge, Mass.: 1952) p. 87.
64. Gibianskii, 'K istorii', 3 (1991) p. 22.
65. Rothschild, *The Communist Party*, p. 257.

9 The Soviet Union and 'the Greek Question', 1946–53: Problems and Appraisals
Artiom A. Ulunian

For a long time, owing to the inaccessibility of materials in the USSR archives, the position taken by the Soviet Union on 'the Greek question' has remained unresearched in both our own and foreign historiography. Moreover, nothing could be said about a very important aspect of this matter, namely, the role and place of the CPSU(B)'s international connections and of the Greek CP during the civil war of 1946–9 and subsequently. In this chapter I do not undertake an exhaustive treatment of this extensive subject, but merely try to touch upon the key problems in the context of the international relations of the CPSU(B) and the principal participant in the 'Greek drama', the Communist Party of Greece.[1]

The end of World War II did not signify the beginning of an era of peaceful development for the Balkans. The involvement of an 'external factor', in the shape of Great Britain, the USSR and, later, the USA, in the affairs of the region meant a prolongation of the policies of the great powers, the foundations of which had been laid during the war. Greece was the only country of the peninsula which lay, geopolitically, in the zone of the West's military-strategic interests. The defeat, in February 1945, of the National Liberation Front of Greece (EAM) which was controlled by the local CP, in an armed conflict with Britain, resulted in an aggravation of the situation in the country. Both of the Greek political forces engaged in the conflict – the CPG and the anti-Communist right-wing politicians – counted on support from without.

In mid-January an official delegation from the National Liberation Front came to Moscow in order to find out from the Soviet leadership what degree of support the CPG and EAM could expect from them. It was led by the General Secretary of the CC of the EAM, a Politburo member and secretary of the CC of the CPG, M. Partsalidis, the other members being the leader of the left wing of the Liberal Party, General Grigoriadis (close to the Communists already during the resistance), and Lules, the leader of the Radical-Democratic Party. However, the several attempts made by the leader of the delegation to have a meeting, 'if this is considered possible, with Comrade Stalin or with Comrade Molotov, so as to inform them about the situation in the country and obtain their advice on the tactics to be employed by the CPG and EAM at this stage' proved unsuccessful.[2] At a time when Britain and USA were actively pursuing their policy in Greece, the Soviet Party-and-State leadership had to be cautious about binding themselves with firm promises. At a meeting arranged by Molotov on 18 January 1946, held in the premises of the All-Union Trade Union Council, those present were the deputy head of that organization's international department, Zhmykov, the deputy head of the International Information Department of the CC of the CPSU(B), L. Baranov, and a *referent* from that department, P. Manchkha. Partsalidis said that EAM and the CPG were not supporting the Sophoulis Government at that time because it had not fulfilled the conditions 'under which EAM promised to give all-round support to this government without participation in it by representatives of EAM'.[3] In order to ascertain the reaction of the Soviet side to possible tough actions by the Greek CP and its attempt to internationalize the conflict, drawing in the USSR and the 'people's democracies', Partsalidis informed the Staraia Ploshchad that 'EAM has now demanded the formation of a representative government with obligatory participation by representatives of EAM, and it will use all the means available to it to enlist support for this demand by the democratic organizations and governments of the allied countries'.[4] However, the Soviet reply regarding the possibility of participation in the conflict by forces friendly to the National Liberation Front (primarily the CPs of the neighbouring countries and the USSR) was already cautious at the beginning of 1946. To discover what Moscow's actual attitude was to the actions planned by the Greek CP, Partsalidis tried to put the question indirectly. He mentioned his talk in London with the leader of the British CP, Harry Pollitt, 'whom he asked how the CPGB would react if civil war were to break out in Greece'. The British Communist leader had replied that 'EAM and the Greek Communists should take account of the fact that relations between the USSR and Britain were very strained, more or less like in 1939, and it was therefore necessary to observe the maximum caution and do everything to ensure that civil war did not break out'.[5]

Molotov knew the result of the meeting already on 18 January, but there could be no question of a visit to the Kremlin. Neither Stalin nor Molotov could sacrifice their relations with the Allies – who, to be sure, were now turning into enemies. Hoping to secure the Soviet leaders' attention to the Greek problem, Partsalidis composed, at the end of January 1946, 'Brief notes on some questions of the work of the Communist Party of Greece'. This document was also an exposition of the positions of the CPG leadership regarding prospective actions by the Party in both the near and the more distant future. It was made clear that, in developing the proposition about the struggle having changed from being 'national-liberationist' to 'national-democratic' (Seventh Congress of the CPG, 1945), the Party's ideologists had radicalized their appraisals still further. It was stated that 'the Party adheres to the policy of *national unity and securing proletarian leadership of the national revolution*' [emphasis in the text – A.U.].[6] Partsalidis's note declared that 'it would be difficult to emerge "peacefully" from the present situation'.[7] The document spoke of a process of preparing 'in a military way, organizationally and technically, for defence against attacks by reaction and for going over to a vigorous offensive'.[8] An important factor here was material and technical provision for the CP and training for its cadres. At this stage, therefore, Partsalidis asked Moscow to supply a printing press and newsprint and also to dispatch to Greece the Greek émigrés who had graduated from the Comintern school.[9]

The measures to be taken by EAM and the CPG if they came to power were set up with particular precision where the national (Macedonian and Thracian) question was concerned. Partsalidis mentioned in this connection that 'in the programme of national demands we were obliged to make some concessions to our allies in EAM and questions were formulated regarding our national demands in relation to Bulgaria and Albania', but, at the same time, 'concessions by our Party [the CPG] on the national demands do not constitute any danger, since all the parties in EAM have accepted the principle proclaimed by the CP, namely, that a democratic, EAM-ruled Greece can and will arrive at agreement on our territorial demands with the neighbouring democratic countries in a spirit of mutual understanding'.[10]

Partsalidis returned to Greece with a message from the CC of the CPSU(B) which contained the concrete recommendation: 'Take part in the elections now. Later, review the situation. In accordance with the way it develops the centre of gravity may move as necessary, either to legal methods or to armed struggle.'[11]

The nearer, however, that the elections to the Greek Parliament approached, the more impatient became the General Secretary of the CPG, N. Zachariades. The Party did not take part in the elections of 31 March 1946. Towards the end of March, Zachariadis, on his way from Greece to Czechoslovakia, visited Yugoslavia, where he met the leaders of the Federal People's Republic – Tito, Ranković and Djilas – who agreed to receive 20 000 men, 'persecuted by the monarcho-fascist forces' – these were future fighters in the Communist partisan bands.[12] Through Dimitrov he sent to the CC of the CPSU(B) several notes which left no doubt as to the CPG's plans. He openly stated that

> the Party's military organization is strictly secret and decentralized and covers the entire country. It combines work in the army and

among the officers, self-defence and specialized groups ... Despite the Varkiza agreement EAM has managed to retain a considerable number of rifles, machine-guns and other military equipment.[13]

The Soviet leadership was asked to 'establish in Yugoslavia, Bulgaria and Albania centres for training officers and fighters to the number of 8000 in Yugoslavia and 2000 in Bulgaria and Albania'. The question was raised of military aid being sent through Yugoslavia and 'organization, in the principal centres of the Balkan countries and of Europe, of bases from which information can pass from and to Greece'.[14]

At the end of August 1946 the Greek CP leaders put forward their plan for settling the internal political conflict in Greece. Its political section consisted of 'declaring Greece neutral, under the protection of UNO and on condition that the British leave.'[15] A report on this was conveyed by Politburo member Y. Ioannidis through Dimitrov to Moscow. Dimitrov himself refrained from answering. The report, entitled 'The situation in Greece and the urgent tasks of our movement', raised rather serious questions. The most important were: How to emerge from the political crisis, and What material and technical help could the CPG expect from Moscow in the event of its entry into armed struggle? The plan for Greek neutrality under UNO supervision was seen by the CPG leaders as what the USSR would find most acceptable and also most to its advantage. As regards material and technical support for the CPG from the Soviet Union, this was to include the granting of monthly subsidies of 150 000 dollars. In addition, it was provided that they should receive from the USSR 8000 rifles, 15 heavy mortars and 50 light ones, 50 heavy machine-guns, the same number of medium machine-guns, 150 light machine-guns, 500 sub-machine-guns and 10 000 grenades of various types.[16] The leaders of the CPG emphasized to the Soviet leadership their hope for aid: 'How the struggle will develop in the days ahead depends not only on internal but also on external conditions. In any case, given the specific difficulties of the winter season, we are not in a position by ourselves to cope with all the demands of partisan struggle...'[17]

Moscow viewed favourably enough the CPG's requests for technical and material aid. In a special note sent by M. Suslov in mid-October 1946 to Stalin, Beria, Mikoian, Molotov, Malenkov and Zhdanov it was said that,

> considering the extremely difficult financial situation of the Greek CP and the impossibility of raising the necessary resources from within the country, and also the difficult situation with respect to clothing and medicines for the partisans, it may be considered possible and necessary to help the CPG with money and also with the clothing and medicines needed by the partisans in Greece.[18]

At the same time the question of the large-scale aid from abroad on which the CPG leaders counted remained unclear in November 1946. Dimitrov acted as intermediary between the Greek CP and the Soviet Party-and-State leadership. At talks in Sofia at the beginning of November between the Bulgarian Communist leaders and representatives of the CC of the CPG Y. Ioannidis and P. Rusos, the latter were given highly evasive answers to their concrete questions. At the outset Dimitrov said that he was going to give his personal view and also that of 'the top', meaning Moscow. His advice amounted to this: hold back from intensifying the partisan movement during the winter and in the prevailing international situation. At the same time he set the task (hardly practicable in the conditions obtaining in Greece in the autumn of 1946) of shifting the centre of gravity 'to mass political work among the people and flexible utilization of the legal possibilities, while also maintaining the Party's links with the masses'. They should 'preserve the Party's cadres and not subject them to risk of annihilation'. Despite the 'restrained' nature of the advice given, Dimitrov's speech was optimistic in spirit and concluded with the words: 'We support the view that the Party's line corresponds to the situation.' He approved the CPG's plan for a 'neutral Greece'.[19]

The obvious inconsistency of Moscow's position, which was what, essentially, Dimitrov was expounding, testified to the absence of a decision by the Kremlin on what its own policy in Greece should be. Moscow had in fact chosen the tactic of operating in Greece through its strongest neighbour, Tito's Yugoslavia. On 31 December 1946 Ioannidis, in Belgrade, received a message in cipher from Dimitrov in which the latter said, frankly: 'At the present time you ought not to count on the help you asked for, and you should wait.'[20] Ioannidis then advised Zachariadis to apply directly to Moscow, so as to get a final answer to his technical and political requests. This was also the advice of the Yugoslavs, who understood that Moscow wanted to lay the whole burden of armed conflict on Belgrade.

Talk of the actual motives of the CPG, striving to seize power in the country, was not allowed in Soviet circles. In the secret 'Bulletin of the Information Bureau of the CC of the CPSU(B): Questions of Foreign Policy', intended for a restricted circle, the same pattern of thinking predominated as in the Soviet Party's open publications: there was talk of 'monarcho-fascist reaction', 'the Greek democrats led by the National Liberation Front', 'measures for armed self-defence', 'raising the banner of partisan struggle for the honour, freedom and independence of the Greek people'.[21] *Frankly disinformational* was the thesis that 'the chief operations of the partisans are carried on in areas which, during the Italo-German occupation of Greece, were for two years the territory of "Free Greece", in which people's power was established.'[22] In covering up the true character of the Communist revolt with words about democracy and people's power, the Soviet Party's experts were fully aware that their readers understood the conventions of Party language.

The aid received from abroad, with the tacit approval given to the actions of the Greek CP and the military-political and moral assistance to the partisans, was probably interpreted by the leaders of the CPG as a signal to them to harden their position. In mid-February 1947 the Greek Politburo 'decided that the democratic movement, while continuing to utilize fully all legal possibilities, must appreciate that armed struggle is becoming the immediate task'.[23] Thus, abandoning for the moment the question of 'Greek neutrality', the CPG's leaders decided to activate pressure on the Government in Athens not as a method conductive to acceptance of the demands of the Party (using the cover of CAM) but as a means of intimidation.

A split was developing in Greece's ruling circles. Even the representatives of conservative, anti-Communist patriotic circles realized that the country was being transformed into an area of confrontation between foreign forces for which Greeks would have to pay with their blood. An influential informer of the CPG who was close to Government circles told Zachariadis on 17 March, at a secret meeting, that one of the political advisers of former Prime Minister Tsaldaris had said to him that

> Tsaldaris will not object to waging a joint struggle along with the CPG to stop the civil war... Tsaldaris is in danger from Zervas-Papandreou and the CPG from Sophoulis. You see that the thinking of Tsaldaris and the CPG coincides in this case and something good for our country can come of that, with an end to the civil war. If the war continues, that will harm both, and strengthen the position of their opponents.[24]

The question of arming the Democratic Army of Greece which the CPG had created, was the subject of special negotiations between the USSR's Foreign Minister Molotov and the Secretary of the CC of the CPY and Yugoslav Minister of Internal Affairs Ranković at the beginning of June 1947. The Yugoslav passed on CPG's request to increase support for the partisan movement in Greece.

Given that the CPG leaders were still obsessed in the spring of 1947 with the idea of getting serious help for the partisan struggle from abroad – and not so much from the 'people's democracies' as from the USSR – it was not surprising that Zachariadis came to Moscow at the beginning of May for a meeting with the Soviet leaders. In accordance with Kremlin protocol, however, he had to send Stalin and Molotov letters requesting to be received by them 'in order to describe the situation in Greece'.[25] As a preliminary, on 13 May Zachariadis prepared, at Suslov's request, an information note 'On the situation in Greece', which was circulated on 19 May to all members of the 'foreign-policy group of seven' – Stalin, Molotov, Zhdanov, Beria, Mikoian, Malenkov and Voznesenskii. This document made clear the way the CPG leaders saw the immediate prospect: the internal situation in Greece was favourable to victory by the Democratic Army of Greece, which was able to mobilize up to 50 000 men: the task of the armed struggle was to establish a people's-democratic regime; aid from the Soviet Union would ensure their victory.[26]

Zachariadis's meeting with Stalin soon after 20 May 1947 was warm enough. Moscow considered that the Greek CP could tie the Anglo-Americans down in Europe, preventing them from actively intervening in the conflict in progress in China. War materials and diplomatic backing were guaranteed by Moscow. Of the CPG leaders' reaction to Stalin's premise we can judge from the cipher-telegram sent by Ioannidis to the members of the Politburo in Greece 'Kukos [Zachariades] met the Old Man [Stalin] and our problems were thoroughly discussed. We should be completely satisfied with the results.'[27] The position of the Soviet leadership on 'the Greek question' was, at this stage, largely determined by the so-called Truman Doctrine which had been proclaimed in March 1947 and which was seen in the Kremlin as a direct threat to the USSR from the south.

The arming and supplying of the Democratic Army was gone into by Molotov and Ranković at the beginning of June 1947, when the Yugoslavs presented the Greek CP's request for the USSR to provide 50 million rounds of rifle ammunition (instead of the 10 million asked for earlier), 15 million rounds of sub-machine-gun ammunition (instead of 10 million) and 20 mountain guns. In a note to Suslov, Molotov mentioned that Yugoslavia was not in a position to furnish the Greeks with military supplies from its own army because their stocks were run down.[28]

In a letter to Tito, Zachariadis gave an optimistic estimate of the CPG's chances: 'Without exaggerating we can say that our prospects for the coming winter and the spring of 1948 are positive.'[29]

On 1 September 1947 Zachariadis said in a letter to Zhdanov, who supervised links between CPs, that 'the prospects before the movement [meaning the CPG/EAM] are good'. He mentioned that Greece's former Foreign Minister Sophianopoulos was in contact with the CPG.[30]

The coming to power in Athens of the liberal Sophoulis, advocate of a policy of 'civil peace', gave the CPG hope. However, the very next day after becoming Prime Minister he called for the Democratic Army to lay down its arms and cease insurrectionary activity. On 3 September 1947 a plenum of the CC of CPG adopted a military-political plan code-named 'Lake' ('Limnes'), which aimed at setting up a Communist rebel government and seizing Salonika, which was to be this government's first seat. This secret document, known only to a narrow group of CPG leaders, had been drawn up with active participation by Yugoslav advisers. The Soviet leadership was at once informed by Zachariadis. This inner-Party information produced for a circle of officials of the Soviet CC apparatus and the Party-and-State *nomenklatura* contained an impartial exposition of the main features of 'Limnes' (though without using the name). It did not question the realism of creating 'compact areas of liberated territory' and 'increasing the numbers of the Democratic Army to 50 000, with transition, in principle, to the formation of a regular army'.[31] At the end of January 1948, however, the Kremlin started to adopt a guarded attitude to 'the events in Greece'. Zachariadis's promised victories seemed, in reality, to be mere projects and, despite the fact that the Greek Government's troops were encountering difficulties in the fight against the Communist partisans, Moscow lost faith in victory by the latter. Consequently the civil war in Greece became a negative factor in the Soviet leadership's calculations for the Kremlin's 'high' politics. They did not want an extreme exacerbation of relations with the West. In a talk with Yugoslav representatives on 10 February 1948, Stalin asked them to tell 'the Greek comrades' that they should 'roll up' the partisan war.[32] This advice-cum-order, having reached the CPG 'at second hand', gave Zachariadis grounds to suppose that he might take an independent decision. At a meeting between Ioannidis and the Yugoslav Party-and-State leaders, in Belgrade after the Yugoslav delegation's return from Moscow, the Greek succeeded in convincing Tito that military operations should continue. He even guaranteed that the Democratic Army would be victorious by August–September 1948.

By the summer a new factor had entered into 'the Greek question', namely, the breakdown of Soviet–Yugoslav relations and the adoption by the Cominform of threatening resolutions on 'the Yugoslav question'. The CPG leaders had to react to the new situation. On 7 July 1948 the CC of the CPG received a special directive from the Cominform Secretariat 'On the attitude of the Parties belonging to the Information Bureau to the invitation by the CC of the CPY to send delegations to the 5th Congress of the CPY'. The directive recommended refusal.[33] At the same time the agents of the CPG in various political circles in Greece were instructed by the Party's leaders to sound out the situation that was being created around Yugoslavia, both in the Party's own interests and to meet Moscow's needs. The information obtained in Athens by the CPG stated:

> The assistant to the Secretary of State ... said that the divergence between Tito and the Cominform is ideological in character. Tito will

come out on top eventually because he has a basis and because he has friends in several Parties. When he was asked why Moscow was revealing and deepening the differences, he replied that Moscow, having war in mind, was interested in clarifying the situation.[34]

In the autumn of 1948 the Greek CP leaders explained to Soviet representatives their plan to transform the partisans into a regular army and their confidence in the military prospects. On 6 September Ioannidis and Rusos met, through the head of the International Department of the CC of the Romanian Workers' Party, Chişinevschi, the deputy head of the Foreign Relations Department of the CC of the CPSU(B), L. Baranov. In conversation with the latter, Ioannidis said that 'we must complete the reorganization of the army (seven divisions have been formed – previously the largest formation was a brigade) and transfer operations to Greek territory [meaning territory controlled by the Athens Government].[35] The task before them, he said, was 'during the winter to solve the problem of reserves of manpower and to create liberated territories along the frontiers, so as to prepare the conditions for carrying out major operations in the spring of 1949'. The CPG leaders counted on receiving aid from the Eastern bloc countries and the USSR. Their gamble on a more active involvement of 'the external factor' in the Greek conflict was not concealed in their talks with the Soviet Party in the autumn of 1948. As Baranov reported to the CC of the CPSU(B),

> Ioannidis also raised the question of establishing a regular link between the Greek CC and the Information Bureau and proposed the convening of a special conference of representatives of certain parties for the purpose of co-ordinating action to bring help to the democratic forces in Greece in their fight against Fascism. Ioannidis said that he had exchanged views on this question with Rákosi, who had reacted favourably to the proposal.[36]

Such a conference was held in Warsaw on 8 September 1948. Present were representatives of Poland, Czechoslovakia, Hungary, Romania, the USSR and the Greek CP. They discussed 'fulfilment by their countries of their duty to meet the needs of the Democratic Army of Greece'.[37] It was decided 'to set up in Warsaw a commission for technical co-ordination of measures, with responsibility for seeing to the fulfilment of the conference's decisions, by creating stocks of material and financial funds.'[38] However, despite these results of the conference, the situation as regards military supplies to the Democratic Army from its northern neighbours became difficult.

The meetings – held on 20–21 January and 15–16 February 1949, in Prague and Budapest – of the commission set up in the autumn of 1948 to co-ordinate aid to the Democratic Army revealed complications that had arisen in this work which were due to both material and political causes. The Soviet representative at the discussions reported to the CC of the CPSU(B):

> Delegates at the conference said that each country would increase its contributions to material support of the Democratic Army of Greece. As regards contributions in money, all the delegates said 'no'. It was calculated that there was a demand for about 30–40 million dollars. The Greek representatives at the conference expressed their dissatisfaction at the delay in establishing a financial fund. The representatives of Poland and Hungary said that they would give money but could not, at the moment, say how much ... The Poles made various proposals for extending aid ...[39]

The curtain of secrecy which covered the question of how much help the USSR was giving to the Greek rebels was so thick that the Soviet representative at the conference, speaking to Baranov and referring to Chişinevschi (who, in turn, passed this on to one of the Greek CP's representatives) revealed, that the question of holding such conferences had been sanctioned by Moscow.[40]

The Communist rebellion in Greece coincided in its later stage with the conflict that broke out within the Cominform, and the CPG leadership found itself, as a result, a hostage in the struggle between Belgrade and Moscow. Plans drawn up in London and Washington for overthrowing Hoxha's regime in Albania (which Moscow knew about) obliged the Soviet Party-and-State leadership to take measures to safeguard the USSR's position in Eastern Europe, avoiding obvious adventures outside its own 'domain'. In April 1949 the Kremlin called on the CPG leadership to end the civil war during May of that year.[41] On 21 April, in the name of EAM and the Provisional Democratic Government which the CPG had created in the mountains of Free Greece, the rebels' radio station located in Romania transmitted the proposals which had been put forward on the previous day by the Politburo member Porphyrogenis. The CPG proposed a ceasefire and the holding of elections in which all the political forces involved in the civil war should participate.

The Soviets' position was confirmed by a number of steps taken which, though logical from the diplomatic standpoint, were inconsistent with the military needs. Already at the end of April aid to the Democratic Army had been substantially decreased. On 26 April the Greek CP's representative in Bulgaria reported to the Party's Politburo on difficulties that had begun to appear in the supply of arms from that country.[42] At the beginning of May the Soviet representative at the UN, Gromyko, had an informal meeting with his British colleague H. McNeil and the deputy to the US Secretary of State, D. Rusk. In this conversation, on 4 May 1949,

Moscow explained its plan to settle the affairs of Greece, which included the proposals by Porphyrogenis which had been broadcast on 21 April by the rebels' radio. The principal element in the Soviet plan was that the USSR, the USA and Britain should all use their influence with the corresponding forces in Greece in order to bring about a ceasefire and the holding of parliamentary elections in which all the political forces in the country should participate. However, the Western representatives, seeing in these demands a potential danger of recognizing thereby the Provisional Democratic Government, rejected the Soviet proposals. The failure of Gromyko's peacemaking effort led to the CPG leadership (probably not without advice from Moscow) repudiating its own proposal of 20 April. This action might have signified either a possible hardening of the Communists' position or readiness to make compromises more acceptable to the West. The subsequent course of events showed that the gesture by the CPS leadership was intended to mislead the USSR's partners in the negotiations. At the moment when, on 14 May 1949, Gromyko again put forward his proposal for settling the affairs of Greece,[43] Zachariadis was advised by Moscow to intensify military pressure on the Government forces,[44] so as, presumably, to show that the CPG was in a position to negotiate from a position of strength. But the USSR's attempt to stabilize the situation in Greece failed to produce positive results for the USSR and its ally, the CPG. To no small degree this happened because of the West's confidence that it could bend Belgrade over to its side. The Yugoslav leadership, which found itself isolated within the Eastern bloc, while at the same time providing the bulk of military-technical supplies to the Democratic Army of Greece and allowing its territory to be used for regrouping by the Army's forces and for the transit of aid from Albania and Bulgaria, was trying to avoid confrontation with Washington and London, the patrons of the Athens Government.

The position of the CPG at the beginning of summer 1949 was affected by rapid loss of territory controlled by the Democratic Army. An unfavourable situation was taking shape also in the foreign-policy arena. The Western countries were increasing their aid to the Athens Government, on the one hand, and, on the other, were preparing, in case of need, to strike a blow at Albania. In these circumstances Moscow could not count on arriving at plans jointly agreed with Washington and London for settling 'the Greek question' as a basis of principles acceptable to the CPG.

Despite the clearly emerging prospect of defeat, the CPG leadership headed by Zachariadis continued to contemplate quite seriously plans for striking blows at the Government forces in the Grammos and Vitsi areas, the last stronghold of the Democratic Army. What the Greek CP leaders did not want to see was obvious, though, to military analysts in the USSR and the 'people's democracies'. On 1 August 1949, CC member Rusos reported from Budapest to Zachariadis on his meeting with Rákosi, who, 'proceeding from the new military situation, the present relation of forces and their geographical distribution, conveyed to us the opinion of the specialists' that the time had come to draw in their horns'.[45] Rákosi had said that 'this was not instruction or advice, but simply an exchange of views with friends, but he would like me to pass it on to you. He showed me a map, pointing out the difference, for example with China, Spain, etc.'[46]

With the end of the civil war in Greece the situation in the Balkans continued to remain favourable for the geopolitical interests of the Soviet Union while considerably improved for the USA and Britain. The USSR strengthened its positions in Albania, Bulgaria and Romania, as well as in Poland, Czechoslovakia and Hungary. Consolidation of the Eastern bloc was accompanied by hardening of the Communist regimes both in the USSR and in the countries within its sphere of influence. On their part the USA and Britain sought to prevent any extension of the *Pax sovietica*. A balance of forces between the USSR and the Anglo-Americans was achieved with the creation in 1949 of NATO, which was joined in 1952 by Turkey and Greece, and with the signing in 1953–4 of a series of treaties between Greece, Turkey and Yugoslavia which laid the foundations for a Balkan Pact. Each side – participants in the 'Cold War' – endeavoured to weaken its rival as much as possible, while nevertheless taking care not to engage in armed actions along the line of confrontation in Europe. Consequently the 'zones of conflict' shifted to the periphery, which at the beginning of the 1950s meant the Far East and Indochina.

In the new conditions, when the 'Greek question' seemed to have been settled without account taken of the USSR's interests, only one possibility remained for Moscow to help the Communists who had been defeated and outlawed in Greece. Out of the political arsenal of the international Communist movement was brought the thesis of the mid-1930s – the need to create a coalition of forces in the form of a 'people's front'. Under the CP's control (or, at least, closely linked with it) a bloc of Lefts should be formed. This line was propagated through the Party's radio station 'Free Greece' in Romania, with the slogan 'unity of all honest democrats and patriots' and the call to form committees of the united democratic front'. The Soviet propaganda organs joined in this activity. Their task was 'to expose the anti-popular character of the Greek Parliament' and also 'the warmongers and their accomplices in the Balkans in the shape of the Belgrade clique and the Greek monarcho-fascists who are trying to turn Greece into a base for aggression', while 'publicising the struggle of the working people of Greece for their political and economic rights'.[47]

Although the continuing armed struggle was not being conducted on a mass scale it was supported very actively by the Greek CP. Eighteen months after the defeat of the Democratic Army more than 100 Party members were sent into Central and Eastern Macedonia and Thrace 'to reinforce and to relieve those partisans who had been more than a year in the mountains'. In the spring of 1951 it was proposed that those men be relieved by another group.[48] All this activity was, of course, supported organizationally and technically by the countries of the Eastern bloc and the USSR. Under the conditions of the 'Cold War', both West and East, while refraining from launching large-scale operations, supported local 'partisan actions' in the opponent's zone.

In Greek internal politics there was sharp confrontation between the Left-and-Centre coalition in which the chief element was General N. Plastiras's EPEK party and the Right-Conservative pro-American forces grouped around the 'Greek Assembly' party of Marshal A. Papagos.

The Greek CP's interpretation of the results of the elections of 15 April 1951 placed it in sharp opposition to both Papagos and Plastiras. Soviet broadcasts to Greece took the same line. The broadcast of 25 April 'On the municipal elections in monarcho-fascist Greece' declared that

> the leaders of EPEK – Plastiras, Tsouderos and their ally Rendis – marched separately from the black front because, once again, they wanted to deceive the electors with democratic phrases ... The marked reduction in the number of votes cast for EPEK compared with last year's parliamentary elections shows that the people have forgotten nothing and see through the double game being played by EPEK's leaders.[49]

The strategy of the CPG was closely followed by the Soviet Party organs. Moscow watched the process of forming a left-wing coalition under CP control, which took shape as a political party called the United Democratic Left (EDA). The attempt to create a strong left opposition which would play the role of a 'third force' in Greek politics was viewed quite seriously on Staraia Ploshchad. Consequently, any slips made by the Greek CP in their appraisal of the situation were noted by the Soviet Party's foreign policy experts. The Soviet 'Review of broadcasts in October 1951' commented critically on the propaganda campaign carried on by 'Free Greece' radio:

> A certain vagueness is observable regarding the antagonism between the King and Papagos. The radio says that, by order of the American imperialists, all the monarcho-fascist parties, from Venizelos to Plastiras, are preparing a dictatorship by Papagos. The only active opponent of this dictatorship, according to the broadcasts, is King Paul. But since the radio does not explain adequately in what way Paul is better than Papagos, a vagueness results from which a favourable situation for the King emerges...[50]

Despite the unfriendly relations obtaining between the leaders of EPEK and those of the CPG, the latter contemplated co-operation with Plastiras. The importance of this question was emphasized in a special letter from Zachariadis to the CC of the CPSU(B). He insistently requested an answer from the Soviets, observing:

> The way that the political situation is developing, it is highly likely that we shall have parliamentary elections ... In the event that these are held under the first-past-the-post system and that we cannot take part as a party or in some other guise [EDA, and so on], we think that we should (a) concentrate all our fire against Papagos, who constitutes the immediate threat, as agent No. 1 of the American state, and whose accession to power, as he himself has declared, will bring the people slaughter and war, and (b) call on the people to vote for Plastiras on the basis of a minimum programme directed against Papagos, while strongly criticizing Plastiras for his irresolution and reactionary policy and supporting those of his henchmen who accept our programme of bread, amnesty, peace, democracy and independence. This means that we should support Plastiras only to keep Papagos out. This political line follows from our basis task, which is to bar the way to Marshal Papagos, strengthen the anti-American, anti-imperialist, democratic and patriotic front in Greece, and prevent the realization of America's plans for war in the Balkans.[51]

To judge by the subsequent tactical positions adopted by the CPG, Moscow's reply to Zachariadis was not in the negative.

The extensive campaign of struggle for peace, which was facilitated by both objective and subjective factors, played no abstractly humanistic role in the plans of international communism but had a quite concrete class purpose. This was made clear in Stalin's work *Economic Problems of Socialism in the USSR*, which was finished at the beginning of February 1952 but published only in October of that year:

> It is possible that in a definite conjuncture of circumstances the fight for peace will develop here or there into a fight for socialism. But then it will no longer be the present-day peace movement; it will be a movement for the overthrow of capitalism ... To eliminate the inevitability of war it is necessary to abolish imperialism.[52]

At the same time Stalin affirmed that a third world war was not so close as it had been two or three years earlier.[53] Definite nuances in the approach to the problems of war and peace were apparent also in relation to 'the Greek question'. Thus, a phrase in the radio commentary of 'Free Greece' on 26 February 1953, saying that 'the feverish haste of the American and local bandits is worrying the popular masses, who perceive a close threat of war', was considered incorrect by the experts of the CC of the CPSU. They concluded that 'such statements spread war-psychosis'.[54] The contradictions between the national interests of the USSR as a world power and the ideological doctrine of its foreign policy as the world centre of communism were particularly obvious where 'the Greek question' was concerned. The foreign-policy experts of the CPSU commented in their review of the 'Free Greece' broadcasts, quoting passages about 'liquidation of the police state and establishment of a democratic government', that this was equivalent to a revolution, which could hardly be accomplished through an election campaign. 'We consider this way of posing the question politically superficial ... It has to be said that the blatant tone adopted by the radio station is not appropriate to progressive propaganda.'[55] The division of Europe into two opposing camps with sharply contrasting military-political doctrines made it difficult to evaluate objectively the situation within the individual particular countries making up these camps. While the Western side saw any instability in its zone as a sign of 'the Communist threat', the Eastern bloc resorted to formulations no less sharp, only the other way round. One official Soviet document stated that 'Greece today is a constitutional monarchy, a state of the fascist type, with feudal survivals, a state in which the American imperialists reign absolutely ...'.[56]

The fading of interest in 'the Greek question' was accompanied by increased attention on the Kremlin's part to a wider complex of problems connected with the Balkan Pact. But that is a subject for special research.

Notes

1. This chapter is based on the materials used for the author's book *Kommunisticheskaia partiia Gretsii. Aktualnye voprosy ideologii, politiki i vnutrennei istorii. (KPG v Nat'sional'nom Soprotivlenii, Grazhdanskoi i 'Kholodnoi' voinakh). 1941–1956gg.* (Moscow: 1994) 424 pp. Original sources used in this chapter represent handwriting copies of the Greek Communist Party documents that have not yet been published. After the KKE split in 1968 into two parallel parties, those who disagreed with pro-Moscow KKE formed the Greek Communist Party (internal) and managed to have many of the Party documents at their disposal. Later, the official organ *E Avgi* (The Dawn) of the Greek Communist Party (internal) started to publish some material from that archive. The author extends his gratitude to those persons who allowed him to look through some unpublished material and to use excerpts from the documents. The author had an opportunity to verify the main bulk of the material in the Russian archives which have not yet been made accessible. Therefore, in the references to the documents the author has used the following form: 'copy in the author's archives' (c.a.a.), and cited them as they had been received from the Greek Communist Party (internal) holdings.
2. Baranov, note to Malenkov, 4 February 1946 (c.a.a.).

3. Report by Baranov to Molotov, 19 February 1946 (c.a.a.).
4. *Ibid.*
5. *Ibid.*
6. Brief notes by Partsalidis on some questions of the work of the Communist Party of Greece, 31 January 1946 (c.a.a.).
7. *Ibid.*
8. *Ibid.*
9. Note by Medvedev and Manchkha to Baranov, 22 February 1946 (c.a.a.).
10. Brief notes on some questions.
11. M. Partsalidis, *Diplé apokatástase tes Ethnikes Antístases*, Vol. 1 (Athens: 1978) pp. 195, 199.
12. *Diáspase tou KKE*, Vol. 1 (Athens: 1975) p. 95.
13. Notes by the General Secretary of the CC of the Communist Party of Greece, Comrade Zachariades (sent through Dimitrov on his return from the Eighth Congress of the KKE) (c.a.a.).
14. *Ibid.*
15. Cipher telegram from Zachariades to Dimitrov, 30 August 1946, *E Avgi*, 2 August 1979.
16. Note by Ioannidis on the situation in Greece and the urgent tasks of the movement, 12 September 1946 (c.a.a.).
17. *Ibid.*
18. Note by Suslov to members of the Politburo of the CC of the CPSU (c.a.a.).
19. *E Avgi*, 2 December 1979.
20. Cipher telegram from Ioannidis to Zachariades, 31 December 1946, *ibid.*
21. 'K sobytiiam v Gretsii' [Biulleten' Biuro Informatsii TsK VKP(B)], *Voprosy vneshnei politiki*, 50 (1 February 1947) 15.
22. *Ibid.*, p. 17.
23. Letter from Zachariades to Stalin, 13 May 1947, *E Avgi*, 7 December 1979.
24. Communication to Zachariades, 17 March 1947 (c.a.a.).
25. *E Avgi*, 12 December 1979.
26. *Ibid.*, 9 December 1979.
27. *Ibid.*, 11 December 1979.
28. Note from Molotov to Suslov, 16 June 1947 (c.a.a.).
29. Letter from Zachariades to Tito, 12 August 1947, *E Avgi*, 25 December 1979.
30. *E Avgi*, 30 December 1979.
31. 'O tret'em Plenume TsK Kommunisticheskoi partii Gretsii' [Biulleten' Biuro Informatsii Tsk VKP(B)], *Voprosy vneshnei politiki*, 22/69 (15 November 1947) 17.
32. D.G. Kousoulas, *Modern Greece. Profile of a Nation* (New York: 1974) p. 219.
33. Minutes of the 5 July 1948 session of the Secretariat of the Information Bureau, RTsKhIDNI, f. 575, op. 1, d. 49, l. 13 (c.a.a.).
34. Information from Athens, 3 October 1948, to the CC of the KKE (c.a.a.).
35. Baranov to Sorokin, 7 September 1948, RTsKhIDNI, f. 575, op. 1, d. 60, l. 10, 11.
36. *Ibid.*
37. Report by Pukhlov to Baranov on talk with Comrade Chişinevschi about the question of a conference for sending aid to democratic Greece, 10 March 1949, RTsKhIDNI, f. 575, op. 1, d. 97, l. 36.

38. *Ibid.*
39. *Ibid.*, l. 37.
40. *Ibid.*
41. Goúsias-Voutítsios, *Oi aitíes gia tis ettes*, Vol. 1, pp. 501, 502; Partsalidis, *Diplé apokatástase*, p. 199 (c.a.a.).
42. Communication to the CC of the KKE, 26 April 1949 (c.a.a.).
43. See also V. Kónte, *E aggloamerimaniké politiké kai to elleniko provlema: 1945–1949* (Thessaloniki: 1948) pp. 384, 385.
44. Goúsias-Voutítsios, *Oi aitíes*, pp. 507, 516.
45. Communication by Rusos to Zachariades, 1 August 1949, RTsKhIDNI, f. 525, op. 1, d. 97, l. 96.
46. *Ibid.*
47. Long-term plan for broadcasts by the Committee on Broadcasting attached to the USSR Council of Ministers, March 1950.
48. Information note, RTsKhIDNI, f. 575, op. 1, d. 197, l. 114, 115.
49. GARF, f. 6903, op. 24, d. 28, l. 76.
50. Review of broadcast from 'Free Greece' radio station, October 1951 (c.a.a.).
51. RTsKhIDNI, f. 575, op. 1, d. 232, l. 228, 229.
52. I.V. Stalin, *Sochineniia*, vol. 3/XVI (Stanford: 1967) pp. 230–1.
53. *Pravda*, 2 April 1952.
54. Review of broadcasts from 'Free Greece' radio station, 14–28 February 1953, RTsKhIDNI, f. 575, op. 1, d. 266, l. 123.
55. Analysis of broadcasts from 'Free Greece' radio station, 7–13 October 1954, RTsKhIDNI, f. 575, op. 1, d. 362, l. 183, 185.
56. RTsKhIDNI, f. 575, op. 1, d. 292, l. 16.

10 The Soviet Union and the Italian Communist Party, 1944–8
Elena Aga-Rossi and Victor Zaslavsky

The purpose of this chapter is to clarify, on the basis of newly available documents from Russian archives, the underlying trends and objectives of Stalin's policy towards Italy and the role the Italian Communist Party played in Italian–Soviet relations between 1944 and 1948.[1] While an analysis of the overall strategy of the Stalinist leadership is obviously beyond the scope of this chapter, two fundamental principles of Stalin's understanding of international relations should be mentioned from the outset. On the one hand, Stalin believed the world to be divided into a Socialist and a capitalist camp in continuous struggle with each other. Prisoners of their ideology, Stalin and Molotov always based the Soviet foreign policy on the assumption of the inevitability of a future war with the capitalist world. Still during the war in his discussions with the leaders of foreign Communist Parties Stalin repeatedly stated that 'the crisis of capitalism manifests itself in the division of the capitalists into two fractions, the Fascist and the democratic ones ... Today we support one of these bourgeois fractions in its struggle against the other, but in the future we will also be against this capitalist fraction.'[2] He deemed inevitable a final conflict between the Soviet Union and the capitalist world, making the consolidation and further expansion of the Soviet sphere of influence as a necessary precondition and, indeed, the only way of meeting Soviet security requirements and advancing the Socialist system. On the other hand, for the immediate post-war years Stalin counted on a period of peace and collaboration with the Western Powers in order to gain time and recover from the destruction caused by the war. To this end, Stalin's post-war policy towards Europe would need to respect the spheres of influence assigned to each member of the victorious Alliance. As a result, Stalinist foreign policy in the aftermath of World War II tried to balance the benefits of continued co-operation with Western Allies with the imperative of consolidating the newly acquired sphere of influence and preparing ground for its future expansion.[3] Soviet policy towards Italy in 1944–8 is especially instructive as an example of a difficult balancing act performed by the Stalinist leadership in combining a rather cautious policy towards Italy (which belonged to the Western sphere of influence) with firm control over one of the major political forces of Italy, the Italian Communist Party (PCI). The Stalinist transformation of the PCI into a major instrument of Soviet geopolitical interests, in turn, precluded the possibility of a left-wing coalition dedicated to economic growth and the defence of Italian national interests from coming to power in the aftermath of World War II.

In presenting its history, the PCI always tried to create an image of a party totally reorganized by Togliatti after his return to Italy in 1944 that pursued policies independent of the USSR. A cornerstone of this myth of independence has always been the so-called *svolta di Salerno*, or the Salerno 'turning-point', the sudden April 1944 reversal of policy when the PCI dropped its insistence on immediate abdication of the king and joined the Badoglio Government. According to the standard historical interpretation, the *svolta di Salerno* was presumably determined by Togliatti's decision, taken independently from Soviet advice and based on the specifics of the Italian situation.[4] Togliatti himself seemed to confirm this interpretation, since he maintained he left Moscow in February and thus knew nothing of the March 1944 Soviet decision to recognize the Badoglio Government.[5] In reality, however, Togliatti must have left Moscow after his meeting with Stalin on 4 March 1944.

Stalin took advantage of the stalemate created in Italy by the anti-Fascist groups' opposition to Badoglio to take a two-pronged initiative in promoting a strong Communist participation in the national unity Government. On the one hand, on the 14 March 1944 the Soviet Union unexpectedly recognized the Badoglio Government; on the other hand, Stalin engineered the 'Salerno turn' policy which resulted in the other political parties' joining the Badoglio Government and the consequent overall strengthening of the PCI position in Italy. In personal meetings with the leaders of the two major Western Communist Parties on the eve of their respective departures to Italy and France, Stalin suggested to Togliatti and Thorez the course of action that he expected the PCI and PCF to follow during the immediate post-war phase when the political parties were being reorganized and relations with other political forces established.[6] The instructions given to both leaders were very similar and shed considerable light on Stalin's post-war plans and intentions. Stalin's point of departure was that both the PCI and PCF were starting out from a position of weakness in countries belonging to the Western sphere of influence. Their first priority was therefore to widen the Parties' base of support as much as possible by following a policy of national unity and forming blocs and alliances with other left-wing forces. At the meeting with Togliatti, Stalin suggested that the Italian Communist Party should abandon for the time being the slogan calling for immediate abdication of the king and join the Badoglio

Government. Togliatti was also advised against publicizing the fact that the national unity line was Stalin's suggestion. In fact, the Soviet leadership never opposed the Badoglio Government and did not raise any objections to the support given by the Anglo-Americans to Badoglio. The plan of action for the PCI which Stalin and Togliatti agreed upon was based on three principles. First, a left-wing coalition led by the PCI was to be constructed. Second, premature mass action, such as an uprising or civil war, was to be avoided, since this would increase tension between the USSR and the Western Allies and prevent the Soviet Union from gaining enough time to stabilize Eastern Europe. Third, a programme for the radical reform of the Italian economy was to be proposed which would enjoy support from broad sections of the country and win elections.

Immediately after the meeting between Stalin and Togliatti, Georgi Dimitrov (who after the Comintern's dissolution had become an official of the CPSU Central Committee's apparatus in charge of the international Communist movement) wrote a directive for the French Communist Party that closely followed Stalin's instructions to Togliatti.[7] It recommended that the PCF should concentrate its efforts on becoming the leading national party in a broad coalition of left-wing forces and defend the Soviet–French alliance as a cornerstone of French foreign policy. Dimitrov referred to the building of Socialism in France as the ultimate objective of the PCF, while stressing that, in the USA, such a task would simply not be feasible in the foreseeable future. Stalin himself discussed the problems facing the PCF in a long meeting with Maurice Thorez on 19 November 1944, imparting the instructions already familiar from the encounter with Togliatti.[8] The main priority of the French Communists, according to Stalin, was the creation of a broad left-wing bloc drawing in the Socialists and Radicals and strengthening links with the trade unions, peasants and youth. According to Stalin, the fact that the resistance troops remained armed undermined the PCF's legitimacy, for the existence of a second army could not be justified when there was a legitimate French Government with its own regular army recognized by the Allies. Stalin thus suggested the resistance troops become a political organization and hide their arms for some possible future use. On the whole, the policies adopted by the Italian and French Communist Parties in the immediate post-war years followed the outlines sketched out by Stalin in 1944.

The entry of Communists into a coalition government created a completely new situation in Italy. As Togliatti pointed out in a conversation with Ambassador Kostylev, 'the PCI is now working in extraordinarily complex conditions where it is very difficult to reconcile the participation in the Government with leading the opposition'.[9] Togliatti repeatedly asked Moscow for advice on the political line of the PCI and kept receiving the suggestion to gather support from the widest possible constituency. The discussions between Kostylev and PCI leaders revolved mainly around the issue of the relationship with other left-wing parties, especially the Socialists. Some leaders of both parties at that time pressed for a merger between PCI and PSI. Togliatti firmly opposed this, believing the disadvantages outweighed the advantages. First, the right wing of the PSI was against the merger and so the Socialist Party would inevitably split. Second, Togliatti argued that merger was not a suitable policy in any case since it would weaken the influence of the left within the Government and leave just one party to defend the interests of the left coalition. Third, he believed that a single party would gather fewer votes than two separate ones, which could appeal to broader sectors of the population.[10] This reasoning led Togliatti even to oppose the transfer of individual Socialists to the PCI, 'so as not to deprive the Socialist Party of its most progressive elements and avoid having to cope with opposition from a rightward-looking PSI'.[11]

Another task of the PCI was to impose a strict discipline on its own membership and thus, indirectly, on all members of the left-wing coalition, to dissuade them from undertaking insurrection at a moment which might be inopportune for the Soviet Union. After the fall of the Fascist regime, the defeated Italy experienced a deep erosion of state power, which in combination with war destruction and growing economic hardship created a situation of explosive political instability. Italy gave the impression of a country on the verge of civil war. In the first 'political letter' (periodic reports to Moscow on the political situation in Italy) sent by Kostylev to Molotov, the Ambassador wrote that the Italian people 'is ready for courageous revolutionary action. Only the moderating influence of its vanguard, the PCI ... can halt this rush of the masses towards premature insurrection'.[12]

Soviet faith in the PCI was not misplaced, for in that turbulent situation Togliatti led the PCI along the path of compromise, pacification and a search for a gradual increase in electoral support. The task was by no means easy, as Togliatti, Longo and other PCI leaders complained in discussions with Kostylev. According to the Soviet Ambassador, Togliatti 'was worried about the alarming degeneration of the partisan movement in the North ... [where] some partisan groups became involved in banditry, expropriation and violence against citizens', causing the PCI a loss of mass support.[13] Togliatti's personal responsibility for preventing the outbreak of outright civil war in Italy should not be underestimated. With great skill the PCI transformed the armed troops of the resistance into a political organization, persuading partisans to hide their arms and abandon violence.

Another recurrent theme of discussions between Soviet representatives and PCI leaders was the Party's programme, aimed to strengthen greatly the central state and its planning and control functions. Control over prices and savings was to be reinforced; control over production was to be exercised by the factory Workers' Councils; certain industries and a number of major enterprises were to be nationalized; and tax policy would 'hit the well-to-do classes'.[14] A battery of measures to limit profits of entrepreneurs had to be introduced, such as a surtax on the sale of shares, rigid limits on dividends and various special taxes on capital. The whole programme was thus redistributive and anti-capitalist, 'a real programme of the Italian democratic-revolutionary movement', as Kostylev characterized it.[15] The leaders of the PCI relied on direct intervention in the economy by the state, not just as a way of coping with the emergency, but as a fundamental Socialist principle, whose validity had been confirmed by the Soviet experience. Without stating it openly, the PCI's economic programme drew on the Soviet model in its broad outlines.

To point out that in the aftermath of World War II the PCI was inspired by the Stalinist system is not to criticize that historically conditioned position with an easy hindsight. In the 1940s it was evident that the Soviet system had transformed a semi-peasant country into a great military power capable of destroying the potent German war machine. It is hardly surprising, therefore, that Italian Communists were particularly vulnerable to the promises of the Soviet project. The major problem for the PCI was the fact that the Stalinist leadership, for the reasons to be discussed below, was unwilling to provide Italy with even a token amount of economic assistance and was stalling off the resumption of economic relations. Confronted with the absence of Soviet aid, the PCI's leadership had to defend the thesis that post-war Italy could base a policy of stabilization and economic reconstruction on internal resources. The strong point of Alcide De Gasperi's Government – a point which drew agreement from broad sectors of the Italian population – was precisely that Italy could not emerge from its post-war crisis without economic aid and large-scale foreign loans.

Of all the issues in Soviet-Italian relations in the 1944-8 period, two are particularly revealing of Stalin's policy towards Italy and the role played by the PCI. The first is the problem of Trieste and the borders between Italy and Yugoslavia in general. On this question there was a sharp difference between the position taken up by the majority in the Italian Government and public, and the PCI leadership. The second is the issue of the resumption of Italo-Soviet economic relations that elicited basic consensus across the whole Italian political spectrum.

Trieste was one of the thorniest problems left by World War II. In the post-war years it became the focus of a three-fold conflict. It was a conflict between the Great Powers, since the presence of Allied troops in the city meant that it was seen as the Western camp's 'last bulwark', psychologically and politically, against Soviet expansionism. Moreover, it was a conflict between Italy and Yugoslavia over the city which Tito with Soviet complicity wanted to turn totally Slav and whose Italian identity was firmly defended by De Gasperi. Finally, it was a conflict within the Italian Government itself between the Communists and the representatives of other parties.

From the first months of the war, Stalin had planned a post-war territorial settlement in Europe, in which the Yugoslav territory would be enlarged at the expense of Italy, that would lose Trieste, Fiume and various Adriatic islands.[16] This position became more accentuated during the course of the war, as Tito's army turned into the strongest of Stalin's allies.[17] In the January 1945 'political letter', Ambassador Kostylev sketched the main outlines of Soviet policy towards Italy, suggesting that 'when the Yugoslavs ask for the territories of Istria, Gorizia, Zara and the nearby islands we will have to support their demand'.[18] Of course, the Soviet leaders had to take into account the attitudes of the Western Powers, but on this point there was a certain amount of optimism. Since 1941, the British Government was willing to accept Yugoslav territorial claims against Italy; and differences between the British and United States Governments over the future of the region probably led the Soviets to believe that the Western Allies would not put up implacable resistance.[19] The Soviet Union's unconditional support for Yugoslav territorial claims left the PCI no room for manoeuvre; it had to accept the Soviet line, even though it was causing serious internal friction within the Party. The leadership of the PCI was placed in the difficult position of demonstrating its determination to put class interests above national ones at the expense of compromising the image of Togliatti's 'new party' as a broadly-based national party. 'Reconciling participation in the Government with leading the opposition' became particularly difficult in the case of Trieste, for although the De Gasperi Government accepted other territorial claims, it was always firm on Trieste's belonging to Italy and made this claim the priority of Italian foreign policy. As the negotiations between the Great Powers developed, the PCI's position changed – but always in accordance with Soviet policy of the moment. In a first phase, starting in autumn 1944, when a German withdrawal from Yugoslavia seemed imminent, Tito's plan to confront the Western Allies with a *fait accompli* by occupying the region of Venezia Giulia was accepted by the PCI leadership. In his frequent and long discussions with Kostylev during these months, Togliatti reassured the Ambassador of his full support of the Soviet–Yugoslav position, stating that the Italian frontiers were imperialist and that Yugoslavia was entitled to total satisfaction of its territorial claims.[20] In October 1944 Togliatti wrote to the representative of the PCI in Slovenia, Vincenzo Bianco:

We must facilitate the occupation of the Julian province by Marshal Tito's troops in every way possible. This means that in this region there will be no British occupation and no restoration of the reactionary Italian administration; thus there will be created a situation radically different from that prevailing in the liberated part of Italy ... this directive applies also, and above all, to the city of Trieste.[21]

The Yugoslavs interpreted this directive of Togliatti as a complete and definitive acceptance of the annexation of Venezia Giulia and Trieste. They underestimated the truly devastating effect such an outcome might have had for the Communists' prestige in Italy. The PCI leadership kept searching for a face-saving solution, however. Togliatti asked Tito to conduct Yugoslav policy in a manner 'acceptable to the Italians'.[22] The Communist leaders of northern Italy, while recognizing that Trieste belonged to Yugoslavia, specifically requested that Yugoslavs postpone any open declaration in this regard until after the war. The Yugoslavs refused this proposal, although such a tactical compromise would have avoided divisions within the Committee for the Liberation of Upper Italy (CLNAI), as well as splits in the partisan movement, and tensions and conflicts within the ranks of the PCI. In their conversations with the Soviet Ambassador, Togliatti and other Communist leaders continued to emphasize serious difficulties that the problem of Trieste created for the PCI. As Ruggiero Greco told Kostylev,

on the problem of Trieste the PCI is isolated in the country. Even within the Party itself we have been obliged from time to time to impose rigid discipline on Party members since not all of them have understood the primacy of class interests over national ones in the case of Trieste and not all have been fully in agreement with the Party's line.[23]

On 1 May 1945 Tito's troops entered Trieste in an attempt to present the arriving Allied troops with a Yugoslav occupation and administration. The PCI leaders immediately requested instructions from Moscow. The Communist Deputy Foreign Minister, Eugenio Reale, hurried to Kostylev, asking him, 'in Togliatti's name and on his request', if Stalin had really promised Trieste to the Yugoslavs, since 'the PCI line on Trieste would depend on this information'.[24] Moscow's reply can be easily inferred from the fact that at the 31 May 1945 meeting Togliatti told Kostylev that he had been in contact with Tito and repeated 'the idea, already stated on a previous occasion, that Trieste had no future as an Italian port city, since it was not connected with the main centres of the country, but that it could prosper by serving the needs of Yugoslavia and the other countries of the Danube basin'.[25]

Even when the Western Allies put pressure on Tito to withdraw his troops and set up their own military administration of Trieste, the Soviet leadership continued to hope that in the end, by playing on British–American differences, it would arrive at the desirable solution of the Trieste problem. So the PCI did not alter its position either. Thus at the August 1945 meeting with Kostylev the Communist Deputy Foreign Minister Celeste Negarville informed the Ambassador about Togliatti's preoccupation with 'the nationalist and imperialist stance' the Italian delegation would presumably adopt at the Paris Peace Conference, and repeated that the PCI leadership considered 'Italian claims on Trieste' unacceptable.[26] Later, however, the unpopularity of this position within Italy and the stalemate in the negotiations between the Great Powers led Togliatti to seek a compromise solution on Trieste which would be acceptable to the Soviet Union and yet prevent the loss of popular support for the PCI. Togliatti had already proposed a direct bilateral agreement between Yugoslavia and Italy on Trieste, but had met with refusal from both the Soviets and De Gasperi. At the 24 May 1946 meeting with Kostylev, Togliatti pointed to the extreme difficulty of the problem and raised again the idea of 'a compromise on the basis of "shared administration" of Trieste by Italy and Yugoslavia'.[27] The Soviet position remained basically unchanged, however, judging by Kostylev's account for Moscow: 'I replied that the Yugoslavs were firm over the annexation of Trieste because all the hinterland belonged to the Yugoslavs and to leave Trieste with Italy would be like separating the head from the body.'[28] During the Paris Conference, on 19 June 1946, Reale, a member of the Italian delegation, met with Molotov asking him, on Togliatti's behalf, to adopt 'an attitude towards the problem of Trieste more favourable to us'. Molotov advised the Italian Communists 'not to give too much importance to Trieste and to concentrate their attention, and that of the Italian people, on the issue of national independence'.[29] During the Conference Molotov put forward a series of unrealistic proposals intended to postpone the decision, but these were rebuffed by the Western representatives. Both sides finally agreed on a compromise solution creating a Free Territory of Trieste. It was only at this point that Togliatti's idea of trying an alternative path via a personal agreement with Tito was considered by the Soviets as a last attempt to avoid a solution which might leave Anglo-American troops in Trieste indefinitely.

Since the talks between Reale and Kardelj in Paris confirmed that the Yugoslavs were open to new proposals, Togliatti asked for Soviet mediation to organize an encounter with Tito. As a result, on 20 October 1946 the Soviet Ambassador in Yugoslavia, Anatolii Lavrent'ev, passed to Tito a letter from Togliatti which proposed a meeting 'of the two politicians in their capacity as leaders of the

Communist movements of their respective countries to solve directly and definitively the problems at issue between the two peoples'.[30] Togliatti emphasized the considerable propaganda advantages of such a meeting: it would 'unmask the Anglo-American imperialists by showing that they are interested in turning Trieste into a base for their imperialist activity and sowing discord between the two peoples rather than in defending the national interests of the Italians' and it would allow the Italian Communists 'to isolate nationalists and Anglo-American agents in Italy' by proposing a reasonable solution of the problems at issue between Italy and Yugoslavia.[31] Tito immediately agreed to the meeting, but made it clear to the Soviet Ambassador that, however interested he was in expelling the Anglo-Americans from Trieste, he could not agree to return the city to Italy. Tito proposed placing Trieste under a common Italo-Yugoslavian administration, in which the Italians might play the predominant role.[32] At the next meeting with Lavrent'ev, Tito repeated that he was ready to receive Togliatti on 2 November in Belgrade but deemed the concession of Trieste to Italy unacceptable.[33] During the negotiations which took place 2–6 November 1946, Togliatti managed to get Tito to recognize that Trieste belonged to Italy, but at the cost of ceding to Yugoslavia the city of Gorizia, whose Italian status had been confirmed at the Paris Conference.

Togliatti apparently viewed the agreement with Tito as very favourable for Italy and for the image of the PCI, as well as his personal success. Even before he informed the Italian Government of the results of his secret negotiations, Togliatti gave an interview to the Party's official newspaper *L'Unità*, in which he proclaimed triumphantly that Tito agreed with the return of Trieste to Italy. In a subsequent message to Molotov, Kostylev defined Togliatti's visit to Belgrade 'a most unpleasant surprise and a serious political blow for the Italian right' and claimed that it resulted in 'full rehabilitation of the PCI, previously accused by the reactionaries of betraying national interests'.[34] In reality the Tito–Togliatti meeting was less successful than Kostylev believed. It may be that in Togliatti's eyes the shift in the PCI position from supporting Yugoslav claims to Trieste to proposing an exchange of Trieste for Gorizia seemed so radical that it led him to misjudge the reaction of the majority of the Italians. The Italian Foreign Minister, Socialist Pietro Nenni, understood the situation better, writing in his diary: 'to tell the truth, Tito is giving up what he does not have in exchange for something we do.'[35] Togliatti was infuriated by the reaction of the Italian press, which, he lamented to Kostylev, 'was making Gorizia out to be a sacred Italian city, a kind of Italian Mecca'.[36] He was also very irritated by the Government statement in which there was 'not a word of thanks to Tito for his magnanimity in returning Italian prisoners of war, and which took up a completely wrong-headed position over the question of the Italian–Yugoslav border'.[37] In addition, a serious conflict was created with the Socialist Party, the major ally of the PCI, that categorically rejected the idea of exchanging Trieste for Gorizia.

The Togliatti–Tito negotiations represented one of the very rare cases where the PCI took the initiative in foreign policy, albeit with the direct authorization of the Soviet Government. From Togliatti's point of view, it was not just an attempt to improve the popular image of the PCI and escape from the isolation, in which the PCI had placed itself by supporting Yugoslav territorial claims and the Soviet line over Trieste. It was also an offensive action aimed at weakening the De Gasperi Government and presenting the PCI as an independent and pragmatic force, capable of obtaining concrete results.[38] However, by accepting to cede Gorizia, Togliatti cancelled a large part of the propaganda credit he might have gained in the negotiations with Tito. The Christian Democrats, and De Gasperi personally, were able to exploit to the full the negative reaction of the Italian population in general, and the Socialists in particular, to the Togliatti–Tito deal and reinforce their image as committed defenders of Italy's territorial integrity.[39]

Analysis of the new documentation on the case of Trieste thus permits some preliminary conclusions. The documents demonstrate that the degree of Soviet control over the PCI leadership was very high, and undoubtedly higher than previously recognized by historians. All major initiatives on the part of the PCI had to receive Soviet authorization. The documents vividly reveal both Togliatti's ability to propose actions that he desired and his dependence on the Soviet Union that imposed significant restrictions on his ability to act. When Soviet geopolitical interests (as they were interpreted by the Stalinist leadership) contradicted such Italian national interests as the defence of the territorial integrity of the country, the leadership of the PCI, sometimes against their will, had to give priority to the Soviet policy requirements. Moreover, the new documentation confirms a high degree of control exercised by the PCI leadership over rank and file members of the Party. The Party was able to preserve its membership and maintain its monolithic structure even when it conducted a policy that was plainly counter-productive to the PCI's popularity in the country. Finally, Stalin's policy on Trieste demonstrates convincingly that the presence of a strong Communist Party in Italy did not lead Stalin to soften his hard-line, often punitive attitude towards Italy. Stalin obviously based his decisions on his calculations of relative cost and benefit to the Soviet Union. An examination of economic relations between the Soviet Union and Italy in the 1945–8 years confirms these conclusions.

The Italian Communist Party proved unable to mediate between Italy and the Soviet Union in the long negotiations conducted by the Italian

Government to re-establish economic relations and sign a trade agreement with the USSR. The issue of economic links with the Soviet Union and Eastern Europe was of great importance to Italy, which urgently needed raw materials and food in exchange for manufactured products and labour. The political advantages of opening up the Italian economy to the East were equally evident. In the time when the country was totally dependent on Western aid for economic revival and even for survival, establishing economic relations with the emerging Eastern bloc would favour economic reconstruction and allow Italy greater autonomy and a more balanced foreign policy. All the major political forces of Italy agreed on the importance of good economic relations with the Soviet Union. For a period of time, even De Gasperi entertained the idea of a 'policy of equidistance' of Italy between the blocs, while politicians and industrialists emphasized the complementarity of the Soviet and Italian economies. As early as August 1945, Prime Minister Ferruccio Parri proposed that Italian industry could build ships and various kinds of machinery for the USSR in exchange for raw materials.[40] In October 1945 Meuccio Ruini, the Minister for Economic Reconstruction, communicated to Kostylev Italy's interest in signing an Italian–Soviet trade treaty, arguing that for the USSR Italy 'could become the tailor that works his customer's cloth'.[41] According to Ruini, trade with the Soviet Union would be 'an important counterweight to the penetration of Anglo-American capital that dominates the Italian foreign trade'.[42] Vittorio Valletta, the Chairman of FIAT, repeated the same idea in almost the same words while stating that Soviet orders would counterbalance 'the FIAT's subordination to Anglo-American interests'.[43] Leaders of the Communist and Socialist Parties, on the other hand, pointed to the advantages to the Italian working class following the resumption of Italian–Soviet economic relations in terms of employment, growth of popular sympathy towards the Soviet Union and electoral gains for the Left. Soviet diplomats in Italy basically agreed with these arguments. As Kostylev pointed out in his 1945 outlines for Soviet policy towards Italy: 'The Americans will try to obtain complete control over Italian foreign trade and consequently over the entire economy of a weak Italy. We should not permit this.'[44] Until the autumn of 1947 the response of the Soviet leadership to the proposals of the Italian Government, the prompting of the Italian Left, as well as their own diplomats, continued to be the same: no reaction. In May 1947 a high-ranking Foreign Ministry official drawing up a summary document on the state of Italian–Soviet economic relations for the Deputy Minister Andrei Vyshinsky, compiled a long list of proposals, initiatives, suggestions and appeals to sign a trade agreement and launch commercial relations on the part of Italian members of Government, politicians and industrialists. He concluded his report with a phrase: 'Until now the Ministry of Foreign Trade has not given any reply.'[45]

Later, in 1947, the Soviet Government, however, began expressing interest in establishing trade relations with Italy. At first glance the fact that the Soviet leadership became more responsive to the idea of trade relations with Italy after the expulsion of the Italian Left from the Government in May 1947 and the escalation of the Cold War, following the announcement of the Marshall Plan and the organization of the Cominform, seems puzzling. Soviet internal documents, however, explain this change in attitude: the Soviets were anxious to receive the substantial sum of 100 million dollars of Italian reparations to the USSR as had been established by the Peace Treaty signed in February 1947. As it was emphasized in the March 1947 political letter from the Rome Embassy to Moscow, 'the sooner we conclude a trade agreement, the easier it will be to exact reparations'.[46] Moreover, the Soviet Government tried to use a trade agreement to force Italy to pay reparations from current production, but the firm resistance of the Italian side to link the resumption of trade with the payment of reparations forced the Soviets to drop this demand.[47] The trade agreement was finally signed in December 1948.

An analysis of the documents from Russian archives regarding Soviet refusal to establish mutually advantageous trade relations with Italy in the period 1945–7 raises three related questions. Why did Stalin's Government make no effort to counter-balance Anglo-American economic influence in Italy?, Why was the PCI leadership so cautious in attempts to use its special relationship with the USSR to promote Soviet–Italian trade? and Why did it never try to use its influence to soften the punitive character of the Peace Treaty or lighten the burden of reparations? To answer the last questions the following considerations are to be taken into account. First, the leaders of the PCI, unlike the Socialists, were bound by iron rules of discipline and subordination reigning in the Communist movement since the times of the Comintern. No criticisms of the Soviet leadership were permitted, and any attempt to intervene on behalf of their own country would in all likelihood have been judged as nationalism and neglect of the class approach, accusations that would signify the end of career for any Communist functionary. Also, many PCI leaders were undoubtedly aware of the extremely low standard of living in the USSR due to wartime destruction and sacrifices and the nature of Stalin's post-war internal policy. In addition, the PCI's reliance on Soviet financial assistance did not allow its leaders to advance further requests. Most importantly, however, the PCI leadership obviously shared the Soviet approach that the Italian Left, led by the Communists, had first to achieve a considerable electoral success and introduce a programme of major political and economic change before large-scale trade and economic aid from the USSR could get under way. Kostylev repeatedly assured the Communist leaders that he anticipated an immediate increase in Soviet–Italian trade in the event of the Democratic Popular Front's victory in the 1948 elections.[48]

It is more difficult to answer the first question, especially since the policy of refusal to establish economic relations with Italy was often misunderstood even by lower-level Soviet diplomats.[49] The newly available documents, nevertheless, suggest that complex economic, political and international considerations on the part of Stalin's leadership (as well as personal characteristics and the way of thinking of such major protagonists as Stalin and Molotov) were in various degrees responsible for the postponement of a Soviet–Italian trade agreement in the immediate post-war years. We need to bear in mind the inflexibility which often marked the policy of Stalin and Molotov, especially with regard to economic issues, as well as the rigidity, inexperience and obtuseness of the Ministry of Foreign Trade bureaucrats who were to design and supervise a Soviet–Italian trade agreement. Moreover, documents from Russian archives demonstrate that Stalin's dealings with the foreign Communists, be they Italian, Chinese or Korean, were always characterized by 'Stalin's crude calculation of material advantage to the Soviet Union'.[50] The objective economic difficulties of the post-war Soviet Union were enormous and Soviet leaders themselves justified the continuous delay of the resumption of economic relations with Italy in these terms.[51] This argumentation should not be taken at face value, since for the Stalinist leadership political considerations always took priority over economic criteria. The Soviet Union had trade relations with a number of countries, but Italy was not one of them. The principal motive behind Soviet lack of interest in economic relations with Italy was perhaps revealed by Kostylev in his reply to the then Italian Foreign Minister, Nenni. At the 16 November 1946 meeting with the Soviet Ambassador, Nenni emphasized that the arrival of Soviet grain would be crucial for the improvement of the position of the Left, and requested reliable information regarding the possibility of Soviet grain deliveries to Italy.[52] To answer Nenni, Kostylev had to ask precise instruction from Moscow, and at the subsequent meeting told Nenni that 'there would be no deliveries because no grain is available, due to drought in some regions of the USSR, and due to exports to Romania, France, Finland and other countries'.[53] The Soviet leaders were seemingly more sceptical than the Italian Left regarding both the very possibility of Italy maintaining a 'position of equidistance' between the Great Powers, and the likelihood that the Left could win the elections with help of Soviet deliveries. The fact is that, notwithstanding its strong Communist Party, Italy was of minor importance for the Soviet Union. The Sovietization of Eastern Europe was obviously Stalin's absolute priority. And among the countries which did not fall within the Soviet orbit, France had clear priority over Italy, for in Stalin's eyes the presence of Anglo-American troops, even if they later were confined to the Trieste zone, was the crucial factor determining Italy's belonging to the Western sphere of influence.

From Stalin's perspective, in an emerging bipolar world the European countries had a simple choice between the 'progressive course of development' within the Soviet sphere of influence and 'the road of capitulation to American capital'.[54] In these terms, the Italian Communist Party, with all its efforts to create a strong left-wing bloc, win the elections and proceed to a radical transformation of the economy after the Soviet model, was too far from reaching these goals in practice. This fact, combined with the Western Allies' military presence in Italy, convinced the Soviet leadership that the investment of scarce Soviet resources in Italy was not justified. Obviously the situation could change in a case of the left-wing victory, and the newly available Soviet documents demonstrate that both Soviet representatives in Italy and leaders for some time took seriously such an outcome. We can only guess what might have been the Soviet reaction had the left-wing bloc led by the Communists come to power. The existing documentation suggests that Stalin in all likelihood would have continued to support a peaceful non-revolutionary development of Italy. Russian archives contain many documents that permit such an interpretation, but the documents pertaining to a possible seizure of power through armed uprising after the April 1948 elections are particularly revealing. According to the PCI leadership's reading of the situation, the Democratic Front's victory would be followed by the cancellation of the election results and big disorders organized by the Christian Democrats. Togliatti himself considered such a scenario so realistic that upon his request the Soviet Embassy arranged the departure of Gramsci's young children to Moscow through Yugoslavia.[55] On 23 March 1948 at a secret meeting with the Soviet Ambassador, Togliatti informed him that the PCI was preparing the masses for armed action, especially in northern Italy, and asked Moscow if the Party should organize an armed uprising to seize power as a response to a 'gross provocation' on the part of the Christian Democrats. In his immediate reply Molotov wrote: 'We think that at the moment the Italian Communist Party must under no circumstances go for a seizure of power through armed uprising.'[56] In the light of new documentation, the issue of the PCI's oscillation between reformism and revolutionism that fascinated historians of the previous generation becomes a secondary problem pertaining mainly to intra-Party factional struggles, since the final decision always remained with the Soviet Union.

The newly accessible documentation demonstrates beyond doubt that in Stalin's time all principal directions and initiatives of the PCI policy were discussed, co-ordinated and approved by the Soviet leadership. The history of the PCI cannot be studied, therefore, without reference to the Party's close links with the USSR, since hard documentary evidence confirms that the Stalinist leadership used the PCI as an instrument of its geopolitical strategy. Moreover, the PCI leadership voluntarily accepted its subordinate position and followed Moscow's instructions. In the period under examination the Italian Communist Party was a Leninist Party in its organization and Stalinist in its leadership. Its structure and organizational principles were in many respects a direct copy of those of the CPSU, the successor of the Bolshevik Party built by Lenin. It was a Stalinist Party insofar its highest leadership was dominated by Stalinists, ready to pursue whatever policy was dictated by the Soviet leader, however counter-productive it might have been for PCI's image and popularity. The PCI leadership skilfully utilized the organizational resources of the Leninist Party to channel its mass membership's energies to accomplish various tasks dictated by the interests of the Stalinist post-war policies, rather than by Italian national interests. The image of the PCI as a 'national party', skilfully cultivated by Togliatti, is particularly damaged by the Soviet documents.

It is well known that the concept of 'national interest' is one of the most polyvalent in the political vocabulary, for different groups and social forces in a particular nation-state can conceive of national interests in very different terms.[57] In the immediate post-war years there was a clear contradiction between the definition of Italian national interests held by PCI leaders and that held by members of other parties, as well as by much of the country. Convinced Communists could always justify unconditional support for the USSR as conforming to the true interests of Italy, since they believed that only Socialism could solve all the country's problems and the Soviet model of Socialism was the only one realized in practice. This ideological belief was enormously strengthened by Soviet successes in World War II. Togliatti and the other PCI leaders realized, however, that the majority of Italians thought of national interests more in terms of defending the territorial integrity of the country, maintaining internal stability and raising the Italian standard of living which depended, in turn, on the country's ability to attract international aid and to create jobs.

In the aftermath of World War II Togliatti and other PCI leaders made considerable efforts to reconcile the Party's internationalist orthodoxy with commonly held ideas concerning Italian national interests. As a mass Party the PCI sought support from broad strata of the Italian population, making frequent appeals to patriotic sentiments, extensively using heroic names from Italian history and referring to national values. Moreover, in the 1943–8 the PCI undoubtedly played a positive national role by organizing the resistance (in which it became a key force), encouraging unity in the anti-Fascist struggle, and exercising a moderating influence in the most turbulent years of post-war Italian history. It not only helped to create a potent trade union movement but also on various occasions supported the politics of economic growth and productivity. When the interests of Soviet foreign policy, as Stalin understood them, contradicted Italian national interests, as understood by the majority of the Italian population or its politically active part, the leadership of the PCI invariably sided with the Soviet Union. The PCI's position on Trieste, on the Italian reparations to the USSR and on Italian–Soviet economic relations, are examples of Italian Communist leadership subordinating Italian interests to those of Stalin's foreign policy. As a consequence, the PCI was constantly undermining the positive results of its own policy initiatives. Many historians saw the roots of the growing autonomy of the Italian Communist Party from Moscow (that culminated in the 1979 'split') in the events connected with the 1947 organization of Cominform, accompanied by Zhdanov's heavy criticisms directed at the Italian and French Communist Parties. The documentation from Russian archives provides no evidence of dissidence on the part of the PCI leadership as a whole or its individual members in the period between 1943 and 1948. The explanation of Zhdanov's attacks on the Western Communists lies, thus, in the political psychology of Stalin and his collaborators. The Italian Communists were accused of an excessive reliance on parliamentarianism and of a reluctance openly to proclaim their firm support of the USSR as the indisputable centre of the international Communist movement. The Italian representatives were taken by surprise – and could easily rebut these criticisms – by stating that this political line had been suggested by Stalin and had never been previously criticized by the Soviet leadership. Later, Pietro Secchia, in his discussions with Soviet leaders, successfully adopted this line of defence. The true fault of the leadership of the PCI consisted in their tardy reaction to the radical change of the international situation created by the Marshall Plan. In the new international conditions, Zhdanov claimed,

> the policy of support for the Soviet Union as the leading force in the struggle for a sound and lasting peace, the struggle for democracy, needs to be pursued by the CP's honestly and frankly. It must be emphasized as firmly as possible that the fraternal CPs' efforts to strengthen the USSR, coincide with the vital interests of their own countries.[58]

The immediate change of the PCI policy and adoption of an intransigent pro-Soviet line occurred without any debate, let alone resistance, within the Party. Almost overnight the low-key opposition to Western Powers, restrained for purely tactical reasons, turned into a fierce propaganda war against the 'world's strongest capitalism,'[59] the American one, while the rejection of the Marshall Plan became the major touchstone of division between Communists and non-Communists.

The most telling example of the disastrous consequences of Communist leaders' subservience to Stalin remains the PCI's rejection of the Marshall Plan without making any reasonable alternative proposal for Italy's economic reconstruction. The decision of the Communist Labour Confederation to redefine its major objective as the struggle against the Marshall Plan provoked an irrevocable split in the Italian labour movement. By slavishly following Stalin's course the Italian Communists 'placed themselves outside the continuum of normal politics'.[60] The PCI leaders were convinced that their redistributive economic programme, combined with the alliance with the Socialists, would be sufficient to win the 1948 elections.[61] Togliatti himself expected a considerable gain for the Left compared with the 1946 elections to the Constituent Assembly, and even on 19 April 1948, the day after the elections but before the results were known, he discussed with Kostylev whether he should put himself forward as Prime Minister.[62]

The Commmunist Party saw the national elections of 18 April 1948 as crucially important, perhaps hoping, as Paolo Robotti put it, that 'victory will give the Party the chance to move on legally to much more determined tactics, as it has happened in Czechoslovakia'.[63] Throughout the country the election took on the significance of a choice of sides on the world political arena. The results were a net victory for the Christian Democrats and a major defeat for the Front. The first reaction of the PCI leadership was incredulity, and all the subsequent analyses of the causes of defeat remained superficial, accusing the victorious parties of electoral fraud,[64] blaming the Socialists for their poor contribution to the electoral campaign or even criticizing the PCI propaganda for a failure 'to spread the truth about the USSR ... its wealth and power, the free life and labour of its people'.[65] Neither the PCI leaders nor the Soviet representatives ever had the courage to analyse the outcome of the national elections. At most, they discussed how the PCI could recover and comforted themselves with the fact that Party organization withstood the blow.[66] No open discussion of political defeats, and no open criticism of leaders by the rank and file, was permitted by Stalinist political culture. A resounding defeat of the Communist-led coalition in the 1948 elections testifies to a realistic judgement passed by the Italian voters on the PCI's attempts to obstruct American aid and paralyse economic reform.

CONCLUSIONS

Historians do not have full access to some important documents regarding Soviet–Italian relations in the period under examination. Much of the ciphered correspondence between Moscow and the Soviet Embassy in Rome cannot yet be consulted, and the documents preserved in the Archives of the President of the Russian Federation have been only partially accessible to scholars. At the same time, the newly available documentation from Russian archives is so massive and detailed that, combined with the materials preserved in American, British and Italian archives, it throws new light on practically all aspects of Soviet–Italian relations in the Stalin period. This chapter's analysis of new documentation indicates the following two basic areas in which certain widely accepted historical interpretations require modification, or sometimes a thorough revision. The first is the character of the relations between the European Communist Parties, the PCI in particular, and the Soviet Party-state, leading to a historical re-evaluation of the role the PCI played in post-war Italy. The second concerns a new interpretation of Stalin's plans for post-war Europe that explains the particular character of Soviet policy towards Italy in the period between 1944 and 1948.

Until now historians have often been inclined to give much credit to the PCI for its contribution to the democratic achievements of post-Fascist Italy. Typically, summing up PCI's accomplishments in the period between 1943 and 1948, David Travis concludes:

> The Party emerged from the war as one of the principal champions of democracy; its support ensured the inauguration of a parliamentary republic and a democratic constitution in Italy. The Communists were instrumental in the resurgence of an active and potent trade union movement.[67]

Travis's paradoxical conclusion that the PCI 'made the decisive contribution to the return of democracy' in Italy illustrates the fallacy of a historical study proceeding with only half the documentation to hand. Most studies by Italian historians accepted at face value the PCI's self-definition as a Party of 'progressive democracy', fighting for renewal and a growing popular participation in Government against the conservative or outright reactionary aspirations of De Gasperi's Christian Democrats or the Liberals. A minority view portrayed the PCI as following a two-track policy in which the acceptance of democratic rules was always combined with the preparation for the imminent revolution. According to this interpretation, PCI's 'two-faced policy' was, in turn, determined by a permanent clash between two basic tendencies within the Party, that is between its reformist and revolutionary factions and policies.[68] The previous absence of documentary evidence, due to the closure of Soviet archives (incidentally, the PCI also kept its most sensitive documentation in Moscow), made impossible an impartial study of the history of the PCI, especially its relations with the USSR in the Stalinist period. The absence of documentation contributed to the proliferation of ideologically biased evaluations of the PCI's historical record.

An historical paradox of post-war Italy, whose strong and popular left-wing parties were incapable of offering a social-democratic alternative to Christian-Democratic rule, can thus be explained by the Stalinist nature of the PCI. Thanks to its superior organization, the PCI dominated the left-wing coalition, while due to its Stalinist nature it precluded the emergence of a viable left-wing democratic, by definition anti-Stalinist, alternative to the Christian Democrats. The new documentation provides important information, previously hidden from the public, on the activities of Togliatti, and gives new clues for the reassessment of this controversial political figure. 'A moderate Stalinist' seems to be the most appropriate political verdict. Togliatti could be appalled by Stalin's recurrent purges and indiscriminate terror, by the sheer counter-productivity of Stalinist excesses, but from the time of the Comintern he followed Stalin's policy unhesitatingly, out of conviction and shared responsibility for many of Stalin's political decisions. His disapproval of Khrushchev's de-Stalinization as harmful for both the Soviet Union and the international Communist movement and his support of the 1956 invasion of Hungary were logical conclusions to Togliatti's Stalinist career.[69]

Newly available documents permit us to analyse the evolution of Soviet thinking from initially fairly concrete plans of defending immediate Soviet security interests based upon some sort of a division of the world into spheres of influence, and the exploitation of a presumed Anglo-American antagonism, to the later policy of Sovietization of Eastern Europe and attempts to extend the Soviet sphere of influence by all means short of a direct military clash with the West. A huge number of internal documents and analytical reports combined with transcripts of confidential discussions between top Soviet leaders and diplomats, and the leaders of the Communist Parties, provide the missing links for a truly historical investigation of the emergence of a bi-polar world – and of the crucial role European problems played in shaping the US–Soviet confrontation. Stalin's strategy towards Europe between 1944 and 1948 was far more complex and sophisticated than it has usually been assumed. An historical hypothesis of the existence of the Soviet leadership's 'minimum and maximum programmes' for post-war Europe seems to have found its documentary confirmation.[70] The minimum programme consisted in the further strengthening of the Communist Parties in the East European countries where Soviet troops were stationed. The maximum programme included laying down the structural foundations for a parliamentary conquest of power by left-wing coalitions dominated by the Communist Parties and a gradual transition to some sort of 'popular democracy regimes' in the countries of Western Europe outside the Soviet sphere of influence. In both cases an active participation of local Communist Parties was taken for granted. The programmes did not envisage the process of total Sovietization, however. Dimitrov's instructions to Czechoslovakian leaders in December 1944 are most revealing in this regard:

> Do not put the Sovietization of Czechoslovakia on the imminent agenda. We must not try to guess when the appropriate moment will come ... As Stalin has rightly said, we must proceed step by step, and before taking any new step we should consolidate positions already conquered.[71]

New documentation from the Russian archives permits a more profound understanding of Soviet post-war goals and throws new light on the controversial problem of the origins of the Cold War. The Cold War did not develop either out of Soviet excessive preoccupation with security or from a 'spiralling cycle of mistrust' between the two superpowers pursuing essentially defensive, security-oriented policies,[72] but rather from the fundamental incompatibility between the nature and the basic characteristics of Western liberal-democratic and Stalinist societies, whose very existence represented a constant challenge and a source of permanent instability for each other.

Notes

1. The crucial characteristic of Soviet–Italian post-war relations was that they took place on two intertwined and overlapping levels – official diplomatic relations between the two Governments, and the relations between the Stalinist leadership and the Italian Communist Party. This chapter seeks to examine the relations between Moscow and the Italian Communist Party in the light of newly available archival documentation that includes records of regular unofficial meetings between Soviet representatives and Italian Communist leaders, as well as internal Soviet documents regarding Soviet–Italian relations in 1944–8. Especially informative are the minutes of hundreds of meetings between Soviet diplomats, first of all the Soviet Ambassador to Italy, Mikhail Kostylev, and Palmiro Togliatti and other Communist leaders preserved among the records of the AVP RF.
2. Quoted in M. Narinskii, 'Togliatti, Stalin i "povorot v Salerno"', in O. Rzheshevsky (ed.), *Vtoraia mirovaia vojna. Aktualnye problemy* (Moscow: Nauka, 1995) p. 130.
3. V. Pechatnov, 'The Big Three after World War II. New Documents on Soviet Thinking about Post War Relations with the United States and Great Britain', Working Paper 13, Cold War International History Project, Woodrow Wilson International Center for Scholars, 1995, p. 22.

4. E. Ragionieri, 'La svolta politica e sociale', in *Storia d'Italia*, Vol. 4 (Turin: Einaudi, 1976) pp. 2371–4; D. Travis, 'Communism and Resistance in Italy, 1943–8', in T. Judt (ed.), *Resistance and Revolution in Mediterranean Europe 1939–1948* (London–New York: Routledge, 1989) pp. 93–4.
5. For Togliatti's statement to this effect see P. Spriano, *Storia del partito comunista italiano*, Vol. 5: *La resistenza. Togliatti e il partito nuovo* (Turin: Einaudi, 1975) p. 283.
6. The substance of the Stalin–Togliatti meeting is given in Dimitrov's 'Diary', entries 4 and 5 March 1944. This extraordinarily rich source is due to be published in English as *The Diary of Georgi Dimitrov, 1939–1949* (Yale University Press, forthcoming). Minutes of Stalin's conversation with Thorez are in the Stalin collection in the APRF. See V. Volkov, 'Sovetskoe rukovodstvo i nekotorye problemy Yugo-Vostochnoj Evropy v poslednij god vojny, 1944–1945 g.', paper presented at the conference 'The Establishment of the Communist Regimes in Eastern Europe, 1945–1950: A Reassessment' (Moscow, 29–31 March 1994).
7. See Dimitrov's Diary, entry 5 March 1944.
8. APRF, f. 45, op. 1, d. 390, l. 85–93.
9. Togliatti–Kostylev meeting held on 3 November 1944, AVP RF, f. 098, op. 26, p. 152, d. 8, l. 6–7.
10. Kostylev–Togliatti meeting, 25 July 1945, AVP RF, f. 098, op. 29, p. 152, d. 9, l. 169–70.
11. Kostylev–Togliatti meeting, 24 January 1946, AVP RF, f. 098, op. 29, p. 164, d. 8, l. 150.
12. Kostylev to Molotov, 15 October 1944, AVP RF, f. 098, op. 27, p. 159, d. 12, l. 6.
13. Kostylev–Togliatti meeting, 26 August 1945, AVP RF, f. 098, op. 26, p. 152, d. 10, l. 20. See also the conversation between Kostylev and Longo, 26 March 1946, AVP RF, f. 098, op. 29, p. 164, d. 9, l. 183.
14. Thus when the Minister of Finance Scoccimarro was explaining to Kostylev the advantages of his principal proposals, such as monetary reform and a tax on property, he stressed above all the fact that these policies would help to identify rich individuals and allow the state to confiscate large-scale capitals. Kostylev–Scoccimarro meeting, 25 October 1945, AVP RF, f. 098, op. 26, p. 152, d. 10, l. 85–6.
15. Kostylev to Molotov, 7 December 1946, AVP RF, f. 06, op. 9, p. 54, d. 810, l. 14–15.
16. See O. Rzheshevsky, 'Vizit A. Edena v Moskvu v dekabre 1941', *Novaja i novejshaja istorija*, 2 (1994) 91.
17. In a telegram to Tito of 15 April 1944, Stalin and Molotov declared that they considered Yugoslavia 'our main bastion in South Eastern Europe', APRF, f. 56, op. 1, d. 1369, l. 129.
18. Kostylev to Molotov, 6 January 1945, AVP RF, f. 098, op. 26, p. 151, d. 2, l. 31.
19. On British–American conflicts over Trieste in the months preceding the German collapse, see B.F. Smith, E. Agarossi, *Operation Sunrise. The Secret Surrender* (New York: Basic Books, 1979) pp. 172–83.
20. See, for example, Kostylev–Togliatti meeting, 19 February 1945, AVP RF, f. 098, op. 26, p. 152, d. 8, l. 64.
21. The text of the whole letter sent to 'Vittorio'–a pseudonym of Vincenzo Bianco – is in the APC, and has been published by Spriano, *Storia del partito comunista italiano*, pp. 437–8.

22. Cf. P. Pallante, 'La politica dei comunisti italiani dopo la "svolta jugoslava"', *Storia Contemporanea*, 18, 6 (December 1987) 1498. See also R. Gualtieri, *Togliatti e la politica estera italiana dalla resistenza al trattato di pace* (Rome: Editori Riuniti, 1995).
23. Kostylev–Grieco meeting, 21 May 1945, AVP RF, f. 098, op. 26, p. 152, d. 8, l. 374.
24. Kostylev–Reale meeting, 4 May 1945, *ibid.*, l. 339–40.
25. Kostylev–Togliatti meeting, 31 May 1945, *ibid.*, l. 403.
26. Kostylev–Negarville meeting, 19 August 1945, AVP RF, f. 098, op. 26, p. 152, d. 9, l. 195–6.
27. Kostylev–Togliatti meeting, 24 May 1946, AVP RF, f. 098, op. 29, p. 165, d. 10, l. 97.
28. *Ibid.*
29. Reale to Togliatti, 19 June 1946, APC, Carte Togliatti, carte dalla scrivania.
30. Togliatti to Tito, AJBT-KMJ, I–2/42, Belgrade. This letter, written in Russian, was found by L. Gibianskii.
31. *Ibid.*
32. Lavrentiev–Tito meeting, 20 October 1946, AVP RF, f. 0144, op. 30, l. 106.
33. Lavrentiev–Tito meeting, 23 October 1946, *ibid.*, l. 113.
34. Kostylev to Molotov, 7 December 1946, AVP RF, f. 06, op. 9, p. 54, d. 810, l. 1.
35. P. Nenni, *Tempo di guerra fredda. Diari di 1943–1956* (Milan: SugarCo, 1981) p. 296.
36. Togliatti–Kostylev meeting, 8 November 1946, AVP RF, f. 06, op. 9, p. 54, d. 811, l. 20.
37. *Ibid.*
38. Kostylev–Togliatti meeting, 12 September 1946, AVP RF, f. 098, op. 29, p. 165, d. 12, l. 24.
39. Soviet representatives Kostylev and Martynov had to recognize that this was the Italian press's predominant reaction to the Tito–Togliatti agreement. See their respective political letters to Molotov, 8 February 1947 and 7 March 1947, AVP RF, f. 06, op. 9, p. 54, d. 810, l. 1–16 and 28–43.
40. Kostylev–Parri meeting, 20 August 1945, AVP RF, f. 098, op. 31, p. 183, d. 41, l. 12.
41. Kostylev–Ruini meeting, 19 October 1945, AVP RF, f. 098, op. 26, p. 152, d. 9, l. 244.
42. *Ibid.*, l. 245.
43. Kostylev–Valletta meeting, 13 November 1946, AVP RF, f. 06, op. 9, p. 54, d. 811, l. 30–6.
44. Kostylev to Molotov, 6 January 1945, AVP RF, f. 098, op. 26, p. 151, d. 2, l. 30. During the whole of the 1945–7 period, Soviet experts kept making similar recommendations to the leadership, repeating that Soviet–Italian trade 'would act as a counter-weight to the total subordination of the Italian economy to British and especially American capital'. See Mikhailov to Vyshinskii, 19 May 1947, AVP RF, f. 098, op. 30, p. 172, d. 29, l. 73).
45. Mikhailov to Vyshinskii, 19 May 1947, *ibid.*, l. 72–3.
46. Martynov to Molotov, 7 March 1947, AVP RF, f. 098, op. 30, p. 171, d. 14, l. 37–8.

47. For the internal discussion of the problem see Kozyrev to Vyshinskii, 11 February 1948, AVP RF, f. 098, op. 31, p. 183, d. 41, l. 114–15.
48. See, for example, Kostylev–M. Secchia meeting, 6 March 1948, AVP RF, f. 098, op. 31, p. 179, d. 14, l. 171.
49. The following episode is quite characteristic. In January 1948, Ivan Martynov informed Moscow that in his talk with the General Secretary of the Italian Foreign Ministry Fransoni, he had mentioned that 'some articles in the Peace Treaty might facilitate the economic reconstruction of Italy, having in mind the possibility of deliveries of our raw materials to facilitate the reparations'. Irritated, the Head of the First European Department of the Soviet Foreign Ministry, Sergei Kozyrev, wrote on the margins of Martynov's communication: 'It has to be explained to the Comrade Martynov that we are not interested in delivering raw materials to Italy.' See AVP RF, f. 098, op. 31, p. 179, d. 9, l. 69.
50. K. Weatherby, 'Korea, 1949–50. To Attack or Not to Attack? Stalin, Kim Il Sung, and the Prelude to War', *Cold War International History Project Bulletin*, 5 (Spring 1995) 3.
51. See, for example, the minutes of the 1 February 1947 meeting between Molotov and the Italian Ambassador Quaroni, AVP RF, f. 098, op. 31, p. 183, d. 41, l. 18.
52. Kostylev–Nenni meeting, 16 November 1946, AVP RF, f. 06, op. 9, p. 54, d. 811, l. 54–5.
53. Kostylev–Nenni meeting, 27 November 1946, *ibid.*, l. 80.
54. For a typical example of this conceptual framework applied to Italy see the 1947 'Memorandum on the Economic Situation in Italy' sent from the Rome Embassy to Moscow, AVP RF, f. 098, op. 31, p. 188, d. 77, l. 199–201.
55. See Bogemsky–M. Secchia meeting, 3 April 1948, AVP RF, f. 098, op. 31, p. 179, d. 10.
56. For the text of Molotov's 26 March 1948 ciphered telegram to Kostylev, see M. Narinskii, 'Stalin, Togliatti, Thorez i politicheskaia liniia kompartii v kontse vtoroi mirovoi voiny', paper presented at the International Conference 'Le relazioni tra l'Unione Sovietica e i partiti comunisti francese e italiano' (L'Aquila, May 1995), p. 21.
57. See Raymond Aron's criticisms of Hans Morgenthau, who placed the concept of national interest at the centre of his theory of international relations. R. Aron, *Paix et guerre entre les nations* (Paris: Calmann-Levy,1984) pp. 97–102.
58. G. Procacci (ed.), G. Adibekov, A. Di Biagio, L. Gibianskii, F. Gori, S. Pons (co-eds), *The Cominform. Minutes of the Three Conferences 1947/1948/1949*, Fondazione Feltrinelli, *Annali*, XXX (Milan: Feltrinelli, 1994) p. 457.
59. Togliatti's phrase, reported in G. Bocca, *Palmiro Togliatti*, Vol. 2 (Bari: Laterza, 1977) p. 395.
60. C. Maier, 'The Politics of Productivity: Foundations of American International Economic Policy after World War II', *International Organization*, 3 (1977) 626.
61. See the meetings Boghemsky–Robotti, 31 March 1948, AVP RF, f. 098, op. 31, p. 179, d. 10, l. 48; Martynov–Platone, 31 March 1948, *ibid.*, l. 43–5; Martynov–Di Vittorio, 2 April 1948, *ibid.*, l. 37–8; Kostylev–M. Secchia, 14 April 1948, AVP RF, f. 098, op. 31, p. 179, d. 15, l. 10–15.
62. Kostylev–Togliatti meeting, 19 April 1948, *ibid.*, l. 53.

63. Boghemsky–Robotti meeting, 31 March 1948, AVP RF, f. 098, op. 31, p. 179, d. 10, l. 48.
64. According to Togliatti, 'the Christian Democrats stole no less than half a million of votes'. Kostylev–Togliatti meeting, 26 April 1948, AVP RF, f. 098, op. 31, p. 179, d. 15, l. 48–9. To rid himself of blame for his predictions of the Front's victory, Kostylev added: 'I personally believe the DC stole between a million and a half and two million votes', *ibid.*
65. Boghemsky–Robotti meeting, 24 April 1948, AVP RF, f. 098, op. 31, p. 179, d. 10, l. 65.
66. Kostylev–Togliatti meeting, 26 April 1948, AVP RF, f. 098, op. 31, p. 179, d. 15, l. 47–8; Kostylev–M. Secchia meeting, 4 May 1948, *ibid.*, l. 20–2.
67. Travis, 'Communism and Resistance', p. 107.
68. P. Di Loreto, *Togliatti e la 'doppiezza'. Il PCI tra democrazia e insurrezione 1944–49* (Bologna: Il Mulino, 1991) p. 27.
69. N. Bocenina, *La segretaria di Togliatti. Memorie* (Florence: Ponte alle Grazie, 1993); *Cold War International History Project Bulletin*, 5 (Spring 1995) 32–3.
70. W. Taubman, *Stalin's American Policy: From Entente to Détente to Cold War* (New York: Norton, 1982) pp. 74–5; Volkov, 'Sovetskoe rukovodstvo', pp. 14–17.
71. Cited in V. Mariina, 'Korreliatsiia politicheskoi strategii VKPb, Kominterna i KPC v gody vtoroi mirovoi voiny', paper presented at the conference 'The Establishment of the Communist Regimes in Eastern Europe, 1945–1950: A Reassessment' (Moscow, 29–31 March 1994), pp. 30–1.
72. M. Leffler, *A Preponderance of Power: National Security, the Truman Administration, and the Cold War* (Stanford: Stanford University Press, 1992) pp. 97–8.

11 Stalin and the Prospects for Post-War Europe: a Comment on Chapters 1, 2 and 7

Alexander Dallin

Reconstructing a particular political actor's perception of a problem facing him, and his calculus regarding it, is always a difficult matter. It is especially difficult half a century later, and uniquely so in the case of Stalin. The best the historian, armed with an awareness of what actually happened, can do is to engage in a form of heuristic triangulation – using whatever documentary record there is, along with memoirs by insiders as well as outside observers, and of course published contemporary sources. None of this is without risk: documents, however authentic, can be vastly misleading; observers and memoirs may provide only a glimpse into another's outlook; logic and coherence need not always be the best guides to reality; and actual events may reflect not only the implementation of policy decisions but unintended consequences as well. Manifestly, history writing requires not only using all available materials but also refraining from taking at face value any or all the evidence at hand. Documents, moreover, tend to be snapshots whereas political reality is often far more fluid, indeterminate, or ambiguous than a piece of paper can, or wishes to, convey. Such caution is indicated, for instance, in using the interesting *Pieck – Aufzeichnungen*[1] to reconstruct Stalin's expectations for post-war Europe and his policies regarding it (see Chapter 2). For example, even if we assume (perhaps rashly) that Pieck correctly recorded what he was told, what Stalin tells Wilhelm Pieck is not necessarily what Stalin thinks. That *caveat* is particularly indicated in view of the conflicting picture that emerges from our general knowledge of how Stalin operated; from his wartime negotiations with the Western Allies; from later reconstructions of Stalin's conversations with other figures (be it Viacheslav Molotov or Milovan Djilas), which must be handled with similar caution; and from Soviet and other archival records now made available by Russian and foreign scholars.

Stalin's policy toward Europe, and in particular the future of Germany, was bound to reflect the sort of conflicting pulls that so often confronted Soviet (and not only Soviet) policy-makers. On the one hand, the victorious advance of the Red Army into Eastern Europe and ultimately the Soviet victory in the war presented Stalin with a unique opportunity to extend the area of his control. Whatever our conclusion about the balance of his motivations – ideological/communist and Russian/geopolitical, defensive and offensive, or whatever else – clearly, given his life-long world view so often reiterated and reaffirmed, it would have been treasonous not to attempt with all possible means to maximize power – and for him international power prominently included territory. At the end of World War II the possible gains were massive indeed – manifestly greater than the bits of territory, such as Petsamo, Klaipeda, or northern Bukovina, that Moscow had fiercely bargained over in 1939–41 – and they needed to be consolidated. As Molotov reminisced many years later, 'My task as minister of foreign affairs was to expand the borders of our fatherland. And it seems that Stalin and I coped with this task quite well.'[2]

On the other hand, Stalin was keenly aware of the constraints imposed on his behaviour by the wartime alliance with the United States and the United Kingdom. For a number of perfectly good reasons – from international security to economic benefit – Stalin was eager to maintain and extend the alliance as long as possible beyond the end of the war. This meant not antagonizing his Western partners by asking for, or indeed advancing, too much too fast. It also meant proceeding at a carefully measured step – and occasional stop – in the transformation of the new East European sphere in the Soviet image. The same strategy was also called for out of the realization that, in Eastern Europe and the future East Germany, there was bound to be a good deal of hostility to the Soviet presence.

Stalin had been aptly described – well prior to World War II – as the master of dosage. Indeed, he knew instinctively how often to administer how many pills to his intended victims (as well as to his partners). He had honed this skill at home, and he was now prepared to apply it abroad. In 1945 Communists in Eastern Europe and East Germany, much to their annoyance, were instructed *not* to strike for power. Moscow sought to restrain Tito from pursuing his territorial ambitions at the expense of his neighbours; and Stalin's advice to the Yugoslav partisans during the war was *not* to put a red star on their caps, which would only 'scare the British'.[3]

This policy of tactical restraint was equally in evidence in regard to the Communist Parties in the West. Indeed, the French Communist Party, though uniquely equipped with weapons at the time, after years in the maquis, after the Allied landing in Normandy in 1944 were well advised *not* to strike for power; there could be little doubt that the decision to participate in the Gaullist Coalition Government had Moscow's unambiguous approval. Likewise, the advice to the Italian comrades to co-operate with the right – even the monarchists – in joining a post-Mussolini Government meant stretching the notion of a popular front and evoked more than a few raised eyebrows in the PCI.[4]

Seen in this light, Soviet policy towards post-war Germany fits well into the broader picture of Stalin's calculations. If the general orientation was to maximize power and control, any given decision was subject to a crude and often instinctive cost/benefit analysis. Stalin's frame of mind is well illustrated by a conversation related by Anthony Eden. It was December 1941, at the height of the German advance on Moscow, and as Stalin received Eden in the Kremlin, they could hear the German artillery booming in the distance, on the outskirts of the capital. 'We should not underestimate Hitler. He is a very able man. But he made one mistake. He did not know when to stop,' Stalin said. As Eden relates it, he must have smiled, whereupon Stalin turned to him and said: 'I know why you're smiling. You think that if we are victorious I shall not know when to stop. You are wrong. I do know.'[5]

This was part of his skill at dosage – not to miss opportunities but also to know when to hold back. Of course, as the following years were to reveal, this did not ensure him against serious errors of judgement. Nor does it imply that Soviet policy was neatly packaged, unanimously adopted (even under conditions of Stalinist controls), or consistently pursued. Indeed, Aleksei Filitov's chapter in this volume (Chapter 1) illustrates some interesting diversity of positions among senior diplomatic planners as well as the espousal, by at least some Soviet officials, of positions quite contrary to those ultimately adopted by the USSR.[6] The bureaucratic struggle over foreign-policy issues as well as confusion and inconsistencies are also dramatically illustrated by Sven Holtsmark in Chapter 7.[7] The relationship between the establishment bureaucracy and the topmost leadership on these issues remains to be studied further.

Perhaps the most difficult issue both for Soviet policy-makers and for later analysts has been the definition of post-war policy towards Germany. One possible approach to it can be explored by pointing to some of the conflicting strands that entered into consideration. At some level of maximum aspirations of course the absorption of all of Germany, or control of it, was bound to be at least an ill-defined goal in Moscow. Such a perspective failed to deal with the dilemma whether to build up a future Germany as an ally or satellite, or whether – in pursuit of an anti-German animus which (as in the West) argued strongly against the recreation of any German state or states – Germany should be deindustrialized and colonized: a view that weakened with the passage of time. More seriously, Soviet policy-makers faced the likely claims of the Western Allies to their share of Germany, claims that –

especially after the Allied landing in Normandy – Moscow could not expect to ignore. Furthermore, there were the wartime agreements on the several zones of occupation which Moscow had accepted; and finally, the Soviet demands for reparations from Germany would presumably permit it to garner considerable resources from the Ruhr and other industrial and mining centres in the West.

The result of such conflicting pulls made not only for some diversity of views within the Soviet administration[8] but the symptomatic dilemma whether to prefer complete control over part of Germany to lesser influence over all of it. Stalin's characteristically hard-headed response was to consolidate control and transformation in the Soviet zone – the future DDR – while continuing to advocate a united Germany to which Moscow would address substantial economic and other appeals and demands. Milovan Djilas cites Stalin as remarking early on: 'This war is not as in the past; whoever occupies a territory also imposes on it his own social system. Everyone imposes his own system as far as his army can reach. It cannot be otherwise.' And in 1948 Stalin is again quoted as remarking: 'The West will make West Germany their own, and we shall turn East Germany into our own state.'[9] By then the two-camp approach in Soviet policy had again become dominant.

We cannot be sure we know what Stalin thought. In particular, we cannot tell to what extent he was responding to, or anticipating, his Western partners' behaviour. Given everything we know about Bolshevik thinking and Stalin's own record, one may best hypothesize that in his mind the distinction between offence and defence, between initiative and response was a purely technical one – a difference perhaps embedded in bourgeois international law, but in his mind, if not altogether obliterated, then hardly a controlling consideration.

In 1945 and the following years, Stalin was far from thinking of marching the Soviet Army westwards to the Atlantic: those American or West German analysts who voiced alarm about such contingencies were missing at least two vital dimensions. One was the enormous cost that the Soviet Union – its people and its economy – incurred during four years of murderous war. The exhaustion and the need to recover were bound to be paramount in the leadership's mind even if Stalin would not let on in dealing with his wartime allies so as not to jeopardize his gains by admitting to weakness. The other aspect of the same problem was the cost incurred by the Soviet armed forces. It had taken an unprecedented effort – and an entirely unique enemy – to mobilize the army (and for that matter, the civilian 'rear') to crawl on their bellies from Stalingrad to Berlin. As Moscow made unmistakably clear to its West European comrades, Communists abroad could not expect the Soviet troops to do the same one more time in support of Communists in Italy or France...[10]

Finally, both Stalin and his successors – with a few notable exceptions, such as Khrushchev's Cuban missile ploy – tended to pursue a foreign policy of relatively low risk. To be sure, this assertion must not ignore the question to what extent Moscow accurately gauged the risks of a given line of conduct. And such a generalization, even if accurate, does not permit us to project it *a priori* onto a particular set of political circumstances. To Stalin, there was little to gain and much to lose from a 'premature' and perhaps unfavourable confrontation with the Western Powers, and the United States in particular. In this sense, a Soviet policy of seeming moderation coupled with *de facto* if gradual *Gleichschaltung* made perfect sense.

The above picture may well need to be refined or corrected in some particulars as additional archival evidence comes to light. It needs to be challenged and, if appropriate, modified. But there is nothing in the record to sustain the argument that, in the long run, Stalin wanted a 'bourgeois-democratic' government anywhere anytime – surely not in the Soviet Union, surely not in Eastern Europe, and surely not in Germany.

Notes

1. R. Badstuebner, W. Loth (eds), *Wilhelm Pieck – Aufzeichnungen* (Berlin: Akademie-Verlag, 1994). See also W. Loth, *Stalins ungeliebtes Kind* (Berlin: Rowohlt, 1994).
2. F. Chuev (ed.), *Sto sorok besed s Molotovym* (Moscow: Terra, 1991) (Engl. edn, with A. Resis, *Molotov Remembers* [Chicago: Ivan R. Dee, 1993]) p. 8.
3. '... by which he meant that we ought to avoid anything that might alarm [the British] into thinking that a revolution was going on in Yugoslavia or an attempt at Communist control.' See M. Djilas, *Conversations with Stalin* (New York: Harcourt, Brace, 1962) p. 73. On the initial go-slow policy, see also, for example, W. Leonhard, *Child of the Revolution* (Chicago: Regnery, 1962), and Z. Brzezinski, *The Soviet Bloc* (Cambridge, Mass.: Harvard University Press, 1967) ch. 3. Examples of Stalinist dosage in regard to Eastern Europe include his advice to Tito to postpone Yugoslavia's absorption of Albania so as 'not to attract the attention of the English and the Americans', especially given his simultaneous push for Trieste; and similarly, his advice that, while he desired a federation of Yugoslavia and Bulgaria, a first step might be a treaty of friendship and mutual assistance between the two states. See 'Poslednii visit i Broza Tito k I.V. Stalinu', 27.5.1946, *Istoricheskii arkhiv*, 2 (1993) 16-35. Reference to Stalin's alleged remark that it might take ten or fifteen years before the Communists could consolidate complete control in Hungary, has been attributed to Mátyás Rákosi. (The references are cited in W. Taubman, *Stalin's American Policy* [New York: Norton, 1982] pp. 79, 263.)
4. In the final stage of Stalinist frenzy, in 1952, the French Communist Party accused two of its prominent veterans, André Marty and Charles Tillon, of a number of sectarian and 'Blanquist' crimes among which

figured prominently having advocated the seizure of power in 1944. For a summary, see J. Fauvet, *Histoire du Parti Communiste Français* (Paris: Fayard, 1965) II, pp. 246–58; A. Rieber, *Stalin and the French Communist Party* (New York: Columbia University Press, 1962) ch. 6. For Marty's own version, see A. Marty, *L'Affaire Marty* (Paris: Deux Rives, 1955). On The West European Parties, see also the bitter partisan perspective in F. Claudín, *The Communist Movement* (New York: Monthly Review, 1975) Vol. 2, ch. 5. See in particular the paper in the present volume by Elena Aga-Rossi and Victor Zaslavsky, 'The Soviet Union and the Italian Communist Party, 1944–8' and the sources cited there. On Soviet 'advice' to Western comrades, see also for example, J. Barth Urban, *Moscow and the Italian Communist Party* (Ithaca, N.Y.: Cornell University Press, 1986), ch. 6.
5. Anthony Eden, in *Time*, 17 July 1950.
6. A. Filitov, 'Problems of Post-War Construction in Soviet Foreign Policy Conceptions during World War II', in the present volume.
7. S. Holtsmark, 'The Limits to Soviet Influence: Soviet Diplomats and the Pursuit of Strategic Interests in Norway and Denmark 1944–7', in the present volume.
8. Cf. N. Naimark's *The Russians in Germany: A History of the Soviet Zone of Occupation* (Cambridge, Mass.: Harvard University Press, 1995). See also *Molotov*, p. 60.
9. Djilas, *Conversations*, pp. 114, 153 and Id., *The New Class* (New York: Praeger, 1957) p. 197. See also W. Pfeiler, *Deutschland politische Optionen der Sowjetunion* (Melle: Knoth, 1987).
10. Royal Institute of International Affairs, *The Soviet–Yugoslav Dispute* (London: RIIA, 1948) p. 51.

12 How much of the Cold War was Inevitable? A Comment on Chapters 4, 6, 8 and 9

William Taubman

Taken together and separately, the four chapters on which I am commenting raise a general question which transcends all of them: Exactly how sharp, enduring and dangerous did the Cold War have to be? In view of a variety of factors ranging from the vacuum of power that followed World War II, to the ideological gulf between Communism and capitalism, to geopolitical conflict between East and West, some sort of conflict was inevitable. So says Mikhail Narinskii on the very first page of Chapter 4, 'The Soviet Union and the Berlin Crisis, 1948-9', and I agree. But did that conflict have to become a military as well as a political struggle fraught with crises and even war? That is the question these chapters can help to answer.

As I read these chapters, I recalled that as World War II came to an end, the two sides – the Soviet Union on one side and the United States and Great Britain on the other – were closer than we may remember on a key issue that later came to divide them, the issue of spheres of influence, and especially of a Soviet sphere of influence in Europe. We all know that Stalin insisted on such a sphere of influence in Europe. We all know that Stalin insisted on such a sphere in Eastern Europe, particularly in the area occupied by the Red Army, and it is often said that this insistence precipitated the Cold War. But it is also true that Winston Churchill and Franklin Roosevelt were generally prepared to allow Stalin such a sphere, provided that the Soviet leader was relatively discreet in how he went about establishing and consolidating it.

In the end, of course, Stalin proved anything but discreet. On the contrary, his tactics in Eastern Europe were crude, brutal and ruthless. And that in turn produced a hardening of Western policy, which in turn hardened the Soviet stance in an escalating spiral of distrust and enmity. Moreover, this cycle was further intensified by various other Soviet errors involving misunderstanding the West or miscalculating its reactions to Soviet moves. Whether these errors were mainly Stalin's, or emerged from the bureaucratic policies of his totalitarian regime, is another tantalizing question that is posed but not fully answered by the chapters under review. None of this is to say, of course, that the West was without sin. But it is not the West, but rather the Soviet Union, which is the subject of these chapters and therefore of these comments.

How exactly do these chapters relate to the larger theme I have defined? Two of them (Jukka Nevakivi's 'The Soviet Union and Finland after the War, 1944–53' (Chapter 6), and Artiom Ulunian's 'The Soviet Union and 'the Greek Question', 1946–53: Problems and Appraisals' (Chapter 9)) relate to places where Stalin behaved with just the sort of discretion which, if applied across the board, might have served to reduce the virulence of Cold War conflict. Chapter 8 – R. Craig Nation's 'A Balkan Union? Southeastern Europe in Soviet Security Policy, 1944–8' – treats an area where Stalin's policies showed some discretion, but also a much grimmer face. Chapter 4, by Mikhail Narinskii, on the Berlin crisis, shows how once the Cold War began in earnest, Stalin made it even worse by miscalculating Western determination to pursue hard-line policies that his own previous moves had provoked.

With that summary, let me turn to each of the chapters in turn.

Rather than being central to the Cold War, Finland is usually considered peripheral to the conflict. But in view of the considerations I have outlined, Soviet relations with Finland are very significant. If Stalin had been willing and able to 'Finlandize' the rest of Eastern Europe (that is, to treat it as he treated Finland), instead of Sovietizing and Stalinizing it, then the West would have been much less alarmed, which raises the main questions of Chapter 6: 'Why did the dictator make this exception to the process of Sovietizing all the other countries concerned in 1945–8? Did he have some sentimental or personal motives in allowing Finland to survive, or did he leave this country out for particular *raisons d'état*?'

Nevakivi's answer to his own questions in Chapter 6 is that various considerations at various moments shaped Stalin's behaviour: the lack of sufficient Soviet troops to defeat Finland militarily, the strength of potential Finnish resistance, self-restraint by the Finns including an early willingness to pay reparations to the USSR. In short, Soviets and Finns behaved very differently in regard to each other than, say, did Soviets and Poles. In the latter case, the Soviets proved far more determined to control Poland, and the Poles far more resistant to Soviet designs. Also relevant, but in a way that is not fully clear in Nevakivi's account, is internecine Soviet bureaucratic strife. Nevakivi demonstrates that there were such disagreements, but not how they affected Soviet policy towards Finland, perhaps an inevitable omission given the paucity of Soviet sources, but one that marks other chapters as well.

In posing the general question illuminated by all four chapters, I stressed Soviet moves in Eastern Europe that alarmed the West. But equally if not more alarming, were presumed Soviet ambitions to expand in what the West regarded as its own sphere. For the most part, however, Stalin proved much more cautious in the West than the East, and Greece is the classic case. What struck me in Ulunian's account in Chapter 9 is how consistently cautious Stalin was in Greece, how (with the exception of a couple instances) he rebuffed continuing Greek Communist pleas to support an all-out armed drive for power on their part.

Like Nevakivi, Ulunian takes note of bureaucratic tensions in Moscow, this time between the Soviet Ministry of Foreign Affairs and the Central Committee department in charge of relations with the other Communist Parties. But once again, the actual influence of these tensions on Soviet policy towards Greece remains unclear.

Turning to the Balkans, the two-sidedness of Stalin's policy mentioned above stands out in Nation's Chapter 8. On the one hand, Stalin tried to rein in the fiery Yugoslavs so as to avoid unnecessarily complicating relations with the West. On the other hand, he treated allied Communist Parties as crudely as he did non-Communist forces in Eastern Europe. If Stalin felt so threatened by autonomous actions undertaken by his Balkan Allies, surely he could never have been reassured that the intentions of his capitalist adversaries were benign. If he used schemes like the Balkan Federation for narrow instrumental purposes – that is, to provoke and expose, and divide and conquer other Communist Parties – how could he have agreed with the West to live and let live?

The Berlin crisis of 1948 doesn't just illustrate Stalin's capacity for miscalculation. It also fits his penchant for self-fulfilling prophecy. Assuming the worst of his adversaries, he ended up provoking them into the very behaviour he had assumed, in the Berlin case, into an even greater determination to strengthen Western unity and to defend West Germany and West Berlin if necessary by military means.

By 1948, Stalin assumed the Western powers were intent on constructing a bloc including West Germany, but also that he could prevent them from doing so, and perhaps oust them from West Berlin, by applying force. Much of the Berlin crisis reminds me of the Cuban missile crisis 14 years later: the secret planning for the blockade of Berlin, the plan to exert political-military pressure while at the same time ruling out actual war, the willingness to retreat when initial aims weren't achieved. But the most striking parallel of all, which underlines Stalin's (and later Khrushchev's) ability to the make the worst of a bad situation, was the way the two crises ended – in a humiliating Soviet backdown and defeat.

One final observation: It used to be thought that however dangerous and deadly dictatorships were, they had the advantage over democracies of being able to conduct more rational and consistent foreign policies. No one denies that Stalin was skilful in his early Cold War diplomacy. But the main point of my remarks is that in the end he was too skilful for his own good, too prone to creating the very united front against him that it was his constant ambition to prevent. Was this pattern primarily the result of his own personal miscalculations? Did it also reflect failures of the bureaucratic system which he dominated but on which he nonetheless relied? None of the hints in the four chapters about Soviet bureaucratic in-fighting suggests the existence of open dissent. But were his advisers divided between those who dared to provide him with realistic information and those who preferred to tell him what he wanted to hear? If he had allowed somewhat more openness, might that have enabled him to avoid unnecessary errors? These questions await further answers from newly opened Soviet archives, even though the overall pattern of the Cold War's origins, illuminated in chapters like those discussed here, seems fairly well established.

Part II

The Cominform and the Soviet Bloc

13 Stalin's Foreign Policy and the Cominform, 1947–53
Nataliia I. Egorova

Archive sources recently made accessible have enabled scholars to study more closely the Soviet Union's use of the Cominform to consolidate the Eastern bloc and complete the 'Sovietization' of the people's democracies.[1] It has become clear, however, that in initiating the Cominform the Soviet leaders pursued aims that reached beyond those limits. An American historian who has worked in our archives uses the concept 'dualism' in relation to the working of the new 'centre for co-ordination'.[2] In this chapter I continue my investigation[3] of the relation between the 'state' and 'party' diplomacy of the Soviet leadership and their mutual influence.

In the materials prepared for Malenkov's report to the founding meeting of the Cominform in September 1947 we find a sentence in which the speaker explains that he is *not* going to refer to those links between the Soviet Party and other CPs which were effected 'by the Soviet state through official channels'.[4]

The most important stimulus to the creation of the Cominform was the Soviet Party's reaction to the expulsion of the Communists from the Governments of France and Italy in May 1947.[5] The Kremlin had been disturbed by the fact that the action of the French CP in voting against the economic programme of the French Prime Minister, Ramadier, hoping to make him resign, 'was quite unexpected'.[6] On Molotov's instructions, the leaders of all the CPs of Western Europe were told this by the respective Soviet ambassadors.[7] These events exhausted Moscow's patience with the independent activities of the French and Italian CPs, particularly in the parliamentary sphere. It was decided to put an end to ideological compromise with the Socialists and the liberal bourgeoisie. At the September 1947 meeting Zhdanov proclaimed both the conception of 'two camps' and a new line of 'exposure' directed against the Socialist Parties. This change of orientation had been adopted in principle even before the events connected with the Marshall Plan, though that development confirmed it.[8] In Zhdanov's drafts for his report he explained the expulsion of the Communists from the Governments of France and Italy as fulfilment of the principal condition for American aid to be given to those countries.[9] Since the French comrades had 'yielded to blackmail' it was not incumbent on the USSR to organize resistance, and the main task of the Western CPs was to strengthen the position of the USSR. This ruled out of order the tendency for those Parties to stress their independence.[10]

The importance of the Marshall Plan in the thinking which led up to the formation of the Cominform is proved by documents prepared by the Foreign Policy Department of the Soviet Party.[11] Because the Plan was seen as a manifestation of American economic and political expansion in Europe, the new international centre had to serve not only a 'Party' but also a 'foreign-policy' function. One of the Department's memoranda for Zhdanov spoke of the USA's intention to implement the programme of John Foster Dulles, 'to create on the basis of the Ruhr a West-European Federation (including Germany, or at least Western Germany) which would become a bastion against Communism and the Soviet Union'.[12] The Truman administration was said to have endorsed Dulles's idea, and Secretary of State Marshall's plan for 'reconstructing' Europe was the result.[13]

Zhdanov's report was composed, accordingly, so as to demonstrate to the West the determination of the USSR to resist anti-Soviet designs. The conception of Soviet foreign relations formulated in the report was based on the idea – originally expressed already in 1946[14] and finally crystallized after the adoption of the Marshall Plan and the Truman Doctrine – that international political forces were divided into two opposing tendencies. This idea now took the form of 'the imperialist and anti-democratic camp, on the one hand, and, on the other, the anti-imperialist and democratic camp'.[15] Both Zhdanov and Malenkov made clear in their reports that though Soviet foreign policy accepted long-term co-existence of the capitalist and Socialist systems, the USSR's readiness to maintain normal relations with Western Powers did not mean renunciation of the ideological struggle. On the contrary, this would be intensified – the main field of class struggle was now the international arena.[16]

At the end of the first Cominform meeting, on 28 September, it was agreed that all the public materials arising from it should be published simultaneously by all the CPs on 5 October.[17] It has been speculated that this date was chosen so as to coincide with statements to be made by Truman and Marshall on international politics.[18] However, publication of Zhdanov's report was held back until foreign reactions to the announcement of the creation of the Cominform became known. This decision was communicated to the participant parties in a letter dated 17 October.[19]

A report from the Soviet Party's Foreign Policy Department sent to the Politburo on 11 October noted that, although most of the foreign

CPs had accepted the Cominform resolutions as a guide to action, they had not been able to utilize 'the dismay among the right-wing Socialists in such a way as to prevent them from quickly recovering from the blow they had suffered'.[20] We can conclude that the 'suddenness' with which the Cominform was launched had had a dual effect. Its purpose had been to crush any possible resistance among the participants to the idea of 'co-ordination' and also to make a powerful impression on opponents in the West, including both the Social-Democrats and the Western Governments. The foreign press did not fail to note the significance of the presence at the foundation meeting of Malenkov, who, besides his Party posts, was Vice-Chairman of the USSR Council of Ministers.

The official Soviet reply to foreign comments on the establishment of the Cominform was given in *Pravda* of 10 October.[21] Against criticism by the Socialists, the right of the Communists was affirmed to 'organize resistance to the American plan to enslave the European countries' – an admission of the Cominform's main purpose. The *Pravda* article was written in consultation with the Soviet Foreign Ministry, as we know from correspondence between P.N. Pospelov and Molotov himself.[22]

The CC of the Soviet Party regarded publication of Zhdanov's report 'On the international situation' as a statement by the USSR of the basic principles guiding it relations with the West in the changed international situation. During the preparations for the first Cominform meeting Dimitrov put up a proposal for an International Committee to Combat the Danger of War and Fascism. L. Baranov, the deputy head of the Party's Foreign Policy Department, counterposed to this a proposal that the Cominform issue a special appeal 'to the democratic organizations of the world', calling on the peoples to fight 'against the warmongers and against attempts by reaction to encroach upon the economic independence and national sovereignty of the peoples'.[23] However, the time had not yet come for an ideological and political campaign to defend peace. The primary task was to oppose the Marshall Plan – though the thesis about the danger of a new war did appear both in Zhdanov's report and in the Cominform's first documents.

After the signing, on 17 March 1948, of the treaty creating the Western Union (the Brussels Pact) and then, at the beginning of 1949 the creation of NATO, 'the war danger' began to be taken as more than a propaganda slogan. The Soviet Government interpreted these moves as being closely connected with the aggressive intentions of the Marshall Plan, as contrary to the Yalta and Potsdam agreements, and as bringing near the danger of a new war.[24]

The first step towards the organization of a movement of partisans of peace was the Congress of Cultural Workers in Defence of Peace which was convened by the CPs of Poland and France at Breslau (Wrocław) in August 1948. In April 1949 came the World Congress of Partisans of Peace, held simultaneously in Paris and Prague. The Soviet Politburo assigned a sum between 70 000 and 100 000 dollars for the preparation of this congress, and on 8 March ordered the launching of a world-wide campaign of support for it.[25] The Foreign Policy Department of the Soviet Party's CC included in the agenda for the Cominform Secretariat's meeting on 14–16 June 'statements by the representatives of the parties on measures for further development of the movement of the partisans of peace'.[26] This was approved by Stalin.

The brief supplied to Suslov, as the Soviet Party's representative in the Cominform Secretariat, was classified 'Top Secret'. It set out frankly the views of the Soviet leaders on the task of the Cominform in the 'peace campaign': 'In the struggle for peace the All-Union CP(B) does not confine itself to the diplomatic and state means which are available to it as a ruling party ... We consider that the CPs can strengthen, with all the resources at their disposal, the rebuff given to Anglo-American and other imperialist propaganda.'[27] The chief task of Communists in the immediate future was to organize the masses 'for struggle against war, for developing the movement of partisans of peace'.[28]

On 14 June, however, the day when the Cominform Secretariat began its work, the Politburo decided to postpone this matter to the next meeting of the Cominform itself. Explaining this sudden change to the agenda (the question of measures to be taken against 'the Tito clique' was also postponed) Suslov referred to 'the great importance' of these matters, which necessitated that they be discussed 'not in the Secretariat but at the next meeting of the Information Bureau,[29] Thus, in the foreign-policy priorities of the Soviet Party, the activity of the Cominform to mobilize the forces of the partisans of peace was seen as being just as important as the struggle, begun at the 1948 meeting, against Tito and his supporters, who were allegedly being used by the Anglo-American imperialists for their aggressive aim.

The November 1949 meeting of the Cominform in Budapest was preceded by another important event in Stalin's 'peace offensive'. On 25–27 August an All-Union Conference of Partisans of Peace was held in Moscow and elected a Soviet Committee for the Defence of Peace. This became a major instrument for mobilizing the forces of the partisans of peace through such organizations as the World Federation of Trade Unions, the International Democratic Federation of Women, the World Federation of Democratic Youth, and so on.

If we remove from Suslov's report to the Cominform's 1949 meeting all the propaganda clichés and then compare it with the Politburo's directive to the Soviet delegation at the fourth session of the United

Nations General Assembly we perceive that all of its propositions repeated the contents of that document. The directive stated, among other things, that the General Assembly should take note of the peoples' will to peace.

How extensive, though, at that time, was the world-wide anti-war movement which was intended to make the UN endorse the Soviet Union's peace initiatives? The Soviet Party's Foreign Policy Commission had a two-fold task – to activate the peace movement through the Cominform and also through the Soviet Peace Committee.[30] That was why the third Cominform meeting accorded this movement such importance. The contribution of the Soviet Party's chief ideologist (in July 1949 Suslov again became head of the CC's Department of Agitation and Propaganda) to the theoretical justification of the fight for peace as the central task, in the given international situation, of the world's CPs consisted in the following thesis. The weakening of the imperialist camp (through a change in the relation of forces favourable to 'the forces of the camp of peace, democracy and socialism') did not signify a reduction in the danger of war. Marxist–Leninist theory taught that war was the means by which imperialism resolved its internal contradictions. And on the CPs of Western Europe, on those countries which the American imperialists sought to use for their aggressive plans, particularly important tasks were incumbent.[31]

How these appeals were received by the representatives of the French and Italian CPs we can judge from the materials of the discussion[32] at the Cominform meeting and from the reports by Togliatti and Duclos. In particular, Duclos stressed, in his report on the Rules for the Cominform, which had to be approved at this meeting, that he was directing the attention of every party to its 'international obligations'.[33] The French CP bore special responsibility in that connection, since Paris was the seat of the Standing Committee of the World Congress for the Defence of Peace, headed by F. Joliot-Curie.

Not only the French and Italian CPs but all the CPs of Western Europe accepted Suslov's report and the resolutions of the Cominform meeting as their direct guide to action. Thus, the Politburo of the Belgian CP adopted on 3 December a resolution that it would use every means to fulfil with honour the task 'which the Information Bureau has assigned to the Communist Parties'.[34]

The brightest page in the Cominform's activity to extend the movement of the partisans of peace is the story of the collection of signatures for the Stockholm Appeal. In accordance with a decision by the Soviet Politburo on 17 January 1950, 'On measures for further development of the movement of partisans of peace', a plenary session of the Standing Committee of the World Congress of Partisans of Peace was held in Stockholm at the beginning of March, at which the well-known Appeal was adopted.³⁵ It called for banning of the atom bomb and condemnation as war criminals of whatever government used it first. A mass campaign was to be launched to collect signatures to this appeal. To the Cominform was assigned, as we see from the materials of its Secretariat's meeting on 20–22 April 1950, the function of centre for co-ordinating the campaign. The Secretariat was originally not to have met till June, but, on Stalin's orders, its meeting was brought forward to April, when the signature-collection campaign was due to begin.³⁶ In his speech at the Secretariat meeting Suslov, while repeating what he had said to the Cominform, added something new. He spoke twice of peaceful competition between the two systems and criticized 'fatalistic' talk of inevitable war.³⁷ He drew attention to the publication in the Soviet press, for the first time, on 22 April 1950, of two documents from 1920 in which Lenin spoke of the possibility of peaceful co-existence between Soviet Russia and capitalist states.³⁸

There are grounds for concluding that the year 1950 saw a turn in Stalin's foreign policy,³⁹ towards reducing confrontation and seeking ways to open a dialogue with the West, especially on Germany. This turn entailed a change in tactics. Togliatti had spoken, in his report to the Cominform's 1949 meeting, of the need for joint action with left-wing Socialists.⁴⁰ However, the Korean War, which began on 22 June 1950, dealt a grave blow to this prospect.

Suslov emphasized the priority to be given to the signatures campaign, especially in the USA and Britain. Hundreds of millions of signatures must be collected, 'otherwise the political significance of this measure will be lost'.⁴¹ The aim was to 'deepen the split' on the war question, to demonstrate to world public opinion who was for peace and who was not, to 'expose the warmongers'. The Politburo decided that the second Congress of Partisans of Peace was to approach UNO with a proposal, supported by the signatures collected, for the atom bomb to be banned.⁴² The Soviet proposals at the UN's General Assembly (in September–December 1950) and the manifesto of the Congress of Partisans of Peace in November were almost identical.

Another important initiative was launched at the April session of the Cominform's Secretariat, by the French member E. Fajon. Referring to the broadcasts by the 'Voice of America' radio station, he urged intensification of counter-propaganda by the Soviet radio, aimed at France, Italy and Belgium.⁴³ The proposal was adopted. J. Duclos had already advocated (9 March 1950) the setting-up in Prague of a powerful transmitter for use by the Cominform.⁴⁴

At the final session of the Secretariat it was decided not to publish a report on how the 1949 Cominform resolution on 'defence of peace' had been carried out, but to make it known to the Socialist Unity Party of Germany and to the CPs of Albania and Finland.⁴⁵

The Italian CP had the greatest success in making less obvious the Communist inspiration of the signatures campaign, bringing to the forefront the 'committees of partisans of peace'.[46] But the outbreak of the Korean War caused difficulties. The Italian Government developed a counter-campaign, alleging that the Soviet Union was using the collection of signatures against war to mask its own aggressive policy.[47] When the second congress of the Partisans of Peace opened in Warsaw (16–22 November 1950) it was announced that 485 735 000 signatures to the Stockholm Appeal had been collected.[48]

Of special importance in the history of the Cominform is the November 1950 session of the Secretariat and preparations for a fourth meeting of the organization, which never took place.[49] On 21 September V.G. Grigorian sent Stalin the agenda prepared by the Soviet Party's Foreign Policy Commission for the next session of the Cominform Secretariat.[50] A resolution by the CC was even prepared.[51] But, a month later, on 26 October, another message to Stalin proposed a new agenda, focused on the idea of extending the functions of the Cominform.[52] The French CP would open a discussion on that subject.[53] There can be no doubt that this idea could have come only from Stalin himself. The French Communist leader, G. Cogniot, was already, on the instructions of the Soviet Party's CC, developing connections with the Latin American countries,[54] and the Cominform Secretariat was regularly informing the CC on the work of CPs which were not members of the Cominform.[55] The Cominform's newspaper *For a Lasting Peace, for People's Democracy!* was published in 14 languages and distributed in 57 countries.[56]

What was to be the last session of the Cominform Secretariat was held in Bucharest on 22–24 November 1950. It was agreed that developments in the international situation demanded a widening of the organization's functions.[57] Fajon spoke of the need for a new structure so as to ensure 'unity of views and actions at every turn of international events'.[58] A reorganized Cominform would better play its role as headquarters for the peace movement and the fight against imperialist aggression.[59] D'Onofrio pointed out that the gigantic world-wide peace movement must not be constricted through failure to advise and help those CPs which were not members of the Cominform.[60] Suslov spoke of the rendering of aid to all the world's CPs as 'our international duty'.[61] However, D'Onofrio, representing the Italian CP, emphasized the difference between the old Comintern and the proposed enlarged and strengthened Cominform.[62]

The Secretariat decided that the Cominform should meet, for the fourth time, on 23 December 1950, in Bucharest.[63] But this was not to happen. Judging by newly available documents, together with what was already known about 'the Togliatti affair',[64] the decisive reason was refusal by the Italian CP leader to become General Secretary of the renovated Cominform. Togliatti's poor state of health and Stalin's wish to discuss with him, personally, such an important question as extending the functions of the Cominform led to the Politburo deciding to postpone the Cominform's meeting to 25 January 1951.[65] Suslov wrote to the member-Parties about this.[66] Togliatti was told through the Soviet ambassador in Rome.[67]

In December Togliatti went to Moscow for medical treatment. His stay in the USSR was prolonged until February 1951 because Stalin was keen to get him to agree to head the renovated Cominform. In the Archives of the President of the Russian Federation, which are still not open to researchers generally, there are two letters from Togliatti to Stalin in which he explains in detail the reasons for his refusal. On 4 January 1951, Togliatti writes of his need to concentrate on leadership of the PCI. But Stalin did not give up hope. On 17 January the Politburo decided to postpone once more the meeting of the Cominform.[68] It was explained that this decision was due to difficulty in appointing a General Secretary.[69] In February a letter to Stalin signed by Togliatti, Secchia and Colombi reaffirmed that the leader of the PCI would not accept the post of General Secretary of the Cominform, out of concern for the interests of his own Party. A certain decline in the Cominform's activity ensued. But this did not affect the peace movement. The second congress of the Partisans of Peace elected a World Council which took over co-ordination of the work. The Berlin Appeal which it issued after its session of 21–26 February 1951, for a peace pact between the Great Powers, had collected by 25 October more signatures than for the Stockholm Appeal – 559 624 293.[70]

The USA State Department regarded Stalin's 'crusade' for peace as an attempt to force the West to give up its 'defence'.[71] The Soviet leadership was now acting through the Soviet Defence Committee and through bi-lateral relations with other CPs. After the Cominform meeting in 1949[72] the tactic chosen was one of operating mainly through non-Communist forces.

The era of the Cominform passed away.[73] This international Communist organization had been engendered by a foreign policy, Stalin's, which underwent revision in Khrushchev's time. Part of the 'Cold War', its existence became pointless when the international situation changed. It was replaced by other, state forms of co-operation between the USSR and the countries of Eastern Europe: the Council for Mutual Economic Aid (1949) and the Organization of the Warsaw Pact Countries (1955). As regards relations between the CPSU and the CPs of France and Italy, Stalin's decision not to extend the functions of the Cominform can be seen as evidence that, by the beginning of the 1950s, these CPs were already carrying out the tasks entrusted to them by the organization in its then-existing form. Not having assumed the likeness of the Comintern, all that remained to the Cominform was to dissolve itself, which was done in April 1956.

Notes

1. L.Ia. Gibianskii, 'Kak voznik Kominform. Po novym arkhivnym materialam', *Novaia i noveishaia istoriia*, 4 (1993) 131–52; G.M. Adibekov, *Kominform i poslevoennaia Evropa* (Moscow: 1949); L.Ia. Gibianskii, 'The Soviet–Yugoslav Conflict of 1948 and the Cominform', paper presented at the Conference 'The Establishment of the Communist Regimes in Eastern Europe, 1945–1950: A Reassessment' (Moscow, 29–31 March 1994); S.D. Parrish, 'Soviet–American Relations. The Marshall Plan and the Division of Europe, 1947', paper, *ibid.*
2. Parrish, 'Soviet–American Relations', p. 44.
3. N.I. Egorova, 'From the Comintern to the Cominform: Ideological Dimension of the Cold War Origins (1945–1948)', paper presented at the conference 'New Documents on the History of the Cold War' (Moscow, 12–15 January 1994); Id., '"Iranskii Krizis" 1945–1946 gg. Po rassekrechennym arkhivnym dokumentam', *Novaia i noveishaia istoriia*, 3 (1994) 29, 33.
4. RTsKhIDNI, f. 575, op. 1, d. 3, l. 24.
5. RTsKhIDNI, f. 77, op. 3, d. 89, l. 3.
6. Zhdanov to Thorez, 2 June 1947, RTsKhIDNI, f. 77, op. 3, d. 89, l. 7.
7. *Ibid.*, l. 5, 6.
8. For more details see: M.M. Narinskii, 'SSSR i plan Marshalla. Po materialam Arkhiva Prezidenta RF', *Novaia i noveishaia istoriia*, 2 (1993) 11–19; S.D. Parrish, 'The Turn toward Confrontation: The Soviet Reaction to the Marshall Plan, 1947', in *Cold War History International Project*, Working Paper No. 9, March 1994, Woodrow Wilson International Center for Scholars, pp. 1–39.
9. RTsKhIDNI, f. 77, op. 3, d. 9, l. 111, 113.
10. *Ibid.*, l. 115.
11. RTsKhIDNI, f. 575, op. 1, d. 3, l. 2.
12. RTsKhIDNI, f. 575, op. 1, d. 13, l. 41.
13. RTsKhIDNI, f. 575, op. 1, d. 35, l. 29.
14. A. Zhdanov, *29–aia godovshchina Velikoi Oktiabrskoi sotsialisticheskoi revoliutsii* (Moscow: 1946) p. 23.
15. A. Zhdanov, *O mezhdunarodnom polozhenii* (Moscow: 1947) p. 16.
16. Malenkov's report on the activity of the CC of the CPSU, 22 September 1947, RTsKhIDNI, f. 575, op. 1, d. 1, l. 30.
17. RTsKhIDNI, f. 77, op. 3, d. 96, l. 9.
18. AVP RF, f. 06, op. 9, p. 12, d. 151, l. 3–4.
19. Zhdanov to Slánský, Gomułka, Gheorghiu-Dej, Chervenkov, Longo, Kardelj, Duclos, Farkas, 17 October 1947, RTsKhIDNI, f. 77, op. 3, d. 97, l. 1.
20. RTsKhIDNI, f. 575, op. 1, d. 4, l. 65.
21. *Pravda*, 10 October 1947.
22. Pospelov to Molotov, 10 October 1947, AVP RF, f. 06, op. 9, p. 12, d. 150, l. 6, 8–15.
23. RTsKhIDNI, f. 575, op. 1, d. 3, l. 3.

24. RTsKhIDNI, f. 17, op. 3, d. 1075, l. 109–10.
25. RTsKhIDNI, f. 17, op. 3, d. 1074, l. 61–2.
26. Suslov, Grigorian, Ponomarev, Baranov to Stalin, May 1949, RTsKhIDNI, f. 575, op. 1, d. 82, l. 85.
27. RTsKhIDNI, f. 575, op. 1, d. 84, l. 148.
28. Ibid., l. 136.
29. RTsKhIDNI, f. 575, op. 1, d. 80, l. 2.
30. At the beginning of January 1950 V. Grigorian appealed to Stalin to enlarge the apparatus of the Foreign Policy Commission (consisting of 70 persons), which was not managing to cope with the huge amount of work given to it. A considerable proportion of this work was connected with problems of the Partisans of Peace movement (see RTsKhIDNI, f. 17, op. 137, d. 165, l. 1–2).
31. Suslov's report 'Zaschita mira i borba s podzhigateliami voiny', 16 November 1949, RTsKhIDNI, f. 575, op. 1, d. 74, l. 1–33.
32. Duclos speech on Togliatti's report, 17 November 1949, RTsKhIDNI, f. 575, op. 1, d. 75, l. 38.
33. RTsKhIDNI, f. 575, op. 1, d. 81, l. 28.
34. RTsKhIDNI, f. 17, op. 137, d. 123, l. 4; RTsKhIDNI, f. 375, op. 1, d. 118, l. 50–3.
35. RTsKhIDNI, f. 17, op. 3, d. 1079, l. 63.
36. Grigorian to Stalin, 17 March 1950, RTsKhIDNI, f. 375, op. 1, d. 129, l. 12; V. Grigorian to I. Stalin, 4 April 1950, ibid., l. 33–5.
37. RTsKhIDNI, f. 375, op. 1, d. 120, l. 3, 13.
38. Ibid., l. 13.
39. In 1949 the 'Berlin crisis' of 1948 was finally settled. This showed that the USA's reliance on 'atomic diplomacy' had not justified itself and that diplomatic negotiations were still an important means for settling international crises. On 25 September 1949 the Soviet Union announced that it had created an atomic bomb. The process of consolidating the Eastern bloc was completed, in the main. The Chinese People's Republic and the German Democratic Republic were established. Thus, a certain 'balance of power' had come about in inter-bloc politics.
40. The Socialist P. Nenni headed the Italian Committee of the movement of Partisans of Peace. In 1952 he received the Stalin Peace Prize.
41. RTsKhIDNI, f. 575, op. 1, d. 120, l. 10.
42. RTsKhIDNI, f. 17, op. 162, d. 44, l. 37.
43. RTsKhIDNI, f. 575, op. 1, d. 120, l. 115, 116.
44. RTsKhIDNI, f. 575, op. 1, d. 127, l. 72.
45. RTsKhIDNI, f. 575, op. 1, d. 120, l. 114.
46. RTsKhIDNI, f. 17, op. 137, d. 383, l. 17.
47. Ibid., l. 30, 31.
48. RTsKhIDNI, f. 17, op. 137, d. 468, l. 46.
49. Owing to lack of archive materials this subject was dealt with quite imprecisely in L. Marcou, *Le Kominform. Le Communisme de Guerre Froide* (Paris: 1977) pp. 110–12. It was studied on the basis of the Cominform Archives in Adibekov, *Kominform i poslevoennaia Evropa*, pp. 205–20.
50. Grigorian to Stalin, 21 September 1950, RTsKhIDNI, f. 575, op. 1, d. 129, l. 12.
51. Ibid., l. 14, 15.
52. Grigorian to Stalin, 26 October 1950, RTsKhIDNI, f. 575, op. 1, d. 129, l. 42.

53. *Ibid.*, l. 43.
54. RTsKhIDNI, f. 575, op. 1, d. 106, l. 34, 153; RTsKhIDNI, f. 575, op. 1, d. 118, l. 5–6, 9; RTsKhIDNI, f. 575, op. 1, d. 82, l. 86.
55. Extract from Grigorian's letter to Molotov, 15 July 1949, *ibid.*, l. 182; Baranov to all members of the Cominform, 30 August 1949, *ibid.*, l. 184.
56. RTsKhIDNI, f. 575, op. 1, d. 80, l. 139; RTsKhIDNI, f. 575, op. 1, d. 120, l. 118.
57. Speech by D'Onofrio, 23 November 1950, RTsKhIDNI, f. 575, op. 1, d. 122, l. 40.
58. Speech by Fajon, 22 November 1950, *ibid.*, l. 7.
59. *Ibid.*, l. 8.
60. *Ibid.*, l. 42.
61. Speech by Suslov, 23 November 1950, *ibid.*, l. 30, 31.
62. *Ibid.*, l. 43.
63. *Ibid.*, l. 100.
64. Marcou, *Le Kominform*, pp. 113–19. This author refers to G. Bocca, *Palmiro Togliatti* (Rome: 1973), and G. Seniga, *Togliatti e Stalin* (Milan: 1961).
65. RTsKhIDNI, f. 17, op. 162, d. 45, l. 8.
66. Telegram from Suslov to Duclos, Gottwald, Bierut, Rákosi, Gheorghiu-Dej and Chervenkov, 8 December 1950, *ibid.*, l. 69.
67. Telegram from Gromyko to Soviet Embassy, Rome, 8 December 1950, *ibid.*, l. 70.
68. *Ibid.*, l. 117.
69. *Ibid.*, l. 138.
70. RTsKhIDNI, f. 17, op. 137, d. 468, l. 47.
71. Marcou, *Le Kominform*, pp. 113–19.
72. RTsKhIDNI, f. 17, op. 162, d. 44, l. 37.
73. Kotelenets to Grigorian, 28 August 1952, RTsKhIDNI, f. 575, op. 1, d. 224, l. 84; Mitin to Khrushchev, 4 and 8 January 1954, RTsKhIDNI, f. 575, op. 1, d. 283, l. 16–19; Mitin to CC CPSU, 28 June 1954, *ibid.*, l. 51.

14 The Marshall Plan and the Founding of the Cominform, June–September 1947
Anna Di Biagio

Among the unresolved questions regarding the genesis of the Cold War and the division of Europe, one of the most important concerns the Cominform. What was the Soviet leadership aiming at when it set up the Informburo (better known as the Cominform) at the 'private information conference' which brought together representatives of nine European Communist Parties at Szklarska Poręba, 22–28 September 1947? Until recently, lack of access to documentary evidence concerning the foundation of this organization made it difficult to answer this question. Recently, however, the Minutes of Conference Proceedings have become available.[1]

The new documents do not give us direct access to decision-making; nonetheless, they do extend our knowledge of relations between Moscow and the European Communist Parties in a period which is crucial for understanding how the Cold War got under way – the period between June and September 1947. This chapter will thus focus on the relationship between the founding of the Cominform and the event which preceded it – the United States' proposal for a programme of aid for European reconstruction; and I will examine what role the Marshall Plan had in the decision to found the new European Communist organization. More generally, I will suggest that Soviet foreign policy in the years following World War II should be re-conceptualized so as to take into account the multiplicity of factors which contributed to the line taken.

The newly available material on the founding of the Cominform, plus recent studies of Soviet reactions to the Marshall Plan,[2] make it fairly plain that the Soviet decision to found the Cominform probably should not be seen exclusively as a direct reaction to the Plan. There were certainly many factors other than Soviet fears regarding the American initiative. The idea of creating a new Communist organization was due above all to internal needs regarding the Soviet sphere of influence, the need to synchronize policies of the various Communist

Parties, and the need to hold back the powerful centrifugal tendencies which were present in this sphere of influence (tendencies which were encouraged by Moscow's uncertainty as to what line to take *vis-à-vis* changes in the post-war international situation). So Soviet fears concerning the Marshall Plan accelerated a project which had already been under consideration, to set up forms of 'co-ordination' for the activities of European Communist Parties. The decision to firmly reject the Marshall Plan made it possible to overcome the wavering of assessments which, until very late on, had bedevilled the Soviet leadership – uncertainties as to whether or not a *cordon sanitaire* around the borders of the USSR should be erected, restoring the isolationism which had fundamentally characterized Soviet foreign policy in the pre-war period.

We do not have the documentary evidence which would enable us to reconstruct a complete and detailed account of relationships between the All-Russian Party and the European Communist Parties in 1946–7. We do have considerable evidence, however, that those relationships were marked by significant differences and conflicts.[3] These conflicts led the Soviet leadership to take initiatives aiming to strengthen control over the various Communist Parties – even before the Marshall Plan had been launched.

So the need to create an 'Information Bureau', which would achieve a 'general co-ordination of activities' and 'the smoothing over of differences between the individual parties', had already been discussed in June 1946, during a meeting in Moscow between Stalin, Tito and Dimitrov. However, a year passed before anything was done to further this plan. At a meeting which took place in late May or early June 1947, Stalin and Gomułka discussed the matter – although we do not know the details. In any case, after this meeting, Gomułka put forward the proposal publicly. However, his initiative was merely for a 'Special Information Conference' for an exchange of information, as preparation for a new journal devoted to 'questions of the workers' movement in the individual countries'. This informal initiative was thus quite limited in scope; and invitations were sent only to nine Parties (in addition to the Soviet and Polish Parties, those of Yugoslavia, Bulgaria, Romania, Czechoslovakia, Hungary, France and Italy).[4] From the evidence we possess, however, at the time of Stalin's meeting with Gomułka, there does not seem to have been any link with American plans for intervention in Europe.

Recent archival research has shown that Moscow originally reacted with interest to the proposals put forward by the American Secretary of State. Moscow hoped that it might be possible to create a zone of economic exchange where internal affairs and foreign affairs could be kept apart – a zone where it would be possible to continue the wartime policy of co-operation between the Big Three, while at the same time avoiding interfering in each others' spheres of influence.[5] Moscow's original openness altered into a stance of firm opposition when it did not succeed in obtaining concessions – particularly on the revision of the point that aid would be conditional on the country in question formulating an 'economic programme'. As is well known, Molotov denounced this condition as a violation of the sovereignty and 'economic independence' of European states – an interference in their internal affairs which would reduce them to a position of virtually colonial subjection (*zakabalenie*)[6] to American economic interests.[7] In reality, Soviet fears concerned mainly the Eastern European states. Newly available archive material makes it clear that all the steps taken by the Soviet leadership in these negotiations were guided by the determination to prevent the West from being able to exercise influence in countries within the Soviet sphere of influence. So Soviet leaders were extremely sensitive to the idea that states of the East might be induced to revise their internal policies, bringing them more in line with the free market, with the result that they would be more tied into a network of interdependence woven by the United States throughout Europe.[8]

Nevertheless, one of Moscow's first reactions seems to have been to play the card of national sovereignty as a way of encouraging friction between the United States and the European countries, and turning this to his own advantage.[9] In a telegram dated 5 July addressed personally to all leaders of the Communist Parties of Eastern Europe, Molotov transmitted a directive according to which the respective Governments should participate in the upcoming Paris Conference on the Marshall Plan in order 'to demonstrate the unacceptability of the Anglo-French Plan, to prevent unanimous adoption of the Plan and then to leave the Conference, taking with them as many delegates from other countries as possible'. Within a few hours, however, Moscow had given up the idea of mobilizing the Eastern countries at the Anglo-French Conference as a way of placing obstacles in the way of what was seen as American expansionism.[10]

No exhaustive solution has yet been given to explain this sudden change of policy. It is very probable that a number of factors affected this decision – a decision which, as has been noted,[11] facilitated American plans to limit its economic aid to Western Europe. Among the factors in question, we should note the peculiar situation in which some coalition governments in Eastern Europe found themselves – making decisions on a foreign policy line which would have major consequences for internal policy. However, the decision to turn down the invitation to attend the Anglo-French Conference would have posed significant problems of sovereignty to the Eastern European Governments – at least as serious as those which Moscow claimed were raised to the Western European Governments by the Marshall Plan provisions.[12] If the Eastern Governments had been obliged to follow Moscow's line over the Marshall Plan, moreover, this would inevitably have created a conflict between national economic interests and loyalty to Moscow. In any case, not all the Eastern Parties were favourable to the Anglo-French Conference; crucially, Tito had always been firmly opposed to the American plan.[13]

In this delicate situation, the vacillating behaviour of the Soviet leadership towards the Eastern European Governments exacerbated the complications which already existed between the Soviet Union and the countries falling within its sphere of influence. It seems likely that the difficulties the Soviet leadership had in imposing their line on coalition governments where Communist Parties did not yet have complete control (particularly in the field of foreign policy) were a factor inducing it to take control over a region which was considered vital for Soviet security interests. So the decision to give up the idea of a boycott of the Marshall Plan was probably the first sign of a return to pre-war policies – the avoidance of involvement in international tensions via an intransigent defence of the principle of non-interference and the determination to refrain from taking part in any collective initiative in Europe.[14]

At the end of World War II the USSR was no longer confined within the limits of 'Socialism in one country'. However, Soviet reaction to this was not to encourage 'a gradual transformation to Socialism' in Eastern Europe, as the Hungarian economist, Varga, had argued as late as March 1947[15]; the official line was rather to accelerate the transformation from 'democracies of the new type' into 'people's democracies'. This involved reinforcing the Soviet Union's control over its strategic domain via the imposition from above of a form of compulsory integration which implied full assimilation of the domestic structure of the Eastern European states to the Soviet model of society.

In any case, it seems very likely that Moscow's decision not to sabotage the American plan had a decisive influence on the decision to transform the Conference of Information into a conference founding a new organization.[16] The first effects of this shift in policy were felt in relations between Moscow and the Eastern Communist Parties. The Soviet Union started to take a harder line towards Parties whose approach had been broadly along the lines of the 'new type of democracy' described by Varga. This is clear from the dossiers drawn up before the Conference up by a team of officials of the Foreign Policy Department.[17] These documents (drawn up for all the Parties invited to the Conference) criticized leaders of all the Parties which had taken this sort of line.[18] It seems clear from the dossiers that Moscow had decided to push ahead with Sovietization: the 'national roads' which had been recommended were now seen as signs of 'national limitedness'.

It was only at the end of the first phase of the Conference that delegates were told about the decision to transform what had started out as an informal initiative into the founding Conference of a new Communist organization.[19] This means that it is possible to make comparisons between the two phases of the Conference – and these shed very significant light on the shift in Soviet foreign policy, and on the effects the shift had on relations between Moscow and the European Communist Parties.[20]

If we read the information reports given by delegates in the first phase of the Conference – especially if we read the original versions, before they were censored for the minutes[21] – it is clear that, with the important exception of Kardelj, the speakers took an approach which was in line with that prevailing in Moscow before the rejection of the Marshall Plan. The Italian delegate, Longo, for example, reiterated the stance towards the Marshall Plan taken up by his Party; and, more generally, he repeated PCI arguments regarding the need for equidistance between the USSR and the USA if the formation of two blocs was to be avoided.[22] Duclos's position was quite different, for he fiercely criticized the anti-Soviet character of the Marshall Plan, and he also took up a stance closer to the most recent Soviet positions *vis-à-vis* the Anglo-French Conference – which he dubbed 'the first step towards the formation of a Western bloc'. He talked about the danger of 'a new war' contained in the Marshall Plan, and expressed the opinion that the Plan should have been the first item on the Conference agenda. However, the second part of his speech was very different in tone. The problem in his view was how to demonstrate to the defenders of the Marshall Plan, and to the 'masses of their countries', that the European Governments would be capable of reconstructing their economies 'even without help from the USA'.[23]

As for the representatives of Eastern European Parties, it is significant that even those which (in July) had showed interest in taking part in the Anglo-French Conference (the Polish and Czechoslovak Parties) lined up formally behind Moscow's intransigent line of complete rejection of the Marshall Plan. At the same time, however, they expressed interest in what was by no means a secondary aspect of the Plan – the fact that it might be capable of relieving the tensions of 'the class struggle' and warding off the danger of civil war which was hanging over all European countries. Gomułka and Slánský were particularly aware of the potential effects that abandonment of the cautious position their parties had hitherto adopted within coalition Governments could have in terms of disrupting internal stability. As for Kardelj, his speech took a very hard line over the international repercussions of the 'internal class struggle'[24]; nonetheless, even he shared worries of other delegates about the consequences of unleashing the 'class struggle' in the countryside.²⁵ Anxiousness to take a moderate line with peasants, and more general concern with internal tension, was in fact shared by most of the East European delegates. This is particularly significant if we remember that the Foreign Policy Department dossiers had criticized the Eastern Parties for being sluggardly over collectivization in rural areas and had called for intensification of the 'class struggle' in the countryside.²⁶

Zhdanov's report to the Conference has traditionally been considered one of the most important documents revealing how the Soviet leadership saw the international situation in the years immediately after the war. We now have access to earlier drafts of the report, and can compare these with the final version.²⁷ This allows us to trace how the theory of the two camps emerged – even though significant gaps in our knowledge remain.²⁸

What were the most significant changes which appeared between what seems to be the first typed draft of the text conserved among Zhdanov's personal papers²⁹ and the final version of the theses on the international situation?³⁰ It must be borne in mind that the final version consisted of the declaration of the two camps, welded onto a text which had not originally contained this idea, and which, indeed, had confined itself to a survey of Soviet foreign policy. So the two-camps theory had to be worked into an original text which had been much more open to the possibility of dialogue. In this survey it had been argued that the Soviet Union's margin for manoeuvre to avoid the formation of two blocs depended on exploiting 'Anglo-American friction', which was seen as a key to international relations. Thus the first draft maintained that the 'first task' which the USA had before it in its 'new expansionist course' was to shift the balance in its long-standing rivalry with Britain.

'The American expansionist course is based on the need to stop Britain from escaping from the dependent position established during the war, and indeed to step up pressure on Britain to let go of its colonies and reduce it to the position of a vassal-power.'³¹ It was only after this first objective that the United States was seen as preventing 'the growing international influence of the Soviet Union, which is the principal obstacle to the United States' plans for world domination; the struggle against the countries of new democracy which have freed themselves from Anglo-American imperialist control'.³²

This interpretation of the international situation was rooted in an analysis of the meaning of the Truman Doctrine. The fundamental aims of the doctrine were listed as follows:

1. Creation of American bases in the Eastern sector of the Mediterranean basin, with the aim of replacing British influence in this region.

214   *The Marshall Plan and the Founding of the Cominform*

2. Demonstration of support to the reactionary regimes in Greece and Turkey in their role as bulwarks against the spread of Communism (giving military and technical aid to Greece and Turkey, and loans).
3. Keeping up constant pressure on the states of new democracy via false accusations of totalitarianism and expansionist ambitions.[33]

This relatively open interpretation of the pattern of international alignments implied that in Soviet eyes a Western bloc had not yet been consolidated. The implication was clearly that the USSR – portrayed as a 'bastion of peace, democracy and Socialism'[34] – might be willing to undertake international commitments, within the framework of the United Nations, to 'consolidate the defence of the interests of genuine people's co-operation'; to affirm respect for the principle of 'all people's equal rights to defence against aggression', without distinctions between 'inferior' and 'superior' races or nations; to ensure that 'colonial aggression' was recognized as a real 'threat to peace and security for all peoples'. The USSR was to act as a guarantor in defence of the 'weaker countries', against attempts by the 'imperialist powers' to impose their will via instrumental use of their economic and military superiority.

So although the Soviet Union clearly deplored the shift in American policy which had occurred with Roosevelt's death, it still wished to encourage attempts which would enable the Communist Parties to set themselves at the head of 'all democratic, anti-Fascist and peace-loving elements in their struggle against the new plans for aggression and war' put forward by the United States.[35] Confidence that this was feasible was also present in the analysis of the first European reactions towards the Marshall Plan. For it was claimed that the Plan would fail since 'it is a larger-scale replica of the well-known Dawes Plan, which failed because it was conceived without considering its host'.[36] In the Soviet view, in other words, the European states would react as they had in the pre-war period, and defend their national sovereignty and independence against American attempts to turn the European continent into a colony.[37] It was thus believed that the 'Molotov approach' had a good chance of obtaining support in the countries of Western Europe. The criticisms made of the PCI and the PCF – which were present in this first draft of Zhdanov's theses – were originally made in this context. They need to be related, that is, to the boycott which Molotov had planned in June. For the criticisms constituted an explicit invitation to make the 'Molotov approach' more effective via determined support for the values of patriotism and national independence, to ward off the American plans for economic integration.

All these passages were eliminated by Zhdanov during the various rewritings of his theses,[38] with the exception of the criticisms of the errors committed by the PCI and the PCF. In the final version, they were replaced by pieces on the theory of the two camps, and the argument that there no longer existed any room for manoeuvre to avoid the crystallization of two blocs. The declaration of a camp opposed to the 'imperialist' camp, and the fact that this was no longer labelled 'anti-Fascist', but rather 'anti-imperialist and democratic', made it necessary to revise the whole orientation contained in the first draft of the theses. For example, the transformation of Britain into an American 'vassal' was now seen as already having come about. Consequently, the possibility of exploiting Anglo-American friction to avoid consolidation of the Western bloc was no longer an option.

In the final version, reference to the possibility of Soviet commitments in the framework of the United Nations was replaced with the concepts of the defence of national sovereignty seen as opposed to 'world government'; this illustrates the new isolationist line which had prevailed in Moscow. From now on, the Soviet leadership gave up the search for multilateral solutions to its security problems (the approach which had been dominant in the period of the anti-Fascist alliance) and relied on unilateral solutions. It is no surprise, therefore, that in the final version of his thesis, Zhdanov reassessed relationships between the Allies during the war – playing down the importance of the 'anti-Fascist' alliance,[39] and stressing continuity with the 'Munich policy' of the Western Governments in the pre-war period. This gave more conviction to his argument regarding the need to break with the line of the anti-Fascist front – the policy which hitherto had been considered as the most suitable to the interests of Soviet foreign policy – and go on the offensive in the name of anti-Americanism.[40] Finally, the label given to the new regimes of Eastern Europe changed; from being 'states of new democracy', they became 'people's republics'.[41]

Neither Zhdanov's conference report, nor the resolutions adopted at the end of the proceedings contained specific indications regarding the orientation the Eastern European Parties needed to adopt if they were to contribute to the 'offensive' against American expansionist plans. Nonetheless, if we examine the debate which followed Zhdanov's report, it becomes clear that the attack on the two Western Parties invited to the Conference also had implications for those of Eastern Europe. For the attack on the PCI and PCF was the first step towards legitimizing the right of the All-Russian Party to interfere in the internal affairs of the other Parties, and to establish disciplinary tribunals for those which committed errors and deviated from the 'correct line'. It was supposed that the other Communist Parties would draw lessons from the mistakes exposed.

The lessons to be drawn were clear enough in any case in Zhdanov's report. The bipolar perspective which he used to reinterpret international relations – including those during the period when the Big Three had co-operated under the anti-Fascist banner – inevitably involved abandoning the Popular Front line which Moscow had until then advocated for the European Parties. In this kind of bi-polar world – which had already been sketched by Stalin in 1927,[42] but now became a general principle for interpreting the international relations – any room for neutral or non-aligned positions, like those favoured by the PCI in particular, disappeared. The same was true for those policies pursued up to this point by the Communist Parties in coalition governments in both Western and Eastern Europe, which aimed at compromise and co-operation with other Parties and other social groups.

Longo was not slow to perceive the unmistakable implications of Zhdanov's downgrading of anti-Fascist co-operation. He saw that it meant the reversal of the previous instructions to 'stay out of any bloc'.[43] Moscow no longer considered that defence of Soviet security required the Western Communist Parties to oppose the division of Europe. In addition, Zhdanov's theory of an 'inseparable connection' between international situation and internal situation made it impossible for the French or Italian Communist Parties to think of going back into governing coalitions. The Western Parties could only be governing parties as long as there was co-operation between the great powers. With the declaration of the two camps, it was clear that the Western Parties would be thrust back into permanent opposition Parties, and would be forced to fall back on the old and not very efficacious methods of agitation and propaganda.[44]

The Conference debate shows, however, that Moscow's indications for the Western and the Eastern Parties differed. The first consequence of Moscow's recognition of the division of Europe was thus a distinction in the tactics recommended for Parties working in the two camps. So in the West, Moscow demanded that the Communist Parties should take up the banner of 'defence of the motherland honour and independence' – which had been outraged by the attempts at *zakabalenie* implied by American expansionist plans.[45] For the Eastern European Parties, on the other hand, the change marked the first step in their transformation from 'democracies of a new type' into 'people's democracies' via a struggle against 'national limitedness'. The new policy put a stop to any attempt to create regional alliances, and was the start of the process whereby Eastern European states were forced into an integration decided and led exclusively by Moscow, and which eliminated autonomy both in foreign policy and in internal affairs.

The relationship between a bi-polar conception of the world and the gradual assertion of total control over the Eastern European countries was made particularly explicit in the speech given by the Hungarian delegate Farkas. Farkas emphasized the negative consequences of the breakup of the Comintern, and attacked the very common tendency among Social Democrats and also among members of his own Party to have 'illusions' that it was possible to build a 'bridge between East and West' – 'the illusion that there is some third possibility between freedom and imperialism'. This was quite unrealistic, according to Farkas, because there could be no 'neutrality' between the two camps. After the declaration of the two camps, in other words, a country's membership of one camp or the other was judged by the question of whether or not it fell within the Soviet sphere of influence. It was this which became the crucial differentiating criterion. In addition, Farkas argued that if Eastern Parties were to overcome their 'national limitedness', this had major consequences for the coalition governments:

> American imperialism's fight against Hungarian democracy is conducted not only by sabotage but also through political parties and, moreover, not only from outside the Government but also within the governmental bloc ... We must boldly steer towards elimination of the American agents from the democratic bloc, towards struggle against the right wing in the parties which collaborate with the Communists.[46]

Gomułka took up a slightly different stance. He toed the line formally speaking over Zhdanov's criticisms of the 'opportunistic mistakes' committed by the PCF and the PCI; but he also expressed serious doubts over the efficacy of the new line. He maintained that a return 'to the old slogan of the united front only from below', and the abandoning of any attempt at working with leaders of the Socialist and Liberal-Democratic Parties, would place again those parties in a very isolated position.[47] Nonetheless, when it came to the 'lessons' to be drawn for his own Party, Gomułka took up the same stance as other Eastern delegates; that is to say, he gave up his own sovereignty, the reasoning being that

> When two antagonistic blocs – imperialist and democratic – have crystallized on the world scale, the problem of the tactics to be adopted by Communist Parties in particular countries cannot be treated as merely a domestic problem for each Party separately, but must be the object of concern and discussion by all the Parties.[48]

The available documentation does not allow us to give definitive answers regarding the objectives which the Soviet leadership hoped to achieve with the founding of the Cominform; in particular, it does not allow us to settle the thorny question, often raised by historians, of whether it was conceived as a successor to the Comintern. However, there is considerable indirect evidence which indicates that at least in the minds of its promoters (especially Zhdanov),[49] the Cominform was conceived as a sort of European Comintern; and, as such, it was seen as implying the subordination of all members to the security interests of the USSR, and also a clear distinction between the Parties of the West and those of the East. For the latter, further and more rigorous 'Bolshevization' was envisaged[50], while the former were to be encouraged to abandon the Popular Front line which had prevailed since the VIIth Congress in the name of anti-Fascism, and reasserted when the Comintern had been dissolved. The old tactic of 'the United Front from below' was to be pushed through among the Western Parties – a line which predictably had similar effects to that of 'the turn to the left' launched at the VIth Comintern Congress in 1928. So rather as in the pre-war years, the new line defending sovereignty and national independence ended up in grand gestures of sectarian intransigence, accompanied by passivity or basic incapacity to work out an independent political line.[51]

So the Marshall Plan destroyed the Soviet leadership's hopes that it would be possible to create a zone where neither side would interfere in countries' internal affairs. The price for obtaining American aid was too high for the USSR and countries belonging to its sphere of influence to pay. They would have had to adopt major changes to the system which had been set up in the homeland of Socialism from 1929 on, and which was intrinsically associated with Stalin personally. As the hope collapsed, Moscow abandoned the cautious gradualism which guided its early post-war policy in Eastern Europe, and it adopted an uncompromising line. This, however, turned out to be counter-productive, both as regards relationships with the West and those with the countries which became part of the Soviet bloc. For far from putting a spoke in the American wheel, the founding of the Cominform actually facilitated the plan to stabilize Western Europe against Communist subversion and Soviet expansion.[52] And in Eastern Europe, the brutal suddenness with which Moscow took total control in its sphere of influence in Eastern Europe exacerbated, rather than attenuated, the powerful centrifugal tendencies which were present in the area; it thus introduced even more instability into an area where the Soviet Union was trying to impose compulsory integration. The appeal to patriotism and national pride as an arm to combat the European Recovery Program (the only weapon which was really suggested) was later to boomerang against Moscow. This became obvious just a few months after the founding Conference of the Cominform, when the conflict with Belgrade broke out.

Notes

1. G. Procacci (ed.), G. Adibekov, A. Di Biagio, L. Gibianskii, F. Gori, S. Pons (co-eds), *The Cominform. Minutes of the Three Conferences 1947/ 1948/1949*, Fondazione Feltrinelli, *Annali*, XXX (Milan: Feltrinelli, 1994).

2. See: G. Takhnenko, 'Anatomiia odnogo politicheskogo resheniia (K 45 – letiyu plana Marshalla)', *Mezhdunarodnaia zhizn'*, 5 (1992) 113–27; M.M. Narinskii, 'SSSR i plan Marshalla. Po materialam Arkhiva Prezidenta RF', *Novaia i noveishaia istoriia*, 2 (1993) 11–19; S.D. Parrish, 'The Turn Toward Confrontation: The Soviet Reaction to the Marshall Plan, 1947', in *New Evidence on the Soviet Rejection of the Marshall Plan, 1947: Two Reports*, Working Paper No. 9, Cold War International History Project, Woodrow Wilson International Center for Scholars, March 1994. For an account of this recent research, and an attempt to draw up a balance sheet of the current state of knowledge, see G. Roberts, 'Moscow and the Marshall Plan: Politics, Ideology and the Onset of the Cold War, 1947', *Europe-Asia Studies*, 46, 8 (1994) 1371–86.
3. An emblematic example is the friction which came out into the open at the Peace Conference between Hungarian and Czechoslovak Communists over national minorities in the two countries. This friction turned into open conflict between delegates of the two states at the Cominform Conference in 1947 (cf. *The Cominform*, p. 343 ff.).
4. L. Ia. Gibianskii, 'Kak voznik Kominform. Po novym arkhivnym materialam. Sekrety i versii', *Novaia i noveishaia istoriia*, 4 (1993) 134–8.
5. That Stalin did nurture hopes of this kind is shown by the content of his interview with the Republican Senator, Harold Stassen (9 April 1947). When Stassen asked him whether the Soviet planned economy and America's free market economy could co-exist, Stalin answered that Lenin himself had put forward the possibility of 'co-operation of the two systems' (I.V. Stalin, *Sochineniia*, tom 3 (XVI), 1946–53 [Stanford: 1967] pp. 75–7).
6. On fears that if the Soviet Union opened up to the West colonial subjection could be the result, see A. Di Biagio, *Le origini dell'isolazionismo sovietico. L'Unione Sovietica e l'Europa dal 1918 al 1928* (Milan: 1990) p. 131 ff.
7. V. Molotov, *Voprosy vneshnei politiki. Rechi i zayavleniya* (Moscow: 1948) p. 473; on the 'Molotov approach', cf. M.J. Hogan, *The Marshall Plan. America, Britain and the Reconstruction of Western Europe 1947–1952* (Cambridge: 1987) pp. 86–7. Molotov rejected the economic integration proposed by the Marshall Plan on the grounds of defence of national sovereignty and concern over the reinstatement of Germany. Western Governments were not entirely impervious to these arguments.
8. Narinskii, 'SSSR i plan Marshalla', 19; see also the material published as an appendix to Takhnenko, 'Anatomiia', 125 ff.
9. Takhnenko, 'Anatomiia', 125.
10. See Molotov's telegram of 7 July in *ibid.*, 126.
11. Narinskii, 'SSSR i plan Marshalla', 19.
12. On 4 July, G. Dimitrov declared to the Soviet Ambassador at Sofia that a refusal by the Government to take part in the Anglo-French Conference would be seen in the West as evidence that Eastern European Governments had lost their political independence (*ibid.*, 17).
13. *Ibid.*, 16–17, where a telegram sent from Moscow to the Soviet Ambassador at Belgrade, 5 June, is quoted. The telegram put pressure on Tito to change his position.
14. This had been the core of the 'Rapallo policy' before the war. Cf. Di Biagio, *Le origini*, p. 33 ff.

15. In an article published in the March number of the journal *Mirovoe choziaistvo i mirovaia politika*, Varga emphasized the differences in the national conditions and tradition of the Eastern countries, in an attempt to show that their 'transformation to Socialism' should not take place on the template of Soviet institutions – but rather respecting their national peculiarities, and 'maintaining the forms of parliamentary democracy'. 'Demokratiya novogo tipa', *Mirovoe choziaistvo i mirovaia politika*, 3 (March 1947) 3–14.
16. On this change in the agenda for the Conference (a change which had occurred by late August), see A. Di Biagio, 'The Establishment of the Cominform', in *The Cominform*, pp. 12–14.
17. On this important department of the CC CPSU – which acted as a centre of information and propaganda between the various Communist Parties, see N.I. Egorova, 'From the Comintern to the Cominform: Ideological Dimension of the Cold War Origins (1945–1948)', paper presented at the conference 'New Evidence on Cold War History' (Moscow, 12–15 January 1993).
18. See Di Biagio, 'The Establishment', p. 19 ff.
19. *Ibid.*, p. 25 ff., for an account of the Conference proceedings.
20. For further details, see *ibid.*, p. 29 ff.
21. The most significant cuts are given in the notes to the Conference minutes. *The Cominform*, p. 423 ff.
22. *Ibid.*, p. 195.
23. *Ibid.*, p. 123. This phrase was faithfully relayed to Stalin in the telegram sent the same day by Zhdanov and Malenkov. The comment was added: 'This is obviously an indirect allusion to the desire for more aid from the USSR and the countries of new democracy' (RTsKhIDNI, f. 77, op. 3, d. 92, l. 8).
24. *The Cominform*, p. 434, note 94.
25. For Kardelj's plea for caution towards peasants, see especially the passages censured out of the minutes, and now reprinted in *ibid.*, pp. 434–5, notes 95 and 96. In their coded telegrams to Stalin, Zhdanov and Malenkov omitted to mention this part of Kardelj's report (cf. *ibid.*, pp. 435–6, note 98).
26. See particularly the criticisms of the Polish and Yugoslav parties: RTsKhIDNI, f. 575, op. 1, d. 3, l. 104.
27. The 'conceptual outline' entitled 'On the International Situation', which Zhdanov mentioned in a letter to Stalin, promising to send it 'by 12 September' (RTsKhIDNI, f. 77, op. 3, d. 90, l. 10) has not yet been located. We cannot tell, therefore, if the alterations were made at the suggestion of Stalin or if they were Zhdanov's own.
28. Thus it should be noted that the numerous drafts of the text preserved in Zhdanov's personal papers are by no means easy to date. Only a few sheets of the first manuscript minute survive (RTsKhIDNI, f. 77, op. 3, d. 94, l. 138–48). These notes seem to be for the first section of the first typed version of the text. The most significant passage of the handwritten minute (and one which was changed significantly in the final version) is that which mentions one of 'the most important results' of World War II. This was that 'a series of countries of Central, South East and East Europe – Yugoslavia, Czechoslovakia, Bulgaria, Romania and Poland – have fallen out of the imperialist system, and states of a new kind have arisen, states of new democracy' (RTsKhIDNI, f. 77, op. 3, d. 94, l. 139). Note that Czechoslovakia was placed second in this list, and that

Hungary did not appear. It is also notable that Zhdanov here defined the regimes of the Eastern European states along similar lines to those employed by Varga in March 1947.
29. RTsKhIDNI, f. 77, op. 3, d. 94, l. 50–92.
30. RTsKhIDNI, f. 77, op. 3, d. 91, l. 74–120.
31. RTsKhIDNI, f. 77, op. 3, d. 94, l. 56.
32. *Ibid.*
33. RTsKhIDNI, f. 77, op. 3, d. 94, l. 72.
34. *Ibid.*, l. 58.
35. *Ibid.*, l. 55, 60–1, 65, 84.
36. *Ibid.*, l. 74.
37. On Soviet reactions to the Dawes Plan, see Di Biagio, *Le origini*, p. 99 ff.
38. See the notes to Zhdanov's report in *The Cominform*, pp. 442–5.
39. On the replacement of the adjective 'anti-Fascist' with 'democratic' in the definition of the 'anti-imperialist camp', see *The Cominform*, p. 441, note 128. It is worth recalling here that in May 1947 the economist Varga was criticized for his defence of the thesis according to which during the period of the anti-Fascist coalition the 'struggle between the two systems' had been suspended. Cf. G.D. Ra'anan, *International Policy Formation in the USSR: Factional 'Debates' during the Zhdanovschina* (Hamden: 1983) ch. 6.
40. The new line – patriotic and anti-American rather than anti-Fascist – is particularly evident in Zhdanov's conclusions. *The Cominform*, p. 353.
41. *Ibid.*, p. 219.
42. On the bipolar image of international relations as an element of continuity going back to before the war, see R.C. Tucker, *The Soviet Political Mind. Stalinism and Post-Stalin Change* (London: 1972) p. 228.
43. *The Cominform*, p. 315.
44. Cf. the comments of F. Claudin, *La crisi del movimento comunista. Dal Comintern al Cominform* (Milan: 1974) p. 362 ff.; also H. Timmermann, 'The Cominform Effects on Soviet Foreign Policy', *Studies in Comparative Communism*, 1 (Spring 1985) 12.
45. See in particular the comments contained in Zhdanov's address on the new tactics proposed for the PCF. *The Cominform*, pp. 453–5.
46. *Ibid.*, pp. 305–7.
47. *Ibid.*, pp. 335, 339.
48. *Ibid.*, p. 333.
49. Cf. Di Biagio, 'The Establishment', pp. 28–9.
50. Cf. P. Spriano, *I comunisti europei e Stalin* (Turin: 1983) p. 283.
51. On the VIth Congress of the Comintern, see Di Biagio, *Le origini*, p. 283 ff.
52. Cf. Hogan, *The Marshall Plan*, p. 44 ff.

The Soviet–Yugoslav Conflict and the Soviet Bloc

Leonid Ia. Gibianskii

Whereas before the Soviet–Yugoslav conflict of 1948 the front of the Cold War ran between the bloc of Communist regimes under Soviet leadership and the Western countries, after that this front ran also inside the disrupted Communist bloc.

From the beginning of the 1950s until the collapse of the former Yugoslavia, the official version of its ruling regime depicted the conflict as a process which began, at latest, during World War II (or even before then) and continued after its end. The cause of it, according to this version, was Soviet dissatisfaction with the special internal and external policy of the CP of Yugoslavia, which ran counter to Moscow's line. This dissatisfaction was manifested in periodically occurring clashes, during and after the war, which increased steadily and eventually developed into sharp Soviet actions directed against Yugoslavia at the end of 1947 and the beginning of 1948, leading to open conflict. A similar scheme, in sundry variants, became widely accepted not only in Yugoslav historiography. It was adopted by a number of Western writers, the most typical example being the well-known publication by Stephen Clissold in which relations between the Yugoslav Communist leadership and Moscow during the war and in the first years after it were presented exclusively as a series of continual and ever-intensifying contradictions and conflict-situations.[1]

This picture, the result of a corresponding selection of factual material, did not, however, square with historical reality. Concrete historical research in a wide range of sources, both published and in the archives, clearly reveals that before the conflict of 1948 relations between the Kremlin and the Yugoslav Communists amounted overwhelmingly to close collaboration and co-operation.[2] These relations were determined by the unity of principle in the socio-political aims of the regime existing in the USSR and those of the Yugoslav CP, which, more than any other of the East European CPs, inclined towards the Soviet model. At the same time, another component in these relations was lack of coincidence in particular concrete tasks, specific strivings and interests on the part of each, and their different tactics in relation to certain concrete questions. The failure to coincide resulted from the different conditions in which the Soviet and Yugoslav Communist leaderships acted, the different problems which confronted each of them, the differences in their experience and their political calculations and, especially, the fact that, within the framework set by common main aims, each, at its own level, endeavoured to strengthen and expand its power and influence. In consequence of this, partial complications occurred from time to time between Moscow and the Yugoslav Communist leaders on particular questions, both during the war and in the first post-war years. These complications – however disproportionately blown up, and even to some extent invented later by Yugoslav official propaganda and historiography – were, in their scale, their significance and their real influence, substantially restricted by the first of the components mentioned in the relations between these partners, namely, the community of basic aims, which played the predominant role. This was greatly strengthened by a third fundamental component in the mutual relations, namely, the fact that the USSR traditionally held the position of world centre of the Communist movement and, at the same time, was the most important foreign-political support of the Yugoslav CP during the war and of the Yugoslav Communist regime after it. Accordingly, the Yugoslav Communists looked to Moscow as their natural centre and ally both in the war and in the post-war years. Any complications that arose were eventually overcome or absorbed by these first and third components and did not damage at all seriously the close alliance and collaboration between the partners, right down to the beginning of 1948.[3]

For evaluating how, in the period preceding the conflict, Moscow viewed Belgrade's policy and its attitude to Yugoslavia compared with that which it adopted towards the other East European 'people's democracies', an interesting source is the information-and-analysis memoranda compiled in the Foreign Policy Department of the CC of the CPSU(B) in August and the first half of September 1947. These were prepared on the instructions of the Party leadership in connection with the then forthcoming constituent conference of the Cominform. Memoranda were compiled on nearly all the Communist Parties then active in the world but, naturally, particular attention was given to the Communist Parties or, more precisely, the 'people's democratic' regimes of the countries of the Soviet bloc: Albania, Bulgaria, Czechoslovakia, Hungary, Poland, Romania and Yugoslavia.[4] In so far as the authors were referents in the Foreign Policy Department of the CC and their chief service function, in each case, was to act from day to day as 'supervisors' of their respective East European countries and CPs, they were among those workers in the apparatus whose duty it was to be *au fait* with the view of Communist leaderships of these countries that was held in Soviet leading circles.

The memorandum prepared on Yugoslavia described in superlative terms the role and success of the KPJ in the armed struggle that developed in the war years and also the Party's achievements in establishing and consolidating Communist authority and creating the appropriate socio-economic model.[5] It was particularly emphasized that the Yugoslavs were the first among the East European countries to lay the foundations of a new order, creating 'people's committees' during the war, and that, for the other countries, this practice was 'to a considerable extent an example for solving the question of people's power in the period of bitter struggle against Fascism and reaction'.[6] There were absolutely no critical comments in the memorandum regarding either the KPJ's conduct during the war or the post-war internal policy of the Yugoslav Communist regime. From this one can, it would seem, deduce that in Moscow at that time they were paying no special attention to the differences on these matters which had arisen earlier. Yugoslav foreign policy was also, as a whole, rated highly in the memorandum, especially Belgrade's firm stand against the West.[7] Yugoslavia was described as 'a bastion of peace and democracy in the Balkans'[8] – in the sense, of course, that Soviet policy used those terms. Specially stressed was the circumstance that 'all the statements by the leaders of the new Yugoslavia ... bear witness to close friendship with and profound gratitude to the Soviet Union' and that, in the international arena, the Yugoslavs 'unwaveringly support all the proposals of the Soviet representatives and uphold its point of view'.[9]

At the same time the memorandum contains some critical comments regarding a few elements in the policy of the Yugoslav leadership. Basically, the criticism relates to questions of foreign policy, in dealing with which, as the memorandum puts it, 'some leaders of the Yugoslav CP sometimes show national narrowness, failing to take account of the interests of other countries and fraternal CPs'. Concretely, this meant, first, that the Yugoslav Government 'took up, for a long time, an incorrect position on the Trieste question, overlooking the common interests of the democratic forces in the fight against the Anglo-Americans where this question was concerned'. Second, mention was made of the presence of 'certain tendencies among the Party leaders to overestimate their achievements and to try to put the Yugoslav CP in the position of a sort of "leading" party in the Balkans'.[10]

On the first point no explanation was given. Evidently it was understood that those for whom the memorandum was intended were sufficiently informed regarding Belgrade's attempts in 1945–7 to obtain greater satisfaction of its demands in the Trieste question and its discontent with what the Yugoslav leaders considered the inadequate support given them by the Soviets. The Yugoslav position had in certain cases evoked rather sharp objections from Moscow which, though supporting Belgrade, nevertheless at the same time, in view of its own concerns, considered it necessary to make some concessions to the West in the matter of Trieste. One of the sharpest Soviet *démarches* in this connection was made secretly at the beginning of June 1945, arising from Tito's speech at Ljubljana which is well known in the historiography from Yugoslav publications issued after the 1948 break.[11] The Yugoslav leadership considered it necessary to respond to this *démarche* with apologies and assurances of its firm alliance with the USSR.[12] Historians were unaware of another case, when, in July 1946, on receiving a telegram from Tito reproaching the Soviet representatives for giving inadequate consideration to Yugoslavia's interests during the examination of the Trieste question at a session of the Council of Foreign Ministers in Paris, Stalin rejected this reproach.[13] On this occasion the reaction of the ruler of the USSR was, however, not as sharp as before, possibly because the Yugoslav's grievance was expressed in a secret telegram, not in a public statement. Given Stalin's response, Tito tried to smooth over this incident.[14] However, as is shown by the memorandum we are discussing, which was written at the end of August 1947, they had not forgotten in Moscow Belgrade's 'incorrect' pretensions to pursue its own specific aims regardless of the interests of Soviet policy. Incidentally, those interests are not named as such, in accordance with the tradition established in the writing of these documents, but are hidden behind the formula 'common interests of the democratic forces'. Concretely, what was referred to in this connection was merely the 'inadmissibly sharp' criticism by the Yugoslav press of the Italian CP, and of Togliatti personally, for their attitude on the Trieste question, which Belgrade found unsatisfactory.[15]

As regards the second point of criticism concerning Yugoslav actions in the sphere of foreign policy, the endeavour to put the KPJ 'in the position of a sort of "leading" party in the Balkans', the memorandum mentioned two instances. One consisted in the fact that, at the end of 1946, in connection with the publication of the draft of a constitution for Bulgaria, the KPJ leadership allowed itself, both through newspaper articles and through confidential contact with a representative of the CC of the Bulgarian CP, to accuse Sofia of taking an incorrect position on the Macedonian question and of encroaching on the rights of the Macedonians.[16] By the time the memorandum was written, however, these events had largely lost their topicality, following the Yugoslav-Bulgarian agreements concluded at the end of July and the beginning of August 1947, which, among other things, dealt with Bulgarian Macedonia.[17] Of much greater topicality was another instance quoted in the memorandum as an example of Belgrade's Balkan ambitions – Yugoslavia's policy towards Albania. Here, besides allegations of delay in the rendering of Yugoslav aid to Albania, what was meant was the Yugoslav–Albanian treaty of friendship and mutual assistance signed on 9 July 1946, the basis of the charge being opposition by Yugoslavia to the development of Soviet–Albanian relations. 'The leaders of the Yugoslav CP', it was said in the memorandum, 'viewed very jealously Albania's desire to have its own direct links with the Soviet Union. According to them, Albania ought to be linked with the Soviet Union only through the Yugoslav Government.'[18] The Yugoslavs' attitude resulted from the role of patron which the KPJ had played in relation to the Albanian CP during the war and which later developed into a similar relationship between the two Communist regimes. The Yugoslav side had shown a desire to strengthen this situation both where Albania's internal affairs were concerned and with respect to its foreign policy. During the war the Soviet leadership had been aware of the Yugoslavs' patronage role and approved of it.[19] In the immediate post-war period links between Moscow and Tirana were also effected through the Yugoslavs, in particular as regards Soviet supplies of armaments.[20] At his meeting with Tito in May 1946 Stalin spoke in favour of retaining this procedure for the channelling of Soviet aid to Albania. On the same occasion he made no objection to the Yugoslavs' desire to include Albania in Federal Yugoslavia, though he warned that such a move would be premature until the Trieste question, important for Belgrade, had been settled. Stalin proposed that, until then, they confine themselves to agreements for further development of the links between Albania and Yugoslavia, and Tito agreed to this.[21] From the documents so far available it is unclear whether Stalin was merely afraid of an untimely union of Albania with Yugoslavia or whether his argument was simply a ruse in order to block such unification in any event. Whatever the case, after this meeting the Soviet side informed the Albanian Government that it favoured 'Albania's orientation on closeness to Yugoslavia' and promoted the conclusion, in the second half of 1946, of the corresponding Yugoslav–Albanian agreements.[22] Later, however, especially after the visit to Moscow by Albania's leaders Enver Hoxha and Koci Xoxe in July 1947, direct links were gradually established between the USSR and Albania, especially in the economic sphere. These links, which included the sending to Albania of Soviet specialists to develop the country's oil resources, caused discontent among the Yugoslavs, as being a violation of their preferential position in Albania.[23] True, after the Albanians' July visit to Moscow the Soviet minister in Tirana told his Yugoslav colleague that Stalin had assured Hoxha of the unalterability of the Soviet position on Yugoslav–Albanian relations and of the USSR's intention to help Albania exclusively through the medium of Yugoslavia.[24] Obviously this must have demonstrated to the Yugoslavs the Kremlin's willingness, as before, to respect Belgrade's ambitions in

Albania. As we see, however, from the memorandum in the Foreign Policy Department of the CC of the CPSU(B) at the end of August, these ambitions, especially the Yugoslavs' endeavour to keep Albania's links with the USSR in their own hands, were viewed negatively by Moscow.

Besides these foreign policy matters, the memorandum also contained very guarded criticism of some internal features of the KPJ – that 'full-blooded Party work is not carried on in its organizations', that the CC, itself of very limited composition, 'fails to hold regular meetings', so that 'all questions of principle regarding the country's leadership are decided by a narrow circle (consisting of Tito, Kardelj, Ranković and Djilas)', and that, although much time had passed since the war ended, no congress of the KPJ had yet been held.[25]

Compared with the descriptions of other countries of the Soviet bloc contained in the memoranda written at that time, the evaluation of the situation in Yugoslavia and the policy of the Yugoslav leadership appears entirely favourable. No other country, perhaps, is spoken of so highly in respect of success achieved in establishing and consolidating the Communist regime and the firmness of the Communist Party's position. The only other Party placed, more or less, on a similar level was the Bulgarian CP, about which what was written also sometimes approached a panegyric.[26] As for critical comments, these are to be found, to one degree or another, in all the memoranda. And the criticism of Belgrade was far from being the harshest. Much more so was, for example, the criticism of the Czechoslovak Communist leadership, while that of their Polish counterparts was particularly sharp. The leaders of the Polish Workers' Party (PPR), and Gomułka personally, were accused of trying 'to ignore the experience of the Soviet Union' and to play down its role and help given in the liberation of Poland and the establishment there of 'people's democracy'. In that connection the memorandum on Poland referred to Gomułka's public statements about the inapplicability to Polish conditions of the Soviet road, with the role, inherent therein, of 'the dictatorship of the proletariat' and collectivization of the countryside. The press organs of the PPR were denounced because, 'speaking about Marxism in general', they 'say nothing about Lenin and Stalin'. Emphasized as criminal were the alleged creation by the Polish authorities of obstacles to the dissemination in Poland of Soviet publications and films and their ignoring and removal from the Polish Army of Soviet officers who had been sent into it earlier.[27] At first the memorandum was composed without these charges being included.[28] They appeared later, obviously on the orders of the head of the Foreign Policy Department of the CC of the CPSU(B) or of Suslov, who directly supervised this department in his capacity as secretary of the CC. In the memorandum on Czechoslovakia the leadership of that country's CP was sharply criticized for its enthusiasm for parliamentary activity and for 'peacefully collaborating with certain reactionary parties which are members of the National Front', instead of mobilizing the masses for struggle against them. It was concluded that the Communists had missed opportunities to secure more extensive nationalization and to conquer more positions in the state apparatus, the army and voluntary organizations. Specially mentioned was the inadequate work of the KSČ to popularize the USSR and Soviet experience, which, as in the case of Poland, was linked in the memorandum with the influence of ideas about a specific Czechoslovak road to Socialism different from the Soviet road. The original statement made by representatives of the KSČ in the Government in favour of Czechoslovakia participating in consideration of the Marshall Plan was described as 'a major political mistake and manifestation of an ill-disposed attitude to the Soviet Union'.[29] And the very much less extensive and sharp criticism of the CP of Hungary nevertheless included charges that 'certain leaders of the Party' were against the transfer of former German assets in Hungary to the Soviet Union, as provided by a decision of the Potsdam Conference, and also against payment of reparations and repayment of Soviet foodstuff loans. In the memorandum on Hungary, this was described not only as manifestation of a 'dependent attitude' towards the USSR but also as slipping into 'narrow-nationalist positions'.[30]

But while comparative analysis of the memoranda does not reveal any exceptionally critical attitude towards Belgrade's policy, it is noticeable that only in the comments on the Yugoslav leadership is a question raised which does not figure in the other memoranda, namely, striving on the part of one of the East European Communist regimes to play a leading role in relation to certain other CPs and 'people's democracies'. Such striving affected negatively the very nature of the Soviet bloc's structure and contradicted the hierarchical model of the bloc upheld by the Kremlin, in which there had to be one centre only, namely, Moscow. The memorandum on Yugoslavia shows that this did give rise to a certain misgiving on the Soviet side, and it may not have been perceived in leading Soviet spheres as a specific problem, but merely as one of the complications that periodically arose with the 'people's democracies', obliging the Kremlin to take the routine corrective measures needed to keep its East European wards under control. Just before this, as the memoranda in question were being put together, in August 1947, such a measure had had to be applied towards Sofia and also Belgrade, in connection with a joint action they had undertaken contrary to a Soviet ban. This was the announcement by the Governments of Bulgaria and Yugoslavia on 1 August 1947 that they had prepared and agreed upon – that is, in fact, initialled – a treaty of friendship, collaboration and mutual aid. Although Tito, through the

USSR's ambassador, and Dimitrov, in a telegram to Stalin, had notified Moscow at the beginning of July of their intention to sign the treaty,[31] the Kremlin considered that it was necessary to wait until the peace treaty with Bulgaria had been ratified. In fact so far back as the spring of 1945, when the question of a Bulgaro-Yugoslav treaty first arose, Great Britain, and the USA along with it, opposed the signing of such a treaty, referring to Bulgaria's status as a defeated enemy country. Although the peace treaty had been signed in February 1947 it had not yet come into force, as it had not been ratified. Consequently Stalin replied to Dimitrov on 5 July that signature of the Bulgaro-Yugoslav treaty should be put off until the peace treaty had come into force.[32] Dimitrov, however, considering that the Bulgaro-Yugoslav treaty could be signed without waiting for ratification of the peace treaty,[33] and Tito, who agreed with Dimitrov,[34] thought it possible, nevertheless, to initial the treaty and announce that this had been done. Taking that step meant disobeying Stalin's instruction. On 12 August, in identical messages sent to Tito and Dimitrov, he condemned their action extremely severely,[35] and this proved sufficient to make them submit in the spirit of hierarchical discipline and proceed thereafter, in the matter of the Bulgaro-Yugoslav treaty, in accordance with Stalin's directives.[36]

This result should have testified to the adequate effectiveness of routine measures by the Kremlin to prevent the 'people's democracies' from slipping into independent action within the Soviet bloc. From the documents, however, it is hard to say definitely the extent to which the Soviet leadership was satisfied with what had been achieved in connection with the Bulgaro-Yugoslav treaty, and whether they regarded this incident, which was kept strictly secret by all involved, as having been completely disposed of. It can be observed, though, that in none of the documents known to us, right down to the end of January 1948, was the incident referred to. In particular, it was not mentioned either in the memoranda on Bulgaria and Yugoslavia written at the end of August 1947 or in the memoranda on these countries and their CPs which were composed, as items in a series of memoranda on CPs and 'people's democracies', in the Foreign Policy Department of the CC of the CPSU(B) at the end of October 1947 and in the second half of January 1948.[37]

As regards the critical remarks contained in the memorandum on Yugoslavia composed in August 1947, to judge by the archive material we have investigated, before 1948 there was only one case of this criticism being repeated, and it related exclusively to the Trieste question. It appeared in one of the drafts for Zhdanov's report at the constituent conference of the Cominform, which was prepared in the first half of September 1947. Strictly speaking, the memoranda composed in August and the beginning of September were also written as materials for this report. In his draft, along with criticism of 'certain activists in the fraternal CPs' for their 'continual stressing' of 'their independence of Moscow' (which was actually directed first and foremost at the French and Italians), mention was also made of 'leftists mistakes', expressed in 'statements to the effect as if the USSR, from considerations of high politics, through willingness to spoil its relations with the great powers, fails to fight vigorously enough in support of the demands of small countries, in particular – Yugoslavia'.[38] We do not know whether this reference to Yugoslavia was inspired by actual intention to point out Belgrade's 'mistakes' or whether it was included for purely tactical purposes, so as to seem to balance the report's sharp criticism of the leaders of the French and Italian CPs for their concessions to 'imperialism and reaction', that is for what was called, in the Communist movement, 'right opportunism'. In the context of the report, however, where criticism of the French and Italians bulked incomparably bigger and constituted one of the most important features, the comment made in passing about the Yugoslavs does rather give the impression of being just a formal 'balancing'. In any case, what is most important is that, in the process of further editing of the report, this comment was completely removed and did not appear in the final text of the report which Zhdanov read at the constituent conference of the Cominform,[39] whereas the charges against the CPs of France and Italy were retained.[40]

At the conference itself, on 22–28 September 1947, the Yugoslavs were among the most active supporters of the delegation from the CPSU(B), and Zhdanov gave, in his reports to Stalin, very favourable accounts of the positions and contributions of the KPJ's representatives.[41] True, the view is held by a number of Western scholars that Zhdanov and the group in Soviet leading circles which he headed, being advocates of a militant 'left' orientation in USSR foreign policy, maintained specially close links with certain radical Communist leaders in Eastern Europe, especially with Tito and his close circle. This view is most fully set out in the book by Gavriel Ra'anan, who says that, in particular, the collaboration at the Cominform's constituent conference between Zhdanov, on the one hand, and Kardelj and Djilas, the KPJ's representatives, on the other, was a manifestation of these links, which amounted to the formation of a group.[42] But neither in Ra'anan's nor in other such works is any factual evidence given for the existence of such links,[43] and the examples quoted of coincidence of the ideological-political positions of Belgrade and those official propositions of Soviet policy (the authorship of which is attributed, in this version, to the Zhdanov group) cannot by themselves serve as proof of such links, testifying as they do merely to the identity of the Yugoslav line with Moscow's line at that period. Moreover, according to Djilas there were in fact no special links between the Yugoslav leadership and Zhdanov's group.⁴⁴ And as for the constituent conference of the Cominform, it is clear from the Soviet and Yugoslav archive documents that, during its preparation, which was directed by Zhdanov, the Yugoslavs, like the leaders of the other CPs participating, knew nothing of the true plans of the Soviets and the purposes of the conference and there was no preliminary agreement on joint action.⁴⁵ Yugoslav policy was described in an extremely positive way after the conference, too, both in public Soviet propaganda, notably in the fundamental articles in the Party's central journal *Bolshevik* at the end of 1947⁴⁶ and also in the memoranda, already mentioned, which were composed in the Foreign Policy Department of the CC of the CPSU(B) in October 1947 and January 1948.⁴⁷ Furthermore, in these memoranda, in contrast to what had been written in August 1947, there were no critical remarks whatsoever.

Yet the USSR's embassy in Belgrade – from which even earlier reports had from time to time been sent which contained critical remarks concerning the Yugoslav leadership – continued to send such information to Moscow. Moreover, precisely between the autumn of 1947 and January 1948 this information became markedly harsher. It did not deal, though, with the matters included in the August memorandum by the Foreign Policy Department of the CC of the CPSU(B). The embassy's reports spoke of the Yugoslavs' exaggeration of the importance of and the experience gained in their own armed struggle in 1941–5, and of their underestimate of Soviet military experience and of the role of the USSR in the liberation of Yugoslavia from occupation. These charges the ambassador, Anatolii Lavrent'ev, aimed particularly at Tito himself, with reference to his report at the Second Congress of the People's Front of Yugoslavia on 27 September 1947. In one of the ambassador's telegrams on this matter sent to the USSR Ministry of Foreign Affairs, Tito's position was described as one of 'national limitedness'. This was repeated in the reports which Lavrent'ev and the Soviet military attaché in Belgrade, Major-General Sidorovich, sent in the first ten days of January 1948 to Moscow concerning several speeches by Tito and leading Yugoslav military men at the end of December 1947. The appraisals contained in these reports were still more severe, going so far as to accuse the Yugoslavs of not understanding 'the essence of Marxism–Leninism', and of lacking a clear-cut ideological-political orientation, while Tito's actual 'leaderism' was directly counterposed by Lavrent'ev to Stalin's 'legitimate' charisma.⁴⁸

When examining these moves by Lavrent'ev and Sidorovich I found myself wondering what gave rise to such very harsh reports, and whether they resulted from the writers' own initiatives or had been encouraged, or even directly inspired, by someone in Moscow.⁴⁹ Clarification of this point is all the more important because, according to the version presented in Ra'anan's book, the Soviet–Yugoslav conflict resulted to a large extent from a struggle within the Soviet leadership against Zhdanov's group which, as already mentioned, was, according to this version, linked with Tito.[50] The archive materials so far studied, however, contain no evidence for the cause of the conflict, nor of the reasons for the steps taken by Lavrent'ev and Sidorovich. All that emerges is that, after Moscow received the telegram from Lavrent'ev about Tito's speech at the Second Congress of the People's Front of Yugoslavia on 27 September 1947, the official in charge of the Balkan Countries Department of the USSR Ministry of Foreign Affairs, Aleksandr Lavrishchev, sent on 8 October to Molotov a report in which he decisively objected to the artificial, purposeful nature of the ambassador's allegations, and showed that these did not square with what Tito had actually said.[51] Lavrishchev was right: this telegram, like other similar reports by Lavrent'ev, was obviously tendentious.[52] We have as yet no data at our disposal on how the higher Soviet spheres reacted to these reports. But proposals from Lavrent'ev and Sidorovich that the Yugoslavs' 'mistakes' be pointed out either to the representative of the CC of the KPJ with the CC of the CPSU(B), or to Djilas, who came to Moscow in mid-January 1948, or through the Cominform, were not acted upon at that time.

Meanwhile, at the end of 1947 and the beginning of 1948 some difficulties arose between Moscow and Belgrade which were not artificially inspired but were real, in connection with the problem referred to in the August 1947 memorandum of the Foreign Policy Department of the CC of the CPSU(B), a problem which affected the nature of the Soviet bloc's structure, namely, correlation of the roles of Yugoslavia and the USSR in Albania.

The Yugoslavs' concern at the establishment of direct links between the USSR and Albania, which began after the visit by Hoxha and Xoxe to Moscow in July 1947, was seriously intensified by reports that an influential member of the Albanian leadership, Nako Spiru, who had been accused by Belgrade in November 1947 of sabotaging economic collaboration with Yugoslavia, maintained special contacts with the Soviet representatives in Tirana. And although Spiru killed himself without waiting for the charge against him to be examined by the Politburo of the CC of the PKSh, the Yugoslavs took up this issue with the Soviet leadership at the beginning of December. They tried to get agreement for withdrawal of Soviet specialists from Albania and for measures to strengthen the predominant role of Yugoslavia in that country.[53] As we know, Stalin's reply was to invite the Yugoslavs to send to Moscow Djilas or some other 'responsible comrade' who was 'best-informed about the situation in Albania', and on 17 January 1948, at a meeting with Stalin, Molotov and Zhdanov, Djilas received the

Soviets' agreement that Albania's development be wholly bound up with Yugoslavia, even to the point of unification, and that the activity of the Soviet military and economic advisers in Albania be co-ordinated with the Yugoslavs. However, as at his meeting with Tito in May 1946, Stalin spoke of the necessity of avoiding haste in the formal unification of Albania with Yugoslavia and of waiting for a suitable moment.[54] The archive documents studied provide no clear answer here, either, to the question whether Stalin was expressing his real intentions or was continuing to play a game with the Yugoslavs.

On 19 January, having received from Moscow Djilas's report on the Soviet position, Tito sent Hoxha a proposal that he offer a base in southern Albania for a Yugoslav division to be sent in, alluding to reports of the danger of a Greek invasion of Albania, supported by 'the Anglo-Americans'. Hoxha replied on 20 January, agreeing.[55] According to Djilas, Tito really wanted to send his troops in to strengthen Yugoslavia's position in Albania.[56] If so, it is not clear whether Tito was encouraged to take this step by Stalin's statement to Djilas supporting Belgrade's preponderant interest in Albania or whether, on the contrary, Stalin's warning against hasty unification made Tito suspicious and impelled him to lose no time in sending in his troops. In any case, Tito took his decision without consulting Moscow, and did not inform it of his appeal to Hoxha.

We know from documents published in recent years that when Moscow learnt of Tito's action it sharply condemned the conduct of the Yugoslav leadership and spoke of 'serious differences' with them 'in how we understand the relations between our countries'. Tito, conforming to the spirit of hierarchical discipline, duly admitted his 'mistake' and refrained from sending his troops into Albania, but the Kremlin was not satisfied with this, and demanded that 'responsible representatives of the Yugoslav Government' be sent to Moscow to discuss their 'differences'.[57] The sharpness of the Soviet leadership's reaction was seriously intensified, it is clear, by the circumstance that, simultaneously with the Yugoslavs, Dimitrov made a foreign policy move not sanctioned by Moscow when, on 17 January 1948, he spoke to journalists about the future creation of a federation of East European countries, including all the 'people's democracies' and even Greece, where the CP was waging war to establish a similar regime. This interview, which became widely known, gave rise to public Soviet condemnation, something unprecedented, in *Pravda* of 28 January, which itself also produced widespread international echoes. Although Dimitrov, who was no less disciplined than Tito, reacted to this criticism by publicly expressing his agreement with it, his attempts to provide some sort of explanation of his position caused still greater misgiving in the Kremlin,[58] where they were disturbed by the simultaneous actions of the Bulgarians and the Yugoslavs, undertaken without the Kremlin's permission. Stalin decided to deal with both of them together, so the Bulgarians and the Yugoslavs were summoned to Moscow at the same time.

What happened at the meeting between Stalin and the Bulgarian and Yugoslav delegations – headed, respectively, by Dimitrov and Kardelj – on 10 February 1948, was known until recently only from the semi-official biography of Tito written by Vladimir Dedijer and the memoirs of Djilas and Kardelj.[59] It has now become known that there are Yugoslav, Bulgarian and Soviet archive documents on this meeting. Using materials from Tito's archive[60] I have already studied the meeting in detail and devoted a special work to this subject.[61] The meeting on 10 February was described by the Bulgarian historian Dobrin Michev more briefly on the basis of the minutes, kept in the archives, that were taken by Kostov, who was present at the meeting.[62] Kostov's minutes, which I was also able to see, and the minutes that were taken by Kolarov, another Bulgarian participant at the meeting,[63] like the still-not-declassified Soviet minutes, correspond on the whole, despite a few nuances, with what was recorded in the Yugoslav archive materials examined by me in the above-mentioned work. While referring the reader to that work, for the details, I will mention that the encounter amounted to a severe slating of the Bulgarians and Yugoslavs by the Soviet leadership for their announcement, unauthorized by Moscow, of the Bulgaro-Yugoslav treaty in August 1947, Dimitrov's statement about a federation in Eastern Europe, and the attempt to send a Yugoslav division into Albania. The criticism made of these actions was justified by their mistakenness in view of the tense relations with the West, but the fundamental sentiment behind it was the inadmissibility of taking such steps without the Kremlin's consent. The Yugoslav and Bulgarian delegations admitted all their 'mistakes'. As a result of the meeting there were signed on 11 February, on the Soviets' initiative, protocols providing for obligatory consultation, where international questions were concerned, between the USSR and Yugoslavia and between the USSR and Bulgaria. As regards Yugoslavia specifically, at the 10 February meeting Stalin firmly reiterated his ban on stationing Yugoslav troops in Albania. He hinted transparently at his suspicion that 'the Yugoslavs are afraid of Russians in Albania and for that reason are hastening to send in their troops'. And to the unification of Albania with Yugoslavia desired by Belgrade he counterposed the idea of the formation, as soon as possible, of a Yugoslav–Bulgarian federation, and, only after that, the unification of Albania with this federation, and not with Yugoslavia alone. This actually put in question Belgrade's intentions towards Albania.

Judging by the available documents, the Yugoslav delegation at the meeting returned no definite answer to this proposal. At the meeting of the Yugoslav Politburo on 19 February, at which the delegation reported, the proposed federation with Bulgaria was firmly rejected.[64] This was confirmed at an enlarged meeting of the Politburo on 1 March, where the conclusion was formulated that, given the Soviets' special influence in Bulgaria, federation with that country could serve as a means of bringing about undesirable control over Yugoslavia as well. At this meeting confirmation was given to the line of continued promotion of Yugoslavia's predominant position in Albania.[65] At the end of February and the beginning of March the Albanian Government, ignorant of the meeting in Moscow on 10 February, again put before the USSR, under the influence of Belgrade, the question of need to bring Yugoslav troops into Albania owing to the danger from Greece, and the Yugoslavs began to persuade Tirana to come forward also with a proposal for uniting Albania with Yugoslavia.[66] Thus, the Yugoslav Government, which had hitherto, as a rule, subordinated itself to the hierarchical relations within the Soviet bloc, was now acting contrary to Soviet instructions.

Along with this, at the enlarged Politburo meeting on 1 March a more general conclusion was drawn, namely, that the USSR was unwilling to take account of the interests of Yugoslavia or of the other 'people's democracies', was trying to subject them to its own aspirations and was exerting pressure on them. Considered as an example of this pressure was the fact that from the end of January and beginning of February 1948 the Soviets, despite their original promises, had begun to delay the solving, desired by the Yugoslavs, of problems connected with fresh supplies of Soviet arms for the Yugoslav Army and with the further development of trade and economic co-operation. The meeting decided to direct policy towards developing the country's economy and strengthening its Army from Yugoslavia's own resources.[67] In fact, the Yugoslav leadership, following its own interests, was thereby taking the road of revolt against Moscow's domination of the Soviet bloc. Meanwhile, a member of the Yugoslav Politburo, Streten Žujović, who was present on 1 March (he had not attended the meeting on 19 February), informed Lavrent'ev in detail about the proceedings.[68]

Up to now we have hardly any direct evidence as to the Kremlin's position in relation to the Yugoslav leadership in the period between the meeting on 10 February and the beginning of March, when Lavrent'ev's report, based on the information supplied by Žujović, was received in Moscow. In Yugoslav historiography and memoirs it is made to appear that, immediately after the 10 February meeting, the Yugoslavs who took part in it and who afterwards remained in Moscow for a few days became aware of an acute estrangement, if not hostility, on the Soviet side, and at the signing on 11 February of the protocol on mutual consultation Molotov was intentionally rude to Kardelj, so that the latter was not able even to have a conversation with him.[69] This presentation has given the impression that the Soviet leaders had already then decided on conflict with Belgrade. From the archive documents, however, it is clear that, on the contrary, a conversation did take place on 11 February between Kardelj and Molotov, during which, besides raising questions of economic and military co-operation, Kardelj spoke of Tito's wish to visit Moscow in March or April, so as to clear up misunderstandings arising from the question of Albania. And on 13 February, when he again met Kardelj (the Yugoslavs, even Djilas, never mentioned this), Molotov said that Stalin would be pleased if Tito came, and also that examination of the military and economic problems would be continued.[70] Something else is also to be noted. On 23 February Djilas, talking with Lavrent'ev in Belgrade, expressed surprise that Tito's report to the 2nd Congress of Yugoslavia's People's Front had not been published in the USSR and asked whether this meant that the Soviets disagreed with some proposition contained in this report.[71] It may be that the Yugoslavs had found something out about the Soviet ambassador's report concerning that speech. On receiving Lavrent'ev's telegram about the question put by Djilas, the Balkan Countries Department of the USSR Ministry of Foreign Affairs, with the sanction of Deputy Minister Valerian Zorin, who had been at the meeting on 10 February, proposed to the publishing house for political literature, at the beginning of March, that they urgently include the speech in question in a collection of Tito's articles and speeches which was at that moment being prepared for publication, in Russian translation, by this central Soviet publishing house.[72] It would seem that all this must tend to show that Moscow, while trying to get Belgrade to submit to its demands, was nevertheless not set on a course towards conflict with Tito.

Žujović's information, sent through Lavrent'ev, about the Yugoslav Politburo meeting of 1 March seemed 'criminal', unacceptable from the standpoint of Soviet dominance in the bloc, and all the more so because it was supplemented by news of Belgrade's ignoring of the instructions given at the 10 February meeting about Balkan affairs and, in particular, about ties with Albania. On 9 March Lavrent'ev telegraphed to Moscow that the Yugoslavs, acting contrary to previous practice, had refused to give the Soviet trade representative information about Yugoslavia's economy. The ambassador's despatch concluded that this 'signals a change' in the attitude of the Yugoslav leaders towards the USSR.[73] As we know, the USSR referred specifically to this incident when it informed Tito on 18 March that it was recalling from Yugoslavia the Soviet civil and military advisers who were working there. And, in the subsequent correspondence between the Soviet and Yugoslav leaderships, the Kremlin, in its letter of 27 March, accused Belgrade of taking an anti-Soviet line, of opportunist mistakes and of revising most important theses of Marxism–Leninism.

The task of preparing this broad political and ideological onslaught was given to the Foreign Policy Department of the CC of the CPSU(B), apparently in the first half of March. In any case, on 18 March the Department had already presented Suslov with a memorandum 'On the anti-Marxist line of the leaders of the Communist Party of Yugoslavia in questions of external and internal policy'.[74] It contained the basic set of accusations which, beginning with the letter of 27 March, were launched by the Soviet leadership when it became clear that Tito, in response to the recall of the Soviet advisers, was showing no sign of repentance. For the framing of these accusations what was utilized was, partly, the matter contained in the reports by Lavrent'ev and Sidorovich mentioned earlier and, partly, the comments made in the August 1947 memorandum, much harshened and inflated. To the latter element was related the thesis included in the memorandum of 18 March about Belgrade's claim to play 'the leading role in the Balkan and Danubian countries'. In the later Soviet letters to the Yugoslav leadership, however, neither this thesis nor the charge concerning Albania was mentioned.

The advancing of general political and ideological accusations against the Yugoslavs meant turning the conflict into a head-on collision, inasmuch as it left Belgrade with one choice only – between complete surrender and resolute resistance. The escalation of the conflict which resulted, expressed in correspondence between the rulers of the USSR and Yugoslavia and leading to the Cominform resolution of June 1948, is sufficiently well known and has been frequently studied in historical writings (although it has to be said that the correspondence published by the Yugoslavs in 1948 was far from complete).[75] Less well known is what happened, simultaneously with this escalation, in the relations between Moscow and the Communist leaders of the other countries of the Soviet bloc.

The archives of the CC of the CPSU(B) show that when they launched their attack on Belgrade the Soviet rulers were at the same time concerned to prevent any inclination appearing, among the other Communist leaders of Eastern Europe, towards independence expressed in taking decisions without previous Soviet sanction, or, worse, contrary to Soviet instructions. Almost parallel with the fabrication of the 'Yugoslav case' in the Foreign Policy Department of the CC of the CPSU(B), broadly similar materials were prepared in relation to some other East European CPs. On 5 April the Department presented Suslov with two memoranda: one 'On the anti-Marxist ideological positions of the leadership of the PPR',[76] the other 'On certain mistakes by the Communist Party of Czechoslovakia'.[77] Both had been written in March: one of the variants of the memorandum on the PPR which preceded the final version was dated 24 March.[78] In March the Foreign

Policy Department composed yet another memorandum: 'On the nationalistic mistakes of the leadership of the Hungarian CP and bourgeois influence in the Hungarian Communist press.'[79] The deputy head of the Department, Leonid Baranov (he actually directed the current work of the Department after Suslov, who had headed it since 1946, became in 1947 secretary of the CC), sent it to Suslov on 25 March.[80] However, like the memorandum of 18 March on the KPJ, the memoranda on the PPR and the KSC were signed not only by the referents who composed them but also by Baranov himself, i.e. they were sent up in the Department's name. The memorandum on Hungary was signed by the referents only.

The basis of all three documents was the criticism that had already been set out in the memoranda on Poland, Czechoslovakia and Hungary which were composed in the Department in August and early September 1947. Now, however, this criticism, as in the Yugoslav case, was, especially with regard to the PPR and the KSC, harshened to the point of incredibility, inflated, and made the pivot of the description given of the leaders of these CPs. Not only the Poles but also the Czechoslovaks (despite the successful Communist coup of February 1948) were accused of 'anti-Marxist positions', and the Hungarians as well, with particular sharpness of 'slipping into a position of nationalism'. In their structure and tone both of these memoranda – to a greater extent in the one on the PPR, and a little less so in the one on the KSC – were similar to the memorandum on the KPJ. In so far as the latter was the political-ideological basis for the fabrication of 'the Yugoslav case', it suggests that there were plans to fabricate similar cases against the Communist leaders of Poland, first and foremost, and possibly those of Czechoslovakia as well. (The memorandum on the PPR certainly contained the bases of the subsequent accusations against Gomułka.) Considerably less sharp was the memorandum on Hungary which might have served as no more than a 'slating' of the Hungarian leadership and for that reason, apparently, was not signed by Baranov.

However, in the situation created by the developing 'Yugoslav case', Moscow eventually did not choose, at that moment, to proceed with the realization of similar 'cases' against the leaders of any of the other countries of the Soviet bloc. Instead, it made efforts to involve them in its action against Belgrade, by circulating among them, unknown to the Yugoslavs, its letter of 27 March. The calculation was obvious: the East European leaders, faced with the necessity of telling the Soviet authorities what their attitude was in the conflict which had begun, were obliged to associate themselves with the condemnation of the Yugoslavs. Thereby, on the one hand, the political pressure on Belgrade would be intensified, while, on the other, the subordination of the other Communist regimes of Eastern Europe would also be intensified. It may be that the materials concerning the Poles, Czechs and Hungarians were made ready for use in case they should prove unwilling to join the attack on Belgrade.

Many of the East European Communist leaders viewed the Soviet accusations against Tito and his circle with scepticism, since they knew them as, precisely, men of the greatest Communist orthodoxy. Misgivings with regard to the accusations were expressed by Gomułka to a representative of the Soviet Embassy and members of the Polish Politburo as soon as he heard them at the beginning of April 1948.[81] According to Djilas, on 19 April Dimitrov, passing through Belgrade, expressed support for the Yugoslavs in a *tête-à-tête* with him.[82] Gheorghiu-Dej, too, judging by his conversation with the Yugoslav Ambassador to Romania on 16 May, did not take the Soviet charges seriously.[83] When they received copies of the Soviet letter of 27 March to the Yugoslavs, signed by Stalin and Molotov, the leaderships of the CPs of Poland, Czechoslovakia and Romania did not at first consider it necessary to adopt special resolutions and send them to Moscow. And the Bulgarian Politburo, though on 6 April it passed a resolution for solidarity with the Soviet position, also did not consider it necessary to send it to Moscow.[84] Explaining this attitude a little later, Gottwald, for example, justified it by saying that the leadership of the KSC immediately and completely supported the Soviet point of view, but did not think that there was need to adopt a special resolution on the matter.[85] It is hard to say whether that was all there was to it, or whether this also implied unwillingness to get involved in the action against Belgrade which the Kremlin had started. In any case, the majority of the Communist leaders of the Soviet bloc countries failed to demonstrate immediately the zeal required by their Soviet patron. The Hungarians alone, after adopting on 8 April a resolution sharply condemning the Yugoslavs, hastened to send it to the CC of the CPSU(B), specially indicating that it could be communicated to the other CPs which had received the Soviet letter of 27 March.[86]

Moscow at once forwarded the Hungarian resolution not only to Belgrade but also to the other CPs concerned, thereby giving the latter clearly to understand what reply was expected from them. Only after receiving this reminder did they follow the Hungarian example.

Gottwald, on receiving on 17 April the copy of the Hungarians' resolution from the official of the Foreign Policy Department of the CC of the CPSU(B) who had brought it to Prague, at once announced that the Presidium of the CC of the KSC would discuss this question in the next few days.[87] And this was done on 19 April when a resolution was adopted which was sent to Moscow on 23 April.[88] Gottwald was unable to conceal from the Soviet representative his annoyance that the Hungarian Communist leadership had hastened to leap ahead in the role of pioneer of loyalty to Moscow, and there and then recalled that, earlier, the Hungarians had often joined with the Yugoslavs in criticizing the KSC.[89] Relations between the Czechoslovak and Hungarian CPs were at that time particularly strained owing to the problem of the Hungarians in Slovakia: this question had even been brought up by the Hungarians at the constituent conference of the Cominform and became the subject there of an acute polemic between them and the Czechoslovaks,[90] and in February 1948 Rákosi had proposed, in a conversation with Suslov, that it be discussed at the next conference of the Cominform.[91] It is not to be ruled out, though, that Gottwald's annoyance was due not only to the contradictions between Czechoslovakia and Hungary but also to the fact that the Hungarian Party leadership's speedy association of itself with the Soviet action against the Yugoslavs made it necessary for Prague to do the same.

Like the leaders of the KSC, those of the other East European countries submitted in a disciplined way to the signal from Moscow. On 18 April Dimitrov sent to the CC of the CPSU(B) the resolution of the Bulgarian Politburo adopted on 6 April; on the following day, 19 April, Gomułka sent the resolution of the Polish Politburo; and on 22 April Gheorghiu-Dej sent to Moscow the Romanian Politburo's resolution. From the CC of the CPSU(B) all these documents, which condemned the leaders of the KPJ and expressed support for the Soviet position, were forwarded to the CC of the KPJ.[92]

The obedience eventually shown by the East European members of the Cominform and later, at the end of April and in the first half of May, by the West European ones as well, enabled the Kremlin to proceed in May to take steps to convene a conference of the Cominform to examine 'the Soviet–Yugoslav differences'. The position taken up already beforehand by all the parties in the Cominform except the Yugoslavs determined in advance that the nature of the examination would be pleasing to Moscow.

This position was due to a complex of causes. The direct resistance of Belgrade to the Soviet charges, and still more the Yugoslavs' subsequent refusal, in May, to participate in the forthcoming conference of the Cominform was incompatible with the attachment of the leaders of the East European countries to the 'bloc' orientation, not to mention that the very establishment and existence of their Communist regimes, unlike that of Yugoslavia, was to a decisive degree ensured precisely by Soviet control over these countries. Consequently, for example, both Gheorghiu-Dej and Gomułka, neither of whom believed in the Soviet accusations, nevertheless considered it necessary to maintain their loyalty to Moscow, and tried to persuade the Yugoslavs to settle the conflict exclusively by way of normalizing relations with the USSR and reaching agreement with it within the framework of 'the camp' and the

Cominform. The Yugoslavs' resistance to Moscow and non-participation in the Cominform conference was perceived by them as a step which would 'help the enemy' and be a 'split from the world revolutionary movement'.[93] In fact their position meant co-operating in the consolidation of a situation of absolute Soviet dictatorship over Eastern Europe.

At the same time, for some of the East European Communist leaders, support of the Soviet accusations against the Yugoslavs was stimulated also by some additional motives. One of these was a rather noticeable endeavour to merit the special favour of the Soviet patron, thereby strengthening their own positions. Judging by the archive materials, this factor was to a considerable degree operative in the conduct of Rákosi, especially. Characteristic was the position taken up, as already mentioned, by the Hungarian Communist leadership in connection with the Soviet letter of 27 March. And in May it even tried to take upon itself the initiative in convening the Cominform conference, though this had already been done by the Kremlin.[94] When the conference took place, in June 1948, Rákosi assumed what was perhaps the most radical attitude, proposing even co-operation in organizing underground anti-Tito struggle in Yugoslavia.[95] After the conference he proposed to Moscow that a group of East European Communist leaders go to Belgrade, to the Fifth Congress of the KPJ, so as to call openly at this congress for the removal of Tito and his circle from the leadership.[96] And not only Rákosi but also almost all the other East European (and also West European) participants in the 1948 conference showed desire to pay back Belgrade for its previous privileged situation in the Soviet bloc and the Communist movement in the first years after the war, for that arrogance and criticism of other CPs and 'people's democracies' by which the Yugoslavs had offended during their period as the Soviets' principal ally.[97] Finally, the Bulgarian delegates at the 1948 conference were noticeably influenced by their disputes with Belgrade on the Macedonian question.[98] All these causes resulted in the leaders of the countries of the Soviet bloc supporting Moscow's position and going along with it in direct opposition to Belgrade – the first split in the bloc.

Notes

1. S. Clissold (ed.), *Yugoslavia and the Soviet Union, 1939–1973: A Documentary Survey* (London: 1975).
2. See: L.Ia. Gibianskii, *Sovetskii Soiuz i novaia Yugoslaviia, 1941–1947gg.* (Moscow: 1987); N. Popović, *Jugoslovensko–sovjetski odnosi u drugom svetskom ratu (1941–1945)* (Belgrade: 1988). This is confirmed, for the war period, by the new Soviet archive documents examined in P. Jukić, 'Soviet Diplomacy, the Comintern and the Partisan Cause: New Perspectives on the Soviet Union and the Yugoslav Revolution', paper

presented at the conference 'The Establishment of the Communist Regimes in Eastern Europe, 1945–1950: A Reassessment' (Moscow, 29–31 March 1994).
3. For more details see L. Gibianskii, 'The Soviet–Yugoslav Conflict and the Formation of the "Socialist Camp" Model', in O.A. Westad *et al.* (eds), *The Soviet Union in Eastern Europe, 1945–1989* (London–New York: 1994) pp. 26–31. See also the works mentioned in note 2.
4. Altogether, 37 such memoranda were composed, RTsKhIDNI, f. 575, op. 1, d. 7–43; Memoranda on East European 'people's democracies', RTsKhIDNI, f. 575, op. 1, d. 9, 11, 14, 32, 33, 39, 41.
5. RTsKhIDNI, f. 575, op. 1, d. 41, l. 1–15, 18–19.
6. *Ibid.*, l. 9.
7. *Ibid.*, l. 15–18.
8. *Ibid.*, l. 15.
9. *Ibid.*
10. *Ibid.*, l. 22.
11. *Pisma TsK KPj i pisma TsK SKP(b)* (Belgrade: 1948) pp. 41–2.
12. AJ-CK SKJ, f. 507, IX, 1–I/22, l. 18, 52; M. Djilas, *Vlast i pobuna* (Belgrade: 1991) pp. 81–2.
13. AJBT-KMJ, 1–3–b/634; AVP RF, f. 0144, op. 30, p. 118, d. 116, l. 28.
14. AVP RF, f. 0144, op. 30, p.-118, d. 16, l. 28–9.
15. RTsKhIDNI, f. 575, op. 1, d. 41, l. 22.
16. *Ibid.*, l. 22–3.
17. On the agreements see D. Michev, *Makedonskiiat v'pros i b'lgaro–iugoslavskite otnosheniia, 9 septemvri 1944–1949* (Sofia: 1994) p. 316.
18. RTsKhIDNI, f. 575, op. 1, d. 41, l. 23.
19. RTsKhIDNI, f. 495, op. 74, d. 599, l. 54, 57; RTsKhIDNI, f. 495, op. 74, d. 178, l. 1; RTsKhIDNI, f. 495, op. 74, d. 31, l. 5.
20. See, for example, 'Novye dokumenty o Velikoi Otechestvennoi voine', *Kommunist*, 7 (1970) 52.
21. 'Poslednii vizit I. Broza Tito k. I.V. Stalinu: Sovetskaia i iugoslavskaia zapisi besedy, 27–28 maia 1946g.' (published by L.Ia. Gibianskii and Iu.G. Murin), *Istoricheskii arkhiv*, 2 (1993) 23, 26.
22. AVP RF, f. 0144, op. 30, p. 118, d. 15, l. 167–8; AVP RF, f. 0144, op. 30, p. 118, d. 16, l. 1.
23. This found expression a little later in a Yugoslav address to Moscow, RTsKhIDNI, f. 77, op. 3, d. 99. l. 2; AJBT-KMJ, 1–3–b/651, l. 3.
24. AJ-CK SKJ, IX, 1/I–143.
25. RTsKhIDNI, f. 575, op. 1, d. 41, l. 20–1.
26. RTsKhIDNI, f. 575, op. 1, d. 11, l. 42–80; another copy of the memorandum on Bulgaria, *ibid.*, l. 2–41.
27. RTsKhIDNI, f. 575, op. 1, d. 376, l. 1–18.
29. Memorandum on Czechoslovakia, RTsKhIDNI, f. 575, op. 1. d. 39, l. 3–30; criticism directed at the leadership of the KSČ, *ibid.*, l. 21–9.
30. RTsKhIDNI, f. 575, op. 1, d. 14, l. 42. On Hungary separate memoranda were composed on the situation in the country (*ibid.*, l. 2–20) and the Communist Party (*ibid.*, l. 21–43); another copy, *ibid.*, l. 44–65.
31. RTsKhIDNI, f. 17, op. 128, d. 294, l. 28; TsDA-TsPA, f. 146, op. 6, a.e. 1064, l. 1.
32. TsDA-TsPA, f. 146, op. 4, a.e. 639, l. 9; the reply is quoted also by Michev, *Makedonskiiat v'pros*, p. 309.
33. AJBT-KMJ, 1–2/17, l. 7; TsDA-TsPA, f. 146, op. 4, a.e. 54, l. 12; TsDA-TsPA, f. 146, op. 6, a.e. 1064, l. 1.

34. TsDA-TsPA, f. 146, op. 4, a.e. 54, l. 12.
35. AJBT-KMJ, I–2/17, l. 70.
36. For more detail see: L.Ia. Gibianskii, 'U nachala konflikta: balkanskii uzel', *Rabochii klass i sovremennyi mir*, 2 (1990) 174; Id., 'K istorii sovetsko–iugoslavo konflikta 1948–1953 gg.: Sekretnaia sovetsko–iugoslavo–bolgarskaia vstrecha v Moskve 10 fevralia 1948 goda', *Sovetskoe slavianovedenie*, 3 (1991) 16–17; M. Isusov, *Stalin i B'lgariia* (Sofia: 1991) p. 70.
37. At the end of October 1947 'brief memoranda' were written on these foreign CPs, which were covered by the memoranda of August–September (RTsKhIDNI, f. 575, op. 1, d. 44); in the second half of January 1948 memoranda were composed, to be presented at the end of January and beginning of February, on the influence of the resolutions of the constituent Conference of the Cominform on these CPs (RTsKhIDNI, f. 575, op. 1, d. 53).
38. RTsKhIDNI, f. 77, op. 3, d. 91, l. 46–7; RTsKhIDNI, f. 77, op. 3, d. 94, l. 90–1.
39. *Ibid.*, l. 44, 90–1.
40. *Ibid.*, l. 40–3.
41. RTsKhIDNI, f. 77, op. 3, d. 92, l. 46–7, 52–4. For more detail see: L.Ia. Gibianskii, 'Kak voznik Kominform. Po novym arkhivnym materialam', *Novaia i noveishaia istoriia*, 4 (1993); L. Gibianskij, 'La costituzione del Cominform (alla luce di nuovi materiali d'archivio)', *Storia contemporanea*, 4 (1993).
42. G. Ra'anan, *International Policy Formation in the USSR: Factional 'Debates' during the Zhdanovshchina* (Hamden, Conn.: 1983) pp. 3, 8, 42–53, 75–6, 101, 103–6, 111–17.
43. The statements about Zhdanov's alleged visits to Yugoslavia in 1944–5 (Ra'anan, *International Policy*, pp. 52–3) are without foundation.
44. Conversation of L.Ia. Gibianskii with M. Djilas, 13 July 1990.
45. For more detail see: Gibianskii, 'Kak voznik Kominform', 139–44; Gibianskij, 'La costituzione', 498–507.
46. Ia. Mirov, 'Kompartii Evropy v bor'be za mir, demokratiiu i nezavisimost' narodov', *Bol'shevik*, 21 (1947); V. Moshetov, V. Lesakov, 'O demokraticheskikh preobrazovaniiakh v stranakh novoi demokratii', *Bol'shevik*, 22 (1947).
47. RTsKhIDNI, f. 575, op. 1, d. 44, l. 160–3; RTsKhIDNI, f. 575, op. 1, d. 53, l. 296–9.
48. For more detail see I.V. Bukharkin, L.Ia. Gibianskii, 'Pervye shagi konflikta', *Rabochii klass i sovremennyi mir*, 5 (1990) 160–3.
49. L.Ia. Gibianskii, 'Vyzov v Moskvu', *Politicheskie issledovaniia*, 1 (1991) 195–6, 200.
50. Ra'anan, *International Policy*, pp. 3, 135–49. For my thoughts concerning this view, see Gibianskii, 'Vyzov v Moskvu', 199–200.
51. AVP RF, f. 0144, op. 31, p. 124, d. 29, l. 7–9.
52. See Bukharkin, Gibianskii, 'Pervye shagi', 161–2.
53. RTsKhIDNI, f. 77, op. 3, d. 99, l. 1–5, 8; AJBT-KMJ, I–3–b/651, l. 1–5; ASSIP-PA, 1947, F-IV, Str. Pov. 1765.
54. For more detail see: Gibianskii, 'U nachala konflikta', 179–81; Id., 'The 1948 Soviet–Yugoslav Conflict', 34–5.
55. AJ-CK SKJ, IX, 1/I–154, l. 1–2; AJBT-KMJ, I–3–b/34; AJBT-KMJ, I–3–b/651, l. 24.
56. Djilas, *Vlast i pobuna*, p. 125.

57. See for more details Gibianskii, 'The 1948 Soviet–Yugoslav Conflict', 36–8.
58. TsDA-TsPA, f. 146, op. 2, a.e. 1766, l. 4–6: TsDA-TsPA, f. 146, op. 5, a.e. 325, l. 3.
59. V. Dedijer, *Josip Broz Tito: Prilozi za biografiju* (Belgrade: 1953) pp. 497–504; E. Kardelj, *Borba za priznanje i nezavisnost nove Jugoslavije 1944–1957: Sećanja* (Belgrade and Ljubljana: 1980) pp. 112–17; M. Djilas, *Razgovori sa Staljinom* (Belgrade: 1990) pp. 111–18; id., *Vlast i pobuna*, pp. 136–40.
60. AJBT-KMJ, I–3–b/651, l. 33–40, 45–6.
61. Gibianskii, 'K istorii', *Sovetskoe slavianovedenie* (from 1992 *Slavianovedenie*), 3 (1991), 4 (1991), 1 (1992), 3 (1992). See also Gibianskii, 'The 1948 Soviet–Yugoslav Conflict', 40–2.
62. Michev, *Makedonskiita v'pros*, pp. 389–93.
63. For Kostov's minutes see TsDA-TsPA, f. 146, op. 2, a.e. 19, l. 103–28; for Kolarov's minutes see TsDA-TsPA, f. 147, op. 2, a.e. 62, l. 1–41. In his minutes Kolarov used Kostov's minutes.
64. AJ-CK SKJ, III/31a.
65. AJ-CK SKJ, III/32; V. Dedijer, *Novi prolozi za biografiju Josipa Broza Tita*, Vol. 3 (Belgrade: 1984) pp. 303–7.
66. AJ-CK SKJ, IX, 1/I–135, 1/I–163, 1/I–164, 1/I–166, 1/I–169; RTsKhIDNI, f. 17, op. 128, d. 472, l. 78–9, 84–6; AJBT-KMJ, I–3–b/35, l. 1, 3.
67. AJ-CK SKJ, III/32; Dedijer, *Novi prolozi*, Vol. 3, pp. 304–8.
68. 'Sekretnaia sovetsko-iugoslavskaia perepiska 1948 g.' (published by L.Ia. Gibianskii), *Voprosy istorii*, 4/5 (1991) 135.
69. Dedijer, *Josip Broz Tito*, pp. 504–5; Kardelj, *Borba*, p. 119.
70. There are Kardelj's telegram to Tito about the 11 February meeting (AJBT-KMJ, I–3–b/651, l. 47) and the Soviet minutes of both conversations, sent by Molotov to Stalin (AP RF, f. 3, op. 66, d. 908, l. 149–50, 152–3).
71. AVP RF, f. 0144, op. 32, p. 128, d. 8, l. 107.
72. AVP RF, f. 0144, op. 32, p. 129, d. 18, l. 7–8.
73. 'Konflikt, kotorogo ne dolzhno bylo byt' (iz istorii sovetsko–jugoslavskikh otnoshenii)' (published by I. Bukharkin), *Vestnik Ministerstva Inostrannykh Del SSSR*, 6 (1990), 60.
74. RTsKhIDNI, f. 17, op. 128, d. 1163, l. 9–24.
75. *Pisma TsK KPJ*; for the more complete correspondence, see 'Sekretnaia sovetsko–jugoslavskaia perepiska', *Voprosy istorii*, 4–5, 6–7, 10 (1992).
76. RTsKhIDNI, f. 17, op. 128, d. 1161, l. 2–19; another copy, RTsKhIDNI, f. 575, op. 1, d. 62, l. 1–18.
77. RTsKhIDNI, f. 17, op. 128, d. 1162, l. 44–73; another copy, RTsKhIDNI, f. 575, op. 1, d. 39, l. 164–93.
78. RTsKhIDNI, f. 575, op. 1, d. 375, l. 143.
79. RTsKhIDNI, f. 17, op. 128, d. 1165, l. 64–8.
80. *Ibid.*, l. 63.
81. RTsKhIDNI, f. 575, op. 1, d. 62, l. 31–2; A. Werblan, *Władysław Gomułka: Sekretarz Generalny PPR* (Warsaw: 1988) p. 521.
82. Dedijer, *Josip Broz Tito*, pp. 528–9; Djilas, *Vlast i pobuna*, p. 155.
83. AJBT-KMJ, I–3–b/549.
84. AJBT-KMJ, I–3–b/142, l. 1–4; AJBT-KMJ, I–3–b/513, l. 1–3; AJBT-KMJ, I–3–b/548, l. 1–5.
85. RTsKhIDNI, f. 17, op. 128, d. 1162, l. 122.

86. AJ-CK SKJ, IX, 1–1/20, l. 2. See also Dedijer, *Novi prilozi*, Vol. 3, pp. 388–9.
87. RTsKhIDNI, f. 17, op. 128, d. 1162, l. 123.
88. Státní ústřední archiv (Prague), f. 02/1, sv. 2, a.j. 115, s. 2; AJBT-KMJ, I–3–b/184.
89. RTsKhIDNI, f. 17, op. 128, d. 1162, l. 122.
90. RTsKhIDNI, f. 575, op. 1, d. 1, l. 266–70. Published in G. Procacci (ed.), G. Adibekov, A. Di Biagio, L. Gibianskii, F. Gori, S. Pons (co-eds), *The Cominform. Minutes of the Three Conferences 1947/1948/1949*, Fondazione Feltrinelli, *Annali*, XXX (Milan: 1994) pp. 342–9.
91. RTsKhIDNI, f. 17, op. 128, d. 1165, l. 60.
92. AJBT-KMJ, I–3–b/142; AJBT-KMJ, I–3–b/513; AJBT-KMJ, I–3–b/548.
93. AJBT-KMJ, I–3–b/514, l. 1, 5, 6; AJBT-KMJ, I–3–b/549, l. 2–3; AAN, ALP, 295/VII–73, K. 12–13a, 16–17.
94. RTsKhIDNI, f. 17, op. 128, d. 1165, l. 96.
95. RTsKhIDNI, f. 77, op. 3, d. 106, l. 13.
96. RTsKhIDNI, f. 575, op. 1, d. 49, l. 42.
97. RTsKhIDNI, f. 77, op. 3, d. 106, l. 5, 13, 15; RTsKhIDNI, f. 77, op. 3, d. 108, l. 18, 29, 30, 31; RTsKhIDNI, f. 575, op. 1, d. 46, l. 54, 72, 75 (published in *The Cominform*, pp. 556–7, 574–5, 578–9).
98. RTsKhIDNI, f. 77, op. 3, d. 106, l. 6; RTsKhIDNI, f. 575, op. 1, d. 46, l. 61–2 (published in *The Cominform*, pp. 564–5).

16 A Challenge Let Drop: Soviet Foreign Policy, the Cominform and the Italian Communist Party, 1947–8
Silvio Pons

Criticism of the Italian and French Communist Parties constituted one of the crucial moments in the founding of Cominform in September 1947. Since Eugenio Reale – one of the members of the Italian delegation at the Szklarska Poręba Conference – revealed these criticisms,[1] historians have pondered their significance. They have been seen as a consequence of the 'two camps' theory in international politics, and of an attempt to induce the Communist Parties to close ranks with the USSR.[2] The archive material to which we now have access allows us to shed light on areas which were obscure until recently. The limits of the documentation available should also be made clear, however: in particular, this sheds no light on the decision-making process in the Soviet leadership which led to the founding of the Cominform. Nonetheless, we are now able to trace more clearly the framework which Soviet leaders gave to the Szklarska Poręba Conference, the positions taken up by representatives of other parties during Conference debates, the reactions of the Italian Communist Party (PCI) to the criticisms, and also developments in relations between the Italian Party and Moscow in the following months. We have enough new evidence to clarify – and sometimes to modify – the interpretations which have been proposed until now. In this chapter I intend to show that although the criticism of the Western Parties had wider consequences for all the other Parties belonging to the Cominform, these were only to a limited extent the corollary of any major reorientation in Soviet foreign policy.

Zhdanov's attack on the Western Parties was not improvised. However, it was not planned in what seems to be the first document setting down the essential points for a conference setting up the Cominform – a memorandum sent to Zhdanov on 15 August 1947 by the head of the Foreign Policy Section of the Central Committee of the Soviet Party, L. Baranov. This document simply mentioned the need to call the 'democratic organizations' to the struggle against the 'Marshall Plan', and the need for 'co-ordination' among the various Communist Parties.[3] It was only a memorandum from Zhdanov to Stalin at the beginning of September which introduced the theme of 'criticism of the errors committed by individual Communist Parties (the French, Italian and Czech Parties and others) – especially regarding lack of reciprocal links between Parties and co-ordination of their actions'. This point did not appear in Zhdanov's first handwritten draft of the memorandum, incidentally: he only added it in the final version.[5] So the decision to make the attack was taken less than a month before the Conference, at the highest levels of the Soviet leadership – as far as we can tell, at the suggestion of Zhdanov. The criticism of the Western Parties appeared in drafts of his report to the Conference and in a dossier of the Foreign Policy Section of the Central Committee of the Soviet Party on the 'international situation of the USSR', which was supposed to provide a 'basis' for the report. This dossier listed four 'errors' committed by the Western Parties: the tendency to 'liquidate themselves', which the American Communists under Browder were accused of; the inability to achieve a 'correct combination' between 'parliamentary struggle and struggle outside parliament', with the result of being 'seduced by parliamentary illusions' (this was one fault that the Italian and French Parties were accused of); the adoption of 'non-Marxist theory' regarding the possibility of achieving a new democracy via 'a peaceful, parliamentary road' (this, once again, was an error of the French and Italian Parties, who were accused of wrongly seeing the situation in their countries as comparable with that present in the 'countries of the new democracy'); finally, the idea of a specific national road to Socialism, different from the Russian road (here the French Party was cited as the example not to be followed, but it was evident enough that the Italian Party could be accused of the same failing).[6] The text of the report took a different angle from the dossier. Right from the first drafts, the report concentrated on the responses of the French and Italian Parties to their expulsion from Government, and to the Marshall Plan. It saw their response as weak and inadequate. The French and Italians were accused of 'over-rating' the strength of the enemy and 'under-rating' their own resources, and the will of the masses 'to defend the vital national rights and interests of their country'. A more adequate assessment of the balance of power would, according to the report, have led Communists to change their alliances and gain the support of 'patriotic elements'.[7] In other words, the criticism had more of a political than an ideological sense – although the basic conceptual framework was very much consistent with that of the dossier, which formed the background thinking. The differences between the various texts we have examined – after the decision to attack the Western European Parties had been taken – seem to be more a question of form than of substance. The most important change in the material prepared for the Conference seems to concern a different issue: it was evidently decided to entirely eliminate criticism of certain Eastern European Parties.[8]

What were the motives for criticizing the Western (and only the Western) Parties so harshly? There is no doubt that the fundamental objective was to achieve mass mobilization and encourage social conflict and opposition to the Marshall Plan, seen as a tool of American expansionism in Europe and the accompaniment of the 'Truman doctrine'. The essentials of the Eastern Parties' attitude towards the Marshall Plan had already been laid down in June 1947, before the Paris Conference. The Soviet leadership had vacillated somewhat and been unsure of the best attitude to adopt at the Conference. But it emerged clearly that it was a priority of Soviet policy to retain firm control over its 'sphere of influence' in Eastern Europe.[9] Influential Soviet figures saw the Marshall Plan as a decisive step towards the setting up of a Western 'bloc'. This was the view of the Ambassador at Washington, N. Novikov.[10] Evgenii Varga expressed the same view in a memorandum to Molotov on the Marshall Plan, written on 24 June 1947.[11] The Soviet decision to forbid the Eastern European states from attending the Paris Conference was rooted in this conviction. Stalin told Gottwald personally that there was 'a more wide-ranging Western plan to isolate the Soviet Union'.[12] Once the Soviet leadership had averted the immediate danger of American influence in Eastern Europe, the logical next steps were to consolidate the Soviet 'sphere of influence', and to use the strength of the main Western Communist Parties to undermine the Western 'bloc'. Consolidation of a Soviet bloc was implicit in the very setting up of the Cominform, in the form this was imposed by the Soviet representatives. The second objective, that of weakening the opposing bloc, was actually made explicit. However, we have seen that the decision to attack the Western Parties openly was only taken in the run-up to the Conference. And even after the decision had been taken, Zhdanov's report avoided the damning accusations of ideological heresy suggested in the dossier of the Foreign Policy Section. In other words, Soviet responses to the Marshall Plan and to the formation of a Western 'bloc' could have taken different directions. So although the remarks made until now seem to explain satisfactorily the decision to involve the Western Parties in the Cominform, we also need to ask ourselves what the Soviet leadership was aiming at when it asked the Western Parties to change their strategy: what were the underlying objectives of Soviet policy and what were its limits?

Evidence from the archives fully confirms that there were differences in the approach taken by Zhdanov in his report and in that taken by the Yugoslav representatives at Szklarska Poręba, Djilas and Kardelj –

divergences remarked upon in Reale's notes, in relation to the Greek question.[13] The most significant difference came out in Kardelj's speech in the discussion of Zhdanov's report. Kardelj focused on aspects of the question which the report never mentioned. Thus he accused Togliatti directly of being part of a revisionist tendency and of believing in the possibility of 'a form of legal path to power for the Communists, and consequently of peaceful transition from capitalism to Socialism'. Kardelj also accused the Italian Party of having let slip a revolutionary opportunity in northern Italy at the end of the war when they failed to follow the Yugoslav example. In addition, he attacked the Italian position over Greece (a position which Kardelj believed had revealed 'the essence of their mistakes'); whereas the Italian Party argued that the war in Greece was in the American interest, he maintained it constituted a serious menace to those interests. So the 'Greek situation' was 'an incomparably better situation than what prevails in France or Italy'. He went on to claim that the creation of a similar situation in France and Italy 'would signify a very severe blow to imperialism, would mean the ruin of the current imperialist offensive against the progressive forces'.[14] Reale's account of these accusations, incidentally, was fairly precise, even though not word-for-word.[15]

As can be seen, the divergence between Zhdanov's position and that of Kardelj were significant. Zhdanov's critique hinged on the categories of governing party and opposition party; his report argued for the advantages of a party of opposition rooted in mobilization of the masses. Kardelj's criticisms, in contrast, explicitly took 'the Greek model' as an example to be followed in Communist strategy. We may wonder whether this combination of a softer and a harder line was planned. The memoirs of both Kardelj and Djilas imply as much, for they both state that Zhdanov personally co-ordinated the attack on the Western Parties.[16] The telegrams sent secretly by the Soviet representatives to let Stalin know how the Conference was proceeding do not mention any direct agreement with the Yugoslavs, but they show that the attack was an organized affair. Even on 23 and 24 September – before Zhdanov had read his report – the Soviet representatives sent Stalin heavily critical accounts of the reports delivered by Duclos and Longo.[17] Longo had made what was in effect a defence of the policies the Italian Party had followed since the war (including its international policy).[18] The Soviet representatives drew the conclusion that 'thanks to the mistakes and wavering of its leadership', the PCI 'does not know what to do and is waiting to see how events will develop'. They maintained that Longo had not given 'any satisfactory reply' to Zhdanov's question as to whether the PCI had 'a plan for counter-attacking reaction'. When Zhdanov had accused the PCI of reacting feebly to De Gasperi's *'coup d'état'*, Longo had defended his Party by referring to 'the objective situation in the country' – a line which cut little ice with the Soviet representatives. They claimed 'Longo's speech made a pitiful impression on the majority of representatives at the Conference'.[19] On 25 September they assessed Djilas's criticisms of the French Party as 'well-founded', and noted that this criticism 'went back to the war'.[20] On 26 and 27 September the Soviet representatives gave Stalin a detailed account of the replies made by Duclos and Longo – both of whom took account of Zhdanov's criticisms, and those of others.[21] The overall assessment of Zhdanov and Malenkov was that in all the speeches the criticisms of the French and Italian Parties 'were very much to the point, and reflected comrades' desire that the French and Italian comrades should correct their errors as soon as possible'.[22]

We should note that the division of labour which allowed the Yugoslavs to make hard-line criticisms, and Zhdanov to take a more moderate line, seemed to have a fairly solid political basis. Yugoslavs and Soviets seem to have shared the conviction that World War II had weakened the capitalist states considerably, and shared commitment to the theory of the 'two camps'. The challenge to the Western 'bloc' and to the USA, which the 'two camps' slogan symbolized, led both Yugoslavs and Soviets to the conclusion that the outcome of the struggle in France and Italy was 'in a sense, the decisive factor in the present phase of the struggle against imperialism' (as Kardelj put it in a phrase which Reale did not record in his notes).[23] Zhdanov could scarcely criticize the PCI for 'letting the revolutionary opportunity slip', as Kardelj was quite able to do, without throwing doubt on the validity of Soviet foreign policy in the previous years. But we have seen that the dossier written by the Foreign Policy Section condemned the concept of a 'peaceful, parliamentary road' in capitalist countries – exactly the same terms used by Kardelj and Djilas. Zhdanov had evaded this issue, but we have no reason to think his view was any different. It seems likely that his silence was rather a consequence of Soviet ambivalence and wavering. It was probably this ambivalence in Soviet attitudes which Togliatti had in mind when he gave Longo and Reale the following advice as they left for the Conference: 'If they criticize us for not taking power, or because we let ourselves be thrown out of the Government, tell them that we couldn't turn Italy into a second Greece. Not only in our interests, but also in those of the USSR.'[24] This was, in fact, the main defence Longo adopted.

What was at stake here can be glimpsed in Djilas's accusation that the French Communists had been 'poor interpreters of Soviet foreign policy' from the time of the war onwards.[25] In the preceding years, both Tito and Togliatti had proposed their own, different readings of Soviet interests and policy in the international field. Both men had stated their opposition to the logic of opposed 'blocs' which was then emerging – but for very different reasons. Togliatti had aligned himself with the moderate line which was the public face of Stalin's declarations – which stressed that any idea of a new war was undesirable and unrealistic. Just recently, in an interview with Stassen in April 1947, Stalin had emphasized a perspective of 'collaboration' between the different social and political 'systems'.[26] Tito, in contrast, was giving voice to a deep-rooted anti-capitalist tradition, rather than the more recent tradition of unity of all anti-Fascist forces. Tito was thus aligning himself with what Stalin is said to have argued privately – views revealed, for example, in Stalin's prophecy (expressed in a conversation with Dimitrov in January 1945) that the USSR would in the future be opposed to the 'democratic fraction of the capitalists', after the defeat of the 'Fascist fraction',[27] or in his appeal to form a 'united front' of Slavs around the Soviet Union so as to prevent another war (a proposal Stalin had made to Tito the last time he had met him, in May 1946).[28] The founding of the Cominform seemed to signal that this second line was in favour. Very probably, however, the Yugoslavs were too rash in posing as in effect the true interpreters of Soviet foreign policy.

Even if there was a kind of division of labour in the roles played by Soviet and Yugoslav representatives at Szklarska Poręba, there were inherent limits to the alliance. For we cannot but wonder whether the Soviet leadership supported unreservedly Djilas's assertion (not reported by Reale) that the armed struggle in Yugoslavia and Greece 'strengthened the position of the USSR as the bastion of the revolutionary forces in the world'.[29] It seems unlikely they would endorse such a position. At least with regard to the international consequences of the civil war in Greece, the Soviet attitude seems to have been extremely cautious. Here it is significant that the Soviet leadership refused to admit the Greek Communist Party to the founding Conference of the Cominform – notwithstanding the pressure exerted by the Yugoslavs.[30] Zhdanov also ignored the appeal to militant and internationalist solidarity with Greek comrades which Kardelj made at the Conference.[31] A few months previously, at a meeting with the Greek Communist leader Zachariadis, in May 1947, Zhdanov had been very cautious.[32] The reasons for this caution should be sought in a conception of foreign policy which traditionally gave first place to security and took full account of the balance of power. In the view of the Soviet leaders, no 'reinforcing' of the USSR's position could be expected from any development which made the Soviets significantly more exposed in the international arena (and any widening of the Greek conflict would inevitably increase this exposure). The Soviet position on Trieste (an issue which affected the Yugoslavs directly) had been consistent with this cautious approach since 1945. We have to remember, in addition, that the Soviet Union could not take it for granted at this time that serious conflicts would not break out within the existing Soviet 'sphere of influence'. There was certainly a risk in Czechoslovakia, but there seem to have been worries about Hungary, too: in April 1947, Molotov cautiously sounded Rákosi on the risk that a 'struggle for power' might break out over the Communists' control of the Ministry of the Interior.[33]

Given this evidence, it seems unlikely that Moscow looked with favour on a scenario of civil war in Italy, at least in the international conjuncture of the years immediately after the war. It seems equally unlikely that, whatever Moscow hoped, it was receiving information from Italy which led it to think insurrection was a real possibility. It is true that Ambassador Kostylev – in a letter to Molotov dated 17 April 1947 – mentioned that 'it is not impossible that the conflict between American reactionary forces and the Greek people may be accompanied by a conflict between the American imperialists and the Italian people'.[34] Kostylev claimed that Togliatti had agreed with this assessment when the two men had met in Rome a few days previously. According to Kostylev, Togliatti confessed that the situation in Italy had become acute, and that revolts might break out – not at the instigation of the PCI, but as the result of provocation.[35] However, as far as we know, Kostylev did not come back to this theme in his diplomatic correspondence with Molotov in May–June 1947. This alarmed note that he sent in April thus seems to be an isolated incident – the mirror image of American fears at the same time that the Communist Parties in France and Italy might take power.[36]

In his closing speech at the Conference, Zhdanov left his own position on the prospective for insurrection vague. (This is a point on which Reale's notes are inaccurate and misleading.) Zhdanov argued that one of the mistakes of the French Party was to have made 'declarations about not being provoked into "adventuristic actions" – since it is hardly expedient to reveal to the enemy one's unwillingness to choose one or another form of struggle'.[37] In other words, insurrection should not be counted out of consideration – it might not be correct today, but things could be different in the future. Assessment of this strategic gap brings out the ambivalence of the criticisms made at the founding conference of the Cominform. A similar gap seems to have been implicit in the moves of Soviet foreign policy – as can be seen in Soviet policy towards Greece.

In any case, criticisms of the Western Parties had a leading part throughout the second part of the Conference, centring around Zhdanov's report. Zhdanov made it clear that the conversion demanded of the Western Parties was 'not a matter of petty corrections and changes of emphasis, but of qualitative changes in policy and in tactics, of a serious reorientation'.[38] Longo was obliged to take these words into account when he reported back to the Direction of the PCI on 7 October 1947.[39] However, Longo took up essentially the same defence which he had improvised at the time of the Conference itself. He reaffirmed unconditional loyalty to complete alignment with the Soviet Union in international policy; but he also made use of the space left him by divergences between Zhdanov and Kardelj, in order to safeguard the essential lines of the PCI's home policies.[40] Togliatti adopted the same approach. He declared unconditionally the need to 'side with the Soviet Union's peace policy', but he was more doubtful about the feasibility of insurrection ('is insurrection possible in the immediate future? I maintain that it is not right to think of the situation in these terms; however, a Communist certainly cannot rule out the question indefinitely').[41] This was the line of defence adopted by the PCI to the criticisms made by the Cominform. Hard-liners within the Party leadership, sympathetic towards the Yugoslav line, did not succeed in altering this position significantly.[42] It may be that the minutes of the PCI's ruling body do not reveal the depth of disagreement which existed, nor the details of which themes were debated. Much fiercer controversy emerges in an account of a meeting of the PCF leadership written by Djilas and conserved in Soviet archives. According to this account of the meeting, Duclos also expressed worry over the centralizing of organization and propaganda at the Cominform's offices in Belgrade. (Among the organizational responsibilities, there figured also the 'distribution and creation of deposits of arms'.) Duclos apparently feared that the French and Italian Parties would be obliged to keep to the decisions made in Belgrade, and that Moscow would thus be able to exercise full control over the PCF's activity.[43] We cannot rule out the possibility that Djilas slanted his account of the meeting, in an attempt to persuade Moscow of the need to keep up the pressure on the Western Parties, or even of the advantages of supporting hard-liners in the PCF and PCI. However, if his account is at least partially accurate, it is natural to think that similar issues may have been no less prominent in the PCI.

At the meeting of the Central Committee, 11–13 November, however, Togliatti repeated the line decided on by the Executive. He lined up behind Zhdanov's analysis of the international situation, and emphasized the importance of mass mobilization; but he made no concessions of substance to any non-peaceful conception of 'progressive democracy', even though he recognized the legitimacy of armed struggle in theory.[44] Before this, on 22 October, Zhdanov's report was published – with the most explicit criticisms of the PCI and PCF censored out. The letter sent to Longo from Moscow (17 October) explained that this had been done 'bearing in mind interventions of enemies of Communism after the publication of the resolutions of the Conference of information'.[45]

The founding of the Cominform did, however, involve the PCI in major public polemics. For a genuine 'incident' arose around statements made by one of the PCI's principal leaders, Umberto Terracini – who at the time chaired the country's Constituent Assembly. I will just draw the broad outlines of the 'incident'.[46] Terracini voiced grave doubts to the PCI Executive about the way in which the Cominform had been founded, arguing that it was wrong to present the national Communist parties with a *fait accompli*. He also disagreed with the specific criticism made of the Italian Party, and denied any need to change the line the PCI had pursued until then. In effect, he also disputed the need to line up closely behind the USSR.[47] Shortly afterwards he gave a press interview in which he claimed that the PCI ought to take up a consistent position of non-alignment with the logic of opposing blocs. If war broke out, he argued, the Italian people should oppose the aggression, wherever it came from (implying that this principle applied to all states, including the USSR). This interview was criticized by Togliatti, and Terracini was forced to partially retract.[48] Togliatti's response was quite harsh in tone – which marked the fact that the PCI was conforming to the logic of the Cold War. His principal criticism, made during the CC meeting on 11 November, was that Terracini presented Soviet policy as if it was 'a complex of actions in reaction to Western policies', thus ignoring the fact 'that the Soviet Union had its own policy of peace, for which it struggles openly for all the world to see'.[49] It is highly likely that Togliatti was not paying merely formal tribute to the Cominform line. He probably believed that it was not in the interests of the USSR to push the challenge contained in Zhdanov's report too far. So Togliatti seems to have reaffirmed his interpretation of the basic co-ordinates underlying Soviet foreign policy. At the same time, however, he relinquished most of what had been his own previous position against the division of Europe and the formation of opposed 'blocs'. Meanwhile, Moscow was kept constantly informed – via Reale's reports to Ambassador Kostylev – of Terracini's statements and on the reaction of the PCI leaders.[50]

The 'Terracini incident' had a wider significance outside the PCI. The case brought out one consequence of the founding of the Cominform, a consequence which Soviet leaders certainly intended: a foreign policy stance of independence from the Soviet Union had come out into the open, where it had, naturally, been condemned. The right to express criticism of Soviet foreign policy – rather than simply offer an 'interpretation' – had also been suppressed. The Terracini 'incident' thus served as a warning for any group in the Western Parties, or even in the 'people's democracies', who were inclined to take an independent line. It should be remembered that views similar to those defended by Terracini had already been attacked by Kardelj at the Cominform

Conference. Kardelj had criticized the slogan 'neither London, nor Washington, nor Moscow, but our own capital' – a rallying-cry he saw as widespread among Communists, but as based on a mistaken idea of the national role of their Parties.[51] It is only apparently paradoxical that a criticism of independence should come from a leader of precisely that Eastern Party which was most active in foreign affairs. For the Yugoslavs tended to place themselves in the front line alongside the Soviet Union. This attitude was evidently associated with the conviction that, with Zhdanov's report, the Soviet leadership had finally decided on a definite line of foreign policy, which would bring about complete harmony between Moscow and Belgrade. If this had been the situation, we might have expected that the conversion undertaken by the PCI in October and November 1947 (and the 'Terracini incident') would be just a first step. So we might have expected the Cominform to exert ever-increasing influence over the PCI. However, this did not come about. The most important passage was probably constituted by Pietro Secchia's trip to Moscow in December 1947. Since the Cominform Conference, the idea of a meeting between Togliatti and the Soviet leadership had been in the air.[52] However, evidently Togliatti did not think it appropriate to go to Moscow personally (unlike Thorez, who met Stalin in November 1947). Of the most influential PCI leaders, Secchia was the one who was most likely to be sympathetic to the founding of the Cominform. At a meeting of the Executive a little more than a year previously, 21 June 1946, Secchia had complained of the lack of a body co-ordinating the Communist Parties internationally.[53] It is interesting to note that this was just a month after the May meeting between Stalin and Tito in Moscow, where the idea of a new organizational structure for the international Communist movement had been floated.[54] In August 1947, during a trip to Poland, it was Secchia who received the news that a conference of the various national parties was about to be convened.[55] After the founding of the Cominform, Secchia seems to have played a relatively marginal role in the discussions within the PCI. However, his statements showed that he was very willing to bend the line of the Party in the direction indicated by the Soviets and also by the Yugoslavs.[56] It is very likely that Secchia's visit to Moscow marked a decisive moment to assess relations between Moscow and the PCI.

Secchia met Zhdanov twice (12 and 16 December) and Stalin, along with Zhdanov and Malenkov, once (14 December).[57] He also gave a speech on the Italian situation to the Foreign Policy Section of the CC of the CPSU on 16 December. Right from his first meeting with Zhdanov, Secchia launched into an exposition 'of the short-term tactics of the Party'. The record of the meeting gives no details of what he said. It contains only Secchia's replies to some questions of Zhdanov's regarding the 'combativeness' of the Italian masses (a reference to the strikes which had taken place in Milan and Rome at the beginning of December).[58] However, there is a note on the meeting in Zhdanov's personal papers, which makes it clear that Secchia had raised questions of the political prospects, and had painted a picture of major social conflict. In particular, he had asked Soviet leaders for their opinion on the prospects for an insurrection, and on the eventuality that civil war might break out – in the light of their reading of the international situation. He also mentioned in this context that Togliatti refused to pose a simple alternative between 'insurrection' and 'peaceful parliamentary development'.[59] Zhdanov was 'deeply interested', and suggested the question be presented to Stalin 'in a more complete form'. Secchia therefore agreed to present a written exposition.[60]

Secchia's report to Zhdanov can also be inferred from a memorandum conserved in the archives entitled 'On the tactics of the Italian Communist Party at the present moment'. Although the paper is not signed and bears no date, its contents leave little doubt that it must have been a transcription of what Secchia said in his first meeting with Zhdanov in December 1947.[61] According to this memorandum, at a meeting of the PCI Direction held at the beginning of December, the problem of what 'perspectives' to follow had been posed in the following terms: whether to keep the Party's approach 'on a democratic basis', going over to armed struggle only in the eventuality of violent action by the 'enemy'; or whether to forestall the 'enemy' and commit oneself to insurrection. The memorandum maintained that Togliatti argued for the first option. To be more precise, he maintained that only a direct threat of war would make civil war inevitable in Italy; however, the international situation was not yet that serious, so it was a mistake to think that the 'democratic road' was not feasible. The author of the memorandum added his own disagreement with such position. He argued that 'a violent, armed struggle' could be seen on the horizon in Italy, and that if past mistakes were to be avoided, it was necessary to 'go over to the offensive'. It was only after this statement that he posed the crucial question to the Soviet leadership –

> whether you consider that the international situation is now such that we should *at the present moment* avoid turning the struggle into civil war, [or whether] you perhaps consider that in the context of the present international situation, open struggle in Italy would be positive and necessary. If you think that we should not hesitate to carry the struggle forward up to the hilt – if necessary, taking up arms, and leading an insurrection – we must start making very serious preparations immediately ... [without leaving the] enemy [the chance] to choose the most favourable moment for them.[62]

This sheds light on what Secchia noted in his *Diaries* – in his account of his first meeting with Zhdanov: 'in that conversation it was evident that I was voicing opinions which were rather different from the tune Togliatti was playing. The Soviets couldn't have been very satisfied with Togliatti's policy.'[63]

Anyway, Stalin personally expressed the opinion that the moment of civil war had not yet arrived in Italy – although he also emphasized the need to redouble preparations for an armed struggle, should it come ('we believe that it is not right to actively plan an insurrection, but it is essential to be ready, should the enemy attack').[64] With regard to Secchia's questions concerning Soviet assessment of the international situation, Zhdanov had already confirmed the statements Malenkov had recently made to Nenni. Zhdanov remarked that 'elements of blackmail prevail over real preparations for war', and argued that the founding of the Cominform had forced the imperialists 'on the defensive', and that 'after the Conference the international situation has changed in our favour'.[65]

There are two other documents which give us an idea of Secchia's explanation of the PCI line: the 'Report on the situation in Italy', conserved in his personal papers (dated Moscow, 14 December 1947),[66] and the stenographer's version of the speech he gave on 16 December (conserved in RTsKhIDNI in Moscow).[67] The two texts differ significantly. In a few words, it can be said that the stenographed version was more critical of the PCI's policy, like the memorandum cited above. Secchia described Italy as the strategic and geopolitical focus of the 'attack' the Americans were preparing against the USSR and the 'new democracy' countries. At the same time, he maintained that the PCI had succeeded in achieving 'almost nothing' in 'reorganizing Italy's economy' or in 'creating a new people's democracy'.[68] These remarks led him to the conclusion that it was necessary to aim at a radical mobilization of the masses. So, echoing the Yugoslavs' criticism, he thought that, in retrospect, Italian Communists had been the victim of 'parliamentary illusions'.[69] On the other hand, Secchia did distance himself from positions which implied that in Italy 'nothing will be achieved' and therefore that it was necessary 'to go over to the armed struggle'.[70] However, on this crucial point, he was not altogether firm or unambiguous. In his conclusions, he argued that the struggle for 'the extension of democracy' was taking place in a country 'where the forces of reaction are still strong', and, hence, the Party needed 'to be ready to take up the armed struggle if it proves necessary'.[71]

The PCI's decision to take the road of 'gradual progress to democracy' and civil peace was not, therefore, a total commitment, but rested on an assessment of objective conditions. If these changed, matters could be reassessed – as Stalin suggested in his meeting with Secchia.

This implied that it was not a strategic option to be counterposed to that 'democratic revolution' cast in the fire of civil war which Kardelj had advocated at Szklarska Poręba.[72] Nonetheless, the PCI's wavering between the two poles of independence from the Soviet Union and insurrection remained resolved for the moment. The solution might be summed up in the formula: neither insurrection nor independence. The Soviet leadership seemed content with this solution, and ceased to exert pressure. It is significant in this context that, in his second meeting with Secchia, Zhdanov gave a largely positive assessment of the French Party's most recent policies.[73] But above all, it is relevant to note that Zhdanov had not pressed Secchia on those 'qualitative changes in policy and in tactics' or on the changes in social alliances which he had demanded three months earlier. From the Soviet point of view, the social conflicts which had already broken out in Italy (and in France) were a satisfactory result. So in the end the impact of the forming of the Cominform had a much less profound and disruptive impact on the PCI than at one time seemed possible. It seems likely, therefore, that this outcome was more than simply the result of the resistance put up by Togliatti.

What effect did the growing conflict between the USSR and Yugoslavia have here? It seems very likely that when the latent divergences between the Soviet and Yugoslav international strategies came to the surface, this led the Soviet leadership to distance itself from the most prominent aspects of the challenge thrown down by the Cominform – hence softening the criticism of the Western Parties. We do not know exactly when this shift in policy became definitely established in Moscow. We do know that when the Cominform Conference was being prepared, Belgrade was already being accused of unjustified intransigence, and of wanting to impose a regional hegemony. As we have seen, it was decided not to bring these criticisms up at the Conference.[74] No criticism of this kind seems to have been in the offing at the time of Secchia's visit to Moscow, or at the time of the VIth Congress of the PCI, a month later. However, signs of serious divergence between the Yugoslav and Soviet attitude towards the Western Parties were growing.

One piece of evidence regarding Yugoslav zeal in the application of a Cominform 'line' is obviously the report on the discussion in the PCF Executive which Djilas sent to Zhdanov – who then passed it on to Stalin.[75] During the VIth Congress of the PCI, while Togliatti reaffirmed the line established at the CC in November, the Yugoslavs tried to persuade the Italians to abandon their 'opportunism', and to take the road of 'open revolutionary struggle'. Togliatti apparently told them bluntly that although he was prepared to accept criticisms, 'when it comes to revolution in Italy, leave it to us'. This, at least, was the version Matteo Secchia related to Kostylev – making amends for his earlier tendency to look towards Yugoslavia 'as our rearguard if conflict should break out with the Americans' – in the wake of Yugoslavia's excommunication from the Cominform, 30 June 1948.[76] Djilas also recalls the Yugoslav attempts to push the Italians towards insurrection at the beginning of 1948.[77]

On the other hand, as we have seen, there is no lack of evidence of cautious attitudes among the Soviet leadership from at least the time of Secchia's visit. It is significant that the proposal of the Italian Communists for an official meeting, to be held before the elections, in which the Soviet Union would promise economic aid if the Left won, was turned down. Zhdanov replied that it would be necessary to avoid giving the impression that the USSR was interfering in Italy's internal affairs, or the impression that the PCI was not independent. Evidently, Moscow was not prepared to expose itself on the Italian question, or push the PCI very far.[78] At the second meeting between the two, Zhdanov told Secchia that Stalin was against the idea on the grounds that it would make the Soviets seem 'too similar' to the Americans, and that it would give rise to 'a violation of national independence and sovereignty'.[79] The Soviet leadership only agreed to provide substantial funding to the PCI for the coming elections.

In the first months of 1948 Soviet caution over Italy became even more marked than it had been in late 1947. The decisive moment came on 23 March, when Togliatti met Kostylev secretly, after the joint Western declaration regarding the restitution of the Free Territory of Trieste to Italy. According to the Ambassador's account, Togliatti said he could not exclude the possibility that there might be attempts to provoke the Popular Front, either before or after the elections (which he predicted would be won by the Front). So he maintained that the Communist Party should be prepared for any eventuality, including an armed uprising in northern Italy. Togliatti himself, according to Kostylev, now asked for the Soviet opinion on the prospects for armed insurrection – as he had three months previously via Secchia. Togliatti apparently made it clear that, even if the Soviet assessment was favourable, the PCI would take active steps only in extreme circumstances. He stated his opinion, indeed, that an uprising could lead to a new world war.[80] Molotov's reply came quickly. On 26 March, he cabled Kostylev, asking him to tell Togliatti that the Soviet leadership advised taking up armed struggle only if there was a military attack from the reactionary forces, and that it considered a Communist uprising highly inappropriate at that point in time. Molotov even warned the Italian Communists not to heed the advice of the Yugoslavs (or that of the Hungarians); he stated that they were not aware of the Soviet stance, even though they claimed to be.[81] It should be remembered that by this time the split between Moscow and Belgrade was being prepared – Stalin and Molotov's first letter of accusations was sent the day after, 27 March 1948.

We have traced Soviet attitudes towards the PCI and over the Italian question between late 1947 and early 1948. This seems to show a slight shift in Soviet foreign policy with respect to the challenge thrown down at the founding Conference of the Cominform. In reality, the logic of this shift lies in the steps taken in September 1947, since even at that time the stakes were not raised beyond a certain level. Renewed attempts were made to increase Soviet influence in the Western 'sphere of influence'; however, in Europe, sensitive areas like Germany or Greece were left alone. So the decision to concentrate Soviet criticisms on the two largest Western Communist Parties was also a sign of self-restraint; it signalled a self-imposed limit to the new turn in foreign policy. There does not seem to have been a complete break with the policy of wait and see, and of reacting to Western initiatives pursued after the end of the war.

In the first two years of peace, Soviet foreign policy did develop an orientation towards a bi-polar world, and away from the old thesis of 'capitalist encirclement'. A first step in this direction was Novikov's secret report to the Soviet delegation in Paris in September 1946 – a report which Novikov has claimed Molotov had a hand in writing.[82] A second step in the same direction took place a year later with Zhdanov's report – which represented the crucial step from an analysis for internal use to an official position of the Soviet Union. However, we may doubt whether the confrontationist tones of Zhdanov's declaration were a consistent source of inspiration for Soviet foreign policy. Even the differences in emphasis between Zhdanov and Malenkov (Malenkov was much more cautious in his assessment of the changes in the international balance of power brought about by the war) show there was also continuity with the kind of policy followed in the previous two years. Probably there was a perception of the bi-polar pattern as still incomplete.[83] An antagonistic attitude, but mainly in a defensive key, was to be established behind the building of an Eastern 'bloc'.

This ambivalence in Soviet foreign policy rendered the 'interpretative' strategies of Communist leaders in Eastern and Western Europe unreliable and vulnerable. European Communists were forced to conform to a rigid alignment with the USSR, without any real links to a clear political project – whether a consistently, confrontational policy, or one aiming at making the most of what chance there was of safeguarding international understanding and peace. Soviet policy pursued neither path with any conviction. What does seem certain is that, from late 1947, the Stalinist leadership effectively decided to de-emphasize the counter-offensive against the Western 'sphere of influence'. This was put off till more favourable times in the future. To this degree, the psychological threat contained in the founding of the Cominform was more significant than the political challenge it launched. On the whole, this was a challenge let drop.

Notes

1. E. Reale, *Nascita del Cominform* (Milan: 1958).
2. Cf. P. Spriano, *I comunisti europei e Stalin* (Turin: 1983) pp. 287–90; A. Guerra, *Gli anni del Cominform* (Milan: 1977) pp. 153–6.
3. RTsKhIDNI, f. 575, op. 1, d. 3, l. 1–3.
4. RTsKhIDNI, f. 77, op. 3, d. 90, l. 14. The Czech party was subsequently taken off the list; see *ibid.*, l. 10.
5. *Ibid.*, l. 3, 12.
6. RTsKhIDNI, f. 575, op. 1, d. 3, l. 74–5.
7. RTsKhIDNI, f. 77, op. 3, d. 91, l. 43–5, 55.
8. Cf. A. Di Biagio, 'The Establishment of the Cominform', in G. Procacci (ed.), G. Adibekov, A. Di Biagio, L. Gibianskii, F. Gori, S. Pons (co-eds), *The Cominform. Minutes of the Three Conferences 1947/1948/1949*, Fondazione Feltrinelli, *Annali*, XXX (Milan: 1994) p. 23.
9. Cf. M.M. Narinskii, 'SSSR i Plan Marshalla. Po materialam Arkhiva Prezidenta RF', *Novaia i noveishaia istoriia*, 2 (1993).
10. Cf. G. Takhnenko, 'Anatomiia odnogo politicheskogo resheniia. Dokumenty', *Mezhdunarodnaia Zhizn'*, 5 (1992).
11. RTsKhIDNI, f. 17, op. 128, d. 408, l. 38.
12. Narinskii, 'SSSR i Plan Marshalla', p. 18.
13. Reale, *Nascita*, p. 39.
14. *The Cominform*, pp. 299–301.
15. Reale, *Nascita*, pp. 116–22.
16. Cf. E. Kardelj, *Memorie degli anni di ferro* (Rome: 1980) pp. 111–12; M. Djilas, *Rise and Fall* (London: 1985) p. 135.
17. RTsKhIDNI, f. 77, op. 3, d. 92, l. 6–15, 47–9.
18. The text of Longo's information report contains no trace of another point which Reale refers to 'regarding military preparations of special squads made ready by the party for the famous X-hour, and on the quantities and location of arms greased and ready for the coming insurrection' (Reale, *Nascita*, pp. 32–3). However, as I show below, other evidence makes it plain that the issue of preparations for the armed struggle was raised at the founding Conference of the Cominform.
19. RTsKhIDNI, f. 77, op. 3, d. 92, l. 48–9. Zhdanov's interruptions and questions during Longo's speech were given in the protocol. See *The Cominform*, pp. 195–7.
20. RTsKhIDNI, f. 77, op. 3, d. 92, l. 54.
21. *Ibid.*, l. 56–67.
22. *Ibid.*, l. 63.
23. *The Cominform*, p. 303.
24. Reale, *Nascita*, p. 17.
25. *The Cominform*, p. 257. The phrase given by Reale is imprecise (Reale, *Nascita*, p. 127).
26. I.V. Stalin, *Sochineniia* (*Works*), XVI (3) (Stanford: 1967) pp. 76–9. Cf. S. Pons, 'L'Unione Sovietica nella politica estera di Togliatti', *Studi Storici*, 33 (1992) 435–56.

27. Cf. M.M. Narinskii, 'Sovetskaia vneshniaia politika i proiskhozhdenie kholodnoi voiny', in *Sovetskaia Vneshniaia Politika v Retrospektive* (Moscow: 1993) p. 122. Cf. A. Ulam's assessment, *Titoism and the Cominform* (Cambridge, Mass.: 1952) p. 85.
28. See 'Poslednii vizit I. Broza Tito k I.V. Stalinu', *Istoricheskii Arkhiv*, 2 (1993) 28.
29. *The Cominform*, p. 257.
30. Cf. L.Ia. Gibianskii, 'Kak voznik Kominform. Po novym arkhivnym materialam', *Novaia i noveishaia istoriia*, 4 (1993) 143.
31. *The Cominform*, p. 303; Reale, *Nascita*, p. 122.
32. RTsKhIDNI, f. 17, op. 128, d. 1019, l. 36.
33. *Ibid.*, l. 13–15.
34. AVP RF, f. 06, op. 9, p. 54, d. 810, l. 60.
35. AVP RF, f. 098, op. 30, p. 170, d. 12, l. 97–8.
36. Cf. M.P. Leffler, *A Preponderance of Power: National Security, the Truman Administration and the Cold War* (Stanford: 1992) pp. 159–64.
37. *The Cominform*, p. 351. Reale's notes, in contrast, read: 'I believe Duclos agrees that we did not mean that it was right to proceed to insurrection. Does it have any sense to reveal one's cards to the enemy?' (Reale, *Nascita*, pp. 147–8).
38. *The Cominform*, p. 351; Reale, *Nascita*, p. 147.
39. See R. Martinelli, M.L. Righi (eds), *La politica del partito comunista italiano nel periodo costituente. I verbali della direzione tra il V e il VI Congresso, 1946–1948*, Fondazione Istituto Gramsci, *Annali*, II (Rome: 1992) pp. 498, 500.
40. Cf.: S. Galante, *L'autonomia possibile. Il PCI del dopoguerra tra politica estera e politica interna* (Florence: 1991) pp. 107, 130–1; A. Agosti, 'Longo e il Cominform', in *Luigi Longo. La politica e l'azione* (Rome: 1992) pp. 69–87.
41. *La politica del partito comunista italiano*, p. 526.
42. See Galante, *L'autonomia*, p. 134 ff.
43. RTsKhIDNI, f. 77, op. 3, d. 98, l. 3.
44. APC, Comitato Centrale, *Verbali*, 11–13 November 1947.
45. RTsKhIDNI, f. 77, op. 3, d. 97, l. 5.
46. Cf. A. Agosti, 'Il partito comunista italiano e la svolta del 1947', *Studi Storici*, 31 (1990) 72 ff.
47. *La politica del partito comunista italiano*, pp. 499–500, 523–4.
48. *L'Unità*, 23 and 24 October 1947; APC, Comitato Centrale, *Allegato n. 4* (1947).
49. APC, Comitato Centrale, *Verbali*, 11 November 1947.
50. AVP RF, f. 098, op. 30, p. 170, d. 13, l. 98–9, 162–3.
51. *The Cominform*, p. 297; Reale, *Nascita*, p. 119.
52. AVP RF, f. 098, op. 30, p. 170, d. 13, l. 96.
53. *La politica del partito comunista italiano*, p. 573.
54. Cf. Gibianskii, 'Kak voznik Kominform', 135–6; cf. 'Poslednii vizit', 28, 34.
55. See *Archivio Pietro Secchia 1945–1973*, Fondazione Feltrinelli, *Annali*, XIX (1978) (Milan: 1979) p. 208.
56. *La politica del partito comunista italiano*, p. 508; APC, Comitato Centrale, *Verbali*, 11–13 November 1947.
57. According to Secchia's 'autobiographical memo', the meeting with Stalin took place on 16 December 1947, and apart from Zhdanov and

Malenkov, Molotov and Beria were also present. See *Archivio Pietro Secchia*, p. 211.
58. RTsKhIDNI, f. 17, op. 128, d. 1101, l. 184.
59. RTsKhIDNI, f. 77, op. 3, d. 90, l. 86–90.
60. RTsKhIDNI, f. 17, op. 128, d. 1101, l. 184.
61. *Ibid.*, l. 6–14. For an identification of this document, see S. Pons, 'Togliatti, il Pci e il Cominform', in E. Aga Rossi, G. Quagliariello (eds), *L'altra faccia della luna. I partiti comunisti francese e italiano e l'Unione Sovietica*, forthcoming.
62. RTsKhIDNI, f. 17, op. 128, d. 1101, l. 13. Emphasis in original. I could not find any record of the meeting of December 1947 in the Archives of the PCI at the Fondazione Istituto Gramsci (October 1995).
63. *Archivio Pietro Secchia*, p. 446.
64. See *Istochnik*, 5–6 (1993) 124. According to this record, Stalin emphasized the need to reinforce the partisans' organizations and to develop a spy service.
65. RTsKhIDNI, f. 17, op. 128, d. 1101, l. 185. For the conversation between Malenkov and Nenni at the end of November 1947, see P. Nenni, *Tempo di guerra fredda. Diari 1943–1956* (Milan: 1981) p. 400.
66. *Archivio Pietro Secchia*, pp. 611–27. From Secchia's memoirs, one infers that this 'report' was the text presented to Stalin on Zhdanov's request: however, as we have seen, also the memorandum cited above was a written exposition, probably at Stalin's disposal when he met Secchia.
67. RTsKhIDNI, f. 17, op. 128, d. 1074, l. 240–60.
68. *Ibid.*, l. 246.
69. *Ibid.*, l. 250.
70. *Ibid.*, l. 254.
71. *Ibid.*, l. 257.
72. *The Cominform*, p. 171.
73. RTsKhIDNI, f. 17, op. 128, d. 1101, l. 190.
74. RTsKhIDNI, f. 77, op. 3, d. 91, l. 47.
75. RTsKhIDNI, f. 77, op. 3, d. 98, l. 1.
76. AVP RF, f. 098, op. 31, p. 179, d. 15, l. 124. Matteo Secchia was Pietro Secchia's brother, and one of Togliatti's secretaries.
77. Djilas, *Rise and Fall*, p. 136.
78. RTsKhIDNI, f. 17, op. 128, d. 1101, l. 182–3.
79. *Ibid.*, l. 189.
80. The records of the secret conversation between Kostylev and Togliatti (23 March 1948), and Molotov's telegram (26 March 1948) are conserved in the Archive of the President of the Russian Federation. I would like to thank Michail M. Narinskii, deputy director of the Institute of World History at the Russian Academy of Sciences, for allowing me to quote these documents.
81. See note 80.
82. See *Mezhdunarodnaia Zhizn'*, 11 (1990) 148–54. Cf. N.V. Novikov, *Vospominaniia diplomata. Zapiski 1938–1947* (Moscow: 1989) pp. 352–3.
83. *The Cominform*, pp. 89–91.

17 Vittorio Vidali and the Cominform, 1947–53
Joze Pirjevec

Analysing Vittorio Vidali's life is an experience reminiscent of watching Kurosawa's film, *Rashomon*; for, as in that film, the truth (or the evidence we have) is so many-sided and ambiguous that it is difficult to believe it makes up a coherent whole at all. Who was Vittorio Vidali? Was he the Communist full of ideals and wary of deviations, as he portrayed himself in his numerous autobiographical writings, or as described in Mario Passi's recent hagiography? Was he (as some Western accounts have it) an NKVD agent trained in Moscow – Stalin's killer sent to Spain and Mexico to fight Trotskyism and then to eliminate Trotsky himself? Or was he, as an outline biography drawn up by the Yugoslav UDB suggests, an adventurer continually willing to play on two or three different chessboards? What is certain is that archive material on Vidali does not allow us to come down unequivocally on one side or the other; for it contains numerous surprises for the historian, complicating matters further and raising still more questions about the 'jaguar' of Muggia.

Take, for example, the letter from the Central Committee of the Spanish Communist Party, sent to the Comintern from Barcelona on 22 February 1938 in reply to a question as to whether Vidali should be given a medal for his part in the civil war. The leaders of the Spanish Party wrote that

> in our opinion, this case cannot be considered since Comrade Carlos never commanded a military unit and never took part in the struggle itself. We do not underestimate his organizational work in the 5th regiment, but we are of the opinion that it is impossible to bestow on him a medal for his heroism at the front.[1]

If we go forward in time nearly a decade, we find further surprises regarding the return to Trieste. Vidali's own account has it that he was unable to leave Mexico before February 1947 because of the obstinate refusal of the local authorities – under pressure from the FBI and the American secret services – to give a visa. Archives in Moscow, in contrast, make it clear that Vidali was well aware that he could not return to Europe before his Soviet superiors had given their consent – for in the spring of 1945 he asked for such permission, although he did not obtain it, for reasons we do not know. He had recently been expelled from the Mexican Party for his opposition to its reformism: is it possible that he was in disgrace in Moscow too? Did Moscow not wish to welcome back someone who had been labelled by the Mexican comrades as an 'agent provocateur, Gestapo spy and conspirator'? Or was it simply a question of creating a smoke screen and waiting until the most appropriate moment to call him back to active service? Whatever the truth, the UDB dossier on him at Ljubljana tells us that his fall from grace led Vidali to ask the Yugoslav consulate at Ciudad in Mexico for its support in obtaining permission for his return to Europe.[2] Everything went smoothly and Vidali embarked in secret on a Soviet ship, which took him to Murmansk, and from there he went to Moscow, then on to Ljubljana and Belgrade. We know nothing of the meetings he presumably had in Moscow, but something of those in Yugoslavia, where he met old friends and acquaintances dating back to his time in the USSR and in Spain – Ivan Regent from Trieste in Ljubljana, and the Serb Veljko Vlahovič Belgrade – and was introduced into the inner circles of the Titoist *nomenklatura*. In both places, he managed to give the impression that he had virtually fled from Moscow and was still *persona non grata* in Soviet eyes – something which at that moment certainly did no harm to his reputation in Yugoslavia.[3]

Ever since Yalta, there had been friction between the KPJ and the CPSU due to the Yugoslav desire to play an independent international role, and to the Soviet conviction that they had a right to be the sole spokesmen for the Socialist camp. This basic difference emerged into the open over the question of Trieste and its territory. As is well known, Stalin did not support Tito in May 1945, when the latter wanted to remain in the city which his troops had liberated and occupied; he gave his support instead to the Anglo-American plan to divide the contested area up into two zones (A and B), to be administered by the Allied and the Yugoslav military authorities respectively, as a temporary solution before the Italian–Yugoslav frontier had been decided at the Peace Conference. In the period which followed, however, Russian and Western suspicions of each other – suppressed by the shared need to defeat Hitler – broke out into the Cold War. This naturally gave the problem of Trieste a new dimension – it turned from a local conflict into one which involved the Eastern and Western spheres of influence as a whole. To cut this new Gordian knot, the Great Powers acted against Italian and Yugoslav interests, and at the peace negotiations forced through an agreement creating the Free Territory of Trieste, covering most of the old A and B zones. According to the agreement, occupying troops were to be pulled out and the United Nations was to nominate a Governor, who would have the task of calling elections for a parliamentary Assembly and appointing an executive which was consonant with the people's vote.

The Yugoslavs resisted this solution fiercely. In the end, Soviet pressure forced them to bow, but they retained claims over Zone A and Zone B. The conflict over Trieste, however, worsened Yugoslav relations not only with the Anglo-Americans and with the Soviets, but also with the Italian Communist Party. For obvious motives of internal policy, Togliatti could not support the Yugoslav claims – even though Italian Communists in Trieste itself did sincerely support them. There had been friction between the Yugoslav and Italian Parties since the time of the resistance; this now worsened and emerged into the open after the PCI was forced out of the governing coalition in Italy. The Yugoslavs failed to take into account the different political situations underlying the resistance movement in the two countries; so when the Italian Party was forced out of government, they saw this as clear confirmation of their thesis that the PCI should follow their revolutionary example and take up arms. When they did not do so, the Italian Communists automatically became 'cowardly opportunists'.[4]

This was the situation Vidali found on his return to Trieste. It is more than probable that he went back to the city at the request of Soviet authorities, who no doubt wanted someone they could trust in a region which was a source of tension with Tito (Vidali himself hints that this was the case in his book *Dal Messico a Murmansk*). The Yugoslavs, for their part, did not notice the trap they were being led into; they believed, indeed, that having a convinced revolutionary in Trieste would usefully reinforce revolutionary tendencies in the PCI. In spite of what Vidali wrote in *Ritorno alla città senza pace*, it is not true that the Ljubljana authorities tried to stop his return to Trieste at the last moment. On the contrary, they encouraged it, reassured as they were by the affirmations of Regent, Vidali's former comrade in Red Aid, that he could swear to his reliability.[5] Why the Anglo-American authorities gave such ready assent to Vidali's return to Zone A (which was under their administration), remains unknown.

In an interview with the journalist Giorgio Bocca, Vidali stated that 'even an internationalist like me, after beating it down for years, ends up spitting out the nationalist blood that remains inside'.[6] In reality, Vidali does not seem to have undertaken such an epic struggle with himself. As soon as he arrived in Trieste in the summer of 1947, he came into conflict with local Party leaders when he declared his intention to follow orders from Togliatti (and thus from Moscow), not from the local representative of the Yugoslav Communist Party, Branko Babič. This clash can be interpreted in various ways. First of all, it should be seen as part of the wider conflict between Tito and Stalin regarding the advisability of extending the revolutionary march in Europe. Secondly, it reflected differences between Slovenian and Italian Communists over their role in Trieste, for Slovenia considered

Trieste part of its sphere of influence not only for nationalist reasons, but also out of ideological conviction, since they believed the Trieste proletariat would naturally look more towards a country where Socialism was being built, than towards Italy, which was becoming more and more of an American backyard. The PCI, on the other hand, could not afford to give up claims to the city, for fear that Parties of the centre and the right cast them in the role of anti-patriots. Finally, there was also a personal element in the rivalry between Vidali and Babič: the two men were the same age, had very similar revolutionary experiences behind them, and even resembled each other physically. It was scarcely surprising, therefore, that they should find themselves like two cocks in the proverbial chicken run – for it was clear that Trieste was too small to give opportunities for both of them. At first, it seemed that Vidali would be forced to give way. Apart from anything else, he was accused of having contacts with Anglo-American intelligence behind the Party's back. And he even seems to have been tempted to return to Mexico. However, in the name of revolutionary discipline, he accepted Togliatti's request that he remain in what was a very exposed situation (we should remember that after the Cominform had been set up in September 1947 the Yugoslavs stepped up their criticisms of the PCI's 'opportunism').[7]

The Yugoslavs did not realize that their display of revolutionary zeal was making them ever more suspect – indeed, frankly dangerous – in Stalin's eyes. In reality, excommunication was approaching; after a heated exchange of letters between Tito and Stalin in spring 1948, this finally came in the well-known Bucharest Resolution on 28 June. In his memoirs, Vidali claims that he only knew about the coming clash a day before the Cominform statement was published in *Rude Pravo* – when he was called urgently to Rome to receive instructions from PCI headquarters.

However, according to one of the UDB spies Vidali was surrounded by, he was already aware of the contents of Stalin's letters – so he must have been prepared for the Resolution, and ready to act on it.[8] In any case, Vidali did act at once. He handed the text of the Resolution over to Western press agencies, and also tried to take over the Slovenian newspaper of the Communist Party of the Free Territory of Trieste, *Primorskj dnevnik*. After just one day, the Titoists (who were also evidently prepared for action) recaptured the paper, and also the Party's funds. On 3 May 1948 there was a stormy sitting of the Executive Committee, which at one point broke out into scuffles. But the vote went Vidali's way, six out of ten members of the Party's supreme body approving a motion condemning Tito. The Free Territory Party then split into two bitterly opposed fractions, each of which claimed the right to represent Communists in both Zone A and Zone B.

Zone B was still occupied by Yugoslav troops, since the Free Territory had never been set up; so here most of the local Communists automatically followed Tito's line. In Zone A, under Anglo-American administration, on the other hand, Trieste Communists were free to choose – indeed they were freer than in many other parts of the supposedly democratic world, since they had two alternative reference points in Vidali and Babič. The crucial issue was that of how the numerous Slovenian Communists in Zone A would react – for victory depended on them. Vidali was fully aware of this, and when he went to Bucharest to confer with the Soviet Cominform leader Iudin at the end of July, he stressed the need to obtain financing for a Slovenian paper. This duly started up early the following year, under the title *Delo* (Labour).[9]

We know little about the meeting between Iudin and Vidali. However, it is clear that Vidali returned from Bucharest (where Cominform headquarters had shifted after leaving Belgrade) with precise instructions, which were put into immediate effect. At the head of the Party of which he was now Secretary, Vidali set up a *troika*, made up of himself and two formidable women – Marija Bernetič, an old Slovenian Communist and – according to the UDB – an agent of the NKVD like Vidali himself, and Laura Weiss, a young Jewish intellectual from a well-known Trieste family (also accused of being a member of the Soviet secret services). In the months and years which followed, this *troika* was frenetically active, struggling against 'the mad dogs of Babič's gang', undertaking spying and sabotage of Yugoslav plans, spreading propaganda against Tito and plotting a coup against the 'Trotskyite' regime in Belgrade. Some aspects of this complicated activity are relatively well known. We know much, for example, of the genuine civil war which broke out in the Trieste working class – clashes where the followers of Vidali, organized in assault gangs, were on the offensive. Vidali's supporters had the advantage also because they were more numerous – since many Slovenes sided with them, probably for reasons of instinct more than of ideology. Having just emerged from 20 years in a Fascist ghetto, many workers, but also many Slovenian peasants, were no doubt unwilling to enter into the new ghetto to which Tito had been consigned when he gave up the safety and the pride of belonging to a great international proletarian movement headed by Stalin. We also have a good deal of evidence about the *troika*'s spying activity against Yugoslavia. Here the *troika* was able to avail itself of Slovenian and Croatian sympathizers as well as many Italians who had moved to Yugoslavia after the war for ideological, economic or political reasons, making up Italian colonies of various sizes in Flume and other industrial towns. There was therefore a very considerable flow of information regarding the situation within Yugoslavia, and this was processed in Trieste and sent on to Rome,

Bucharest, Sofia and headquarters in Moscow. Much of this information was also exploited for the purposes of anti-Yugoslav propaganda. The mouthpiece for this was a special Bulletin, published in French so as to be more accessible to press agencies and the mass media of East and West. This publication did not invariably win Soviet approval, however. The official who had the responsibility for assessing it for the Central Committee of the CPSU criticized its propagandistic style and the weakness of its arguments.[10] On other occasions, when Vidali sent highly valuable information (such as on Yugoslav prisons, and especially on the notorious Goli Otok, a prison camp on Auschwitz lines for Cominform members), this was not exploited for propaganda purposes. The fact that Vidali complained about this to the Soviet Ambassador in Rome shows his basic naivety.[11]

Unfortunately, we know much less about other activities to which Vidali dedicated himself after the summer of 1948. Vladimir Dedijer mentions an attempt at a *coup d'état* in the Yugoslav Navy – a rebel unit of which was to occupy Spalato and then make an appeal to the Soviet Union for assistance.[12] The archives of the Yugoslav secret services mention frequent contacts between Vidali and Fedor Moloskovsky, military *attaché* to the Soviet Embassy in Rome; it seems the purpose of these meetings was to lay plans for the part Italian partisans could play if the Soviet Union should attack Yugoslavia. The same source also mentions similar contacts with Italian troops stationed in Friuli to inform the soldiers which side they would be expected to take in the eventuality of a clash between the two blocs.[13]

In December 1948, Vidali wrote to Elena Stasova, Lenin's former secretary and later Vidali's superior in Red Aid (a person whom he admired enormously throughout his life), to say:

> At the moment, we are working on a present for comrade Stalin [who was about to have his sixtieth birthday]. Guess what it is! Thousands and thousands of signatures of the people, men and women of Trieste affirming they want peace and will never be prepared to take up arms against the Soviet Union. The Anglo-Americans and Tito's gang are furious.[14]

There is little doubt that 'Tito's gang' must have been furious, for the petition was an enormous success, gaining more than 96 000 signatures – showing once and for all that the real Communist Party of the Free Territory of Trieste was the one headed by Vidali. The Allies were naturally less furious. Indeed, after they had noted with satisfaction the split in the Trieste working class, they could contemplate with equanimity the prospect of elections; these had been put off precisely because of fears that a Party too sympathetic to Yugoslavia might emerge from the ballot box. In these elections, held on the 12 and

19 June 1949, Vidali obtained 42 587 votes, as against just 5344 for the Titoists. All things considered, this result did not displease Trieste's pro-Italian bourgeoisie either, for Vidali had given a strong patriotic slant to his propaganda. Of course he had to be sensitive to his Slovenian electorate. And at that time he argued that the Free Territory should be set up, in accordance with what had been planned at the Peace Conference and with Moscow's position. Yet it was clear enough that he regarded this as a provisional solution which would snatch Zone B away from the hated Yugoslavia in order that, later on, the whole territory could be reunited with Italy. Diego De Castro, representative of the Italian Government as the Allied military Governor in Trieste, also interpreted Vidali's position in these terms; in July 1951 he wrote to Andreotti to reassure him that an 'alliance' between the feared champions of Trieste independence and Vidali's Communists was out of the question.[15] Vidali's position was so 'firmly pro-Italian', in fact, that this even damaged his Party at the elections on 25 May 1952. The Party lost over 4000 votes – earning sharp criticism from Luigi Longo in a conversation with the Soviet Ambassador in Rome.[16] This criticism did not, however, deflect Vidali from his visceral anti-Yugoslav policy. He was so fixed in this track that he was not even able to notice the first signs of the thaw between Belgrade and Moscow – and therefore between Togliatti and Tito – which got under way after Stalin's death. So in October and November 1953, when a serious crisis broke out over Trieste, which was threatening to degenerate into an armed clash between Italy and Yugoslavia, Vidali did not hesitate to solemnly proclaim that his followers would fight against Yugoslavia (a declaration which caused much relief among Italian nationalists).[17] However, this was one of the last roars of the 'jaguar'. In the years which followed, Khrushchev went to Canossa, then in May 1955 to Belgrade, and at the Twentieth Congress of the CPSU the personality cult of Stalin was denounced. Vittorio Vidali had been overtaken by history.

Notes

1. RTsKhIDNI, f. 195, op. 221, d. 3776.
2. ANM, Vidali Dossier, pp. 205–7.
3. *Ibid.*, p. 208.
4. RTsKhIDNI, f. 17, op. 128, d. 494, p. 27.
5. ANM, Vidali Dossier, p. 62.
6. D. De Castro, *La questione di Trieste. L'azione politica e diplomatica italiana dal 1943 al 1954*, Vol. 1 (Trieste: 1981) p. 377.
7. Drzavni Arhiv Republike Slovenije, Ljubljana, f. 60K PKJ, st. 10.
8. ANM, Vidali Dossier, p. 67.
9. RTsKhIDNI, f. 17, op. 137, d. 386.
10. RTsKhIDNI, f. 17, op. 137, d. 933.
11. *Ibid.*

12. V. Dedijer, *Novi prilozi za biografiju Josipa Broza Tita*, Vol. 3 (Belgrade: 1984) p. 463.
13. ANM, Vidali Dossier, pp. 63–5.
14. RTsKhIDNI, f. 356, op. 1, d. 111.
15. De Castro, *La questione*, Vol. 2, p. 253.
16. RTsKhIDNI, f. 17, op. 137, d. 933.
17. De Castro, *La questione*, Vol. 2, pp. 592, 656, 660.

18 Revolution Released: Stalin, the Bulgarian Communist Party and the Establishment of the Cominform
Vesselin Dimitrov

The relationship between the great powers and the Eastern European countries has usually been perceived as a one-way flow; the latter have been portrayed, and have portrayed themselves, as hapless victims of great power politics. Thus, historians have concentrated on events such as Yalta and Potsdam, which were seen as predetermining the future of the region and leaving little room for manoeuvre to domestic political forces. The Soviet Union, in particular, has been presented as manipulating local politics through obedient Communist Parties.

The top-down institutional view is usually matched by a similarly one-dimensional view on the flow of policies. The Soviet Union has been seen as a fixed factor pushing towards 'Communization'; wherever moderation and ambiguity have been perceived, they have been attributed to the Eastern Europeans. In this view, the establishment of the Cominform in September 1947 marked the final triumph of the rigid Soviet view over the more flexible Eastern European ideas of 'people's democracy'. In essence, the establishment of closer Soviet control and the intensification of revolution have been regarded as two facets of the same process.

In this chapter, I will argue that, at least in the case of Bulgaria, both the institutional and policy relationships were far more complex; more often than not, the domestic political forces enjoyed independence from, and indeed sometimes managed to manipulate, their great power patrons. Rather than creating and directing the internal political conflict, the great powers were sucked into it. Furthermore, the intransigence of the locals (including the local representatives of the great powers) often undermined the attempts of the Governments to resolve their differences amicably.

My focus will be on the relationship between the BRP(k), the Bulgarian Workers' Party, and the Soviet leadership (which, given the autocratic nature of Soviet decision making, usually meant Stalin). My analysis is based on newly available documents from the Bulgarian and Soviet archives, which make it possible to investigate empirically what could previously be only enlightened guesswork. I will demonstrate that the flow of people's democracy ideas proceeded from Stalin, and their realization was blocked by BRP(k)'s narrow-minded drive for maximum power. The Soviet failure to maintain control over the BRP(k), and the ability of the latter to manipulate Soviet policy can be explained by the fact that there was no unified Soviet policy-making process, either institutionally or conceptually. Institutionally, there were a number of different agencies working independently of each other, and often at cross purposes. Conceptually, Soviet policy tried to meet simultaneously several objectives, which were difficult to achieve within one framework. The BRP(k) was able to exploit these differences to further its own aims.

THE POPULAR FRONT IN 1935–44: AN AMBIVALENT LEGACY

The BRP(k)'s first attempt to construct a popular front came in the mid-1930s, after the Seventh Congress of the Comintern. The new line promoted by Georgi Dimitrov, the Comintern's General Secretary, met with virtually insurmountable obstacles. It was obstinately resisted by both the leadership and the rank-and-file of the BRP(k), as it went against the grain of the Party's radical and doctrinaire heritage. It took a number of years, and the destruction of several hundred 'left-sectarians' in the great purges, to break down the resistance.[1] On the other hand, it was proving hard to find allies for the popular front. Most Agrarian and 'bourgeois' democratic politicians preferred to rely on the perceived sagacity of King Boris rather than pursue active confrontationalist policies. The efforts that did emerge were stifled quite effortlessly by the authoritarian regime. In 1939–41, under the influence of the Nazi–Soviet Pact, the links between the BRP(k) and the politicians whose sympathies lay with the Western democracies were all but broken.

The German attack on the Soviet Union in June 1941 and the emergence of a world anti-Nazi coalition brought the popular front back on the agenda. The Comintern urged its member Parties to undertake an armed struggle against the Germans and their local collaborators, and to form broad anti-Fascist fronts with all patriotic elements.

In Bulgaria, a relatively leniently treated German satellite, the two strands of Comintern's policy worked at cross-purposes. Since the German contingent in Bulgaria was quite small, the armed struggle could only be conducted against the Bulgarian Government which not only had all its machinery intact but also enjoyed the support of the majority of the population due to its success in achieving the country's traditional revisionist aspirations while sparing it the ordeals of war. It is a reflection of the radicalism of the BRP(k)'s leadership that, in the face of all these obstacles, they contemplated organizing an armed uprising in 1941. Stalin promptly put an end to their daydreams and instructed them to postpone the uprising until the moment when it would be possible to combine 'action from within and without'.[2] The party's efforts to organize sabotage and later to develop a partisan movement did not attain the success of their Yugoslav comrades and never seriously threatened the Government's control of the country. Nevertheless, by September 1944 the Party had under its command several thousand armed partisans who were to prove an explosive element after the seizure of power.[3] Politically, the BRP(k) was able to establish links with some leftist Agrarians, Social Democrats and members of *Zveno* (a group of anti-monarchical officers) on the basis of a programme for a 'Patriotic Front' worked out by Dimitrov and Kolarov in Moscow. The programme contained demands for a break with the Germans, the restoration of democratic rights and measures to promote economic welfare. From BRP(k)'s point of view, the Front was only a limited success: some prominent democratic politicians steadfastly refused to join it, and even those who were already members quite often acted outside its framework. The Patriotic Front did not coalesce into a coherent organization until the beginning of September 1944 when the Soviet Army reached Bulgaria's borders.[4]

The Front's seizure of power was due not so much to its own meagre resources as to larger international developments. The Soviet Union's assumption of a dominant role in Bulgaria was curiously improvised; until September 1944 alternative scenarios were still possible, if not more likely. The fact that Bulgaria was at war with Britain and the United States but not with the USSR meant that the country could leave the war by concluding an armistice with the Western powers only. This opportunity was not realized, however. The responsibility lay mainly with Bulgaria's wartime Governments which, for various reasons, procrastinated until the very end and embarked on serious negotiations only at the end of August. The Western powers, for their part, were content to leave the initiative to the Bulgarians. Indeed, on a number of occasions the British sought to discourage any false hopes of an easy peace.

Soviet policy towards Bulgaria, hitherto confined to a barrage of diplomatic notes, began to take a more active turn in early September. It was too much to expect Stalin not to take advantage of the opportunities opened by Romania's unexpectedly rapid collapse to assert his presence in Bulgaria. In this he was encouraged and abetted by a steady stream of letters from Dimitrov.[5] On 5 September, with barely half-an-hour prior notice to the American and British ambassadors in Moscow, the Soviets declared war on Bulgaria, and three days later their troops entered the country. The Bulgarian Government was mesmerized by the Soviet declaration of war, and complete paralysis ensued. The Patriotic Front was thus able to organize a bloodless *coup d'état* in the early hours of 9 September 1944. The coup was carried out by military units loyal to *Zveno;* the partisans came into the city only subsequently. The BRP(k)'s position as the initiator of the Patriotic Front and the fact that only it had been engaged in an armed struggle allowed it to claim, over the objections of its partners, the key post of Interior Minister. *Zveno*'s links with the army secured for it the next strongest position, with the posts of Prime Minister, Foreign Minister and Defence Minister. The numerical distribution of posts in the cabinet was quite equitable, with the Communists, *Zveno* and the Agrarians gaining four ministries each, and the Social Democrats and independents two each.

REVOLUTION AND PATRIOTIC FRONT: THE UNTENABLE COMBINATION (SEPTEMBER 1944–AUGUST 1945)

The BRP(k)'s Revolution

Although it was not responsible for bringing down Bulgaria's last 'bourgeois' Government, the BRP(k) was not slow to take advantage of the resulting political vacuum. In the next few months, the BRP(k)'s long-dwarfed revolution finally seemed to be taking place. Partisans, rebellious soldiers and newly minted 'Communists' went on the rampage throughout the country, killing an estimated 10 000 to 30 000 people.[6] Although the party leadership sought to put an end to the uncoordinated killings, it was not averse to using the purge, this time in the form of organized 'people's trials', to destroy the country's political élite which had survived largely intact during the war. This probably accounts for the particular ferocity of the 'people's trials', the most far-reaching in Eastern Europe: 11 122 people passed through the courts, with 2730 sentenced to death. This included all the ministers of Bulgaria's wartime Governments, the Regents, the late King's advisers and most of the members of Parliament.[7] Some of the local Soviet representatives were all too eager to promote the purges; indeed, one of them complained that they had not gone far enough.[8] The Soviet high command initially attempted to put a limit to the purges of the officer corps in order to preserve the fighting capability of the Bulgarian Army; Molotov said as much to the Bulgarian Foreign Minister in October 1944.[9] The Communists, however, were able to persuade

General Biriuzov, the commander of the Soviet occupying forces and the effective head of the Allied Control Commission, that an attempt by the *Zveno* Minister of War, Damian Velchev, to save persecuted officers by sending them to the front and empowering them to defend themselves against unauthorized arrest, amounted to protecting the 'Fascists'. Biriuzov faced down Velchev and threatened that all Bulgarian troops would be thrown out of the capital.[10] The Communists proceeded to take advantage of Velchev's climbdown by purging 1100 officers, 30 per cent of the officer corps, appointing Deputy Commanders on the model of Soviet commissars at all levels and commissioning 700 reliable Party members.[11]

The 'conquest' of the army was but one side of the BRP(k)'s determined drive to gain control over the instruments of power. By December 1944, 54 per cent of the members of the Patriotic Front committees, a network which encompassed almost all localities and places of work, were Communists.[12] The BRP(k)'s control of the Interior Ministry allowed it to carry out a complete overhaul of the local administration. At the end of 1944, 63 out of 84 cities had Communist mayors, as did 879 out of 1165 villages.[13] The old police was disbanded on 10 September 1944 and replaced by a 'people's militia', packed with former partisans and Party members. The militia was used to intimidate political opponents, often at the discretion of the local BRP(k) committees.[14]

One other aspect of the BRP(k)'s build up was its enormous numerical expansion. On 20 October 1944 the Politburo decided 'to create a mass party which would include all the healthy and militant elements from the working class, the toiling peasantry and the people's intelligentsia'.[15] By January 1945 the Party had mushroomed to over 250 000 – a 30-fold increase in comparison with 9 September 1944.[16] The Communist Youth League attracted more than 400 000 members while the General Workers' Professional Union, which the Communists helped to set up in March 1945, had around 300 000.[17] Through these colossal organizations – in a population of barely seven million people – the Communists were able to introduce an unprecedented level of political activism in a country which had barely known mass politics before. As Kostov put it, undoubtedly reflecting an almost universal feeling in the party's ranks: 'the strength of the revolutionary explosion was such that we could have established Soviet power on 9 September 1944.'[18]

Breakdown of the Patriotic Front

It was not part of Stalin's plans, however, to allow a Communist revolution to be carried out in Bulgaria. While accepting that the Communist Party would be in control, he insisted that the other political parties participating in the Patriotic Front should also be given a degree of influence. This two-fold strategy would create a hegemonial rather than a monolithic system; in the Communist jargon, a 'people's democracy' rather than a 'Soviet' system. In February 1945 he told the Bulgarians that 'your Patriotic Front Government has turned out to be quite a good thing. It should be strengthened and possibly broadened a bit. Do not reject any people who could be used in the struggle against Fascism.'[19] Earlier he had noted that 'perhaps we are making a mistake when we consider Soviet power as the only road to Socialism. Perhaps some other forms – a democratic republic or in certain cases even a constitutional monarchy – might lead to it.'[20]

Stalin's foreign policy also tried to reconcile two elements. On one hand, he was clearly determined to safeguard Soviet control of Bulgaria. In the long and tortuous negotiations on the Bulgarian armistice in September–October 1944 he insisted on and finally obtained a recognition of the leading role of the Soviet chairman in the Allied Control Commission for Bulgaria. With the British, that was backed up by the infamous 'percentages' agreement, allocating the Soviet Union 75 per cent influence in Bulgaria. Stalin did not see the Yalta and Potsdam Conferences as in any way affecting the *status quo* in Bulgaria. As Molotov, who usually acted as Stalin's mouthpiece, assured Dimitrov with regard to the Potsdam Conference: 'In general these decisions are favourable to us. In practice our sphere of influence there has been recognized.'[21] On the other hand, Stalin was anxious not to antagonize his Western Allies and thus endanger the all-important common struggle against Nazi Germany. In October 1944, when the Bulgarians speculated that the Western powers might try to undermine Soviet interests, Molotov firmly emphasized that the three great powers were united in a common cause and would be able to resolve all their differences amicably. It seems that Stalin envisaged that the relationship would continue even after the removal of the common danger, on the basis of the West recognizing his sphere of influence while he undertook not to provoke Western public opinion by strong-arm methods. That was not so far fetched as it might seem in retrospect; John Gaddis, for example, has suggested that what brought about the Cold War was not so much American opposition to spheres of influence *per se*, as disgust with the Soviets' brutality in achieving that.[22]

Stalin's plans for compromise settlements, both internally and externally, demanded very fine balancing and a high degree of control. Unfortunately, they were not forthcoming. First, he was not able to control the activities of the BRP(k). The steady stream of moderating directives from Moscow, usually passed through Dimitrov, produced nothing more than lip-service to Patriotic Front co-operation; the party was either unable or unwilling to restrict its drive for power and its determination to carry out a revolutionary overhaul of the country. Even if the leadership was willing to compromise, the message coming from the middle-ranking activists was overwhelmingly radical. As Kostov reported to Dimitrov: 'it is a fact that at our conferences the militant speeches calling for decisive action are met with storms of applause, while the calls for order and discipline are received with coldness and reserve.'[23]

Secondly, the Communist drive for power and the excesses of the purges naturally brought about a negative reaction in the other Patriotic Front Parties. The conflict centred on the Agrarian Union, a Party which saw itself as the rightful representative of the Bulgarian village. The Agrarians had long traditions and had ruled the country almost single-handedly in 1919–23 and as part of a coalition in 1931–4. The Agrarian Union's development in late 1944 was directed by Dr G.M. Dimitrov (often called the 'G.M.', to distinguish him from his Communist namesake) who aimed to restore the organization of the Union and to make it ready for independent power. By the end of 1944 the Union had over 100 000 members, with a growth rate almost as rapid as that of the BRP(k). The Communists were naturally alarmed by the emergence of a rival for power and used G.M. Dimitrov's unenthusiastic attitude towards the use of the Bulgarian Army against Germany and his alleged links with the British intelligence (he had spent the war years in Cairo) to organize a smear campaign against him. They were able to gain Biriuzov's co-operation, and the Soviet general allegedly threatened the Agrarian leader with the dissolution of his entire organization if he did not resign. In January 1945 G.M. Dimitrov bowed to the pressure and was replaced by Nikola Petkov.[24]

The new Agrarian leader disappointed the hopes placed on him and soon began distancing himself from the Communists. The conferences of the Agrarian Youth League and the regional Agrarian organizations in the spring of 1945 showed the survival of what the Communists called 'G.M.-ism', that is the propensity to see the Agrarian Union as an independent force outside the framework of the Patriotic Front.

The Communist reaction was to organize an internal coup against the 'reactionary' elements. The process took place at all levels. Locally, the Communists identified collaborationist elements in the Agrarian organizations and endeavoured to place them into the leadership. The campaign was quite extensive and totally cynical, as the reports of the regional Communist organizers indicate; all methods were used, including blackmail, militia intimidation and the ambitions of unscrupulous upstarts.[25] Once enough local organizations had been captured and forced to declare themselves against 'G.M.-ism', the Communists proceeded to organize a 'national' conference of left-wing Agrarians in May 1945. As the top Agrarian leadership remained loyal to Petkov, the Communists were hard pressed to find anyone of prominence to head the conference. The only one who proved susceptible was Alexander Obbov, a man whose personal weaknesses were despised by the Bulgarian Communists and the Soviets alike, and were probably used to blackmail him.[26] The Conference condemned 'G.M.-ism', elected an entirely new leadership and called for a purge of doubtful elements. Petkov refused to associate himself with the Conference and by July 1945 was organizing a separate Agrarian Party and was on the point of leaving the Government. The Social Democratic Party also split into pro- and anti-collaborationist wings.

By the summer of 1945 the combination of BRP(k)'s high-handed tactics and the other Parties' reassertion of their interests had thus brought the Patriotic Front system to the brink of collapse. At this point Stalin decided to intervene personally.

On 11 July Dimitrov wrote to Kostov:

Our Big Friend [Stalin] ... considers the removal of Petkov and his friends from the cabinet to be premature ... He points out that not enough has been done, either at home or abroad, to unmask them on the basis of concrete facts ... He stressed that our party should ... not be afraid of differences of opinion and criticism in the Government and the Patriotic Front because it is impossible to have total unanimity on all questions in a government composed of several parties.[27]

Stalin's advice fell on deaf ears. Indeed, some members of the Politburo initially suggested that Dimitrov's telegram be concealed from the Party![28] Although the Party leadership later paid lip-service to the instructions in their internal discussions, they found it impossible to resist the momentum of their own maximalism. They refused to grant Petkov the right to publish an independent newspaper and on 19 July decided to break off the talks. The crisis continued to intensify. The Western representatives in Bulgaria, in a mirror-process, had been increasingly associated with the emerging opposition. This was especially true of Maynard Barnes, the American political representative. As early as December 1944 he had formed an opinion that the Communists were establishing a dictatorship behind the Patriotic Front veneer.[29] It was Barnes's sincere conviction, reinforced by the Yalta declaration, that the United States should seek to promote democratic values in Eastern Europe.[30] His personal involvement grew with the sheltering of G.M. Dimitrov, who was threatened by the Communist militia and sought refuge in the American mission. On one occasion, Barnes told the militia-men trying to break into the building that they could do so only over his dead body.[31] By July, Barnes had regular meetings with Petkov as well, and reported his pleas for help to the State Department.[32] The British representatives were more occupied with strategic considerations, especially those relating to Greece, but tended to support the mercurial Americans.[33]

On 26 July 1945 Petkov appealed to the Western Governments for an international supervision of the elections due to be held in a month's time. In August the American and the British Governments sent notes declaring that no government resulting from the elections would be recognized. Although the notes were intended as a statement of intent rather than to make any specific request, the Western representatives in Sofia took matters into their own hands and in a series of meetings of the Allied Control Commission pressed the Soviet chairman for a postponement.[34] At the crucial point Petko Stainov, the Bulgarian Foreign Minister, a member of *Zveno,* stated at a press conference that it was the Commission, and by implication the Russians, who had the power to settle the issue, and not the Bulgarian Government. Stainov was clearly seeking to transfer the responsibility for antagonizing the West to the Soviet Union. The Communists were not informed and did not seem to have realized the importance of the statement.

Presented with the insistent demands of the Western representatives in Bulgaria (and evidently not realizing that their post-war Governments were preparing to repudiate their hasty actions), taken together with Stainov's statement, Stalin decided to give way and postpone the elections.

Kostov's telegrams to Dimitrov hours before the postponement on 24 August indicate that the Bulgarian Communists were not consulted about the move.[35] The next day the shocked Bulgarians flew to Moscow. There they listened to a lecture by Stalin stressing the need of maintaining good relations with Britain and America: 'You must never ignore England and America. You must have normal relations with them – I am absolutely serious about that. You must not shout too, much about your eternal friendship with the USSR.' The Soviet dictator helpfully provided a theoretical justification of the change of course towards the opposition:

> An opposition is unavoidable in a society consisting of antagonistic classes ... You might even find it profitable to have an opposition of 50–60 men: you can then say to Bevin that you too have an opposition. The opposition will act as a whip and would not allow you to slacken and take things easy ... You can allow some parties to exist outside the Patriotic Front.[36]

The Patriotic Front system was thus unable to survive the crisis occasioned by the August 1945 elections. At this point of time, perhaps under the influence of a moderating 'Potsdam' spirit, Stalin decided to resolve the crisis by partially opening the political system and allowing the existence of an opposition. The Soviet dictator seems to have perceived the opposition in an essentially 'decorative' or at most a consultative function, not challenging the Government's control of the country in any practical way.

On their return to Sofia, the Bulgarian Communists implemented the changes suggested by Stalin. The process was quite painful for them, especially in psychological terms. The Politburo session discussing the postponement of elections was the longest on record in the entire postwar period and involved an unprecedented number of participants. Symptomatically enough, only two or three out of the nearly 60 people present showed any realization of having pushed things too far; all the others blamed the complex international situation.[37] Managing an opposition was clearly not going to be easy for the Bulgarian Communists.

'PATRIOTIC FRONT + OPPOSITION': THE FAILURE OF THE NEW FORMULA (AUGUST 1945–JUNE 1947)

The new political framework also proved unable to contain the aspirations of the major actors; all of them sought to change the terms in their favour. For the first six months, it was the opposition which took the initiative. The opposition saw the concessions it had obtained as evidence that the tide had turned against the Communists and as an opportunity to rout them out of the 'commanding heights'. Petkov's conditions for re-entering the Government amounted to, among other things, the post of a Prime Minister, the transfer of the Ministries of the Interior and Justice to non-Communists and free elections. Petkov's defiant personality was an important factor in the adoption of such an uncompromising stance by the opposition Agrarians. Since he had been a consistent fighter against the former authoritarian regimes, and had tried sincerely to co-operate with the Communists, he was impervious to accusations of 'reaction' with which many prominent politicians had been silenced. His father and brother had fallen victims to political assassins, and this had given him a virtual immunity from fear.

Despite the fact that there were now no formal obstacles to its taking part in the elections scheduled for 18 November 1945, the opposition refused to oblige and announced that it would be boycotting them. Its newspapers violently denounced the Government, and soon surpassed the circulation of their official counterparts.[38]

The local Western representatives continued to articulate the opposition sentiments, and at first it seemed that their Governments would follow suit. Faced with the Soviets' unyielding position at the London Foreign Ministers' Conference, however, the American Secretary of State James Byrnes began to search for a compromise. His efforts to resolve the conflict through sending an 'impartial' observer to Bulgaria (the liberal journalist Mark Ethridge) brought little result. The Soviets' attitude towards Ethridge's meddling in their zone of influence was reflected in Dimitrov's spiteful comment that the journalist was behaving as 'some sort of a messiah'.[39] At the Moscow Conference in December 1945, Byrnes tried another approach, securing from Stalin an undertaking to 'advise' the Bulgarian Government to take in two members of the opposition.

Petkov regarded the terms as a whitewash, and showing his usual intransigence, refused to enter the Government unless his conditions were satisfied. Stalin reflected that 'perhaps it was a mistake to leave the conduct of the negotiations to the Bulgarian Government' and decided to make his own wishes known to the opposition directly. Deputy Foreign Minister Vyshinsky was sent to Sofia to impress on the opposition that all they had to do was to join the Government without setting any conditions.[40] The former public prosecutor flew to Sofia on 9 January, fresh from his success in Bucharest where he had accomplished a similar mission the day before, and raised the leaders of the opposition from their beds at 2 a.m. Petkov and Lulchev, the leader of the opposition Social Democrats, refused to budge and the talks broke down. A second attempt three months later to bring the opposition into the Government also ended in failure. Stalin was beginning to find the opposition's obstinacy quite irritating and advised the Bulgarian Communists to 'take a series of thought-out and well-organized measures to smother the opposition'.[41]

Stalin's hopes of an understanding with the West were also wearing thin. Barnes shared Petkov's view of the Moscow decisions and sought to persuade the State Department to return to the policy of non-recognition.[42] The Soviets made a special protest to the State Department at Barnes's 'instigation' of the opposition. Although Byrnes cautioned Barnes, and even considered recalling him for consultation, he himself gradually drifted towards acceptance of the opposition's contention that its representatives could enter the Government only on the basis of 'mutually-satisfactory' conditions.[43] The Soviets considered that the Americans were going back on their own word and were destroying the compromise they themselves had agreed to in Moscow. From March 1946 onward, the Soviets made no further concessions to the Americans, but were not yet ready to provoke them as long as the peace treaty with Bulgaria had not been signed.

The BRP(k) in the meantime was doing all it could to convince the Soviets that no compromise with the opposition was possible. Despite Stalin's 'theoretical' justification, the Communists never accepted the legitimacy of the opposition's existence. The opposition was depicted, even in discussions at the highest level, as a collection of Fascists and reactionaries who had only two possible options, either to go back to the Patriotic Front and co-operate loyally within its framework, or turn to conspiracy. The local Soviet diplomats shared this opinion: the leader of the opposition Agrarian Youth movement was described as a repulsive Fascist who in different circumstances would engage in sabotage and terrorism.[44] Although it was not yet able to persuade the Soviets to allow it to destroy the opposition by physical force, the BRP(k) was quite successful in gaining Soviet support in the defence of its established positions. In November 1945, after repeated pleas from the comrades at home, Dimitrov was finally able to persuade Stalin to allow him to go home. Previously, Stalin had refused that on the ground that it would give rise to rumours of 'Sovietization'. On his arrival, Dimitrov made it clear in two virulent speeches that there would not be a second postponement of the elections now scheduled for 18 November. On 12 November, in a telephone conversation with Lavrischev, the head of the Balkan Department of the Soviet Foreign Ministry, Dimitrov urged the Soviet Government to realize that another postponement would be a 'disaster' for the Patriotic Front.[45] When in March 1946 it appeared that the *Zveno* members of Government were wavering in their determination and might concede important positions to the opposition, the BRP(k) sought and received Soviet support for its hard line.[46]

Against *Zveno*, the BRP(k) was able to secure more active Soviet support. After August 1945, an active right wing had formed within the Party, which the left-wing leadership was barely able to contain. The Soviet representatives' reports alleged that Stainov was turning the Foreign Ministry into a reactionary fortress while Velchev was promoting his own people into positions of power and looking for a pretext to remove the Communist officers.[47] Stalin was not prepared to tolerate such an exposed position, especially where the instruments of power were concerned. During the March 1946 reorganization of the Government, he insisted in a series of telegrams to Dimitrov that the *Zveno* 'doubledealers' be dismissed from their posts. When the Bulgarian Communists for once proved hesitant, Stalin acidly remarked that 'We are surprised at your modesty and lack of initiative in this matter. The Yugoslav Communists are acting far better and more militantly than you are.'[48]

The Yugoslav factor evidently had a growing appeal to Stalin. Possibly it was not a coincidence that it was during a joint visit of Bulgarian and Yugoslav delegations to Moscow in June 1946 that he authorized the Bulgarians to take on *Zveno* and even criticized them for 'insufficiently decisive measures'.[49]

Stalin's criticism was probably undeserved. Dimitrov's call at the central committee meeting in August 1946 for a general political offensive against the reactionary elements in the Patriotic Front[50] was met with enthusiasm by the Party grassroots, indeed excessively so.

Dimitrov was forced to speak at length against the orgy of beatings and imprisonments and stress that the offensive was to be accomplished by means of agitation and propaganda.[51] In a more organized way, the Communists were able to oust Velchev from his position and carry out a thorough purge of the army dismissing nearly 2000 officers.[52]

Stalin, however, evidently was still under the sway of contradictory emotions, and on a number of occasions spoke of the need for moderation and new ways. In September 1946 he advised the Bulgarians to form a 'Labour' Party:

> You have to unite the working class with the other toiling masses on the basis of a minimalist programme; the time for a maximalist programme has yet to come ... In essence, the party would be Communist, but you would have a broader base and a better mask for the present period. This would help you to achieve Socialism in a different way – without the dictatorship of the proletariat. The situation has changed radically in comparison with our revolution, it is necessary to apply different methods and forms ... You should not be afraid of accusations of opportunism. This is not opportunism but an application of Marxism to the present situation.[53]

That Stalin's ideas were more than a mere freak is indicated by the fact that he developed similar ideas to Tito and the German Communists, as well as to Morgan Phillips of the British Labour Party.[54] To the Bulgarian Communists, however, Stalin's ideas appeared somewhat idiosyncratic. At the central committee meeting in September 1946, Dimitrov mentioned them only as proposals which might be implemented in the distant future after careful consideration and evaluation of their merits.[55] Although he was approved of the concept of a transition to Socialism without the dictatorship of the proletariat, Dimitrov apparently preferred to realize that within the existing Patriotic Front framework.

The increasing polarization of society made such pious hopes unrealistic and led to a showdown between the Communists and the opposition. At the October 1946 elections to a Grand National Assembly, which were conducted with different coloured ballots thus allowing each Party's strength to be judged, BRP(k) gained 54 per cent of the vote while its Patriotic Front partners managed only 17 per cent. The opposition gained 1 250 000 votes, a third of the total. According to Rothschild, 'this was the largest proportion recorded for any real opposition in any post-war East-Central European election'.[56] Even now Dimitrov was not able to accept the legitimacy of the opposition's existence: he thought that it would be possible to attract the 'misled' supporters of the opposition and reduce it to a hard core of some 200 000 Fascists and reactionaries.[57] The emphasis was still on political methods, persuasion as well as internal intrigues.

These sanguine expectations proved wrong. As Soviet intelligence reports make it clear, the opposition perceived its performance as a victory.[58] Furthermore, the non-Communist Front Parties, disappointed by their results and fearful of open Communist domination, began to draw closer to the opposition. This process was especially marked in the Agrarian Union, where Obbov embarked on a full-scale revision of his collaborationist policies and began to work towards a *rapprochement* and eventual union with Petkov.[59] The opposition's spirit had not been dented; they denounced the Government vehemently both in Parliament and in their newspapers. In his verbal duels with Petkov, Dimitrov was often reduced to making sinister threats.[60]

REVOLUTION RELEASED (JUNE–DECEMBER 1947)

The failure of the attempt to isolate the opposition by political means prompted the Bulgarian Communists to look at more forceful methods. The international situation was no longer a significant obstacle. Although Barnes had been encouraged by the opposition's performance in the elections and had seen its 100 deputies as the basis for preserving some degree of pluralism in Bulgarian politics,[61] the Western Governments' attention was turning away from Eastern Europe towards preventing further outward expansion of Communism. The Truman doctrine, with its emphasis on the defence of Greece and Turkey, showed clearly that the new demarcation lines lay to the south of Bulgaria. The Western Governments' main concern now was to conclude the peace-making process as soon as possible so that Soviet troops would leave Bulgaria and pose no further threat to Greece and Turkey. The peace treaty was signed on 10 February 1947, and recognition of the Government followed inevitably. The British recognition came immediately after the signature; the United States decided to delay theirs until after the treaty came into force.[62]

Stalin's policies were similarly shifting. Although it is difficult to follow the exact stages, or outline the relative weight of the different factors in the process, there can be little doubt that in the spring and summer of 1947 Stalin was moving towards retrenchment. In the Balkans, the increasing American involvement in the Greek civil war made Bulgaria a front line of defence and the Bulgarian Communists could no longer be restrained in their drive against 'the enemies within'. Nor were the Bulgarian Communist slow to link the opposition with external reaction; on a number of occasions Dimitrov claimed that the opposition's boldness was only due to their hopes of an American offensive in the Balkans. Dimitrov might have half-believed that himself: in a letter to Stalin of 31 May 1947 he expressed his fears of an intensified Western pressure; given the fact that the Soviet troops were due to withdraw from Bulgaria by the end of the year, it was all the more imperative to secure the Communists' undivided control over the country. Faced with such assessments, Stalin not surprisingly gave his approval for the liquidation of the opposition.[63]

No longer feeling Moscow's restraining hand, the Communists could hardly wait to deal with their opponents. Petkov was arrested in parliament the very day the United States Senate ratified the peace treaty. The possibility of retaining some sort of 'loyal' opposition was initially considered, and the BRP(k) engaged in talks with the remnants of the Agrarian leadership. It proved impossible to arrive at a common basis and by August 1947 it had been decided to disband Petkov's organization entirely.[64] A similar development could be observed with respect to the fate of the arrested opposition leader. The initial plan was to sentence him to death and then commute the sentence to life imprisonment. Petkov's valiant conduct at the trial combined with the Western Governments' public pressure on his behalf, led to a hardening of attitudes and Petkov was duly executed on 23 September 1947.[65]

The Communists also dealt with the doubtful elements in the Patriotic Front Parties. A comprehensive campaign was organized against Obbov, with the Communist regional secretaries bringing pressure on their Agrarian counterparts to declare themselves against their leader.[66] The right-wing leaders of *Zveno* were neutralized by despatching them as ambassadors to various European capitals, while the local organizations began to die out.[67] Thus the political system allowing the existence of a 'decorative' opposition had also proved untenable by the summer of 1947. In contrast to the summer of 1945 when they had to deal with the crisis provoked by Petkov by making further concessions, the emerging Cold War now allowed the Bulgarian Communists to solve the problem by sheer physical force. With the liquidation of the opposition, and the emasculation of the Patriotic Front, the Communists were substantially able to complete their revolution.

Many Bulgarian historians have argued that it was the formation of the Cominform in September 1947 that caused the BRP(k) to abandon its 'people's democracy' ideas.[68] The facts do not bear out that contention: although there had been a lot of rhetoric about Patriotic Front co-operation, especially at leadership level, a clear drive for monopoly power could be perceived ever since 9 September 1944. There is little evidence that the need for genuine compromises which even a hegemonial system would have implied was ever understood or accepted. Furthermore, the Bulgarian report at the Cominform foundation meeting, prepared by the Party ideologist Chervenkov in consultation with Dimitrov, already contained most of the measures which are claimed to have originated as a result of that meeting, such as the nationalization of 'big industry' and the 'consolidation' of the Patriotic Front.[69] The role of the Cominform meeting was thus to authorize as well as to provide a theoretical framework for the Bulgarian Communists' 'revolutionary offensive'.

The BRP(k)'s Politburo had little difficulty in approving the open transition to Socialism. Indeed, the Central Committee session in October 1947 witnessed a comprehensive attack on the Party's alleged 'moderation' in the past. Kostov was forced to point out that the Patriotic Front strategy had been made necessary by the 'circumstances' then present, and had been supported and indeed imposed by the Soviet Union.[70]

By early 1948, the Communists had finally achieved their internal revolution. Their radicalism occasionally spilled over externally, which Stalin was less prepared to tolerate. Their increasing association with Yugoslavs, and events such as Dimitrov's unauthorized speech on a grand federation stretching from Poland to Greece in January 1948, gave rise to concern in Moscow. In Tito's case, Soviet pressure led to a fierce counter-reaction which was eventually to take Yugoslavia out of Stalin's grasp altogether. In Bulgaria, the ailing Dimitrov was neither able nor willing to offer sustained resistance, and the other Party leaders eagerly jumped on the anti-Titoist bandwagon. Having curbed their external ambitions, the Bulgarian Communists proceeded to turn their energies to internal transformations, to the towering problems of industrialization and collectivization.

While not denying the fact that the USSR, the USA and Britain were the major protagonists on the post-war European scene, the chapter has sought to highlight the importance of local factors. Although both the Communists and the opposition managed to attract support from abroad, the former's manipulation of their great power patron was much more extensive and effective. In 1944–7, Stalin's wish for a non-antagonistic relationship with his wartime allies placed a check on the ambitions of the unruly local radicals; by the summer of 1947 he was no longer willing to restrain them. The formation of the Cominform rather than initiating revolutionary transformations was, in many ways, merely a formalization of a *fait accompli*.

Notes

1. N. Oren, *Bulgarian Communism: The Road to Power, 1934–1944* (New York: 1971) pp. 64–100.
2. D. Daskalov, *Zhan Suobshtava* (Sofia: 1991) p. 36.
3. Oren, *Bulgarian Communism*, pp. 169–87, 200–20.
4. *Ibid.*, pp. 220–58.
5. TsPA, f. 146, op. 2, a.e. 1965, l. 54, 86.
6. L. Ognianov, *Durzhavno-Politicheskata Sistema na Bulgariia, 1944–48* (Sofia: 1993) p. 27.

7. *Ibid.*, p. 33.
8. AVP RF, f. 074, op. 34, p. 114, d. 6, l. 185–6.
9. AVP RF, f. 06, op. 6, p. 34, d. 404, l. 7–8.
10. TsPA, f. 1, op. 7, a.e. 140.
11. TsPA, f. 1, op. 5, a.e. 2, l. 237–8.
12. M. Isusov, *Politicheskite Partii v Bulgaria, 1944–1948* (Sofia: 1978) p. 24.
13. P. Ostoich, *BKP i Izgrazhdaneto na Narodnodemokraticheskata Durzhava, 9 Septemvri 1944–Dekemvri 1947* (Sofia: 1967) pp. 76–7.
14. TsPA, f. 1, op. 5, a.e. 2, l. 241.
15. TsPA, f. 1, op. 6, a.e. 2, l. 2.
16. TsPA, f. 1, op. 5, a.e. 2, l. 6.
17. Ognianov, *Durzhavno-Politicheskata*, p. 54.
18. TsPA, f. 1, op. 5, a.e. 2, l. 268.
19. TsPA, f. 1, op. 9, a.e. 12, l. 11–12.
20. TsPA, f. 146, op. 2, a.e. 15, l. 18, quoted in M. Isusov, *Stalin i Bulgariia* (Sofia: 1991) p. 161.
21. TsPA, f. 146, op. 2, a.e. 15, l. 87, quoted in Isusov, *Stalin*, p. 87.
22. J.F. Gaddis, *The Long Peace: Inquiries into the History of the Cold War* (Oxford: 1987) pp. 29–30.
23. Quoted in M. Isusov, *Komunisticheskata Partiia i Revoliutsionniia Ptrotses v Bulgariia* (Sofia: 1983) p. 53.
24. C.A. Moser, *Dimitrov of Bulgaria: A Political Biography of Dr. Georgi M Dimitrov* (Ottawa, Il.: 1979) is a detailed account, partly based on Dr G.M. Dimitrov's personal papers, of the long and stormy career of the Agrarian leader.
25. TsPA, f. 146, op. 5, a.e. 217.
26. AVP RF, f. 074, op. 35, p. 125, d. 8, l. 37.
27. TsPA, f. 1, op. 7, a.e. 398, l. 1.
28. *Ibid.*, l. 5.
29. Barnes to Secretary of State, 1 December 1944, in *FRUS, 1944*, Vol. 3, p. 495.
30. Acting Secretary of State to Barnes, 3 March 1945, in *ibid.*, p. 169.
31. Moser, *Dimitrov of Bulgaria*, p. 227.
32. Barnes to Acting Secretary of State, 30 July 1945, in *FRUS, 1945*, Vol. 2, p. 728; Barnes to Secretary of State, 28 February 1945, in *FRUS, 1945*, Vol. 4, p. 272.
33. Houstoun-Boswall to Foreign Office, 31 July 1945, PRO, FO 371/48128.
34. M. Boll, *Cold War in the Balkans: American Foreign Policy and the Emergence of Communist Bulgaria, 1943–1947* (Lexington, Ky.: 1984) pp. 134–55, reviews the events from the point of view of the Western representatives and their Governments.
35. Even Kostov's last telegram before the announcement of the postponement, sent at 4.45 p.m. on 24 August 1945, reveals no knowledge of what was to take place within the next few hours, TsPA, f. 1, op. 7, a.e. 464, l. 1–2.
36. TsPA, f. 146, op. 4, a.e. 639, l. 26–8.
37. TsPA, f. 1, op. 6, a.e. 71.
38. RTsKhIDNI, f. 17, op. 128, d. 759, l. 221.
39. TsPA, f. 1, op. 7, a.e. 539, l. 2.
40. TsPA, f. 1, op. 7, a.e. 675, l. 7.
41. TsPA, f. 146, op. 2, a.e. 16, l. 54; quoted in Isusov, *Stalin*, p. 46.

42. Barnes to Secretary of State, 15 January 1946, in *FRUS, 1946*, Vol. 6, p. 54.
43. *Department of State Bulletin*, (17 March 1946) 447.
44. AVP RF, f. 074, op. 34, p. 115, d. 10, l. 88.
45. AVP RF, f. 06, op. 7, p. 28, d. 350, l. 18.
46. TsPA, f. 146, op. 2, a.e. 16, l. 54; quoted in Isusov, *Stalin*, p. 45.
47. TsPA, f. 146, op. 4, a.e. 420, l. 26.
48. TsPA, f. 146, op. 2, a.e. 16, l. 53; quoted in Isusov, *Stalin*, pp. 43-5.
49. TsPA, f. 146, op. 2, a.e. 16, l. 63–4; quoted in Isusov, *Stalin*, p. 46.
50. TsPA, f. 1, op. 5, a.e. 7, l. 12.
51. *Ibid.*, l. 16.
52. *Ibid.*, l. 64.
53. TsPA, f. 1. op. 2, a.e. 16, l. 78–9; quoted in Isusov, *Stalin*, pp. 49–50.
54. See G. Swain, 'The Cominform: Tito's International?', *The Historical Journal*, 3 (1992); W. Loth, 'Stalin's Plans For Post-War Germany', in this volume.
55. TsPA, f. 1, op. 5, a.e. 9, l. 86.
56. J. Rothschild, *Return to Diversity: A Political History of East-Central Europe Since World War II* (Oxford: 1989) p. 118.
57. TsPA, f. 1, op. 5, a.e. 11, l. 2–7, 56.
58. TsPA, f. 146, op. 5, a.e. 1224, l. 12.
59. I. Zarchev, *BZNS i Izgrazhdaneto na Sotsializma v Bulgariia, 1944–1962* (Sofia: 1984) pp. 177–90.
60. *Izgrev*, 17.1.47.
61. Barnes to Secretary of State, 5 November 1946, in *FRUS, 1946*, Vol. 6, pp. 166–7.
62. Boll, *Cold War in the Balkans*, pp. 182–8.
63. TsPA, f. 1, op. 7, a.e. 902, l. 2.
64. TsPA, f. 1., op. 5, a.e. 15, l. 8.
65. TsPA, f. 146, op. 2, a.e. 17, l. 51; quoted in Isusov, *Stalin*, pp. 190–1.
66. TsPA, f. 1, op. 7, a.e. 1157, l. 2.
67. I. Dimitrov, 'Naroden Suiuz Zveno (1 Oktomvri 1944–19 Fevruari 1949g.)', in *Bulgariia na Balkanite i v Evropa* (Sofia: 1983) pp. 301–3.
68. Originally expressed by Isusov, this view has become standard in Bulgarian historiography; see: Isusov, *Stalin*; Id., *Politicheskite Partii*; Id., *Komunisticheskata Partiia*.
69. RTsKhIDNI, f. 77, op. 3s.
70. TsPA, f. 1, op. 6, a.e. 365, l. 9–11; TsPA, f. 1, op. 5, a.e. 17, l. 56–7.

Part III

The Relations between the Soviet Union and Western Europe

19 From 'Ally' to Enemy: Britain's Relations with the Soviet Union, 1941–8
Geoffrey Warner

When Nazi Germany invaded the Soviet Union on 22 June 1941 it also threw the latter into a temporary alliance with Britain. The implication in this sentence that the alliance was accidental is intentional. Certainly no one would have confidently predicted it even a matter of weeks before the German attack. Anglo-Soviet relations since the Russian revolution of 1917 had never been good, let alone close. Britain had taken a leading part in the futile and misguided allied intervention on the side of the 'Whites' in the Russian civil war; diplomatic relations, opened in 1924, were broken off by the British Government in 1927 on the grounds of Russian interference in Britain's domestic affairs; and although these relations were restored in 1929, the Soviet Union continued to be the object of suspicion and barely disguised hostility on the part of the right-wing Governments which ruled Britain in the 1930s. Russian attempts to build an anti-Fascist coalition from 1935 onwards were never taken seriously by these Governments, partly because the Red Army was deemed to be capable only of defensive operations – a sentiment heightened by the Stalinist purges of 1936–8 – and partly because it was feared that Russia's Communist rulers were anxious to embroil Britain in a war for their own selfish purposes.

The events of 1939–41 did nothing to modify these sentiments. Indeed, there were now fresh grounds for suspicion and hostility: the Molotov–Ribbentrop non-aggression Pact of August 1939 itself, the Soviet occupation of Eastern Poland (a corollary of the pact), its invasion of Finland, its annexation of the Baltic States and its supply of raw materials to Nazi Germany. Although Britain was never as enthusiastic as its French ally to send troops to help the Finns or to bomb the Russian oil fields in the Caucasus, plans to do both were seriously examined and might have been implemented but for Finland's collapse in March 1940, the disastrous Norwegian expedition in April and the German offensive in the West in May. Even as the German onslaught upon the Soviet Union was clearly looming in the summer of 1941, the opinion in the Foreign Office was that any resultant pressure to treat the latter as an ally should be resisted.[1]

It was too much to expect this atmosphere of suspicion to vanish overnight. Although Winston Churchill's famous broadcast speech on the day of the German invasion proclaimed that '[a]ny man or state who fights on against Nazidom will have our aid', and that '[i]t follows therefore that we shall give whatever help we can to Russia and the Russian people',[2] Gabriel Gorodetsky has pointed out that the Prime Minister – in accordance with the Foreign Office's attitude – 'refrained from using the term "ally" throughout the speech' and that assistance was offered in qualified terms.[3] Churchill's fierce anti-Communism – he had denounced the ideology in 1920 as 'a pestilence more destructive of life than the Black Death or the Spotted Typhus'[4] and had been the leading advocate inside the Government of intervention to destroy it – was never far below the surface. At the end of August 1941 he asked his Minister of Information, Brendan Bracken, to consider what action was needed 'to counter the present tendency of the British public to forget the dangers of Communism in their enthusiasm over the resistance of Russia'[5] and told his Foreign Secretary, Anthony Eden, on 14 November 1941 that when he became Prime Minister, he could do as he liked about relations with the Soviet Union, 'But while I am here we fight strictly on [the] basis of two people who have come together just to do this job.'[6] Things were not improved by the Russian diplomatic style, which thoroughly exasperated and annoyed the British. A comment by Eden's private secretary, Oliver Harvey, in his diary for 10 February 1943 expressed a common reaction: 'The Russians are very tiresome allies, importunate, graceless, ungrateful, secretive, suspicious, [and] ever asking for more', although he graciously added that in military terms they were 'delivering the goods'.[7] It was thought, no doubt with some justification, that one reason for the Russian attitude was the nature of the Soviet political system, which left individual diplomats and soldiers with little room for manoeuvre. Churchill, for one, was therefore always pleased to deal with Stalin directly. 'If only I could dine with Stalin once a week,' he said in January 1944, 'there would be no trouble at all. We get on like a house on fire.'[8] To be fair, the Russians were not the only ones at fault. The three heads of the British military mission in Moscow, for example, were all disasters and Stalin complained personally to the British Ambassador in September 1944 about the last of them. The officer in question, he said, 'had no respect for the Russian leaders or for the Red Army, and they had none for him'.[9] The fact remains that the degree of co-operation between Britain and the Soviet Union never even remotely approached that between Britain and the United States, before or after the latter entered the war in December 1941. If the late Christopher Thorne could describe the British and the Americans between 1941 and 1945 as 'Allies of a Kind',[10] how then should we refer to the British and the Russians?

Between 1941 and 1944 there were two main issues between Britain and the Soviet Union: the 'second front' and post-war Russian objectives in Europe. I shall say very little about the first because I believe it was more significant in relation to Russian perceptions of Britain than vice-versa. There is certainly no evidence that the British deliberately delayed the opening of the 'second front' in order to bleed the Soviet Union white, and the principal consequence of continual Russian pressure upon Britain's perception of the Soviet Union was to heighten that feeling of exasperation and annoyance to which reference has already been made.

Post-war Russian objectives in Europe were much more influential in moulding British perceptions of the Soviet Union. When Stalin first set them out in conversations with Eden in Moscow in December 1941, the British Foreign Secretary was clearly impressed by his relative moderation. He told the editor of the *Manchester Guardian* on 15 January 1942 that people had to make up their minds whether Russia was motivated by Communist ideology or by the ideas of Peter the Great. 'Personally he was convinced that Stalin's policy was that of a Peter-the-Great Russia and that we could, and therefore must, live with her in Europe.' When the editor wondered how far a Peter the Great's ambitions might extend, Eden said that 'Stalin had convinced him that Russia was, and would be, reasonable in her aims'.[11] At the same time Eden was well aware that a Russian victory on the Eastern front would put temptation in Stalin's way and he therefore wished to commit him as far as possible in advance. As he put it on 8 February 1942,

> ... [A] German collapse this year will be an exclusively Soviet victory with all that implies. Therefore clearly we must do all in our power to lessen grievances and come to terms with him for the future. This may not prevent him from double-crossing us, but it will at least lessen pretexts. He has them now.[12]

Stalin had insisted that any treaty with Britain must include, as a minimum, British recognition of the annexation of the Baltic States by the Soviet Union, together with the modifications in the Russo-Finnish border following the 'Winter War' of 1939–40. Beyond that the Russian leader had made it clear that his ultimate objective was the restoration of the entire Western frontier of the Soviet Union at the time of the German invasion, that is including Eastern Poland, Bessarabia and Northern Bukovina. Initially, Churchill was totally opposed to Soviet incorporation of these territories. 'They were acquired', he reminded Eden on 8 January 1942, 'by acts of aggression in shameful collusion with Hitler.'[13] Eden eventually won him and the rest of the cabinet round to accepting Stalin's minimum demands, but then the Russians introduced a new condition which set off the alarm bell of mistrust: a secret protocol authorizing treaties of guarantee between the Soviet Union and Finland and Romania which would permit the Russians to station troops on their territories. Even Oliver Harvey, who was relatively sympathetic to the security needs of the Soviet Union, jibbed at this. On 21 May 1942, the day the Soviet Foreign Minister, Viacheslav Molotov, arrived in London to complete the negotiation of the proposed Anglo-Soviet treaty, Harvey noted in his diary that 'we cannot possibly give way over Finland and Romania. To acquiesce in these guarantee pacts would be tantamount to handing them over body and soul to Russia.' As he pointed out, the absorption of the Baltic States had begun with just such pacts.[14] The issue was in effect shelved because Molotov dropped his insistence upon a treaty incorporating territorial provisions in favour of an alternative draft put forward by the British which established a 20-year alliance between Britain and the Soviet Union but contained no mention of frontiers. Just over a year later, in June 1943, Eden approached the Soviet and American Governments with the proposal that those enemy countries which fell away from the Axis alliance should be controlled on a tripartite basis under the aegis of a tripartite 'United Nations for Europe'. Eden explained to the British cabinet that the reason for this proposal was to avoid the creation of an exclusive Soviet sphere of influence in Eastern Europe.[15] The Russians did in fact accept the proposal, although its rationale was obviously not put to them, and it was the British and the Americans who almost immediately reneged on it in practice if not in theory in the case of Italy, albeit on military grounds.

By the time the British Foreign Secretary had put forward this proposal the problem of Russian ambitions in Eastern Europe had of course become more acute as a result of the break in diplomatic relations between the Soviet Union and the Polish Government-in-exile over the Katyn massacre. Eden, as his private secretary recorded at the time, was 'at a loss to know what Stalin is up to',[16] but that did not lessen the need for an agreement with him. Quite the reverse. Although there was little doubt in London that the Russians were responsible for the killings, *raison d'état* dictated the need not to split the anti-German alliance. Press and radio were asked to play the issue down and the Foreign Office was strengthened in its belief that the Poles should be compelled to accept the Curzon Line as their astern frontier, in their own best interests as well as those of the British Government. As Bell has noted, however, Katyn did mark an important step in the evolution of British public opinion. During the preceding year the latter was dominated by what he calls 'Russomania', an atmosphere in which no one could doubt 'the extent and intensity of admiration for the Soviet Union, concentrated primarily upon its military performance, and rubbing off on the regime and the personal reputation of Stalin'. Katyn precipitated a division in public opinion and although the majority supported the Russian position, a sizeable minority took the side of the Poles and the crisis fuelled anxieties about post-war relations.[17]

Although they did not resolve the Russo-Polish problem, the tripartite foreign ministers meeting in Moscow in October 1943 and the subsequent 'summit' Conference in Teheran in December led to an improvement in Anglo-Russian relations. Eden reported to Churchill from Moscow on 29 October 1943 that '[t]here have been many signs during our Conference that the members of the Soviet Government are sincere in their desire to establish relations with ourselves and the United States on a footing of permanent friendship'.[18] The previously cited remark of Churchill's that he got on with Stalin 'like a house on fire' was made in the aftermath of the Teheran Conference, and in an exchange of minutes with Eden in January 1944 both men agreed that the Russians should have their 1941 frontiers in Europe, which in fact fell short of those of the Russian empire of 1914.[19] At the same time Churchill admitted that the principal motive for acceding to Soviet demands was one of *Realpolitik*: the Red Army would soon be moving into these disputed areas and there was no means of getting them out. The real issue was how much farther the Russians would go. Alarmed by the Soviet Union's recognition of the Government of Italy, from which country's control it had been effectively excluded by the British and the Americans, he asked on 3 April 1944:

> Why are they [that is the Russians] gate-crashing in Italy in this way? Their conduct could be explained as a calculated attempt to smash all left parties and centre parties save the Communists ... I confess to growing apprehension that Russia has vast aims, and that these may include the domination of Eastern Europe and even the Mediterranean and the 'communising' of much that remains.[20]

A month later Churchill called for a paper on

> the brute issues between us and the Soviet Government which are developing in Italy, in Romania, in Bulgaria, in Yugoslavia, and above all in Greece ... Broadly speaking the issue is: are we going to acquiesce in the Communisation of the Balkans and perhaps of Italy?[21]

Both Churchill and Eden were reflecting the importance of the Mediterranean in British policy. It had long been regarded as crucial to Britain's position in the Middle East and India. It had been the principal theatre of operations for the British during the war so far and much effort had been expended to prevent the Axis powers from extending their control from its northern to its southern shore. The British

Government had no intention of permitting any other power to threaten its hegemony in the Mediterranean at the end of the war. It is in the light of this consideration that the genesis and content of the notorious 'percentages agreement' of October 1944 must be seen. In Romania, which was not a Mediterranean country, part of which had formerly belonged to Russia and which had fought on the Axis side to boot, the Soviet Union would predominate. On the other hand, in Greece, a Mediterranean country *par excellence*, the position was reversed and Britain would predominate. In Bulgaria, moreover, which bordered on Greece and on whose territory British post-war planners had pointed out the Russians could 'establish airfields within 100 miles of the [Turkish] Straits',[22] Britain would have a more important stake than in Romania. If a determination to preserve its position in the Mediterranean was one guiding principle of the British Government's foreign policy, another was that the ultimate test of Britain's and the Soviet Union's ability to continue their wartime co-operation into the post-war period lay in their treatment of Germany. This is why there was so much concern in the Foreign Office when, during the course of 1944, the Post-Hostilities Planning Staff of the Chiefs of Staff put forward the proposal to build up Germany as a potential ally after the war in order to guard against the possibility of a breakdown of the Anglo-Soviet alliance. The rationale behind this view, which was shared by the Chiefs of Staff themselves, is clearly set out in a diary entry of 27 July 1944 by their chairman, Field Marshal Sir Alan Brooke. 'Should Germany be dismembered or gradually converted to an ally to meet the Russian threat of twenty years hence?' Brooke asked, and in answer to his own question

> suggested the latter and feel certain that we must from now onwards regard Germany in a very different light. Germany is no longer the dominating power in Europe – Russia is. Unfortunately Russia is not entirely European. She has, however, vast resources and cannot fail to became the main threat in fifteen years from now. Therefore, foster Germany, gradually build her up and bring her into a Federation of Western Europe.[23]

To the Foreign Office any attempt to implement such a policy, which could hardly remain secret, would bring about the very threat it was designed to forestall. It would be much better to join with the Soviet Union in holding Germany down.

Much has been made of this disagreement by some historians in order to contrast the prophetic insight of Britain's military as opposed to the purblind 'appeasement' of its diplomats.[24] This is to go too far. As the Foreign Office representative on the PHPS pointed out on 28 July 1944, the Chiefs of Staff do not dispute that it would be in our interest to achieve a World Organisation, or anyhow an alliance between the three Great Powers, but they are ... 'profoundly sceptical' of a World Organisation ever coming into being and ... of the United States ever coming to our assistance in time if we should get into serious trouble on the continent.[25]

In other words, they did not wish to treat the Soviet Union as an actual enemy, but merely as the only potential one. In practice this was not very different from the Foreign Office's own position. As one of the officials most commonly dubbed an appeaser remarked on 10 August 1944, it agreed with the military that the Soviet Union was 'the only power in Europe that can be a danger to our security' and was, as we have seen, resolved to hold the line against the Russians in the Mediterranean. 'The difference between us', this official continued, 'is ... one of method and not of principle, though we may take different views as to the imminence of the Russian danger.'[26]

As far as the treatment of Germany was concerned, considerable agreement was in fact reached during 1944 in the European Advisory Commission, the only relic of Eden's 1943 proposal for a tripartite body to supervise post-war policy in former Axis Europe. In particular, agreements were drawn up on the instrument of German surrender, the machinery for allied control of the occupied country and the boundaries of the zones of occupation themselves. The chief obstacle in the way of these agreements was not Anglo-Soviet antagonism, but the inability of the United States Government to get its act together.

Throughout 1944 the British put enormous pressure on the Polish Government-in-exile in London to accept the Russian proposals concerning Poland's Western frontier in the hope that this concession would dissuade the Soviet Union from imposing a puppet regime on the liberated country. The Poles refused and the Russians recognized the Communist Lublin Government on 5 January 1945. Two days later Cadogan told the Polish Ambassador that it looked as though the Lublin Government would impose the collective farm system among other things. 'Each successive development would make it harder to turn the clock back,' he added; 'but he did not see how one could do anything about such events except deplore them, since Britain was in no position to deflect Russia from her course.'[27]

A cosmetic solution to the problem of the Polish Government was eventually reached on the eve of the Potsdam Conference in July 1945. As this conference approached, the British vainly urged the Americans to push on as far and as fast as possible into Germany, Austria and Czechoslovakia in order to stem the outflow of Russian power. The Chiefs of Staff were even instructed to draw up a military plan for opposing the Soviet Union, but as Brooke commented in his diary for 24 May 1945, 'The idea is, of course, fantastic and the chances of success quite impossible. There is no doubt that from now onwards Russia is all-powerful in Europe.'[28]

By this time, the Soviet Union was also pushing for territorial concessions in Turkey, a United Nations trusteeship in North Africa and further improvements to the already substantial gains in East Asia promised to Stalin by President Roosevelt at Yalta in return for Russian entry into the war against Japan – an agreement which Eden had urged Churchill not to sign. 'You mentioned in conversation yesterday', the Foreign Secretary wrote to the Prime Minister on 17 July, 'that the Russian policy was one of aggrandizement. This is undoubtedly true.'[29] In view of its waning economic and military strength, what was the British Government's response to be?

It fell to a new Labour Government, elected by a landslide in July 1945, to solve this problem. Its solution, according to some scholars, was 'to compensate for relative weakness by manoeuvring the USA against the USSR within the "Big Three" framework'.[30] This 'manoeuvring' took the form of enlisting American support for British interests which were felt to be under threat from the Soviet Union. The key figure in this process is seen to be the new Foreign Secretary, the bluff and belligerent former trade union leader, Ernest Bevin, whose policies led to a degree of reverence among Conservatives for a politician of the opposition party which was matched only by the contempt of those on the left-wing of his own.

It was certainly true that Bevin was greatly concerned by the Russian threat in the Mediterranean and the Middle East. He told two influential American Republicans, Senator Arthur Vandenberg and John Foster Dulles, on 24 January 1946 'how the Russians were trying to wrap one arm to the west round the Straits and the other arm round the eastern end of Turkey by acquiring the provinces of Kars and Ardahan' and that 'after undermining the Persian province of Azerbaijan the Russians hoped to penetrate through Kurdistan and so further wrap the arms of the bear round the eastern end of Turkey, as well as imperilling the oilfields of Mosul [in Iraq]'.[31]

Vandenberg and Dulles were in London as members of the American delegation to the first session of the new United Nations Organization. This promised to be a lively affair, since the Iranian Government had appealed to the Security Council about Russian policy in Azerbaijan and the Soviet Union had retaliated by tabling complaints about the conduct of British troops in Greece and also in Indonesia, where they were helping the Greek Government and the Dutch respectively to re-establish control in the face of armed opposition from local Communists and nationalists. After a tough session on Indonesia in the

Security Council on 10 February 1946, Bevin's principal private secretary recorded, 'Hardly any doubt any longer that Russia is intent on the destruction of the British Empire'.[32]

On 1 March 1946 the Joint Intelligence Committee of the Chiefs of Staff reported that the Soviet leadership 'will consider it important to create and consolidate round the frontier of Russia a "belt" of satellite States with Governments subservient to their policy', which would extend into Turkey and 'the major parts of Persia'. Although the Soviet Union would probably seek to avoid major war for at least another five years, a conflict brought about by miscalculation could not be ruled out.[33] The British *chargé d'affaires* in Moscow, Frank Roberts, went even further. He thought, for example, that Russia's ultimate objectives included 'a Germany looking East and under Soviet influence', the whole of Iran and the extension of its influence 'throughout [the] Arab world and in [the] Aegean and [the] Eastern Mediterranean'.[34]

According to one historian, 2 April 1946 may be seen as the 'precise date' upon which Britain's Cold War policy towards the Soviet Union was born.[35] Two important developments did take place on the date in question. The first was that Christopher Warner, the Superintending Under-Secretary for the Northern and Southern Departments of the Foreign Office (which dealt with the Soviet Union and the Mediterranean), wrote a memorandum entitled 'The Soviet campaign against this country and our response to it'. The second was the first meeting of the so-called 'Russia Committee' of Foreign Office officials. In his memorandum, Warner wrote that 'the Soviet Government, both in their recent pronouncements and in their actions, have made it clear that they have decided upon an aggressive policy, based upon militant Communism and Russian chauvinism. They have launched an offensive against Social Democracy and against this country.' In retaliation he called for 'a defensive–offensive' campaign which would take the form of attacking and exposing Communism wherever it showed itself.[36] Warner spoke to this memorandum at the meeting of the 'Russia Committee', the task of which was '[t]o review ... the development of all aspects of Soviet propaganda and Soviet activities throughout the world, more particularly with reference to the Soviet campaign against this country' and to come up with the necessary counter-measures.[37]

Like Frank Roberts and Churchill before him, Warner mentioned Russian policy in Germany. Under the agreements reached during the war, culminating at the Potsdam Conference, Germany was occupied by British, French, Russian and American troops. Each power had its own separate occupation zone, together with its own sector of Berlin, which was situated inside the Soviet zone. At the same time, jointly agreed policies designed to prevent Germany from again becoming a threat to world peace were meant to be implemented throughout the country. In other words, Germany was not to be dismembered, as had been suggested at various stages during the war, but treated as a single country. The Soviet Union, however, effectively sealed off its zone from contact with the others and, in February 1946, set about enforcing a merger between the Communist and Socialist Parties inside it.

These developments gave rise to considerable alarm in Britain. There were two main reasons for this. The first was economic and financial. The British zone in Germany was predominantly industrial and it could not feed itself. Food had therefore to be imported and, ideally, much of it should have come from the Soviet zone in exchange for industrial products. But if the Russians sealed off their zone, this exchange was impossible and the British occupation authorities had to find the food from elsewhere, which added to their already considerable costs. The second reason was political. It was felt that Russian policy was designed not only to consolidate Soviet control in Eastern Germany, but to cause problems in the Western zones which the newly fused (and Communist-dominated) Socialist Unity Party would exploit in order to take over the rest of the country. On 23 March 1946 Sir Orme Sargent, who had just taken over from Cadogan as the senior official in the Foreign Office, wrote to Bevin that the time had come to decide what policy to pursue in Germany. 'Should we', he asked, 'proceed on the assumption that we must prepare for a German government which will govern the whole of Germany from Berlin or should we merely concentrate on ensuring that anti-Communist forces are strongly established in our own zone?'[38]

What Sargent was in fact asking was: should Britain, by continuing to support the wartime agreements, run the risk of handing over Germany to Soviet control through the agency of a Communist-dominated central Government, or should it try and save as much of Germany as possible by abandoning those agreements and partitioning the country? The Foreign Office was clearly in favour of the latter, but Bevin was not so sure. At a meeting on 3 April 1946 to discuss the issue, his immediate reaction was that the proposal to divide Germany 'meant a policy of Western Bloc and that meant war'.[39] Some of his cabinet colleagues were even less enthusiastic. When they discussed the issue, a Foreign Office official told a meeting of the 'Russia Committee' on 14 May 1946, '[s]ome ministers ... took the line that it would be wrong to consider Russia to be "hostile" to this country, that we should not treat the Soviet Union as an "enemy" and so on'.[40]

Moreover, when the US Secretary of State, James F. Byrnes, suggested at the Paris meeting of the Council of Foreign Ministers on 11 July 1946 that those occupation zones which were willing to work together should go ahead and do so, Bevin told the cabinet that the

Americans wanted to exclude the Russians and he thought 'that it would be a mistake at this stage to commit ourselves irrevocably to a measure which implied a clear division between Western and Eastern Germany'. He only accepted the American proposal, in fact, after he was assured by his officials that it was the only practical solution to the problem of the financial drain caused by the deficit in the British zone and that it did not foreclose the possibility of the eventual unity of Germany.[41]

Similarly, although the Warner memorandum of 2 April 1946, with its call for a 'defensive–offensive' campaign against the Soviet Union, was approved for wider circulation, this did not mean that its contents were wholeheartedly endorsed by the Government, and when a detailed programme was drawn up along the lines proposed by Warner, Bevin vetoed it. He eventually agreed to a limited operation in Iran, but commented: 'I am not going to commit myself to the whole of ... [this] scheme in order to tackle Persia...'[42] Despite his earlier attempts to frighten Senator Vandenberg and John Foster Dulles about the extent of Soviet ambitions in the Middle East, moreover, it was none other than Bevin who appeared to panic in March when, in response to Russian troop movements in northern Iran, the Americans took a strong line and the troops were subsequently withdrawn. At the height of the crisis a cabinet colleague recorded that he found the Foreign Secretary 'in a great state, saying that the Russians were advancing in full force on Teheran, that "this means war", and that the US were going to send a battle fleet to the Mediterranean'.[43]

When, in December 1946, Bevin returned from the New York meeting of the Council of Foreign Ministers, which had finally reached agreement on peace treaties with Italy, Romania, Bulgaria, Hungary and Finland, according to Christopher Mayhew, one of his junior ministers, he was 'full of repressed optimism and delight and self-congratulation...', cited the remark of the Soviet Foreign Minister, Viacheslav Molotov, on the boat back to Europe – 'I think we are learning now to co-operate' – and attributed much of the toughness and bitterness of Russian diplomatic methods to the inexperience of their officials.[44] None of this provides any support for the view that Bevin took the lead in fomenting the Cold War. If Bevin was less of a Cold War hawk than some have argued, the Labour Prime Minister, Clement Attlee, was positively doveish. During the first 18 months of the Labour Government the Prime Minister fought hard for a fundamental revision of British policy which involved nothing less than complete withdrawal from the Eastern Mediterranean and the Middle East. His arguments were four-fold. The first was military and based upon his conviction that the British position in the Mediterranean had been based upon sea power and that in an age of air power and the atomic bomb it was simply not possible to maintain it in wartime. Secondly, he felt that Britain could only rely upon a 'congeries of weak, backward and reactionary States', in order to sustain its present policy.[45] Thirdly, the policy was too expensive anyway; and, finally, it was unnecessarily provocative towards the Soviet Union, which must feel threatened by the deployment of British forces so close to its borders. The Prime Minister's own policy, as summarized by a colleague on 9 March 1946, was that '[w]e should pull out ... from all the Middle East, including Egypt and Greece, make a line of defence across Africa from Lagos to Kenya, and concentrate a large part of our forces in the latter ... We should [then] put a wide glacis of desert and Arabs between ourselves and the Russians.'[46] In addition, at the end of 1946, Attlee proposed negotiations with the Russians for the neutralization of the Middle East.

Opposition to Attlee came principally from the Chiefs of Staff and from Bevin. The former regarded the Prime Minister's attitude as 'past belief' and 'defeatist'.[47] They based their views on the belief set out in a memorandum of 2 April 1946 that '[a] conflict with Russia is the only situation in which it at present seems that the British Commonwealth might again become involved in a major war' and that it was therefore vital to hold the Middle East, not least because it was one of the few areas from which a counter-attack – by bombing Soviet oil fields and industrial centres – could be mounted.[48] Bevin, as we saw earlier, was also concerned about Russian pressure in the Mediterranean and the Middle East. Apart from the economic importance of oil, however, he chose as Foreign Secretary to emphasize the political importance of holding the area. Abandoning it, he argued, would leave a power vacuum into which the Russians would inevitably move and this would in turn threaten the stability of the whole of Southern Europe. Negotiation with the Soviet Union would achieve nothing, but the effect of withdrawal upon the United States would be 'disastrous', the United Nations would be 'imperilled' and the consequences for the Dominions 'incalculable'.[49] Against this powerful coalition of interests, Attlee felt compelled to give in.

He did, however, obtain two important concessions from his opponents: agreement on the need to withdraw British troops from Greece and Palestine. It was as a consequence of this agreement that two notes were presented to the United States Government on 21 February 1947 announcing that in view of the country's financial position Britain could no longer provide aid for either Greece or Turkey. This in turn precipitated the formulation and enunciation of the so-called 'Truman doctrine' by the American President in a speech to Congress on 12 March. This speech was undoubtedly another milestone on the road to the Cold War. Although it was also undoubtedly brought about by British policy, Robert Frazier has demonstrated that the British

Government did not deliberately set out to provoke a shift in American policy, but was merely responding to its own economic imperatives.[50]

The 'Truman doctrine' was proclaimed shortly after the beginning of the Moscow meeting of the Council of Ministers (10 March–24 April 1947). Not surprisingly, it did little to improve the atmosphere of this meeting, which was devoted largely to the quest for a solution to the problem of Germany, where the British and the Americans had formed their 'bizone', the French were hesitating and the Russians standing pat. In contrast to the US Secretary of State, George Marshall, who told his official biographer in 1956 that it was at Moscow that he finally came to the conclusion that it was impossible to reach a settlement with the Russians,[51] Bevin's attitude was more sanguine. Indeed, he wrote that 'Mr. Molotov was beginning to come to a better understanding of the attitude of His Majesty's Government and ... to show some sympathy for it'.[52] But his patience was not inexhaustible, and after his return from Moscow he told Christopher Mayhew – who recorded it in his diary for 26 May 1947 – that Stalin was 'a dreadful fellow' and that if things went on as they were, he would give up hope of a settlement with the Russians after the next meeting of the Council of Foreign Ministers in London in November.[53]

This surely implies, however, that – unlike Marshall – he had not given up hope yet, an interpretation which is supported by his initial reaction to the latter's famous Harvard speech on 5 June 1947, in which he floated the idea of an economic recovery programme for Europe to be drawn up by the European countries themselves with American assistance. The Soviet Union was invited to take part along with all other European countries, but it was neither expected nor indeed hoped that it would. When the Russians agreed to attend the initial conference which Britain and France had convened in Paris in order to discuss Marshall's offer, however, Bevin took a completely different view. 'Perhaps they *will* play after all,' he optimistically told a ministerial colleague.[54]

They did not. To have accepted American aid or to have permitted their Eastern European satellites to do so would, as Pierson Dixon noted on 2 July 1947, 'introduce western methods and ideas into the Eastern European systems, and thus undermine Soviet influence. It might even undermine the Soviet regime itself.' And when Molotov attacked Marshall's proposal, Bevin murmured to Dixon: 'This really is the birth of the Western bloc.'[55] As the year progressed East–West relations continued to deteriorate. The Western European countries and the United States sought to put flesh on the bones of Marshall's original proposal in the shape of the 'Marshall plan', while the Soviet Union set up the Cominform in reply in September 1947. Finally, the London meeting of the Council of Foreign Ministers broke down without agreement in December.

Both the speed and nature of Bevin's reaction to this last development indicate that, in contrast to his position the previous June, he anticipated failure and had given a great deal of thought to what should be done next. Early in January 1948 Bevin presented four separate memoranda to the cabinet in which he set out the nature of the Soviet threat and his proposals for dealing with it. These included the creation of 'some form of union in Western Europe ... backed by the Americas and the Dominions',[56] the establishment of a West German state on democratic lines, which would not only prevent a Soviet takeover of the whole country but also act as a powerful magnet for the Germans in the Russian zone, and an all-out propaganda offensive against Communism, the basis for which should be Britain's social democratic ideology. All his proposals were accepted. Two months later, following the Communist takeover in Czechoslovakia, Bevin informed his cabinet colleagues that despite all the efforts which had been made since the war to reach an amicable settlement with the Soviet Union,

> not only is the Soviet Government not prepared at the present stage to co-operate in any real sense with any non-Communist or non-Communist controlled Government, but it is actively preparing to extend its hold over the remaining part of continental Europe and, subsequently, over the Middle East and no doubt the bulk of the Far East as well. In other words, physical control of the whole World Island is what the Politburo is aiming at – no less a thing than that.[57]

Public opinion was completely behind the Government. A poll in August–September 1948, for example, showed that no less than 91 per cent of Britons believed that the Soviet Union wanted to dominate the world, compared with only 38 per cent of Italians and 30 per cent of French people.[58] In so far as these developments marked the abandonment of any hope of an accommodation with the Russians together with the determination to mobilize the 'free world' against the threat of Communist aggression and subversion, they may be said to mark the British Government's declaration of the Cold War.

One major American book on the origins of the Cold War is entitled *From Trust to Terror*.[59] This implies that the Cold War was an aberration, the unfortunate outcome of the breakdown of the wartime alliance. It would be more accurate to see the latter as an enforced and uneasy four-year truce in seven decades of suspicion and hostility between the Soviet Union and the capitalist world. As this chapter has endeavoured to show, there was not much in the way of 'trust' between Britain and Russia at any stage during the period it covers. There was always a suspicion on the British side that the Soviet Union represented a threat to Britain's interests and that suspicion progressively hardened into certainty. By 1946 the Foreign Office and the military were united in their view that Soviet hostility was implacable. It was another 18 months, however, before ministers were entirely persuaded. Suggestions that Britain somehow engineered the Cold War confrontation between the United States and the Soviet Union in order to further its own interests are wide of the mark. Britain was more willing than the United States not only to accept but to endorse an expanded Russian sphere of influence. What it was not prepared to accept was any encroachment upon its own.

Notes

1. M. Kitchen, *British Policy towards the Soviet Union during the Second World War* (London: Macmillan, 1986) p. 53.
2. M. Gilbert, *Finest Hour: Winston S. Churchill 1939–1941* (London: Heinemann, 1983) p. 1121.
3. G. Gorodetsky, *Stafford Cripps' Mission to Moscow 1940–42* (Cambridge: Cambridge University Press, 1984) p. 176.
4. R. Edmonds, 'Churchill and Stalin', in R. Blake, W.R. Louis (eds), *Churchill: A Major New Assessment of his Life in Peace and War* (Oxford: Oxford University Press, 1993) p. 311.
5. P.M.H. Bell, *John Bull & The Bear: British Public Opinion, Foreign Policy and the Soviet Union 1941–1945* (London: Edward Arnold, 1990) p. 43.
6. J. Colville, *The Fringes of Power: Downing Street Diaries 1939–1955* (London: Hodder & Stoughton, 1985) p. 436.
7. J. Harvey (ed.), *The War Diaries of Oliver Harvey 1941–1945* (London: Collins, 1978) p. 219.
8. M. Gilbert, *Road to Victory: Winston S. Churchill 1941–1945* (London: Heinemann, 1986) p. 664.
9. Clark Kerr to Foreign Office, 25 September 1944, Avon Papers, Birmingham University Library, FO 954/26/461-2. [Cited by permission of the Countess of Avon.]
10. Ch. Thorne, *Allies of a Kind: The United States, Britain, and the War against Japan, 1941–1945* (London: Hamish Hamilton, 1978).
11. A.J.P. Taylor, *Off the Record: Political Interviews of W.P. Crozier 1933–43* (London: Hutchinson, 1973) p. 266. See also Eden to Halifax, 22 January 1942, Avon Papers, FO 954/29/360-2.
12. G. Ross (ed.), *The Foreign Office and the Kremlin: British Documents on Anglo-Soviet Relations 1941–45* (Cambridge: Cambridge University Press, 1984) pp. 89-90.
13. W.S. Churchill, *The Second World War*, Vol. 4, *The Hinge of Fate* (Boston: Houghton Mifflin, 1950) p. 695.
14. *The War Diaries*, p. 126.
15. Sir L. Woodward, *British Foreign Policy in the Second World War*, Vol. 5 (London: H.M.S.O., 1976) pp. 46–50.
16. *The War Diaries*, p. 251.
17. Bell, *John Bull and the Bear*, pp. 96, 99.
18. Eden to Churchill, 29 October 1943, Avon Papers, FO 954/26/187.
19. Sir L. Woodward, *British Foreign Policy in the Second World War*, Vol. 3 (London: H.M.S.O., 1971) pp. 112–15.

20. V. Rothwell, *Britain and the Cold War 1941–1947* (London: Cape, 1982) p. 125; Woodward, *British Foreign Policy*, Vol. 3, p. 109.
21. Woodward, *British Foreign Policy*, Vol. 3, p. 115.
22. *The Foreign Office*, p. 143.
23. Sir A. Bryant, *Triumph in the West* (London: Collins, 1959) p. 242.
24. For example, J. Lewis, *Changing Direction: British Military Planning for Post-War Strategic Defence, 1942–47* (London: The Sherwood Press, 1988).
25. *The Foreign Office*, p. 160.
26. *Ibid.*, p. 161.
27. E. Raczynski, *In Allied London: The Wartime Diaries of the Polish Ambassador in London* (London: Weidenfeld & Nicolson, 1962) p. 262.
28. Bryant, *Triumph in the West*, pp. 469–70.
29. The Earl of Avon, *The Eden Memoirs: The Reckoning* (London: Cassell, 1965) p. 546.
30. P.J. Taylor, *Britain and the Cold War: 1945 as Geopolitical Transition* (London: Pinter, 1990) p. 107.
31. R. Bullen, M.E. Pelly (eds), *Documents on British Policy Overseas*, Series I, Vol. 4, *Britain and America: Atomic Energy, Bases and Food 12 December 1945–31 July 1946* (London: H.M.S.O., 1987) No. 18.
32. Pierson Dixon diary, 10 February 1946, Pierson Dixon Papers in the possession of Mr P. Dixon and cited with his permission.
33. *Documents on British Policy Overseas*, Series I, Vol. 6, *Eastern Europe 1945–1946* (London: H.M.S.O., 1991) No. 78.
34. *Ibid.*, Nos. 84, 85, 86.
35. J. Zametica, 'Three Letters to Bevin: Frank Roberts at the Moscow Embassy, 1945–46', in Id. (ed.), *British Officials and Foreign Policy 1945–50* (Leicester: Leicester University Press, 1990) p. 87.
36. *Eastern Europe 1945–1946*, No. 88.
37. R. Merrick, 'The Russia Committee of the British Foreign Office and the Cold War, 1946–7', *Journal of Contemporary History*, 20 (1985) 255.
38. R. Steininger (ed.), *Die Ruhrfrage 1945/46 und die Entstehung des Landes Nordrhein-Westfalen* (Düsseldorf: Droste Verlag, 1988) No. 112, fn. 1.
39. Unsigned 'Notes on Meeting held at the Foreign Office on the 3rd April, 1946', PRO, FO 945/16.
40. Howe minute, 17 May 1946, PRO, FO 371/56784/N6733/G.
41. Cabinet minutes, C.M.(46) 68, 15 July 1946, PRO, CAB 128/6; Dean minute, 23 July 1946, PRO, FO 371/55589/C8643).
42. R. Smith, 'A Climate of Opinion: British Officials and the Development of British Soviet Policy, 1945–7', *International Affairs*, 64 (1988) 639–41.
43. B. Pimlott (ed.), *The Political Diary of Hugh Dalton, 1918–40, 1945–60* (London: Cape, 1986) p. 368.
44. Christopher Mayhew diary, 20 December 1946, Christopher Mayhew Papers, in the possession of Lord Mayhew and cited with his permission.
45. R. Hyam (ed.), *British Documents on the End of Empire*, Series A, Vol. 2, *The Labour Government and the End of Empire 1945–1951*, Part 3, *Strategy, Politics and Constitutional Change* (London: H.M.S.O., 1992) No. 281.
46. H. Dalton, *Memoirs 1945–1960: High Tide and After* (London: Frederick Muller, 1960) p. 105.

47. R. Smith, J. Zametica, 'The Cold Warrior: Clement Attlee Reconsidered, 1945–7', *International Affairs*, 61 (1985) 245–6.
48. *British Documents*, Part 3, *Strategy, Politics*, No. 321.
49. *Ibid.*, No. 282.
50. R. Frazier, 'Did Britain Start the Cold War? Bevin and the Truman Doctrine', *Historical Journal*, XXVII (1984) 715–27.
51. F.C. Pogue, *George C. Marshall: Statesman 1945–1959* (New York: Viking, 1987) p. 196.
52. Undated Bevin memorandum, PRO, FO 800/447.
53. Mayhew diary, 26 May 1947, Christopher Mayhew Papers.
54. F. Williams, *Ernest Bevin* (London: Hutchinson, 1952) p. 265.
55. Dixon Diary, 2 July 1947, Pierson Dixon Papers.
56. *British Documents on the End of Empire*, Vol. 2, Part 2, *Economics and International Relations*, No. 142.
57. *Ibid.*, No. 145.
58. G. Warner, 'The United States and France and Italy', Unit 6 of The Open University's Course A324, *Liberation and Reconstruction: Politics, Culture and Society in France and Italy, 1943–1954* (Milton Keynes: The Open University, 1990) p. 11.
59. H. Feis, *From Trust to Terror: The Origins of the Cold War 1945–1950* (New York: Norton, 1970)

20 General de Gaulle and the Soviet Union, 1943–5: Ideology or European Equilibrium

Georges-Henri Soutou

De Gaulle's policy towards the USSR during World War II has been the subject of various explanations and appraisals. The most commonly encountered is what might be called 'realism'. According to this version, the General considered that Eternal Russia was more important than the Soviet regime, which was either a mere historical avatar or, at most, an instrument serving Russia's permanent imperial ambitions. As a result, he is supposed to have thought that Moscow's support was indispensable to France during the war and also looking forward to the post-war period, both against Germany and against the Anglo-Saxons. In this interpretation, de Gaulle had a very classical idea of the balance of power in Europe which took no account of the specific revolutionary element embodied by the USSR, or else he regarded this as nothing more than a means to achieve Russia's traditional aims.[1]

It is to be observed, however, that a witness who knew the USSR well and who had the opportunity to follow closely the General's policy towards that country during the war, and particularly in 1944, namely, Jean Laloy, saw the matter as much more complex and subtle, and I regard his view as being nearer the truth. While he agrees that de Gaulle wanted to make use of the USSR as a 'counterweight', in a classical French policy of playing-off the great powers against each other, he also saw a 'duality' in the General's outlook: 'with his right eye de Gaulle saw Russia, but with his left he saw the international Communist movement.'[2]

THE FIRST CONTACTS, 1941–2

We know that when Germany attacked Russia, de Gaulle declared, on 22 June 1941: 'We are quite frankly with the Russians, since they are fighting the Germans.' We recall that when the French National Committee was set up, on 24 September 1941, the USSR recognized it, using the same terms as the British ('as representing all free Frenchmen, wherever they may be, who have rallied to the service of the Allied cause'), but also added a promise of aid.[3] There can be no doubt that, from then on, de Gaulle ascribed the greatest importance to France's relations with the USSR, in relation both to the war and to the post-war period. On 20 January 1942, in a speech hailing the Soviet victory before Moscow, he said:

> From the political standpoint, Russia's certain emergence in the forefront of tomorrow's victors brings to Europe and the world an assurance of equilibrium which no power has better reason than France to welcome. To our common misfortune, alliance between France and Russia has too often, over the centuries, been prevented or thwarted by intrigue or misunderstanding. It remains, nevertheless, a necessity which we see reappearing at every turn of history.[4]

It has been possible to show the element of illusion which, at that time at least, this policy required: Free France mattered little to Moscow and Stalin had no intention of sacrificing his relations with the Anglo-Saxons to the French General's desire for a restoration of world-equilibrium.[5] That de Gaulle did suffer from illusions at that time, illusions which he was to shake off after 1943, seems to me to be obvious from his conversation with Molotov on 24 May 1942, the first high-level exchange between the two sides.[6] The General, who was accompanied by his Commisioner for Foreign Affairs, Maurice Dejean, thought good not only to speak of his differences with the Anglo-Saxons but also to emphasize 'the disquiet caused to us by the imperialistic tendencies which are becoming manifest in America'. Molotov's statements (together with the Soviet version of the conversation)[7] did not confirm the optimistic conclusions for the future of Franco-Soviet relations, and on the importance accorded them by Moscow, which figure in the telegram about the meeting which was sent to Garreau, who represented Free France at Kuibyshev, or in the General's *Mémoires de guerre*. Molotov had been free with assurances which cost him nothing, but his only remark of any importance was a warning uttered in reply to the French complaints about the Anglo-Saxons: 'Russia is the ally of Great Britain and of America.'

The reason for this desire by the French to put an optimistic interpretation on relations with the USSR has doubtless to be sought in the difficult relations that prevailed between Free France and the Anglo-Saxons during most of 1942, culminating in the decision by Washington and London, after the landing in North Africa in November, to recognize Darlan. It is noteworthy that Moscow did not condemn the Clark–Darlan agreements, and there is even evidence that the USSR would have been just as happy to deal with Giraud, who proved easier for the French Communist Party to handle, as appeared, for example, in connection with the liberation of Corsica.[8]

1943: FIRST FUNDAMENTAL REFLECTIONS ON THE FUTURE OF FRANCO-SOVIET RELATIONS

Before 1943 there is no evidence of any fundamental thinking among the leaders of Free France about the future of Franco-Soviet relations, apart from the immediate advantage of Soviet backing for the French National Committee and the General's statements about the importance of the Franco-Russian alliance and his obvious and lasting conviction that this alliance was needed both as a safeguard against Germany and as a counterweight to the Anglo-Saxons. True, it was only in 1943 that Stalin seemed to take de Gaulle seriously and that genuine diplomatic exchanges began. Nevertheless, it seems to me, contrary to a frequently met opinion, that the fact that he took the Algiers Committee seriously did not mean that, from then on, Stalin basically and unambiguously supported de Gaulle – far from that. As I see it – and here, too, I distance myself from a widespread view – de Gaulle noticed this, and that helps to explain why his attitude to the USSR from 1943 onward was less marked by lyrical illusions than it had been in 1941–2.[9]

Moreover, at the Conference of Foreign Ministers held in Moscow the USSR proposed the creation of what came to be the European Advisory Commission, meeting in London, without suggesting that France should be a member.[10] For well-informed members of Free France, at least, the illusions of 1941–2 on the possibility of escaping right away, thanks to Russia, from the burdensome protection of the Anglo-Saxons, were no longer fashionable, and this doubtless accounts for the more prudent tone adopted thereafter by de Gaulle, as we shall see.[11]

In any case, the French Committee of National Liberation (CFLN) was emerging as a real Government, replacing the French National Committee which had until then been organized very primitively, and it began to devote some long-term thinking to the problem of Franco-Soviet relations. There were three tendencies in this thinking. First, one which aimed to keep these relations strictly at the level of inter-state dealings and the advancement of French interests, avoiding any possibility of Soviet interference in France's domestic politics. This was how René Massigli, Commissioner for Foreign Affairs after January 1943, telegraphed on 21 May to Garreau, rebuking him for agreeing to discuss France's domestic politics with Soviet representatives:

> We hope that, in external affairs, our actions will converge. Believing that, when peace comes, Soviet diplomatic support may

be very valuable to us, it is our duty, while seeking to improve our relations with the Western powers, to take full account of Russian interests in our policy in Europe. On the other hand, we must put aside the idea that we ought to cultivate Soviet co-operation for purposes of domestic politics ... Our domestic affairs must be settled between Frenchmen and only between Frenchmen.[12]

A second tendency which was rather different and which doubtless commanded a majority in Free France was well represented by Maurice Dejean, who represented the CFLN with the refugee Allied Governments in London. On 13 October and 3 November 1943 he composed two memoranda on Soviet policy and Franco-Soviet relations, in the context of the Conference of Foreign Ministers held in Moscow.[13] For Dejean, Stalin would agree to collaborate lastingly with the West on condition that the latter abandoned any form of *cordon sanitaire* and allowed the USSR to recover former Russian territory, particularly the Baltic states, Poland up to the Curzon Line, and Bessarabia. Furthermore, the USSR wanted 'permanent access to the open seas – the North Sea, the Mediterranean, the ... Gulf'. Also, the West should agree to Moscow's establishing, on the periphery of Russia in both Europe and Asia, a 'security zone' comprising Finland, Poland, Czechoslovakia, Romania, Bulgaria, Yugoslavia, Persia, Chinese Turkestan, Outer Mongolia and Manchuria. According to Dejean the Soviets were prepared to respect the independence of these countries and would not insist on having exclusive influence in them, but would not tolerate regimes there which were 'systematically hostile to the USSR'.[14]

Dejean, then, went very far in the direction of concessions to Moscow. He fully shared an illusion that was common in Free France, that of a special relationship between Russia and France, based on common interests and a degree of complicity against the Anglo-Saxons. He put the blame for the German–Soviet Pact of 1939 very largely on the mistakes committed after 1933, and even after 1918, by the Western powers in their relations with the USSR, while stressing that in the case of France, unlike that of the Anglo-Saxon countries, Soviet mistrust was not directed against the nation as a whole, but only against 'the ruling class', which fitted in with the predominant ideology of Free France. Dejean's tone was thus very different from Massigli's. He advocated a close and special alliance with the USSR. This alliance was, of course, supposed to enable France to realize her objectives in the Empire and against Germany, but it would oblige France to approve all the Soviets' aims pursued in Europe in the name of security. It would be based on condemnation of the policy followed by the French ruling classes since 1918 and on common opposition to 'reactionaries', that is, on a certain form of ideological solidarity against the Anglo-Saxons, regarded as suspect in that quarter. The entire policy of the Soviets from 1917 was thus justified and the dominant position of the USSR in post-war Europe accepted and approved in advance, as a result of a guilt complex about the past and with the prime purpose of controlling Germany jointly.

There existed in Algiers, of course, especially in the Consultative Assembly, an ideological tendency that was even more favourable to the USSR. The mission of Pierre Cot, a member of the Assembly's Foreign Affairs Commission, to Russia in March–July 1944, on which he composed a report that was extremely laudatory about the USSR and Moscow's ideas on world affairs,[15] illustrates this tendency and the problem it presented to the CFLN.

AUTUMN 1943: THE FIRST ORIENTATIONS OF THE CFLN REGARDING THE FUTURE OF FRANCO-SOVIET RELATIONS

The CFLN devoted its meeting on 12 October 1943 to the main orientations of post-war foreign policy, on the basis of a survey by René Massigli. He advised leaning on Britain, the USA and the USSR, but with caution where the last-named was concerned, because of the risk of interference in French domestic politics. At this meeting some members of the CFLN expressed quite divergent opinions, tending either to give priority to an understanding with the USA or with the USSR, or to withdraw upon France itself, or else to prepare for a European Federation. At the next meeting de Gaulle drew the conclusions from this discussion and put forward a sort of synthesis, a compromise between the different views expressed, which was printed in edited form in a circular sent on 30 October to the representatives of Free France.[16] This compromise was doubtless due to de Gaulle's wish to take account, to a certain extent, of the different views expressed by the national commissioners, but it also corresponded to his own obvious and prudent evolution since 1941–2 in his attitude to the USSR.

From de Gaulle's declarations and the circular of 30 October there emerge belief in the imperialistic tendencies of the principal Allies and certainty that the USA and the USSR would come out of the war as the predominant powers, and as hostile to each other. It was not out of the question that a German danger would reappear in the post-war world, either as such or through the effect that evolution of the German question might have on the antagonism which was foreseeable between the USA and the USSR, an antagonism that could result in 'new conflicts kindled on account of Germany'. (Noteworthy here is the appearance of the link between the German problem and the East–West antagonism: this was to play a big role in the evolution of France's attitude to the USSR later.)

Under these conditions, France's security would depend primarily on a Franco-Soviet treaty of alliance, but this treaty would be subject to certain precautions. It would not apply in Asia, and in Europe it would be related exclusively to Germany, so as not to risk obliging France to support Soviet policy in all circumstances, and it would guarantee noninterference by the USSR in French domestic affairs. It is noteworthy that, in accordance with Dejean's views, Algiers was ready to make big concessions to the Soviets in Eastern Europe. Massigli observes in his memoirs:

> France would have to defend itself against the entreaties that would reach us from Warsaw and Bucharest. Our activity in those countries would be restricted to the cultural and economic planes. The formation of a Balkan Federation and of a Polono-Czechoslovak Federation would meet with no objection from us, but the carrying out of these plans would require the USSR's agreement.[17]

We can see where the wish to please the USSR in order to secure its support against Germany was tending – to abandonment of the policy followed by France in Eastern Europe since 1919. There was, nevertheless, a balancing factor, as it was understood that an attempt should be made to set up a 'Federation of Western Europe' embracing France, the Netherlands, Belgium, Luxembourg, the Ruhr and the Rhineland, and perhaps Great Britain and Italy as well. This federation was presented as a means of controlling Germany, but it is clear that it was also conceived, implicitly, as a means of counter-balancing Soviet influence in Europe after the war. To control and divide Germany with the USSR's help, but, through dividing the former Reich, to unite Western Europe round France, with inclusion of the Ruhr's industrial potential, so as to counter-balance the power of the USSR – that is what seems to me to have been de Gaulle's plan from 1943 onward.

AUTUMN 1943–SUMMER 1944: DIFFICULTIES AND MENTAL RESERVATIONS

The period from the autumn of 1943 to the Liberation was a difficult one for Franco-Soviet relations, essentially because Stalin continued to give precedence to his relations with the Anglo-Saxons. Yet in this period Algiers wanted to put Franco-Soviet relations on a contractual basis. They were very interested in the Soviet–Czech treaty of December 1943.[18] Massigli proposed on 14 December 1943 to Bogomolov to look into the question of a Franco-Soviet treaty,[19] but the Soviet diplomat's response was dilatory.

Generally, Soviet policy for the post-war period seemed to the leaders in Algiers, during that winter of 1943–4, to be rather worrying. They began to realize that Moscow would definitely refuse to have any further dealings with the London Polish Government, even if Dejean thought that the latter, provided it made the necessary concessions without delay, could still manage to re-establish relations with the USSR.[20] They observed the marked hardening of all the Soviet objectives in Central and Eastern Europe, now that Moscow was sure of ending the war with a great victory.[21]

This explains, no doubt, the evolution in the spring of 1944 of the question of the Western European Federation, thereafter often referred to as 'the Western bloc'. At the beginning of 1944 France's plans assumed definite shape. In them we see appearing, explicitly, the twofold function which, in my view, the Western bloc was meant to serve: both to facilitate control of Germany and to restore the balance of Europe after the East of the continent had become dominated by the USSR.[22] de Gaulle himself gave official status to the idea of a Western grouping in a speech he made on 18 March 1944 before the Consultative Assembly.

On 20 March, however, Bogomolov called on Massigli to protest against this speech.[23] He was particularly offended by the phrase in which the General justified the 'Western grouping' as a factor 'in an equilibrium that corresponds to the conditions of our epoch': Bogomolov evidently saw there an allusion to the USSR, and we may think that he was right. After the Soviet protest the plan for a 'Western bloc' was buried, for the time being at least.

JUNE 1944–NOVEMBER 1944: WARMING OF RELATIONS AND PREPARATION FOR VISIT TO MOSCOW AND FRANCO-SOVIET PACT

After D-Day relations between Free France and the USSR seemed gradually to become warmer. At his press conference on 25 October de Gaulle denied ever having spoken of a 'Western bloc'. The states of Western Europe obviously had common interests in security and economic matters which justified 'organizing their relations', but 'there could be no question of separating the rest of Europe from any part thereof ... because Europe is one'.[24]

On 8 November de Gaulle asked for an invitation to Moscow and received a positive reply from Bogomolov on 14 November.[25] The Provisional Government of the French Republic had been pressing the question of a Franco-Soviet treaty ever since the beginning of July. Clearly, the General ascribed the highest importance to the visit he was going to make to Moscow, even if he may have undertaken it with some illusions. There seems, nevertheless, to have been a certain lack of preparation. It was only on 23 November, on the eve of the General's departure, that Dejean, now political director at the Quai d'Orsay, composed a memorandum on 'revision of the treaty relations between France and the USSR'[26] and a 'draft of a Franco-Soviet agreement'.[27]

These documents are very interesting in that they enable us to understand the position of the French delegation to Moscow on the proposed treaty. In his memorandum on 'revision of the treaty relations', Dejean advised that the pact sought should have a preamble referring to the non-aggression pact of 1932, regarded as being still valid (this pact was of interest to the French because it contained a clause on non-interference in domestic affairs); to the mutual assistance pact of 1935, also regarded as being still valid; and to the exchange of letters between de Gaulle and Maisky on 20 September 1941. To recall the treaty of 1935 was not sufficient, though: it had been surrounded by so many reservations, references to the League of Nations, and so on, that it was inoperative, as subsequent events had shown. Besides, it would seem quite insufficient to the Soviets, whose ideas were clearly apparent from the treaties they had signed with Britain in 1942 and with Czechoslovakia in 1943. There would therefore have to be a convention restating the provisions common to those two treaties: commitment not to make a separate peace with any German Government whatsoever; commitment to coordinate policies after the war so as to bar the way to further aggression by Germany; and mutual assistance against any attack by Germany or a state associated with Germany. These were very far-reaching commitments. But that was just the way Paris wanted it:

> As for the spirit in which a new pact should be concluded between France and the USSR, if the two countries mean to forge an effective instrument, it must be quite different from the spirit in which the agreement of May 1935 was negotiated and concluded, and more akin to the spirit which presided over the Franco-Russian convention of 1892.

This is extremely important. It has often been observed that the pact of 10 December 1944 was far-reaching and rigorous, automatic and preventive, and imposed substantial obligations on France in certain circumstances – to which point we shall return.[28] But that was precisely what they wanted. In order to keep Germany under control it was thought necessary to go back to the Franco-Russian alliance of 1892–4, which was simple, direct, plain-spoken. It was the French who proposed such hard terms for the treaty, contrary to what has long been believed, and this is the key to the Moscow negotiations.

The 'draft of a Franco-Soviet agreement' which was also composed by Dejean on 23 November followed the line advised in the memorandum on 'revision of treaty relations' and corresponded to the idea mentioned above. The preamble referred to the 1935 treaty. Articles 1 and 2 provided for common struggle until victory over Germany, without negotiations or separate peace. Article 3 provided for 'immediate consultation' between the parties in the event of 'threat or danger of aggression from Germany'. Article 4 provided for immediate assistance in the event of German aggression against a partner (it was worded very broadly and could lend itself to a very generous interpretation of the concept of aggression). Article 5 (due, obviously to memory of the problems of 1939, and expressing France's recognition of the USSR's strategic preponderance in Eastern Europe) provided that France would use its influence with the Romanians and the Poles to get them to allow passage to Soviet troops. Article 6 provided that Articles 4 and 5 were to remain valid until a system of collective security had been established which was accepted as adequate by both parties. Article 7 reaffirmed the validity of the 1932 treaty.

DE GAULLE'S VISIT TO MOSCOW AND THE TREATY OF 10 DECEMBER 1944

I shall not give a detailed account of the General's visit,[29] but merely mention the outstanding points, while observing straightaway that he seems, from what we read in the archives, to have made more concessions to Stalin than (a) might have been expected from the prudent attitude he had adopted since 1943 or (b) are admitted in his *Mémoires* or the reports published as appendices to them (in some cases subtly corrected when Volume 2 appeared in 1959). However, these concessions and this fresh evolution by de Gaulle, this return to his positions of 1941–2, were due to the importance that the General ascribed to the Franco-Soviet treaty, which was certainly greater than what it meant for the Soviets. In particular, the treaty was to allow for permanent control of Germany after the war, something that the British, and still less the Americans, were not willing to ensure fully, together with realization of the French plan for annexation of the Saarland, and separation of the Rhineland and the Ruhr from Germany. De Gaulle subscribed absolutely to Dejean's analysis on the point that the treaty must be as effectual as the pre-1914 Franco-Russian alliance. This accounts for the features of the treaty which imposed strict constraints on France, features which have often surprised commentators but which were largely sought by the French themselves, as we have learnt from the archives now accessible. Only a few diplomats were to mutter and say that the French had gone too far, but no attention was paid to them – at least before the summer of 1945.

Three essential questions were discussed in Moscow: France's demands from Germany, the Franco-Soviet pact, and recognition of the Lublin Committee. On Germany, de Gaulle put before Stalin France's aim to annex up to the Rhine when they had their first meeting, on 2 December. Stalin replied that this question could not be settled otherwise than by agreement with London and Washington and he did not quit his position when de Gaulle pointed out that he lacked the same scruples where Germany's Eastern frontier was concerned.

Faced with Stalin's resistance, de Gaulle made three important concessions during his meeting with the Soviet leader on 8 December. He accepted the Oder–Neisse frontier (which had until then been mentioned only between the Soviets and the Anglo-Saxons at Teheran, and had not been agreed to in principle until the Yalta and Potsdam Conferences, and then only on a provisional basis). And he proposed that the Ruhr – which, like the Rhineland, was to be separated from Germany – be internationalized, so that the USSR would share in its administration. This was the first time that the French had envisioned internationalizing the Rhur.

There is no need to dwell on the importance of this proposal. It has not been sufficiently observed that the French thesis on internationalization of the Ruhr was born of the need to please Stalin in order to obtain his acceptance of France's aims in Germany. It will be remembered that the Ruhr was to be one of the poles of the West European Federation which had been conceived in Algiers to balance the USSR's power in the East. The French had now moved a long way from that idea, and, indeed, de Gaulle again repudiated the 'Western bloc' concept when Stalin questioned him on it on 6 December. It is clear that, after his period of prudence in 1943–4, de Gaulle had returned to a much more dynamic view of Franco-Soviet relations.

But Stalin did not abandon his reserve, despite de Gaulle's tempting offers – though he did bring up at Potsdam the idea of internationalizing the Ruhr, much to the Anglo-Saxons' disquiet. Yet acceptance by Stalin of the French demands on Germany was the General's essential objective, together with conclusion of the pact, as is proved by a note which he wrote himself during his stay in Moscow.[30] He failed in that, and at various times in Moscow he voiced his regret that they had not had a fundamental discussion about Germany. This was doubtless one factor in the process which was to bring him back in the succeeding months to a more cautious attitude towards Moscow.

The discussion on the treaty went more easily, but, even so, was marked by revealing incidents. On 2 December Stalin and de Gaulle agreed on the principle of this treaty, and next day the French handed over their draft.[31] It was based on Dejean's draft of 23 November, but, as we shall see, had been considerably strengthened and hardened. This hardening expressed the will of the General, who had studied Dejean's text with him on 1 December (in the train that took the French delegation from Baku to Moscow) and again in two sessions during the morning of 3 December.[32] The essential new element was an Article 5 which brought the *casus foederis* into play not only in the event of aggression by Germany but also if the partner 'found itself involved in hostilities with Germany' as a result of measures which had been taken in accordance with Article 4 and which were therefore intended to 'cope with any threat from Germany' and to 'wreck any attempt at aggression by Germany'. Articles 4 and 5, taken together, made the French draft of the treaty a preventive pact. This feature went very far and was similar to the Soviet–Czech pact of 13 December 1943. Contrary to what has hitherto been supposed, it was not the Soviet side that wanted, at the outset, a pact of this type, but the French. As Molotov said to Bidault on 5 December, the Soviets themselves had thought of a treaty like the Anglo-Soviet treaty of 1942 much more moderate.[33]

Another example of the General's desire to toughen up the original draft treaty is a new Article, No. 6, which provided for the negotiation 'without delay' of a military convention. This was no up-in-the-air proposal. Juin, the Chief of Staff, was with the delegation and had a working meeting on 6 December with the Soviet General Staff. He said that France expected to have, after the war, an army with between 16 and 20 immediately available divisions, so as to safeguard the security of the West against Germany within the framework of the Franco-Soviet treaty. He proposed that the two General Staffs should engage in extensive exchange of information and raised the possibility of constructing Soviet aircraft under licence in France.[34]

Two working meetings between Molotov and Bidault on 5 and 7 December, together with the Soviet counter-draft presented to the French on 6 December (exactly the same as the pact eventually signed on 10 December) provide perfect illustrations of the motives of both sides. Molotov repeated that the Soviets had not thought, at first, where the essential question of the *casus foederis* was concerned, of a pact of the Soviet–Czech type, more of the Anglo-Soviet type, but he had no difficulty in accepting the French text on this point, and Article 5 of the French draft appeared unchanged (but as Article 4) in the Soviet draft, and so in the final text. On the other hand, Molotov proved immovable on a number of very revealing points which Bidault had to accept without being able to alter a jot. There would be no military convention at first, to Bidault's great astonishment and without even the shadow of a credible explanation from Molotov (except that no such convention had been concluded with the British). There was no recalling of the

1935 treaty, which the French accepted without difficulty, but no recalling, either, of the 1932 treaty, which the French found much harder to accept, obviously because of its useful clause about non-interference. (This shows, once more, that the French delegation was perfectly aware that there was a problem of ideological proselytism, and also doubtless points to the reticence of a section of French public opinion.) There was a passage in the preamble, much weakened, from Article 3 of the French draft of 3 December, which linked the Franco-Soviet treaty with the future international security system. And Molotov demanded and obtained a commitment not to join any alliance or coalition directed against the partner (Article 5).

Let us dwell on the problem of the link between the treaty and the future security system, to which the French attached a great deal of importance and to which they frequently returned in attempts to move their partners (for example, Bidault during the Stalin–De Gaulle meeting on 6 December). As the General explained to Stalin on 8 December, for Paris collective security was 'the third tier of security', the first being the Franco-Russian alliance and the second the Anglo-Russian treaty and the future Franco-British treaty. For the French, the collective-security tier would make it possible to bring America into the system, as de Gaulle said to Stalin. The 'equilibrium game' which de Gaulle wanted to play of course included the USA: there was no question of keeping them out of it, whatever quarrels Free France might have had with them. For Stalin, however, and this seems to me very revealing, while he expressed agreement with the general idea of organizing collective security, there was no question of accepting dependence of the Franco-Soviet pact on such an international organization, which would mean the Americans having a say in the way it worked.

On all these points, then, the Russians made no concessions. As against that, as we have seen, Moscow welcomed the essential feature of the pact as proposed by the French themselves: it would be a preventive pact. The Soviets had evidently not supposed at first that the French might prefer a treaty like the Soviet–Czech one to a treaty on the Anglo–Soviet pattern. It has often been commented that, given the difference in relative strengths between the two countries, a preventive pact placed a very heavy obligation on the smaller partner. On all the other aspects, however, it was the Soviet point of view that prevailed. In fact, France risked entering into the European diplomatic system centred on Moscow which Stalin sought to construct, not only against Germany but also against the Anglo–Saxons. The sole difference from the Soviet–Czech pact of 1943 was that France avoided incurring the obligation to support the USSR also against a country indirectly associated with Germany (meaning the USA). We know, though, from

Stalin's statements to the Czechs in July 1947, that he considered that difference as having been a mistake.[35] Yet, let me say this once more, it was the French who had wanted the essential character assumed by the pact, very vigorous and even preventive, through their fierce determination to bring Germany finally under control.[36]

This having been said, and even though the pact was, in the end, largely to the advantage of the USSR, the Soviets insisted on conditions, to such a point that we must suppose either that they were, if need be, ready to refuse to sign, or because they knew (for example, through bugging the train from Baku to Moscow and the French Embassy in Moscow) that the French would end by making the concessions required, so as to get the pact. First there was the episode of Churchill's proposal, on 7 December, of a tripartite pact, which was warmly approved by Stalin and Molotov, outwardly at least, but which angered the French. The latter considered that it would be much better to have three bilateral pacts between London, Paris and Moscow (and in Paris they still counted on signing a treaty with London as soon as agreement had been reached on Germany and the Middle East) rather than a three-sided pact. For the latter to function, agreement would be needed by all three parties, whereas in a triangle of bi-lateral pacts there would always be two parties agreed on action, most probably the USSR and France, 'continental states, neighbours of Germany'.[37] De Gaulle himself set out to Bogomolov, on 7 December, imprudently perhaps, France's grievances against London and his doubts regarding Britain's future policy towards Germany. It is highly probable that Stalin supported, briefly, the British proposal only so as to facilitate his essential blackmail, namely, that the pact would not be signed unless Paris recognized the Lublin Committee.[38] This was obviously a crucial question for the USSR's entire policy in Poland and in Eastern Europe generally, given France's historical role in relation to Poland and the echoes that recognition would evoke.

Molotov indicated on 5 December that the fate of the pact depended on an exchange of official representatives between Lublin and Paris. Bidault replied that this would depend on the attitude of the British and the Americans, and both he and de Gaulle emphasized to Stalin next day that just as they wanted, and would do what they could to encourage, friendship between Poland and the Soviet Union, so they no less wanted a Poland that was really independent. De Gaulle was especially eloquent and even sharp on this point on 6 December (more than was allowed to appear in the report published in his *Mémoires de guerre*, deprived of an ironical remark addressed to Stalin). In general he defended, that day, the principle of free elections to be held throughout Eastern Europe, under Allied supervision. Yet on 7 December Bidault made France's first two concessions to Molotov: Lublin would be allowed to send a semi-official representative to Paris, and it was 'perfectly possible' that 'some day' Paris would likewise send a semi-official representative to Lublin. But that was not the last concession. De Gaulle was, in fact, determined to pay any price for the pact and, as we shall see, on this point the appendices to the *Mémoires* are actually falsified. On 8 December Stalin, during a talk with de Gaulle, suddenly dropped his support for the British 'tripartite' proposal and agreed to a bilateral treaty, but required, in exchange, that France come to an agreement with Lublin. The text published in the *Mémoires* tells us:

> From what Marshall Stalin has just said, General de Gaulle believes he may conclude that Russia will not sign a pact with France unless an official arrangement is come to with the Lublin Committee. He finds that this proposal is of no great interest. He repeats that the French Government is quite ready to send a delegate to Lublin and to accept a delegate from Lublin in Paris, but without these delegates having the status of diplomatic representatives.

The original text of the report, however, reads quite differently.

> The interpreter having expressed himself not very clearly, General de Gaulle understands that what is being referred to is a tripartite pact, on condition that an official arrangement is come to with the Lublin Committee. He considers that this proposal is of no great interest.

But it was indeed a tripartite pact that would not have been very interesting. A bilateral pact would be something else, as subsequent events were to show, despite the version published in the *Mémoires*, even at the price of an arrangement with the Lublin Committee. (It must be added that the words 'without these delegates having the status of diplomatic representatives' do not appear in the original version.) The original report goes on, a passage totally absent from the *Mémoires*:

> On his return to the Embassy, General de Gaulle learns that M. Bidault and M. Garreau have understood differently what Stalin said about the conclusion of a pact and an arrangement with Lublin. According to M. Bidault and M. Garreau, Stalin was referring to the bilateral Franco-Soviet pact and not to the tripartite pact.
>
> At 11 p.m. M. Bidault and M. Garreau have another interview with M. Molotov, who confirms this interpretation. Stalin had indeed offered to conclude the bilateral pact if the Lublin Committee and the Provisional Government of the French Republic exchanged delegates.
>
> Thereupon the General decides that next day, Saturday, at 13 hours, M. Garreau will receive at the Embassy the representatives of the Polish Committee of National Liberation, who arrived in

Moscow a few days ago. During the interview General de Gaulle will come to the Embassy and see them.

There is no need to stress the importance of this newly available version. On 9 December, at 13 hours, de Gaulle did indeed receive the Polish ministers and agreed to the exchange of delegates. The Poles then put the crucial question: will these delegates enjoy official status? de Gaulle then hinted at a possible further concession, which the version given in the *Mémoires* again camouflages. The Poles having declared that if representatives were to be exchanged (de Gaulle had again said that he was agreeable to this), it was necessary that a protocol be drawn up, for publication, the *Mémoires* version makes him say that 'he did not see that such a protocol would serve any useful purpose'. But the original version of the report is different again – itself, moreover, containing deletions and corrections. The first text has 'General de Gaulle repeats that he cannot move so quickly and will study the question'. The final text of the original report has already been sweetened: 'General de Gaulle repeats that he cannot move so quickly. He does not see that such a protocol would serve any useful purpose.'

With Molotov, four hours later, Bidault continued down the road of concession. He agreed that the delegates' mission would not be merely technical 'but would also possess a political competence', which practically amounted to giving them official status. Molotov at once increased the pressure, which made Bidault complain: a communiqué and an exchange of letters would be required. Thereafter the battle was to be fought over that issue. Clearly, though, the French delegation was ready to yield on the essential point. A handwritten note of Dejean's dated 9 December, evidently connected with the discussions within the French delegation, indicates the reservations that they felt concerning the Lublin Committee, but adds that they must prepare themselves for 'immediate recognition' of the Committee (when the Anglo-Saxons recognized it as the Government of Poland, apparently): 'attention must be paid to our interests [in Poland].'[39]

The famous night of 9–10 December, so dramatized by de Gaulle in his *Mémoires*, is the subject of a report in the archives of the Quai d'Orsay which finally clears up the question.[40] The Soviets dropped their demand for an exchange of letters but gave battle on the communiqué. In the end the French yielded: besides the exchange of representatives there would indeed be a communiqué. (The history of the negotiations shows that it was not so much the exchange, in itself, that mattered from then on, contrary to what is usually believed, but the communiqué, which gave it an official character that went further than the technical exchanges which had evidently been provided for some time previously, for the prisoners of war, and so on.) Garreau and Dejean composed a document which de Gaulle watered down a little, deleting an opening phrase which stated that the Provisional Government of the French Republic and the Polish Committee of National Liberation had decided to exchange delegates. Thus altered by the General the communiqué became: 'M. X ... has arrived in Lublin as delegate from the Provisional Government of the French Republic. M. Y... has arrived in Paris as delegate from the Polish Committee of National Liberation.'

But the General was perfectly well aware of the implications of this document, even when thus modified. The *Mémoires*, after giving a false version of the document prepared by Garreau and Dejean, present just this as the text decided on for the communiqué: 'Commandant Fouchet has arrived in Lublin.'[41] Nothing offers better proof of the extent of the concessions made by the French to Moscow than the falsifications of the *Mémoires de guerre*. Some diplomats, notably Massigli in London and Chauvel in the General Secretariat, were very unhappy about the way the negotiations had proceeded, without proper preparation and without keeping the British informed.[42] As for the General, he summed up the situation perfectly in the train going home: 'Yes, we're stuck with those people for a hundred years...'[43]

WINTER TO SPRING 1945: THE FIRST DISILLUSIONMENTS

If de Gaulle made important concessions to Stalin it was to obtain the USSR's support, first against Germany and secondly against the Anglo-Saxons. But disillusionment came quickly, in fact at the Yalta Conference, where absent France was accorded a zone of occupation in Germany only on Churchill's insistence. Also bitterly resented in Paris, of course, was the holding of the Potsdam Conference in July without France, and without Stalin lifting a finger to have France invited. Stalin obviously had no desire to allow France to become a dominant power in Western Europe by helping it to get control of the Ruhr and the Rhineland. In the words of the American diplomat Bohlen, who had an excellent grasp of Soviet policy, addressed to a French colleague at the end of August 1945: '[the Soviets] do not want to see a second great power arise on the Continent. They think that such a power would inevitably be used as a counterweight against them.'[44] That phrase is probably the best summary of what was at the back of Stalin's mind, as also of de Gaulle's.

Garreau's successor in Moscow, General Catroux, was soon obliged to accept that the USSR did not seem to set much store by the pact of 10 December – for example, when it failed to back the French request to participate in the Executive Committee of the Reparations Commission. The interview that Catroux had with Stalin on 20 March 1945 gave no grounds for seeing any marked change in that situation.[45] And on 4 May the European Directorate of the Quai d'Orsay was able to draw up a list of difficulties put in the way of the French by the Soviets even in technical spheres: refusal to give the Air Attaché a visa to enter the USSR, obstacles to the despatch of French representatives into Eastern Europe, difficulties concerning French deportees and prisoners of war, establishment of a government for Austria without consulting Paris, handing over by the Soviet authorities of the Bor mines (French property) to Marshal Tito's administration.[46] On 7 May a memorandum to the General from the cabinet listed the Soviets' 'harassments and insults' in dealings with France, including the matter of repatriation of prisoners of war.[47]

It seems, though, that during the spring of 1945 it was, above all, Soviet policy in Eastern Europe and the Middle East – two regions which we know de Gaulle regarded as being very important – that worried Paris, led it to consider that there was a Soviet threat to be faced, and prepared the way for the gradual evolution of policy which becomes clearly apparent from the summer and still more so from the autumn of 1945. I cannot enlarge on these aspects here, but the archives show, from the spring of 1945, a growing disquiet in Paris regarding Soviet policy in Eastern Europe and the Middle East.

THE VISIT TO WASHINGTON IN AUGUST 1945 AND THE BEGINNING OF THE REORIENTATION OF FRENCH POLICY

There was never any question for de Gaulle of not taking account of America in his conception of the post-war world, even if he feared its isolationism as much as its 'imperialist' tendencies. In the 'instructions from the Government to the delegation to the San Francisco Conference', composed in April and entirely revised and corrected by the General, we find this revealing phrase: '... the most concrete result we can expect from this conference is that in future the United States will associate itself with Europe's security and that, thanks to their presence, the conditions will be created for a necessary balance of power in Europe.'[48]

It is clear to me that the 'necessary balance of power', though it undoubtedly refers to Germany, refers also to the USSR. At the beginning of June the conditions were completed for the visit to Washington which the General was to make at the end of August. To be sure, for most of the officials in Paris and for the great majority of public opinion, it was not yet a question of forming a Franco-American front against the USSR. Generally speaking, the spirit of the alliance of 10 December had not been abandoned and there was a desire to bring it back into the concert of the Allies. As we shall see, however, de Gaulle and Bidault showed themselves to be more pessimistic and went noticeably further during their visit to Washington. They were entering that phase, which was to last until 1947, in which, although the French Government continued officially and publicly to follow the line of collaboration between the wartime Allies, in deepest secrecy certain political, diplomatic and military personages were beginning to think of a Western alliance against the USSR.[49]

De Gaulle's visit to Washington at the end of August 1945 went off well, as the *Mémoires de guerre* testify. The new administration seemed to the French to have a more realistic view of the world than Roosevelt's team. All the same, they did not yet share the French Government's worries about the USSR. In his conversation with Truman on 22 August, de Gaulle reasserted France's claims for the Rhineland and the Ruhr and opposition to the reconstitution of central administrations for Germany, but added a new argument: 'A reconstituted united Germany would still be dangerous. And it would be subject to influence from the great and powerful Slav bloc which has been formed in the East.' Bidault pursued this theme next day with Byrnes: 'That would mean that Soviet influence exerted in Berlin would extend to Germany's Western frontiers. The French do not want that, and they think that it would not be good for anyone... . We may therefore fear that a reunited Germany would fall under Soviet influence.'

There was here, of course, also an argument aimed at the Americans with a view to persuading them to agree to the French objectives in Germany. But the argument corresponded also to a sincere apprehension. This transition from perception of a German threat (still regarded as the only one at the time when the Franco-Soviet treaty was signed) to perception of a threat from a German–Soviet bloc was an essential dialectical moment in the process that led the French into the Cold War, a moment determined by all the disillusionments and increasing anxieties of the first six months of 1945.

At first the Americans declined to listen to this talk, while at the same time pointing out, cruelly, the major contradiction in French policy: how could France's German policy be justified by reference to a Soviet menace when France was supporting inclusion of the Russians in international control of the Ruhr, an idea put forward by de Gaulle in Moscow and taken up by Stalin in Potsdam, and which greatly alarmed the Americans?

The Americans gave, in private, some hints that they were, all the same, ready to contemplate rendering de Gaulle a minimum of aid.[50] The visit to Washington had therefore not been entirely fruitless.

AUTUMN 1945: TOWARDS RETURN TO THE WESTERN BLOC AND TOWARDS A WESTERN ALLIANCE AGAINST THE USSR?

Disillusionment with the USSR advanced further during the autumn of 1945 and the General seemed to be considering different ways to counter what, apparently, looked to him increasingly like a Soviet threat. Neither at the London Conference in September nor during the Franco-Soviet negotiations in Moscow in December did the Soviets offer the slightest support for the French positions on Germany, whereas de Gaulle (in disagreement with Bidault, who was now convinced that the Anglo–Saxons were right on this matter) continued to advocate Soviet participation in control of the Ruhr.

Meanwhile, the French Communist Party had clashed with the General since July, first on the major question of the powers of the future constituent assembly (in demanding that this assembly be fully sovereign the Communists sought to open the way for the establishment of a people's democracy) and then, in September, on promotion for officers from the resistance, which had implications for control of the armed forces.[51] The Communists' opposition was to be the basic reason for the General's resignation in January 1946. In the same period Soviet officials began reproaching their French counterparts for their obsession with the Soviet threat, and stressing that the USSR would ensure peace and prosperity in Europe, not the American capitalist system, which was committed to imperialism and threatened the independence of France.[52] This was a language quite different from that which Moscow had spoken since Teheran, giving France lessons in solidarity with America.

In face of the steady worsening of Franco–Soviet relations and of an ever clearer perception of the Soviet threat (even in the form, mentioned above, of a German–Soviet threat), de Gaulle reacted in two ways. First, he revived his idea of a 'Western bloc', put to sleep in April 1944 and publicly repudiated in the autumn of that year. He brought it up again in an interview in *The Sunday Times* of 10 September 1945. And, during a visit to Germany at the beginning of October, he made it once more an essential axis of his policy. He evoked a West European grouping that would include the Western part of Germany and constantly used the expression 'Western Europeans'.[53] This was, indeed, the concept of a Western bloc embracing France, the Benelux countries, Italy, the Rhineland and the Ruhr, and perhaps Britain. Such a bloc was undoubtedly conceived by him, primarily as a means of controlling Germany, but it was also evidently meant to counter-balance the USSR. de Gaulle certainly considered that, even though things had changed since his visit to Moscow, his treaty with the Soviets was still of use against a possible German resurgence. Nevertheless, speaking to China's Prime Minister, Soong, on 19

September 1945, the General said that Eastern Europe was 'in vassalage ... partly under constraint' to the USSR and that France was trying to form in Western Europe an 'association of interests'.[54]

The Soviets understood quite well what this reappearance of the 'Western bloc' idea meant. The Polish and Czechoslovak press launched a strong attack on the idea,[55] and on 13 October Bogomolov had a revealing conversation with Catroux. Besides bringing up some minor complaints, Bogomolov stressed above all the 'altered orientation' of French policy, following the General's 'recent statements', evidently referring to those which mentioned the 'Western bloc' idea. Catroux replied that, since the treaty of 10 December 1944, Paris had not received the slightest support from Moscow on any matter whatsoever (French participation in the Executive Committee of the Reparations Commission or in the major inter-Allied conferences). This encounter marked the end of the Moscow-oriented policy initiated by de Gaulle in 1941–2 and again after the Liberation.[56]

The extent to which that policy had died in the General's thinking is confirmed by the second axis of his conduct towards the USSR up to the autumn of 1945, one less well-known than that of the 'Western bloc' idea and, moreover, still somewhat mysterious. To political disappointments and anxieties were now added concerns on the strictly military plan. General Billotte (a hero of Free France and Governor of the Rhineland and Hessen-Nassau) warned de Gaulle on 17 August that the Soviets were not demobilizing their forces, whereas the Americans were demobilizing theirs, and very quickly too. He sent the General a memorandum on 15 September advocating a secret military agreement between France, Britain and the USA. On 20 October he met de Gaulle, who expressed approval of his plan and decided to appoint him Deputy Chief of Staff of France's armed forces, in order to prepare for negotiations to bring about the proposed agreement.[57] At the same time, in the French General Staff, Colonel Lassalle, in a memorandum of 22 October which was approved by Juin, advocated a system for the defence of Western Europe with a unified command and participation by 450 000 American soldiers.[58]

De Gaulle stepped down in January 1946. With his consent, however, Billotte at once told the new head of the French Provisional Government, Gouin, about his plan. Gouin did not endorse it. Here we must remember that the 'three-party' political combination (including the Communists) still survived and that the French Socialists' policy of neutrality between Moscow and Washington was, in 1946, still firmly upheld by them, Blum included. However, Michelet, the Christian Democrat Minister of Defence, decided to send Billotte to the French delegation at the United Nations, actually as cover for exploratory talks with the American authorities.[59] Billotte set off, with the backing of

Juin and de Gaulle, and was destined to play an important role in 1947–8 in preparing what became NATO. We can suggest, therefore, without being too paradoxical, that the General was one of the remote begetters of that alliance.

CONCLUSION

One is struck by the presence of very diverse tendencies within Free France on the subject of Franco-Soviet relations, much more so than might have been thought, ranging from mistrust to ideologically based enthusiasm. The majority tendency seems to have been that of Dejean (who played a far from negligible role, especially in drawing up the treaty of 10 December 1944). He was willing to abandon Eastern Europe to Soviet influence, above all because he wanted to bring Germany finally under control through agreement with Moscow, the Anglo-Saxons being seen as too lukewarm on that question. The postwar control of Germany was, in fact, the essential driving-force in France's policy towards the USSR in that period, even more than the wish to escape from 'the Anglo-Saxon hegemony'.

This was certainly the case with de Gaulle himself. To a certain extent he went along with Dejean, as when he indicated to the Soviets that the new France would show a better understanding of the USSR than the Third Republic had shown – but only to a certain extent. He undoubtedly agreed with Dejean on the need to come to an understanding with Moscow about Germany, but with much more reticence on the surrender of Eastern Europe. The General passed through phases that were more sharply contrasted than has been supposed – a degree of illusion in 1941–2 and again in the autumn of 1944, but in 1943–4 and again in 1945 a measure of mistrust which eventually became very marked, when it became for him a question of parrying the Soviet threat by leaning on America and reviving the idea of a Western bloc. The whole process was accompanied by sharp turns and sometimes even contradictions.

De Gaulle was more aware, at least in 1945, than has often been claimed, of the threat from the USSR – primarily in its geopolitical aspect, in Eastern Europe and the Middle East, but also in its ideological aspect, which he did not overlook (much less, certainly, than the *Mémoires de guerre* allow to appear). The General was, in fact, quite conscious of the ideological issues in the world-wide conflict and, while wishing to separate the problem represented by the French Communist Party from that of Franco-Soviet relations, he did not ignore the connection between these problems. This did not prevent him from making many concessions to Stalin during his visit to

Moscow, especially on Poland: more than was long supposed and more than the *Mémoires* admit. The binding and preventive aspect of the Franco-Soviet treaty was sought by the French, not by the Soviets, and, again, this was in order to bring Germany under better control.

That constituted, indeed, the central axis of de Gaulle's policy, and it allowed him to pass over many awkwardnesses in Stalin's behaviour. At the same time the General appreciated the problems that the USSR might cause, and that was the source of his plan, maintained constantly in spite of a few meanderings, which recalls the combinations and methods of the Concert of Europe before 1914, to keep Germany under control and detach the Rhineland and the Ruhr with the USSR's aid, and then to build a bloc of West European states under French leadership which would counter-balance the power of the USSR. In my view this plan was always at the heart of de Gaulle's policy, even if sometimes it was kept in the background, and despite some contradictions, such as the General's wish for Soviet participation in the international control of the Ruhr, which would have singularly reduced the value of the Western bloc, as the Americans did not fail to point out.

Yet this contradiction resulted from the fact that France did not possess the strength to impose a more ambitious policy. de Gaulle wanted to persuade Stalin, by all possible means, to back him where Germany was concerned, but the Soviet leader never took the General quite seriously and did not want to sacrifice to him, in the short term, his relations with the USA, and, in the long term, the opportunities open to the French Communist Party and for the establishment of a European diplomatic system centred on Moscow and directed against America. As Bohlen observed straight away, Stalin had no intention of helping de Gaulle in his game of weight and counter-weight, symbolized by the 'Western bloc' affair, and allow France to play an important role in Europe.

Notes

1. This view of things is well summarized by P. Lefranc in J. Lacouture, R. Mehl, *de Gaulle ou l'éternel défi* (Paris: Seuil, 1988) p. 159.
2. *Ibid.*, p. 159 ff.
3. J.-B. Duroselle, *L'Abîme 1939–1945* (Paris: Imprimerie Nationale, 1982) p. 313.
4. N. Moltchanov, *Le Général de Gaulle* (Moscow: Editions du Progrès, 1988) p. 143.
5. H. Rollet, 'Ambiguïtés diplomatiques. La France Libre et l'URSS en 1942', *Commentaire*, 64 (Winter 1933).
6. Telegram of 13 June to Garreau at Kuibyshev, MAE, Papiers Dejean, vol. 74.
7. Quoted by Rollet, 'Ambiguïtés'.
8. Duroselle, *L'Abîme*, pp. 505–7.

9. It will be observed that Moltchanov himself pointed out this evolution (*Le Général*, p. 170).
10. H. Feis, *Churchill, Roosevelt, Stalin* (Princeton: 1957) pp. 213–14.
11. A very thought-provoking telegram from Vienot to London, 28 October, MAE, Algiers, vol. 1472.
12. *Ibid.*
13. MAE, Papiers Dejean, vol. 74.
14. Garreau, at Kuibyshev, agreed with this analysis: cf. telegram of 23 November 1943, MAE, Algiers, vol. 1262.
15. Pre-report of 23 April, MAE, Algiers, vol. 1472, and 'Compte-rendu de mission en URSS', *ibid.*, vol. 1267–8.
16. R. Massigli, *Une comédie des erreurs 1943–1956* (Paris: Plon, 1978) p. 37 ff.
17. *Ibid.*, p. 42.
18. Dejean, telegram of 26 November 1943, MAE, Algiers, vol. 1262.
19. Note of 14 December 1943, MAE, Algiers, vol. 1472.
20. Note from the Political Directorate, 6 December, telegram from Dejean, 21 December 1943, MAE, Algiers, vol. 1262.
21. Telegram from Dejean, 13 January 1944, following a talk with Ripka returning from Moscow, MAE, Algiers, vol. 1263.
22. *Ibid.* See, for example, a note from the Economic Affairs Directorate of the Foreign Affairs Commissariat, 2 March 1944.
23. Massigli, note of 21 March 1944, MAE, Algiers, vol. 1263.
24. Henri-Christian Giraud, *de Gaulle et les communistes*, 2 Vols (Paris: Albin Michel, 1989) Vol. 1, p. 336.
25. Telegram from Garreau, 16 November, and letter from Bogomolov to the General, 14 November, MAE, Europe 1944–1960, vol. 51.
26. MAE, Papiers Dejean, vol. 74.
27. *Ibid.*, vol. 75 (several rough drafts by Dejan).
28. J. Laloy, *Yalta* (Paris: Laffont, 1988) p. 88 ff.
29. Cf. *Mémoires de guerre* and appendices (reports of de Gaulle's conversations in Moscow), and J. Laloy, 'A Moscou: entre Staline et de Gaulle', *Revue des études slaves*, (1982). A collection of the original reports is in MAE, Papiers Dejean, vol. 75, together with the file on the negotiations.
30. C. de Gaulle, *Lettres, Notes et Carnets, Juin 1943–Mai 1945* (Paris: Plon, 1983) pp. 359–60.
31. MAE, Papiers Dejean, vol. 75.
32. Diary kept by Dejean during Moscow visit, MAE, Papiers Dejean, vol. 75.
33. Report in *ibid.*
34. MAE, Europe 1944–1960, URSS, vol. 51.
35. G.-H. Soutou, 'Georges Bidault et la construction européenne 1944–1945', in S. Berstein, J.-M. Mayeur, P. Milza (eds), *Le MRP et la construction européenne* (Bruxelles: Complexe, 1993).
36. It was precisely in this way that the French delegation justified the severe clauses of the treaty. Telegram to Comert, who was in charge of the London publication *France*, 18 December, MAE, Papiers Dejean, vol. 75.
37. Note of 8 December, MAE, Papier Dejean, vol. 75.
38. This was, moreover, the conclusion drawn by the French. Telegram from Cairo to London, 15 December, MAE, Papiers Dejean, vol. 75.
39. *Ibid.*

40. *Ibid.*
41. *Ibid.*, p. 97.
42. Massigli, letter to Chauvel, 11 December, and Chauvel's reply, 13 December, MAE, Papiers Massigli, vol. 94.
43. Laloy, 'A Moscou'.
44. Note of 31 August 1945 on conversations in Washington, MAE, Papiers Massigli, vol. 59.
45. General Catroux, *J'ai vu tomber le Rideau de Fer* (Paris: Hachette, 1952) p. 49 ff.
46. MAE, Europe 1944–1960, URSS, vol. 51.
47. MAE, series being rearranged.
48. De Gaulle, *Lettres, Notes*, p. 420.
49. G.-H. Soutou, 'Les dirigeants français et l'entrée en Guerre froide: un processus de décision hesitant (1944–1950)', *Le Trimestre du Monde*, 3rd quarter (1993).
50. Cf. the reports of the conversations in MAE, Papiers Massigli, vol. 59, as well as the note of 31 August on talks with American diplomats, including Bohlen, already quoted (see note 44).
51. J. Lacouture, *de Gaulle*, Vol. 2 (Paris: Seuil 1990) pp. 184–202, and Ph. Buton, *Les lendemains qui déchantent. Le Parti communiste français à la Libération* (Paris: Presses de la FNSP, 1993) p. 200 ff.
52. Statements by a diplomat at the Soviet Embassy, 3 September, MAE, Europe 1944–1960, URSS, vol. 31.
53. De Gaulle, *Lettres, Notes*, especially his speech at Baden-Baden on 5 October.
54. *Mémoires de guerre*, Vol. 3, p. 496.
55. Telegram from Warsaw, 19 October, MAE, Europe 1944–1960, Pologne, vol. 59, and telegram from Prague, 28 December, MAE, Europe 1944–1960, Tchécoslovaquie, vol. 60.
56. On the way the Soviets saw the evolution of de Gaulle's policy, cf. Moltchanov, *Le Général*, p. 219.
57. P. Billotte, *Le Temps des armes* (Paris: Plon, 1972) p. 395 ff., and note by Billotte, s.d., mentioning de Gaulle's reservations on points of detail but implying his overall agreement, MAE, series being rearranged (the note of 15 September has not been found).
58. *De Gaulle et la nation face aux problèmes de défense 1945–1946* (Paris: Plon, 1983) pp. 117–18.
59. Billotte, *Le Temps*, pp. 423–37.

21 Britain and the Death of Stalin
Antonio Varsori

Stalin's death in March 1953 marked a new development in East–West relations and in a few years the Cold War appeared to give way to what has been called the 'early *détente*'.[1] In this connection Britain, in particular the Tory leader Winston Churchill, who had come back to power in October 1951, played a leading role in promoting a dialogue between the West and the Kremlin's new leaders. The role Churchill played in trying to overcome the worst aspects of the Cold War, his speech at the House of Commons in May 1953, his attempts at convening a summit conference, the difficulties he had to cope with as a consequence of the American authorities' suspicions, and also of the doubts nurtured by Anthony Eden and the Foreign Office, and by several members of the Tory cabinet, are well known; scholars' attention has already focused on these issues.[2] Nonetheless if these episodes are examined in a broader perspective, they seem to offer some food for thought, in particular they may throw some light on the changes in Britain's policy towards Moscow between late 1952 and mid-1953, on early contrasting reactions to Stalin's death, as well as on the reasons which led Churchill in May 1953 to openly launch his project for renewed dialogue with the Soviet Union.

Dialogue with Moscow had been a main goal for Churchill from the moment he came back to Downing Street in October 1951.[3] His hopes surfaced both in an official telegram he sent to Stalin and in the inaugural speech he delivered at the House of Commons on 7 November.[4] The Prime Minister's aspirations were confirmed during 1952, even if he understood his ambitious goals could not be achieved without a radical change in the attitude of the American administration, but it was very unlikely the Washington authorities could work out such a dramatic development on so thorny an issue, in particular since in 1952 American foreign policy was heavily influenced, almost paralysed, by the impending presidential elections. In mid-June Churchill confided to his private secretary and close adviser, John Colville, '... that if Eisenhower were elected President, he [Churchill] would have another shot at main peace by means of a meeting of the Big Three'.[5] A few months later Churchill confirmed his opinion, according to which, if Eisenhower were elected, the new President would be ready to start some dialogue with the Kremlin's leader.[6]

In spite of these hopes, as John Young has argued, 'the first year of the Conservative Government saw no easing in the Cold War'. Among the reasons for such a deadlock Young has singled out the Truman administration's steady opposition to any initiative on the part of the West.[7] The continuing American intransigence was not the only element which frustrated the Prime Minister's aspirations: the Soviet attitude did not justify any optimism. On the other hand, the Soviet note on the future of Germany, issued in March 1952, had been rejected by the Western powers, which had labelled the Soviet document as a mere propaganda device.[8] In late December 1952 the British Ambassador in Moscow, Sir Alvary Gascoigne, sent Eden a secret and personal despatch, which aroused the Foreign Secretary's attention. In sketching out the main patterns of Soviet foreign policy in 1952, Gascoigne stressed the negative attitude the Soviet Foreign Minister Vyshinsky had shown on the Korean question. The British Ambassador added:

As viewed from Moscow the Kremlin's attitude towards the West seems to have crystallised during the year. The proceedings of the Communist Congress in October, and the implications of Stalin's various statements at that time, seem, undoubtedly, to show that the Soviet Government have definitely, as far as one can see, turned their faces against any agreement with the non-communist world.[9]

Gascoigne, who was aware of Churchill's hopes, pointed out the Western European leaders' eagerness to renew some form of dialogue with Moscow, but he ruled out any chance of 'high level talks'. In the opinion of the British Ambassador, the Soviet Union did not want an armed conflict with the West; at any rate he believed the existing situation played into the hands of the Soviets both in Asia and in Europe. Furthermore, Stalin appeared to be able to control the tensions in the Communist bloc. As a conclusive remark, Gascoigne took into consideration the Republican electoral success. In this connection, on the basis of the 'warmongering' statements by some Republican leaders, Gascoigne wrote:

As regards the future, I suggest that we can but continue to deal with the leaders of Soviet communism as we have in the past. Patience is of the essence; that and a willingness to listen to any Soviet suggestion which may be made for an easing of the tension, be it made directly or indirectly. Any hasty action taken for instance with regard to the Eastern European satellites, or in Asia against China, might well, I feel, bring upon us the great calamity of a general war. It is to be hoped that the new leaders in the United States will bear this very much in mind, and that they will not be pushed by certain elements to take hasty action which we should regret.[10]

In the context of a pessimistic approach, Gascoigne suggested a very cautious attitude, which appeared to be very far from either the aggressive boasting of some members of the new Eisenhower administration or Churchill's hopes; it is very likely that such an attitude was at least partially shared by both Eden and the Foreign Office.

A week after this message had been despatched, on 30 December, Churchill left for the United States, where he was scheduled to meet Eisenhower. The British Premier had two informal meetings with the newly elected President, on 5 and 7 January. The conversation Churchill had with Eisenhower on the evening of the 7th was of some relevance. On this occasion the American President asked for the Prime Minister's opinion about the hypothesis to insert in his inaugural speech some reference 'to the effect that he would be glad to meet anybody who could help him establish the peace of the world and would be prepared to go to a neutral country for this purpose'. The Republican leader added that '... if Mr. Churchill wanted to meet Stalin anywhere, he himself would have no objection at all: would Mr. Churchill have any objection to his meeting Stalin alone?'[11] The Prime Minister replied that, if such a question had been posed to him during World War II, when 'the British Empire and the United States had roughly similar forces, he would have objected to such a proposal, but now it was not his intention to raise any objection'. In spite of that, the Tory leader advised Eisenhower against pursuing such an initiative and he argued:

> ... that surely it would be unwise to take any action 'before his reconnaissance was in'. General Eisenhower ought to spend some months learning all the facts about the present position before he embarked on such a momentous adventure. It would seem therefore that the inaugural speech was not an occasion on which to say anything of this kind.[12]

At first glance it appears somewhat puzzling that Churchill showed so cautious an attitude towards such an opportunity of dialogue with Moscow and we may wonder whether his reaction did not conceal the fear of a unilateral American initiative to the detriment of Britain's role. At any rate Churchill's statement seemed to pour cold water on Eisenhower's hopes. In spite of that, in Washington there were rumours about plans for a meeting between the US President and the Soviet leader and such rumours, even if for different reasons to Churchill's, aroused some concern in Whitehall. In a memorandum, drafted in the second half of January, Paul Mason, a top Foreign Office official, wrote that the Kremlin might be worried about the possibility of an armed conflict with the West, but he thought it very unlikely the Soviet Union could make concessions on the numerous issues which opposed the West to the Soviet bloc and he cautiously stated:

... for the next few months we ought to practice a policy of great reserve towards the Soviet Government. At the same time we ought to watch developments in that country as closely as possible. It is quite conceivable that the progress of internal events in Russia (and in the satellites) during the coming months will show a degree of weakness in the internal structure which up till now we have not felt justified in assuming. If this is so, consciousness of it may result in the Soviet Government being more ready than I believed to be at present to treat with the outside world on terms which offer some prospect of success, both for a high level approach and for some resulting agreement at least on important subsidiary matters.[13]

Mason's views were shared by Sir Frank Roberts, Deputy Under-Secretary of State for Foreign Affairs, who did not reject the possibility the Soviet leaders could exploit from a propaganda viewpoint the likely aspiration by the new US administration to start some direct contact between Eisenhower and Stalin. Furthermore, Roberts remarked that 'Stalin has every reason to recall General Eisenhower's rather naive and over-simplified approach to the Russian problem in 1945 and would no doubt hope to turn a meeting to his own advantage'.[14] He also hinted that the vague plan for a meeting between the two leaders might conceal an initiative by Charles Bohlen, who had been appointed US Ambassador in Moscow. Both the Permanent Under-Secretary, Sir William Strang, and Eden agreed with these suggestions for a cautious attitude.[15] In fact some State Department officials appeared to be interested in finding different ways in Washington's policy towards Moscow; such an attitude seemed to be prompted by the opportunities offered by the settling in of a new administration. On the other hand, some US diplomats did not rule out the possibility that in the Soviet Union a new political balance could surface if Stalin had disappeared.[16]

As a consequence of the US administration's attitude, in early February Mason wrote to the British Ambassador in Washington, Sir Christopher Steel. In his letter the Foreign Office official rejected the vague project for a meeting between Eisenhower and Stalin as mere wishful thinking. Furthermore, he confirmed that the West 'for the next few months ... should practice a policy of great reserve towards the Soviet Union'.[17] On the other hand, the news coming from Moscow seemed destined to reinforce the cautious 'wait and see' attitude developed by Whitehall. In a personal message he sent to Eden in February, Gascoigne reported two episodes which, in his opinion, were of some relevance: the request on the part of the Soviet authorities, following which the British had to move from the building where their Embassy was located, and the so-called 'doctors' plot'. As for the former episode, he stated with some humour:

> ... Stalin, or one of his cronies, may have become annoyed by reason of the fact that every time they look out of their windows in the Kremlin they can see the British Embassy (complete with flag on Sundays), and that Stalin, or somebody at his level, has told Vyshinsky to get the British out 'of my sight and get them out quickly'.[18]

Obviously Gascoigne paid more attention to the most recent Stalinist 'purge' and, even though he thought it difficult to ascertain the real roots of Stalin's decisions, the British Ambassador wrote:

> ... I would like to stress that it is my definite opinion that, while these precautions are being taken for 'clearing the decks' in the Soviet Union, they are not being adopted because this country is planning to take an initiative for war. I still think, as I always have, that Stalin's main objective is to avoid a general conflict. But, as I said above, I believe that he is now apprehensive lest the Americans may force the pace to such an extent that an eventuality of this kind may become unavoidable.[19]

In that same period the US administration also received gloomy reports about Stalin's attitude towards the Western world.[20] Furthermore, on 25 February, on the occasion of a press conference, President Eisenhower was asked for his opinion about a meeting with Stalin. He stated:

> I wouldn't want to just say, 'Yes, I will go anywhere'. I would go to any suitable spot, let's say halfway between, and talk with anybody, and with the full knowledge of our allies and friends as to the kind of thing I was talking about, because the business of defending freedom is a big job. It is not just one nation's job.[21]

A few days later the international situation changed dramatically. On 4 March it was publicly announced that Stalin was affected by a serious illness; on the evening of the following day the Soviet leader's death was announced.[22] In the early afternoon of the 4th, Gascoigne reported to London his opinions about the most likely successors to the Soviet dictator. If Molotov was singled out as 'the logical immediate successor', Malenkov appeared to the British Ambassador as 'the most influential of the younger generation'. Gascoigne concluded:

> Perhaps all that can reasonably be conjectured at the moment, is, firstly, that there may be a struggle for power which the announcement of a successor to Stalin as Chairman of the Council of Ministers ... will not necessarily resolve. Nor will it necessarily give us a final clue to the problem. ... Secondly, however, this struggle for power need not assume the proportions of the conflict after

Lenin's death since there is not, as now so far as we know, any well marked rival groups corresponding to the Triumvirate of Stalin, Zinovief and Kamenev on the one hand, and Trotsky and his associates on the other.[23]

In the afternoon of the 6th, 24 hours after Stalin's death had been announced, Gascoigne sent a further telegram to Whitehall; in his message the British Ambassador tried to look into the most recent events which had taken place in Moscow. As a preliminary remark, he wrote:

Firstly, I do not ... look with satisfaction on Stalin's disappearance. He and he alone wielded the power in this country, and there is nobody who can really take his place. Despite his dogged determination to pursue his Communist policy to the bitter end, and to have no compromise with the West, he was a man of great experience and caution who did not wish to promote an armed conflict between the two worlds. He had much common sense and a certain understanding of foreign mentality.[24]

In his opinion Molotov would be appointed Chairman of the Council, but power would be shared by a small group formed by Molotov, Malenkov, Beria, Bulganin and Kaganovich.[25] As for Kremlin's policy, in the British diplomat's view, it would not be too different from that pursued by Stalin either in internal or foreign affairs. In this connection it is of some relevance that Gascoigne appeared to be more concerned about the American attitude towards the Soviet Union. He feared Washington might give up the policy of 'containment' and could favour 'more forward and positive' initiatives, in the false hope the Soviet leadership could be weaker. Gascoigne strongly suggested 'that the *greatest possible caution* should be taken in our dealings with this country during the weeks and months that lie ahead, until at least we can see which way the wind is blowing'.[26] Stalin's funeral, held on 9 March, offered Gascoigne the opportunity to confirm his opinions, as well as to sketch out the Soviet leaders' rites and habits. It is impossible to quote in full this long despatch, which gave a detailed picture of the funeral with its numerous odd, if not humorous, episodes; at any rate Gascoigne remarked with some surprise:

The most striking features of these remarkable ... days have been the ordinary Russian's apparent indifference to this historical event: the air of relaxed expectancy and excitement in the crowds during the Lying-in-State, to the exclusion of the more sober sentiments: and, perhaps most of all, the remarkable success with which the troops and militia prevented all but a moiety of the $7\frac{1}{2}$ million population of Moscow from seeing either Stalin's Lying-in-State or his funeral.[27]

As for the funeral orations delivered by Malenkov, Beria and Molotov, Gascoigne wrote:

> These were devoted of course, in part, to eulogies of Stalin's activities in laying the foundations of the Soviet State. They stressed the necessity for solidarity between the Soviet people and the Party, and the close links between the Soviet Union, China and People's Democracies. Malenkov, in particular, dwelt on the longing of the people for peace, and the fact that Soviet foreign policy was designed to promote peace. At the same time he emphasized that the Soviet Union's defence forces must be in state of preparedness and should be strengthened to meet any hostile attack. But these speeches heralded no new tendencies, neither did they contain any clue as regards future policy.[28]

One week later, Gascoigne singled out an important public statement by Malenkov, who, once appointed Chairman of the Council of Ministers on the occasion of the meeting of the Supreme Soviet held on 15 March, had stated that there was no international issue, however difficult, that could not be solved through peaceful means on the basis of mutual interest of the parties concerned. In the British Ambassador's opinion such a conciliatory move might be regarded as a mere propaganda instrument for internal consumption, but it could also aim 'to allay and/or *confuse* opinion in the West, and especially in the United States'.[29] A few days later Sir Alvary Gascoigne developed further his analysis. Once again the British Ambassador recommended the Foreign Office make use of the utmost caution in dealing with Moscow and he believed that, at least in a short-term perspective, it would be very unlikely that the Soviet attitude towards the Western world would radically change, even though he thought there could surface some symptom of resilience. But Gascoigne did not seem to ignore that Stalin's death could revive Churchill's hopes in *détente*, and in this connection he wrote:

> After considerable thought I have the honour to submit with all respect that, as seen from here, it would be better not to force the pace but to let things take their course at any rate for the next few months. After some time has elapsed we should be able to determine whether or not the new men at the helm will really be disposed to show any more inclination towards a softening of the cold war than did Stalin, and I believe that to suggest a meeting now would be a false move.

He added:

> Of course if the Soviet Government ... were to take a clear initiative ... (I do not place Malenkov's recent statement at the Fourth Section

of the Supreme Soviet in this category) that would require most careful consideration. But I do not believe that this is likely to take place in the immediate future, and I think that we can afford to keep an open mind on the subjet since the Russians can easily make further gestures if they really mean business – they are not dumb and we are not deaf.[30]

A few days later, as a consequence of some minor friendly gestures on the part of the Russian authorities, and also because he envisaged some move by his Government, Gascoigne confirmed his prudent opinions. In a further despatch to Eden, even though he did not rule out the possibility that the Western world could exploit the Kremlin's new attitude, the Ambassador stated:

> I personally ... think that the new policy of a temporary easing of the cold war, without giving anything away of importance, may prove to be much more dangerous than the former straightforward and brutal policy exercised by Stalin. I feel convinced that these minute olive branches are not extended in sincere fashion, and that there is little prospect of anything in the Soviet Government's *basic* policy towards the West being changed.[31]

On the morrow of Stalin's death, then, Gascoigne's attitude towards a dialogue with Moscow was characterized by scepticism, if not open mistrust.[32] The Foreign Office's early views meanwhile appeared to be mainly influenced by a steady cautiousness. This perhaps was also the consequence of Eden's absence, as in mid-March the Foreign Secretary had left for the United States in order to hold conversations with the American authorities about the situation in Egypt. On 7 March Paul Mason drafted a minute dealing with the appearance of a collective leadership in the Soviet Union; in his opinion such a development was not 'unpromising' for Western interests, for the new Soviet leaders seemed to be interested in reassuring their own public opinion, as well as in pursuing 'a conservative foreign policy'.[33] Furthermore, it is of some relevance that the head of the 'Northern Department' of the Foreign Office, Henry Hohler, singled out as an important development Khrushchev's appointment as First Secretary of the CPSU. But the British diplomat added: 'The real sources of power may now lie more in the control of the leading Ministries than in the control of the Party apparatus. Much must obviously depend on whether Khrushchev is Malenkov's man or not.'[34]

On 28 March, as a consequence of the early symptoms of an easing in the relations between Moscow and the West, the Foreign Office appeared to take up a more hopeful stand, and Hohler suggested the Ambassador in Moscow could give Molotov a brief message on the part of Eden, which could identify a series of issues the two Governments could deal with. Such a move seemed to be an early step 'for direct contact between the Secretary of State and the Soviet Minister of Foreign Affairs'.[35] Nevertheless Hohler stressed that it was Eden's intention to avoid any discussion about the German question, as a way of confirming Whitehall's cautiousness towards Moscow. While in the Soviet capital Gascoigne went on drafting worried messages, and the Foreign Office tried to develop a cautious policy, Churchill took a bold initiative. On 11 March the Prime Minister wrote a personal letter to Eisenhower. On the basis of the conversation he had had in early January with the American President, Churchill put forward, even if in somewhat vague terms, a plan for a Western move towards the new Soviet leaders.[36] In Washington, after the announcement of Stalin's illness, the Eisenhower administration started a series of careful analyses sketching out a coherent policy towards the likely developments in the Soviet Union.[37] Among the many options which were taken into consideration, there appeared a definite tendency on the part of the American authorities to exploit autonomously with regard to their allies the opportunities which the death of Stalin seemed to offer to the Western world. It is not surprising that Eisenhower replied to Churchill's letter in a non-committal way.

> Even now I tend to doubt the wisdom of a formal multilateral meeting since this would give our opponent the same kind of opportunity he has so often had to use such a meeting simultaneously to balk every reasonable effort of ourselves and to make of the whole occurrence [*sic*] another propaganda mill for the Soviet.

Eisenhower's only concession to Churchill's arguments was: 'It is entirely possible, however, that your government and ourselves should agree upon some general purpose and program under which each would have a specific part to play.'[38] On the same day Eisenhower sent this letter, the National Security Council held an important meeting. On this occasion the Secretary of State, John Foster Dulles, was able to impose his opinion according to which there was no advantage in a meeting with the Soviet leaders, as it could be exploited by Moscow and could entail divisions among the Western Allies.[39] Churchill was in the dark about this meeting and on 19 March sent a further message to Eisenhower. Churchill reported the view of Tito (who was then in London) that the new Soviet régime 'will probably feel their way cautiously for some time' and would be weakened by internecine divisions. That was an implicit invitation to exploit a situation which appeared to be favourable to Western interests.[40]

As a consequence of Eisenhower's non-committal attitude, Churchill looked for a different solution, and on 28 March he wrote to Eden. The

Prime Minister pointed to the interest the Soviet leaders had shown in favouring the release of British diplomats kept prisoners in North Korea, and he suggested the delivery of a personal message to Molotov, as a first step towards direct contacts between Eden and the Soviet Foreign Minister. In the draft of this message, Churchill stressed the close ties which had characterized the wartime relations between London and Moscow, and put forward the project for 'another friendly and informal meeting', which would have perhaps concurred in leading 'us all farther away from madness and ruin'. In order to urge a positive reply on the part of the Foreign Secretary, Churchill did not hesitate to resort to flattering Eden: 'I do not want an interview between Gascoigne and Molotov, but between Molotov and you. At a later stage, if all went well and everything broadened, I and even Ike might come in too.'[41]

Eden's reply was almost immediate. He wondered whether it was possible to tackle with the Soviet leaders important and thorny issues such as Germany, Austria, and Korea without taking into consideration the opinions of Britain's Allies. Furthermore, the Foreign Secretary did not rule out the possibility the Russian leaders hoped to break up the Western alliance easily through a 'policy of moderation and concession in minor matters and perhaps in some major matters too'. Eden suggested a thorough discussion with the Prime Minister about this question and he conceded that 'Our own tactics will have to be to respond as freely as we can without surrendering vital positions like the North Atlantic Treaty'.[42]

In spite of these cautious remarks, the idea of a meeting with Molotov appeared to awaken Eden's ambition. He ordered Foreign Office officials to study the idea, and also recalled Gascoigne for an exchange of views. On 1 April a meeting was held at the Foreign Office which saw the participation of Eden, Mason, Strang, Hohler, Gascoigne and Evelyn Shuckburgh, Eden's private secretary. Shuckburgh's diaries offer a lively picture of the bewilderment and hostility of Foreign Office diplomats at Eden's apparent 'hankering after a meeting with Molotov', which, in their opinion, would have been tantamount 'to a willingness, for the sake of popularity, to abandon policies hitherto pursued'. The Foreign Office officials were able to pour cold water on Eden's hopes, and it was decided that Whitehall would limit itself to 'Tell Gascoigne to take up the minor Anglo-USSR questions with Molotov on his return'; furthermore, Eisenhower would be informed of this initiative, and he would be asked for his opinion about the possibility of 'any more direct contacts'. On 2 April, Eden seemed able to persuade Churchill of the need to act very cautiously.[43] Three days later, Churchill wrote Eisenhower a further letter. In his message the Prime Minister referred to the conversations he had had with Eden, and he stated it was of a fundamental relevance to ascertain Malenkov's apparent goodwill. Churchill reported that Gascoigne, after his short stay in London, was going back to Moscow with instructions which aimed at solving some minor difficulties between Britain and the Soviet Union. In Churchill's opinion, this was a way to test the Kremlin's real intentions and, he hopefully concluded:

> It may be that presently the Soviets will make overtures for some form of direct discussion of world problems, whether on a Four Power basis or in some other manner. I assume of course that we shall deal in the closest collaboration with any such overtures if they are made.[44]

The President replied in a positive way, even though he appeared to limit the scope of the British initiative. Eisenhower also informed the Prime Minister that he was working out the text of a public statement, whose aim was to show 'before the world the peaceful intentions of this country'.[45] It appeared clear to Churchill that Eisenhower's move[46] would weaken the significance of the projects worked out in London in that same period. In addition, we must not forget that the scope of such projects had already been reduced in comparison with Churchill's early proposals. At any rate, on 8 April the Foreign Office instructed Gascoigne to raise with Molotov, on Eden's behalf, a series of problems which affected the relations between London and Moscow.[47] Three days later, the British Ambassador met Molotov, and informed him of Eden's message.[48] In reporting his conversation with the Soviet Foreign Minister, the British Ambassador did not conceal his continuing scepticism:

> I did not ... expect at this interview to obtain answers from him to the cases which I raised. Whether we shall get any satisfaction or not remains to be seen. He gave no sign either positive or negative, but I have some hope at least that we shall not be wholly unsuccessful. These hopes, however, are only prompted by the *manner* in which Molotov received me, and the conspicuously friendly *atmosphere* of the meeting.[49]

Gascoigne's distrust of the new Soviet leaders was confirmed in a further telegram he sent to the Foreign Office on 22 April. In his message he raised the by then usual arguments and, in spite of some symptoms of *détente*, he argued that:

> ... their [Soviet] basic objectives remain the same and that present period is but a change of tactics chiefly manifested in questions connected with Korea ... While all efforts must be made to profit by this 'softer atmosphere', I have no reason to believe that it need mean more than a temporary change of air.[50]

In the meantime, the Foreign Office had some contact with Paris and Washington in the attempt to ascertain the characters and goals of the new Soviet leaders' policy, especially those of Malenkov.[51] In this connection, it must be noticed that the French authorities appeared to be worried about Moscow's initiatives and eager for an exchange of views among the three Western powers.[52] There was also some anxiety in Paris about Churchill's hopes for a dialogue with Moscow.[53] The Prime Minister, for his part, seemed to be concerned about the speech Eisenhower was going to deliver on 16 April. In a series of personal messages, Churchill made every effort to influence the content of the President's speech. The Prime Minister appeared eager to avoid the risk the President's speech would threaten better relations between East and West. So he wrote, for instance: 'Would it not be well to combine the re-assertion of your and our inflexible resolves with some balancing expression of hope that we have entered upon a new era?'[54]

Churchill, meanwhile, on the occasion of a speech he delivered in Glasgow on 17 April in front of an audience of Conservative Party members, reaffirmed his belief in a dialogue with Moscow.[55] As for Eisenhower's address, the so-called 'The Chance for Peace' speech, it received a wide echo both in the United States and abroad. In Stephen Ambrose's opinion:

> The specific charges, demands, and proposals in 'The Chance for Peace' ... were little more than a restatement of some of the oldest Cold War rethoric. They were not what made the speech great. What did make it great was Eisenhower's warning about the dangers and the cost of continuing the arms race.[56]

The President's words concurred in enhancing Eisenhower's stand in international opinion; the speech inevitably damaged London's attempt to play a leading role in a renewed dialogue with the Soviet Union. A further blow to Churchill's hopes was the attitude taken by the Soviet leaders. On 23 April Gascoigne met Molotov, who, in the Ambassador's opinion, showed no will to comply with Britain's cautious 'avance'.[57] In spite of that, Churchill was not deterred from pursuing his policy: on 21 April he wrote Eisenhower a further letter. In his message the Prime Minister took profit from the President's speech and, after some flattering remarks, he stated:

> I should like to know what you think should be the next step. Evidently we must wait a few days for their reply or reaction. It is not likely that the Soviets will agree about the release of the Satellites or a unified Korea. There will, however, be a strong movement here for a meeting between Heads of States and Governments. How do you stand about this? In my opinion the best would be that

the Three victorious Powers, who separated at Potsdam in 1945, should come together again ... I am sure the world will expect something like this to emerge if the Soviets do not turn your proposal down abruptly.

Churchill concluded: 'If nothing can be arranged I shall have to consider seriously a personal contact.'[58]

Eisenhower replied politely but in the negative. He suggested Churchill should take a cautious stand towards Moscow, and also rejected the plan for a unilateral initiative on the part of the Prime Minister.[59] Eisenhower's very cautious attitude towards Moscow was shared by the Foreign Office, which, in spite of Churchill's position, in a telegram to the High Commissioners in the Dominions confirmed that the British cabinet was 'bound to proceed on the assumption that the ultimate objectives of Soviet policy have not been changed'.[60]

Moscow's reaction to Eisenhower's speech was not slow to come: on 25 April the Soviet newspaper *Pravda* published a precise and complete translation of the President's words. In the same issue, a front-page article thoroughly replied to Eisenhower's arguments in a way which was not prejudicially hostile. This unprecedented event became the object of lively discussion and careful analysis in Western capitals. The American Ambassador in Moscow, Bohlen, appeared to develop a positive view of the episode,[61] while the Department of State and the CIA came to the following pessimistic conclusions:

> The Soviet statement of 25 April 1953 is a defense of Soviet policy and of the world Communist movement, and a condemnation of US policy. The statement gives no indication that the rulers of the USSR will modify their stand on any of the issues outstanding between East and West.[62]

It was these views which prevailed in Washington.[63] As for the French authorities, their reactions were contradictory. At a meeting held on 25 April at the Quai d'Orsay between Bidault, Dulles and the British Chancellor of the Exchequer, R.A.B. Butler, the French Foreign Minister appeared to be very much interested in the possibility of a new Soviet diplomatic initiative for a Four Power conference on Korea or on Germany. On that same occasion Bidault hinted that the Western powers might begin to work out a tentative agenda for such a conference.[64] A few days later, however, French evaluations appeared far more cautious.[65]

In London the Foreign Office did not rule out the possibility the Soviet authorities wished to start some form of negotiation with the West, but 'they appear in no hurry for genuine talks of general scope'. On the other hand, the article published by *Pravda* was mainly regarded as a piece of 'political warfare'. Even though it was believed some changes had taken place in the Soviet leaders' attitude in the aftermath of Stalin's death, the Foreign Office stated: 'Basic Soviet aims and policy remain unchanged, but tactics have become more cautious and realistic.'[66] This instance reflected Eden's attitude. Even if the Foreign Secretary disagreed with Gascoigne's deep mistrust, and with some biased American interpretations of the Kremlin's goals, he thought it useful for the West – and in Britain's interest – to pursue a cautious policy towards the new Soviet leaders, which did not rule out some initiative.

Eden's prudent stand was not shared by the Prime Minister, who believed it was his duty to take some bold initiative. On the other hand, Churchill could suddenly take profit from the serious illness which affected the Foreign Secretary. On 12 April Eden had undergone an operation which went wrong and had serious consequences for his health, so that on the 29th, he was compelled to undergo a further operation.[67] A third operation in the United States became necessary, as well as a long period of leave; Eden was out of his office till late 1953. These events led Churchill to play a more active role in Britain's foreign policy. At a cabinet meeting held on 28 April, the Prime Minister drew his Ministers' attention to a statement by Molotov, in which the Soviet Foreign Minister appeared to favour the convening of a Five Power conference (the Soviet Union, the United States, Britain, France, and Communist China) in order to draft a 'peace pact'. It is very likely the ministers feared Churchill might take some hasty initiative, so they pointed out the mere propaganda character of Molotov's statement. On that occasion the cabinet decided that 'it would be premature to draw any conclusions from this announcement, and it would be unnecessary for the Government to volunteer any public statement about it at this stage'.[68] As a consequence of this non-committal, if not hostile, attitude which cabinet members had taken towards the hypothesis of a dialogue with Moscow, Churchill resolved to approach Eisenhower once again. On 4 May the Prime Minister sent the President a message, to which he attached the tentative draft of a telegram to Molotov putting forward the plan for an informal meeting with Malenkov 'to restore an easy and friendly basis between us such as I have with so many other countries'.[69] Eisenhower's reaction was immediate and negative. Backed by Dulles, Eisenhower made a number of objections to Churchill's scheme: the choice of Moscow as the venue for the meeting, the lack of reference to any role for the French Government, the lack of any evidence of real goodwill on the part of the Soviet authorities.[70] Two days later, in a further message to Eisenhower, Churchill tried to defend his project, even if he accepted postponement of a unilateral British initiative.[71] In reality Eisenhower's position compelled the Prime Minister to drop his scheme.

Churchill fully realized that only clear-cut support on the part of the American administration would allow him to overcome the obstacles his Ministers and the Foreign Office were opposing to his project for direct contacts with the Soviet leaders. One way only was left open to Churchill: a public statement on the model of Eisenhower's 'The Chance for Peace' speech. On 11 May, in a debate on foreign affairs at the House of Commons, Churchill proposed that 'a conference on the highest level should take place between the leading powers without long delay'.[72] As is well known, Churchill's speech aroused deep enthusiasm and strong hopes in Western European public opinion. The Prime Minister's position caused far less enthusiasm in Washington, and Churchill's proposals compelled the Eisenhower administration to comply with a French request for a meeting of the three major Western powers in order to examine the prospect of a dialogue with Moscow.[73] The reaction of both leading Tory Ministers and the Foreign Office officials was negative. In a memorandum drafted in late May, Henry Hohler took advantage of an article published by *Pravda* to speak of a 'highly disappointing reaction to the Prime Minister's speech'. Furthermore, he stressed that Moscow aimed at creating a wedge between Washington and London. Hohler concluded: 'I think it is now beyond doubt that the Soviet leopard has not changed its spots, and it would be unwise to encourage any public belief to the contrary.'[74]

These opinions were shared by Gascoigne,[75] who thought it wise to write a long 'personal and secret' letter to Churchill informing the Prime Minister of his views on Soviet foreign policy. In the hope of influencing Churchill, the British Ambassador wrote:

> ... at present, Soviet foreign policy seems to be more or less static; it is possible that they may, in due course, become a bit more reasonable; although I do not feel that we can expect them to make any substantial concessions on Germany or Austria, or as regards a final political agreement in Korea. I believe that the Kremlin are not in a hurry for a four power conference; and that they have probably made up their minds that the present division of Germany suits them quite well, or at least constitutes as good an arrangement of the German question as they are likely to get.[76]

The prevailing feeling among cabinet members found expression in a question the Parliamentary Under-Secretary for Foreign Affairs, Anthony Nutting, posed in a letter to a Foreign Office official. He stated that the Soviet leaders had no interest whatsoever in a Four Power conference and he thought their main goal was the division of the Western world. Then he wrote: 'In other words, are we not now getting pretty full proof that the bear has not changed?'[77]

In spite of the many difficulties and obstacles, Churchill wished to persevere in his aims.[78] It is a little ironical that Churchill's goals were to be achieved only after his retirement as a consequence of Eden's initiatives. The long-coveted summit conference was held in July 1955; far from confirming Britain's leading role on the international scene, the Geneva Conference provided clear evidence of the emergence of a bi-polar world, so confirmation of Britain's decline.[79]

The analysis of this episode may lead to some concluding remarks of a more general character. First of all it should be noticed that Britain's Soviet policy in the aftermath of Stalin's death was marked by a series of inconsistencies and misunderstandings: many experienced decision-makers appeared unable either to realize the real meaning of the events which took place in Moscow or to forecast developments in the Soviet Union; the effectiveness of London's policy was seriously impaired by the deep contrasts between the Prime Minister and the Foreign Office; Churchill seemed to be unable to work out a coherent policy towards the Soviet Union and his ambitious goals often bordered on some sort of senile mania. In addition, the object of the proposed conversations with the new Soviet leaders was always very vague and it was impossible to tackle the most difficult international issues, such as Korea, Indo-China, Germany and disarmament, without taking into consideration the opinions of the other major Western powers. On the other hand, the events which have been examined in this chapter confirm the growing influence Washington was exerting in East–West relations. Both Churchill and the Foreign Office clearly realized that some sort of dialogue with Moscow was feasible only with the Eisenhower administration's consent. The only difference was that Churchill believed it was possible to mend the fences with the American Government through his personal relationship with Eisenhower, while the Foreign Office and Eden appeared to rely on their diplomatic skills and on the 'special relationship', two elements which appeared to be worn out. So it became evident that the British authorities had no effective means to convince the Eisenhower administration to make up their minds about the Western attitude towards Moscow. As far as the British evaluations of Stalin are concerned, the Soviet dictator's death led the British decision-makers to focus their attention on the Kremlin's new leaders. Gascoigne's overall judgement on the man who had ruled the Soviet Union for about three decades was shelved for the record – and for future historians – in the British archives. In this connection we may stress the way in which the British Ambassador concluded his long despatch on Stalin's funeral:

> Stalin will, I presume, rank in history as a cruel, cold-blooded and ruthless tyrant. And yet there is no gainsaying the fact that he was a

350 Britain and the Death of Stalin

great man. I thought of his humble birth at Gori ... and of all the vicissitudes through which this 'man of steel' had passed during his long life. I thought also of the heroic part which he played in defeating the Germans in the Second World War when, inter alia, in the face of almost overwhelming odds, he personally refused to leave Moscow. As I looked for the last time on his face, I evinced the bitterest feeling of regret that he should have chosen because of the canker of Marxism and of his overweening desire for power, the path which has led him and his country away from the comity of the civilian nations.[80]

Notes

1. See, for instance, R. Ashton, *In Search of Détente. The Politics of East–West Relations since 1945* (London: Macmillan, 1989), in particular pp. 66–104, and J. Van Oudenaren, *Détente in Europe. The Soviet Union and the West since 1953* (Durham–London: Duke University Press, 1991) pp. 5–63, as well as *Relations Internationales*, 71 (Autumn 1992): this issue dealt with the following topic: 'Est–Ouest. 1955-1958: la première détente'.
2. See in particular: M. Gilbert, *'Never Despair' Winston S. Churchill 1945–1965* (London: Heinemann, 1988) pp. 653–1130 *passim*; J.W. Young, 'Churchill's Bid for Peace with Moscow', *History* (1988) 425–48; Id., 'Cold War and Détente with Moscow', in Id. (ed.), *The Foreign Policy of Churchill's Peacetime Administration 1951–1955* (Leicester: Leicester University Press, 1988) pp. 55–88; A. Varsori, 'Britain and Early Détente: 1953–1956', in G. Schmidt (Hrsg.), *Ost–West Beziehungen: Konfrontation und Détente 1945–1989*, Vol. 2 (Bochum: Brockmeyer, 1993) pp. 175–97.
3. See the statements by Churchill in September 1951 on the occasion of a dinner offered in Paris by the British Ambassador in the French capital, Sir Oliver Harvey, quoted in Gilbert, *'Never Despair'*, p. 636.
4. *Ibid.*, pp. 659–60.
5. J. Colville, *The Fringes of Power. Downing Street Diaries*, Vol. 2, *1941–April 1955* (London: Sceptre, 1987) p. 306.
6. *Ibid.*, p. 310.
7. Young, 'Cold War', p. 57. There had been some minor symptoms of *détente* on the part of the Soviet authorities towards Britain in Autumn 1952. See, for example, Minute by E. Shuckburgh, 2 September 1952, PRO, FO 371, NS 1051/32 (100839); as for the British attitude see, for example, FO to UK Del. United Nations (New York), 17 November 1952, PRO, FO 371, NS 1051/40 (100839). [Transcripts of documents in the Public Record Office subject to Crown copyright appear with the permission of Her Majesty's Stationery Office.]
8. As far as this aspect is concerned see S. Dockrill, *Britain's Policy for West German Rearmament 1950–1955* (Cambridge: Cambridge University Press, 1991) pp. 121–3. On the Soviet Note see for instance R. Steininger, *Eine Vertane Chance* (Berlin/Bonn: Dietz Nachf., 1986); W. Loth, *The Division of the World 1941–1955* (London: Routledge, 1988) pp. 258–62. As for a British evaluation see, for example, 'Minutes

of the Meeting of the Russia Committee held on 18 March 1952', PRO, FO 371, NS 1052/10 (100841).
9. Sir A. Gascoigne (Moscow) to A. Eden (FO), 23 December 1952, PRO, FO 371, NS 1021/8 (106524). On 1st January Eden minuted 'Interesting. I think that copies of this letter should be circulated to my Cabinet colleagues.'
10. *Ibid.*
11. Minute by J. Colvile, 8 January 1953, PRO, FO 371, NS 1071/29 (106537). See also Gilbert, *'Never Despair'*, p. 790. Gilbert quotes a telegram from Churchill to the Foreign Office. Furthermore see E. Shuckburgh, *Descent to Suez. Diaries 1951–56* (London: Weidenfeld & Nicolson, 1986) p. 74.
12. Minute by J. Colvile, 8 January 1953, PRO, FO 371, NS 1071/29 (106537).
13. Memo 'The Question of a Top-Level Meeting with Marshal Stalin', by P. Mason, 19 January 1953, PRO, FO 371, NS 1071/30 (106537). It is likely that this interpretation was not too far from reality; see for example V.M. Zubok, *Soviet Intelligence and the Cold War: The 'Small' Committee of Information, 1952–53* (Washington: The Woodrow Wilson International Center for Scholars, 1992) pp. 10–11.
14. Minute by Sir F. Roberts, 20 January 1953, PRO, FO 371, NS 1071/30 (106537). On Roberts' attitude in this period see F. Roberts, *Dealing with Dictators. The Destruction and Revival of Europe 1930–70* (London: Weidenfeld & Nicolson, 1991) pp. 165–8.
15. Minute by Sir William Strang, 20 January 1953, and minute by A. Eden, 20 January 1953, PRO, FO 371, NS 1071/30 (106537). Eden, among other things, wrote: 'I have no confidence in Mr Bohlen and had rather hoped he might disappear with this new administration' and he added: 'It is quite possible that this is largely a Bohlen exercise *pour se faire valoir.*'
16. See in particular *FRUS, 1952–54*, Vol. 8, pp. 1071–3 and 1075–7.
17. Letter from P. Mason (FO) to Sir C. Steel (Washington), 3 February 1953, PRO, FO 371, NS 1071/30 (106537).
18. Sir A. Gascoigne (Moscow) to A. Eden (FO), 4 February 1953, PRO, FO 371, NS 1021/17 (106524).
19. *Ibid.*
20. J. Beam (Moscow) to State Department, 19 February 1953, in *FRUS, 1952–54*, Vol. 8, pp. 1078–9.
21. Quoted in *ibid.*, p. 1079.
22. On Stalin's death see, among others, M. Geller, A. Nekrich, *L'utopie au pouvoir* (Paris: Calman Levy, 1982). On Soviet foreign policy following Stalin's death see, among others: A.B. Ulam, *Expansion and Coexistence. The History of Soviet Foreign Policy, 1917–1967* (New York: Praeger, 1968); Id., *The Communists. The Story of Power and Lost Illusions 1948–1991* (New York: Scribners, 1992); J. Nogee, R.H. Donaldson, *Soviet Foreign Policy since World War II* (New York: Macmillan, 1992).
23. Sir A. Gascoigne (Moscow) to FO, 4 March 1953, PRO, FO 371, NS 10110/2 (106515). The early US reactions were similar to these of Gascoigne: see Department of State Intelligence Estimate, 4 March 1953, in *FRUS, 1952–54*, Vol. 8, pp. 1086–90.
24. Sir A. Gascoigne (Moscow) to FO, 6 March 1953, PRO, FO 371, NS 10110/12 (106515).

25. As is well known, Malenkov was appointed Chairman of the Council of Ministers, Molotov became Foreign Minister and Khrushchev First Secretary of the CPSU.
26. Sir A. Gascoigne (Moscow) to FO, 6 March 1953, PRO, FO 371, NS 10110/12 (106515). The British Ambassador added: 'If there is to be any eventual change for the better in the Soviet Government's external policy, brought about possibly by internal difficulties, the one way, as I see it today, to consolidate the Soviet people behind their new chiefs would be ill advised hostile action or propaganda against them.'
27. Sir A. Gascoigne (Moscow) to A. Eden (FO), 13 March 1953, PRO, FO 371, NS 10110/59 (106516). This despatch contrasts with the '500 casualties caused by a panic-striken multitude' described in Geller, Nekrich, *L'utopie*. Among the humorous episodes Gascoigne wrote that all the diplomatic representatives of the non-Communist nations had concurred in the order for the same funeral wreath 'except the Swiss colleague, who had been to great trouble and expense to preserve neutrality only to have his wreath snatched from the flower shop at the last moment by the Albanian Minister'.
28. Sir A. Gascoigne (Moscow) to A. Eden (FO), 9 March 1953, PRO, FO 371, NS 10110/53 (106516). See also Sir A. Gascoigne (Moscow) to FO, 9 March 1953, PRO, FO 371, NS 10110/31 (106515).
29. Sir A. Gascoigne (Moscow) to FO, 16 March 1953, PRO, FO 371, NS 1021/21 (106524). As for the reasons for the Soviet initiative see, for example, the recent evaluations in Zubok, *Soviet Intelligence*, pp. 11–17, and J. Richter, *Reexamining Soviet Policy towards Germany During the Beria Interregnum* (Washington: Woodrow Wilson International Center for Scholars, 1992) *passim*.
30. Sir A. Gascoigne (Moscow) to A. Eden (FO), 20 March 1953, PRO, FO 371, NS 1021/23 (106524).
31. Sir A. Gascoigne (Moscow) to A. Eden (FO), 26 March 1953, PRO, FO 371, NS 1021/29 (106524).
32. It is very likely that Gascoigne's attitude had been largely influenced by the experience he had had in his capacity of British representative at Budapest in the immediate post-war period; see the interesting remarks in B. Arcidiacono, *Alle origini della divisione europea. Armistizi e Commissioni di controllo alleate in Europa orientale 1944–1946* (Florence: Ponte alle Grazie, 1993) pp. 306–90.
33. Minute 'The Kremlin Changes', by P. Mason, 7 March 1953, PRO, FO 371, NS 10111/3 (106517).
34. Minute 'N.S. Khrushchev', by H.A.F. Hohler, 21 March 1953, PRO, FO 371, NS 10111/11 (106517). Mason remarked that: '... Khrushchev is a man to watch', while Hohler thought there might be some family ties between Malenkov and Khrushchev as the family name of Malenkov's wife appeared to be Khrushchev.
35. Minute by H.A.F. Hohler, 28 March 1953, PRO, FO 371, NS 1071/40 (106537). It is very likely this plan was influenced by the Prime Minister's attitude; see *infra*, document quoted in note 41.
36. P.G. Boyle (ed.), *The Churchill–Eisenhower Correspondence, 1953–1955* (Chapel Hill–London: The University of North Carolina Press, 1990) p. 31. See also Gilbert, *'Never Despair'*, pp. 806–7, and Young, 'Cold War', p. 59.
37. See the documents in *FRUS, 1952–54*, Vol. 8, pp. 1091–115. See also D. Meyers, 'After Stalin: The Ambassadors and America's Soviet Policy, 1953–62', *Diplomacy and Statecraft*, 5, 2 (July 1994) 213–47.

38. Eisenhower to Churchill, 11 March 1953, in *The Churchill-Eisenhower*, p. 32. It must be noticed that the project for a Foreign Ministers conference had been put forward with some vigour by one of Eisenhower's close advisers; Memorandum, E.J. Hughes to D.D. Eisenhower, 10 March 1953, in *FRUS, 1952-54*, Vol. 8, pp. 1113-15.
39. Memorandum of Discussion at the 136th Meeting of the National Security Council, Washington, 11 March 1953, in *ibid.*, pp. 1117-25.
40. Churchill to Eisenhower, 19 March 1953, and Eisenhower to Churchill, 19 March 1953, in *The Churchill-Eisenhower*, pp. 32-4.
41. Message from the Prime Minister, 28 March 1953, PRO, FO 371, NS 1071/41 (106537).
42. Message telephoned to Prime Minister from Secretary of State, 28 March 1953, PRO, FO 371, NS 1071/41 (106537).
43. Shuckburgh, *Descent*, pp. 83-5.
44. Churchill to Eisenhower, 5 April 1953, in *The Churchill-Eisenhower*, pp. 36-7.
45. Eisenhower to Churchill, 6 April 1953, in *ibid.*, pp. 37-8.
46. Memorandum of telephone conversation with the President, by the Secretary of State, 16 March 1953, in *FRUS, 1952-54*, Vol. 8, pp. 1130-1.
47. FO to Moscow, 8 April 1953, PRO, FO 371, NS 1051/18 (106533).
48. Sir A. Gascoigne (Moscow) to FO, 11 April 1953, PRO, FO 371, NS 1051/22 and NS 1051/23 (106533); Sir A. Gascoigne (Moscow) to FO, 11 April 1953, PRO, FO 371, NS 1051/24 (106533).
49. Sir A. Gascoigne (Moscow) to FO, 11 April 1953, PRO, FO 371, NS 1051/25 (106533).
50. Sir A. Gascoigne (Moscow) to FO, 22 April 1953, PRO, FO 371, NS 1021/50 (106525).
51. See in particular FO to Washington, 8 April 1953, PRO, FO 371, NS 1021/31 (106524); minute, Sir F. Roberts to Sir W. Strang, 9 April 1953, PRO, FO 371, NS 10345/9 (106532); Sir O. Harvey (Paris) to FO, 11 March 1953, PRO, FO 371, NS 1021/37 (106525).
52. Letter, F.R. Hoyer Millar (Paris) to Sir P. Dixon (FO), 13 April 1953, PRO, FO 371, NS 1071/45 (106537).
53. See in particular the statements by Maurice Schumann on the occasion of a conversation with the Parliamentary Under-Secretary for Foreign Affairs Anthony Nutting; see minute by Sir A. Nutting, 22 April 1953, PRO, FO 371, NS 1021/52 (106525).
54. Churchill to Eisenhower, 12 April 1953, in *The Churchill-Eisenhower*, pp. 43-4. See also other messages in *ibid.*, pp. 40-5.
55. Gilbert, *'Never Despair'*, pp. 815-16.
56. S.E. Ambrose, *Eisenhower The President*, Vol. 2, *1952-1969* (London: Allen & Unwin, 1984) p. 84. For the text of this speech see *FRUS, 1952-54*, Vol. 8, pp. 1147-55.
57. Sir A. Gascoigne (Moscow) to FO, 23 April 1953, PRO, FO 371, NS 1051/33, and NS 1051/35 (106534).
58. Churchill to Eisenhower, 21 April 1953, in *The Churchill-Eisenhower*, p. 46.
59. Eisenhower to Churchill, 25 April 1953, in *ibid.*, p. 47. For the constraints of an internal nature which influenced Eisenhower's foreign policy during 1953 and 1954, see the interesting remarks in J. Broadwater, *Eisenhower and the Anti-Communist Crusade* (Chapel Hill-London: The University of North Carolina Press, 1992) pp. 112-36.

60. FO to UK High Commissioners (Canada, Australia, New Zealand, South Africa, India, Pakistan, Ceylon), 23 April 1953, PRO, FO 371, NS 1021/44 (106525).
61. C. Bohlen (Moscow) to State Department, 25 April 1953, in *FRUS, 1952–54*, Vol. 8, pp. 1165–6. On the role played by Bohlen, see the recent article by D. Meyers, 'After Stalin' 213–47.
62. Special Estimate, 30 April 1953, in *FRUS, 1952–54*, Vol. 8, pp. 1168–9.
63. At any rate we must discard any simplistic interpretation of America's policy towards the Soviet Union as an example of a mere 'Cold Warrior' mentality. In this connection see some recent evaluations of the Eisenhower administration's position: R.A. Melanson, D. Mayers (eds), *Reevaluating Eisenhower. American Foreign Policy in the Fifties* (Urbana–Chicago: University of Illinois Press, 1987); R.H. Immerman (ed.), *John Foster Dulles and the Diplomacy of the Cold War* (Princeton: Princeton University Press, 1990). See also P.G. Boyle, *American–Soviet Relations from the Russian Revolution to the Fall of Communism* (London–New York: Routledge, 1993) pp. 121–4. Some Foreign Office officials appeared to understand the motives of the American attitude: see Sir R. Makins (Washington) to Sir W. Strang (FO), 4 June 1953, PRO, FO 371, NS 10345/2 (106532).
64. 'Record of a Tripartite Meeting at the Quai d'Orsay on April 25, 1953', PRO, FO 371, NS 1071/61 (106538). The reactions of both the American delegation and the British delegation were very prudent. On the other hand in London there had already been some rumours following which Bidault favoured the convening of a four power conference: see minute by H.A.F. Hohler to the Prime Minister, 25 April 1953, PRO, FO 371, NS 1071/57 (106537).
65. Minute by Sir F. Roberts to Sir W. Strang, 1 May 1953, PRO, FO 371, NS 1071/70 (106538). For France's reactions to Stalin's death see, for example, G. Elgey, *Histoire de la IVe République*, Vol. 2, *La République des contradictions 1951–1954* (Paris: Fayard, 1968) pp. 323–4.
66. FO to UK High Commissioners (Canada, Australia, New Zealand, South Africa, India, Pakistan, Ceylon), 1 May 1953, PRO, FO 371, NS 1071/65 (107538).
67. Gilbert, *'Never Despair'*, p. 820.
68. PRO, CAB 128, C.C.(53)29th Conclusions, 28 April 1953.
69. Churchill to Eisenhower, 4 May 1953, in *The Churchill–Eisenhower*, p. 48.
70. Eisenhower to Churchill, 5 May 1953, in *ibid.*, pp. 49–50.
71. Churchill to Eisenhower, 7 May 1953, in *ibid.*, pp. 50–1.
72. *Parliamentary Debates – House of Commons*, Vol. 515, column 897. The whole text of Churchill's speech in columns 883–98. For a careful analysis of the Prime Minister's speech see Gilbert, *'Never Despair'*, pp. 827–33.
73. See, for instance, Young, 'Cold War', pp. 60–2.
74. Memorandum 'Pravda's Article, May 24, 1953', by H.A.F. Hohler, PRO, FO 371, NS 1071/106 (106538). Hohler conceded: 'It is true that the article does not actually "slam any doors". It preserves the new matter-of-fact manner and leaves room for hope that the Soviet Government will eventually be ready to treat on some issues.'
75. Sir A. Gascoigne (Moscow) to FO, 25 May 1953, PRO, FO 371, NS 1071/92 (106538).

The Soviet Union and Germany in the Late Stalin Period, 1950–3

Gerhard Wettig

Until a few years ago, analysis and interpretation of Stalin's foreign policies had to be based almost exclusively on such statements, notes and similar documents as had been intended for public consumption. While these materials are most relevant for Soviet interaction with the outside world given the fact that the effort to influence foreign audiences was a crucial part of the USSR's foreign policy, particularly after the Cold War had begun in mid-1947, evidence from private government sources is essential for both information on intrabureaucratic detail and assessment of underlying intent. It therefore adds considerably to previous historical knowledge that documents from Russian archives have recently become available, if only in bits and pieces.[1] The following attempt to assess and to interpret the general traits of Stalin's policy towards post-war Germany in the early 1950s is based on such a number of detailed studies for which material from Russian archives has been utilized. This basis includes results from my own research and from that of other historians.[2]

STALIN'S POLICIES IN POST-WAR GERMANY DURING THE PRECEDING YEARS

Stalin's policies in occupied Germany were dual-track in character from the very start. On the one hand, they were both unilaterally designed by the USSR and directed at Communist transformation. The Soviet occupation authorities spared no effort to fill all crucial political and administrative positions by reliable Communist cadres, to secure a dominant role for the KPD and hence to prevent the other parties from developing their activities, to create a united 'anti-Fascist' front which practically obliged the 'bourgeois' parties to loyalty *vis-à-vis* the Communists, to prepare for state ownership of industry under the pretence of 'de-Nazification', and to enforce land reform for destroying the 'class enemy's' social basis in the countryside as well. These measures, taken as early as 1945, marked the beginning of Soviet-type 'democratic transformation' in the Soviet zone. In 1946, the KPD took over the SPD in an act of imposed 'unification of the two workers' parties'. One year later, a process of intensifying Sovietization was initiated when Stalin had decided for all-encompassing confrontation with the Western countries. On the other hand, however, the Soviet leader displayed political caution, professed adherence to four-power cooperation in Germany for a while, and continued to declare his willingness to abide by 'all-democratic' principles in Germany even after the open breach with the West had occurred. Until his death, he never wavered in presenting himself as a partisan of German unity and in saying that he was willing to press the West for appropriate policies. At the end of World War II, the Soviet authorities also denied any intention to introduce Communism in the defeated country. After the cesura of 1947, the Kremlin embarked upon a course of more open Sovietization in its part of Germany but continued to stick to the claim that its policies conformed to the agreements reached by the four powers and that they provided a basis for East–West consensus for this reason.

Underlying was a concept of how Soviet power was to extend beyond the USSR's borders when victory over Hitler allowed the Red Army to occupy foreign territories. Stalin not only decided to renounce the other lands' incorporation into the Soviet state; he also felt that he had to create at least an appearance of taking into account Western, particularly American, interests by postulating structural differences between the countries under Soviet domination and the USSR itself. To suit this purpose, the Soviet leader invented the category of 'people's democracy' as a socio-political order which allegedly provided a connecting link between Western and Soviet 'forms of democracy'. The political objective was not only to neutralize Western objections against the Soviet effort to remodel the East European countries; it was also intended as a rationale which would allow a pro-Soviet order to expand westward if the correlation of power would permit that to occur in the future. Stalin appears to have hoped that such possibilities would open themselves after Roosevelt had told him at Yalta that US troops would stay in Europe for but a few years.[3] If the Americans would withdraw, the West European countries would certainly be unable to provide a sufficient counterweight to Soviet power on the Continent. The concept of 'people's democracy' which de-emphasized the Soviet element in the socio-political structure of the East European countries but shaped the crucial patterns of power along Soviet lines, might then become a useful tool of expanding Moscow's political influence which, in Stalin's perception, was invariably linked to changes in the domestic power structures of the countries concerned.

In the case of Germany, there was even more need to display caution and hence to avoid the image of socio-political transformation in an anti-Western sense. This is why Stalin felt that it was inappropriate to profess any pursuit of Communist aims and decided in favour of an 'all-democratic' policy line which was said to be compatible with the 'bourgeoisie's' interests. While the image thus intended required some concessions to the Western idea of democracy such as, in particular, the acceptance of a multiparty system, these concessions were largely more apparent than real. For instance, the multi-party system established in East Germany was largely stripped of the elements of both the parties' individual independence and their mutual competition. A political consensus resulting from policy-making on the basis of the Communists' *de facto* leading role was made obligatory; political divergence among parties was stifled by common 'anti-Fascist' principles being imposed on all of them; the Communists were given the crucial political positions in public administration with only limelight and largely uninfluential positions being reserved for the other parties. 'It must look democratic, but we must have everything in our hands', Ulbricht instructed his fellow-Communists.[4] The political structures in the Soviet zone were clearly devised with a view towards all of Germany. It was for this purpose that, previous inter-Allied agreement on allowing but local political activities to the Germans at the beginning notwithstanding, Stalin unilaterally ordered a German Party system to be established in Soviet-occupied Berlin shortly after the war had ended: he intended to fix crucial political patterns not only in his own sphere of influence but in the Western zones as well.

The Soviet leader's attempt to make Berlin the determining centre of German political life and to shape German politics on the basis of the USSR's predominant influence in the Berlin region failed, however. The emerging political forces in Germany outside the Soviet-occupied territory refused to follow the lead from Berlin. This made Stalin increasingly rely on the claims he derived from the USSR's role as an occupation power. To the extent that his Western partners proved unwilling to accept these claims, Stalin was bound to direct his demands also against them. It is in this context that Soviet diplomacy reinterpreted the Potsdam Agreement so as to turn it, since July 1946, into a political instrument which was to delegitimatize Western occupation policies. The socio-political order established in the Soviet zone was explicitly presented as the very model of how the inter-Allied agreements had to be put into practice. Foreign Minister Molotov tabled demands which implied that, on this basis, the USSR was to exercise a right of political intervention in West German affairs. Also, Soviet participation in control over the Western zones' industrial heartland, the Ruhr District, was postulated.

The crucial point was to oblige the three Western powers to make decisions on the Western zones only on the basis of preceding agreement with the USSR. It was this claim which triggered the open outbreak of East–West conflict in Germany more than anything else. Both Britain and the United States increasingly felt that co-operation with Moscow was possible only when punitive measures against the Germans were on the agenda.[5] But whenever constructive measures were discussed which would allow for the Western zones' problems of material sustenance to be solved, the Soviet side would prevent any decision. This came to be increasingly seen as intolerable in Western capitals – all the more so since any Western influence on matters in the Soviet zone was *a priori* excluded. Washington eventually decided that there was no possibility but to go forward solving the problems in West Germany without Soviet consent. When this decision was finalized and the Marshall Plan with West Germany to be included was announced, Stalin perceived this as a declaration of political war to himself and reacted by embarking upon a course of anti-Western confrontation.[6]

It would have been logical if Moscow's display of open hostility against the West[7] had resulted in discontinuation of insistence on inter-Allied co-operation and hence in renunciation of the previous dual-track policy. In the Soviet zone, transition to a 'people's democratic' order of a distinctly Soviet type was initiated.[8] But at the same time, Stalin did not renounce his claim that decisions on West Germany could be made only in agreement with him and therefore stuck to his demand for four-power co-operation. Given the current East–West relationship of confrontation, the Soviet side felt that such co-operation had to be imposed on unwilling Western powers. To generate the necessary political pressure, the Kremlin appealed to the Germans to unite with the USSR in taking an anti-Western stand and to make the Western occupants accept German unity and evacuate their troops from German soil. What Stalin thus sought was to restore the situation of the early post-war years and to produce a development which he had then hoped for. The crucial point was restoration of the Soviet veto on West German matters so as to allow for no unapproved action outside the USSR's sphere of control.

There were two postulates which were designed to advance this aim: conclusion of a peace treaty with Germany and restoration of German unity. Either demand was presented as Soviet advocacy of the German national interest – an advocacy which allegedly could not but make the Germans identify with the Soviet cause. To the extent that the Germans were free to make their political choice, however, they decided in their overwhelming majority to side with the West, as was clearly demonstrated during the Berlin Blockade. In mid-1949, the Soviet Government indicated by the stand it took at the Paris Conference that it realized its political defeat.[9] But Stalin did not relinquish his hopes altogether but was waiting for new opportunities.

SOVIET ADVOCACY OF GERMAN UNITY, 1950–1

In the light of some archival evidence which has become available in recent years, it seems clear that Stalin has never contemplated military attack which he felt might involve him in military conflict with the United States.[10] On the contrary, it can be concluded that the Soviet leader was quite fearful of the possibility that an armed clash might occur. It may seem paradoxical, therefore, that the intensification of East–West confrontation which occurred in 1950 resulted from Communist military aggression approved by Stalin. The explanation is that the Soviet leader, who had initially been unwilling to support Kim Il-Sung's plan of attack against South Korea, eventually allowed himself to be persuaded that this would be a risk-free action which was certain of instant success.[11] But this assumption was falsified when US President Truman decided that what he saw as the beginning of a global Communist attack had to be stopped before it could develop further. This perception was largely shared by America's allies. It entailed Western concerns that Communist aggression had to be expected soon in Europe as well. As a consequence, the need for both a sizeable Western defence force with US participation on the Continent and a West German military contribution to the Western effort imposed itself on the minds of crucial leaders in Washington, London and, increasingly so, also in Paris. Chancellor Adenauer in Bonn was willing to go along with such demands feeling that this would give the Federal Republic a good chance to get better protection and more sovereign rights than it had enjoyed so far.[12]

This turn of events terrified Stalin. There are indications that he saw himself trapped by the Korean War. After all, the US Secretary of State had stated in January 1950 that Korea was outside his country's defence parameter and then the US President had responded to North Korea's attack by military intervention.[13] This seemingly deceitful provocation by the United States appears to have been perceived by the Soviet leader as part of a political manoeuvre designed to create domestic conditions in Western countries which would allow large-scale military preparations for attack against the USSR.[14] While the Kremlin had seen formation of German military cadres in the Soviet zone to be imperative as early as in 1947–8,[15] prospective inclusion of German soldiers into military forces built up by the Western powers was deemed absolutely unacceptable. Therefore, Stalin perceived the Korean War's political impact as being disastrous indeed. At the same time, however, he saw a chance resulting from the challenge with which he had been confronted. Rearmament was very unpopular among the West Germans. It appeared to the Soviet leader that this would allow Moscow to protest against Western plans for West German 'remilitarization' a strong political weapon in the ongoing struggle for the Germans' allegiance, particularly if the USSR would find some way of linking positive promise to rejection of Western rearmament plans.

It was this rationale which shaped Soviet policies since autumn 1950. An incipient statement made by the three Western Foreign Ministers, saying that West German contribution to the Western defence was under consideration, was almost instantly followed by Eastern appeals to the West Germans that they resist the occupants' designs.[16] On 21 October 1950, the Eastern Foreign Ministers were called together in Prague to voice their protest against West German 'remilitarization' and to advocate both quadripartite decision on 'conditions for the formation of a united peaceloving democratic German state' and quadripartite conclusion of a 'peace treaty with Germany' which would provide for 'restoration of the unity of the German state'.[17]

Mere repetition of Moscow's long-standing intention to conclude a peace treaty and have Germany united, however, seemed insufficient. Therefore, the DDR's Prime Minister Grotewohl was instructed to come up with a public proposal for German unification which had been put together in Moscow.[18] On 30 November 1950, the East German Head of Government sent a much-publicized letter to Chancellor Adenauer suggesting that peaceful understanding among the Germans rather than West German participation in preparing war had to be put on the agenda. An All-German Constituent Council to be formed by representatives of the two German states on the basis of parity, was to prepare simultaneously both the formation of an all-German Government and the conditions for holding all-German elections.[19] Such a step would not oblige the Eastern side to anything since the leaders of the DDR – and through them Stalin and the other Soviet foreign policymakers – would not have to make any concession when practical details came under discussion, whereas the West German side would have been put in the situation of standing up against the Western powers by the very fact of its willingness to enter into negotiations which would lack Western approval. On this basis, Stalin would have got the say in West Germany he had wanted ever since 1945 without having to give anything in return.

The proposal submitted by Grotewohl was clearly not a serious offer for negotiation. It was a propaganda ploy which served the purpose of mobilizing West German pro-reunification sentiment for the Soviet cause. It cannot have come as a surprise to Stalin, therefore, that Adenauer's Government was not impressed by the offer but continued political co-operation with the Western powers as before. But among the more national-minded West Germans, some feeling emerged that the proposal might open a chance for East–West interaction in Germany which might eventually result in German unity. The

Chancellor of the Federal Republic had to take this into consideration and hence was obliged to take issue with this view. The appropriate way to do this was to exploit the issue of free elections. After all, it was precisely those elections which both the SED leaders and their Soviet masters had shunned in recent years, and there was hardly anyone in West Germany who was willing to accept unification on the basis of submission to Moscow. In addition to that, there was already much public discussion in West Germany focusing on Eastern unwillingness to allow for free unification which would have to be based on unimpeded all-German elections.

From a democratic perspective, the East German leaders' failure to accept that their rule's legitimacy be tested by elections had to be the crucial motive for rejection. A large majority of the West German population felt indeed that political freedom was more important than national unity and that, for this reason, reunification was desirable and acceptable only if the power structures in the future Germany would be based on the free will of the people as expressed in free elections. Grotewohl's letter did not contain anything which would have taken this prevailing attitude into account. For this reason, it was comparatively easy for Adenauer's Government to decline the offer saying that it did not provide for Germany's reunification through free elections. To be sure, this did not imply West German acceptance of a military contribution to Western defence. What was more, the prevailing anti-'remilitarization' mood in the country left Stalin with a psychological lever in the Federal Republic even when he failed to come to meet West German unification requirements.

Western plans for the Federal Republic's rapid inclusion into the Western defence system were increasingly delayed due to problems of intra-Western decision-making. So Stalin continued to have a chance of making impact on West Germany. By summer 1951 at latest, the Soviet leader seems to have understood that free all-German elections were relevant in providing political credibility to Eastern reunification offers. It was in September 1951 that his capacity to draw the necessary conclusions was first tested. After the summer pause, the Western powers and Adenauer's Government made a new start in getting the West German defence contribution going. On 14 September 1951, the Foreign Ministers of the United States, Britain and France announced a detailed programme on how agreement on both Federal Republic's military integration and its prospective status as an ally with equal rights was to be negotiated. The Kremlin reacted instantly. Grotewohl was ordered in great haste on the following day to counter the Western declaration by another reunification offer.[20] Addressing the DDR *Volkskammer*, the Prime Minister advocated convocation of an All-German Consultation which largely resembled the body he had proposed on 30 November 1951. There were, however, two new elements: The task of talking about free all-German election was emphasized, and the Eastern side no longer insisted on the number of representatives being necessarily equal for both sides.[21] At a closer look, the differences were more apparent than real. The DDR failed to commit itself to both concrete procedures which would have guaranteed freedom of all-German elections. Also, there were no provisions that all-German elections would be the basis for both the crucial decisions on the socio-political order and the ruling personnel of the prospective all-German state. So everything remained open to negotiations, which would have to be conducted with an Eastern veto always being around the corner. For Grotewohl's second modification was a concession only in semblance. It is true that the Eastern side was now willing to accept fewer negotiators than the Federal Republic would have, but as was expressly stated this did not mean that the DDR leadership would accept any decision to which it would not have given its full consent. In essence, the Eastern position had not changed at all.

During the following months, Eastern propaganda was seeking to make the West German public believe that the principle of free elections had been given full approval by the DDR. So, previous West German objections were said to have been met. There was no longer any reason to have doubts about the possibility of German reunification along the lines which had been formulated by the Federal Republic. If Adenauer's Government declined negotiations nonetheless, it was added, this demonstrated that the West German rulers did not want reunification under any conditions and allowed themselves to be guided by Western rather than German interests. In an effort to persuade the West German public, the DDR *Volkskammer* prepared a draft for a law on all-German elections which was presented to the public on 9 January 1952. As was alleged, this draft made clear beyond doubt that free elections would be guaranteed in all of Germany if only the Federal Republic was willing to allow for their being held. A closer look, however, reveals that a number of clauses were built into the draft which provided for vagueness and/or maintenance of DDR practices.[22] The other crucial issue – whether both the system and the regime of the future Germany would be determined by the elections or not – was not given any attention.

To sum up, Stalin's policy in 1950–1 basically continued along traditional lines. Just as during the period of 1947–50, the Soviet demands for a peace treaty with Germany and for restoration of German unity served the function of claiming back the chance which had been lost when the Western powers had decided to go forward in West Germany irrespective of the designs of the Soviet side. This concept presupposed emergence of a prevailing trend among the West Germans to side with the USSR against the Western powers. But as events had shown prior to 1950, German sympathies were in an overwhelmingly strong measure with the West wherever they could be voiced freely. It was this obstacle which Stalin sought to overcome by exploiting the anti-military mood which prevailed in the Federal Republic. The slogan of German reunification was used to bolster the Eastern appeal by providing a positive goal which rejection of 'militarism' allegedly served.

Only gradually did the Soviet decision-makers realize that the effectiveness of reunification appeals greatly depended on West German confidence in the Eastern side's willingness to allow for the prospective united German state to be built on free elections. At that point, the Kremlin was clearly in a difficult position. After all, Stalin saw extension of his power and influence to be essentially proportional to his ability to install 'friendly' regimes, the dependability of which he felt depended on authority established from above and on the effectiveness of Soviet control mechanisms. Neither would be possible if free elections were allowed to determine policies in the respective countries. In this case, spontaneity and unpredictability were bound to prevail. It is logical, therefore, that the Kremlin failed to produce convincing proposals on German reunification through free elections. This was a crucial dilemma which prevented Soviet counteraction against Western integration policies from making any decisive impact. Adequate perception of the problem by the Kremlin was hampered by ideological assumptions according to which any people, including the West Germans, were bound to be essentially in sympathy with the USSR's policies unless misguided by the enemy's disinformation which, however, can be effectively countered by one's own effort at political enlightenment. It would not be surprising if future historical evidence would show that Stalin and the other Soviet leaders (whose policy assessments were guided by ideas which could not be applied to the Western world) failed to grasp the full extent to which they were trapped in the free elections' dilemma.

THE CLIMAX OF STALIN'S POLITICAL EFFORT IN GERMANY IN 1952

Were the Soviet decision-makers capable of understanding their problem and changing their policies accordingly? The occasion for this to reveal itself was not far off. In winter 1951–2, the negotiations between the Western powers and West Germany on both a defence contribution and a sovereign status entered a decisive stage. After one last crucial issue between the Western partners had been settled, the foreign policy-makers in Moscow felt that the time had come to initiate some counteraction. Stalin authorized a procedural agenda worked out by Soviet diplomats under the aegis of Deputy Foreign Minister Gromyko.[23] In accordance with that, the East German Government sent a note – the wording of which had been received from the Foreign Ministry in Moscow – to the four powers on 13 February 1952 asking them to accelerate the conclusion of a peace treaty with Germany so as to allow the German people to unite.[24] The next step was that, on 20 February 1952, the Soviet Government gave a positive reply to this request.[25] Two and a half weeks later, on 10 March 1952, Moscow directly addressed Washington, London and Paris sending a note which demanded a peace treaty with Germany to be concluded within a short period of time. On this basis, both restoration of a united German state and withdrawal of the occupation troops from German territory was to be effected. While these demands had been central points of the USSR's agenda for Germany ever since 1947, the new element in the note was that principles to guide the prospective agreement on Germany were spelt out. What was conspicuously missing, however, was any indication on how German unity was to be achieved under the umbrella of the peace treaty sought.[26] It was only from other statements, mostly from those of SED leaders, that the Kremlin's insistence on its previous demand for reunification through negotiations between the two German states became clear.[27]

Thus Moscow was unwilling to allow for a procedure of reunification other than one which would imply an unlimited veto, and hence full co-determination, to be given to the SED leaders. This was tantamount to Soviet refusal to consider unification along democratic lines. This conclusion is fully confirmed by the provisions entering the 10 March 1952 note. To be sure, the wording of the final version may be seen as somewhat vague, but comparison with preceding drafts makes it clear that the note's final verbiage (which is identical with the terminology traditionally used to describe the DDR's socio-political order) simply provides substitutes for the unambiguous Communist requirements stated in the first drafts. As Soviet policy-makers expressly stated on that occasion, they felt it was inexpedient to be too clear about the underlying purpose.[28] There are also other indications of Soviet intransigence with regard to concessions to West German democratic demands such as, in particular, reunification on the basis of free elections:

- In their private discussions, the decision-makers in Moscow referred to the note as an instrument of political struggle being waged against the Western Governments and their partner in Bonn. They neither expected nor hoped a positive Western response to result.[29] They rather aimed at mobilizing the West German population against Adenauer's Government, at bringing it down and at thereby wrecking the Western powers' political and military position in the Federal Republic.[30]

- Private discussions among the policy-makers in Moscow also clearly reflected the dichotomic world view which Stalin's envoy Zhdanov had announced as mandatory at the Cominform founding session in September 1947: There were two camps opposing each other in absolute hostility.[31] Such a perception of global politics did not allow for the idea of concession and compromise. In accordance with that, the non-Communist political forces in the Federal Republic who refused unconditional submission to cadres under Soviet control, were seen and treated as enemies even if they accepted crucial tenets of Moscow's position on German unification. In this perspective, not only the social democratic opposition but also Heinemann's Fundamentalist Reunification Party were not viewed as potential partners in prospective negotiations.

- It is equally significant that the leading SED circles who were traditionally haunted by the fear of being sacrificed to divergent Soviet foreign policy priorities (as notably the Polish Communist Party's fate in the inter-war years suggested), did not show the slightest discomfort in spring 1952. On the contrary, the East German Communists then displayed confidence that things went their way.[32] Also, those Soviet leaders who are on the historical record as staunch hard-liners in the German problem were happy. For example, Molotov who participated extensively in preparing the text for the 10 March 1952 note, clearly felt that it was absolutely innocuous as can be gauged not only from his willing co-operation at the time but equally from his remark when, one year later, he perceived Beria to be willing to abandon the DDR: such a thing would have been unthinkable as long as Stalin had been alive![33]

- It fits into the picture that the DDR's subsequent openly confrontationist course against West Germany and Western democracy was initiated in Moscow at the very time when the March note put a peace treaty with Germany and the restoration of German unity on the East–West agenda.[34] The measures then prepared for the DDR under the label of 'building Socialism' gave East Germany the status of a fully-fledged 'people's democracy' in analogy to the other countries of the Soviet-dominated bloc in Europe. Not by coincidence, it was also envisaged to have the East German military cadres, which had been secretly put up since mid-1948, transformed into an undisguised national army – a plan which was dropped only later.[35]

- The fact that the 10 March 1952 note was not initiated by Stalin but by executives at a level even below Gromyko, simply indicates that the previous policy line was being continued. If a political change would have been intended, no one but Stalin himself would have been entitled to take the first step. Subordinate officials in one of the Soviet Foreign Ministry departments were free to submit proposals only when they offered to make a contribution to implementing policies already established.

Obviously, the Soviet decision-makers had not concluded in March 1952 that they had to satisfy the West German demand for reunification on the basis of free elections. This triggers the question: What political purpose was the note to serve if no concessions were offered to buy what the Soviet side was seeking: that is, prevention of West Germany's inclusion into the West European defence system? The difficulty of finding a persuasive answer to this underlies much of Western observers' speculation on what the note was allegedly bound to mean. One side felt that Stalin simply made an exercise in propaganda since there were clearly no substantial concessions the West Germans could hope for. The adherents of the opposing school of thought, however, argued the other way round. Assuming that the Soviet leader could not possibly have meant no political business at all, they concluded that he must have had substantial concessions in mind even though he did not indicate them. The picture which emerges on the basis of the evidence now available from the Russian Foreign Ministry archive, does not conform to either of these views. The Soviet note of 10 March 1952 was designed to foster neither diplomacy nor propaganda. The intended objective was to give a 'mighty impetus' to the 'movement for democratic unity and a just peace' which Communist cadres in the Federal Republic were ordered to organize against Adenauer's policies and Adenauer's Government.[36] This, on its part, indicates a fundamental Soviet misperception of the political situation in West Germany. How could the decision-makers in Moscow believe that the note might serve as a powerful instrument to influence the country's public against Western policies and make it susceptible to Communist appeals when the note did not even hint at Soviet preparedness for allowing a free and democratic united Germany to emerge? Seen from a German perspective, the Soviet side wanted the Federal Republic to abandon everything it had thus far acquired – integration into an increasingly prosperous Western world, Western protection against the Soviet threat and, last but not least, the benefits of a democratic order – without offering anything in return.

One can argue, of course, that national reunification as such was an interest which would move the Germans to make great sacrifices. While the Soviet decision-makers appear to have felt that this was precisely the mood they would be able to exploit, the order of priorities which prevailed in the Federal Republic was actually putting national unity behind political freedom and presumably also behind material welfare. There were more than ten million West Germans who had poured into the country from the East after having directly suffered from Soviet power and/or the SED regime. They expounded what the Eastern alternative to the Western model would be like. This was an unsurmountable obstacle to the Eastern effort at influencing, mobilizing and organizing the West German 'masses' for Soviet goals against the West.

To be sure, there was widespread West German antipathy to rearmament, which resulted from the policies pursued by the Adenauer Government and the Western powers. Opposition against it was indeed sufficiently strong in the country that, for some time, the West German Chancellor was in acute danger of being ousted.[37] But the Soviet leaders misread the message when they concluded that the West German public would be willing to identify itself with Moscow and East Berlin on this basis. As the subsequent political development was to demonstrate, it was just the other way round: the prevailing antipathies against both the USSR and Communism were helpful to Adenauer in combatting those of his opponents who wanted no military contribution towards Western defence. It was only later, after Stalin's death, that the ruling circles in Moscow grasped at last how much they had alienated the Germans: on 17 June 1953, the Germans in the USSR's own power sphere demonstrated that they were willing to take a great risk once they felt they might be able to rid themseves of Eastern repression. It was not coincidental that this became the turning point of Soviet policies towards Germany: from then on, all-German rhetoric was largely abandoned. The decision to do so was easy, since the Kremlin had failed to come close to the objective it had vainly sought on the basis of German unity being preserved, or respectively restored, ever since 1945: to secure a decisive say in West German affairs.

THE CAUSES OF STALIN'S FAILURE IN GERMANY

Stalin's mind was shaped by a dichotomic world view. In his perspective, the Soviet Union was the product of a fundamentally new order which was bound to challenge the old one. While the other side represented by the Western powers was seen as doomed in the end, it was clear that, for the time being, the USSR was both isolated in the global context and inferior to US capabilities. On the basis of this situation assessment, the Soviet leader devised a policy concept which was inherently contradictory. He was willing to exploit the opportunities provided by victory in World War II to the maximum extent possible.

His ambition could be satisfied without too many difficulties to the extent that the respective foreign countries were conquered by the Red Army. In Germany, however, things were more complicated. The Soviet military forces occupied only one, if central, part of the country. As long as the United States were present in the German theatre, the Kremlin leader felt unable to seek extension of influence and power by force. Under these premises, it appeared that the choice was between either restricting ambitions to the territory occupied or seeking to exercise influence on all of Germany in the context of inter-Allied co-operation. But Stalin wanted neither. He appeared to opt for co-operation, but only seemingly so. He intended that influence would only be exercised in an East–West direction, and was unwilling to accept reciprocal rights of the Western powers. This was the first inherent contradiction in Soviet policy which, after two years, resulted in total disruption of the four-power relations which, in Moscow's perspective, had always been basically antagonistic in character.

Soviet failure to enforce the exploitation of four-power co-operation to the partners' systematic detriment, entailed a change of policy which was also inherently contradictory. From then on, it was not the Western powers but the German people whose support the Soviet side wanted. But again, it was simply the other side's utilization for the USSR's purpose which was sought. The alleged partner was to provide any necessary political strength, and was not given any prospects that its own interests would be served. Stalin and the policy-makers around him did not cease to regard the Germans as objects of political control and material exploitation, and hence saw no need to allow German self-determination on the basis of free elections; he nonetheless expected the German people to attain the anti-Western political breakthrough which the Kremlin sought in Germany. If Stalin had traded German unification through free elections in return for the Federal Republic's abstention from integration into the West, he would have had an excellent chance to crucially weaken the West's geopolitical position in Western Europe. He would also, however, have run the risk of having Germany drop out of his power sphere. But in the wake of the open East–West confrontation he had initiated, Stalin felt it was paramount to consolidate control in Eastern and Central Europe rather than allow Soviet domination to be weakened, let alone jeopardized.[38]

Another crucial inherent contradiction in Stalin's policy lay in the clear divergence between Moscow's unification rhetoric and separation measures. At the very moment when the Soviet leader had decided to treat the US announcement of the Marshall Plan as a profoundly hostile act against the USSR, he began to systematically prepare his part of Germany for both full Communization and the establishment of separate statehood. Even at a time when, in the spring of 1952, he publicly displayed particular interest in German unity, he had also ordered measures to be taken for the physical seclusion of the DDR from the Federal Republic. As a result, the demarcation line between the two German states was largely closed at the end of May, allowing but a trickle of what had previously been a stream of inter-German border traffic. In late autumn 1952, the Soviet Foreign Ministry proposed a similar border regime for traffic between the two parts of Berlin.[39] In this case, however, Stalin felt inhibited by caution: he thought that he could not afford to disregard the City's special status which the Western powers had successfully defended during the blockade.

The fact that the USSR's leader was unwilling to pay a substantial price for the support against the Western powers that he sought from the German people – particularly the West Germans – requires explanation. Why was he nonetheless confident of enlisting all the Germans on his side? After all, he refrained from luring the Germans with anything other than the prospect of what in fact would have become Communist unification, but hoped nonetheless to have the Germans join in, while actually an overwhelming majority of the German people detested both the Soviet Union and the Communist regime. There was an underlying situational assessment in Moscow which was at extreme variance with the real situation. How can this be explained?

On the basis of the scant evidence thus far available, the question can be answered only by formulating some hypotheses:

1. The priority Stalin accorded to consolidation of control over his own power sphere, is likely to have absorbed his attention to such an extent that he became unable to realistically assess evidence from the other world in the West that was so different from everything he had become used to. It appears plausible that the natural outcome was impaired assessment of Western developments.
2. Stalin appears to have adhered to ideas absolutely opposed to the Western compromise ideal, which requires striking a balance of benefits among negotiating partners. As it seems, the Soviet leader saw himself in the role of a protagonist in an ongoing political struggle against the West. If this is correct, the natural consequence was that it was inconceivable for him to see the DDR as something which might potentially be traded against some other benefit. Instead, the East German state appeared as a bulwark designed to promote both defence and attack against the West's political positions.
3. Another element underlying Stalin's policies towards Germany may have been a large measure of ideological autism which was further increased by the fact that the executives in Moscow cherished an unconditional belief in their leader's superhuman wisdom.

Whatever Stalin said and did, no one among the Soviet policy-makers would have considered openly that it might possibly be an error. The god-like *vozhd* (a term for 'leader' which has connotations similar to that of the 'Führer' in Nazi terminology) was always right; questions could not be asked once his authority had settled the problem.

To sum up, Stalin's inability to understand German feeling made him come up with allegedly gracious offers to the German nation which were bound to be perceived by the addressees as predominantly threatening rather than essentially attractive. What resulted was a fundamentally wrong political approach to the German problem. A number of Western, particularly West German, observers, however, have felt that such an able politician as Stalin could not conceivably have erred to such an extent. The fact that he offered unification to the Germans and that he did so with emphasis, is then seen as an indication that some serious plan must have been behind his plea for unification even though it was never spelt out. The 'mere propaganda' hypotheses being dismissed, these observers conclude that the Soviet leader could not but have thought of serious business, that is genuine negotiations. Since respective evidence on the basis of Soviet sources is missing, all kinds of other arguments are put forward to make the point.[40] The logic underlying such considerations is that, on the basis of the kind of judgement we are used to in the West, Stalin's policy would have to be seen as irrational – an idea discarded as unimaginable. The possibility that Stalin may have acted on premises and perceptions quite different from those of the West, and that his judgement may have been grossly at variance with realities in Germany, is not taken into account. But this is precisely the conclusion which the evidence now available from ex-Soviet archives suggests to us. And it is not uncommon in history that individuals and groups who are alienated from each other by great ideological differences, are particularly prone to mutual misperception. This is to say, it is not a matter of Stalin's political and/or intellectual capacity if one concludes that he failed to see and to understand German attitudes correctly.

Notes

1. Thus far, hardly any documents on Soviet policies towards Germany have been published from Eastern archives. A notable exception is R. Badstübner, W. Loth (eds), *Wilhelm Pieck – Aufzeichnungen zur Deutschland-Politik 1945–1953* (Berlin: Akademie Verlag, 1994).
2. While quite a few studies on details of Stalin's post-war policy towards Germany have been written on the basis of new archival documents, efforts to evaluate this policy as a whole in the light of the emerging

evidence are conspicuously lacking. An exception to this is W. Loth, *Stalins ungeliebtes Kind. Warum Moskau die DDR nicht wollte* (Berlin: Rowohlt Verlag, 1994). In this book, Loth seeks to reaffirm his previous idea that Stalin wanted Germany's democratic unification all the time. For this purpose, he refers to the Pieck notes which, however, do not bear this out in the judgement not only of this author but overwhelmingly of other historians. There is also much other archival evidence against Loth's thesis. For review see, *inter alia*, P. Zolling, 'Mut ist oft sehr dumm', *Der Spiegel*, 25 (1994) 68–72; H. Köhler, 'Stalin – ein deutscher Demokrat', *Frankfurter Allgemeine Zeitung*, 2 August 1994.
3. *FRUS*, 'The Conferences at Malta and Yalta', *1945*, pp. 701–2.
4. W. Leonhard, *Die Revolution entlässt ihre Kinder* (Cologne–Berlin: Kiepenheuer & Witsch, 1955) pp. 357–8.
5. The fact that the Soviet side had been clearly heading towards confrontation in Germany before the open rift occurred in mid-June 1947 has been emphasized on the basis of new archival evidence by J. Laufer, 'Auf dem Weg zur staatlichen Verselbständigung der SBZ. Neue Quellen zur Münchener Konferenz der Ministerpräsidenten 1947', in J. Kocka (ed.), *Historische DDR-Forschung. Aufsätze und Studien* (Berlin: Akademie Verlag, 1993) pp. 27–56.
6. Cf. G. Wettig, *Entmilitarisierung und Wiederbewaffnung in Deutschland 1943–1955. Internationale Auseinandersetzungen über die Rolle der Deutschen in Europa* (Munich: Oldenbourg, 1967) pp. 192–8.
7. For the relevant official decisions taken at the constituent Cominform meeting (22-27 September 1947) see *Bol'shevik*, 19 (1947) 9–14.
8. G. Wettig, 'All-German Unity and East German Separation in Soviet Policy, 1947–1949', *Jahrbuch für Historische Kommunismusforschung* (1994) 122–39; G. Wettig, 'Die KPD als Instrument der sowjetischen Deutschland-Politik. Festlegungen 1949 und Implementierungen 1952', *Deutschland Archiv*, 8 (1994) 816–25.
9. Wettig, *Entmilitarisierung*, pp. 255–9.
10. See, for example, the evidence for Soviet defensive military planning in the German theatre in winter 1946-7 as provided by M.A. Garelow [M.A. Gareev], 'Woher droht Gefahr?', *Einheit*, 6 (1989) 573–89. The conclusion that Stalin sought to avoid war with any coalition in which the United States would participate, can also be drawn from Soviet behaviour during the Berlin Blockade of 1948–9 when precisely those steps were carefully avoided which carried the risk of war. See Wettig, *Entmilitarisierung*, p. 219; V. Gobarev, 'Soviet Military Plans and Activities during the Berlin Crisis, 1948-1949', paper presented at the conference 'The Soviet Union, Germany, and the Cold War, 1945–1962: New Evidence from Eastern Archives' (Essen, 28–30 June 1994), and M. Narinskii, 'Soviet Policy and the Berlin Blockade, 1948', paper presented at the same conference.
11. K. Weathersby, 'The Soviet Role in the Early Phase of the Korean War: New Documentary Evidence', *Journal of American-East Asian Relations*, 2, 4 (Winter 1993) 425–58.
12. Wettig, *Entmilitarisierung*, pp. 306–52.
13. Cf. Soviet Foreign Minister Vyshinskii's remark as quoted by G.D. Paige, 'Comparative Case Analysis of Crisis Decisions – Korea and Cuba', in C.F. Hermann (ed.), *International Crises* (New York: Free Press, 1972) pp. 48–9.
14. Cf. the evidence contained in documents of the Italian Communist Party as published in German translation in *Osteuropa* (1970) 699–706, A 703–718.

15. See my article 'Neue Erkenntnisse aus sowjetischen Geheimdokumenten über den militärischen Aufbau in der SBZ/DDR 1947–1952', *Militärgeschichtliche Mitteilungen*, 53 (1994) 199–219.
16. *Dokumente zur Aussenpolitik der Regierung der DDR*, Vol. 1 ([East] Berlin: Rütten & Loening, 1954) pp. 153–65.
17. *Dokumente zur Deutschlandpolitik der Sowjetunion*, Vol. 1 ([East] Berlin: Rütten & Loening, 1957) pp. 244–53.
18. Evidence for this can be found in the paper by M. Lemke, 'Eine deutsche Chance? Die innerdeutsche Diskussion um den Grotewohlbrief vom November 1950', presented at the conference 'The Soviet Union, Germany, and the Cold War, 1945–1962'.
19. Bundesministerium für gesamtdeutsche Fragen (Hrsg.), *Die Bemühungen der Bundesrepublik um Wiederherstellung der Einheit Deutschlands durch gesamtdeutsche Wahlen. Dokumente und Akten*, Teil 1, 4th edn (Bonn: 1958) pp. 21–2.
20. This can be concluded from a report by UP correspondent Zolling on 18 September 1951 resulting from information he had received in East Berlin. In 1963–4, I found a document containing direct information to this effect in the archives of the Ostbüro der SPD. The correctness of the conclusion is corroborated by display of great uncertainty and confusion among leading SED officials during the first days: there had obviously been no timely information and/or instruction to the relevant cadres on the proposal's intentions and implications.
21. O. Grotewohl, *Im Kampf um die einige Deutsche Demokratische Republik. Reden und Aufsätze*, Vol. 2 ([East] Berlin: Dietz Verlag, 1959) pp. 444–64.
22. *Die Bemühungen*, pp. 63–70.
23. G. Wettig, 'Die Deutschland-Note vom 10. März 1952 auf der Basis diplomatischer Akten des russischen Außenministeriums', *Deutschland Archiv*, 7 (1993) 786–805, particularly 797–8; Id., 'Stalin and German Reunification: Archival Evidence on Soviet Foreign Policy in Spring 1952', *The Historical Journal*, 2 (1994) 411-19; Id., 'Die Deutschland-Note vom 10. März 1952 nach sowjetischen Akten', in *Die Deutschlandfrage von der staatlichen Teilung Deutschlands bis zum Tode Stalins* (Berlin: Duncker & Humboldt, 1994) pp. 83–111; V. Mastny, 'Stalin's German Illusion', paper presented at the conference on 'The Soviet Union, Germany and the Cold War, 1945–1962', and L. van Dijk, 'The Stalin Note: Last Chance for Unification?', paper presented at the same conference.
24. *Dokumente zur Aussenpolitik*, pp. 73–5.
25. *Dokumente zur Deutschlandpolitik*, pp. 288–9.
26. *Ibid.*, pp. 289–93.
27. Cf., *inter alia*, DDR Prime Minister Grotewohl's official declaration before the *Volkskammer* on 14 March 1952 (Grotewohl, *Im Kampf*, pp. 79–80, 88–9); statement by Grotewohl on 21 March 1952 (*ibid.*, pp. 95–6, 100–1); remark made by Soviet Foreign Minister Vyshinskii when US *Chargé d'affaires* Cummings handed him the Western reply on 25 March 1952 (AP, 27 March 1952); Radio Moscow in Russian, 25 March 1952 at 9.25 a.m.; statement by SED Secretary General Ulbricht on 3 May 1952. See W. Ulbricht, *Zur Geschichte der deutschen Arbeiterbewegung. Aus Reden und Aufsätze*, Vol. 4 ([East] Berlin: Dietz, 1960) p. 336.
28. See Wettig, 'Die Deutschland-Note', pp. 793–5.
29. Cf. Soviet Foreign Minister Vyshinskii's reaction after having glossed over the Western reply handed to him by US *Chargé d'affaires* Cummings

on 25 March 1952 as reported by Cummings to the State Department. See H. Graml, 'Die Legende von der verpassten Gelegenheit', *Vierteljahreshefte für Zeitgeschichte*, [1981] 329.
30. Wettig, 'Die Deutschland-Note', pp. 798–803.
31. See the relevant documents in *Bol'shevik*, 19 (1947) 9–14.
32. See, for example, F. Schenk, 'Der lange Schatten Stalins. Erinnerungen an die Deutschland-Note 1952 und das Scheitern der Berliner Aussenministerkonferenz', *Frankfurter Allgemeine Zeitung*, 10 March 1994.
33. *Sto sorok besed s Molotovym. Iz dnevnika F. Chueva* (Moscow: Terra, 1991) p. 335.
34. Cf. Wettig, 'Die Deutschland-Note', pp. 802–3; *Wilhelm Pieck*, pp. 391–402.
35. See Wettig, 'Neue Erkenntnisse', 399–419.
36. Cf. G. Wettig, 'Die KPD als Instrument der sowjetischen Deutschland-Politik. Festlegungen 1949 und Implementierungen 1952', *Deutschland Archiv*, 8 (1994) 826–9.
37. H.-P. Schwarz, 'Adenauer als politischer Neuerer', in G. Langguth (ed.), *Macht bedeutet Verantwortung* (Cologne: Verlag Wissenschaft und Politik, 1994) p. 31.
38. This attitude had become quite plain when Stalin, shortly after the open outbreak of East–West confrontation in mid-1947, decided to forgo his considerable chances to prevent, or at minimum to delay, implementation of the Marshall Plan by obstructive participation in the Paris negotiations but rather to strengthen his control over the countries within his power sphere by not allowing them to get diplomatically involved with the West: cf. M.M. Narinskii, 'SSSR i plan Marshalla. Po materialam Arkhiva Prezidenta', *Novaia i noveishaia istoriia*, 2 (1993) 11–17.
39. M. Gribanov, 'Spravka obustanovlenii okhrany na sektornoy granitse v Berline', 4 December 1952, AVP RF, f. 082, op. 40, p. 98, d. 266, l. 15; Vyshinskii and Semënov to Stalin, 20 December 1952, *ibid.*, l. 18–22.
40. See, for example, R. Steininger, 'Eine Chance zur Wiedervereinigung? Darstellung und Dokumentation auf der Grundlage unveröffentlichter britischer und amerikanischer Akten', *Archiv für Sozialgeschichte*, 12 (1985).

23 Soviet–Italian Relations, 1945–8
Nina D. Smirnova

Post-war Soviet historiography lacks special works on the history of Soviet–Italian relations in the first phase of the Cold War.[1] Nor have many of the relevant documents been published in the USSR. In Italy, however, much has appeared on the subject. Of prime importance is the work by R. Morozzo della Rocca, *La politica estera italiana e l'Unione Sovietica (1944–1948)*.[2] Also noteworthy is the diary of Manlio Brosio, who was Italy's ambassador in Moscow in 1947–51.[3] The question of Italy's relations with Moscow and with Washington has been dealt with in numerous works by Italian historians.[4] In this chapter I have used documents from the Archive of Russian Foreign Policy (AVP RF) and also from the Russian Centre of Conservation and Study of Records for Modern History (RTsKhIDNI) which were not available to those Italian scholars.

In the first months after the re-establishment of diplomatic relations (25 October 1944) the prospects for Soviet–Italian relations looked good, especially after the end of the war.[5] Discontent with the policy of the Anglo-American occupying authorities led Italy's ruling circles to turn towards the Soviet Union and Eastern Europe. Symptomatic was the appointment as Foreign Minister of Count Carlo Sforza, who had shown himself, when in the same post in 1920–21, to be favourable to a 'Slavophil' line: he had sought to secure for Italy domination of the Adriatic through alliance with Yugoslavia and to counter-balance Britain's power in Europe through friendship with Russia. In a new preface to a pre-war book of his, reprinted in 1945, Sforza wrote that Russia would seek a peaceful future in order to develop her huge natural resources, so as to become a great industrial power comparable to the USA.[6] Sforza was a professional diplomat who had broken with Mussolini's regime at its very outset and gone abroad.[7] Unfortunately for him, however, the fact that he spent the war years in the USA caused both Churchill and the Soviet leaders to see him as an American agent.

The Prime Minister at that time, De Gasperi, also looked amicably upon Russia, whose right he recognized to be the protector of the Balkan peoples, a role in which he thought Russia represented no threat to Italy.[8] That his Government sought *rapprochement* with the USSR is shown by many conversations between Italian and Soviet diplomats which are recorded in the AVP RF.[9] Until 1947 it was customary to give the post of deputy Foreign Minister in the Italian Government to a Communist. Italy's ambassadors to the USSR were persistent in their efforts to develop friendly relations between these two countries.[10]

The Soviet Ambassador to Italy, M.A. Kostylev, set out in a letter to Molotov a detailed programme for diplomatic activity in Italy and the Mediterranean region generally.[11] In this letter he noted that the Bonomi Government enjoyed little authority in the country, having been installed by the Anglo-American military administration, and said that the immense prestige of the Soviet Union should be used to influence political developments in Italy, including support for the campaign to replace the monarchy by a republic. The USSR should do what it could in the sphere of trade to frustrate America's plan to dominate the Italian economy. As regards territorial problems, Kostylev thought that Istria, Gorizia, Gradisca, Zara and the adjoining islands should be ceded to Yugoslavia, though he did not mention Trieste. Similarly, Italy's islands in the Aegean should be ceded to Greece. The island of Saseno (Sazan), in the Strait of Otranto, should be returned to Albania: this was important from the strategic standpoint, especially for Yugoslavia. In the post-war period the USSR proved unable to play the economic role advocated by Kostylev, but the climate of friendship continued, as can be seen from the record of Molotov's talk with the Italian Ambassador on 13 September 1945.[12] A few months later, in May 1946, Molotov met De Gasperi to discuss some questions that had arisen at the Peace Conference. The Soviet leader supported Italy's application for membership of the United Nations.[13] Actually, Italy was accepted as a member only in December 1955, and it was the USSR that prevented its acceptance until then. In the spring of 1946, however, the Communist leader Togliatti was in the Italian Government and it looked as though his Party might be victorious in the parliamentary elections: Molotov naturally favoured admission to UNO for Italy in those circumstances.

Among attempts to develop Italo-Soviet trade relations in the 1945–7 period was the initiative taken by Professor G. Pazzi, in February 1945. This economist proposed to Kostylev that an Italian trade mission visit the USSR to discover possibilities for economic exchanges.[14] He also expressed hope that the Soviets would help Italy to resist American attempts to get control of Italy's oil requirements.[15] The Soviet Ambassador's cool response seems to have been due to his Government's expectation that the Left would soon come to power in Italy and their consequent unwillingness to enter into such commitments with the existing 'bourgeois' Government. The stonewalling is illustrated by incidents recorded in Kostylev's diary in which he rebuffs

Italian requests for coal and oil by referring to the damaged condition of the Donbas mines and the USSR's own domestic needs. When the Italians offered to send specialists to help in Russia's reconstruction, the Soviet Ambassador changed the subject, complaining about hostile articles in Italy's newspapers. Other Italian initiatives in this sphere were similarly rebuffed.[16]

When the Soviets persisted in their protests about the attitude of certain Italian newspapers, the official head of the Italian Foreign Ministry explained the difference between a totalitarian and a democratic regime. 'Under Mussolini a single telephone call would have been enough for no more to be seen not only of the publication in question but also of its publisher.'[17] Suspicion on Moscow's part was not reduced by Italian diplomats' protestations that their Government wanted to stay clear of blocs and to maintain equally good relations with both the USA and the USSR.[18] Italy's attitude did not alter even after her acceptance of the Marshall Plan.[19]

The desire of Italy's ruling circles for closer relations with the USSR coincided with that of the Left elements.[20] The latter counted on winning the parliamentary elections of 18 April 1948, provided that the Soviet Union showed understanding of Italy's national interests, particularly with regard to the fate of Trieste. The Soviets had moved from support of Yugoslavia's claim to Trieste to the compromise arrangement of the 'Free Territory of Trieste' and the position of the Italian CP had changed accordingly. In 1945 and until early 1946 the Party had suffered isolation through its pro-Yugoslav stance on Trieste, which, indeed, lacked enthusiastic backing even among its members.[21] The situation was complicated by the Yugoslavs' reference to the assurance given by Stalin to Tito that he would get Trieste.[22] Already at the beginning of 1946, however, the Italian CP's position began to change. The Soviet Party leaders had decided that 'Trieste must be given to the Italians so that the Italian Communists can win the elections'.[23]

The Italian Communists also hoped for a Soviet gesture in the realm of economic aid to their country. In May 1947 a Soviet women's delegation had visited Italy, and one of its members, an official of the Soviet Party's Foreign Policy Department, talked with Togliatti. In her report she said that, being aware of the USSR's economic difficulties, he had not officially asked for economic aid, but she pointed out that, in view of the forthcoming elections, 'any step taken in that direction by the Soviets would have enormous importance for us'.[24] However, this hint seems to have met with no response.

In December 1947 the Italian Communist leader Secchia visited the USSR and had talks with Zhdanov. From the Soviet archives we know that he asked not only for Soviet subsidies for his Party but also for economic aid to Italy from the USSR.[25] The pro-Communist leader of the Italian Socialists, Nenni, had been assured by Malenkov that if 'the democratic forces' came to power in Italy, the USSR would send wheat and coal, but Secchia urged that this aid be given *before* the elections. 'We are very much afraid that, if the popular bloc wins, America will strangle us economically. A public announcement of aid from the Soviet Union would guarantee us against that.' To which Zhdanov replied that such a guarantee would have to be thought about carefully, 'lest it be taken as interference in Italy's internal affairs'.[26] Secchia tried to argue, saying that many Italians thought that only the USA was able to help Italy and that the USSR could not, because it lacked the material possibilities. At first it seemed that Zhdanov had been moved by this argument, and when Secchia met him some days later the Italian began by saying: 'We have no doubt that, with the aid of the CPSU(B), we shall achieve complete victory.' But Zhdanov told him that he had discussed the matter 'with our great leader, Comrade Stalin', and the latter had ruled against Secchia's proposal, saying that if they acted on it they would be seen as behaving like the Americans, interfering in Italy's domestic affairs.[27]

Probably, Stalin did not want to encourage the Italian Communists' 'parliamentary illusions', which had been criticized at the first meeting of the Cominform. Nevertheless, the Communists and Socialists were able to make something, in their election campaign, of the Soviet note of February 1948 which favoured the return to Italy of her (pre-Fascist) colonies. This retreat from the 'anti-colonial' position was dictated by pragmatic calculations: the USSR preferred to see in the Mediterranean region a weak Italy rather than a strong Anglo-American bloc.[28]

In that same month Moscow began to come round to the idea that there should be economic negotiations with Italy, after all.[29] The Italian Government had asked for such negotiations in a note of 12 January 1948. S.P. Kozyrev, the deputy head of the First European Department of the USSR's Ministry of Foreign Affairs, advised his principals to respond favourably. He referred to the long-drawn-out affair of Italy's reparations payments. At that time the Italians saw no possibility of fulfilling them before 1949. After presenting proposals for dealing with this problem, Kozyrev put these aside for future consideration. For the present he favoured entering into trade talks with Italy, and considerably softened the reply to the Italian note which had been prepared in Mikoian's department. 'The arrival of an Italian trade delegation in Moscow and the opening of negotiations would undoubtedly produce favourable echoes in Italian democratic circles, which is especially important just now, with the parliamentary elections coming up. These negotiations could also help Italy's democratic forces in their struggle against the Marshall Plan.' Not until August 1948, however, was agreement reached on the composition and date of arrival of the Italian delegation, to be headed by a well-known economist and leader of the Republican Party, U. La Malfa. He signed with Molotov a treaty on trade and navigation. Signed also were documents on the payment of reparations to the USSR out of the current production of Italian industry.

The agreements arrived at in December 1948 marked the highest point in Soviet–Italian relations in the first post-war years. Unfortunately, the period in which they were prepared and signed coincided with the period when Italy abandoned neutrality and opted for 'Atlanticism'. A bi-polar system became established in international relations, and Soviet–Italian relations finally sank into the background. Sforza, who had been such a keen promoter of a new Eastern policy, radically reviewed his system of values. On 15 November 1948, in a speech at Carrara, he put forward two tasks as having priority – struggle for revision of the peace treaty, as Italy's immediate aim, and, after that, the creation of a European federation.

Once Italy joined the group of countries bound together by the Marshall Plan there was no choice open to her but the one she made. Only for the period 1945–6 can one speak of opportunities lost by Soviet foreign policy. The year 1947 was the turning-point in relations between the two countries. The notorious 'class approach' hindered the development of normal, mutually beneficial relations. The Italians could not understand why it was not possible to go to the USSR to help restore what had been destroyed during the war, or why the Russians refused their tempting offer to create a mixed Italo-Soviet airways company for the Moscow–Rome route – their fear of getting infected by the bourgeois way of life 'over there', or of allowing foreign spies to fly over Soviet territory. All that was far from helpful to the improvement of relations: and both the USA and the USSR built firm structures within which to contain their respective allies ...

Notes

1. The only work dealing with Soviet–Italian relations in the period concerned here – A.S. Protopopov, *Vneshnaia politika Italii posle vtoroi morovoi voiny* – appeared 30 years ago. Reflecting as it does the official view of these relations held at that time in the USSR Ministry of Foreign Affairs, it has itself become an historical document. Naturally, the three-volume *Historiia Italii* (Vol. 3, published in 1971), in the little it had to say about foreign policy, denounced the 'Atlanticism' alleged to have been inherent in De Gasperi's cabinet from the outset.
2. This book was published in Rome in 1984. It was reviewed by N.D. Smirnova in *Novaia i noveishaia istoriia*, 1 (1988). On the ideas regarding Eastern policy held by Count Sforza, De Gasperi's Foreign Minister, see G. Petracchi, 'Carlo Sforza e il mondo sovietico 1917–1950 (Apparenze diplomatiche e realtà psicologiche)', *Il Politico*, 2 (1984).
3. M. Brosio, *Diari di Mosca, 1947–1951* (Bologna: 1986).

4. E. Ortona, *Anni d'America. La ricostruzione 1944–1951* (Bologna: 1984); P. Quaroni, *Valigia diplomatica* (Milan: 1956); Id., *Il mondo di un ambasciatore* (Milan: 1965); B. Vigezzi (ed.), *La dimensione atlantica e le relazioni internazionali nel dopoguerra (1947–1949)* (Milan: 1987); E. Di Nolfo, *Le paure e le speranze degli italiani, 1943–1953* (Milan: 1986); P. Pastorelli, *La politica estera italiana del dopoguerra* (Bologna: 1987); R. Quartararo, *Italia e Stati Uniti. Gli anni difficili, 1945–1952)* (Naples: 1986).
5. The Parri cabinet of 15 June to 24 November 1945 was succeeded by five cabinets between December 1945 and 1948, all headed by A. De Gasperi, who was thus at the head of Italy's foreign policy throughout the period 1945–6, having been Foreign Minister under Parri. From October 1946 to February 1947, P. Nenni was Foreign Minister. In De Gasperi's third cabinet, that is, from 2 February 1947, and in all his remaining cabinets, Count Sforza was Foreign Minister.
6. R. Morozzo della Rocca, *La politica estera italiana e l'Unione Sovietica (1944–1948)* (Rome: 1985) p. 417.
7. Like many other Italian politicians, Sforza did not understand the Soviet politico-economic system. Brosio recalls, on the first page of his Moscow diary, that he met in Warsaw, on his way to the Soviet capital, an Italian engineer who had spent a long time in Russia, knew the country well, and depicted Moscow life under the Stalin regime in the darkest of colours. He spoke of the incapacity of a regulated economy, at least as regulated by Russians, to meet the elementary needs of the people's well-being, confirming this by facts within his knowledge. 'His pessimistic views failed to shake the firmness of my ideas', noted the newly-appointed Ambassador. (Brosio, *Diari di Mosca*, pp. 19–21.)
8. Morozzo della Rocca, *La politica estera*, p. 19.
9. In one of his talks with the Soviet Ambassador to Italy, M.A. Kostylev, the official head of the Italian Foreign Ministry, said that, in his opinion, 'the revival of Europe after the recent ruinous conflict must come from the East: it will bring to the aid of ruined Europe a new and mighty force, the Soviet Union'. He denied that it was possible for Italy to have close, friendly relations with Britain, 'because Britain is too interested in making absolute its domination of the Mediterranean, and further strengthening of Britain's position in the Mediterranean is not in Italy's interests'. Kostylev to Prunas, 18 April 1945, AVP RF, f. 098, op. 26, p. 7, d. 152, l. 294–5.
10. P. Quaroni arrived in Moscow as Ambassador at the end of 1944. He had been at the Italian Embassy there before, in 1925. In those days he had saved from the torture-chambers of the GPU a young Russian noblewoman who became his wife. He knew the country and its language. In the AVP RF is his letter of congratulations to Molotov – written by hand, in good Russian, probably by his wife – on the occasion of the award to the Minister, in November 1946, of the Order of Lenin.
11. AVP RF, f. 06, op. 7, p. 34, d. 479, l. 2–17.
12. AVP RF, f. 06, op. 7, p. 74, d. 486, l. 1–2.
13. AVP RF, f. 06, op. 8, p. 37, d. 580, l. 9–11.
14. Kostylev to Pazzi, 11 February 1945, AVP RF, f. 098, op. 26, p. 8, d. 152, l. 26.
15. *Ibid.*, l. 27.
16. 'Dnevnik i zapisi besed posla v Italii M.A. Kostyleva za 1945g.', AVP RF, f. 098, op. 26, p. 152, d. 8; Gorshkov to Santia, 28 June 1945, AVP RF, f. 098, op. 26, p. 152, d. 6, l. 139–42; Dekanozov to Quaroni,

15 January 1946, AVP RF, f. 098, op. 31, p. 41, d. 183, l. 15; Dekanozov to Quaroni, 11 March 1946, *ibid.*, l. 13; Molotov to Quaroni, 6 April 1946, AVP RF, f. 06, op. 8, p. 37, d. 580, l. 4–5 and AVP RF, f. 06, op. 9, p. 55, d. 816, l. 1–2. Morozzo della Rocca quotes (*La politica estera*, p. 126) from a confidential note from Prunas to Quaroni which was probably the basis of the Ambassador's talk with Molotov. Prunas wrote of the importance of restoring economic relations with the USSR 'not only for the immediately-expected results but also because only after we have established good economic ties with Russia will we be able to sign trade treaties with the East-European and Balkan countries'. Also: AVP RF, f. 06, op. 9, p. 55, d. 816, l. 1–2.

17. Martynov to Prunas, 5 May 1945, AVP RF, f. 098, op. 26, p. 152, d. 8, l. 81.
18. Kostylev to Prunas, 1 February 1946, AVP RF, f. 098, op. 29, p. 11, d. 165, l. 7; AVP RF, f. 06, op. 9, p. 55, d. 816, l. 3–6.
19. In a conversation with Kostylev on 1 April 1944 Sforza spoke very critically of the policy of the Americans, who 'though they like a republic, actually favour the monarchy'. On Churchill's Futon speech he expressed himself in the same spirit, saying that 'Churchill's last two speeches have buried him as a statesman. These speeches are manifestations of Churchill's madness.' AVP RF, f. 098, op. 29, p. 8, d. 165.
20. The Italian Communist Party advocated an exclusively Eastern orientation. The RTsKhIDNI contains a report, received from Dimitrov, of a conversation between Togliatti and an unnamed Bulgarian comrade in which the Italian gives his view of his country's place in the world economy: 'The present orientation of the Italian economy on Western Europe and America is based on a mistaken foundation. Italy is an industrial country which lacks the raw materials it needs for its industry. Our industry cannot compete with American, British or French industry. At the moment, Western Europe needs our industry because it has not yet completed its reconversion from war to peace. This process cannot, however, take long. The only correct oientation for our industry is towards the East: from there we could obtain the raw materials we need, and the countries of Eastern Europe, especially the Balkan countries, could use our industrial potential.' When Suslov received this document from Dimitrov, he regarded it as so important that he circulated it to nearly all the members of the Politburo. RTsKhIDNI, f. 17, op. 128, d. 1101, l. 4.
21. Kostylev to Grieco, deputy chief commissioner for the purge, 21 May 1945, AVP RF, f. 098, op. 26, p. 8, d. 152, l. 374; Kostylev to Reale, 4 May 1945, *ibid.*, l. 384.
22. Kostylev to Reale, 4 May 1945, *ibid.*, l. 339.
23. Lesakov to Baranov, 1 March 1946, RTsKhIDNI, f. 17, op. 128, p. 1, d. 905, l. 10.
24. Suslov to Zhdanov, *ibid.*, l. 97.
25. *Archivio Pietro Secchia, 1945–1973*, Fondazione Feltrinelli, *Annali*, XIX, 1978 (Milan: 1979); Zhdanov to Secchia, 12 December 1947, RTsKhIDNI, f. 17, op. 128, d. 1101, l. 181. The same file number was given to Secchia's meeting with Stalin on 14 December. The Italian had asked for 600 000 dollars for his Party's need. Stalin agreed at once to supply the sum required, in two bags, each weighing 40–50 kg. Some technical difficulties arose in connection with the conveyance of this load. See 'Zapis' besedy I.V. Stalina s P. Sekk'ia, 14 dekabria 1947g.', *Istochnik* 5–6 (1993) 123–6.

26. RTsKhIDNI, f. 17, op. 128, d. 1101, l. 183–4.
27. Zhdanov to Secchia, 16 December 1947, *ibid.*, l. 188–9.
28. The Americans, in their turn, wagered on Italy. In a review of Italy's foreign policy composed in November 1948 by the First Secretary of the Soviet Embassy, G.N. Dul'ian, the view was expressed that Marshall had not tried very hard to draw Italy into his bloc, keeping it in reserve as 'the chief cog' in an inner Mediterranean system. The USA's plans contemplate variants of two blocs functioning in parallel: (1) A North-Atlantic alliance composed of the USA, Canada, Britain, Norway, France, Holland and Portugal, and (2) a Mediterranean bloc, under America's aegis, made up of Greece, Turkey and Italy. AVP RF, f. 098, op. 31, p. 37, d. 170, ch. II, l. 125.
29. Kozyrev to Vyshinskii, 11 February 1948, AVP RF, f. 098, op. 31, p. 41, d. 183, l. 1–2.

24 Negotiating a Settlement for Italy and the Minor Axis Powers: Peace Diplomacy and the Origins of the Cold War, 1945–7

Ilaria Poggiolini

I should like to begin by making it clear that the aim of this chapter is basically to elaborate the idea of 'agreement on disagreement'. I readily admit, right at the start, that this is quite a paradoxical definition which does, however, help us significantly in understanding the rules of peace diplomacy in the years 1945–7. Secondly, my aim is not to provide a detailed reconstruction of day-to-day diplomacy at the CFM, but rather to isolate those issues which contributed to force the negotiators to make their positions clear – even at the cost of a breakdown in negotiations – and those compromise solutions which were elaborated in order to reduce the danger of such a disappointing conclusion of the CFM's meetings. I shall also hint at the historiographical debate on the origins of the Cold War from the point of view of my specific interest in post-World War II peace-making. Indeed, the crucial passage from wartime peace thinking to post-war practices of pacification has not been fully explored by diplomatic historians. The reason for this is, of course, apparent: the Cold War cast a dark shadow on post-war Allied peace-making strategies as a whole. However, the failure of the former wartime Allies to elaborate an overall settlement after World War II should not lead us to conclude that the study of peace diplomacy in itself is irrelevant. As I shall demonstrate, the importance of the issue can be seen in a different perspective today, because the need to cast light on the phase of transition from wartime to post-war international relations is much clearer in the present unstable scenario. Let me then attempt to summarize, briefly, some crucial passages in peace negotiations as far as Italy and the former Axis powers are concerned. This will provide us with relevant examples of what I have termed 'agreement on disagreement'. It is my intention to select those peace issues which either accelerated or slowed down the break-up of the Great Alliance, and I shall suggest that the balance between these conflicting issues was, in the end, more favourable to mediation than to competition.

At the first session of the CFM meetings, previous procedural arrangements elaborated at the Potsdam Conference[1] were challenged by the Soviet Union. Moscow refused to accept the participation of France and China in the discussions over the Balkan and Finnish treaties and also Chinese participation in the negotiations over Italy. Furthermore, the Western positive approach to the Italian question, the so-called 'just peace' approach, was immediately confronted by Soviet obstructionism coupled with Soviet requests for reparations, a share of the Italian navy and colonies[2] and, even more important, Soviet support for Yugoslav claims regarding Trieste. The Italian case was also immediately turned into a 'test case' of any decision regarding military restrictions, length of military occupation and theoretical mechanisms of enforcement of the European treaties. Furthermore, as far as Finland, Bulgaria and Romania were concerned, Moscow made it clear that she would consider them 'as one and the same question'[3] and that she would regard the armistice agreements as the basis for a definitive settlement. The extent and the areas of East–West disagreement had not been anticipated, particularly as regards Moscow's refusal to acknowledge the procedural rights granted to Italy at Potsdam, Soviet claims of a share of the Italian colonies, and Moscow's tenacious support of the Yugoslav side as regards the future of the Trieste area. It has to be pointed out that Italian diplomacy was certainly not ready to confront such an offensive from the Soviet side. Actually, on 17 September 1945, the Italian Ambassador in Moscow wrote to the Secretary General of the Foreign Office in Rome, Mr Prunas, debating if Italy's policy of neutrality between the two blocs should be stretched up to the point of formally promising Moscow that Italy would not enter any anti-Soviet alliance.

This document is very interesting because it shows very clearly how little Italy was ready to commit herself one way or another; but it also shows that, at least from the point of view of the Italian Ambassador in Moscow, the international alignment of the country should not be perceived as decided, yet.

According to Ambassador Quaroni, Moscow could be willing to enter a pact with Italy on the same lines as the Franco-Soviet alliance of 1942, even if the explicit anti-German character of the latter had been completely superseded by events. This analysis was based on the assumption that a Soviet–Italian pact of this sort could mitigate Soviet opposition towards Italy at the peace negotiations. However, even if Quaroni felt that an alliance with Moscow might produce short-term benefits, he was not inclined to abandon his neutralistic stance. A few days later, the Italian representative in London wrote to Prunas showing an even stronger awareness of the limited choices open to Italy, given the emerging confrontation between the two blocs. Indeed, Western attitudes towards the Bulgarian and Romanian Governments had already produced Soviet diplomatic retaliation as regards the issue of the democratic character of the Government in Italy.[4]

In any case, the crucial issue at the peace negotiations was no longer the extent of Italy's independent initiative, but rather the atmosphere emerging between the members of the CFM. Paradoxically, the Italian case did contribute to make East–West relations difficult, but not as much as the numerous questions already at stake in Eastern Europe. Only over the question of Italian reparations (where the Americans refused to accept Soviet and Yugoslav claims), did the harshness of the discussion between Molotov and Byrnes resemble the tone which characterized the debate over the Eastern European cases. Notwithstanding relative agreement over the future of Finland, the Soviets insisted on negotiating the peace treaties in the same order in which they had signed the armistices: first Romania, then Bulgaria, finally Finland and Hungary. As far as the internal regime in Hungary was concerned, Western recognition was conditioned to a set of internal political reforms which were not openly obstructed by Moscow. In Bulgaria conditions for obtaining Western recognition did not exist, but the Soviets were not held completely responsible for such an unsatisfactory state of affairs. Indeed, Romania and Bulgaria were the real bones of contention and, unfortunately, these countries came first on the agenda, according to the order which the Soviets insisted on maintaining.

Byrnes did not hesitate to describe the Romanian Government as Moscow's 'puppet' and this was only the beginning of a remarkable escalation in East–West confrontation which could provide no basis for a productive debate on Western diplomatic recognition of Bulgaria or Romania. Finally, Molotov brought up the issue of French and Chinese participation in the discussions, and denied his previous consent to the procedural arrangements which granted their presence.[5]

So no significant agreement came out of the very first session of the CFM meetings. On the contrary, the extent of East–West disagreement emerged very plainly. Back in Washington, Secretary Byrnes and the American delegation reassessed this result and pondered a set of possible explanations for Soviet behaviour. They felt that their own stubborn refusal to recognize Romania and Bulgaria had contributed to the deadlock, but they also became increasingly convinced that the exclusion of the Soviet Union from the administration of Japan had been the main cause of Moscow's unwillingness to become involved in a real process of diplomatic bargaining. This analysis prompted the Americans to suggest that an exchange of views over the most important areas of dissent in Western–Soviet relations was urgently needed.

At Moscow, during ten days in the middle of December 1945, therefore, various crucial questions were debated at length – international control of Japan, diplomatic recognition to the Balkan states, control over the production of atomic energy, and procedure for the elaboration of the peace treaties.[6] From the point of view of negotiating practices, the most notable result was Byrnes's willingness to abandon 'atomic diplomacy' in favour of a traditional '*do ut des*' diplomatic approach. As result, the premature breakdown of peace negotiations was avoided and vague assurances of Moscow's intention to improve 'democracy' in the East achieved. However, this mediation had a price: that of unifying the discussion over the future of Italy and the other minor Axis powers, thus depriving Italy of the right to be the first to have her peace treaty discussed and hammered out by the CFM.

Furthermore, even though an agreement over the structure of the Peace Conference and of the final session of the CFM was achieved at the Conference in Moscow, and this did represent a step forward in the process of achieving a settlement for Italy and Eastern Europe, the overall balance of costs and benefits of the meeting in the Soviet capital could not be easily assessed. Byrnes, and those at the State Department who were still operating along the lines of the previous administration, felt that the balance was on the side of the benefits, while an increasing number of figures within the new administration, including the President himself, could not accept the costs of keeping diplomatic dialogue with Moscow open.[7] Particularly, they could not take lightly the way in which the Potsdam procedural rules for peace negotiations had been adapted to Soviet priorities: negotiations over Italy had been levelled to those of the Eastern European countries, and France and Chinese participation in the settlement had been openly questioned.

Those who were responsible for the compromise could not deny that those costs were high, nor that Soviet–Western relations were deteriorating day by day; but they attempted to isolate peace issues from the numerous areas of conflict with the Soviet Union and, in particular, from the ideological side of this confrontation. This attempt finally failed during the first months of 1946.[8]

Negotiations were continuously on the verge of total deadlock and this made Washington even more inclined than before to reject Byrnes's approach in a frantic search for a possible way out. This was a time when talks of a separate peace with Italy were heard more and more often in Washington.[9]

However, the real dilemma underlying any decision to amend Italy's status was perceived very clearly both in Washington and at the CFM (meetings of the Deputies included). It was a matter of choice between abandoning any hope of achieving an overall settlement for all the former Axis powers, or keeping open, at any price, a last opportunity to negotiate with Moscow.

Since the autumn of 1945 all Western attempts to introduce significant revisions into the Italian armistice had demonstrated that Soviet consent was very unlikely. This meant there was only one solution: a unilateral decision of the United States and Great Britain to end the state of war between the victorious Western powers and Italy. However, the Moscow Conference had already produced an ambiguous situation because it had ushered in a diversion to the previous trend towards bilateral agreements. The Conference had succeeded temporarily in keeping the diplomatic option open but, in the long-run, there did not seem to be a way out of the dilemma; both the projects for a separate peace with Italy and the hypothesis of negotiating the future of Italy and the minor Axis powers with Moscow, needed to be maintained.

However, even though the American delegation was forced to keep the diplomatic channel of communication with Moscow open, was there any real chance of turning this dialogue into productive discussion? Let us look at the basic assumptions on the basis of which both the Western and the Soviet sides were operating. The West, and particularly the United States, supported the view that Italy had 'worked her passage' from enemy into ally at the end of World War II as a result of her 'cobelligerency'. Thus she was entitled to a lenient settlement. The Soviets opposed this view fiercely and stuck to the idea that Italy should pay for her involvement in the hostilities as one of the major Axis powers. Moscow also aimed at conveying the idea that a positive approach should inform the Allies' attitude towards the minor Axis powers in the East, thus acknowledging Soviet interests in pacifying the area and avoiding the resurgence of nationalistic feelings, contrary to her plans to exert influence on friendly neighbouring states.[10] However, America's 'positive' attitude towards Italy had been one of the most well-established themes in American foreign policy after World War II.

Therefore, neither the West nor the Soviet Union had much flexibility and there seemed to be very little room for manoeuvre at the CFM negotiating table. As a result, American plans to revise the Italian armistice and to achieve a separate peace constantly re-emerged. The British ended up reluctantly supporting such plans but Moscow continued to oppose them fiercely. Therefore, even though alternative options to peace negotiations were taken into consideration, the idea of abandoning plans for an overall peace was not quite allowed to go through in Western quarters.[11] Certainly, the rigidity of East–West positions made diplomatic mediation very difficult, but the final breakdown of the CFM meetings would have left issues of great interest for both sides without a settlement. Two negative results would have been achieved in this case

– the end of peace diplomacy (thus making Germany's and Austria's futures even more uncertain) and the spreading out of potential competition between the two superpowers in both Eastern and Western Europe.

It is not surprising that, if this was the alternative, both sides felt that they should somehow revive the diplomatic option. They also felt that time had come to make clear what could or could not be challenged in each other's positions at the CFM. In other words, the negotiators were determined to narrow down the area of their disagreement. From the American point of view, the question was how to reconcile signs of an increasingly 'tough' attitude towards the Soviet Union with their renewed effort to negotiate at the CFM. A way out of this dilemma was found when the different approaches put forward by the Secretary of State and the President finally emerged into the open. This divergence of views was made public when Secretary of State Byrnes promised to resign at the end of the peace-making process, thus making it clear that he was the one, within the administration, who was committed to a policy of diplomatic mediation.[12] By now Washington had come down on the tough side in dealing with the Soviet Union, and this meant it could take an explicit wait-and-see attitude as regards Byrnes's diplomacy at the CFM meetings.

As a result, it was clear that Byrnes would no longer be Secretary of State; but at the same time, he was able to go back to the negotiating table as the protagonist of a 'peace offensive' which was based on both 'firmness' and 'patience'.[13] This ambiguous but rather effective diplomatic method succeeded in isolating the areas of East–West dissent, and paved the way for a set of compromise solutions. These were designed so as not to upset the most essential goals of both sides (namely, American commitment to provide Italy with a 'just' peace, and Soviet security interests in the East).

However, once the areas of dissent and basic interests had been made clear, a possible area of consensus still had to be identified. This was the scenario when the session of the CFM closed.[14] Italy had obtained an important revision of the armistice clauses, namely the abolition of the Allied Control Commission and of a number of military clauses. Byrnes, back in Washington, declared that if the CFM did not reach an agreement about the date of the peace conference by the following summer, the American administration would support active involvement of the UN in the peace process.[15] Vandenberg, the Republican representative of the Senate at the CFM meetings, made it clear that the US delegation would accept a fair deal for Trieste only if satisfied by Soviet policy in Poland, Bulgaria and Romania.[16] As far as Italy was concerned, the Americans could hardly afford to lose their role as sponsor of a just settlement for Italy, nor sit back and watch the Soviet Union improving her image in the eyes of the Italians as result of their failure. Indeed, this was precisely what seemed to happen in the course of the summer session of the CFM when a compromise over the Italian treaty was finally worked out. For border rectifications, the creation of the Free Territory of Trieste, the loss of the Italian colonies, the imposition of reparation and military limitations were very punitive clauses.[17]

Rather than being seen as diplomacy informed by a strategy of 'firmness' and 'patience', the Italian settlement was perceived in Italy (but paradoxically also in the USA) as a sell-out. The architects of the settlement argued, however, that Italy's position within the Western sphere of influence was already out of the question, and that the agreement they had negotiated was the best available at the time. Indeed, it did serve the purpose of normalizing Italy's status and elaborating peace treaties for the minor Axis powers in the East.[18]

As far as the Eastern countries were concerned, the question of military limitations and of the withdrawal of Allied troops was crucial. These issues could have easily led to the breakdown of negotiations. It was not only a matter of the difficulties in evaluating each country's military capabilities and potentialities, but also a question of handling a discussion over the national defence policies of states which, in the future, were very likely to be controlled by the Soviet Union. Furthermore, Moscow was clearly interested in keeping troops in Romania in order to safeguard lines of communication with her occupying forces in Austria. Washington and London had a similar interest in avoiding the emergence of too strong a Bulgaria, which could have threatened the stability of Greece.[19] Thus, mediation was finally possible because both sides recognized the need to isolate refractory disputes and made an effort to restrain ideological dissent.

It became much more difficult to avoid open confrontation, and the break-up of negotiations, at the Peace Conference in Paris in the summer of 1946, where the drafts of the peace treaties could still be amended. By this time, both sides had exhausted their capacities to ensure that their long-term interests would not impair the peace effort. As a result, American intentions of stabilizing Western Europe, and Soviet plans to safeguard most of her security requirements, now emerged forcefully, as can be easily detected in the positions taken by the two sides regarding the most important peace issues. As the Italians had painfully realized in connection with the Italo-Yugoslav border question, 'the real confrontation was now between the United States and the Soviet Union, and not between the two countries directly concerned'.[20]

Even Secretary Byrnes, the protagonist of a policy of constant mediation at the CFM, took a sharply different attitude at the Paris Conference. He became caught up in the ideological escalation which characterized East–West relations on that occasion, aligning himself with Washington's tough attitude towards the Soviet Union.[21] Before the opening of the Paris Conference, Secretary Byrnes had balanced a certain intransigence, always exercised with much restraint, and a very flexible compromise diplomacy. Now he moved over to the approach favoured by the President and the rest of the administration. However, the price of this shift was Byrnes's recognition that his former favourite approach was unfit for the purpose of ameliorating the draft treaties at the Paris Conference.[22]

This shift can be explained only if one keeps in mind the judgement of the political parties and American public opinion, regarding the results of peace diplomacy. This judgement had been negative, due to the general disbelief in the assumption underlying Byrnes's efforts: the continuation of East–West dialogue. He had assumed that peace diplomacy should aim at maintaining the diplomatic channel of communication open for at least as long as would be needed in order to normalize relations between the victorious powers and all the defeated countries, Germany and Japan included.

At Paris, Molotov made it very clear that the Soviets were willing to leave the substance of the draft treaties unchanged but he also pointed out that East–West relations could not be described simply as the inevitable competition between two conflicting views of the post-war world. Therefore, he appealed to the West not to take the inevitability of the present crisis in international relations for granted. Stalin maintained a similar attitude.[23] Byrnes, instead, was ready to cast aside what had been left of his willingness to negotiate with Moscow. He evidently preferred to direct American public opinion against the continuation of Soviet–American collaboration, retracting his previous faith in compromise diplomacy, and all he had achieved thanks to this method.[24]

The last act of peace-making was performed at the CFM held in New York in November. The Italian draft treaty was the first item in the agenda, but even now agreement was not easy to reach. Notwithstanding Western firmness in maintaining the draft as the basis for discussion, Soviet amendments caused a new wave of arguments. The result was, once again, a compromise which, however, did not alter the substance of all previous agreements.[25]

The odd combination of 'patience and firmness' from the side of the American delegation at the CFM, had produced debatable results. Was this a complete diplomatic failure, as many in Italy and even Washington, argued? The Italian treaty certainly could not be perceived as mild: Italy was to lose her colonies, pay reparations, see her frontiers altered at her expense, and be subjected to military limitations. Furthermore, the Italian Government was forced to accept the establishment of the 'free territory' of Trieste.[26]

However, Washington made it very clear that Rome should not be ashamed of being subjected to this remarkable set of punitive clauses because the entire treaty already belonged to the past. As now openly stated by the American administration, the future of the West was going to be shaped according to a new, global, Western-oriented plan for reconstruction and integration. Italy would not be left out of this, upon condition of signing the treaty, thus performing an act which symbolized the overcoming of her wartime responsibilities. Furthermore, normalization of Italy's status would be followed by Western initiatives aimed at revising the Italian Peace Treaty. This was going to be a very peculiar procedure because Soviet support could hardly be expected especially when it came to the issue of returning Trieste to Italian sovereignty.[27] One can argue that competition between the superpowers on the future post-war order was finally recognized by both sides once the peace treaties had been signed. During the previous years East–West relations maintained a certain degree of flexibility as much as ambiguity. The peace-makers operated within this sort of 'free diplomatic area' with very clear national goals in their minds, but also making an effort to keep the channels of communication open. Thus, peace-making after World War II did not coincide, either temporally or conceptually, with the planning of one single overall scheme of post-war pacification.

By 1947 there were two such schemes which could be referred to 'Pax Sovietica' and 'Pax Americana'.[28] The latter coincided with two parallel principles – 'containment' of the Soviet Union and political and economic 'stabilization' of the West. The former consisted of Sovietization of that part of Europe where Moscow's influence was paramount, and with a determined quest for security at regional level. Thus, while 'co-operation' was the source of inspiration on which peace-making diplomacy during the years 1945 to 1947 was based, 'competition' informed East–West plans of post-war pacification after 1947. However, what is of interest here is how much longer that we commonly think diplomacy maintains, after the end of World War II, a classic *do ut des* pattern and, therefore, some ground for mediation and understanding between the two blocs.

Until 1947, the two sides avoided pushing their ideological and strategic dissent to the extreme, even though they never succeeded in achieving a conciliatory level of discussion in the course of peace negotiations. However, informal understanding between East and West about the long-term advantages of jointly ending the state of war with the former minor Axis powers, explained why the Western Allies were willing to negotiate with Moscow and adapt their diplomatic behaviour accordingly, until it became clear that no diplomatic tool could help in bridging East–West differences. Thus, what was missing in 1947 should not be searched for in the area of diplomacy but in the realm of political and strategic goals. Diplomacy became out-of-date because the new uncompromising attitude of both sides could not, by definition, be expressed by a classic *do ut des* diplomatic practice. However, up until 1947, the odd formula of *agreement on disagreement* had expressed the desire of the victorious powers to maintain goodwill. Actually, the parties might have wanted 'to clarify what they disagreed about so as to better focus future negotiations on the unsettled disputes'. The conclusion of compromise agreements, unlikely to hold for long (such as the creation of the Free Territory of Trieste), between powers whose relations were strained, were 'constructed as though these powers had exchanged promises to be more accommodating toward each other in the future'.[29] In normal circumstances, given the fact that negotiating positions are usually flexible, if a conference ends without agreement the same issue is taken up again in later negotiations. This was the case at the numerous sessions of the CFM meetings, and could have been an opportunity again in later years.

In conclusion, one can argue that diplomatic methods could hardly be held responsible for the failure to keep East–West negotiations alive in 1947. Disregard for diplomacy, like that which characterized the early Cold War years, can only be explained with a misperception of the role played by mediators at the CFM. Without the carry-over effects which normally follow the shift in positions between the beginning and the end of a conference, mediation is no use. However, those carry-over effects were prevented at the CFM meetings by major changes in the world scenario, not by the negotiators' inability to capitalize on their *agreement on disagreement*.

Notes

1. At Potsdam, an American project, submitted to Stalin and Churchill, called for a Council of Foreign Ministers composed of the representatives of the United States, Great Britain, France, the Soviet Union and China. The Foreign Ministers were to negotiate the draft treaties for Italy and the minor Axis powers. Both Churchill and Stalin objected to the idea of asking France and China to join the CFM. As a result, the role of these two countries was limited. As far as France was concerned, participation would be allowed only during discussions of the Italian treaty and possibly of the German treaty in the course of subsequent sessions. As far as China was concerned, only matters relating to the Far East would be negotiated with her participation.
2. I. Poggiolini, *Diplomazia della transizione. Gli Alleati e il problema del trattato di pace italiano (1945–1947)*, (Florence: Ponte alle Grazie, 1990) pp. 84–5.
3. *FRUS, 1945*, Vol. 2, p. 112.
4. Quaroni a Prunas, 17 settembre 1945; Carandini a Prunas, 27 settembre 1945, in *I documenti diplomatici italiani*, Decima serie 1945–8, Vol. II, pp. 732, 778.
5. Quaroni a De Gasperi, 12 ottobre 1945, in *ibid.*, p. 836 ff.
6. R. Dennet, J.E. Johnson, *Negotiating with the Russians* (Boston, Mass.: World Peace Foundation, 1951) pp. 5–14.

7. Poggiolini, *Diplomazia*, pp. 38–9.
8. P. Dawson Ward, *The Threat of Peace* (Kent, Oh.: Kent State University Press, 1979) p. 87.
9. Dunn to Matthews, 27 February 1946, *FRUS, 1946*, Vol. 2, p. 16.
10. The Assistant Secretary of State to the Secretary of State, London, 13 March 1946, *FRUS, 1946*, Vol. 2, p. 28.
11. Poggiolini, *Diplomazia*, p. 49; see also Dowling to the Secretary, 9 April 1946, NA, R.G. 59, box 1.
12. On Byrnes's resignation see R.L. Messer, '"Et tu Brute", James Byrnes, Harry Truman and the Origins of the Cold War', in K.A. Clements (ed.), *James F. Byrnes and the Origins of the Cold War* (Durham, N.C.: Carolina Academic Press, 1982) pp. 19–49.
13. Poggiolini, *Diplomazia*, p. 55.
14. A.H. Vandenberg Jr (ed.), *The Private Papers of Senator Vandenberg* (Boston, Mass.: Houghton Mifflin, 1952) p. 284.
15. Dawson Ward, *The Threat*, p. 99.
16. *The Private*, p. 289.
17. J.F. Byrnes, *Speaking Frankly* (New York: Harper & Brothers, 1947) p. 131.
18. *The Private*, p. 297; see also *Remarks of Hon. Arthur Vandenberg, Senator of the State of Michigan, in the Senate of the United States relative to the Peace Treaties which will finally terminate World War II, July 16, 1946* (Washington, D.C.: United States Government Printing Office, 1946); *Remarks of Hon. Tom Connally, Senator of the State of Texas, in the Senate of the United States relative to the Peace Treaties which will finally terminate World War II, July 19, 1946* (Washington, D.C.: United States Government Printing Office, 1946).
19. M. Fulop, 'The Military Clauses of the Paris Peace Treaties with Rumania, Bulgaria and Hungary', in F. Tanner (ed.), *From Versailles to Baghdad: Post-War Armament Control of Defeated States* (New York: United Nations, 1992) pp. 39–54.
20. 'Seduta del 12 agosto 1946', Ambasciata Italiana di Parigi, ASMAE, Affari Politici, Italia Conferenza della Pace, 1946, b. 57, f. 2.
21. Poggiolini, *Diplomazia*, pp. 80–1.
22. P. Dawson Ward, 'James F. Byrnes and the Paris Conference of the Council of Foreign Ministers, April 25–July 12, 1946', in *James F. Byrnes*, pp. 59–74.
23. Cited in Poggiolini, *Diplomazia*, pp. 95–6.
24. 'Paris Peace Conference', 29 July to 15 October 1946, 'Report by Secretary Byrnes', 18 October 1946, in *A Decade of American Foreign Policy, Basic Documents 1944–1949* (Washington, D.C.: United States Government Printing Office, 1950) pp. 86–92.
25. R. Messer, *The End of an Alliance. James F. Byrnes, Roosevelt, Truman and the Origins of the Cold War* (Chapel Hill, N.C.–London: The University of North Carolina Press, 1982) p. 214.
26. 'Third Meeting of the Council of Foreign Ministers', New York, 4 November to 12 December 1946, 'Report by the Department of State', in *A Decade*, pp. 92–7.
27. Poggiolini, *Diplomazia*, pp. 149–51.
28. See V. Mastny, 'Pax Sovietica', in R. Ahmann, A.M. Birke, M. Howard (eds), *The Quest for Stability. Problems of West European Security 1918–1957* (New York: Oxford University Press, 1993) pp. 379–88, and

Id., 'The Making of "Pax Americana": Formative Moments of United States Ascendancy', in *ibid.*, pp. 389–434.
29. F.C. Ikle, *How Nations Negotiate* (New York–London: Harper & Row Publishers, 1964) pp. 16–22.

25 The Search for Symmetry: a Tentative View of Trieste, the Soviet Union and the Cold War
Giampaolo Valdevit

The post-war conflict over Trieste has been seen as significant by second-generation studies[1] for two main reasons. It is seen as a test case of the early Cold War and later as a microcosm of the Cold War. So a source of conflict between the United States and the Soviet Union (at least up to the split between Tito and Stalin in June 1948), and at the same time the battlefield of a domestic Cold War. At any rate, the issue is recognized as a minor issue rather than a major point of observation of the Cold War, as the first-generation studies preferred to see it.[2] The second-generation studies have found, in US diplomatic history, the framework that was previously lacking, and have been strongly influenced by post-revisionist historiography. So the crisis of May–June 1945 has been portrayed as the first confrontation between the 'Riga axiom' and the 'Yalta axiom' or as a prologue of containment (the sources of inspiration of these interpretations are Daniel Yergin and John F. Gaddis respectively).[3]

Thus the problem of Trieste lies at the intersection of geopolitical, ideological, and strategic frameworks. Trieste now appears as an area where US interests took shape, and a project was designed and carried out. In the end it became part of the building of a security belt in Southern Europe.

However, the wider context – the origins of the Cold War – has yet to be completely described. In other words, what remains to be clarified is the interplay between the internal and external determinants of American and Soviet foreign policy, interests and underlying assumptions. This problem, obviously, goes well beyond the geographical limits considered here. The most recent interpretation – which sees national security as the motivating force (at least of US foreign policy) – is too general to be a useful conceptual tool.[4]

A major impulse to redraw the wider context of the Cold War and its origins comes from the opening of the Soviet archives. We could use the new documentary evidence simply to update the debate going on within American diplomatic history; but it would seem more profitable to rethink the Cold War in its essence – that overall interaction of challenge and response, on both sides of the fence. At any rate we are faced with a very difficult task. In fact the first steps in this direction leave us with mixed feelings: they certainly allow us to address the problems better, but we are not able, as yet, to give satisfactory answers. This is doubly clear if we reconsider the problem of Trieste in the light of the new Soviet sources. Even though the exploration of the archives here has been very partial, we can now at least try to understand the intertwining motivations leading to US and USSR intervention in the dispute. One further warning is needed: this chapter is much more focused on the Soviet attitude. For the American and British side a large body of historiographical literature on the problem of Trieste – and its wider implications – has been made available in the last ten years by American and especially Italian scholars. Therefore in this chapter the behaviour of the Western powers will merely be sketched in its main outlines.

Where should we start if we wish to identify symmetries and asymmetries in American and Soviet conduct? I believe a useful starting point is the problem of the vacuum of power. As some German revisionist historians, Hillgruber in particular, have emphasized, this problem was shared by all conflicting parties.

In the last stage of the war (from November 1944) in north eastern Italy, Allied Force Headquarters (AFHQ) assumed that a vacuum of power would result in Venezia Giulia as the consequence of the final German collapse. Allied plans for occupation of the disputed territory were also very uncertain.

Alerted by the British missions on the spot to the sharp political polarization existing in Venezia Giulia, the Foreign Office feared that the 'Greek experience' could be repeated there. In order to avoid such an unwelcome contingency, by the end of 1944 the Foreign Office preferred to seek Tito's consent to a demarcation line across Venezia Giulia. According to this plan, the Allied forces would occupy the Western portion of the region, including the port of Trieste and the lines of communication towards Austria. Control of these was of the utmost importance if military operations were to be extended into Austria.

The American component of the AFHQ, on the other hand, opted for a policy based on the principles of liberal internationalism that was a part of Roosevelt's Grand Design. According to these principles, war was not the right time to adjust border lines, since this was a job of the peace-makers. The Americans also noted that the Italian armistice provided for Allied military occupation of the whole Italian territory included within the 1939 borders. The two approaches were naturally irreconcilable; a dispute broke out, but remained unsettled. So Field Marshal Alexander, the Supreme Commander of the AFHQ, was left without any clear guidance from the Combined Chiefs of Staff. He therefore decided to seize control of what was absolutely necessary if military operations were to be continued – the port of Trieste and the lines of communication northwards. In fact the Allied troops entered Trieste just a few hours later than the Yugoslav partisan army. So at the end of the war Trieste and the surrounding area were left in a very singular situation. Two armies – the Allied troops and the Yugoslav IVth Army – occupied the same territory; but only one imposed political control (the Leninist revolutionary pattern of control imposed by the Yugoslavs). Incidentally, as the Slovenian and Croatian partisans were also strongly motivated by ethnic antagonism, the Communist takeover in Venezia Giulia was accompanied by acts of intimidation and persecution against the Italians and the anti-Communist political parties. Thousands were deported and some of these immediately executed and thrown into Carsian pits (*foibe*).[5]

The vacuum of power produced by the German collapse had thus been filled, but the normal state of affairs, according to which military occupation and political control of a territory go hand in hand, was violated. This is the substance of the crisis of Trieste in May–June 1945. How could the normal state of affairs be restored? This was the problem that American diplomacy pondered in early May (while the Foreign Office was almost completely paralysed). On 10 May the problem was settled by Truman's decision to 'throw them [the Yugoslavs] out'. The inconsistent attitudes of Truman in the early days of his presidency suggests we should not take this statement at face value. What is surely more important is to understand the background in Department of State thinking. The State Department drew a parallel between Trieste and Poland. In Poland – so the reasoning went – the Red Army had occupied the territory and imposed its own political rule on it; in contrast, in Trieste and the surrounding area, British and American troops were on the spot, but the civilian government was completely in the hands of the Yugoslav Army. Therefore Truman's statement should be read as an appeal to redress the balance, to fill the power vacuum in Trieste, applying the same rules as in Poland.[6]

The parallel between Trieste and Poland has a crucial meaning in the evolution of US foreign policy from wartime to post-war politics. After the Yalta Conference the political situation in Poland was carefully monitored in order to ascertain whether Soviet behaviour there was consistent with the principles of the Yalta declaration on liberated Europe. Therefore Poland became a kind of litmus test of Soviet intentions regarding the restoration of international order in Eastern Europe, and Soviet adherence to the principles of liberal internationalism. In the last weeks of his life Roosevelt experienced doubts after doubts in this regard, and the idealism of his Grand Design openly clashed with the realism which was also present in his foreign policy. In fact the USSR was exercising tight political control over the Polish internal situation, considering the Yalta declaration mostly as a dead letter.[7] The Polish theme, taken as a benchmark by the Department of State in its thinking over the Trieste crisis, seems to represent an example of continuity in US foreign policy, even though – unlike Roosevelt – Truman preferred to follow the so called *quid pro quo* approach, and tended to interpret it on a geopolitical basis. Therefore he preferred symmetry to be applied in particular to the cases in which the course of events had brought about asymmetry.

But how, concretely, was the Yugoslav Army 'thrown out' of Trieste? To force them to the negotiating table, military pressure was exerted: at the end of May the British and American troops moved a few miles eastward – up to the proposed demarcation line. But at the same time the Yugoslavs were offered a temporary solution (pending a final settlement at the Peace Conference): the partition of Venezia Giulia into two occupation areas. The Eastern (and larger) zone – Zone B – was to be administered by a Yugoslav Military Government, the Western area – Zone A, including Trieste, the lines of communication towards Austria, and the enclave of Pola in Southern Istria – by an Allied Military Government (AMG). This arrangement was eventually sanctioned by the Belgrade agreement of 9 June 1945. Remarkably, such a compromise solution was supported even by the Under-Secretary of State, J. Grew, one of the cold warriors around Truman. At this stage even the cold warriors were not yet what they later became.[8]

At this point the dispute was settled, at least temporarily. Retrospectively it can be seen that it was not a dispute between Italy and Yugoslavia, in which the great powers acted as their proxies: and indeed the Department of State made this point very clearly at the time.[9] Neither was it a confrontation between the United States and the Soviet Union. Nonetheless, during the crisis a message was sent to Stalin via Tito: the USSR – it stated implicitly – was a power with which compromise agreements were still possible (and, in particular, being in a position of strength made them easier to reach).

Trieste, therefore, was one of the first areas where the guiding principles of US foreign policy towards the USSR during the second half of 1945 were put into practice – the *quid pro quo* approach and negotiation from strength. The approach contained a measure of unilateralism, and this eventually paved the way for confrontation. But we should not mistake the prelude to a phenomenon for the phenomenon itself. Basically the American approach had a geopolitical meaning – it aimed at maintaining the connection between military occupation and military government in the disputed territory. The ideological content of the crisis was present only on the surface (as when Field Marshal Alexander publicly accused Tito of being 'reminiscent' of Hitler and Mussolini).

The Belgrade agreement ensured a strong British–American presence in Zone A of Venezia Giulia. The vacuum of power was thus filled through a compromise between idealism and realism. However, this was only temporary – since the future of Venezia Giulia was to be decided at the Peace Conference. Moreover, Article 3 of the Belgrade agreement did not grant the Allied authorities full powers in the administration of the territory. The consequence was that the diplomatic negotiating process was intimately bound up with a local issue: who should have political control over Zone A?

When we shift our attention to the Soviet side, discussion focused for a long time on the question of who pushed whom. Did Stalin push Tito to go ahead or, was it rather Tito that forced Stalin to give him support? This question was posed in particular in the memoirs of Yugoslav leaders, and was strongly influenced by the subsequent split between Tito and Stalin. Fortunately we now can move beyond it. A background paper produced in early July by the Soviet Ministry of Foreign Affairs allows us to address the issue from a different perspective – that of symmetries and analogies between American and Soviet conduct. The vacuum of power, in fact, was also the starting point in the Soviet analysis of the so-called race for Trieste between the Allied and the Yugoslav troops. The sequence, seen from the Soviet side, was as follows: German defeat – Yugoslav occupation; vacuum filled – problem settled in an 'absolutely lawfully' way. *Realpolitik* was the guiding principle; and it inspired the analysis of the historical background to Yugoslav territorial claims as well. It was denied that, historically, Venezia Giulia had any specifically Italian identity. The territories claimed by Yugoslavia – the document asserted – 'almost continuously from the Seventh Century until 1918 ... shared a common history with the people of today's Yugoslavia'. Therefore – the reasoning went on – Italy was alien to Venezia Giulia, and Italian annexation of the whole region at the end of World War I was motivated purely by power politics. By the same logic, Italy should be forced out.[10]

Besides *Realpolitik*, the other component of the Soviet approach was ideology: 'the correction of history's injustice', the theme of the 'just war' and 'the just punishment of Italy' all called for a territorial settlement favourable to the Yugoslav claims. So the connection between *Realpolitik* and ideology appears much closer on the Soviet side than among the Allies. This was the content of Stalin's message to Truman on 21 June .[11] It is, of course, widely accepted that Soviet foreign policy grew out of a combination of *Realpolitik* and ideology. Soviet analysis of British and American conduct in the early stage of the crisis is much more interesting, however. Up to the race for Trieste, Allied policy was defined as 'self-restrained' – in other words, no clear British (or American) line of conduct was perceived. But in its conjecturing of why the Western Allies were interested in Trieste, the Soviet paper – if we read between the lines – is revealing of Soviet conduct as well. The British and Americans – the document states – were forced to intervene in Venezia Giulia by the 'stormy reaction of the Italian Government and of the whole of Italian society'. In the Soviet view, it was for this reason that 'they started to get uneasy, to support the Italians and to take issue with Yugoslavia'.[12] Moreover, a later Soviet paper on the Italian position at the first session of the Council of Foreign Ministers in London, again stressed this point: 'We can surely say that, before laying down their claims, the Italians had already obtained the approval, and even a promise of support, from the British side.'[13]

This Soviet language implies, in my opinion, a reference to spheres of influence, and hence to the search for clients – the Yugoslavs – who could counter-balance the supposed British clients, the Italians. Soviet perceptions were misplaced, since at that time there was no British alignment on Italian territorial claims. However, the Soviet Foreign Ministry does seem to have believed that the Western Allies were establishing a patron–client relationship with Italy, and that *Realpolitik* therefore forced them to take a similar stance towards Yugoslavia. Obviously their decision was also influenced by ideology; Tito was a Communist leader, who was building a Communist society in Yugoslavia. But the Soviet–Yugoslav alignment also seems to have been dictated by the tendency to act symmetrically *vis-à-vis* the Western Powers.

Let us try to explore further instances of symmetry. In evaluating the Allied conduct during the May crisis, the Soviet memorandum states that it was 'moderate enough and did not oppose the Yugoslav territorial claims, but called only for the establishment of an Allied Military Government in the region, plus postponement of the final decision regarding the new border line to the Peace Conference'. At this time, therefore, the USSR did not yet perceive a patron–client relationship between the Western powers and Italy as being firmly established. Moreover – the memorandum goes on – 'the Yugoslav Government has been forced by the Anglo-Americans to consent to the withdrawal of its own troops'.[14] It implied that the USSR did not give all-out support to the Yugoslav territorial claims. In other words, the Soviet–Yugoslav patron–client relationship paralleled the Western one: once again, we find symmetry. *Realpolitik* (the other face of the coin) is still the dominant approach in the last part of this memorandum, which considers the Belgrade agreement. In particular, the Soviet Foreign Ministry perceived 'a great fear on the part of the Yugoslav authorities as far as both the future of this territory and the Slav population are concerned'.[15] In other terms, the power vacuum filled by the Belgrade agreement marked the end of that combination of military occupation and political control of a territory which was typical of the Communist takeover in Eastern European countries.

This does not mean that Soviet diplomacy was already reasoning in terms of an iron curtain in Venezia Giulia (or elsewhere in Europe). However, beyond any doubt it was implicitly recognized that the pattern of government based on 'people's powers', the pattern introduced by the Yugoslav Army, was over. Actually a conflict was still in being, because Article 3 of the Belgrade Agreement did not clearly define the mutual relationship between the Allied Military Government and the Communist-dominated system of local committees, installed during the Yugoslav occupation. But, according to the Soviet point of view, this dispute 'affected only the mutual relations between the Yugoslav authorities and the Allied military authorities'[16]; the Soviet Union had no role to play. This does not mean that Soviet interest towards Venezia Giulia disappeared, but simply that it was seen as one more issue in the bargaining over post-war territorial settlements. Another symmetry existed here. For the Allied authorities on the spot also considered that the Yugoslavs were the only Party in the dispute over the pattern of local government.[17]

Only after an agreement was reached in Paris at the beginning of July 1946, creating the Free Territory of Trieste (FTT), did the symmetries start to disappear. The Department of State considered the AMG in Trieste as the bulwark to Soviet ambitions to take over Zone A.[18] So when the Soviet delegation at the Peace Conference proposed self-government as a pattern of administration for the FTT, the British and Americans opposed this, seeing it as a weak arrangement, liable to being overrun by Yugoslav pressure. In the end – it was feared – the FTT would be annexed to Yugoslavia.[19] From mid-1946 on, therefore, Trieste was caught up in the challenge–response framework in which Soviet–Yugoslav encroachment was confronted by American containment. The continued presence of the AMG was intended to display American determination not to let the Trieste domino collapse.[20]

Was this an accurate perception of Soviet plans regarding Trieste? To decide this question, documentary evidence on the Soviet side is still too poor, virtually non-existent. At any rate what we can take for granted is the fact that in February 1946 the Yugoslavs started a war of nerves against Zone A, especially by moving troops close to the demarcation line. In July 1946 the AMG was also the main target of a general strike called by pro-Yugoslav organizations. Yugoslav pressure on Zone A of the FTT was thus undeniable. Was Yugoslav pressure exerted upon the Soviet Government as well? Did Tito perceive (or misperceive) a Soviet tendency to react to the strengthening of the American presence in Zone A? We come here to the crucial issue of Soviet-Yugoslav relations. It is now a common view that the two countries basically differed in the perception of their national interests, especially with regard to the Balkan area as a whole.[21] On the Yugoslav side, in particular, it is likely that specifically national interests dictated the vision of the international order much more than the other way round. For instance, at the first meeting of the Cominform in September 1947 Kardelj openly stated his preference for a 'Greek situation' in France and Italy (which, obviously, would have paved the way to the fulfilment of Yugoslav territorial ambitions).[22] But did this correspond to Soviet plans? Probably the disorder within the Soviet camp in the field of foreign policy had already reached a critical stage.

The split between Tito and Stalin rapidly and radically altered the scenario in which the problem of Trieste had been inserted. Once a minor Cold War issue, it became a Cold War erratic boulder. From 1950 on, American policy towards Yugoslavia became part of the process of redefining Western security. Considering Yugoslavia as a possible target of Soviet expansion on the Korean pattern, at the end of 1951 the Truman Administration started a programme of military aid as part of the policy of 'keeping Tito afloat' which had been decided immediately after the split had come into the open. To justify American military aid to Yugoslavia, the Joint Chiefs of Staff maintained that the Yugoslav Army would resist a Soviet (or Soviet-satellite) invasion, and in particular defend the Ljubljana gap, the gateway to the northern Italian plains. The step from military aid to military planning was not a long one; discussion of the issue got under way in Belgrade in November 1952.[23]

In this way, Trieste was forced out of the framework of containment; and the idea that the Allied presence in Trieste was 'the last barrier against infiltration from the East towards Northern Italy' was concurrently abandoned. Policy was directed towards different aims, in particular towards 'cooling off tensions'. This was a framework which could help to push both Italy and Yugoslavia towards the negotiating table. By early 1950 the United States and Great Britain started to cautiously push both parties in this direction.[24]

The USSR was also forced to make some change in its course. Soviet diplomacy repeatedly urged that the provisions of the Peace Treaty in regard to the FTT should be enforced. For instance in April 1950 they called for the appointment of a governor as the first step leading to the creation of the Territory. In reality, the problem of Trieste had become part of a quadrilateral relationship (involving the USA, the UK, Italy and Yugoslavia), and the Peace Treaty provisions had no weight in this framework. Therefore the USSR was excluded from the possibility of interfering in the four-corner relationship. Probably Soviet diplomacy was not unaware of this. It is therefore not unexpected to find that Soviet policy tended to consider the problem of Trieste exclusively in the framework of that ideological confrontation between East and West which was a substantial part of the Cold War. Trieste was defined as a 'base of American imperialism'; diametrically opposed to it was the institution of the FTT, which offered the only chance of 'destroying one of the bases of armed aggression in Europe'.[25]

The Soviet demands were backed by Togliatti. His stance put the Italian Communist Party (PCI) in a position where it risked becoming isolated within Italy, and being considered a Party strongly opposed to the Italian national interest – an anti-national Party. For at that time the Italian Government was aiming at bringing at least Trieste and Zone A of the FTT back under Italian sovereignty. Togliatti, however, preferred not to consider foreign policy as a divisive issue in Italian politics. For instance, in February 1951, he suggested a 'new' Italian foreign policy (new in the sense of more independent).[26] In regard to the problem of Trieste he tried, very cautiously and not openly, to put some distance between the PCI and the Soviet positions.

In November 1951, when discussion between the Italian and Yugoslav delegations was officially opened, the USSR sent a diplomatic note to the US, British and French Governments with the intent of 'unmasking the plot over the partition of the Free Territory of Trieste'. The note called for Allied withdrawal from Trieste and the enforcement of the Peace Treaty provisions. The Soviet declaration was nothing new: it simply confirmed the Soviet tendency to play the Trieste card in the context of the ideological struggle between East and West.

More interesting is the origin of the Soviet initiative, as this was later explained by the Ministry of Foreign Affairs.

> One of the reason inducing the Soviet Government to issue this note was Togliatti's initiative requesting the Soviet Government to restate once more its own position on the question of Trieste. But, as the Soviet Ambassador to Italy, comrade Kostylev, later communicated, the Italian friends made poor use of it, and added unsatisfactory comments both quantitatively and qualitatively.[27]

How can we explain Togliatti's contradictory attitude? It was, in my opinion, the expression of his attempt to cautiously distance himself from the Soviet position. It is widely known that Togliatti played tactics very skilfully; on this occasion, he basically ignored the Soviet statement even though the substance of the Soviet position was not openly rejected.

Some months later, Togliatti played the same role and again distanced himself from the official Soviet line. During 1951 the Italian Government and the pro-Italian political parties in Trieste put growing pressure on the AMG to try to force it to grant some authority in Zone A to Italian officials. The AMG resisted this pressure, considering it as an attempt to 'undermine' its own authority (incidentally, the same term had been used in 1946–7 to describe Communist plans for infiltration and subversion of Zone A).[28] The AMG's attitude generated tensions, which came to a head in March 1952 when riots broke out in Trieste. The Italian Government requested 'the Italian character of Zone A be fully recognized'. In order to relieve some pressure, official talks were opened in London. Some minor Italian officials were introduced into the AMG apparatus as a result of these talks, and an Italian political adviser was appointed. The Italian Government interpreted the outcome of the London negotiations as a step towards future annexation of Zone A to Italy.[29]

In Moscow the London agreement was basically interpreted as a plot between Italy, the United States and Great Britain, aimed at 'reducing the growing mass discontent over De Gasperi's policy'. According to the Soviet account, the Italian Government first staged nationalistic demonstrations in Trieste and elsewhere; the Western powers then demonstrated at least partial support for the Italian claims; and the London talks constituted the last act of the plot. Soviet diplomats reached the conclusion that the Western powers had offered the Italian Government a useful card to play during the coming local elections.

The Soviet reaction to what they saw as a plot was motivated by symmetry – the USSR tried to produce a card which the PCI could play in the electoral campaign. The Soviet Ambassador in Rome suggested 'sending a note of protest against the infringement of the Peace Treaty provisions relating to Trieste' in order to 'help the Italian friends in the campaign for the local elections'.[30] However the PCI's reaction to the proposed Soviet note turned out to be much more important than the note itself. Both the local Communist leader, Vidali, and Togliatti opposed it (and in the end it was never sent). The former was 'strongly against it', while the latter displayed his tactical ability. According to the report of the Soviet Foreign Ministry, Togliatti said that the note

> from the point of view of the electoral campaign either in Italy or in Trieste, would neither be of any use nor cause any damage; while from the international point of view ... it would not be timely [because] it would distract international public opinion away from the very crucial issue raised by the Soviet Government of a peace treaty with Germany.[31]

Togliatti was fully aware of Soviet sensibilities, and of the fact that in Moscow the German question carried a very different weight to the problem of Trieste (which at that time was only a subject of the ideological dispute). Weighing the two questions against each other, the result was assured: if the diplomatic note on Trieste risked prejudicing Soviet policy regarding the German question, as Togliatti hinted it might, the Soviet Foreign Ministry would immediately drop it.

What lay behind Togliatti and Vidali's statements? No documentary evidence exists, but we may hazard an informed guess, bearing in mind the background to the London talks. Togliatti and Vidali were aware that the Italian Government and the pro-Italian Parties in Trieste expected a successful outcome to the talks, and were over-sensitive to the issue of gaining more influence within the AMG. They probably feared that reaffirming the Soviet position at that time would cause strong antagonism between the pro-Italian forces and the Communist Party in Trieste, and between the Italian Government and the PCI in Italy, an antagonism which could end up in the isolation of the PCI as a party opposed to the defence of the national interest. Even though a domestic Cold War did exist in Italy and in Trieste, Togliatti and Vidali preferred not to have their own Party cast in these terms.

The final phase of the problem of Trieste lasted a little more than one year, from August 1953 to October 1954, when a nominally provisional settlement was reached with the partition of the two zones of the FTT between Italy and Yugoslavia.

The framework for this last crisis was provided by Eisenhower's 'New Look', in particular by his (and Dulles') attempt to give territorial continuity to the line of Western security in Europe by attracting Yugoslavia over to the West. The Eisenhower Administration quickly removed the ambiguities in Yugoslav–American defence relations left open by the previous administration, and in August 1953 offered Yugoslavia logistic and operational support in the case of Soviet (or Soviet-satellite) attack.

In this framework, Trieste rapidly became something more dangerous than the 'sore spot' that it had been defined as. It now became a 'stumbling block' to Yugoslav attraction to the Western security system. The American and British Governments therefore decided to intervene directly to settle the dispute. On 8 October 1953 they issued a diplomatic note stating their intention to discontinue the AMG, to withdraw the troops from Zone A, and transfer it to Italian administration.[32]

Soviet diplomacy followed this last stage of the controversy very carefully and produced some position papers, drafted by Gromyko and some junior diplomats and addressed to the Politburo. On the whole, they reveal what might be defined as a Soviet policy of impotence. In early September, Gromyko defined the American plan as an attempt to settle the dispute by partitioning the two zones of the FTT, to draw Italy into a Balkan alliance, and to ensure the presence of an American base in Trieste.[33] This was a glaring misconception, for the Americans, and even more the British, were eager to remove their troops from Trieste. But this is not the most interesting point. From Gromyko's point of view, the American project was not threatening at all since it was bound to be frustrated by mutual hostility between Italy and Yugoslavia, both considered to be strongly opposed to a compromise solution.

Gromyko argued that acceptance of a compromise settlement by the Yugoslavs 'would deny them the possibility of playing the role of "defender" of the national interest, which represents a substantial part of their demagoguery in domestic politics'.[34] In other words, Gromyko perceived national interest as the main driving force behind Yugoslav policy. Even after Stalin's death, this was probably still commonplace in Moscow (and incidentally confirms what is now a widely held assumption – that the split of June 1948 occurred over two conflicting definitions of national interest). Gromyko also saw another characteristic in Yugoslav foreign policy: he suspected it of being provocative (again, this is reminiscent of 1948). So he thought that the American–British note of 8 October 1953 sprang from Yugoslav determination 'to test the Allied powers and Italy', forcing them to make their own intentions manifest.[35]

In Gromyko's view, Italy would also oppose a compromise solution. 'Having followed an unpopular pro-American policy, no Italian Government', he wrote, 'could stay in power if it abandoned its position on the problem of Trieste.' On the contrary, the Italian Government badly needed a successful outcome to the territorial dispute with Yugoslavia, in which Italy was backed by the USA. As Gromyko saw it, this was the only chance of making a pro-American policy acceptable to Italian public opinion.[36] So it was thought that 'Yugoslav demagoguery' and 'Italian unpopular policy' would conspire to frustrate the American plan. 'The Western Governments could not openly take either the part of Italy or that of Yugoslavia,' stated Gromyko – they were paralysed.[37] Moreover, this paralysis was an inherent feature of the four-cornered relationship between the US, the UK, Italy and Yugoslavia – the framework in which the problem of Trieste was inserted.

A simplified, Leninist vision of international relations is easily discernible in Gromyko's analysis. It was an ideological vision, motivated by an inner logic and therefore self-confirming. The USSR can sleep easy, seemed to be Gromyko's conclusion. But that was not enough. He looked for further insurance: let's fan the flames, this is his last call. The impulse came again from the inner logic:

it would be appropriate to publish in the Soviet press an article stressing that non-fulfilment of agreements (in this case the Peace Treaty with Italy) is a cause of serious worsening of international relations; that the USSR has made considerable efforts to solve the problem of Trieste pacifically; that the Western countries have rejected these efforts; and that the USSR is nonetheless ready to repeat them.[38]

These suggestions paved the way to a Soviet note, requesting the Security Council promptly to re-examine the problem on the basis of the Peace Treaty provisions. Gromyko seemed to prefer a diplomacy of optimism. But if we look at the matter more carefully, it proves rather to be a diplomacy of impotence. His own vision of international relations was a source of confidence but to a certain extent a trap, as the actors on the international scene were imagined to play unchangeable roles. If they eventually turned out to be not so stereotyped, the only way to adapt Soviet behaviour to the new circumstances was by a U-turn.

At the end of November a new position paper was produced by the Soviet Ministry of Foreign Affairs. In the meantime the Italian and Yugoslav reactions to the diplomatic note of 8 October had brought about a stalemate. The Italian Prime Minister publicly interpreted the note as support for Italian claims, and a first step towards eventual annexation of the whole FTT. For his part, Tito threatened to move Yugoslav troops into Zone A, if the Allies withdrew handing administration over to Italy. Nonetheless, after the 8 October declaration, British and American determination to bring AMG control of Zone A proved to be irreversible. A few weeks later they proposed an international conference open to five participants (USA, UK, France, Italy and Yugoslavia) as the forum where a final agreement could be reached.[39]

Soviet diplomacy did not fail to perceive that the obstacles to a compromise solution were not as insuperable as Gromyko had presented them. They therefore put aside the ideological framework preferred by Gromyko. In fact they considered that the United States was moving in the opposite direction to that identified by Gromyko. The American intention – as they perceived it – was to withdraw the troops from Trieste; the project to keep a military base in Trieste was not even mentioned. Moreover they did not ignore that Tito 'would face a domestic political setback, if he accepted the 8 October declaration as a basis for the settlement of the question of Trieste'. As far as the Italian Government was concerned, they simply noted that 'some preparation was necessary' before they could abandon their claims to the whole FTT. In the end Gromyko's optimism disappeared. He now argued that the 'Western Governments may be able to get out of the stalemate'.

Tito's inner circle was said to perceive a determination 'to speed up the initiative leading to the international conference'. The partition of the FTT and the granting of some institutional autonomy to both of its zones 'could furnish the basis for an agreement between Italy and Yugoslavia. Even though to reach such an agreement was still difficult', nonetheless 'some preliminary steps had been taken.'[40]

However, the final recommendation of the Soviet diplomats revealed the same ideological approach which ran through Gromyko's paper. The concluding remark is basically the same as Gromyko's, and even the language closely resembles his. It is suggested that a 'statement on the illegal actions of the Western countries on the question of Trieste ... contradicting the provisions of the Peace Treaty' be placed in the Soviet press. In this way, it was claimed, 'the illegal actions of the Western countries over the question of Trieste will be unmasked, and the double-crossing position of the Yugoslav Government as well'.[41] Probably, what could be defined as the return of ideology was motivated by the force of habit. In a retrospective analysis (written after a compromise agreement had been reached in October 1954), the American Ambassador in Moscow, Bohlen, wrote that Soviet conduct had been marked by 'caution'. Soviet diplomacy, echoed the Policy Planning Staff of the State Department, 'remained more or less quiet on the issue, both in regard to official statements and propaganda output', even though they were informed about the last stage of the negotiations.[42] This was the only path which the diplomacy of impotence, inherent in Gromyko's approach, left open to the USSR (as events moved towards a compromise solution). Basically they had to accept the idea of being deprived of any role in the settlement of the dispute. So after the signing of the London agreement in early October 1954, the USSR simply 'took cognizance' of it.

The Soviet note to the Security Council marked a U-turn with regard to the former Soviet policy, which had aimed at the institution of the FTT. The Policy Planning Staff interpreted the Soviet shift 'in the context of Soviet policy towards Yugoslavia'; and they noted that 'the tempo of normalization [in USSR-Yugoslav relations] increased sharply' in September 1954.[43] At any rate, the Soviet position paper of November 1953 did not fail to notice a Yugoslav tendency to accept compromise settlements, and to abandon what Gromyko had called 'demagoguery'. Naturally, this new tendency needed to be confirmed by positive acts; and from this perspective we can now understand why Soviet diplomacy 'remained more or less quiet on the issue'. Before relations with Yugoslavia could be normalized, the first Soviet perceptions of a shift in Yugoslav foreign policy needed to be corroborated.

From this point of view, the problem of Trieste in its last stage now seems to have a further dimension, which has been largely ignored in the historiographical literature. On the Soviet side it was considered as a litmus test of developments in Yugoslav foreign policy; in parallel, on the Yugoslav side it was a card to be played in order to expedite reconciliation with the USSR.

Notes

1. G. Valdevit, *La questione di Trieste 1941–1954. Politica internazionale e contesto locale* (Milan: 1986); Id., 'La Labour Policy del Governo Militare Alleato (1945–1954)', in L. Ganapini (ed.), ...*anche l'uomo doveva essere di ferro. Classe e movimento operaio a Trieste nel secondo dopoguerra* (Milan: 1986) pp. 245–79; Id., 'Fra Balcani e Mediterraneo. Contesti della politica britannica e americana sul problema di Trieste (1944–1948)', *Qualestoria*, 1 (1988) 109–26; Id., 'Conflitti di interesse fra Italia e Inghilterra: Trieste e i Balcani 1943–1945', *Qualestoria*, 1 (1992) 33–54; Id., *Trieste 1953–1954. La crisi finale?* (Trieste: 1994). See also: R. Rabel, *Between East and West. Trieste, the United States, and the Cold War, 1941–1954* (Durham–London: 1988); R. Pupo, *Fra Italia e Jugoslavia. Saggi sulla questione di Trieste (1945–1954)* (Udine: 1989); M. de Leonardis, *La 'diplomazia atlantica' e la soluzione del problema di Trieste (1952–1954)* (Naples: 1992); D. De Castro, *La questione di Trieste. L'azione politica e diplomatica italiana dal 1943 al 1954*, 2 Vols (Trieste: 1981).
2. J.B. Duroselle, *Le conflit de Trieste, 1943–1954* (Brussels: 1966); B.C. Novak, *Trieste, 1941–1954. The Ethnic, Political and Ideological Struggle* (Chicago, Ill.: 1970).
3. Valdevit, *La questione di Trieste*; Rabel, *Between East and West*, referring respectively to D. Yergin, *Shattered Peace. The Origins of the Cold War and the National Security State* (Boston, Mass.: 1977), and J.L. Gaddis, *Strategies of Containment. A Critical Appraisal of Postwar American National Security Policy* (New York: 1982).
4. H. Jones, R.B. Woods, 'Origins of the Cold War in Europe and the Near East: Recent Historiography and the National Security Imperative', *Diplomatic History*, 2 (1993) 251–76.
5. Valdevit, *La questione di Trieste*, p. 89 ff.
6. Memorandum of conversation between Truman, Grew *et al.*, 10 May 1945, in *FRUS, 1945*, Vol. 4, pp. 1154–5; memorandum by Cannon, 6 May 1945, NA, RG 59, 740.00119 Control (Italy).
7. R.C. Lukas, *Bitter Legacy: Polish–American Relations in the Wake of World War II* (Lexington, Ky : 1982).
8. Grew's draft of a message by Truman to Churchill, n.d., Truman Library, Independence, Mo., Truman Papers, PSF, b. 181.
9. Memorandum by Cannon, 6 May 1945, NA, RG 59, 740.00119 Control (Italy).
10. Memorandum by Ivanov, first referent for European Affairs, and Kozyrev, chief of the division of European Affairs, 3 July 1945, AVP RF, f. 098, op. 26e, p. 208, d. 4.
11. Stalin to Truman, 21 June 1945, in *FRUS*, 'The Conference of Berlin', *1945*, Vol. 1, pp. 846–7.
12. Memorandum by Ivanov and Kozyrev, 3 July 1945, AVP RF, f. 098, op. 26e, p. 208, d. 4.

13. Report by Ivanov on the First Session of the Conference of Foreign Ministers, 25 December 1945, AVP RF, f. 098, op. 29, p. 165, d. 165.
14. Memorandum by Ivanov and Kozyrev, 3 July 1945, AVP RF, f. 098, op. 26e, p. 208, d. 4.
15. *Ibid.*
16. *Ibid.*
17. Valdevit, *La questione di Trieste*, p. 102 ff.
18. Report by the State-War-Navy Coordinating Committee, 6 August 1946, in *FRUS, 1946*, Vol. 4, pp. 822–7.
19. Waldock (Paris) to the Foreign Office, 5 August 1946, PRO, FO 371/59355R/11480/3/92; memorandum by Waldock, 17 August 1946, in *FRUS, 1946*, Vol. 4, pp. 844–7.
20. Staff Study by the War Department (Norstad), 12 July 1947, NA, RG 319, P&O, 092 TS 12/29/47.
21. L. Gibianskii, 'La costituzione del Cominform', *Storia contemporanea*, 4 (1993) 489–516; A. Guerra, 'L'esportazione dello stalinismo nell'Europa dell'Est', in A. Natoli, S. Pons (eds), *L'età dello stalinismo* (Rome: 1991) pp. 311–12. On the relations between Stalin and Tito, see J. Pirjevec, *Il gran rifiuto. Guerra fredda e calda fra Tito, Stalin e l'Occidente* (Trieste: 1990).
22. A. Agosti, 'Il Partito Comunista Italiano e la svolta del 1947', *Studi storici*, 1 (1990) 66.
23. G. Valdevit, 'Italia, Jugoslavia, sicurezza europea: la visione americana (1948–1956)', in M. Galeazzi (ed.), *Roma e Belgrado. Gli anni della guerra fredda* (Ravenna: 1995) pp. 39–61.
24. Valdevit, *La questione di Trieste*, p. 206 ff.
25. M. Galeazzi, 'Togliatti fra Tito e Stalin', in *Roma e Belgrado*; see also S. Pons, 'L'Unione Sovietica nella politica estera di Togliatti (1944–1949)', *Studi storici*, 2/3 (1992) 441.
26. M. Galeazzi, 'Luigi Longo e la politica internazionale. Gli anni della guerra fredda', *Studi storici*, 1 (1990) 129 ff.
27. Memorandum from Sergeev to Vyshinskii and Bogomolov, 9 May 1952; Bogomolov to Vyshinskii, 5 May 1952, AVP RF, f. 098, op. 35, p. 326, d. 26.
28. Unger, US political advisor in Trieste, to the Department of State, 3 January 1951 and 28 March 1951, and Webb to US Embassy Rome, 26 February 1951, in *FRUS, 1951*, Vol. 4, pp. 206–8, 222–4, 216–17.
29. De Castro, *La questione*, Vol. 2, pp. 182–5.
30. Memorandum by Sergeev, 9 May 1952, AVP RF, f. 098, op. 35, p. 326, d. 26.
31. *Ibid.*
32. Valdevit, *Trieste 1953–54*, p. 12 ff.
33. Memorandum by Gromyko, 8 September 1953, AVP RF, f. 098, op. 36, p. 234, d. 29 (the memorandum was addressed to the whole Soviet '*nomenklatura*': Malenkov, Molotov, Voroshilov, Khrushchev, Bulganin, Kaganovic, Mikoyan, Saburov, Pervuhin).
34. *Ibid.*
35. *Ibid.*
36. *Ibid.*
37. *Ibid.*
38. *Ibid.*
39. Valdevit, *Trieste 1953–1954*, p. 29 ff.

40. Memorandum by Tugarinov (deputy chief of the Information Committee), Zimianin (chief of the 4th European Department), Yershov (deputy chief of the 1st European Department), 21 November 1953, AVP RF, f. 098, op. 36, p. 234, d. 29.
41. *Ibid.*
42. Bohlen to the State Department, 14 October 1954, in *FRUS, 1952–54*, Vol. 8, p. 581; memorandum by Campbell (Policy Planning Staff), 29 October 1954, in *ibid.*, pp. 586–8.
43. Memorandum by Campbell, 29 October 1954, in *FRUS*, 1952–54, Vol. 8, pp. 586–8.

26 Security and Perceptions of Threat in Italy in the Early Cold War Years, 1945–53
Leopoldo Nuti

This chapter analyses the main concerns of those institutions which, for the period from 1945 to 1953, were responsible for defining and shaping Italian security policies. Its main purpose is to assess whether the Italian military and the Italian Government ever perceived the threat of Soviet military aggression as real, or whether for them the Cold War took a different, subtler, dimension. It concludes that for most of the period under consideration (the main exception being the months that followed the outbreak of the Korean War) the Italian military, and the Allied occupation authorities before them, focused their attention on the domestic dimension of the Cold War rather than on the strategic problems posed by a Soviet military menace. If any external threat was perceived as serious, this was the Yugoslav rather than the Soviet one.

In the first section the chapter looks at the plans and ideas of the Allied Military Government and discusses the main framework in which the problem of Italian security was conceived in the early post-war years. After analysing the withdrawal of the Allied occupation troops, the chapter then looks at the security problem as it was perceived by the Italian General Staff in the crucial period immediately before and after the political elections of April 1948. The last section in the chapter looks at Italy's inclusion in the Atlantic Alliance and at the outbreak of the Korean War. The chapter is based on a variety of sources, drawn from Italian, American and British archives. The picture it draws, however, is somewhat incomplete, since some of the Italian military records that would be necessary for a thorough study are not available for research.[1] The records that can be consulted, however, make it possible to sketch out a general framework of how the Italian military regarded the security problem of their country during these years. What is not possible is to assess how wrong, or how right, were the perceptions that shaped these military plans, as very little documentation is available about the insurrectional plans of the Communist Party or about Soviet policy towards Italy.[2]

THE END OF THE WAR AND ITS IMMEDIATE AFTERMATH

As World War II was slowly coming to an end after the bitter campaign fought by the Allies on Italian territory, the main concern of the Supreme Allied Commander in the Mediterranean was that the military victory that had long been sought in the Mediterranean might be spoiled by political turmoil if no agreement could be worked out with the resistance forces in northern Italy. The Greek experience of December 1944, when British and Commonwealth troops had to be called in to crush a sudden Communist insurrection after the Germans had been expelled from the country, loomed large in the minds of all the Allied military and political authorities in Italy.[3] Most observers of the Italian scene perceived a clear swelling of a revolutionary tide, in the wake of institutional collapse which might burst into the open once the war was over.[4] Even after an agreement with the partisans was reached in late 1944, the Allied command was still afraid that the end of the war might be followed by a period of anarchy and lawlessness, in which Allied military forces would be the only authority available to guarantee law and order in the newly liberated territories of northern Italy.[5]

To the concern about law and order another major source of apprehension was added immediately after the end of hostilities, when the Allied troops entered the city of Trieste only to find it partially occupied by Marshal Tito's Yugoslav People's Liberation Army. An uneasy truce was reached when the mounting crisis was settled by the compromise of 15 June, but the tension in the Julian region remained high and a military showdown was regarded as quite likely by all the parties involved.[6]

So to the Allied Headquarters the situation in Italy seemed ripe for a period of serious unrest. Field Marshal Alexander and Chief Allied Commissioner Rear Admiral Ellery W. Stone appreciated the importance of retaining Allied forces in the peninsula until the Italian Government was able to stand on its own, and emphasized the importance of retaining a large number of Allied troops until a stable democracy had been established. In the stormy political atmosphere of the early aftermath of the war, the presence of Allied forces could be critical in steering Italy – which was at the crossroads between 'democracy and a new totalitarianism' – in the desired direction.[7] Nevertheless this bid for a strong military posture in order to make Italy 'a bulwark of democracy' in the Mediterranean contrasted sharply with pre-established demobilization plans. Thus the suggestions of the Allied authorities in Italy went largely unheeded, and the number of Allied occupation troops was sharply reduced between May 1945 and the summer of 1947. By late 1945 there remained in Italy only the 56th

British division and the US 88th infantry division, plus the Polish Corps, that was soon to be redeployed in Great Britain. This early withdrawal clearly made the replacement of these troops by an alternative force all the more urgent.[8]

Allied military leaders in Italy decided that the only solution lay in helping the Government of Italy, however limited its powers might be under the occupation regime, to rebuild its armed forces. The Allied Headquarters in the Mediterranean felt that the control of a substantial amount of troops would make the present Italian Government stronger, capable of dealing with domestic upheavals and with minor threats to its security from the outside: besides, the availability of a reliable force to protect the fragile Italian Government was regarded as crucial in the process of growth of a democratic, Western-oriented political system in Italy. In the summer of 1945, therefore, while the war in the Far East was still being fought, the Supreme Allied Commander in the Mediterranean asked the Combined Chiefs of Staff for authorization to continue supplying the Italian combat groups (which had fought alongside the Allies after the armistice) even after the end of hostilities, in order to build up a force which might be used to restore order if need be – a gesture which, with a little stretch of imagination, might be described as the first step towards post-war rearmament of a defeated country. On 30 September 1945, the CCS met SACMED's request by granting him the authorization to dispose of Allied surplus material to help rebuild the Italian Army.[9] In late 1946 a similar decision was taken about the reconstruction of the Italian Air Force.

The debates held by the Allied Control Commission and by the Military Mission to the Italian Army about the reconstruction of the Italian armed forces, and in particular of the Italian Army, clearly reveal the dual purpose of the Allied decision: when the choice had to be made whether the new Italian Army should be structured either as a sort of an expanded militia with domestic policing tasks or as a true army with real fighting capabilities, the MMIA basically adopted a compromise that veered towards the first solution.[10] The new divisions that began to be set up in 1946, therefore, were structured in such a way as to make them more akin to a large police force than anything else. As an aside, it might be noted that Italian officers serving in the Combat Groups and in the General Staff were afraid that the Allies might turn their units into some kind of town militia, and often voiced their scant appreciation for such a role.[11] The rearmament of the Italian Army was therefore conceived and implemented by the Allied authorities in Italy as a stop-gap measure necessary to deal with a contingent problem, and not as part of a general strategy of confrontation with the Soviet Union – a strategy which in mid-1945 and early 1946 had yet to be formulated. In short, throughout this early post-war period Allied planning rotated around two major issues, namely the fear of domestic disturbances and that of a border clash with the Yugoslavs over the destiny of Trieste. There was no serious discussion about the risk of a major war, in which in any case Italy could have played a role only as a minor, powerless ally.

THE WITHDRAWAL OF THE OCCUPATION TROOPS

The Peace Treaty between Italy and the Allied powers was signed on 10 February 1947, and ratified by all parties concerned by 15 September, thereby necessitating the final departure of all the remaining occupation troops within 90 days.[12] In between the signature of the treaty and its ratification, however, there was some concern lest the Yugoslav Government should not ratify the treaty, thus causing an 'indefinite delay' in the conclusion of the peace settlement. While the tension with Belgrade was mounting, the British advised the State Department that for a number of reasons they would have to immediately recall all their occupation troops from Greece and Italy. Both the US military in the field and the State Department reacted sharply against this decision, stressing that the presence of the Allied troops had been crucial in preventing a Communist uprising supported by Yugoslavia, and that 'the removal of present forces in Italy would facilitate Yugoslav assistance to Communists in Italy if the latter should attempt a coup against the Italian Government'. Eventually, however, the USA decided that 'the withdrawal would not affect the situation in Italy and in Venezia Giulia to a substantial degree', but that it would 'place on the United States the entire burden of providing a stabilizing influence on the Italian and Greek Governments'.[13] The creeping crisis was terminated by the Yugoslav ratification of the Peace Treaty on 15 August 1947, but it had lasted long enough to drive home to the attention of the Truman Administration the fact that the withdrawal of the occupation troops would create in Italy a vacuum of power whose consequences could be very serious indeed. An evaluation of the Special Intelligence Group concluded that the

> withdrawal would seriously affect US interests and security in Italy by: a) throwing open to Communist pressure the important area of Northern Italy where the proximity of Yugoslav Communists makes it possible for the USSR to create a situation on the border similar to that prevailing in Northern Greece; and b) leaving the entire country and the weak De Gasperi Government ill-prepared to cope with the powerful Communist Party in the national elections scheduled for April 1948.[14]

The Italian Government could not openly request the continued presence of the occupation troops since this was tantamount 'to political suicide', the document continued, and the only realistic alternatives were seen in a further strengthening of the Italian security forces and in the reaching of an agreement which would allow the USA to use certain port and railway facilities 'in order that maintenance and supply troops may protect the lines of communication from the Free Territory of Trieste to the US zone [in] Austria'. It was argued by the CIG that 'the presence of these troops ... would lend the moral support greatly needed by the anti-Communist forces, and would greatly strengthen the non-Communist Italian Government by enabling it to cope with the critical period leading to the national elections'. As a stop-gap initiative, the Truman Administration resolved to study the option of reinforcing the Italian Army; and shortly after the last ratification was deposited, the US Army sent to Italy an American military mission under Colonel Charles R. Bathurst, who closely examined the Italian armed forces to find out whether a programme of military assistance could be effective in strengthening the Italian Government and its military posture.[15]

The Italian Government of Prime Minister Alcide De Gasperi was also fully aware of the significance of the Allied withdrawal. The domestic political situation had been quickly deteriorating since the late spring of 1947 – when the left-wing forces had been expelled from the Government coalition; and during the fall the tension reached a dramatic climax when the Communist Party launched a violent campaign of massive strikes. By the end of the year, therefore, De Gasperi suggested that the Allies delay the departure of occupation troops to the very last moment, strengthen the occupation forces in Austria and perhaps 'maintain a reserve of troops in some position in the Mediterranean from which, in case of need, they might be quickly sent into the peninsula'.[16] Shortly afterwards, De Gasperi sent a military representative to US Ambassador James Clement Dunn, presenting him with a dramatic estimate of the situation: according to several studies by Italian intelligence, the Communists were losing hope of carrying the day at the polls, and were preparing to take action by force. The Italian Prime Minister, however, believed that the Italian security forces would be capable, if properly equipped, of dealing with an insurrection, and suggested therefore that the USA continue to provide them with the necessary military assistance.[17]

At midnight of 14 December 1947, when the final departure of the occupation troops eventually occurred, it was staged as a spectacular demonstration meant to impress upon the Italian population the might and strength of the Allies.[18] At the same time, the Truman Administration began to discuss how to implement a secret programme of military assistance to help the De Gasperi Government in rebutting any attempt to overturn democratic institutions before – or even after – the incoming political elections of April 1948.[19]

THE ELECTIONS OF 18 APRIL 1948

The growing US concern for Italian security before the political elections of April 1948, and the importance it had in shaping US policies in the Cold War, has been the subject of several studies, and need not be recalled here.[20] Much less is known, on the other hand, about the perception of the problem of Italian security by the Italian General Staff in the early months of 1948, when the problem of a common strategy for the containment of Soviet power began to be discussed by the other Western countries. At this time the Italian Government and the military were mostly concerned with the impending political elections of April 1948, and with the possible Communist reaction to their outcome: an electoral defeat for the left-wing forces, in fact, was regarded as likely to trigger an attempt to seize power by force; the attention of military planners was therefore concentrated on how this could be prevented.

Studies drafted by the Italian General Staff in the spring of 1948, and sent to Washington shortly afterwards, shed some light on the main trends of thought in the Italian military at the time.[21] A first paper tried to persuade the United States of the strategic importance of the Italian territory in any future global conflict with the Soviet Union, and called for aid and support to be given to the Italian armed forces. It was the only document which tackled the problem of a general war, but it did so in a very sketchy and superficial way, repeating some of the main *clichés* about a Soviet military offensive without any original contribution.[22]

Far more interesting, on the contrary, are the detailed studies of the Italian domestic situation, whose length and depth clearly expose the order of priorities of the Italian High Command. Some of the most interesting observations come from a document titled 'Potentialities of Internal Security in Italy', which appraises all the possible consequences of the incoming political elections.[23] It anticipates that in case of a defeat or, even worse, if there was a marginal victory in only one of the two Chambers, the Communist Party might stage a series of initiatives ranging from local riots to isolated armed uprisings, up to a general revolutionary insurrection supported by the armed intervention of the Eastern bloc and of Yugoslavia in particular. The study analysed in some depth the paramilitary structure of the PCI – the *apparato*, whose total strength according to the figures available to the General Staff went from a minimum of 50 000 to a clearly exaggerated maximum of 200 000 – as well as the potential aggressive capabilities of the Yugoslav armed forces, which could sustain the insurrection either by a sizeable landing on the Adriatic coast of Italy or by threatening its northeastern frontier, be it by infiltrating weapons and small paramilitary formations or by a large-scale attack. If the insurrection spread and was supported by the dreaded Yugoslav intervention, it would engage the Italian armed forces in a full-scale military operation, and it was quite likely that they would not be able to prevent the insurgents from taking over most of northern Italy. In this case the study concluded that it would be necessary to leave this part of the country to the Communists and gather the Italian armed forces south of the Apennines in order to retain the control of the west coast, whose ports were regarded of crucial strategic relevance.[24] Thus, according to the Italian General Staff, the Italian armed forces were faced with a veritable dilemma. To preserve law and order across the country, the Italian Army had to scatter its small forces across the whole national territory, but this dispersion hampered that concentration of forces in the northeast which was essential to prevent a Yugoslav attack. If they had to cope with both these assignments, the study concluded, the Italian armed forces required the supply of a massive amount of foreign equipment, and above all close co-operation with Allied occupation troops in Austria and in the Free Territory of Trieste. These would be crucial in thwarting a Yugoslav thrust during the early stages of the operations.

Worry about an insurrection decreased temporarily after the Christian Democrats won by a large margin at the polls. But only three months later, apprehension resurfaced with the riots that followed the attempted assassination of the PCI Secretary, Palmiro Togliatti. In several days of serious fighting, a large number of Communist militants challenged law and order in many Italian cities, strengthening the belief of the political and military authorities in the existence of a masterplan for a national insurrection.[25] A document drafted by the Office of Operations of the Army General Staff in early August 1948 clearly stated that

> the recent events undoubtedly reinforce the thesis of the existence of an insurrectional plan aiming at subverting the official powers of the state, and they also reveal something of the techniques which would be used to put it into effect. These allow to understand the full gravity of the situation that could be created if the whole plan should be implemented. It seems that plan will entail: firstly, the provoking of isolated riots between masses of demonstrators and the police, with the purpose of dividing and wearing down the security forces by leading them to intervene in separate locations at some distance from each other; secondly, as soon as favorable conditions have been

created, the intervention of the formations of the left-wing paramilitary apparatus.[26]

It is hard to establish if such a plan actually existed, since Communist historians have always vehemently denied its reality.[27] According to the confessions of the Party's Vice-Secretary, Luigi Longo, in the tense aftermath of the assassination attempt, the Party had made preparations to ward off a coup which the Government might stage after the elections, but was not itself ready to implement one.[28] It may well have been the case that both sides were so caught up in the apocalyptic atmosphere of the moment as to attribute to each other the worst possible intentions. What is clear, however, is that the Government and the military authorities firmly believed in the existence of the insurrectional plan, and that they were not just using it as a mere propaganda tool to frighten the Italian bourgeoisie.[29]

As for the fears of a Yugoslav attack, the schism between Stalin and Tito did not substantially affect the perception of the threat: in Rome it was widely believed that the break between the two Communist states was nothing but a ruse, and that if it was real it would be short lived, since the Soviet Union could not allow such a blatant challenge to its power to grow and develop. By mid-1948 the main threat to Italian security was therefore regarded by the Italian General Staff as a subtle combination of insurrectional outbursts and real military operations, or as a sort of continuum going from limited local riots to a general uprising supported by foreign intervention. In none of the documents of the time, however, is general war mentioned as a likely possibility, or as an impending threat: when such an issue was mentioned, it was dealt with in a theoretical, abstract way which suggests concern was rather remote. Limited threats seemed therefore to require limited responses. It seems justifiable to posit a connection between this moderate assessment of the dangers facing the country and the caution with which the Italian General Staff and Government viewed the early stages of the debate about the creation of the Atlantic Pact. The Government regarded this as difficult to present to Italian public opinion and possibly unnecessary, from the point of view of Italian security, as well.

What defence policy was held to be necessary to meet this configuration of possible threats?[30] For a few months after the elections of 1948, both the Government and the General Staff regarded the continuation of the informal relationship of military assistance which had developed between the United States and Italy in the preceding months as more than sufficient. If the Italian armed forces could count on a steady flow of American supplies, and on co-operation with the occupation troops in Trieste and in Austria in the eventuality of a Yugoslav attack, the security of the country could be reasonably guaranteed. Furthermore, a defence policy based on the informal support of the United States featured the additional advantage that it could be implemented quietly and without the fuss of a parliamentary debate, which would be necessary if Italy decided to join a formal alliance such as the Brussels Pact.[31] By the end of the year, however, the continuation of an informal bilateral military relationship with the United States turned out to be much more difficult than anticipated, and the United States made it clear that they gave the highest priority to the establishment of the Atlantic Alliance.[32] The Italian Government was eventually forced to revise its policy of 'armed neutrality' and ended up demanding to be included among the signatories of the Atlantic Pact, a request which met strong resistance from many of the other countries involved in the negotiations, and was only eventually accepted thanks to French insistence.

DEFENCE PLANNING IN THE EARLY YEARS OF THE ATLANTIC ALLIANCE, 1949–53: A DIFFERENT ORDER OF PRIORITIES

In the spring and summer of 1949 the conclusion of the Atlantic Pact negotiations, and the widening of the rift between Yugoslavia and the Soviet Union, modified the conditions under which the Italian military had to face the key issues of national security. Membership in the Atlantic Alliance basically implied two major consequences: (1) a more stable pro-Western orientation of the Government, and thereby a sharp reduction of concerns about a revolutionary uprising; (2) a partial reorientation of the attention of the Italian armed forces towards the role they would play in the overall Atlantic strategy, and away from purely domestic issues. From 1949 onwards, the papers of the General Staff focus more and more on issues of general strategy rather than on matters of domestic security. This does not mean, of course, that the problem was solved once and forever, but rather that internal security was becoming the separate concern of specialized bodies and institutions, in particular the swelling police force of Minister of Interior Mario Scelba.[33] The crucial issue of Italian security, however, remained a possible confrontation with Yugoslavia rather than a general war. The inclusion of Italy in the Atlantic Alliance did not entail any immediate integration of Italian defence plans with those of its Allies. This was mostly due to the fact that the only Allied troops which could concretely co-operate with the Italian armed forces in case of war were the occupation troops in Austria and Trieste, and these were not included in the Alliance's chain of command and their commanders were prevented by their original instructions from discussing their plans with the Italians. Nevertheless, the fact that Italy had become a member of the

Alliance had important consequences for the definition of a general Allied strategy, since it compelled Allied planners to take into account the possible role Italy might play in a general war and, above all, to dismiss the possibility of Italian neutrality. It is true that, at the strategic level, US and British planners continued to disagree about the feasibility and advisability of defending Italy, and therefore about the importance of assisting the Italian armed forces; at the local level, however, by the summer of 1949 the Allied Planning Staff in Austria completed a first draft of the ('Pilgrim') plan for the withdrawal of the occupation troops in case of war, and in all of its three versions ('Able', 'Baker' and 'Charlie') Plan Pilgrim clearly envisaged some role for Italy – even if the Italian High Command was not informed of it.[34]

The plan concluded that the decision on which option should eventually be adopted largely depended on an event over which none of the Allies had much influence – namely the future behaviour of the Yugoslav Government. The attitude of the Tito Government, in fact, was considered the crucial factor for shaping the outcome of the early stages of a future war in this region. If the Government in Belgrade decided to side with the Soviet Union in a general war, a joint Soviet–Yugoslav attack could easily penetrate the Julian Alps and establish Soviet control over Italy, and eventually over the entire Mediterranean basin. If, on the other hand, the split between Moscow and Belgrade became permanent, and Yugoslavia decided to remain neutral, the Soviet forces would be forced to attack with smaller forces on a much narrower front, giving Allied troops a better chance to withdraw safely into Italy and stage a successful defence there.[35]

Thus already in late 1949 Allied military planning looked at the security issues of the region from a broad, global perspective, basically discarding the risk of an Italian–Yugoslav confrontation, and hoping to bring about some degree of co-operation between the two countries. Neither the Italian Government nor the Italian High Command, however, seemed to share this approach: the hostility and suspicion caused by the claims that both Rome and Belgrade laid to the Free Territory of Trieste made it impossible for Italy to seriously consider any possible co-operation with the Yugoslavs. In short, Italian security policies remained, at least until the outbreak of the Korean War, deeply influenced by the issue of Trieste. If a general war had been a major concern, or if it had been regarded as imminent, the Government and the military might have tried to reach at least a compromise with the Yugoslavs in order to improve the overall strategic situation. The lack of any effort in this direction seems to indicate that the main Italian concern was still a different one.

The onset of the Korean War impressed a different pace upon NATO activities, and slightly altered the approach of the Italian military, but did not bring about substantial change regarding the diffidence towards Belgrade. The initial Italian reactions to the Far Eastern conflict were rather cautious: in early July 1950, for instance, a meeting of the Army Staff debated the possible consequences of the war and concluded that although other Far Eastern countries might be dragged into the conflict Italy was unlikely to be. The European situation, however, was far from being entirely reassuring, and in order to meet any future threat the Chief of the Army Staff called for an increased build-up of the armed forces and of the Army in particular.[36] The first impact of the war, therefore, was to spur the military to intensify their requests for a larger defence budget. Prime Minister De Gasperi initially met these demands with some scepticism, and warned the cabinet that it was the United Nations (to which Italy did not belong) that was involved in the conflict, while the Atlantic Pact was not a part in it.[37] The deterioration of the international situation, however, forced the Government to revise this first appraisal of the situation, and by the end of July it had already agreed to ask Parliament for an extraordinary allocation of 50 billion lire for the defence budget.[38] As the war went on and threatened to turn into a truly global conflict after the intervention of troops from the People's Republic of China, this first figure was raised by the end of the year to the sum of 250 billion lire; even the usually circumspect De Gasperi, by then, talked to his cabinet about the need to set up a 'pre-war economy' with tough measures which might include the freezing of prices and salaries.[39] For a few months, therefore, both the Government and the military felt that the chances of war had become more real than they had ever been, and reacted accordingly.

The sensation of impending danger sharpened by the Far Eastern conflict also encouraged a further revision of the Allied plans so as to finally establish some degree of co-operation between the Italian Army and the Allied occupation troops in Austria and in the Free Territory of Trieste. In July 1950 the Italians were informed for the first time that the occupation troops in Austria and Trieste had devised a number of plans which envisaged their withdrawal into Italy, and it was also agreed that the UK, the USA and France would make available the order of battle of their forces in the region.[40] Shortly afterwards, the NATO/EMMO Regional Planning Group adopted its first short-term strategic plan, which was a slightly different version of 'Pilgrim/Charlie', and in early February 1951 the commanders of the occupation troops in Austria and Trieste decided that in case of war they would try to defend as much of Austria as possible in order to 'give the greatest possible time and encouragement to the Italians to mobilize and fight on their frontiers'.

The pattern defined in this early example of Atlantic co-operation was continued in a more formalized fashion after the creation of the integrated military structure of NATO in early 1951 and the appointment of a Supreme Commander for the Allied Forces in Europe in the person of General Eisenhower.[41] SHAPE's strategic thinking, in fact, not only encompassed the presence of the occupation troops in Austria and the FTT, but above all insisted in trying to incorporate Yugoslavia into Atlantic planning – by assuming either that it would be neutral or even a cobelligerent.[42] If Yugoslav cobelligerence could be counted upon, in particular, SHAPE could work on a scenario in which the initial phases of the battle for Italy would be waged on Yugoslav rather than on Italian territory – an option which would greatly improve the Western strategic position, as the very nature of the terrain along Italy's eastern frontier made it very difficult to stop an aggressor at the border for the time necessary to mobilize Italian resources.

Whenever a forward strategy in Yugoslavia was discussed, however, the Italian General Staff always remained very sceptical that it could be implemented, and regarded it at best as a rather theoretical possibility.[43] A similar scepticism was displayed by both the military and the Government towards the idea of creating of a Balkan alliance. From the beginning of the negotiations between Yugoslavia, Greece and Turkey in late 1952 to their conclusion in the summer of 1954, the Italian Government always maintained a strongly suspicious attitude towards the whole initiative. For Rome, Belgrade's insistence on the creation of a Balkan military alliance was only a shrewd scheme conceived to strengthen its negotiating strength in order to achieve a favourable settlement over Trieste. Thus the Italian reply to the Allied pressures to acknowledge the strategic relevance of the tentative Balkan alliance was that the issue could be discussed only after the problem of Trieste had been solved once and forever.[44] During his visit to Greece in January 1953, De Gasperi told Greek Prime Minister Marshal Papagos that this order of priorities could not be altered for any reason.[45]

In spite of the benevolence which Greece and Turkey displayed towards a possible Italian adhesion to this pact, therefore, the Italian Government voiced many reservations about a Balkan alliance and reacted with hostility when the three Balkan countries signed a Treaty of Friendship in Ankara on 28 February 1953.[46] Not having been able to prevent it being signed, Italy then tried to prevent the Treaty from developing even further, and to slow down any progress towards an actual pact of mutual assistance until the issue of Trieste had been solved. Such a policy clearly shows how the Italian Government was following an agenda of its own, which had a thoroughly different set of priorities from that of the other NATO powers.

Eventually this Italian attitude clashed with the intention of both NATO/AFSOUTH and the United States to support a Balkan military alliance in order to link the military potential of Yugoslavia to NATO.[47] Faced with the perspective of the conclusion of the Balkan Pact before a final settlement of the dispute over Trieste, the Italian Government began to display a certain resentment towards NATO, and in particular towards the American CINCSOUTH.[48] Eventually De Gasperi sent an indirect signal to the Americans that if the ties between Yugoslavia and the West were strengthened much further, Italy would be compelled to revise its attitude towards the creation of a European Defence Community, which De Gasperi's Government had hitherto strongly supported.[49]

In short, for the whole period that goes from the beginning of the Korean War to the Italian–Yugoslav crisis of the late summer of 1953 and beyond, no conclusive and definite defence planning could be established for the Julian region. This was mostly due to the diffidence, if not outright hostility, between Rome and Belgrade, which prevented the adoption of the only military course of action which was regarded as strategically sound. Even though the outbreak of the war in the Far East had somewhat altered for a brief moment the Italian perceptions of the Cold War, for Rome it was still the local problem rather than the big strategic picture which dictated the country's defence and security policies.

CONCLUSIONS

Throughout the early Cold War years, the Soviet threat was rarely perceived in purely military terms by the Italian military: only for a short span in the summer and fall of 1950 did the Government and the High Command share the belief that there was a serious risk of a general war. This does not imply, however, that the ruling class felt that there was no threat at all to its control over the country. Quite the contrary, the records of these years convey a feeling of utmost instability, and the presence of a constant menace hangs over most Government activities; but the menace was mostly perceived in domestic rather than military or strategic terms. Even the problem of Trieste was probably regarded as a top priority because of the possible domestic repercussions of a prolonged stalemate over the future of the city (let alone its possible loss), rather than as a purely foreign policy issue.

The Italian perspective about the nature of the Soviet threat was therefore bound to be different from that of its Western partners, many of which in those early Cold War years had direct experience of military confrontation – and quite often of actual fighting – against either the Soviet Union or some of its satellites, from the Berlin blockade to Korea, to the Malayan insurgency, to Indochina. For Italy, on the other hand, the Soviet threat was embodied by the awkward presence in its territory of the largest Communist Party in the Western world. As the risk that the PCI might unleash an all-out insurrection decreased, the threat took an entirely political outlook which called for a very different set of counter-measures. With the exception of the months that followed the outbreak of the Korean War, the Italian Government was therefore rather hostile to a course of increasing militarization of the Cold War; and in the years which followed it made clear to its Allies whenever possible its preference for an anti-Communist strategy that took into account politico-economic, rather than military, issues.[50]

Notes

1. I would like to express my gratitude to two Directors of the Historical Office of the Army Staff, Brig. Gen. P. Bertinaria and Col G. Gay, for allowing me full access to previously classified records of the Army Staff; the records that are not available are those from the Ministry of Defense. This chapter draws on several previous works of mine: *L'esercito italiano nel secondo dopoguerra, 1945-1950* (Rome: USSME, 1989); 'The Italian Military and the Atlantic Pact', in E. Di Nolfo (ed.), *The Signature of the Atlantic Pact Forty Years afterwards: A Historical Reappraisal*, Proceedings of the International Conference held in Florence, 3–5 April 1989 (Berlin: Walter de Gruyter, 1991); 'Italy and the Defence of NATO's Southern Flank, 1949–1955', in K.A. Maier, N. Wiggershaus (eds), *Das Nordatlantische Bündnis, 1949–1956* (Munich: Oldenbourg Verlag, 1993).
2. The official reply of PCI leaders is of course that there never was such a plan; see for instance the declarations that followed the aborted uprising after the attempted assassination of Togliatti: P. Secchia, *Lo sciopero del 14 luglio* (Rome: Rinascita, 1948) p. 27; L. Longo, 'La risposta del popolo', *Rinascita*, 7 (July 1948) 234–5; see also *Archivio Pietro Secchia 1945–1973*, Fondazione Feltrinelli, *Annali*, XIX, 1978 (Milan: Feltrinelli, 1979) p. 427. A similar denial can be found, *inter alia*, in M. Caprara, *L'attentato a Togliatti. 14 luglio 1948: il PCI tra insurrezione e programma democratico* (Venice: Marsilio, 1978), or in G.C. Marino, *Guerra fredda e conflitto sociale in Italia, 1947–1953* (Palermo: S. Sciascia editore, 1991) ch. 1. A similar conclusion, but in a much more balanced presentation, is offered by P. Spriano, *Le passioni di un decennio, 1946–1956* (Milan: Garzanti, 1986) p. 98.
3. See, for instance, the reflections of H. Macmillan, *War Diaries. Politics and War in the Mediterranean, January 1943–May 1945* (London: Macmillan, 1984), under the entries of 25 March and 15 April 1945. On the 'Greek perspective', see also P. Spriano, *Storia del partito comunista italiano*, Vol. 5, *La Resistenza. Togliatti e il partito nuovo* (Turin: Einaudi, 1975) ch. 16. On the relations between Italy and the Allied powers after the armistice of 8 September 1943, see *inter alia*: D. Ellwood, *Italy 1943–1945* (Leicester: Leicester University Press, 1985); N. Kogan, *Italy and the Allies* (Cambridge, Mass.: Harvard University Press, 1956); J.E. Miller, *The United States and Italy, 1940–1950. The Politics and Diplomacy of Stabilization* (Chapel

Hill–London: The University of North Carolina Press, 1986); H. Stuart Hughes, *The United States and Italy*, 2nd edn (Cambridge, Mass.: Harvard University Press, 1965).

4. E. Di Nolfo, 'The US and Italian Communism, 1942–1946: World War II to the Cold War', *Journal of Italian History*, 1, 1 (1978) 74–94.
5. See, for instance, the concerns of SACMED, Field Marshal Alexander, in his letter to the Combined Chiefs of Staff of 3 August 1945, NA, Record Group 165, ABC 420 Italy (30 October 1943), Sect. 1–B.
6. On Trieste, see: D. De Castro, *La questione di Trieste: l'azione politica e diplomatica italiana dal 1943 al 1954*, 2 Vols (Trieste: LINT, 1981); M. de Leonardis, *La 'diplomazia atlantica' e la soluzione del problema di Trieste (1952–1954)* (Naples: ESI, 1992); A.G. de' Robertis, *Le grandi potenze e il confine giuliano, 1941–1949* (Bari: Laterza, 1983); J.-B. Duroselle, *Le Conflit de Trieste, 1943–1954* (Brussels: Institut de Sociologie de l'Université Libre de Bruxelles, 1966); B. Novak, *Trieste 1941–1954. The Ethnic, Political and Ideological Struggle* (Chicago: University of Chicago Press, 1970); R.G. Rabel, *Between East and West. Trieste, the United States, and the Cold War, 1941–1954* (Durham: Duke University Press, 1988); G. Valdevit, *La questione di Trieste 1941–1954. Politica internazionale e contesto locale* (Milan: Angeli, 1986).
7. 'Future Policy toward Italy', memorandum by Chief Commissioner Ellery Stone, 23 June 1945, in *FRUS, 1945*, 'The Conference of Berlin' [The Potsdam Conference], Vol. 1, pp. 688–94.
8. For more information about Allied demobilization plans, see the exchange of letters between Churchill and FM Alexander, on 17 June 1945, PRO, War Office, 193/280.
9. The Supreme Allied Commander in the Mediterranean to the Combined Chiefs of Staff, 3 August (NAF 1051) and 22 August (NAF 1059) 1945; CCS to SACMED (FAN 621), 30 September 1945, NA, Record Group 165, ABC 420 Italy (30 October 1943), Sect. 1–B.
10. Minutes of a MMIA Conference, 2–3 November 1945, Federal Records Center, Suitland, Record Group 331, #10000/120/5293.
11. Lettere del Generale Utili al Ministro della Guerra e al Capo di Stato Maggiore Regio Esercito, 21–2 luglio 1945, AUSSME, Diario Storico Stato Maggiore Regio Esercito, 1945, Allegato 174.
12. By mid-1947 US forces in Italy proper (that is, not counting those deployed in Trieste) amounted to one tank battalion (the 752nd) and one infantry division (the 88th), while the British had six tactical units (unbrigaded infantry battalions) for a total of 5000 men, and supply and administrative units for a total of 7800, plus a military mission of about 500 men. For the data on US troops, see H.J. Schraut (with J.D. Hefferman, A.M. Karber, P.A. Karber, M.D. Yaffe), *The United States Army in Europe, 1945–1955* (Nuclear History Program, 1990). For the data on the British troops, see the report by the Joint Intelligence Committee to the JSSC 'Estimates of the Situations in Greece and Italy', NA, RG 165, ABC 370.5 Greece Italy (20 August 1947), Sect. 1–A.
13. *Ibid.*
14. 'Consequences of Allied Troop Withdrawals from Italy', Central Intelligence Group Special evaluation no. 30, 16 September 1947, Declassified Documents Reference Service, 1976, 16 D.
15. 'US Military Assistance to Italy. Report by the US Army Survey Group to Italy', 13 October 1947, NA, RG 319, P and O 091 Italy TS

(13 October 1947), Sect. 1, Case 1, Part 1. For a more detailed analysis of the Bathurst mission, see Nuti, *L'esercito italiano*, pp. 122–5.

16. The request to delay the withdrawal is mentioned in 'Note of Record, Delay in Departure of US Forces from MTO', 28 November 1947, NA, RG 319, P and O 384 (Sect. VII), Cases 91/103. The other suggestions are in The Ambassador in Italy [James Dunn] to the Secretary of State, 5 December 1947, in *FRUS, 1948*, Vol. 3, pp. 736–7.
17. The Ambassador in Rome [James Dunn] to the State Department, 7 December 1947, in *ibid.*, pp. 738–9.
18. Lovett to Royal, 28 November 1947, in *ibid.*, p. 729. On that very day the US Congress passed a bill providing Interim Aid for France and Italy as a stop-gap measure before the Marshall Plan begun to be implemented: Miller, *The United States and Italy*, p. 236.
19. For the details of this debate, see Nuti, *L'esercito italiano*, pp. 127–8.
20. J.E. Miller, 'Taking Off the Gloves: the US and the Italian Elections of 1948', *Diplomatic History*, 7, 4 (1983) 33–55. On the role played by the CIA in the elections, and the 'sense of omnipotence' generated by its success, see P. Grose, *Gentleman Spy. The Life and Times of Allen Dulles* (Boston: Houghton Mifflin, 1994) pp. 284–5. On Great Britain and the Italian elections, see A. Varsori, 'La Gran Bretagna e le elezioni italiane del 18 aprile 1948', *Storia Contemporanea*, 13, 1 (1982) 5–70. On the curious role of Ireland, see the fascinating essay by D. Keogh, 'Ireland, the Vatican and the Cold War: The Case of Italy, 1948', *The Historical Journal*, 34, 4 (1991) 931–52.
21. As the US Military Attaché suggested at the time, these studies must be interpreted with great caution, since they were prepared shortly before the elections of 18 April and were therefore conceived to put some pressure on the Truman Administration. The studies were consulted by the author (in the English translation made by the US Embassy at the time) at the National Archives thanks to the Freedom of Information Act. No copy of the original version could be located in the archives of the Army Historical Office in Rome. The Italian origin of these documents seems to deny the charge made by Massimo Caprara that Scelba's statements were all based on the work of the PWB and the OSS: M. Caprara, *L'attentato a Togliatti*, p. 138, note 50.
22. The paper stressed the importance of the control of Italy for the Russian strategy in the Mediterranean in order both to disrupt the Allied lines of communication with the Middle East and to outflank the Allied forces in Central Europe, threatening France directly: Office of the Military Attaché, American Embassy in Rome, to Director of Intelligence, GSUSA, Dept. of the Army: Italian General Staff Studies, 'Function of Italy in the Anglo-American Strategic Plan for the Mediterranean', 28 April 1948, NA, RG 319, P and O 091 Italy TS, Box 17–Tab. 21–STAT.
23. Office of the Military Attaché, American Embassy in Rome, to Director of Intelligence, GSUSA, Dept. of the Army: Italian General Staff Study, 'Potentialities of Internal Security in Italy', 28 April 1948, NA, RG 319, P and O 091 Italy TS, Box 17–Tab. 21–STAT.
24. Part 1, 'Probable Military Repercussions as Result 18 April Elections in Italy'; Part 2, 'Outline of the Organization of the Italian Communist Military Apparato'; Part 3, 'Possibilities of Landings on the Adriatic Coast', Italian General Staff Study, 'Potentialities Internal Security in Italy'.

25. See the report of General de Giorgis to the Ministry of the Interior, 26 August 1948, quoted by Marino, *Guerra fredda e conflitto sociale*, p. 44.
26. Ministero della Difesa, Stato Maggiore Esercito-Ufficio Operazioni, 'Insegnamenti da trarre dai recenti disordini', 6 agosto 1948, AUSSME, I–4, racc. 59, cart. 10.
27. See for instance the writings by Pietro Secchia quoted in Marino, *Guerra fredda e conflitto sociale*, pp. 46–50. It should be remembered that Secchia himself had put forward a very ambiguous proposal to Stalin in December 1947, hinting at the possibility that the Party should adopt an all-out revolutionary course: *Archivio Pietro Secchia*, p. 426. On this issue see also Spriano, *Le passioni*, pp. 90–2.
28. Caprara, *L'attentato*, pp. 54–5.
29. See, for instance, the conclusions of a high-level meeting of members of the Ministries of the Interior and Defence, August 1948, where it was decided that the closest co-ordination between all the security forces was necessary in order to cope successfully with possible large-scale disturbances of public order: Stato Maggiore della Difesa, 3 Sezione, 'Verbale della Riunione che ha avuto luogo il 12 agosto presso lo S.M. Difesa allo scopo di esaminare se le norme in vigore per l'ordine pubblico rispondano ad ogni esigenza e di proporre al ministro della difesa eventuali aggiunte o varianti', 24 August 1948, AUSSME, I–4, racc. 59, cart. 10.
30. The following paragraph is taken from Nuti, 'The Italian Military'.
31. A. Varsori, 'La scelta occidentale dell'Italia (1948-1949)', *Storia delle Relazioni Internazionali*, 1–2 (1985) 95–159, 303–68, and L. Nuti, 'La missione Marras, 2–22 dicembre 1948', *Storia delle Relazioni Internazionali*, 2 (1987).
32. Nuti, 'La missione Marras'.
33. For the growth of the Italian police force, see A. Sannino, 'Le forze di polizia nel secondo dopoguerra (1945–1950)', *Storia Contemporanea*, 16, 3 (1985) 427–85.
34. For the debate at the strategic level, see B. Heuser, 'Yugoslavia in Western Military Planning 1948–1953', in M. Milivojevic, J.B. Allcock, P. Maurer (eds), *Yugoslavia's Security Dilemmas. Armed Forces, National Defence and Foreign Policy* (Oxford: Oxford University Press, 1988) pp. 132–5. For plan 'Pilgrim', see 'Plans for the Withdrawal of Allied Forces from Austria'. Copy of a memorandum dated 22 July 1949 from the War Office to the Secretary, Chiefs of Staff Committee. Annex II, Digest of Plan 'Pilgrim' – 'Evacuation of Allied Forces from Austria. Note from the War Office', PRO, DEFE 11/23.
35. *Ibid.*
36. Sintesi della riunione dei Capi Reparto e dei Capi Ufficio SME tenuta il 3–4 luglio 1950, AUSSME, L–13, Fondo Marras, racc. 52, b. 4.
37. Riunione del Consiglio dei Ministri, 27 giugno 1950, ACS, Verbali delle riunioni del Consiglio dei Ministri.
38. Nuti, *L'esercito italiano*, pp. 232–5.
39. Riunione del Consiglio dei Ministri, 12 dicembre 1950, ACS, Verbali delle riunioni del Consiglio dei Ministri.
40. Extract of meeting of Principal Staff Officers of the EMMO Region on 13 July, PRO, DEFE 11/23.
41. Chiefs of Staff Committee, 'Strategy to be Adopted in Northern Italy in an Emergency'. Copy of a letter dated 18 September 1951 from the

British Military Representative, SHAPE, to the Secretary, Chiefs of Staff Committee. 21 September 1951, PRO, DEFE 11/24.
42. Heuser, 'Yugoslavia', p. 139.
43. Chiefs of Staff Committee, 'Strategy to be Adopted in Northern Italy in an Emergency', PRO, DEFE 11/24. According to the Italian Secret Service, the Yugoslavs were thinking of deploying 14 to 16 divisions along the 530 km of the Bulgarian border in order to defend Macedonia, and another 16 along the 1200 km of the border with Hungary and Romania. This was seen as evidence of Yugoslav intention not to defend the Ljubljana gap: 'Stato Maggiore Esercito–Ufficio Operazioni, a Stato Maggiore Difesa. Oggetto: riunione delle delegazioni militari jugoslavo-greco-turca (Belgrado, 9–20 settembre 1953)', 7 January 1954. See also 'Sintesi degli argomenti trattati nella riunione dei capi di SM con il Maresciallo Montgomery', 30 January 1954, AUSSME, I–5, Carteggio Ufficio Operazioni SME.
44. Tarchiani a De Gasperi, 25 dicembre 1952, in M.R. De Gasperi (ed.), *De Gasperi scrive. Corrispondenza con capi di Stato, cardinali, uomini politici, giornalisti, diplomatici*, 2 Vols (Brescia: Morcelliana, 1974) Vol. 2, pp. 150–1.
45. The Ambassador in Greece [Peurifoy] to the Secretary of State, De Gasperi–Papagos Conversation, 12 January 1953, NA, RG 59, 740.5/1-1253. See also the impressions of the Turkish Foreign Minister on this regard in The Ambassador in Turkey [McGhee] to the Department of State, 6 January 1953, in *FRUS, 1952–54*, Vol. 8, pp. 603–5. As for US interest in the creation of the Balkan Alliance, see *ibid.*, pp. 590–673.
46. The Ambassador in Turkey [McGhee] to the Department of State, 6 February 1953, in *ibid.*, pp. 616–19. For Yugoslav resentment about the late revisions of 'critical paragraphs' in the treaty as a result of US and British insistence, see The Ambassador in Greece [Peurifoy] to the Department of State, 26 February 1953, in *ibid.*, pp. 625–6.
47. For Admiral Carney's support of a Balkan alliance, see Naples (American Embassy Special Liaison Officer) to the State Department, Bi-Weekly Review for NATO Southern Region, 16 April 1953, NA, RG 59, 740.5/4–1653. References to CINCSOUTH's role also in the Ambassador in Italy [Luce] to the Department of State, 20 July 1953, in *FRUS, 1952–54*, Vol. 8, pp. 633–4.
48. In June 1953 the Italian Defence Minister Pacciardi felt it necessary to write a letter directly to the SACEUR, 'significantly bypassing admiral Carney', in which he criticized any military association between NATO and Yugoslavia: The Ambassador in Rome [Luce] to the Secretary of State, 13 July 1953, NA, RG 59, 740.5/7–1353.
49. The Ambassador in Bonn [Conant] to the Secretary of State, 23 July 1953, NA, RG 59, 740.5/2353.
50. For a similar argument, see also A. Varsori, 'L'Italia e la difesa dell'Occidente, 1948–1955: l'alleato sfuggente', in Id., *La politica estera italiana nel secondo dopoguerra (1943–1957)* (Milan: LED, 1993). On Italian security and defence policies see also L. Nuti, 'Appunti per una storia della politica di difesa italiana nella prima metà degli anni' 50', in E. Di Nolfo, R. Rainero, B. Vigezzi (eds), *L'Italia e la politica di potenza in Europa negli anni, 50* (Milan: Marzorati, 1992).

Index

Note: page numbers in **bold** indicate contributed material.

Abramov, A.N. 111–12
Acheson, D. 28
Ackermann, A. 33, 44, 49
Adenauer, K. 44, 360, 361–2, 363, 365, 367, 368
Aegean, control of 9, 301
Afghanistan 13, 15
Africa, North 300, 304
Aga-Rossi, E. **161–84**
Albania
  Balkan States, federation of 133, 134
  Bulgaria and 234–5
  Cominform and 202
  Communism in 125, 126, 134, 223
  Greece and 146, 233
  Italy and 376
  Macedonia 125, 127, 130–1, 132
  Soviet Union and 11, 16, 92, 155, 225–7, 232–3, 234–5, 236, 237, 376
  UK and 153, 154, 233
  USA and 153, 154, 233
  Yugoslavia and 126–7, 131–2, 133, 134, 137, 138, 225–7, 232–3, 234–5, 236
Alexander, H. 397, 399, 413
Allied Control Commissions
  Bulgaria 277, 280
  Finland 91, 92, 93–4, 95, 96–7, 98, 100–1
  Italy 388, 412–17
Allies, Western
  Austria and 396, 418, 419, 421, 422
  Bulgaria and 274–5, 277, 279–80, 281–2, 285–6, 385
  Germany and 24, 25, 26, 28–9, 30–1, 33, 46, 47, 53, 59–60, 61–2; Berlin crisis 62–74; currency reform 66–7, 68–9, 70, 71, 73; West Germany, establishment of 62, 68–9, 70–1, 72, 73
  Greece and 285

Italy and 162, 174, 396–7, 412–17, 422; Trieste 165–70, 259, 265, 269–70, 396–401, 402–3, 404, 405–6, 407–8, 413, 415, 418, 419, 420, 422
  Romania and 385
  Soviet Union and 57, 58, 62, 63, 145, 161–2, 186, 189, 209–10, 215, 216, 291–429
  Stalin, attitude of to 58, 145, 161–2, 186, 189, 191–2, 315
  Turkey and 285
  Yugoslavia and 421
  see also individual countries
Ambrose, S. 345
Arkad'ev, G.P. 4
Arnold, K. 47
Atom bomb 57, 202, 386
Attlee, C. 303–4
Auriol, V. 15
Austria
  Allies and 396, 418, 419, 420–2
  peace negotiations with 388
  Soviet Union and 13, 389
  USA and 416

Babarin, E.I. 4
Babič, B. 266–7, 268
Badoglio, P. 162
Bakarič, V. 135
Balkan States
  Balkan Pact 155, 158, 423–4
  China and 384
  Communism in 125, 138, 297
  federation of 125–32, 138, 193, 287, 315
  France and 315, 384
  Germany and 128
  Italy and 375, 423–4
  peace negotiations with 384, 386
  Soviet Union and 8, 9, 13, 15–16, 58, 125–43, 144, 155, 158, 192, 193, 297, 375, 384, 402
  UK and 125, 129–30, 132, 137, 144, 155, 297
  union of 132–6

431

432   Index

Balkan States – *cont'd.*
  USA and 132, 144, 155, 285–6
  see also individual countries
Baltic States
  Soviet Union and 5, 92, 295, 296
  UK and 295
Baltic Straits 107–12, 119–20, 121
Baranov, L. 145, 152, 153, 199, 238, 246
Barnes, M. 279, 285
Barthou, L. 15
Bathurst, C.R. 416
Belgium
  Cominform and 201
  France and 315
  Germany and 62
  Soviet Union and 9, 10, 13, 202
Bell, P.M.H. 296
Beneš, E. 136
Beria, L.P. 339, 340, 366
Berlin Appeal 204
Berlin crisis 29, 30, 57–75, 359, 370
  'air-bridge' 64, 71–2, 73
  Soviet Union and 57–75, 136, 192, 193
  United Nations and 72–3
  Western Allies and 62–74
Bernetič, M. 268
Bevin, E. 112, 300, 302–3, 304, 305–6
Bianchini, S. 132
Bianco, V. 166
Bidault, G. 67, 320–1, 322–3, 324, 327, 328, 346
Billotte, P. 329–30
Blum, L. 329
Bogomolov, A. 315, 316, 322, 329
Bohlen, C. 325, 331, 337, 346, 408
Bonomi, I. 376
Bornholm, 108, 109–10, 111–12, 119–20, 121
Bracken, B. 294
Britain *see* United Kingdom
Brooke, Alan 298
Brosio, M. 375
Brussels Pact 199
Bulganin, N.A. 62, 109, 339
Bulgaria
  Albania and 234–5
  Agrarian Union in 274, 275, 278–9, 281, 286

Allies, Western, and 274–5, 277, 279–80, 281–2, 285–6
Balkan States, federation of, and 134, 287
Cominform and 209, 286–7
Comintern and 273
Communism in 126, 127, 223, 227, 272–89, 297; army 275–6; BRP(k) 272–3, 274, 275–6, 277, 279, 281–2, 283, 284, 286, 287; Communist Youth League 276; General Workers' Professional Union 276; Patriotic Front 274, 275–85
elections in 280, 281, 283, 284, 285
Germany and 273–4
Greece and 133–4, 146, 148
'Labour' Party in 284
Macedonia and 125, 127, 130–1, 241
monarchy in 273
Patriotic Front and breakdown 276–81; elections 284; formation 274, 275; opposition 281–5, 286; revolution 285–7; Stalin and 276–8, 279–81, 282, 283, 284, 286, 287
peace negotiations with 303, 384, 385
purges in 275–6, 283–4, 286
reparations from 133
revolution in 285–7
Social Democratic Party and 274, 275, 279
Soviet Union and 9, 11, 15–16, 58, 92, 134–5, 155, 227, 228–9, 233–4, 235, 272–89, 297, 298, 313, 384, 385, 388; invasion 274–5
Stalin and 276–8, 279–81, 282, 283, 284, 286, 287
Turkey and 133
UK and 129–30, 274–5, 279–80, 297, 298, 389
USA and 274–5, 279–80, 389
Yugoslavia and 127–30, 131, 132–7, 228–9, 234–5, 239, 241, 268–9, 287
Zveno in 274, 275, 276, 280, 283, 286

Index

Butler, R.A.B. 346
Byrnes, J.F. 28, 281–2, 302, 327, 385, 386, 388, 389–90

Cadogan, A. 299, 302
Catroux, G. 325, 326, 329
Chervenkov, V. 128, 286
China
 Balkan States and 384
 Finland and 384
 Italy and 384
 Korean War and 422
 Soviet Union and 12, 13, 15, 313, 340, 347, 384, 385
Chişinevschi, I. 152, 153
Christian Democratic Union *see* Germany: CDU
Churchill, W.S.
 Balkan States and 129, 297
 Cold War and 191, 334–50
 Communism and 294
 Eisenhower and 334, 336, 342, 343–4, 345–6, 347, 348, 349
 France and 322, 325
 Germany and 18, 294
 Greece and 130, 138
 Italy and 129, 297
 Mediterranean and 297–8
 retirement of 349
 Roosevelt and 129
 Sforza and 375
 Soviet Union and 18, 129, 191, 294, 295, 297, 300, 322, 334, 342–4, 345–8, 349
 Stalin and 18, 130, 138, 191, 294, 297, 322
 summit, call for 348
 Tito and 342
 USA and 334–6
 Yalta Conference and 300
Clay, L. 64, 66, 68
Clissold, S. 222
Cogniot, G. 203
Cold War
 Churchill and 191, 334–50
 de Gaulle and 327
 definition of xviii–xix, xxiv
 historiography of xviii, xx–xxiii, 3, 178–80, 185, 189, 194, 197, 208–9, 222, 306, 356, 375, 383, 396, 409
 inevitability of 57, 180, 191–4
 Italy in 412–29
 origins of xviii–xxiv, 21, 33, 52–3, 180, 191–4, 208, 277, 301, 304, 306–7, 327, 383–94, 395
 period of xviii–xix, 301, 304, 327, 356, 412
 political geography of xix, xxii, 222
 Stalin and 185–94, 334
 Trieste in 395–411, 413, 415, 417, 418, 419, 420, 421, 422, 424
 see also individual countries
Cominform 153
 Albania and 202
 Belgium and 202
 Berlin Appeal 204
 Bulgaria and 209, 272–89
 creation of 59, 136, 138, 172, 176, 198–9, 211–12, 223, 229–30, 246–7, 248, 251, 252, 254–5, 259–60, 286–87, 305, 366
 Czechoslovakia and 209, 240
 dissolution of 205
 Eastern bloc and 195–289
 extension of functions of 203
 Finland and 100, 202
 France and 200, 201, 203, 204–5, 209, 230, 246, 253
 Germany and 29, 202
 Greece and 251
 Hungary and 209, 217, 240, 268
 Italy and 201, 203–4, 205, 209, 230, 246–63, 378
 Marshall Plan and 208–21, 246–7, 305
 'peace campaign' and 199–203
 Poland and 200, 209, 217
 purpose of 199, 208–21
 Romania and 209
 Stalin and 197–207, 209
 Stockholm Appeal 201–2, 203
 Vidali and 264–71
 Yugoslavia and 209, 229–30, 231, 232, 237, 240–1, 248–51, 253, 255, 258–9, 269
Comintern 76, 78, 91, 126, 127, 163, 273, 286
Communism
 Albania 125, 126, 134, 223
 Balkan States 125, 138
 Belgium 201
 Bulgaria 126, 127, 209, 223, 227, 272–89

Communism – *cont'd.*
  Czechoslovakia 209, 223, 227–8, 237, 238, 306
  Finland 89, 93, 98, 99–100, 101–2, 103, 202
  France 163, 176, 186, 197, 201, 203, 204–5, 209, 214–15, 216, 328, 331
  Germany 23–6, 32, 37–53, 186, 202, 356–7, 358, 365, 366, 367, 368, 370
  Greece 125, 131, 133, 135, 136, 137–8, 144–60, 193
  Hungary 209, 223, 228, 238
  Italy 161–80, 187, 197, 201, 203–4, 205, 209, 214–15, 216, 246–63, 376, 403–5, 412–13, 415, 416, 417–19, 425
  Poland 76–87, 209, 223, 227, 237–8
  Romania 209, 223
  Spain 264
  Trieste 267–70, 405
  UK 145, 202, 306
  USA 202, 247
  Yugoslavia 125, 126, 209, 222–3, 224–7, 228–41, 248–51, 253, 255, 258–9, 267–70
Cot, P. 314
Council of Foreign Ministers (CFM)
  atomic energy and 386
  Austria and 388, 389
  Balkan States and 384, 386
  Bulgaria and 303, 384, 385, 388, 389
  China and 384, 385
  Finland and 303, 384, 385
  France and 384, 385
  Germany and 302–3, 305, 388, 390
  Greece and 389
  Hungary and 303, 385
  Italy and 303, 383, 384, 385, 386, 387, 388–9, 390–1, 400
  Japan and 385, 386, 390
  London meeting 29, 384–5, 400
  Moscow meeting 29, 305, 386, 387–8
  New York meeting 303, 390–1
  Paris meeting 302–3
  Paris Peace Conference 389–90
  peace negotiations and 303, 383–94
  Poland and 388
  role of 392
  Romania and 303, 384, 385, 388, 389
  Soviet Union and 29, 63, 305, 384–92, 400
  Trieste and 388, 389, 391
  UK and 387, 389
  USA and 385, 386–7, 388–9, 390–1
  Yugoslavia and 385
Creuzberger, S. 50
Currency reform (Germany) 19, 60–1, 65–7, 68–9, 70, 71
Cyprus 5
Czechoslovakia
  Balkan States, federation of, and 134
  Cominform and 209, 240
  Communism in 223, 227–8, 237, 238, 247, 306
  France and 315
  Greece and 152
  Hungary and 240
  Marshall Plan and 212, 228
  Soviet Union and 7, 9, 10, 13, 15, 102, 136, 155, 180, 227–8, 237, 238–9, 247, 252, 313
  Western bloc and 329
  Yugoslavia and 239

D'Onofrio, E. 203
Dallin, A. **185–90**
Darlan, J. 311
DDR *see* Germany: DDR, creation of
De Castro, D. 270
De Gasperi, A. 165, 166, 168, 170, 171, 178, 249, 375–6, 404, 415, 416, 417, 422, 423, 424
de Gaulle, C.
  Communism and 310, 328, 330–1
  Europe, balance of power in 310–33; Western bloc 315, 316, 326–7, 328–30
  Germany and 310, 312, 314, 315, 318–20, 322, 327, 328, 330, 331
  Middle East and 330
  Poland and 322–5
  Soviet Union and 314; attitude to 311, 312, 316–17, 325–7, 328, 329, 330; Free France

Index 435

310–11, 330–1; Moscow, visit to 318–25; treaty 316–25
Stalin and 311, 312, 318–25, 330–1
UK and 310, 311, 312, 321, 322, 329
USA and 310, 311, 312, 314, 321, 326–7, 329–30
Dedijer, V. 234, 269
Dejean, M. 311, 313–14, 316, 317, 319–20, 324, 325, 330
Dekanozov, V.G. 3, 18, 20–1, 100, 108–10, 114, 119
Denmark
  Danish Freedom Council 108–9
  Germany and 108, 110
  Soviet Union and 9–10, 13, 106–12; Baltic Straits 107–12, 119–20, 121, 121; Bornholm 107, 108, 109–10, 111–12, 119–20
  UK and 108
  USA and 108
Dertinger, G. 38, 48, 49, 51
Deutsche Demokratische Republik *see* Germany: DDR, creation of
Di Biagio, A. **208–21**
Dimitrov, G.M. 40, 76, 77, 81, 82, 85, 86, 92, 127, 129, 130, 133, 134–5, 136, 137, 146, 147, 148, 163, 180, 199, 209, 229, 233–4, 239, 240, 273, 274, 277, 279, 282, 283–4, 285–6, 287
Dimitrov, G.M. ['G.M.'] 278, 279
Dimitrov, V. **272–89**
Dixon, P. 305
Djilas, M. 29, 100, 126, 127, 134, 135, 146, 227, 230–1, 232–3, 234, 236, 239, 248, 249, 250, 251, 253, 258
Dornhofer, H. 47
Døssing, T. 108
Duclos, J. 201, 202, 212, 249, 250, 253
Dulles, J.F. 198, 300, 342, 346, 347, 405

East Germany *see* Germany: DDR, creation of
Eastern bloc *see* Europe: Eastern bloc
Ebgen, E. 44
Eden, A. 11, 90, 107, 114, 129–30, 187, 294, 295, 296, 297, 300, 334, 337, 341, 342–3, 347, 349
Egorova, N.I. **197–207**
Egypt 304, 341
Eisenhower, D.D. 28, 334, 336, 337, 338, 342, 343–4, 345–6, 347, 348, 349, 405, 423
Enckell, C. 99
Erusalimsky, A.S. 5
Ethridge, M. 282
Europe
  de Gaulle and 310–33
  Eastern bloc 136, 137, 155, 174, 186, 189, 191, 192, 193, 279, 326, 330; Cominform 195–289; Marshall Plan 210–11, 212, 214–18, 248, 305; rural policies/problems 212–13
  Litvinov Commission view of 12–13, 14–15, 20
  Maisky Commission view of 7–12, 14–15, 20
  Socialism in 7, 11–12, 14, 24–27, 163, 164, 178–9, 186, 211
  Western bloc 315, 316, 326–7, 328–30
  see also individual countries; spheres of influence

Fagerholm, K.A. 101
Fajon, E. 202, 203
Farkas, M. 216–17
Filitov, A.M. **3–22**, 187
Finder, P. 76, 78, 81–2
Finland
  Allied Control Commission and 91, 92, 93–4, 95, 96–7, 98, 100–1
  China and 384
  Cominform and 209
  Communism in 89, 93, 98, 99–100, 101–2, 103
  economy of 96–7
  France and 293, 384
  Germany and 89, 94–6, 97
  Mannerheim and 94, 95–6, 97–9
  Olympic Games in 102
  Paris Peace Treaty and 91
  peace negotiations with 303, 384–5
  reparations from 96, 102–3
  Soviet Union and 5, 7–8, 11, 13, 89–103, 111, 173, 192, 295,

Finland – *cont'd.*
296, 313, 384, 385; armistice 91; Friendship, Co-operation and Mutual Assistance Treaty 89–90, 102; Moscow Peace Treaty 89, 90; Winter War 89, 90; Zhdanov 91–2, 93–5, 96, 97–8, 99–101
Teheran Conference and 90–1
UK and 90, 91, 293, 295–6
UN and 102
USA and 90
France
Balkan States and 315, 384
Belgium and 315
CFLN 312–15
Cominform and 200, 201, 203, 204–5, 209, 230, 246, 253
Communism in 163, 176, 186–7, 197–8, 214–15, 216, 246, 250, 258, 328, 330, 331; Marshall Plan 247
Czechoslovakia and 315
Finland and 293, 384
foreign policy of 314–15
Franco-Soviet Treaty 316–25
Free France 310–11, 312–14, 330–1
Germany and 24, 29, 60, 62, 305, 313–14, 315, 317–18, 319–20, 322, 325, 327, 328, 330, 331, 346, 360–1; Berlin crisis 64–5
Hungary and 315
Italy and 315, 420, 422
Luxembourg and 315
Marshall Plan and 247, 305
Middle East and 322
NATO and 330
Netherlands and 315
Poland and 315, 318, 322–5
Potsdam Conference and 325
Romania and 318
Soviet Union and 5, 6, 8, 10, 12, 13, 60, 163, 173, 174, 186–7, 188, 202, 247, 250, 258, 306, 310–33, 345, 346, 347, 348, 360, 384, 385, 403
Trieste and 403, 407
UK and 310, 311, 312, 313–14, 315, 322, 328, 329, 330, 345, 348

UN and 329–30
USA and 252, 310, 311, 312, 313–14, 326–7, 328, 329–30, 346, 348
Yalta Conference and 325
see also De Gaulle, C.
Frazier, R. 304–5

Gaddis, J.F. 277, 395
Garreau, 311, 312–13, 323–4, 325
Gascoigne, A. 335–6, 337–8, 339–41, 343, 344, 345, 347, 348, 349–50
Germany
Allies, Western, and 24, 25, 26, 28–9, 30–1, 33, 46, 47, 53, 59–60, 61
Balkan States and 128
Berlin crisis 29, 30, 57–75, 136, 192, 193, 359, 370; role of 358, 370
Bulgaria and 273–4
CDU creation 37–8; DBD and 50–1; DDR, role in 51–3; Dertinger 38, 48, 49, 51; Hermes 38, 39, 40, 41, 42–4, 52; Kaiser 38, 42, 43, 44–8, 52; land reform 39–40, 41; Lemmer 38, 44, 47, 49–50, 52; Nuschke 47, 48, 49, 51, 52; People's Congress 47–8, 49, 50; popularity 44–5, 50–1; religion 40, 41, 46, 52; SED and 48–51; Soviet Union and 37–53
Cominform and 29, 202
Communism in 23–6, 29, 32–3, 186, 356–7, 358, 365, 366, 367, 368, 370; CDU and 37–53; *see also* Soviet Union and
currency reform in 19, 60–1, 65–7, 68–9, 70, 71
DBD 50–1
DDR, creation of 30, 31–3, 51–3, 73, 369–70
defence of 360–1, 362, 364, 367
democratization of 59
de-Nazification of 33, 39, 59, 356
Denmark and 108, 110
disarmament of 8, 59
economy of 96

elections in 362, 363, 364, 365, 366, 367, 369
Finland and 89, 94–6
France and 24, 29, 60, 305, 313–14, 317, 318–20, 322, 325, 327, 328, 330, 331, 360–1, 365
Fundamentalist Reunification Party 366
KPD *see* SED
'Labour' Party in 284
land reform in 39–40, 41
LDP 38, 39, 41, 46, 51
Marshall Plan and 46–7, 62, 359
nationalization in 33
NDPD 51
neutrality of 16, 20
NKVD 32
Norway and 106, 113, 116
occupation of 8, 28, 325, 356–7, 358–9
partition of 3, 5, 8, 12, 16–18, 19–21, 23–33, 59–60, 72, 73, 301–3, 305, 369
party system of 358
peace negotiations with 302–3, 305, 388, 390
People's Congress in 47–8, 49, 50
rearmament of 360–1, 362, 364, 368
religion in 40, 41, 46, 52
reparations from 6–7, 8, 17–18, 26, 46, 59, 60, 188
Romania and 97
SED 23, 24, 28, 29, 30–1, 32, 33, 37, 38–9, 44, 45, 47, 49, 50, 356, 362, 365, 366, 368
Socialism in 24, 25, 26–7, 29–30, 31–2
Soviet Union and 4, 5, 11, 13, 16–18, 19–21, 23–33, 58–9, 111, 185–6, 189, 301–3, 335, 356–74; Berlin crisis 57–75, 136, 192, 193, 359, 370; role of 358, 370; CDU 37–53; Cominform 29; Communization 356–7, 358, 369; currency reform 19, 65–7, 68–9, 70, 71; DDR, creation of 30, 31–3, 72, 73, 369–70; disarmament 8; land reform 39, 356; Molotov–Ribbentrop Pact 293; neutrality 16, 20; occupation 8, 28, 356–7, 358–9; partition 3, 5, 8, 12, 16–18, 19–21, 23–33, 72, 73, 187–8, 299, 301–3, 305, 369; party system 358; rearmament 360–1, 364; reparations 6–7, 8, 17–18, 60; unification 3, 16–17, 19–20, 28–9, 32, 33, 301–3, 357, 359, 360–4, 365, 366, 367–8, 369–70, 371
SPD 26, 27, 38, 41, 44, 45, 52
Stalin and 4, 18, 20–1, 23–33, 51, 52, 59, 185–6, 188, 189, 319, 327, 356–74; Berlin crisis 62, 65, 68–70, 72, 73, 192, 193; policies, failure of 368–71
SVAG 32–3, 37–8, 40, 42–3, 44, 49, 50
UK and 18, 29, 293, 298, 299, 302–3, 305, 359, 360–1, 365
unification of 3, 16–17, 19–20, 24–5, 28–9, 30, 32, 33, 301–3, 327, 357, 359, 360–4, 365, 366, 367–8, 369–70, 371
Unity Party 44
USA and 19, 26, 28, 29, 46, 59, 198, 299, 302–3, 305, 359, 360–1, 365
Vatican and 46
West Germany, creation of 62, 68–9, 70–1, 73, 198, 363, 364
Yugoslavia and 126
Gheorghiu-Dej, G. 239, 240
Gibianskii, L.Ia. **222–45**
Giraud, H. 311–12
Girenko, Iu.S. 134
Gniffke, E.W. 33
Golikov, F.I. 116
Gomułka, W. 76, 77, 78, 82, 83, 86, 209, 212, 217, 227, 238, 239, 240
Gorodetsky, G. 294
Gottwald, K. 239–40, 248
Greece
Albania and 146, 233
Allies, Western, and 285
Balkan States, federation of 125, 133, 134
Bulgaria and 133–4, 146, 148

Greece – cont'd.
civil war in 131, 133, 135, 136, 137–8, 145, 146–55, 233, 249, 251, 285
Cominform and 251
Communism (partisans) in 125, 131, 133, 135, 136, 137–8, 144–60, 193, 297, 300; Democratic Army of Greece 149, 150, 151, 152–3, 154, 156; 'Limnes' 150–1
Czechoslovakia and 152
EDA and 156
EPEK and 156, 157
Hungary and 152, 153, 155
Italy and 249, 376, 423
Macedonia 127
monarchy in 156, 158
NATO and 155
Poland and 152, 153
Romania and 152
Soviet Union and 9, 11, 13, 15–16, 137, 144–60, 192, 193, 251, 252; aid 147–8, 149, 150, 152–3, 156, 297, 298, 376; elections 146; 'Free Greece' radio station 155, 156, 157–8
Turkey and 155, 423
UK and 129–30, 131, 137, 138, 139, 145, 147, 153–4, 156, 297, 298, 300, 304, 389, 415
UN and 147
USA and 137, 145, 153–4, 156, 214, 249, 285, 389, 415
Yugoslavia and 125, 127, 131, 133–4, 139, 148, 150, 151–2, 153, 154, 155, 249, 251, 423
Greco, R. 167
Grew, J. 398
Grigorian, V.G. 203
Gromyko, A. 153–4, 365, 405–8
Grotewohl, O. 24, 49, 361, 362–3

Hackzell, A. 93–4
Harvey, O. 294, 296
Hebrang, A. 130
Heller, W. 42–3
Hermes, A. 38, 39, 40, 41, 42–4, 50
Hohler, H. 341–2, 343, 348
Holland *see* Netherlands
Holtsmark, S.G. **106–24**, 187

Hoxha, E. 127, 133, 153, 226, 232, 233
Hungary
Balkan States, federation of, and 134
Cominform and 209, 217, 240, 268
Communism in 223, 227, 238
Czechoslovakia and 240
economy of 96, 155
France and 315
Greece and 152, 153
Italy and 259
peace negotiations with 303, 385
Soviet Union and 9, 11, 13, 155, 227, 238–9, 252, 385
USA and 216–17
Yugoslavia and 134, 238–40, 241, 268–9

Iceland 9–10
Indonesia 300, 349
Ioannidis, Y. 147, 148, 150, 151, 152
Iran
Soviet Union and 8, 13, 15, 300, 301, 303, 313
UK and 303
UN and 300
Iraq 300
Italy
Allied Control Commission and 388, 412–17
Balkan States and 423–4
China and 384
Cold War and 412–29; *see also* Soviet Union and
Cominform and 201, 203–4, 205, 209, 230, 246–63, 378
Communism (PCI) in 161–80, 187, 197–8, 214–15, 216, 246–63, 297, 415, 425; achievements 178–9; civil war, possibility of 250, 252–8, 259, 412–13, 415–16, 417–19, 425; elections 177, 377, 415, 416, 417; government posts 376, 416; ideology 175–7; Leninism 175; Marshall Plan 176–7, 247; monarchy 187; 'peace campaign' 203; reparations 176; Stalinism 165, 175, 179;

Index 439

strength 417; strikes 416;
svolta di Salerno 162;
Togliatti 162–4, 166–7,
168–70, 174, 175, 177, 179,
203–4, 250, 256, 257, 258,
259, 376, 377, 403–5, 418;
trade unions 176; Trieste
165–70, 176, 225, 259,
265–7, 377, 403, 405
economy of 164, 165, 171, 172,
176
elections in 177, 377, 412, 415,
416, 417–20
FIAT 171
France and 315, 420, 422
Greece and 249, 376, 423
Hungary and 259
Korean War and 412, 421–2, 424,
425
Marshall Plan and 176–7, 247,
377, 378, 379
NATO and 419, 420–2, 423–4
occupation of 413–17
peace negotiations with 303,
383–91, 415
post-war situation in 164, 413–14,
417–18
rearmament of 414–15,
416–17
reparations from 172, 176, 378,
384, 390
Soviet Union and 11, 13, 161–84,
188, 246–63, 297, 306,
375–82, 384–5, 386, 388–9,
390, 391, 407, 412, 424–5;
African possessions 8; civil
war, possibility of 250,
252–8, 259; economic
relations 165, 170–4, 176,
376–7, 378–9; elections 177,
377; ideology 175–7;
Leninism 175; Marshall Plan
176–7, 247, 377, 378;
monarchy 187;
'peace campaign' 203; radio
counter-propaganda 202;
reparations 176, 378, 384;
Sicily 5, 8; Stalinism 165,
175, 179; Togliatti 162–4,
166–7, 168–70, 174, 175,
177, 179, 203–4, 250, 256,
257, 258, 259, 376, 377,
403–5; trade unions 176

Trieste and 165–70, 176, 225,
259, 265–7, 377, 384, 388,
389, 390, 391, 396–7, 398–9,
400, 402, 403–5, 406, 407,
413, 415, 417, 418, 419, 420,
421, 422, 424
Turkey and 423
UK and 129, 166, 167, 171, 172,
174, 296, 297, 376, 387, 400,
402, 404, 406, 415, 421, 422
UN and 376, 422
USA and 166, 171, 172, 174, 177,
252, 257, 259, 296, 375, 376,
377, 386–7, 388–9, 400, 402,
406, 415–17, 419–20, 421,
422
Vidali and 270, 404, 405
Yugoslavia and 165–70, 249,
258–9, 266–7, 268–9, 376,
377, 402, 405, 406, 407–8,
412, 413, 415, 417–18, 419,
420, 421–2, 423–4
Iudin, M.M. 4, 268

Japan
Soviet Union and 10, 11, 12, 385,
386
USA and 390
Joliot-Curie, F. 201
Juin, A. 320, 329, 330

Kaganovich, L. 339
Kaiser, J. 38, 42, 43, 44–8, 50
Kardelj, E. 128, 129, 134, 135, 136,
137, 168, 212–13, 227, 230,
234, 235–6, 248–9, 250, 251,
253, 254–5, 402
Katyn massacre 296–7
Kekkonen, U. 102
Khrushchev, N. 193, 204, 341
Koch, W. 41
Koenig, M.-P. 66
Kolarov, V. 135, 234, 274
Kolesnichenko, ??? 50
Kollontai, A. 108
Korean War 202, 203, 343, 344, 348,
349, 360, 412, 421–2, 424, 425
Kostov, I. 128–9, 130, 135, 234,
276, 278, 287
Kostylev, M.A. 163–4, 166, 167,
168, 169, 171, 173, 177, 252,
259, 376–7, 403
Kozyrev, S.P. 378

Kratin, A. 38, 48, 50
Kucherov, S.G. 116
Külz, W. 41
Kurile Islands 7
Kuusinen, H. 93, 97
Kuusinen, O.V. 89
Kuznetsov, N.D. 117
Kuznetsov, V.V. 4
La Malfa, U. 379
Lake Bled declaration 133–4, 135, 139
Lalkov, M. 132
Laloy, J. 310
Lavrent'ev, A. 168–9, 231–2, 235
Lavrishchev, A. 232, 283
Lebedev, V.Z. 102
Leino, Y. 98, 99, 102
Lemmer, E. 38, 44, 47, 49–50
Lie, T. 10, 113, 114, 118
Lippmann, W. 15
Litvinov, M.M. 3
Litvinov Commission 4–6, 7, 12–17, 18–19, 20, 107–8, 111
Lobedanz, R. 48
London conference [on Germany] 62, 68–9, 71
Longo, L. 164, 212, 216, 249–50, 252–3, 419
Loth, W. 3–4, **23–36**
Lozousky, S.A. 4, 5, 108, 110, 117
Luxembourg 62, 315

Macedonia 125, 127, 130–1, 132, 225, 241
Maclean, F. 126, 130
McNeil, H. 153
Magill, J.H. 103
Maisky, I.M. 5, 18, 114, 317
Maisky Commission 4, 6–12, 13–15, 17–18, 19, 20
Malenkov, G. 62, 135, 197, 198, 199, 250, 257, 260, 338, 339, 340–1, 344, 345
Malik, J. 72
Manchkha, P. 145
Manchuria 313
Mannerheim, C.E.G. 94, 95–6, 97–9
Manuilsky, D.M. 4, 5
Marshall, George 60, 198, 305
Marshall Plan 29, 46–7, 58, 59, 62, 172, 176–7, 197–8, 199, 248, 305, 359, 369, 377, 378, 379

Cominform and 208–21, 246–7
Mason, P. 336–7, 341, 343
Massigli, R. 312–13, 314, 325
Mayhew, C. 303, 305
Mediterranean, control of 297–8, 299, 301, 303–4, 313, 376, 378, 421
Meissner, B. 23
Michev, D. 234
Middle East
 France and 322, 326, 330
 Soviet Union and 10, 300, 304, 326, 330
 UK and 300, 303–4
Mihailovič, D. 126
Mikoian, A. 4
Mikołajczyk, S. 84, 85–6
Mil'khiker, 42–3
Moloskovsky, F. 269
Molotov, V.M.
 Balkan States and 134, 135–6
 Baltic Straits and 107
 Berlin crisis and 62, 63, 68, 69, 70–1
 Bornholm and 109, 112
 Bulgaria and 275
 Byrnes and 28, 385, 390
 CFM and 29, 30, 305, 385, 390
 China and 385
 Cominform and 197, 199
 De Gaulle and 311, 322–3
 Denmark and 107, 109, 112
 Finland and 100, 296
 foreign minister, as 186
 France and 311, 320–1, 322–3, 385
 Germany and 293, 313, 366
 Greece and 144–5, 149, 150
 hardliner, as 3
 Hungary and 259
 ideology of 161, 173
 Italy and 168, 173, 259, 376, 385
 Kardelj and 235–6
 Litvinov and 4, 5
 Maisky and 7, 17
 Marshall Plan and 210, 214, 305
 Norway and 113–19
 Poland and 322–3
 post-war construction and 20–1
 Potsdam Conference and 277
 Romania and 296
 spheres of influence and 277

Stalin, death of, and 338–9, 340
Svalbard and 113–19
Trieste and 168
UK and 296, 305, 311, 322, 338–9, 343–5
UN and 376
USA and 210, 214, 311, 390
Yugoslavia and 134, 135–6, 235–6, 259–60, 366
Molotov–Ribbentrop Pact 293, 313
Morawski, E.O. 82
Morozzo della Rocca, R. 375
Moscow Peace Treaty 89

Naimark, N.M. **37–56**
Narinskii, M.M. **57–75**, 191, 192
Nation, R.C. **125–43**, 192, 193
NATO 155, 199, 330, 343, 419, 420–4
Negarville, C. 168
Nenni, P. 32, 169, 173, 378
Netherlands
  France and 315
  Germany and 62
  Indonesia and 300
  Soviet Union and 9, 10, 13
Nevakivi, J. **89–105**, 192, 193
NKVD 7
North Sea, access to 313
Norway
  Germany and 106, 113, 116
  Soviet Union and 10, 13, 106, 112–24; agreement 109; border areas 115–18, 119; Svalbard 113–14, 115, 116, 117–18, 119
  UK and 113–14, 116, 293
  USA and 120
Novikov, N. 248, 260
Nowotko, M. 81, 85
Nuschke, O. 47, 48, 49, 51, 52
Nuti, L. **412–29**
Nutting, A. 348

Obbov, A. 279, 285, 286
Oil 293, 304
Orlov, P.D. 93, 100, 108, 113
Outer Mongolia
  Soviet Union and 313

Paasikivi, J.K. 98, 102
Papagos, A. 156, 157
Palestine 304

Paris Peace Conference/Treaty 91, 133, 168, 248, 260, 359, 389–90, 401
Parri, F. 171
Partsalidis, M. 144, 145–6
Passi, M. 264
'Pax Americana' 391
'Pax Sovietica' 391
Pazzi, G. 376–7
'Peace campaign' 199–203, 204
Petkov, N. 278, 279–80, 281, 282, 285, 286
Petranovič, B. 126, 132
Pieck, W. 4, 23–4, 25, 27, 28, 29, 30, 31, 38, 40, 41, 65, 185
Pijade, Moša 129, 130
Pirjevec, J. **264–71**
Plakhin, A.I. 110–12, 120–1
Plastiras, N. 156, 157
Poggiolini, I. **383–94**
Poland
  AK in 77, 78, 81, 84–5, 86, 87
  AL in 81, 84, 85, 86, 87
  Balkan States, federation of, and 134
  BCh in 77, 81, 84–5, 86, 87
  CKL in 83–4
  Cominform and 200, 209, 217
  Communism in 76–88, 223, 227, 237, 238
  CSDSiS in 83
  France and 315, 318, 322–5, 331
  Germany and 78, 79, 84
  Government-in-exile of 77, 78–9, 80, 81, 83, 84, 85–6, 296, 299, 315
  Greece and 152, 153
  Jews in, attitude to 79
  Katyn massacre 296
  KPP in 76, 81
  KRN in 78, 82, 83, 84, 85
  land reform in 76–7, 79, 80–1, 85, 299
  Lublin Committee 318, 322–5
  Marshall Plan and 212
  PPR in 76–8, 81, 82, 83–4, 85, 86, 87
  PPS in 77, 78–9, 81, 84
  PPS-Lewica in 83, 86
  PS in 80
  religion in 81
  RJD in 83–4
  RPPS in 80–1, 82–3, 84

Poland – cont'd.
  SL in 77, 78, 81, 83, 84–5, 86
  Soviet Union and 7, 8–9, 11, 13, 15, 76–88, 111, 112, 155, 227, 237, 238–9, 296, 299, 313, 315, 318, 319, 322–5, 331, 388, 397–8
  UK and 299, 322
  USA and 322
  Warsaw Uprising 84
  Western bloc and 329
  WRN in 79–80
  Yugoslavia in 239
  ZPP and 77, 84, 86
Pollitt, H. 145
Pons, S. **246–63**
Popovič, K. 134
Popovič, V. 129
Portugal 8, 13
Pospelov, P.N. 199
Potsdam Conference 58, 59–60, 199, 272, 277, 299, 319, 325, 327, 358, 384, 386
Prazmowska, A.J. **76–88**
Prisoners of war 326

Quaroni, P. 384–5

Ra'anan, G. 230, 232
Rákosi, M. 155, 240, 241, 252
Ramadier, P. 197
Rankovič, A. 146, 149, 150, 227
Reale, E. 168, 246, 249, 250, 252, 254
Regent, I. 265, 266
Religion
  Germany 40, 41, 46, 52
  Poland 81
Reparations
  Bulgaria 133
  Finland 96, 102–3
  Germany 6–7, 8, 17–18, 26, 46, 59, 188
  Italy 172, 176, 378, 384
  Romania 96
Ribbentrop, J. von 107, 293
Roberts, F. 301, 337
Robotti, P. 177
Romania
  Balkan States, federation of, and 133, 134
  Cominform and 209
  Communism in 223, 297
  economy of 96
  France and 318
  Germany and 97
  Greece and 152
  peace negotiations with 303, 384, 385
  reparations from 96
  Soviet Union and 7–8, 9, 11, 13, 15, 130, 137, 155, 173, 239, 296, 297, 313, 318, 384, 385, 388, 389
  UK and 296, 297
  Yugoslavia and 134, 239, 297
Roosevelt, F.D. 28, 129, 191, 300, 357, 396, 398
Rothschild, J. 284
Ruini, M. 171
Rusk, D. 153
Rusos, P. 148, 152, 154–5
Russia *see* Soviet Union

Saburov, M.Z. 4
Sakhalin 7
Saksin, G.F. 4
Sargent, O. 302
Savonenkov, G.M. 101
Scandinavia 9–10, 13, 106–24
Scelba, M. 420
Schneider, G. 47
Schreiber, W. 39–40, 42, 44
Schwarz, H.-P. 23
Secchia, P. 176, 204, 255–7, 258–9, 377–8
Semenov, V.S. 20, 28, 30, 33, 51, 59, 61, 62, 63, 64–5, 108–10
Senin, M. 67, 69, 73
Sforza, C. 375, 379
Shoup, P. 125, 136
Shtein, B.E. 4, 16, 17
Shuckburgh, E. 343
Sidorovich, G. 231–2, 237
Siewert, R. 39–40
Sikorski, W. 84
Siluianov, N.M. 4
Simič, S. 130
Smirnov, A. 20, 59, 62, 63–4
Smirnova, N.D. **375–82**
Smodlaka, J. 129
Sinkiang *see* China
Socialism, European *see* Europe, Socialism in
Sokolovsky, V. 46, 59, 61, 62, 63, 64, 66, 68

Index

Sophoulis, 145, 150
Soutou, G.-H. **310–33**
Soviet Union
  Aegean and 301
  Afghanistan and 13, 15, 223
  Albania and 11, 16, 92, 134, 135,
    155, 225–7, 232–3, 234–5,
    236, 237, 376
  Allies, Western, and 57, 58, 62,
    63, 145, 161–2, 186, 189,
    209–10, 215, 216, 291–429
  Austria and 13, 389
  Balkan States and 8, 9, 13, 15–16,
    58, 92, 125–43, 155, 158,
    192, 193, 375, 384, 402
  Baltic States and 5, 92, 295, 296
  Belgium and 9, 10, 13, 202
  Berlin crisis and 57–75, 136, 192,
    193, 359
  Bulgaria and 9, 11, 15–16, 58, 92,
    155, 223, 227, 228–9, 233–4,
    235, 239, 272–89, 298, 313,
    384, 385, 388
  CFM and 29, 63, 305, 384–92,
    400
  China and 12, 13, 15, 313, 340,
    347, 384, 385
  Cominform and 195–289, 305; see
    also Cominform
  Cyprus and 5
  Czechoslovakia and 7, 9, 10, 13,
    15, 102, 136, 155, 180, 223,
    227–8, 237, 238–9, 247, 252,
    313
  de Gaulle and 310–33
  Denmark and 9–10, 13, 106–12
  East Asia and 300
  Eastern bloc and 136, 137, 174,
    178, 193, 248, 272, 296, 326,
    330, 357; Cominform
    197–289
  economy of 101–2, 157
  European Socialism and 7, 11–12,
    14, 24–7, 92–3, 155, 163, 178
  Finland and 5, 7–8, 11, 13, 15,
    89–103, 111, 173, 192,
    295–6, 313, 384, 385
  foreign policy of 3, 4–21, 58–60,
    161–2, 399–400; Cominform
    197–207, 246–63
  France and 5, 6, 8, 10, 12, 13, 60,
    163, 17, 258, 306, 310–33,
    345, 347, 348, 384, 385, 403
  Germany and 4, 5, 11, 13, 57–75,
    111, 185–6, 187–8, 299,
    301–3, 305, 317–18, 319,
    335, 356–74
  Greece and 9, 11, 13, 15–16, 131,
    137, 138, 144–60, 192, 193,
    251, 252, 298, 376
  Hungary and 9, 11, 13, 155, 217,
    223, 227, 238, 252, 385
  Iceland and 9–10
  Iran and 8, 13, 15, 300, 301, 303,
    313
  Iraq and 300, 303
  Italy and 5, 8, 11, 13, 161–84,
    187, 188, 197–8, 201, 202,
    214–15, 216, 246–63, 306,
    375–82, 384–5, 386, 387,
    388–9, 390, 391, 399, 404,
    407, 412, 424–5
  Japan and 10, 11, 12, 385, 386
  Katyn massacre and 296–7
  Korean War and 202, 203, 343,
    344, 348, 349, 360
  Kurile Islands and 7
  Manchuria and 313
  Marshall Plan and 59, 197–8, 199,
    208–21, 246–7, 248, 305,
    359, 369, 378
  Mediterranean and 297–8, 299,
    300, 301, 304
  Middle East and 10, 300, 304,
    326, 330
  military strength of 57–8
  Netherlands and 9, 10, 13
  NKID, Scandinavia and 106–21
  North Africa and 300
  Norway and 10, 13, 106,
    112–24
  Outer Mongolia and 313
  'Pax Sovietica' 391
  Poland and 7, 8–9, 11, 13, 15,
    76–88, 111, 112, 155, 217,
    223, 227, 237, 238–9, 296,
    313, 316, 318, 319, 322–5,
    331, 388, 397–8
  Portugal and 8, 13
  post-war construction and 295–6;
    problems of 3–21
  Romania and 7–8, 9, 11, 13, 15,
    130, 137, 155, 173, 223, 239,
    296, 297, 313, 318, 384, 385,
    388, 389
  Sakhalin and 7

Soviet Union – *cont'd.*
  Scandinavia and 9–10, 13, 106–24
  Spain and 8, 13
  spheres of influence and 3, 13–16, 58, 191, 193, 248, 252, 260, 277, 296, 307, 358, 359, 370; *see also* Europe; Litvinov Commission; Maisky Commission
  Stalin, death of, and 338–48, 349; view of 370–1; *see also* Stalin, J.
  Sweden and 5, 13, 111, 112
  Trieste and 165–70, 224–5, 229–30, 251, 225, 265, 266–70, 377, 384, 391, 395–411
  Turkestan and 313
  Turkey and 10, 13, 137, 300, 301
  UK and 5, 6, 60, 293–309, 334–55, 359, 378, 400, 403, 404; post-war construction, plans for 8, 9, 10, 11, 12–13, 15–16, 20, 107, 112, 130, 137, 138, 186, 322, 323
  UN and 200–1, 202, 300, 407, 408
  USA and 8, 10, 11, 16, 24, 28, 46, 57–8, 59, 60, 96, 102, 186, 189, 210, 213–14, 300, 307, 328, 331, 337, 340, 342, 345–6, 347, 357, 359, 360, 378, 385–92, 395–6, 398–9, 400, 403, 404, 405–6
  Vidali and 264–71
  Western bloc, formation of, and 329, 331
  Yugoslavia and 9, 11, 13, 16, 92, 102, 103, 130, 138–9, 148, 151, 155, 165–70, 193, 200, 218, 222–45, 248–52, 255, 258–60, 265–6, 267, 268–70, 313, 376, 377, 384, 399, 400–3, 406, 407, 408, 409, 419, 420, 421
  see also individual countries; Stalin, J.
Spain
  Communism in 264
  Soviet Union and 8, 13
Spheres of influence 3, 13–15, 20, 58, 191, 193, 210, 248, 252, 260, 277, 296, 307, 358, 359, 370; *see also* Europe; Litvinov Commission; Maisky Commission
Spiru, N. 134, 232
Stainov, P. 280, 283
Stalin, J.
  aims of 58, 157, 173, 186
  Albania and 134, 226, 232–3
  Allies, Western, attitude to 58, 145, 161–2, 186, 189, 191–2, 315
  Balkan States and 126, 128, 132, 134–5, 136–7, 138–9, 192, 193
  Baltic Straits and 107, 111
  Bevin and 305
  Bulgaria and 229, 272–89
  CFM and 28–9
  Churchill and 294, 297, 322
  Cominform and 197–207, 209, 255
  de Gaulle and 311, 312, 318–25, 330–1
  death of 270, 334–55
  'dosage' 186, 187
  Economic Problems of Socialism in the USSR 157
  Eastern bloc and 173, 179–80, 186, 189, 191, 357
  Eisenhower and 337, 338
  evaluation of 349–50
  Finland and 89–91, 92, 95–6, 102, 192
  foreign policy of 161–2, 173, 176, 179–80, 185–90, 202, 251, 277, 356
  France and 163, 174, 257, 313, 318–25, 326
  Germany and 4, 18, 20–1, 23–33, 51, 52, 59, 185–6, 188, 189, 319, 327, 356–74; Berlin crisis 62, 65, 68–70, 72, 73, 192, 193
  Greece and 131, 137–8, 145, 150, 151, 157, 192, 193
  ideology of 161, 186, 364, 370
  Italy and 161–3, 165–6, 170, 171, 175, 176, 178, 255, 257, 378
  Katyn massacre and 296–7
  Korean War and 360
  Labour Parties and 284
  Marshall Plan and 359
  militarism of 57

Paris Peace Conference and 248, 390
'peace campaign' and 200
Poland and 77, 84
post-war construction and 3, 23–33, 92–3, 166, 178, 179–80, 185–90, 295–6
priorities of 136
Roosevelt and 300, 357
Socialism, view of 26, 27
Tito and 27, 93, 127, 130, 133, 135, 138, 209, 225, 226, 229, 233–4, 251, 255, 265, 266, 267, 395, 398, 399, 402, 419
Togliatti and 203–4
Trieste and 165–70, 225, 265, 395, 398, 399, 402
Truman and 399
UK and 294–7, 311, 315, 319, 321
USA and 311, 315, 319, 321, 331, 357, 360, 398, 399
Western bloc, formation of, and 331
Yalta and 300
Yugoslavia and 129, 130, 132, 133–4, 135, 136, 138, 151, 166, 167, 193, 226, 229, 232–3, 259, 266, 267, 399
see also Soviet Union
Stasova, E. 269
Stavrakis, P. 131
Stockholm Appeal 201–2, 203, 204
Stone, E.W. 413
Strang, W. 20, 337, 343
Šubašić, I. 128
Surits, G.Ia. 4, 150
Suslov, M. 91, 135, 147, 200, 201, 202, 203, 237–8, 240
Svalbard 113–14, 116, 117–18, 119
Sweden
Soviet Union and 5, 13, 111, 112
Stockholm Appeal 201–2

Tarle, E.V. 4
Taubman, W. **191–3**
Teheran Conference 90–1, 297, 319, 328
Terracini, U. 254
Thorez, M. 162, 163, 255
Thorne, C. 294
Tito, J.B. 102, 103, 125, 126, 128, 132, 134, 136, 146, 151–2, 167–70, 200, 211, 227, 231, 232, 236, 237, 239, 250–1, 270, 243, 377, 396, 399, 407, 408
Stalin and 27, 93, 127, 130, 133, 135, 138, 209, 225, 226, 229, 233–4, 251, 255, 265, 266, 267, 395, 398, 399, 402, 419
Tiul'panov, S.I. 29, 33, 38, 40, 41–2, 45, 46–9, 50, 52
Togliatti, P. 162–4, 166–7, 168–70, 174, 175, 177, 179, 201, 202, 203–4, 225, 249, 250–1, 252, 253, 254, 255, 256, 258, 259, 266, 270, 376, 377, 403–5, 418
Travis, D. 178
Trieste 165–70, 224–5, 229–30, 251, 259, 265–70, 377, 384, 388, 389, 390, 391, 392, 395–411, 413, 415, 417, 418, 419, 420, 421, 422, 424
Truman, H.S. 46, 327, 335, 360, 388, 390, 397, 398, 399, 402, 415, 416
Truman Doctrine 59, 150, 198, 213–14, 248, 285, 304–5
Turkestan 313
Turkey
Allies, Western, and 285
Bulgaria and 132
Greece and 155, 423
Italy and 423
NATO and 155
Soviet Union and 10, 13, 137, 300, 301
UK and 304
USA and 214
Yugoslavia and 132, 155, 423

UK *see* United Kingdom
Ulam, A.B. 102, 138
Ulbricht, W. 24, 25, 26, 31, 33, 47, 358
Ulunian, A.A. **144–60**, 192, 193
Union of Soviet Socialist Republics (USSR) *see* Soviet Union
United Kingdom (UK)
Africa and 304
Albania and 153, 154, 233
Balkan States and 125, 129–30, 132, 137, 155
Bulgaria and 129–30, 274–5, 277, 279–80, 281–2, 285, 298
CFM and 387, 389

United Kingdom (UK) – *cont'd.*
  Communism and 145, 202, 306
  de Gaulle and 310, 311
  Denmark and 108, 120–1
  Egypt and 304
  Finland and 90, 91, 101, 293, 295–6
  France and 313–14, 315, 345, 348; *see also* de Gaulle and
  Germany and 18, 29, 60–1, 62, 293, 298, 299, 301–3, 305, 306, 318, 359, 360–1, 365; Berlin crisis 64–5
  Greece and 129–30, 131, 137, 138, 139, 145, 147, 153–4, 156, 298, 300, 304, 415
  Indonesia and 300
  Iran and 303
  Italy and 129, 166, 167, 171, 172, 174, 296, 387, 400, 402, 404, 406, 415, 421, 422
  Kenya and 304
  Marshall Plan and 305
  Mediterranean and 297–8, 299, 300, 303–4
  Middle East and 300, 303–4
  Norway and 113–14, 115, 116, 120, 293
  Palestine and 304
  Poland and 299
  Romania and 296, 297
  Socialism and 27, 93
  Soviet Union and 5, 6, 60, 293–309, 334–55, 359, 360, 378, 400, 403; Katyn massacre 296–7; Mediterranean 297–8, 299, 300, 378; post-war construction 8, 9, 10, 11, 12–13, 15–16, 20, 107, 112, 130, 137, 138, 186, 277, 295, 321, 322, 323; Stalin's death, results of 334–55; wartime alliance 293–300; *see also individual countries*
  spheres of influence and 3, 13–16, 20, 191, 193, 210, 277, 296, 307
  Trieste and 165–70, 266, 269–70, 396, 397, 398, 399, 400, 401, 402, 403, 404, 405–6, 407
  Turkey and 304
  UN and 304
  USA and 10, 11–12, 13, 14, 15, 213–14, 294, 299, 300, 304–5, 307, 334–6, 341, 342, 345–6, 347–8, 349, 415, 421
  Vidali and 266, 267, 269–70
  Western [European] Union 306
  Yugoslavia and 126, 128, 129–30, 154, 166, 266, 398, 400, 401, 402, 405
  see also Allies, Western; *individual countries*
United Nations (UN)
  Berlin crisis and 72–3
  creation of 300–1
  Finland and 102
  France and 329
  Greece and 147
  Iran and 300
  Italy and 376, 422
  Korean War and 422
  Soviet Union and 200–1, 202, 300, 407, 408
  Trieste and 407
  UK and 304
  USA and 388
United States of America (USA)
  Albania and 153, 154, 233
  atom bomb and 57
  Balkan States and 132, 155, 285–6
  Bulgaria and 274–5, 279–80, 281–2, 285–6
  CFM and 385, 386–7, 388–9, 390–1
  Cominform and *see* Marshall Plan and
  Communism in 202, 247
  de Gaulle and 310, 311, 326–7, 330
  Denmark and 108, 120–1
  Finland and 90, 101, 102
  France and 252, 313–14, 326–7, 329–30, 346, 348; *see also* de Gaulle and
  Germany and 19, 26, 28, 29, 46, 59, 60–1, 62, 198, 299, 302–3, 305, 318, 359, 360–1, 365, 390; Berlin crisis 64–5, 71–2
  Greece and 137, 145, 153–4, 156, 214, 249, 285
  Hungary and 216–17
  Iran and 303

Italy and 166, 171, 172, 174, 177, 252, 257, 259, 296, 375, 377, 386–7, 388, 390–1, 400, 402, 404, 406, 415–17, 419–20, 421, 422
Japan and 390
Korean War and 360
Marshall Plan and 29, 46–7, 58, 59, 62, 197–8, 208, 209–10, 218, 248, 305
NATO and 419
Norway and 120
'Pax Americana' 391
'peace campaign' and 202, 204
Soviet Union and 8, 10, 11–12, 16, 24, 28, 46, 57–8, 59, 60, 96, 102, 186, 189, 204, 299, 300, 307, 321, 328, 331, 337, 340, 342, 347–8, 357, 360, 378, 385–92, 395–6, 398–9, 403, 405–6
spheres of influence and 3, 13–16, 191, 193, 210, 277, 296, 307
Trieste and 165–70, 266, 269–70, 395, 396–7, 398–9, 400–1, 402, 403, 404, 405–6, 407
Truman Doctrine and 59, 150, 198, 213–14, 248, 304–5
Turkey and 214
UK and 10, 11–12, 13, 14, 15, 213–14, 294, 299, 300, 304–5, 334–6, 341, 342, 345–6, 347–8, 349, 415, 421
UN and 388
Vidali and 266, 267, 269–70
'Voice of America' radio station 202
Yugoslavia and 128, 154, 166, 266, 385, 397, 398, 400–1, 402, 405
see also Allies, Western; *individual countries*
USSR *see* Soviet Union

Valdevit, G. **395–411**
Valletta, V. 171
Vandenberg, A. 300, 388
Vansittart, R. 17
Varga, E.S. 4, 26, 27, 58, 211, 248
Varsori, A. **334–55**
Vasilevsky, A.M. 4, 91
Vatican 41, 46

Velchev, D. 276, 283, 284
Venizelos, E. 156
Vetrov, M.S. 100, 109, 110–12, 116–17, 118, 119
Vidali, V.
Babi\c and 266–7, 268
Cominform and 264–71
elections, success in 269–70
Italy and 270, 404–5
Mexico, in 264–5
peace petition and 269
Soviet Union and 264–70, 404–5
Spain, in 264
Tito and 269, 270
Togliatti and 266, 267
Trieste, in 266–70, 404–5
UK and 266, 267, 269–70
USA and 266, 267, 269–70
Yugoslavia, in 265
Vlahovič, V. 129, 265
Volnukhin, P.I. 113
Voroshilov Commission 4
Vukmanovic-Tempo, S. 125–6, 134, 137
Vuolijoki, H. 101
Vyshinsky, A.Ia. 4, 19, 20–1, 110, 130, 171, 282, 335

War crimes 98
Warner, C. 301, 303
Warner, G. **293–309**
Warsaw Uprising 84
Weiss, L. 268
Welles, S. 17
West Germany *see* Germany: West Germany, creation of
Western bloc *see* Europe: Western bloc
Western European Union 199, 306
Wettig, G. **356–74**
Witte, S. 48
Wolf, E. 42
Wolf, W. 42
Woodhouse, C.M. 131

Xoxe, K. 226, 232

Yalta Conference 18, 21, 28, 60, 62, 132, 199, 265, 272, 277, 279, 300, 319, 325, 357, 397, 398
Yergin, D. 395
Young, J. 335

Yugoslavia
  Albania and 126–7, 131–2, 133, 134, 137, 138, 225–7, 232–3, 234–5, 236
  Bulgaria and 127–30, 131, 132–7, 225, 228–9, 234–5, 239, 241, 268–9, 287
  Cominform and 209, 230, 231, 237, 240–1, 248–9, 253, 255–9, 269
  Communism in 125, 126, 222–3, 224–7, 228–41, 253, 255, 258–9, 265–71, 297
  Czechoslovakia and 238–9
  Germany and 126
  Goli Otok 269
  Greece and 127, 131, 132, 133, 139, 148, 150, 151–2, 153, 154, 155, 249, 251, 423
  Hungary and 134, 238–40, 241, 268–9
  Italy and 165–70, 225, 249, 258–9, 266–7, 268–9, 376, 377, 402, 405, 406, 407–8, 412, 413, 415, 417–18, 419, 420, 421–2, 423–4
  'Labour' Party in 284
  Macedonia 125, 127, 130–1, 132, 225, 241
  Marshall Plan and 211
  NATO and 423–4
  Poland and 239
  Romania and 134, 239
  Soviet Union and 9, 11, 13, 15, 16, 92, 102, 103, 128, 148, 151–2, 153, 155, 165–70, 193, 200, 218, 222–45, 248–52, 255, 258–60, 265–6, 267, 268–70, 297, 313, 376, 377, 384, 400–3, 406, 407, 408, 409, 419, 420, 421; Friendship, Cooperation and Mutual Assistance Treaty 130
  Trieste and 165–70, 224–5, 229–30, 251, 265–70, 377, 384, 396–7, 398–401, 402, 405, 406, 407, 413, 415, 421, 424
  Turkey and 133, 155, 423
  UK and 126, 128, 129–30, 131, 154, 297, 400, 401, 402, 405
  USA and 128, 154, 385, 400–1, 402, 405
  Vidali and 264–71
  see also Balkan States; Tito, J.B.
Zachariades, N. 137, 138, 146–7, 148, 149–50, 151, 154, 157, 251

Zaslavsky, V. **161–84**
Zhdanov, A.A. 4, 91–2, 93–5, 96, 97–8, 99–101, 135, 136, 150, 176, 197–8, 199, 213, 214–16, 217–18, 229–31, 232, 246–7, 248–9, 250, 251, 252–3, 255–7, 258, 259, 260, 366, 377–8
Zhdanova, T.L. 115, 116–17, 118, 119
Zhukov, G. 32, 43–4, 59
Zorin, V. 68, 135, 236
Žujović, S. 235, 236
Zverev, A. 61

Lightning Source UK Ltd.
Milton Keynes UK
UKHW010628161119
353650UK00005B/6/P